Charlotte Brontë:
The Imagination in

Charlotte Brontë: The Imagination in History

HEATHER GLEN

OXFORD

UNIVERSITY PRESS

*This book has been printed digitally and produced in a standard specification
in order to ensure its continuing availability*

OXFORD
UNIVERSITY PRESS

Great Clarendon Street, Oxford OX2 6DP

Oxford University Press is a department of the University of Oxford.
It furthers the University's objective of excellence in research, scholarship,
and education by publishing worldwide in

Oxford New York

Auckland   Cape Town Dar es Salaam   Hong Kong   Karachi
Kuala Lumpur Madrid Melbourne Mexico City   Nairobi
New Delhi Shanghai Taipei Toronto
With offices in
Argentina Austria Brazil Chile Czech Republic France Greece
Guatemala Hungary Italy Japan South Korea Poland Portugal
Singapore Switzerland Thailand Turkey Ukraine Vietnam

Oxford is a registered trade mark of Oxford University Press
in the UK and in certain other countries

Published in the United States
by Oxford University Press Inc., New York

ISBN 0-19-927255-7

In memory of
THOMAS

and for
CHARTY

Acknowledgements

I AM GRATEFUL to the Humanities Research Board of the British Academy for the grant of a term's leave in January 1996, without which this book would have been even longer in the writing; and to the staff of the Brontë Parsonage Library, Haworth, and of the English Faculty Library and University Library in Cambridge for their unfailing helpfulness.

Like all future Brontë scholars, I owe an immense debt to Margaret Smith, whose thoughtful, scrupulous, and erudite edition of Charlotte Brontë's letters has at last made it possible to reconstruct something of her subject's intellectual life. I am grateful too to Juliet Barker, whose biography of the Brontë family is a similarly indispensable resource, for her readiness to answer questions. Kim Scott Walwyn's belief in the project, her quick intelligence, and her generosity of spirit have been a constant inspiration to me. My debts to other friends are too numerous to record, but I should like to single out for special thanks Marilyn Butler, Anne Green, Jill Matus, Claire MacDonald and David Trotter, each of whom read portions of the manuscript and made helpful suggestions. Above all, I should like to thank Stephen Fender, who read and commented thoughtfully on the whole.

This book is dedicated to my sons, each of whom in his different way played a very large part in its shaping.

Earlier versions of portions of Ch. 1 have appeared in *Opening the Nursery Door*, of Ch. 2 in my introduction to *The Professor* (Penguin edition), and of Chs. 6 and 7 in *The Cambridge Companion to the Brontës* (Cambridge: Cambridge University Press, 2002).

Contents

Abbreviations

Except in the case of the following abbreviations, full details of works referred to are given after each chapter, either in the notes or in a list of works cited.

Barker   Juliet Barker, *The Brontës* (London: Weidenfeld & Nicolson, 1994)

BPM   Brontë Parsonage Museum

BST   *Brontë Society Transactions*

CBL   Margaret Smith (ed.), *The Letters of Charlotte Brontë* (3 vols.; Oxford: Clarendon Press, 1995–)

CBP   Tom Winnifrith (ed.), *The Poems of Charlotte Brontë: A New Annotated and Enlarged Edition of the Shakespeare Head Brontë* (Oxford: Blackwell, 1984)

CH   Miriam Allott (ed.), *The Brontës: The Critical Heritage* (London: Routledge, 1974)

EBP   Janet Gezari (ed.), *Emily Jane Brontë: The Complete Poems* (London: Penguin, 1992)

EEW   Christine Alexander (ed.), *An Edition of the Early Writings of Charlotte Brontë* (Oxford: Basil Blackwell, vol. i, 1987; vol. ii, parts 1 and 2, 1991)

Gaskell Elizabeth Gaskell, *The Life of Charlotte Brontë*, ed. Alan Shelston (London: Penguin, 1975)

JE   Charlotte Brontë, *Jane Eyre*, ed. Margaret Smith, with an Introduction and revised notes by Sally Shuttleworth (Oxford: World's Classics, 2000)

LL   T. J. Wise and J. A. Symington (eds.), *The Brontës: Their Lives, Friendships and Correspondence* (4 vols.; Oxford: Basil Blackwell, Shakespeare Head Press, 1933)

P   Charlotte Brontë, *The Professor*, ed. Margaret Smith and Herbert Rosengarten, with an Introduction by Margaret Smith (Oxford: World's Classics, 1991)

S   Charlotte Brontë, *Shirley*, ed. Herbert Rosengarten and Margaret Smith (Oxford: World's Classics, 1981)

V   Charlotte Brontë, *Villette*, ed. Margaret Smith and Herbert Rosengarten, with an Introduction and Notes by Tim Dolin (Oxford: World's Classics, 2000)

WH   Emily Brontë, *Wuthering Heights*, ed. Ian Jack, with a new Introduction by Patsy Stoneman (Oxford: Oxford World's Classics, 1995)

Introduction

FOR GENERATIONS, Charlotte Brontë's novels have stirred their readers to intense and passionate response. Theirs is a world very different from those configured by the great Victorian social novelists: a world not of subtle moral discriminations, but of black-and-white difference and life-and-death struggle, of primitive emotion and 'feverish disquiet'.[1] The experience they offer is of suspense, of excitement, of repulsion; one takes sides with the hero or heroine, or recoils in dislike or 'pain'. 'We feel no art in these remarkable books', wrote Margaret Oliphant in 1855.

What we feel is a force which makes everything real—a motion which is irresistible. We are swept on in the current, and never draw breath till the tale is ended. Afterwards we may disapprove at our leisure, but it is certain that we have not a moment's pause to be critical till we come to the end.[2]

'We open *Jane Eyre*; and in two pages every doubt is swept clean from our minds'; thus Virginia Woolf in 1916. 'Nor is this exhilaration short-lived. It rushes us through the entire volume, without giving us time to think, without letting us lift our eyes from the page.'[3] 'The power of *Jane Eyre* . . . needs no further adjectives. Readers still respond . . . and critics still follow them; sometimes critic following reader a bit uneasily in the same personality,' Raymond Williams observes, fifty years later yet.[4] The voice of these novels, it seems, demands unquestioning assent, rather than calling upon the reader to consider, to discriminate, to reflect. Again and again the sense is of an intensity of identification that threatens to overwhelm the critical faculties: to 'be critical', it seems, has been in some way to 'disapprove'. If the sense that there is 'no art in these remarkable books' has been countered, since the 1960s, by a series of distinguished formalist studies, if new historicist and feminist critics have more recently begun to challenge the view that these novels speak simply of 'private experience' by tracing the presence within them of specifically early nineteenth-century discourses of class and gender and race, in crucial respects the diagnosis remains unchanged. Indeed, as Brontë's first reviewers' uneasy sense of her novels' 'blasphemy' and 'painfulness' has been replaced in more recent criticism by a charting of her ideological blind spots, it has become perhaps more severe. Her works are now more confidently judged as responses to a 'history' whose essential questions and contours are assumed to be well known.

[1] Leslie Stephen, *Cornhill Magazine*, December 1877, in *CH* 420.
[2] 'Modern Novelists—Great and Small', *Blackwood's Magazine* 77 (1855), 558–9.
[3] '*Jane Eyre* and *Wuthering Heights*' (1916), in *The Common Reader: First Series* (London: Hogarth Press, 1925), 196–7.
[4] Raymond Williams, *The English Novel from Dickens to Lawrence* (London: Chatto & Windus, 1973), 63.

Yet the novels of Charlotte Brontë, so passionately loved, so intimately appropriated, have seemed also to their readers to speak in accents teasingly different from theirs. Apparently universally shared experiences—ambition, loneliness, vulnerability, desire—appear within them in sharply particular inflections, shaped by, responsive to, circumstances that their readers have often—if inarticulately—felt to be different from that which they know. That sense, shared by readers in widely different times and places, that the concerns of Brontë's novels are, most intimately, *their* concerns, has been accompanied, always, by a fascination with the alterity of their author's life. And the naïve impulse of identification has been complicated, for many, by the recurrent sense that these novels are abrasive, embarrassing, enigmatic: not unproblematically assimilable, but curiously unsettling to read. 'That's a plaguey book that *Villette*. How clever it is,' declared Thackeray:[5] 'We are left with the sense of an unsolved discord,' wrote Leslie Stephen, of the ending of *Jane Eyre*.[6]

Critics have tended to treat this recalcitrance not as meaningful, but as symptomatic; as evidence of Brontë's clumsiness in handling those subjects with which they take her to be concerned. Yet it is the cumulative experience of generations of readers, far more than academic criticism, that constitutes these novels' continuing cultural life. And that experience poses a persistent challenge to confident judgement of this kind. There is something in these works that continues to stir and disconcert their readers, that speaks not of familiarity but of difference: the difference of Charlotte Brontë's concerns from ours, the difference of her mode of conceiving of her world.

In the chapters that follow I seek to track down the sources of this feeling, in those 'plaguey' features of Brontë's works that impede the reader's progress to the expected destination—but that complicate and question the questions we bring to them. For as one resists that almost overwhelming impulse to identify with the central character and find out what happens in her story, as one pays close attention to that which is subliminally constitutive of every reader's experience—the particulars of form and of language through which character is articulated and narrative framed—much in these novels that has been judged to be awkward, random, disruptive, begins to appear significant. They are much more intelligently crafted than is usually allowed. And they are much more aware of and responsive to a multifarious and changing early nineteenth-century world. What we shall find in them is not a naïve or neurotic or ideologically blinkered attempt to tell a well-known story. They speak in unexpected and sharply percipient ways of concerns that are rather different from those that we bring to them.

We need less to reconstruct a 'history' that will make these familiar works seem strange than to read the 'history' we think we know through the prism of that 'strangeness' which readers still find in them. A prism breaks light into a spectrum: it brings a different version of reality into view. Just so, I shall be suggesting, each of Charlotte Brontë's novels can be seen to point, in a different way, towards different early nineteenth-century phenomena—from romantic gift books for women to the

---

[5] *CH* 198.   [6] Ibid. 421.

writings of the sanitary reformers, from the spectacle of bourgeois prosperity represented in the Great Exhibition to discourses upon happiness. Yet these novels do not merely disclose a 'history' more particular, more variously inflected than that which we have been accustomed to see. Like a prism, they refract and configure it in a quite distinctive way.

For the intelligence that is manifest within them is a specifically literary one. It does not present a single discursive message, but invokes and plays with a whole range of differing discourses, representing, emphasizing, estranging them; interrogating them, inflecting them ironically and critically. It abstracts patterns, exposes faultlines, points towards questions and significances in peculiarly fictional ways. Above all, perhaps, it is characterized by a constant sharp attentiveness to the medium within which it works. 'Her style present[s] the finish of a piece of mosaic,' Mrs Gaskell said. She was pointing to the 'singular' precision of Charlotte Brontë's 'choice of words'. But Brontë's concern with language goes beyond that expressive 'felicity' of which her biographer speaks. She foregrounds and contemplates words from different registers of the language—'It might be provincial,' says Gaskell; 'it might be derived from the Latin'—playing with and upon their meanings, sometimes bringing their etymology suggestively into view. She thinks within and about the cultural discourses of her time, pointing to contradictions and to parallels, re-animating clichés, literalizing metaphors, making those discourses seem strange. What we shall find in her writings is less that 'strong practical regard for the simple holy truth of expression' of which Mrs Gaskell speaks than a differently 'practical' sense of language as a socially constructed medium, a medium with a history, freighted with social significances, used by different speakers in diverse and divergent ways.[7] Hers is not the voice of escapist romance, but that of one almost 'preternaturally' alert to the complex actualities of the world of which she writes.[8] Her novels are not 'self-centred and self-limited', or lacking in 'powerful intellect'.[9] Their imaginative engagement with history is an extraordinarily wide-ranging and piercingly intelligent one.

What is the difference of the 'literary' from other forms of discourse? What does the literary imagination do with the materials with which it works? What kinds of understanding of history does it yield? These are questions that contemporary theorists have evaded rather than explored.[10] They are questions sharply raised both by Charlotte Brontë's novels and by the history of their reception—the seeming critical consensus that hers is not a powerful intellect; the ordinary reader's sense that her novels are not exhausted by the confident placing judgements that critics have made of them. And the student of Charlotte Brontë is peculiarly well placed to explore them. Brontë knew, not in the abstract, but as a matter of concrete

---

[7] All these quotations are from Gaskell, 307.

[8] 'I have been reading *Villette*, a still more wonderful book than *Jane Eyre*,' writes George Eliot to a friend in February 1853. 'There is something almost preternatural in its power' (*CH* 192).

[9] Virginia Woolf, '*Jane Eyre* and *Wuthering Heights*', 199; Leslie Stephen, quoted in *CH* 422.

[10] For discussion of this, see George Levine, 'Introduction: Reclaiming the Aesthetic', in George Levine (ed.), *Aesthetics and Ideology* (New Brunswick: Rutgers University Press, 1994), 1–30.

practice, that for a work to announce itself as 'literary', and demand a 'literary' reading, is a matter of cultural convention. And she knew that convention as a liberating and enabling one. For her, the literary does seem to have been a privileged space—a 'free place', as Mrs Gaskell called it, in describing the Brontë sisters' mutual discussions of their fictions[11]—within which differing versions of reality might be played with, contemplated, understood. Moreover, she left a body of writings that offer an unparalleled insight into the ways in which such a space may be appropriated and used: records not of an imagination free of the constraints of history, or of transcendent, isolated genius, but of a lively group of children exploring the conventions of their culture and seizing the possibilities it offered at a particular historical moment, through a consciously deliberated entry into the fictive arena of play.

[11] Gaskell, 308.

CHAPTER ONE

The Mighty Phantasm

In 1829, at the age of 12, Charlotte Brontë began to write a 'history'. The document still survives at Haworth Parsonage—a blotted scrawl on scrap paper, erratically punctuated and spelled:

The History of the Year

Once papa lent my Sister Maria A Book it was an old Geography and she wrote on its Blank leaf papa lent me this Book. the Book is an hundred and twenty years old it is at this moment lying Before me while I write this I am in the kitchin of the parsonage house Haworth Taby the servent is washing up after Breakfast and Anne my youngest sister (Maria was my eldest) is kneeling on a chair looking at some cakes which Tabby has been Baking for us. Emily is in the parlour brushing it papa and Branwell are gone to Keighly Aunt is up stairs in her Room and I am siting by the table writing this in the kitchin. Keighly is a small town four miles from here papa and Branwell are gone for the newspaper the Leeds Intelligencer is a most exellent Tory news paper edited by Mr Wood the proprieter Mr Hernaman we take 2 and see three Newspapers as such we take the Leeds Inteligencer party Tory and the Leeds Mercury Whig—Edited by Mr Bain and His Brother Soninlaw and his 2 sons Edward and Talbot. We see the Jhon Bull it is a High Tory very violent Mr Driver lends us it as Likewise Blackwoods Magazine the most able periodical there is the editor is Mr Christopher North an old man 74 years of age the 1st of April is his Birthday his company are Timothy Ticklar Morgan Odoherty Macrabin Mordecai Mullion Warrell and James Hogg a man of most extraordinary genius a Scottish Sheppard. Our plays were established Young Men June 1826 Our fellows July 1827 islanders December 1827. those are our three great plays that are not kept secret Emily's and my Bed plays where Established the 1st December 1827 the other March 1828 Bed plays means secret plays they are very nice ones all our plays are very strange ones there nature I need not write on paper for I think I shall always remember them. the young men play took its rise from some wooden soldiers Branwell had Our fellows from Esops fables and the Islanders from several events which happened I will skecth out the origin of our plays more explicitly if I can 1 Young mens papa bought Branwell some Soldiers at Leeds when papa came home it was night and we where in Bed. so next morning Branwell came to our Door with a Box of Soldiers Emily and me Jumped out of Bed and I snatched up one and exclaimed this is the Duke of Wellington it shall be mine. when I had said this Emily likewise took one and said it should be hers and when Ane came down she said one should be hers Branwell likewise took one to be his Mine was the prettiest of the whole and the tallest and perfect in every part Emilys was a grave looking fellow and we called him Gravey Ane's was a queer little thing much like herself he was called waiting Boy Branwell chose Bonuparte

March 12 1829[1]

---

[1] BPM: MS Bon 80 (11).

The story whose beginnings are here 'skecthed out' is now well known. To the motherless children in that Yorkshire parsonage, the soldiers became the original dramatis personae of an imaginary world that was to allure and preoccupy each of the four throughout adolescence and beyond. Seven years later, in uncongenial employment as a teacher of young ladies, 'sinking from irritation & weariness into a kind of lethargy', Charlotte Brontë was to testify to the continuing power of that 'mighty phantasm'—'conjured from nothing from nothing to a system strong as some religious creed'.

> I felt as if I could have written gloriously—I longed to write. The spirit of all Verdopolis—of all the mountainous North of all the woodland West of all the river-watered East came crowding into my mind. if I had had time to indulge it I felt that the vague sensations of that moment would have settled down into some narrative better than any thing I ever produced before. But just then a Dolt came up with a lesson. I thought I should have vomited.[2]

Brontë seems here to be invoking a familiar trope—the transcendent romantic imagination, with its promise of liberation from an intolerable actual world. It is a trope that her later novels—especially *Jane Eyre*, with its imagery of straining beyond limits—appear to develop and endorse. And it seems to be artlessly prefigured in the first of these autobiographical fragments, where the child abandons 'History' as she becomes caught up in the excitement of 'our plays'.

   Yet the truth, as both these pieces attest, was rather more complicated than this. 'I longed to write,' recalls Brontë. 'I felt that the vague sensations of that moment would have settled down into some narrative better than any thing I ever produced before.' The longing is not for an unrestrained 'indulgence' in subjective fantasy, but for the shaping and objectifying of fantasy in shared cultural form. If the writer's sense of the dream as 'conjured from nothing' points back to that childish fiat—'this is the Duke of Wellington'—and its implicit invocation of a quasi-supernatural power, this points back, too—to the 'History' that situates her account of 'the origin of our plays'. For that 'History' begins with a book—'an old Geography . . . an hundred and twenty years old': at once a material object 'lying before me while I write', and—like the volume of Bewick that engrosses the child Jane Eyre—transporting her beyond her immediate situation, to time past and places far away. This book, too, belongs to the male head of the household; this too seems to testify to unquestioned patriarchal power. Yet, like that which fires Jane's dreams of elsewhere, it speaks also of possibility. Indeed, within this 'History' it figures in a pivotal way. For what the writing child records is not the passive reception of a benefit ('Papa lent my Sister . . . A Book . . . she read what it contained'), but the seizing of a space—however circumscribed—of agency: 'Papa lent my Sister . . . A Book . . . she wrote on its Blank leaf . . .' And the drama outlined here is echoed in the longer description of the children's 'play' at the end, where 'papa lent . . . she wrote' becomes 'papa bought Branwell some Soldiers at Leeds . . . I snatched up one and exclaimed this is the Duke of Wellington'. The description is not of escape into a

---

[2] BPM: MS Bon 98 (8).

space of abstract freedom but of an active appropriation of that which 'History' offered, in a manner to which this fragment provides a clue.

For the 'mighty phantasm' in which those 'plays' were elaborated was by no means 'conjured from nothing'. It was made possible, shaped and constrained by the specificities of a quite particular culture, one that is a potent presence in 'The History of the Year'. The whole of that 'History' is coloured by the child's ingenuous fascination with what Byron, in a journal entry of 1812, had called 'the mighty stir made about scribbling and scribes, by themselves and others' at this time.[3] The periodicals she reads and the opinions of those who write for them are as real, to her, as that which actually happens in 'the parsonage house Haworth': to her, men of letters—no less than the Duke of Wellington—are the heroes of the day. That which compels her, however, is not the high romantic ideology of transcendent 'poetry' and 'genius' later to be invoked by her heroine Jane Eyre (*JE* 370).[4] As their half self-advertising, half self-mocking nicknames indicate, 'Timothy Tickler Morgan Odoherty Macrabin Mordecai Mullion Warrell and James Hogg' are not solitary original geniuses, above or outside society, but the consciously created, semi-fictional personae of a lively public sphere. Literary endeavour here is not heroic self-making but improvisatory self-promotion, not lonely aspiration but entry into a world of spirited controversy—a world altogether more ironic and heteroglossic than that 'golden age' of 'poetry' and 'genius' which Jane so resonantly recalls.

Such a world certainly existed in the 1820s and 1830s; and it was, as Charlotte's 'History' makes clear, one that the Brontës knew well. Their first acquaintance with it seems to have been through *Blackwood's Magazine*, singled out here as 'the most able periodical there is': they were soon to become familiar with *Blackwood's*' follower and rival *Fraser's*, which 'Morgan Odoherty' (William Maginn) was to help to found in 1830, and which was received in the Parsonage from 1832.[5] The character of these journals is worth pausing to consider, for they were enormously important in shaping the nature and the dynamics of the Brontës' childhood 'plays'. Each was written by a small group of regular contributors, whose foibles and opinions their readers came to know well. Each issue was produced with a rapidity that gave it a peculiar immediacy, and which, as this 'History' suggests, ensured the reader's involvement in the minutiae of their concerns. Each promoted and throve upon literary and political controversy, and included material of extraordinarily diverse kinds. Essays on topical issues, lengthy philosophical and critical reviews, pseudo-scientific fiction, biography, tales of terror and anecdotes of travel jostled for position in their pages amongst squibs, comic character sketches, parodies, and burlesques. 'A real Magazine', *Blackwood's* proclaimed itself, 'of mirth, misanthropy, wit, wisdom, folly,

---

[3] Thomas Moore, *Works of Lord Byron, with his Letters and Journals, and his Life* (17 vols.; London: John Murray, 1833), ii. 277.

[4] On this strain of romanticism, see Jerome McGann, *The Romantic Ideology: A Critical Investigation* (Chicago: University of Chicago Press, 1983); and Marlon Ross, *The Contours of Masculine Desire: Romanticism and the Rise of Women's Poetry* (New York and Oxford: Oxford University Press, 1989), ch. 1.

[5] See Christine Alexander, 'Readers and Writers: *Blackwood's* and the Brontës', *The Gaskell Society Journal*, 8 (1994), 54–69; Barker, 149–50, 861 n. 101. On *Fraser's*, see *CBL* i. 112–14.

fiction, fun, festivity, theology, bruising and thingumbob';[6] a 'dog's meat-tart of a periodical', *Fraser's* was called by Carlyle (who published many of his early writings there).[7] Certainly, both journals were oddly conglomerate, both in contents and in style. They were most distinctive, perhaps, in their oscillation between sobriety and levity, between that 'poetry of language' which Branwell Brontë recalled finding in Professor Wilson's articles in *Blackwood's*, 'read and re-read while a little child'[8] and the subversive raillery of the same journal's famous 'Noctes Ambrosianae'—imaginary conversations on topical and literary themes; between *Fraser's* serious essays on the issues of the day and the swift retorts, the comic lampoons, the many-targeted ridicule of that

> Magazine most quizzical,
> Sublime and metaphysical;
> Conducted with sagacity,
> And wondrous perspicacity,
> By famous OLIVER YORKE, sir—
> Good at the knife and fork, sir

—as a squib on the reverse of its table of contents for January 1832 proclaimed it to be. Reverential paeans to romanticism—such as *Blackwood's* early description of Scott, Wordsworth and Byron as poets 'of perfectly original genius . . . drinking inspiration from fountains far apart' and ruling 'each by a legitimate sovereignty, over separate and powerful provinces in the kingdom of Mind'[9]—alternate in their pages with deflation of its pretensions: 'Yon lakers . . . Great yegotists; and Wordsworth the worst o' ye a'; for he'll alloo nae merit to ony leeving creatur but himsel'. He's a triflin' cretur in yon Excursion; there' some bonny spats here and there, but nae reader can thole aboon a dozen pages o't at a screed, without whumming ower on his seat.'[10] Indeed, Jane Eyre's sense that 'the golden age of modern literature' has vanished, that 'poetry' and 'genius' must take their stand against 'Mammon', is prefigured in *Fraser's* concern with what it saw as the commodification and debasement of romanticism—its attacks on the annuals, and on 'fashionable novelists' such as Bulwer Lytton and his 'feminine followers', its caustic view of sentiment, its parodies of figures such as Southey, Coleridge, Mrs Hemans, and Thomas Moore, its scorn for the cult of Byron and the overproductivity of Scott. 'We cannot overestimate the tremendous influence that these periodicals play in establishing and sustaining romantic, especially Wordsworthian, ideology, and in supporting the myth of poetry-writing as a powerful vocation', writes one twentieth-century critic.[11] But if the early *Blackwood's* and *Fraser's* spoke of heroes, it was not solely in a spirit of solemn admiration, but also more ironically. Their satiric

---

[6] *Blackwood's Magazine* 12 (1822), 105–6.
[7] Miriam Thrall, *Rebellious Fraser's* (New York: Columbia University Press, 1934), 9.
[8] Branwell Brontë to John Wilson ('Christopher North'), 8 December 1835 (*LL* i. 133–4).
[9] 'Essays on the Lake School of Poetry. No. 1 Wordsworth's "The White Doe of Rylstone"', *Blackwood's Magazine* 3 (1818), 369.
[10] 'Noctes Ambrosianae', *Blackwood's Magazine* 14 (1823), 486. The speaker is the 'Ettrick Shepherd'.
[11] Ross, *The Contours of Masculine Desire*, 54.

literary portraits, their constant lampooning of their own contributors, even the comic pseudonyms of those who wrote for them, all testify to their interest in character as performance, their sense of 'fame' as construction of public image, and of literary 'Genius' as perhaps no more than a pose.

As that list of the *Blackwood's* coterie in 'The History of the Year' suggests, it was to this variety and iconoclasm, this ebullient self-invention, that the young Charlotte Brontë was drawn. It is clearly not insignificant that that list is succeeded in her 'History' by her 'skecth' of 'the origin of our plays'. For the influence of *Blackwood's* and of *Fraser's* is evident in her earliest surviving works. Prominent amongst these, indeed, is a periodical mimicking *Blackwood's*, apparently begun in January 1829 by Branwell, and continued by Charlotte until the end of the following year. Most of the contents of this miniature journal—at first called *Blackwood's Young Men's Magazine* and later simply *The Young Men's Magazine*—were modelled on those of its prototype—poems, book reviews, letters to the editor, and stories and articles by various hands. 'Noctes Ambrosianae' (in which all the figures named in 'A History of the year' took part) are imitated, too, in a series of 'Conversations' between the worthies of the Brontë children's Glass Town. And *Blackwood's* self-reflexive playfulness, its oscillation between seriousness and raillery, is echoed throughout—most notably, perhaps, in the contrast between two of Charlotte Brontë's favourite personae, the sentimental Marquis of Douro and the sardonic Lord Charles Wellesley, each of whom contributes extensively to these little magazines. Thus, the former waxes lyrical over winter, 'when the crystal icicles are hanging from the eaves of the houses & the bushy evergreens are all spangled with snow-flakes, as if twas spring & they were flourishing in full blossom' in *The Young Men's Magazine* for 10 December 1830; 'when all the old women traverse the streets in red woollen cloaks & clacking iron pattons. When apothecarys are seen rushing about with gargles & tinctures & washes for sprained ancles chilblains & frost-bitten noses,' the latter sardonically replies.[12]

The ironic anti-romanticism, as well as the straightforward 'romance', of *Blackwood's* and of *Fraser's* is a prominent feature not merely of the little journals of Glass Town, but of most of the writings that survive from Charlotte Brontë's early years. The buffoonery of *Blackwood's* 'Noctes Ambrosianae' is echoed in 'The Poetaster', her only attempt at a full-length drama, a slapstick satire of romantic effusiveness and Gothic melancholia, which she wrote at the age of 14.[13] *Fraser's* debunking character-sketches—as, for example, its portrait of Theodore Hook, 'just descended from the grand vestibule of the Athenaeum, where he has been enjoying Praed's rhymes of the morning, a well-cayenned mutton-chop, and a glass of the Murchison sherry'[14]—have counterparts in such portraits as that of the 'most noble Richard Marquis of Wellesley . . . reposing in gouty chair & stool with eyelids gently closed by the influence of the pious libations in claret with which he has concluded the dinner of rice-currie devilled turkey and guava' in her later 'Stancliffe's

---

[12] 'Conversations', *Young Men's Magazine*, 10 December 1829, reprinted Barker, 162.
[13] 'The Poetaster, A Drama in Two Volumes by Lord Charles Wellesley', *EEW* i. 179–96.
[14] *Fraser's Magazine* 9 (1834), 435.

Hotel' (1838).[15] Brontë's juvenilia are full of echoes of other reading, from the 'Geography' and the newspapers mentioned in her 'History', to Shakespeare, Scott, and Byron—who, as a figure not simply of romantic aspiration but also of cynical worldliness, in his single person encapsulated much of the contradictory variety of the magazines. But the influence of the multi-voiced *Blackwood's* and *Fraser's* is central. And it may be traced not merely in her mimicry of these journals' protean contents, their quicksilver changes of tone, but in the sense that pervades all her youthful writings, of the literary world as a place not of artless self-expressiveness but of artful self-presentation, in which different roles may be tried out, contemplated, explored and satirized; a place not of monologic fantasy but of heteroglossic and self-reflexive 'play'.

And 'play', as all children intuitively know, is quite different from actual life. That knowledge is evinced in the striking difference between the appearance of the Glass Town writings and that of 'The History of the year'. Whereas the latter is a careless, unfinished scrawl on loose paper, the fictional volumes of Glass Town (testifying to that fascination with the glamour of literary culture—indeed, with the book as object[16]—which Brontë's 'History' records) are sewn into paper wrappers, with tables of contents and title pages, like real journals and books. The childish copperplate of that factual 'History' is in them replaced by a script designed 'to look as like print as possible'—'a hand', Mrs Gaskell complained, 'which it is almost impossible to decipher without the aid of a magnifying glass'.[17] The origins of this miniscule hand lie, of course, in the fact that the earliest Glass Town volumes were designed to be 'read' by wooden soldiers only twelve inches high. (It was possibly also, more prosaically, prompted by the scarcity of paper in the Parsonage). But it seems to signal also a sense of the fictional as writing of a quite distinctive kind: a sense that is manifest not merely in the appearance but also in the nature of the writings of Glass Town. For the stories and articles, dialogues and verses that make up that 'mighty phantasm' have none of the autobiographical directness of 'A history of the year'. They are narrated, usually, through the voices of fictional personae, who are sharply and variously characterized and often mockingly seen. Within the fictional world these personae become the objects of one another's admiring or critical regard: their viewpoints are questioned and ironized, their limitations made clear. In this, the ethos of Glass Town is like that of *Blackwood's* and of *Fraser's*. But in Glass Town, albeit childishly, one finds a questioning of the conventions and premises of early nineteenth-century realism that is scarcely approached by the ironies of the magazines.

For if the highly elaborated writings of the Glass Town saga may seem very far from that game with toy soldiers of which Brontë writes in her 'History', they do not forget their origin: that most ordinary yet extraordinary of all human activities—the entry of the child into the fictive space of 'play'. The denizens of Glass Town are

---

[15] Unpublished MS, June 1838, BPM: MS Bon 114.
[16] On such 'secular bibliolatry' in the early 19th cent., see Richard Altick, *The English Common Reader: A Social History of the Mass Reading Public 1800–1900* (Chicago: University of Chicago Press, 1957), 139.
[17] Gaskell, 112.

not merely objects of a deflating, sometimes slapstick humour. Right through these early writings (rather different, in this respect, from those of their author's twenties) runs a rather more radical sense that these figures of power and pretension are in reality mere fictions, created by beings far more powerful than they. It is a sense for which other of the young Brontës' reading was to provide a resonant image—an image that Charlotte was to invoke throughout her later writings, even to the very last of her published works.[18] 'I took a book—some Arabian tales', recalls Jane Eyre, of her attempt to escape the dreariness that overhelms her after her rebellion against Mrs Reed (*JE* 38). Like countless others in the early nineteenth century, the Brontë children were fascinated by 'Arabian tales'.[19] Inspired by *The Arabian Nights' Entertainments* and also, it seems, by James Ridley's *Tales of the the Genii*, quite early in the development of their 'plays' they assumed for themselves the roles of mighty 'Genii', who wielded control over the imaginary world and could intervene within it in decisive, coercive ways. But whereas in the Arabian tales with which the children were familiar the intervention of the Genii was a device for ensuring closure, magically resolving conflict, and snapping shut the plot, the presence of the Genii in Glass Town has a strangely disruptive effect.

Thus, in a story written, like 'The History of the Year', in 1829, the climactic event of that 'History' appears in a different light. 'A Romantic Tale' is a travel narrative, of a kind familiar to the children from *Blackwood's Magazine*.[20] It tells, from the viewpoint of one of their number, how 'twelve adventurers' journeyed to an 'immense continent', battled with the natives and established a colony there. The intrepid heroes make their way to the middle of a great desert, where they come upon 'the palace of the Genii', 'the pillars of which were ruby and emerald illuminated with lamps too bright to look upon':

The Genius led us into a hall of sapphire in which were thrones of gold. On the thrones sat the Princes of the Genii. In the midst of the hall hung a lamp like the sun. Around it stood genii and fairies without, whose robes were of beaten gold sparkling with diamonds. As soon as their chiefs saw us they sprang up from their thrones, and one of them seizing Arthur Wellesley exclaimed, 'This is the Duke of Wellington!'[21]

And even in this simple little story the identification with the perspective of the teller is such that it is with a shock that the reader realizes that this bold adventurer is in reality but a little wooden soldier, and that the mighty Prince of the Genii of whom he tells is none other than the childish author herself.

For if the magical plots, the rapid changes of scene and the sudden denouements of Glass Town bespeak the child's heady assertion ('This is the Duke of Wellington!') of a coveted fictional power, the world she creates in these writings is one within which the perspectives of the powerless are realized and elaborated; in which power is not simply exercised, but contemplated—and contemplated in potentially disturbing ways. 'How long has it taken to rear the Grand Hall where we now are?' asks Arthur

---

[18] See *V* 167, 209.   [19] Jane Stedman, 'The Genesis of the Genii', *BST* 14: 75 (1965), 16–19.
[20] Barker, 155 and notes.   [21] 'A Romantic Tale', *EEW* i. 14.

Wellesley, as he surveys the marvels of Glass Town. 'Have not these marble pillars and that solemn dome been built by supernatural power?' and he urges his countrymen to believe that 'if the genii have built our city', they will help to defend it too.[22] In another early story, the two protagonists enter an underground passage in the hope that 'perhaps we may find happiness here', but a stone is rolled across its entrance, shutting out all but a single ray of light. 'What is that?' asks one, and the other replies, 'I cannot tell, but never mind, I suppose it is only some Genius playing tricks.'[23] A letter to the editor of the *Young Men's Magazine* in July 1829 begins:

Sir—it is well known that the Genii have declared that unless they [presumably the Young Men] 'perform certain arduous duties every year, of a mysterious nature, all the worlds in the firmament will be burnt up and gathered together in one mighty globe, which will roll in lonely grandeur through the vast wilderness of space, inhabited only by the four high Princes of the Genii, till time shall be succeeded by eternity.'[24]

Sometimes in the Glass Town writings the controlling Brontë children appear in more comic guise. Thus, in the Fourth Volume of *Tales of the Islanders* the Little Queens (as the three female Genii sometimes termed themselves) pretend to be 'the Three Old Washerwomen of Strathfieldsaye', 'knitting with the utmost rapidity and keeping their tongues in constant motion all the while'. But even these humorously diminished figures prove to be strangely disquieting when seen from Lord Charles Wellesley's point of view:

They . . . glided noiselessly into the midst of the river and there, turning three times round amidst the shivered fragments of brilliant light in which the moon was reflected, were swallowed up in a whirlpool of raging surges and foam. He stood a moment powerless with horror, then springing over the mound dashed through the trees on the other side and, gaining the open path, beheld Little King and the three old women walking whole and sound a few yards before him. More surprised than before, he viewed them in silence for an instant and then concluded that they were other fairies whom Little King had brought with him to this earth. He strove to satisfy himself with this conjecture, but, notwithstanding his endeavours, he still felt an uneasy, vague, and by no means pleasant, sensation when he looked at their little sharp faces and heard the shrill, disagreeable tones of their voices (for they were now chatting away as merrily as before) for which he was unable to account.

The narrator who has decided to eavesdrop on their conversation, 'promising himself much amusement from the scheme' appears here as 'powerless with horror', 'uneasy', at a loss.[25]

Of course, like the *Arabian Nights*, such moments are 'entertaining': the child's enjoyment of her joke is manifest throughout. But one, at least, of the tales of this early period, explores its darker implications in a more extended way. The story, which appeared in the December 1830 number of *The Young Men's Magazine*, is entitled 'Strange Events'.[26] It is an imitation of a genre familiar to the children from

[22] 'A Romantic Tale', 13.   [23] *EEW* i. 45–6.   [24] Ibid. 39.   [25] Ibid. 197–9.
[26] Ibid. 256–60. The manuscript was transcribed by Davidson Cook in 1925: its present whereabouts are unknown. Cook describes it as a hand-sewn booklet of twenty pages, 5 cm × 3.5 cm, in a brown paper cover. (Davidson Cook, 'Brontë Manuscripts in the Law Collection', *The Bookman*, November 1925, 100–4.) In my discussion, I deal only with the first of the two 'strange events' the story records.

Blackwood's—a first-person account of the macabre, such as that journal was popularizing in these years.[27] Indeed, its opening paragraph bears a striking resemblance to that of 'The Mysterious Bride', a story by that 'man of most extraordinary genius', the 'Scottish Sheppard', James Hogg, published in *Blackwood's* in the very same month. 'A great number of people now-a-days are beginning broadly to insinuate that there are no such things as ghosts, or spiritual beings visible to mortal sight', Hogg's narrator begins.

Even Sir Walter Scott is turned renegade, and . . . is trying to throw cold water on the most certain, though most impalpable, phenomena of human nature. The bodies are daft. Heaven mend their wits! Before they had ventured to assert such things, I wish they had been where I have often been; or, in particular, where the Laird of Birkendelly was on St Lawrence's Eve, in the year 1777, and sundry times subsequent to that.[28]

'It is the fashion nowadays to put no faith whatsoever in supernatural appearances or warnings', declares Charlotte Brontë's Lord Charles Wellesley, in apparently similar vein. 'I am, however, a happy exception to the general rule, and firmly believe in everything of the kind. Instances of the good foundation I have for this obsolete belief often meet my observation, tending to confirm me in it. For the present I shall content myself with mentioning a few.'

Yet if each of these anecdotes begins by attacking a contemporary 'fashion' for rational explanations of the supernatural,[29] the narrative which follows is directed in each to a very different end. Hogg's is a ghost story, drawing—as his choice of a Scottish peasant-narrator suggests—on the superstitious legends of the Borders, and catering unambiguously to that appetite for terror which *Blackwood's* in these years both created and fed. But on closer inspection 'Strange Events' is rather more complicated than this.

Its 'author', Lord Charles Wellesley, the younger son of the Duke of Wellington, is a favourite narrator of Brontë's: a cynical outsider who throughout the Glass Town saga surveys the passions of others from a mocking point of view. He is himself throughout the object of considerable authorial irony—an irony that is evident in the comic pomposity of the opening paragraph here. The scorn for 'fashion' of which he boasts appears as itself an affectation: this speaker is clearly sharply aware of the figure he cuts in the world. And his studied Byronic disaffectedness is increasingly, humorously exaggerated as he continues with his tale:

---

[27] See Robert Morrison and Chris Baldick (eds.), *Tales of Terror from Blackwood's Magazine* (Oxford: Oxford World's Classics, 1995). The influence of such stories on the young Charlotte Brontë is evident in the images of supernatural voices, strange apparitions, and premonitory dreams that recur in her early works.

[28] *Blackwood's Magazine*, December 1830; repr. Morrison and Baldick, 115–30. The reference is to Scott's *Letters on Demonology and Witchcraft* (1830), which had attacked superstition from a rationalist point of view.

[29] For an account of scientific and philosophical attacks of this kind at the beginning of the 19th cent., see Terry Castle, *The Female Thermometer: Eighteenth-Century Culture and the Invention of the Uncanny* (New York and Oxford: Oxford University Press, 1995), chs. 9 and 10.

One day last June happening to be extremely wet and foggy, I felt, as is usual with Englishmen, very dull. The common remedies—razor, rope and arsenic—presented themselves in series, but as is unusual with Englishmen, I did not relish any of them. At last the expedient of repairing to the Public Library for diversion entered my head. Thither I accordingly went, taking care to avoid crossing the great bridge lest the calm aspect of the liquid world beneath it might induce me to make a summary descent.

The pose of ennui is a modish one, as is his flippant entertainment of the idea of suicide: jokes about Young Werther were in the 1820s commonplace in the magazines.[30] Yet if Brontë is mocking her hero here, his story is beginning to acquire a more disquieting edge. The world-weary individual who began his tale so grandiloquently is, it seems, an oddly precarious entity. And this sense becomes more prominent as his narrative proceeds:

When I entered the room a bright fire flickering against the polished sienna hearth somewhat cheered my drooping spirits. No one was there, so I shut the door. Taking down Brandart's *Finished Lawyer*, I placed myself on a sofa in the ingle-cheek. Whilst I was listlessly turning over the leaves of that most ponderous volume, I fell into the strangest train of thought that ever visited even my mind, eccentric and unstable as it is said by some insolent puppies to be.

It seemed as if I was a non-existent shadow, that I neither spoke, eat, imagined or lived of myself, but I was the mere idea of some other creature's brain. The Glass Town seemed so likewise. My father, Arthur and everyone with whom I am acquainted, passed into a state of annihilation; but suddenly I thought again that I and my relatives did exist, and yet not us but our minds and our bodies without ourselves. Then this supposition—the oddest of any—followed the former quickly, namely, that WE without US were shadows; also, but at the end of a long vista, as it were, appeared dimly and indistinctly, beings that really lived in a tangible shape, that were called by our names and were US from whom WE had been copied by something—I could not tell what.

'It seemed as if I were a non-existent shadow': Byronic attitudinizing gives way to something very different here, as the speaker's confidence in his whole familiar world, and indeed, in his own very being, falters and fails. His sense of his own and others' coherence disappears. Instead, there is a disconcerting glimpse of a split between their existence as subjects—'WE'—and as objects—'US'. Substantial reality seems to belong elsewhere, with 'beings that really lived in a tangible shape'—'at the end of a long vista, as it were'. And beyond all this, and virtually unintelligible, comes an apprehension of that 'something' to which he and his world owe such being as they have.

As in a dream, he sees this 'indistinctly'. In the paragraph that follows, the dreamlike quality takes over, as features of the real England of 1830 (Wellington as Prime Minister, his sons living at his home at Stratfield Saye, George IV as king) are distorted and recombined in a bizarre phantasmagoria, where the familiar is inverted and estranged:

---

[30] On England's reputation in the early 19th cent. as 'la terre classique du suicide' see Barbara T. Gates, *Victorian Suicide: Mad Crimes and Sad Histories* (Princeton: Princeton University Press, 1988), 23–4.

Another world formed part of this reverie in which was no Glass Town or British Realm in Africa except Hindoustan, India, Calcutta. England was there but totally different in manners, laws, customs and inhabitants—governed by a sailor—my father Prime Minister—I and Arthur young noblemen living at Strathaye, or something with a name like that—visionary fairies, elves, brownies, the East Wind, and wild Arab-broken horses—shooting in moors with a fat man who was a great book. But I am lost, I cannot get on.

'I am lost, I cannot get on': for, as the disintegrating syntax of this paragraph attests, the unitary, linear subject on which the coherence of his narrative depends has been thrown into question by the experience he relates. And when that subject reappears in control, it has an odder and odder story to tell:

For hours I continued in this state, striving to fathom a bottomless ocean of Mystery, till at length I was aroused by a loud noise above my head. I looked up and thick obscurity was before my eyes. Voices, one like my own but larger and dimmer (if sound may be characterized by such epithets) and another which sounded familiar, yet I had never, that I could remember, heard it before, murmuring unceasingly in my ears.

I saw books removing from the top shelves and returning, apparently of their own accord. By degrees the mistiness cleared off. I felt myself raised suddenly to the ceiling, and ere I was aware, behold two immense, sparkling, bright blue globes within a few yards of me. I was in [a] hand wide enough almost to grasp the Tower of All Nations, and when it lowered me to the floor I saw a huge personification of myself—hundreds of feet high—standing against the great Oriel.

That dimly intuited 'other creature' here comes gradually into focus—first as a sound, at once familiar and unfamiliar; then as a magically animating force, at last as an 'apparition', imperfectly seen and not at all understood. There are echoes here of *Gulliver's Travels*, which the Brontë children appear to have read at this time,[31] and which Charlotte Brontë was later to present as fascinating the child Jane Eyre: this figure has clear affinities with the giant farmer who lifts a suddenly dwarfed Gulliver in Brobdignag. But unlike that farmer, it is not an other with whom it seems possible to interact. For in face of its unchallengeable potency the narrator's sense of his own unreality seems absolutely confirmed: 'This filled me with a weight of astonishment greater than the mind of man ever before had to endure, and I was now perfectly convinced of my non-existence except in another corporeal frame which dwelt in the real world, for ours, I thought, was nothing but idea.'

'I felt myself raised suddenly to the ceiling'. With a cooler, more clinical realism than Hogg's this tale records the detailed 'sensations' of a first-person narrator undergoing an extraordinary ordeal. And in this it cleverly imitates what Poe was later to call parodically 'a genuine Blackwood article of the sensation stamp'.[32] Yet it is

[31] The August 1829 issue of *Blackwood's Young Men's Magazine*, 'Edited by the Genius CB', carries an advertisement for '*Tales of Captain Lemuel Gulliver in Houynhmhm Land* price 10 shillings 6d.' (*EEW* i. 61).

[32] Poe's 'How to Write a Blackwood Article' was published eight years after 'Strange Events'. Its narrator, Signoria Psyche Zenobia, receives instructions on writing a typical *Blackwood's* tale of terror from Mr Blackwood himself: 'There was *The Dead Alive*, a capital thing! the record of a gentleman's sensations when entombed before the breath was out of his body—full of taste, terror, sentiment, metaphysics and erudition. You would have sworn that the writer had been born and brought up in a coffin. . . . Then

not just an imitation. For (as Poe in his own way was later to do) it exploits both the serious and the comic possibilities of the form to precise and striking effect. In one way, of course, it is simply a childish joke—an elaboration of that 'play' with the perspective of the created which we saw in 'A Romantic Tale'. To himself, this narrator is Lord Charles Wellesley, unconforming, self-assertive, independent: free to choose at a whim whether to live or to die. His cockiness is comically stressed throughout—in his opening assertion of indifference to 'fashion'; in his inability to see his creator except as 'a huge personification of myself'; in the affected boredom with which he ends his account, complaining that he gazed at this astonishing shape for 'an unconscionable time'. But in fact he is a little wooden soldier, whose fictional identity has been 'copied' from that of the Duke of Wellington's son. His 'strange' intuition comes upon him (a nice comic touch) as he turns the pages of a book: such life as he has is dependent upon 'some other creature's brain'. For, as the story's first readers would have recognized with delight, the figure who lifts him is none other than the 'Chief Genius Tallii'—his all-powerful creator, Charlotte Brontë herself. Dwarfed by her mightiness, indeed, created by her, the strutting Lord Charles is revealed to be a provisional creature, the mere puppet of forces immeasurably greater than he.

    Yet 'Strange Events' is rather more than a joke. For, despite the irony with which he is seen, it is with Lord Charles—his vertigo, his doubts, his 'astonishment'—that the reader identifies. Comic as it is, his narrative offers also a disquietingly intimate glimpse of a moment in which existential assurance suddenly disappears. The experience is one that the teller finds 'strange' and, yet more strangely, 'familiar': for the voices he hears and the shape he sees are not exactly unknown. In this, the story accords with Freud's later, famous account of the uncanny as 'that class of the frightening which leads back to what is known of old and long familiar', 'nothing new or alien, but something which is . . . old-established in the mind'.[33] But whereas for Freud the uncanny speaks of apparently timeless psychic realities— 'primitive beliefs which have been surmounted' and 'infantile complexes which have been repressed'[34]—the import of 'Strange Events' is suggestively different

there was '*The Involuntary Experimentalist*', all about a gentleman who got baked in an oven, and came out alive and well, although certainly done to a turn. . . . And then there was '*The Man in the Bell*' . . . the history of a young person who goes to sleep under the clapper of a church bell, and is awakened by its tolling for a funeral. The sound drives him mad, and, accordingly, pulling out his tablets, he gives a record of his sensations. Sensations are the great things after all. Should you ever be drowned or hung, be sure and make a note of your sensations—they will be worth to you ten guineas a sheet. . . . The first thing requisite is to get yourself into such a scrape as no one ever got into before. . . . "Truth is strange", you know, "stranger than fiction"—besides being more to the purpose' (pp. 273–5). (The tales referred to are all first-person accounts of terrifying ordeals from the early *Blackwood's*.) Zenobia attempts to follow these prescriptions, and dies grotesquely, in the act of reporting her own decapitation. ('How to Write a Blackwood Article' and 'A Predicament' (1838) in Edwin Markham (ed.), *Works of Edgar Allan Poe* (10 vols.; New York: Funk & Wagnall's Company, 1904), x. 115–44).

[33] Sigmund Freud, 'The Uncanny', in Albert Dickson (ed.), *The Penguin Freud Library*, 14: *Art and Literature* (London: Penguin, 1990), 340, 363. Hoffmann, Freud's main example of the 'uncanny' effect in literature, was a favourite in the early *Blackwood's*, and a potent influence on the tales of terror to which Brontë is responding here.

[34] Ibid. 372.

from this. For that which Brontë's hero confronts is, as her readers would have recognized, not simply a subjective trauma but the real condition of his being: he is in truth 'nothing but idea'. His 'strange' apprehension, so at odds with 'common sense', points, in truth, to the facts of an actual history—a 'history' on the repression of which his functioning as a confident subject depends.

'While her description of any real occurrence is . . . homely, graphic and forcible, when she gives way to her powers of creation, her fancy and her language alike run riot, sometimes to the very borders of apparent delirium': such was Mrs Gaskell's verdict on the Glass Town and Angrian writings, which she was the first outside the Brontë family to see.[35] It is not hard to see how a story like this, with its central 'strange event' and its bewildering descent into surrealism, might have led her to such a view. Yet beside 'The History of of the Year', 'Strange Events' begins to appear in a rather different light. For each of these two childish documents illuminates the other in an extraordinarily suggestive way. Most obviously, of course, that 'History'—'homely, graphic, forcible'—tells of the 'real occurrence' that Lord Charles Wellesley intuits: how a number of wooden soldiers were brought to life by a group of children at play. To the reader aware of this, 'Strange Events' is not mindless 'delirium', but a clever little joke. Yet its narrator's recollected experience of radical ontological insecurity is by no means merely comic in effect. And in this 'Strange Events' comments also on that 'History', and points to significances within it which might otherwise go unremarked.

Nothing could be further from Lord Charles Wellesley's studied worldweariness than the child Charlotte Brontë's lively interest in her world. There is nothing, in her account of life in the Parsonage, like the 'strange' dilemma that Lord Charles Wellesley confronts. Yet within her 'History' one can see, unstressed, yet clearly registered, something akin to that intuition of provisionality and powerlessness which is brought into focus in his tale. The first person she mentions is 'papa'. It is he, it seems, who determines events: he takes the newspapers, he buys the soldiers; he is the owner and the lender of the book. Indeed, the child Maria's one reported act might be seen as merely an acknowledgement of this: 'she wrote on its Blank leaf papa lent me this Book'. It is true that the actions of the other children appear at first very different. They do not complete a closed circle, but open out into possibility: the whole second half of the 'History' is charged with the excitement of their still developing 'plays'. But if it ends with an account of a heady act of creation, it traces also, unillusionedly, the limits within which that act is framed.

For the world it configures is one within which the writing child has little effective power. Those whom she admires—literary and political figures, the military heroes of the day—move in spheres quite remote from hers. Her 'Duke of Wellington' is in reality nothing but a little toy soldier, given to her brother by 'papa'. And if in relation to these, their creatures, she and her siblings are mighty Genii, namers and givers of life, in actuality they are subject to laws beyond their control. This fact is not stressed, but it is registered from the beginning. For if the first figure in this

---

[35] Gaskell, 112.

'History' is 'papa', the second is 'Maria'—the vanished sister, whose death is acknowledged only obliquely, in the past tense of a parenthesis. And it is in the light of a consciousness of that death—a death which even 'papa' could not prevent—that the whole of that which follows unfolds.

Unsystematic as it is, this 'History' is more than a random series of facts. In its own unpretentious way, it evinces an acute awareness of what it meant to *be* in this child's particular circumstances. The feelings of which it speaks are perhaps, in essentials, common to all human childhoods: the attraction to powers that one does not possess; the apprehension that one inhabits a world that one does not control. Here, these universal problems can be seen in a particular inflection: that of a specific childhood, in a specific time and place—a childhood in which, we may infer, they might have been felt with unusual sharpness. For in early nineteenth-century England the cultural celebration of power—whether of literary 'genius' or military heroism or romantic conquest—was extraordinarily compelling. 'In all senses we worship and follow after Power', says Carlyle, in his *Signs of the Times*, published in the same year.[36] Yet the childhood of which Charlotte Brontë writes was one in which actual powerlessness might have been more than usually evident. For it was one in which the authority of others appeared in peculiarly unsoftened form: that of a girl within an early nineteenth-century patriarchal family (in this 'History', the girls attend to household duties while the boy goes abroad, adventurously, with papa),[37] in which the father was also a priest of a religion that made its own uncompromising claims. And it was a childhood more shadowed than most by that ultimate proof of human impotence, the fact of mortality: a childhood spent in a house surrounded by graves, in a place in which more than 40 per cent of the population died before reaching the age of 6,[38] and in a family that had lost three of its eight members—mother and two older sisters—by the time the writer reached the age of 9.

Nothing like this analysis is offered in Charlotte's 'History': the young historian scarcely reflects upon the material she presents at all. But the parenthetical reference to Maria's death at the beginning, the delighted creation of 'the Duke of Wellington' at the end, map out a more elemental drama than might at first be

---

[36]   The 'papa' who figures in this history must have provided the child with a peculiarly potent example of such Power-worship. For a suggestive discussion of 'the mirage ... of the heroic life', which Patrick Brontë kept 'ever before him as he trod his own pedestrian way', see Winifred Gérin, *The Brontës*, i. *The Formative Years* (London: Longman & Green, 1973), 10–11, 14.

[37]   Branwell's proprietorial account of the origin of the Young Men's Play is suggestively different from that given in 'The History of the Year': 'when I first saw them in the morning after they were bought I carried them to Emily Charlotte and Anne they each took up a soldier gave them names which I consented to and I gave Charlotte Twemy [i.e. Wellington] to Emily Parre [Parry] to Anne Trott [Ross] to take care of them though they were to be mine and I to have the disposal of them as I would—shortly after this I gave them to them as their own—P B Brontë.' (Patrick Branwell Brontë, *The History of the Young Men*, 15 December 1830–7 May 1831: MS Ashley 2468, 9, British Library. I am grateful to Juliet Barker for supplying me with this transcript.)

[38]   See Benjamin Herschel Babbage, *Report to the General Board of Health on a Preliminary Inquiry into the Sewerage, Drainage, and Supply of Water, and the Sanitary Condition of the Inhabitants of the Hamlet of Haworth* (London: HMSO, 1850).

apparent: one in which an assertion of absolute power, the power to determine existence itself, is made in the face of an apprehension of absolute powerlessness, potential non-existence. At the end, creative confidence seems to triumph over awareness of creaturehood. But the 'I' that creates is, it seems, premised on a repression of that annihilating awareness.

And something like that awareness is writ large in 'Strange Events'. In one sense, of course, this little story speaks only of creative potency. Its confident humour, its carefully printed pages, its skilful imitation of a fashionable contemporary genre, are all tangible signs that its youthful author has herself appropriated something of the glamour of that enticing literary sphere. Here, as she could expect her fellow Genii to recognize with delight, Charlotte Brontë is manifestly in command of events. Yet if that portrait of herself from Lord Charles Wellesley's perspective— 'hundreds of feet high—standing against the great Oriel', and filling her hero with 'astonishment'—would to them have been comically entrancing, within his first-person narrative it is more unnerving than this. For what one finds in this little tale is not, most prominently, identification with power, but, far more centrally and intimately, the imagining of powerlessness: an imagining that offers a peculiar challenge to that 'feeling of security' which such an account of a 'strange event' might be expected to provide.[39] Here, what had started as a childish 'play'—the contemplation of the Genii by their creatures—seems to have enabled the young author to objectify and explore that which is inscribed but not confronted in her 'History': a sense of self not as autonomous and free, but as dependent and determined, not as omnipotent, but as potentially not existing at all. The ironic joke that is the mainspring of the fiction permits the entertainment of feelings that the 'realistic' mode of the 'History' could not accommodate—feelings that question and problematize its most fundamental assumption, the sense of reality itself.

Such feelings are more amenable, it might seem, to psychoanalytic than to historicist analysis. And it would clearly be possible to interpret Lord Charles Wellesley's story as a representation of the predicament of one whose parent was a somewhat distanced and mysteriously powerful figure, whose sense of self was perhaps inadequately recognized or confirmed; or as expressive of a more primitive terror at the parent's intuited power to decide between the being and the non-being of the child. But to read it simply thus is, I think, hardly to begin to account for the nature of the expression such feelings here receive. For what we see in this little story is very far from unmediated psychic fantasy. Within it, the disturbing is objectified and contemplated in a form that its author could be confident her readers would recognize. Lord Charles Wellesley, the flippant Byronic hero, is, after all, a familiar figure

---

[39] 'The feeling of security with which I follow the hero through his perilous adventures is the same as the feeling with which a hero in real life throws himself into the water to save a drowning man or exposes himself to the enemy's fire in order to storm a battery,' writes Freud, of the reading of popular adventure stories. "It is the true heroic feeling . . . Nothing can happen to me!" It seems to me, however, that through this revealing characteristic of invulnerability we can immediately recognize His Majesty the Ego, the hero alike of every day-dream and every story.' ('Creative Writers and Daydreaming', in Freud, *Art and Literature*, 137).

of early nineteenth-century masculinity.[40] His studied world-weariness, his affected dissidence are, as the young author's shorthand way with them suggests, virtually clichés of the contemporary literary scene. If his first-person account of an alarming experience is an imitation of a well-known *Blackwood's* genre, the sardonic irony with which he is portrayed likewise owes a good deal to that journal's irreverent treatment of contemporary fashions and fads. This is a mode of writing quite different from that 'trance-like' confessional outpouring often attributed even to the mature Charlotte Brontë:[41] it is flexible, witty, assured. And it is a mode of writing that enables not so much an escape from that real world which its author portrays in her 'History' as an engagement with 'History' of a quite distinctive kind.

For it enables the articulation of intuitions that the realism of 'History' must, it seems, suppress. Indeed, its young author's 'History of the Year' suggests quite sharply why the feelings objectified in 'Strange Events' might by this child be expressed so clearly only in fictional form. In most Western cultures, perhaps, human beings do to a large extent repress the awareness that they are contingent beings, who do not control the world in which they find themselves.[42] The public culture of early nineteenth-century England—the largely masculine culture of individual genius, romantic assertion, military heroism, that the young Charlotte Brontë's 'History' so artlessly evokes—was certainly one in which such awareness was rarely entertained. ('The language of poetry naturally falls in with the language of power', Hazlitt had written twelve years earlier, in an attempt to characterize the spirit of the age.)[43] Yet the experiences that led to that awareness could scarcely be escaped. For some (the emotionally, socially, economically, or sexually disadvantaged) such experiences might be more various, more mutually reinforcing, less softened, than they were for the more fortunate: but none could avoid the powerlessness and vulnerability of childhood, or the fact of mortality. The impotence, the marginalization, the disconfirmation imaged in 'Strange Events' were arguably as central to life in early nineteenth-century England as were the confidence, the success, the heroic achievement celebrated in 'The History of the Year' and promoted as the self-image of the age. And in this fantastic little story, quite at odds with that society's 'realism', this denied sense of creaturehood is confronted and explored.

Here, the twentieth-century reader is afforded a privileged glimpse of something that can seldom be seen with such intimacy from such a historical distance: that most ordinary and yet extraordinary of happenings—a moment of childish play. But because that child was no ordinary child, and this no ordinary play, it offers also

---

[40] On the Byronic pose amongst the young intelligentsia of the 1820s and 1830s, see Edward Lytton Bulwer, *England and and the English* (1833), ed. Standish Meacham (Chicago and London: University of Chicago Press, 1970), 356–7.

[41] For the claim that Brontë was a 'trance-writer' see Winifred Gérin, Introduction to Charlotte Brontë, *Five Novelettes* (London: Folio Press, 1971), 16; and Sandra Gilbert and Susan Gubar, *The Madwoman in the Attic: the Woman Writer and the Nineteenth-Century Literary Imagination* (New Haven and London: Yale University Press, 1979), 311.

[42] See Ernest Becker, *The Denial of Death* (New York: Macmillan, Free Press, 1975).

[43] William Hazlitt, *The Complete Works of William Hazlitt in Twenty-One Volumes: Centenary Edition*, ed. P. P. Howe (London: Secker, 1930–4), iv. 24.

an arresting insight into the ways in which the aesthetic space of fiction can enable intuitions that challenge 'official' versions of reality to be entertained, contemplated, understood. This child, as her 'History' so disarmingly reveals, was in one way quite uncritically compelled by that which her culture valorized and her childhood reading offered: the glamour of military heroism, of literary fame and achievement, the power of the written word. But what one sees in a story such as 'Strange Events' is not a naïve attempt to 'become the hero, the king, the creator, the favourite [s]he actually desired to be',[44] but a rather more complex play, which pivots not on identification with power, but on its objectification—'this is the Duke of Wellington', not 'I shall be the Duke'. It is a play that offers its own distinctive and unexpected comment on that public 'language of power' which Brontë herself found so enticing, and which Hazlitt saw as the inevitable voice of the age.

'I have now written a great many books', Charlotte Brontë was to declare, at the age of 23. 'I long to quit for a while that burning clime where we have sojourned too long—its skies flame—the glow of sunset is always upon it—the mind would cease from excitement and turn now to a cooler region where the dawn breaks grey and sober, and the coming day for a time at least is subdued by clouds'. The untitled fragment that contains these words has become known as the future novelist's 'Farewell to Angria', and read as 'a clear statement' of Charlotte Brontë's 'future intention'.[45] Certainly, no Angrian manuscripts dated after this survive: the fervid plots and exotic settings of Glass Town and of Angria give way to the nineteenth-century England of *Ashworth, The Professor, Jane Eyre.*[46] The sense—which has become established in Brontë criticism—is of a definitive break. Her imaginary world may have been the sphere in which Charlotte Brontë served her literary apprenticeship, but, it is argued, she had to 'struggle out of romance' in order to write the novels on which her reputation rests.[47] 'The hypnotic attraction of Angria had stunted her development as a writer of realistic fiction', says Christine Alexander, summing up her definitive work on these early writings. 'It was only grudgingly, and over a period of years, that childhood romance gave way to the balanced perception of reality that marks her mature work.'[48]

---

[44] Sigmund Freud, 'Formulations of the Two Principles of Mental Functioning', in Albert Dickson (ed.), *The Penguin Freud Library* 11: *On Metapsychology* (London: Penguin, 1991), 42.

[45] Christine Alexander, *The Early Writings of Charlotte Brontë* (Oxford: Basil Blackwell, 1983), 199.

[46] *Ashworth*, written in 1840–1, does contain some Angrian figures, but it is not set in that 'burning clime'. See Charlotte Brontë, *Unfinished Novels* (Stroud: Alan Sutton in association with the Brontë Society, 1993), 18–62.

[47] This phrase is from Karen Chase, *Eros and Psyche: the Representation of Personality in Charlotte Brontë, Charles Dickens, George Eliot* (New York and London: Methuen, 1984), 8. For examples of this view see Kathleen Tillotson, *Novels of the Eighteen-Forties* (Oxford: Clarendon Press, 1954), 265 n. 3; David Lodge, *The Language of Fiction* (London: Routledge & Kegan Paul, 1966); Mary Jacobus, 'The Buried Letter: Feminism and Romanticism in *Villette*', in Jacobus (ed.), *Women Writing and Writing about Women* (London: Croom Helm, 1979); John Kucich, *Repression in Victorian Fiction: Charlotte Brontë, George Eliot, and Charles Dickens* (Berkeley and Los Angeles: University of California Press), 34–5; Lyndall Gordon, *Charlotte Brontë: A Passionate Life* (London: Chatto & Windus, 1994), 85.

[48] Christine Alexander, *The Early Writings of Charlotte Brontë* (Oxford: Basil Blackwell, 1983), 246.

Yet that to which generations of Brontë's readers have responded most power-fully in her novels is not exactly a 'balanced perception of reality'. The choked-off violence of *The Professor*, the elements of fairy tale and Gothic romance that play through *Jane Eyre*, the peculiar centrifugal energies of *Shirley*, the strange mixture of bathos and surrealism in *Villette* speak less of maturity and balance than—as Leslie Stephen complained—of 'feverish disquiet'.[49] Such features of the novels seem closer to the 'wild weird writing' of Glass Town and of Angria than they do to 'The History of the Year'. Indeed, to the reader alert to the irreverent ways in which these youthful writings appropriate and play with contemporary literary forms, there is something a little spurious in the resonance of Brontë's 'Farewell' to the landscapes of her 'youth'. For such farewells to youth and romance were common in the early nineteenth century. Thus, for example, Brontë's hero, Byron, in *Hours of Idleness* (1807):

> Parent of golden dreams, Romance!
>   Auspicious Queen of childish joys,
> Who lead'st along, in airy dance,
>   Thy votive train of girls and boys;
> At length, in spells no longer bound,
>   I break the fetters of my youth;
> No more I tread thy mystic round,
>   But leave thy realms for those of Truth.[50]

Like many such announcements in the writings of Glass Town and Angria, Brontë's 'Farewell to Angria' might perhaps be most accurately read less as a direct expres-sion of authorial intent than as a self-conscious 'specimen' of a well-known literary trope.[51]

Perhaps it is time to question the prevalent view—based partly on that eloquent 'Farewell'—that the replacement of Glass Town and Angria with the world of *Jane Eyre* and *Villette* was a straightforward progression from naïvely diverting romance to a realistic engagement with 'Truth'. It is not merely that the 'realism' of the later novels is rather more disrupted, more self-reflexively problematized, than this ac-count implies. The writings that made up that 'mighty phantasm' are rather more interesting than this. For even the earliest and most fantastic question the easy equation of 'romance' with escape from the 'real'. This seemingly 'wild weird writ-ing' in fact has its own kind of logic, which articulates intuitions at odds with the

---

[49] *CH* 420.

[50] More substantial literary examples include Coleridge's 'Reflections on Having Left a Place of Re-tirement', Wordsworth's account in Book V of *The Prelude* (ll. 560–5) of crossing the 'isthmus' from 'our native continent' [of childhood romance] to 'earth and human life', and Keats's *Fall of Hyperion*. Char-lotte Brontë herself was to rework the theme in *Shirley* (pp. 97–8) to entirely serious effect. But the for-mulaic nature of Byron's lines, evident in rhythms and imagery, bespeaks less introspective seriousness than the conscious adoption of a pose. (For a different view, see Ross, *The Contours of Masculine Desire*, 36–7.)

[51] 'Upon my Christian d—n—n, I do think a man who is really interested in politics the greatest fool the sun looks on', declares the narrator of 'Henry Hastings' (1839), at the end of a long account of the opening of the Angrian parliamentary session. 'I wrote merely as a specimen of a certain style' (Gérin (ed.), *Five Novelettes*, 184).

'realism' of its time. And in this, it might lead us to ask whether those peculiarities of the later novels that have proved so obstructive to attempts at realist reading might not themselves be meaningful as are the 'strange events' of those fantastic little plays.

The story of Lord Charles Wellesley's confrontation with his Genius-creator is one of the most suggestive of Brontë's surviving juvenilia, not merely because it offers a particularly clear example of the way in which the young author drew on and reworked that which her culture offered, but also because it shows particularly sharply how this youthful 'play' prefigures the distinctive conformations of the writings of her later years. 'I saw a huge personification of myself—hundreds of feet high—standing against the great Oriel': that 'shape', at once determining and annihilating, was to reappear in differently troubling guises throughout her published works. 'He stood between me and every thought of religion,' says Jane of Rochester during their courtship, 'as an eclipse intervenes between man and the broad sun' (*JE* 274). When Caroline Helstone, reflecting on marriage, looks back to her traumatic childhood, she sees there the 'half-remembered image' of the father who tried to kill her: 'a strange shape; dim, sinister, scarcely earthly' (*S* 102). Asked if she finds Graham Bretton 'beautiful', Lucy Snowe gives a typically enigmatic yet revealing reply. 'I looked at him twice or thrice about a year ago, before he recognized me, and then I shut my eyes; and if he were to cross their balls twelve times between each day's sunset and sunrise—except from memory, I should hardly know what shape had gone by'. 'Lucy, what do you mean?' asks her confidante, Paulina. 'I mean that I value vision, and dread being struck stone blind' (*V* 424–5). If each of these moments, and each of these 'shapes', is different, and different from that which Lord Charles Wellesley sees, they are as characteristic of their author, and as pregnant with implication, as are Wordsworth's 'spots of time', or those nodal 'combinations' that de Quincey called 'involutes'. Yet they are not, like these two latter, a series of formative images, 'impressed' upon or 'carried imperceptibly into' an individual subjectivity,[52] but an echoing succession of very different fictional scenes. Just as the point of 'Strange Events' lay not simply in its recreation of a peculiar 'state of mind' but in its comic recognition of the circumstances underwriting that state—Lord Charles's creation by the Genii in a moment of childish 'play'—so the significance of such fictional moments as these lies not merely in their rendering of private experience—that 'strange power of subjective representation' for which Lewes praised Charlotte Brontë[53]—than in their charged and revelatory sense of self not merely as subject but as object within a distinctly realized world.[54]

---

[52] On 'spots of time', see William Wordsworth, *The Prelude* (1850), Book 12, 208–23. In his *Autobiography*, de Quincey speaks of 'involutes of human sensibility; combinations in which the materials of future thought or feeling are carried as imperceptibly into the mind as vegetable seeds are carried variously combined through the atmosphere, or by means of rivers, by birds, by winds, by waters, into remote countries' (David Masson (ed.), *The Collected Writings of Thomas de Quincey* (14 vols.; Edinburgh: A. & C. Black, 1897), i. 128.

[53] *CH* 86.

[54] This is, of course, in one sense true also of Wordsworth's 'spots of time', but these stages in 'the growth of a poet's mind' have a quite different function and status in the work in which they appear.

In *Jane Eyre*, in *Shirley*, in *Villette*, the shape that the speaker confronts is no longer an oddly familiar 'huge personification of myself', but an other of a more overtly threatening kind. Indeed, as the examples I have given may suggest, it might be seen simply as a well-known Gothic figure: the looming power of patriarchy, casting its shadow over the female protagonist and imperilling her in both material and psychic ways. Yet *Jane Eyre*, *Shirley*, *Villette* are much more interesting than this. In each of those quoted moments that threatening, inevitable other is presented in sharply particular, quite differently suggestive terms. Thus, Jane's image of Rochester takes its charge from the novel's recurrent emphasis on her desire for a 'power of vision' that will see beyond her present state: its resonances are quite different from the suggestions of devastating dazzle, of the Gorgon-like power of 'sunshine', that play through Lucy's half-admission of her attraction to Dr John. And the intuitions thus focused, so at odds with the 'realist' project, can be traced in these novels not merely in striking images but more subtly, more pervasively, in the minute configurations of the prose.

For even the most accessible, most apparently transparent of Charlotte Brontë's novels is rather less straightforward than might at first appear. *Jane Eyre*, it is true, has conventionally been read as a psychologically realistic narrative of an unprecedented kind. 'Common reader' and critic alike have taken their cue from the novel's subtitle in abstracting and paying attention to the narrator-character Jane—her choices, her feelings, her fears, and her desires. And Jane is very different from the ironized Lord Charles—a figure of triumphant self-affirmation, of survival, of choice and control. 'I care for myself,' she declares. 'I married him.' Yet it is also true that even the most uncritically absorbed of readers, spurred on by eagerness to discover whether this heroine will survive her hardships and marry Mr Rochester, must negotiate a prose in which she appears as something quite other than an effective, substantial presence—a prose that resonates with the dilemma evoked in 'Strange Events'.

Thus, Jane tells of her first day at Lowood:

As yet I had spoken to no one, nor did anybody seem to take notice of me; I stood lonely enough, but to that feeling of isolation I was accustomed; it did not oppress me much. I leant against a pillar of the verandah, drew my gray mantle close about me, and, trying to forget the cold which nipped me without, and the unsatisfied hunger which gnawed me within, delivered myself up to the employment of watching and thinking. My reflections were too undefined and fragmentary to merit record: I hardly yet knew where I was; Gateshead and my past life seemed floated away to an immeasurable distance; the present was vague and strange, and of the future I could form no conjecture. I looked round the convent-like garden, and then up at the house; a large building, half of which seemed gray and old, the other half quite new. The new part, containing the schoolroom and dormitory, was lit by mullioned and latticed windows, which gave it a church-like aspect; a stone-tablet over the door bore this inscription:

'Lowood Institution.—This portion was rebuilt A.D.—, by Naomi Brocklehurst, of Brocklehurst Hall, in this county'. 'Let your light so shine before men that they may see your good works, and glorify your Father which is in heaven.'—St. Matt. v. 16.

I read these words over and over again: I felt that an explanation belonged to them, and was unable fully to penetrate their import. (*JE* 48–9)

And thus, of the eve of her projected marriage:

The month of courtship had wasted: its very last hours were being numbered. There was no putting off the day that advanced—the bridal day; and all preparations for its arrival were complete. *I*, at least, had nothing more to do: there were my trunks, packed, locked, corded, ranged in a row along the wall of my little chamber; to-morrow, at this time, they would be far on their road to London: and so should I (D.V.),—or rather, not I, but one Jane Rochester, a person whom as yet I knew not. The cards of address alone remained to nail on: they lay, four little squares, on the drawer. Mr Rochester had himself written the direction, 'Mrs Rochester, — Hotel, London,' on each: I could not persuade myself to affix them, or to have then affixed. Mrs Rochester! She did not exist: she would not be born till tomorrow, some time after eight o'clock a.m.; and I would wait to be assured she had come into the world alive before I assigned to her all that property. It was enough that in yonder closet, opposite my dressing table, garments said to be hers had already displaced my black stuff Lowood frock and straw bonnet: for not to me appertained that suit of wedding raiment; the pearl-coloured robe, the vapoury veil pendent from the usurped portmanteau. I shut the closet, to conceal the strange, wraith-like apparel it contained; which, at this evening hour— nine o'clock—gave out certainly a most ghostly shimmer through the shadow of my apartment. 'I will leave you by yourself, white dream,' I said. 'I am feverish: I hear the wind blowing: I will go out of doors and feel it.' (*JE* 275)

Each of these passages is crucial in Jane's story of struggle and survival. In each, she confronts an unknown future with apprehension, which subsequent events are to confirm. Each can certainly be read as part of a coherent 'autobiography', in which, in defiance of challenging circumstances, self is defined and affirmed. Yet within each one can also trace a configuration of a rather different kind.

The narrating 'I' is prominent in the first of the passages I have quoted: in its opening few sentences, the first-person pronoun occurs sixteen times. In one way the effect is of self-assertion, made against isolation and deprivation—'the cold . . . without' and 'the hunger . . . within'. Yet the self thus asserted appears under the sign of negation, invisibility, absence: the terms in which it presents itself stress non-presence and ineffectiveness. Just as for Lord Charles Wellesley 'everyone with whom I am acquainted, passed into a state of annihilation', so for this later narrator past and future evaporate: the former seems 'floated away', of the latter she can 'form no conjecture'. This is a self contracted into a mere point of consciousness, neither sure of its own situation ('the present was vague and strange'; 'I hardly yet knew where I was') nor actualized in relation to others ('As yet I had spoken to no one, nor did anybody seem to take notice of me'), its thoughts 'undefined and fragmentary'; a self that indeed disappears as the paragraph comes to an end. And as it does so, suddenly, negatives are replaced by positives; the 'undefined and fragmentary' by solidity and fixity—a large 'church-like' building, an inscription on a tablet of stone. Insubstantiality gives way to clarity, concreteness, definition, as the focus shifts from subjective sensation to an apprehension of that which is incontestably there. Instead of the child's shaky sense of a hazy past, a 'vague and strange' present, and an unguessable future, there is a concrete testimony to definite achievement, a confident command to generations to come.

The text that the tablet bears speaks of the manifest, the recognized, the effective. But the child who confronts it is baffled by what she sees. 'I read these words over and again: I felt that an explanation belonged to them, and was unable fully to penetrate their import.' There is, of course, an obvious irony in this. Jane, after all, is starving and cold precisely because she is dependent on the 'charity' here vaunted: the chapter thus far has been devoted to a graphic description of the rigours of Lowood school. Yet the emphasis is not so much on the hypocrisy of the claim the tablet makes as on its authoritative solidity; and less on a childish confusion that will be resolved with time (such as Dickens presents in *Great Expectations*) than on a state of existential bewilderment, more akin to Lord Charles Wellesley's 'astonishment' than to mere immaturity. The child whose inner and outer worlds present themselves in negatives, who speaks to no one and is noticed by no one, and the tablet with its positive, public record and injunction, seem of quite different orders of being. Those questions of individual growth and development, of moral judgement and choice, which are so prominent in other Victorian novels, so often attributed to this, seem oddly peripheral here. The dilemma portrayed in this passage comes closest to temporary resolution not when the real conditions at Lowood school are exposed and rectified, but when Jane, beginning to be known by those about her, learns, we are told, to conjugate the first two tenses of the French verb *to be*.

Yet in the larger scheme of the novel, that resolution is only a temporary one. Differently but no less distinctively, in the second of these passages the same configuration recurs. Here, once again, the occasion is one that might be expected to provoke anxiety—the eve of the marriage that is to transform the governess-protagonist into the mistress of the house. Here, once again, the prose is marked by negatives—negatives that are in fact forebodings: as the reader is soon to learn, there will indeed be no 'Jane Rochester' on the morrow of this day. Yet, like the ironies that can be read into Jane's account of her first day at school, these premonitory hints seem less prominent than the existential disturbance of which they speak. It is a disturbance rather more radical than that which such a situation might rationally be expected to evoke. The fulfilment of courtship in marriage is figured as the approach of death, and the wedding day as an 'advancing' threat; the images that follow are images not merely of a change of state, but of the vanishing and usurpation of self. The narrator is held in a strange suspense: only obliquely, in an ineffectual negative—'There was no putting off the day that advanced'—does any glimpse of her possible agency appear. It is not until the third sentence of the paragraph that she introduces herself, and then it is in a terminally negative way: '*I*, at least, had nothing more to do.' Her 'trunks, packed, locked, corded, ranged in a row' have far more solidity than she. Indeed, such objects (the subjects of most of the verbs of the passage) appear here as participants in a drama from which she herself is excluded—at once as results of activity ('packed, locked, corded, ranged in a row') and with a surrealistic agency of their own ('they would be far on their road to

London', 'garments said to be hers had already displaced my black stuff Lowood frock and straw bonnet'). The projected journey to London—in conventional terms one of the most decisive acts of the narrator's life—is figured less as a choice she makes than as an irresistible occurrence, in which 'I' is carried along as a kind of appendage to her trunks—'or rather, not I, but one Jane Rochester, a person whom as yet I knew not.'

Here, as in 'Strange Events', the self at the centre of the narrative is strangely indeterminate; less an agent than the object of processes beyond its control. Here, as there, solidity and reality seem to reside elsewhere. It is not 'I', but 'Mrs Rochester', who will go to London; it is to her that the clothes hanging in the closet belong. Yet even 'Mrs Rochester' is an indeterminate figure ('She did not exist: she would not be born till to-morrow'), one who by the end is abandoned as a 'white dream'. And here, as in 'Strange Events', there appears an other more substantial and more effectual than this divided and impotent (and ultimately fleeing) self—an other whose name occurs four times in the passage, transforming the protagonist's, and appearing, like that earlier biblical text, in the reified form of a written command: 'Mr Rochester had himself written the direction, "Mrs Rochester,— Hotel, London," on each.' (Indeed, an Other more mighty even than Rochester is evoked in that quiet 'D.V.'). Here, again, when one examines the fine grain of this 'autobiography', one finds articulated an intuition at odds with that sense of coherent, self-actualizing identity one might expect to find at its centre. Here, as in 'Strange Events', the narrating self comes face to face with the determining conditions of its being: not, as there, in a sudden, surrealistic 'event', but through a destabilizing apprehension of that which its society constructs as 'real'.

Yet if these passages have some of that childhood story's disturbing power, they are altogether richer in their suggestiveness. For here a coherent sense of some of the social determinants of the powerful but bewildering feelings that had there found fantastic expression structures and informs the prose. To the experience of a dependent child, Charlotte Brontë had added that of a governess—that first attempt at 'independence' of which she had written to her sister Emily, 'I see now more clearly than I have ever done before that a private governess has no existence, is not considered as a living and rational being except as connected with the wearisome duties she has to fulfil.'[55] The childhood 'play' with the soldiers and the Genii had given way to a much more elaborated 'play' with one of the most compelling of early nineteenth-century discourses, that of Byronic romantic love. In an extraordinary series of novelettes, written in her early twenties, Charlotte Brontë had explored the dynamics of such love not merely from the perspective of the romantic hero, who travels and returns unpredictably to a series of waiting mistresses, but as the latter might experience it. 'I have never in my life contradicted Zamorna—never delayed obedience to his commands', one such heroine declares: 'I could not! he was sometimes more to me than a human being—he superseded all things—all affections, all

[55] *CBL* i. 191.

interests, all fears or hopes or principles—unconnected with him my mind would be a blank—cold, dead, susceptible only of a sense of despair.'[56] 'Strong-minded beyond her sex—active, energetic and accomplished in all other points of view—here she was as weak as a child—she lost her identity—her very life was swallowed up in that of another': this is the narrator's view.[57] The desire to lose self in another was, of course, commonplace in the discourse of romantic love. But one's sense that that cliché is here being critically foregrounded and contemplated is confirmed by Brontë's ironic handling of the figure in her rather different description of another romantic heroine, written in the following year:

> fresh, naive & romantic, really romantic—throwing her heart and soul into her dreams, longing only for an opportunity to do what she feels she could do—to die for somebody she Loves—that is, not actually to become a subject for the undertaker—but to give up heart, soul, sensations to one adored Hero—to lose Independent Existence in the perfect adoption of her Lover's Being.[58]

As Brontë well knew—her portrayal of Jane's reflections on her wedding eve resonates with the awareness—such metaphors had a peculiarly literal meaning for women in early Victorian England: 'The wife loses all her rights as a single woman, and her existence is entirely absorbed in that of her husband', Barbara Leigh Smith Bodichon was to explain in 1854. 'He is civilly responsible for her acts; she lives under his protection or cover, and her condition is called coverture.'[59] In the words of an Owenite writer in 1834, the married woman was 'an invisible woman—a species of ghost, who haunts her husband, and only becomes half solidified when he is no more'.[60]

The uncanny experience of de-realization described in 'Strange Events' may have been expressible, by the 13-year-old child, only in fantastic form. But it had objective correlatives in early Victorian England of which the adult Charlotte Brontë was clearly aware. And as, in *Jane Eyre*, she contemplates situations in which her heroine occupies a position of real disadvantage (as an 'unregenerate' and unloved child, as a 'dependent', a governess, a woman in love in a patriarchal world), something of that earlier intuition of the self's precariousness enters to complicate the telling and provide a distinctive counterpoint to Jane's story of survival and fulfilment. Of course, as generations of readers have attested, what one hears most compellingly throughout is the voice of that central subjectivity. Yet the intimations of an impinging otherness that enter the narrative at points such as these are more subliminally, but no less powerfully, an essential part of its import: that which the reader apprehends is not merely figure, but its ground. And the result is not merely a reanimation of the existential truth implicit in some of the most familiar of the depicted society's clichés ('a private governess has no existence'; 'her very way

---

[56] 'Mina Laury' (1838), MS in Robert H. Taylor Collection, Princeton University Library, 9.
[57] Ibid. 17.   [58] 'Caroline Vernon', ibid. 364.
[59] Barbara Leigh Smith Bodichon, *A Brief Summary in Plain Language of the Most Important Laws Concerning Women; Together with a Few Observations Thereon* (London, 1854), 6.
[60] Quoted in Barbara Taylor, *Eve and the New Jerusalem* (London: Virago, 1983), 35.

of life was swallowed up in that of another'; 'Mrs Rochester! She did not exist') but—it is beginning to seem—the configuring of a 'history' different from and obstructive to that narrative of self-definition conventionally assumed by the 'auto-biographical' form.

What we might call Lord Charles's dilemma—that intuition of a paramount other, in the face of which existential certainty falls away—seems to have been for Charlotte Brontë an imaginative configuration of a quite compelling kind. (It appears, indeed, at the very end of *Villette*, as with a report of the stories of her enemies, the narrator, her own story unfinished, bids the reader abruptly 'Farewell'). Yet it was, as these passages demonstrate, by no means simply a shape into which her writing habitually, unreflectingly fell. Rather, as befits its origins in those self-reflexive childhood plays, it is in each objectified, contemplated, elaborated, in significantly different ways. And this sense is borne out when one considers (to take just one other example) its recurrence in *Villette*. For here, once again, what one finds is not an involuntary repetition of a familiar constellation of feeling, but the coherent aesthetic reworking of it to a quite distinctive end.

At a pivotal moment in the novel, the narrator lies prostrate on a sofa, powerless in face of an unintelligible world. 'At first I knew nothing I looked on: a wall was not a wall—a lamp not a lamp', she recalls:

I saw myself laid, not in bed, but on a sofa. I looked spectral; my eyes larger and more hollow, my hair darker than was natural, by contrast with my thin and ashen face. It was obvious, not only from the furniture, but from the position of windows, doors, and fire-place, that this was an unknown room in an unknown house.

Hardly less plain was it that my brain was not yet settled; for as I gazed at the blue arm-chair, it appeared to grow familiar . . .   (*V* 166)

The sense is not, as in 'Strange Events', of the familiar growing strange, but of the strange growing strangely familiar. Yet the effect, here as there, is an uncanny and startling one:

What was there in this simple and somewhat pretty sleeping-closet to startle the most timid? Merely this—these articles of furniture could not be real, solid arm-chairs, looking-glasses, and wash-stands—they must be the ghosts of such articles; or, if this were denied as too wild an hypothesis—and, confounded as I was, I *did* deny it—there remained but to conclude that I had myself passed into an abnormal state of mind.   (*V* 168–9)

'Mine was the strangest figment with which delirium had ever harrassed a victim', says Lucy, as she tells of her conviction that 'these articles of furniture could not be real' (*V* 169). The phrase—like her predicament—is charged with memories of Lord Charles Wellesley, lying bewildered in the library of Glass Town, victim of 'the strangest train of thought that ever visited even my mind'. 'It seemed as if I were a non-existent shadow', that earlier hero had declared: here, she whom others perceive as a 'shadow' becomes the 'spectral' object of her own dissociated gaze. Here, as for that Glass Town hero, the world takes on a hallucinatory aspect, and subjective assurance drains away. 'Had a Genius . . . borne me over land and ocean, and laid me quietly down beside a hearth of Old England?' Lucy asks wildly, in a curious private echo of that childhood 'play', which now no others remained to share (*V* 167). And the vertigo of that intuition (imaged, in 'Strange Events', in the hero's decision to 'avoid crossing the great bridge') is registered throughout her account of her awakenings at La Terrasse, in a syntactic seesaw between the presentation of self as subject, offering a rational analysis of its experience ('abnormal', 'delirium'), and the recollection of self as object, 'harrassed', 'confounded', 'baffled', 'alarmed'.

Of course, there is a soon-to-be-offered rational explanation for this sense of the unreality of the real. And Lucy's obsessively detailed elaboration of her 'alarm', if odd, is entirely characteristic: she has by now been established as one who passes all too easily into 'an abnormal state of mind'. Yet if in this her own judgement concurs with that of others, she is no more simply pathologized here than was the 'eccentric' Lord Charles. Just as his intimations of his own unreality are confirmed by evidences of another more effective, more substantial than he, so as this scene unfolds the helpless narrator is 'confounded' by that which comes into focus before her: a collection of objects, which in their sharpness of outline, their elaborated detail, have all the authority of 'fact':

at last I took in the complete fact of a pleasant parlour, with a wood-fire on a clear-shining hearth, a carpet where arabesques of bright blue relieved a ground of shaded fawn; pale walls over which a slight but endless garland of azure forget-me-nots ran mazed and bewildered amongst myriad gold leaves and tendrils . . . as I gazed at the blue arm-chair, it appeared to grow familiar; so did a certain scroll-couch, and not less so the round centre-table, with a blue covering, bordered with autumn-tinted foliage; and, above all, two little footstools with worked covers, and a small ebony-framed chair, of which the seat and back were also worked with groups of brilliant flowers on a dark ground.   (*V* 166)

There is nothing here of the Gothic suggestiveness of *Jane Eyre*'s depiction of the child on her first day at school, of the woman on the eve of her wedding day. That which confronts this narrator is not a forbidding institution, or sense of impending doom, but the busily decorated furniture of a bourgeois drawing-room. The seeming supernaturalism of 'Strange Events' ('I saw books removing from the top shelves and returning, apparently of their own accord'), *Jane Eyre*'s hints of surrealism ('garments said to be hers had already displaced my black stuff Lowood frock and straw bonnet'), are here replaced by a mere turn of phrase: 'as I gazed at the blue arm-chair, *it appeared to grow familiar*' (my emphasis). Yet here, once again, as the description proceeds, something akin to that earlier intuition of a determining other appears:

My bed stood in a little alcove; on turning my face to the wall, the room with its bewildering accompaniments became excluded. Excluded? No! For as I arranged my position in this hope, behold, on the green space between the divided and looped-up curtains, hung a broad, gilded picture-frame enclosing a portrait. It was drawn—well drawn, though but a sketch— in water-colours; a head, a boy's head, fresh, life-like, speaking, and animated. It seemed a youth of sixteen, fair-complexioned, with sanguine health in his cheek; hair long, not dark, and with a sunny sheen; penetrating eyes, an arch mouth, and a gay smile. On the whole a most pleasant face to look at, especially for those claiming a right to that youth's affection— parents, for instance, or sisters. Any romantic little school-girl might almost have loved it in its frame. Those eyes looked as if when somewhat older, they would flash a lightning response to love: I cannot tell whether they kept in store the steady-beaming shine of faith. For whatever sentiment met him in form too facile, his lips menaced, beautifully but surely, caprice and light esteem.   (*V* 170)

Unlike that stony inscription, that soon-to-be-husband's 'directions' this image is 'life-like' and 'animated' in its 'broad gilded picture-frame'. Yet the narrator's attempts to construe it convey an unnerving sense of its potency—a potency of a less public, more insidiously 'menacing' kind. 'On the whole a most pleasant face to look at,' she decides; yet the observation is followed with a more disquieting hint of the aspect this image might present to one with no 'right' to this youth's 'affection', for whom its 'charm' might be a more dangerous thing. This perspective is evoked only obliquely, and is never acknowledged as the teller's: it is followed by the generalized third person of 'Any romantic little schoolgirl might almost have loved it in its frame.' But the oddity of that 'almost' and of the final phrase bring to the fore the fear that lurks within this fascination: this image can be 'loved' safely only as it is contained, like a wild animal in a cage. This is no controlling Genius, or figure of public authority, but the conventional enough object of a barely admitted 'love'. But here, once again, we find something akin to that sense of the other as potentially annihilating confronted in 'Strange Events'. For implicit in this description is an almost unspeakable fear of what it might mean for the one to whom this 'youth' is a specular object to become herself the object of his disconfirming gaze.

Lord Charles's confessional candour, Jane Eyre's frank disclosure of feeling have here been replaced by a peculiarly tense indirectness: the mode of telling bears witness to the teller's traumatized state. Yet if this might seem to invite a psychological reading, here, once again, the concern is not simply with the narrating subject but also with the world that she confronts. And here, that world assumes a distinctive configuration, bespeaking preoccupations rather different from those of *Jane Eyre*. This passage tells not of public authority—admonitions, institutions, instructions—but of the 'pleasant', the comfortable, the elaborate; not of the 'ghostly' shape of an unknown future, or of 'cold without and hunger within', but of apparently safe enclosure (a parlour, a sofa, a 'little alcove') and an all too well-known past. Yet whereas in face of manifest threat, Jane withdraws self-defensively—drawing her mantle close about her, shutting her closet and going outside—Lucy, immobilized on her sofa, is powerless to escape. *Jane Eyre*'s dialectic of coercion and self-assertion has here been replaced by a sense of paralysed exclusion, as before the 'spectral', displaced narrator appear a collection of 'household gods' (167). And as the too too solidly tantalizing 'signs and tokens' of 'home' lead, inexorably, to the attractive image of a 'well-remembered . . . form', the unloved, unrecognized narrator is 'confounded' not by the authority of a text-bearing tablet or 'approaching' husband, but by the more intimately threatening potency of one who is the object of unconfessed and unanswered desire.

If Brontë's later novels have little of the straightforward comedy of Lord Charles Wellesley's 'Strange Events', they carry within them, like a signature tune, echoes of their origins in their author's childhood play. But theirs is not simply 'the voice of special pleading': it is more searching, more flexible, more disinterested than that. What such passages as these disclose is not an obsessive return to a private structure of feeling—the insistent 'first-person stress' that Raymond Williams found in Brontë's writings—but an imaginative intelligence at work.[61] Theirs is the 'eccentric' viewpoint (to borrow Lord Charles Wellesley's word) of history's 'spectral' others—those excluded from official narratives, without effective agency, those who have 'no claim'. The focus in each is on the private experience of a solitary individual, unable to shape or even to understand the world in which she finds herself; the perspective not that of the authoritative, but of the uncomprehending, the situated, embodied gaze. 'I looked up,' says Lord Charles in 'Strange Events', 'and thick obscurity was before my eyes': 'the returning sense of sight came upon me,' says Lucy, 'red, as if it swam in blood' (*V* 165). Yet in each there comes also into focus the quite distinctive outline of that which the narrator confronts. And the presence of that looming other, impenetrable or impervious, points, it is beginning to seem, to their author's imaginative concern with a 'most real and substantial' world (*V* 171).

---

[61] Raymond Williams, *The English Novel from Dickens to Lawrence* (London: Chatto & Windus, 1973), 73, 74.

CHAPTER TWO

'Calculated abruptness':
The Professor

The Professor was written alongside *Wuthering Heights* and *Agnes Grey*, as one of
'three distinct and unconnected tales' with which the erstwhile Genii of Glass Town
hoped to enter the early Victorian literary market-place. If, unlike its two companions, it failed to find a publisher, like them it displays a sharp awareness of the literary fashions of its day. 'I had not indeed published anything before I commenced
The Professor,' Charlotte Brontë announced in an author's Preface written several
years after the novel itself. 'But in many a crude effort, destroyed almost as soon as
composed, I had got over any such taste as I might once have had for the ornamented and redundant in composition':

> I said to myself that my hero should work his way through life as I had seen real living men
> work theirs—that he should never get a shilling he had not earned—that no sudden turns
> should lift him in a moment to wealth and high station—that whatever small competency he
> might gain, should be won by the sweat of his brow . . .   (1)

Like Brontë's 'Farewell to Angria', this Preface has usually been read as a straightforward eschewal of 'romance'. Yet to the reader familiar with those comments on
the nature of the narrative enterprise that punctuate the writings of Glass Town and
of Angria, it seems not quite so straightforward: less a direct announcement of authorial intent than a signal that the novel which follows is to be a perhaps ironic exercise in what was in the 1840s becoming a new fictional vogue.[1] If it is addressed to
a wider public than those youthful addresses to the reader, it is—as its closing self-
image of exaggerated self-abasement suggests—equally tongue-in-cheek: 'it . . .
leans on the staff of a moderate expectation—and mutters under its breath—while
lifting its eye to that of the Public, "He that is low need fear no fall" ' (2).

For *The Professor* is more ironic and considerably more sophisticated than has
often been supposed. The circumstances of its publication—after Charlotte
Brontë's death, and in the wake of Mrs Gaskell's *Life*—meant that it was from the
first overshadowed by Brontë's more successful later novels, and read as a veiled
account of the trials of its author's life. Its first reviewers saw it as 'a mere study for
Jane Eyre or *Shirley*'; or a clumsy attempt to handle material that was later, more

[1] The romance of 'high life' was going out of fashion in the 1840s. Brontë would have been familiar
with Thackeray's mockery of the genre in *Fraser's* (see Kathleen Tillotson, *Novels of the Eighteen-Forties*
(Oxford: Clarendon Press, 1954), 85–6). She would also have been familiar with the growing vogue for
the story of the self-made man.

successfully, reworked in *Villette.* More recent, influential critics have echoed these opinions, often attributing the novel's 'flaws' to the difficulties Brontë found in writing of her experience in the voice of a male narrator—difficulties she was to surmount in her later, less abrasive, works.[2] Yet as Brontë takes pains to inform her reader in the second sentence of her Preface, *The Professor* is the work not of an inexperienced writer, but of one who had 'worn [her pen] . . . down in a practice of some years' (1). It is not a clumsy fictionalization of autobiographical concerns; or a draft for its author's later, more popular works, but a novel of a very different kind.

For the voice of the novel's narrator is as distinct from that of its author as is Lockwood's in *Wuthering Heights.* And in this, it bears a clear relation to the 'practice' to which Brontë's Preface refers. Even the earliest of the narrating personae of Glass Town are by no means figures of unquestioned masculine power, or vehicles for the expression of their creator's point of view. They are themselves objects of representation; they are often mockingly characterized, and their weaknesses and inadequacies exposed. And *The Professor* seems from the first to have been conceived as a fiction of this kind. A surviving fragment by Charlotte Brontë, which appears to be an early draft for the beginning of the novel, proposes just such an ironic view of its narrator, and draws attention to the clumsiness of his narrative:

I had the pleasure of knowing Mr Crimsworth very well—and can vouch for his having been a respectable man—though perhaps not altogether the character he seems to have thought he was. Or rather—to an impartial eye—in the midst of his good points little defects and peculiarities were visible of which he was himself excusably unconscious . . . I suppose the succeeding narrative was the work of his leisure hours after he retired from business—in its original form it extended to nearly twice its present length—but upon his trusting it to me for correction and retrenchment (which he did after finding that the various publishers to whom he offered it regarded the M.S. as a gnat and strained at it accordingly) I took the liberty of cutting out the whole of the first seven chapters with one stroke of the scissars [*sic*]— A brief summary of the import of these chapters will content the reader—[3]

Intrinsic to the novel's conception, it seems, was an objectification of its teller and an alertness to fictional form. Its awkwardness and 'abruptness' is, like Crimsworth's, 'calculated' (132); not evidence of authorial uncertainty, but indicative of the author's critical distance from the narrative she presents.

'You ask me if I do not think that men are strange beings—I do indeed, I have often thought so,' wrote Charlotte Brontë to her former teacher, Margaret Wooler, in January 1846.[4] And in *The Professor* she casts a cold eye on what was beginning to be a familiar contemporary masculine type.[5] The exemplary life of the self-made

---

[2] *CH* 344, 355, 361–3. Twentieth-century examples include Sandra Gilbert and Susan Gubar, *The Madwoman in the Attic: The Woman Writer and the Nineteenth-Century Literary Imagination* (New Haven: Yale University Press, 1979), 335; and Terry Eagleton, *Myths of Power: A Marxist Study of the Brontës* (London: Macmillan, 1987), 34.

[3] BPM MS Bonnell 109; printed in the Clarendon edition of *The Professor* as app. III, 295–6.

[4] *CBL* i. 448.

[5] For an illuminating discussion of *The Professor* as charting a 'struggle for coherent masculine identity' see Sally Shuttleworth, *Charlotte Brontë and Victorian Psychology* (Cambridge: Cambridge University Press, 1996), ch. 7.

man was becoming a well-known genre in the England of the 1840s. In 1829 the Society for the Diffusion of Useful Knowledge had launched its Library of Entertaining Knowledge with George Lillie Craik's *Pursuit of Knowledge Under Difficulties*, a compendium of biographies of scientists, scholars, engineers, and inventors, intended to inspire those without birth or connections who sought to improve their station in life. Craik's volume went into several editions (one 'with female examples') in the 1830s and 1840s, and was well known enough to be mocked by Thackeray in *Vanity Fair* (ch. 37). Similar 'lives' quickly became popular in periodicals such as the *Penny Magazine* and that favourite of the Brontës, *Chambers's Edinburgh Journal*, designed for the self-improving artisan.[6] The form was to reach its apogee in 1859 in Samuel Smiles's best-selling *Self-Help*. Despite Craik's 'female examples', in the early nineteenth century the literature of self-making was a distinctively masculine genre;[7] and it may well have had a peculiar resonance for Brontë in 1844–6. For these were years during which she and her sisters were struggling to find ways of becoming economically independent—producing the prospectus for a school (*CBL* i. 365); seeking literary publication; becoming 'Currer, Ellis and Acton Bell'. And they were also the years in which it was becoming all too evident that (as Charlotte Brontë put it in that letter to Miss Wooler) Branwell Brontë's disastrous lack of 'the faculty of self-government' was rendering him 'incapable of filling any respectable station in life'.[8] As the terms she uses to describe her brother suggest, the discourse of self-help was to her a familiar one. Indeed, the lectures that formed the basis of Smiles's best-seller of the genre were first delivered to a young men's mutual improvement society in Leeds in 1845—the year in which, very probably, only a few miles away, *The Professor* was conceived.[9]

On the surface, Brontë's first novel appears to be a fictional, first-person version of the narrative of self-help. Such ties as her protagonist has with inherited privilege are cut in the opening pages. 'Born with a wooden spoon in [his] mouth' (192), unaided and unencouraged, he must 'work his way through life' (1). His, almost too emphatically, is the story of a self-made man. Like the heroes of Craik and of Smiles, of *Chambers's Journal* and the *Penny Magazine*, he 'conquers the . . . difficulties inseparable from the commencement of almost every career' (59). The values he invokes are those of the self-help tradition—'effort' and 'application' (166, 110), 'punctuality' and 'industry' (25), 'perseverance' and 'self-control' (25, 245). And as in those exemplary 'lives', these values are vindicated by his narrative. 'Unostentatious' in 'habits' and 'temperate' in 'desires', he ends with a modest 'independency' (236–7), in comfortable country retirement with a loving helpmeet by his side.

Yet, as generations of readers have felt, there is something strangely repellent in this apparently simple story of obstacles surmounted, effort rewarded, and victory

---

[6] On the Brontës and *Chambers's Journal*, see Barker, 484; *CBL* i. 484–5; *Shirley*, 445.
[7] See Marianne Farningham, quoted in Ch. 3, 52.   [8] *CBL* i. 448.
[9] Samuel Smiles gives an account of the origins of *Self-Help* in his Introduction to the First Edition; it is reprinted in subsequent editions. On the permeation of the ideology of self-improvement and self-help into local Haworth culture, and Charlotte Brontë's connections with it, see Shuttleworth, *Charlotte Brontë and Victorian Psychology*, ch. 2.

won. Crimsworth himself is a more disquieting figure than the heroes of the self-help narratives—anxiously watchful, coolly domineering, a prey to 'Hypo-chondria' and unease. He tells his story not in the 'plain and homely' style an-nounced in the author's Preface but in a strangely agitated prose, full of suggestions of barely suppressed violence, instability, sexual threat. Moreover, the sense is inscribed at the outset that, unlike the heroes of the self-help narratives, this narrator is not one with whom the reader is straightforwardly invited to identify. For the opening pages of the novel offer an emphatic check to the inti-macy usually assumed by the first-person form. The first chapter consists almost entirely of a letter, sent, the narrator tells, 'to an old school-acquaintance'. 'To this letter', he says, 'I never got an answer'; and in a manner that suggests little confid-ence that he will find a sympathetic recipient, he proposes instead to address him-self to 'the public at large' (11). Abrupt, abrasive, distinctive, the image of the letter that is answered only by silence stands at the outset of his story less as a mark of authorial ineptness than as an exact and ironic pointer to the import of the whole.

For the world of *The Professor* is one less of reciprocity and sympathy than of estrangement and 'Antipathy' (25). And that letter to the vanished 'school-acquaintance' is like a tensely wound spring. 'I think when you and I were at Eton together, we were neither of us . . . popular characters,' says Crimsworth in its first sentence. 'You were a sarcastic, observant, shrewd, cold-blooded creature; my own portrait—I will not attempt to draw.' The adjectives describing his friend seesaw between positive and negative: of himself, he refuses to speak. And refusal becomes the energy that is the mainspring of the prose:

What animal magnetism drew thee and me together—I know not; certainly I never experi-enced anything of the Pylades and Orestes sentiment for you, and I have reason to believe that you, on your part, were equally free from all romantic regard to me . . . your sardonic coldness did not move me—I felt myself superior to that check *then* as I do *now*. (3)

The negativism of this prefigures the narrative to come. The essential configura-tion, to be repeated throughout the novel, is not of expressiveness, or relationship, but of unceasing defensive opposition: of negation, denial, repulsion, and the an-tagonistic assertion of self. This is a configuration very different from that peculiar sense of a threat to the very existence which disrupts Brontë's later first-person nar-ratives. Here, there is no looming other; not collapse of but insistence on self. The perspective is quite unlike that of the defenceless Jane Eyre or the marginalized Lucy Snowe. Yet here, as in those later novels, the 'insistent first-person stress' of the nar-rative is not merely presented, but problematized. Here, too, one can see an imagin-ative intelligence at work, but in a quite different way.

Crimsworth's story is framed throughout in imagery of resistance, rejection, re-fusal. 'I declined both the church and matrimony'; 'I do not think that my turn of mind qualifies me to make a good tradesman'; 'my uncles did not remonstrate—they and I parted with mutual disgust'; 'I form[ed] . . . a resolution no more to take bread from hands, which had refused to minister to the necessities of my dying mother'; 'my refusal of their proposals will I fancy operate as a barrier against all future intercourse'—thus his account of leaving the relatives with whom he spent his childhood (4–8). 'I repressed all—even *mental* comment on his note'; 'I anticipated no overflowings of fraternal tenderness'; 'I felt an inward satisfaction that I had not, in the first moment of meeting, betrayed any warmth, any enthusiasm'— thus, his first encounter with his brother (6–8). These quotations are taken from the opening pages of the novel, but they are characteristic of the whole. Not merely the narrator but all whom he meets habitually oppose, repulse, deny. 'Human nature is perverse,' he says (43). Even supposedly non-hostile encounters are portrayed in conflictual terms, from Crimsworth's first glimpse of his brother and his wife—'she *chid* him, half playfully, half poutingly, for being late . . . Mr Crimsworth soon *checked* her animated *scolding* with a kiss . . . She and Edward talked much—always in a vein of playful *contention*' (9, my italics)—to the novel's closing portrait of Crimsworth's relation with his son. Awareness of difference leads not to interaction but to antagonism and rejection. 'Once convinced that my friend's disposition is incompatible with my own . . . I dissolve the connection,' says Crimsworth (102). If his pupils are disobedient, he offers 'but one alternative; submission and acknowledgement of error or ignominious expulsion' (61). Teaching is a battle. The students at M. Pelet's school 'recoil with repugnance from any occupation that demand[s] close study' (60); their 'insubordination' has 'effected the dismissal of more than one English Master' (60). Those at Mdlle. Reuter's show 'a point-blank disregard of all forbearance towards each other or their teachers; an eager pursuit by each individual of her own interest and convenience, and a coarse indifference to the interest and convenience of every one else' (88). The task of the teacher there is 'to enter into conflict with this foreign will, to endeavour to bend it into subjection to her own' (120).

Even the love that sweetens Crimsworth's story is portrayed in terms akin to these. Thus, when he praises Frances Henri's work, she appears to him not gratified but 'triumphant', and he feels impelled to check her by 'reproof' (126). The scene in which he proposes to her is charged with half-suppressed violence: he holds his beloved in 'a somewhat ruthless grasp' and insists that she speak his language, not her own. She, for her part, is 'as stirless in her happiness, as a mouse in its terror' (207): the moment in which the marriage 'compact' is made is portrayed not as one of expressive interaction, but in imagery which confirms the separateness of each:

She and I were silent, nor was our silence brief. Frances' thoughts during this interval, I know not, nor did I attempt to guess them; I was not occupied in searching her countenance, nor in otherwise troubling her composure; the peace I felt, I wished her to feel; my arm, it is true, still detained her; but with a restraint that was gentle enough, so long as no opposition tightened it; my gaze was on the red fire; my heart was measuring its own content; it sounded and sounded, and found the depth fathomless.   (204)

The only 'peace' Crimsworth can offer is relief from his 'troubling' attention; his 'content' is a private treasure, to be reckoned and hoarded up within himself.

For all interaction is abrasive in the world the novel portrays. 'Her flatteries irritated my scorn, her blandishments confirmed my reserve,' says Crimsworth, characteristically, of Mdlle. Reuter (118); just so, the 'British English' at the Belgian

Pensionnat 'ward off insult with austere civility and [meet] hate with mute disdain' (94). It is by the suppression, not expression, of impulse—'forbearance'—that positive feeling is expressed (88, 215, 231, 245). Even the mild Frances Henri's first words are a series of negatives, 'uttered with emphasis, nay with vehemence': ' "Amélie Mullenberg—ask me no question and request of me no assistance for a week to come; during that space of time I will neither speak to you nor help you." ' 'A comparative silence' follows. 'Whether the calm was permanent I know not,' says Crimsworth; 'two doors now closed between me and the carré' (114). Rare moments of accord are marked by comments such as 'I put no obstacle in her way' (229); 'I agreed with him—but did not say so' (21). Good will is either so arbitrary and inexplicable as to seem a kind of perversity (Hunsden's assistance to Crimsworth is presented thus), or part of a complex system of constantly calculated 'accounts' (41, 187, 182). 'Are you grateful to me?' asks Hunsden. Crimsworth's response is telling. 'Impossible to answer his blunt question in the affirmative, so I disclaimed all tendency to gratitude' (43).

For if there is no disinterested feeling, there is equally no indifference. People watch one another continually in the world of which Crimsworth tells. 'I regarded them all with a steady . . . gaze', he says, of his Belgian pupils. 'A dog, if stared at hard enough and long enough, will show symptoms of embarrassment'; and so, at length, do they (57). 'Caution, Tact, Observation' are, he says, his 'natural sentinels', whose 'lynx-eyes' cannot be baffled by his brother's 'malignity' (26). The school to which he goes is a place of 'staring eyes' (126), in which his strategy is to watch more sharply and from a more 'commanding' position than those who are watching him. 'I carefully and deliberately made these observations before allowing myself to take one glance at the benches before me . . . I found myself cool enough to admit of looking calmly up and gazing deliberately round me' (75). 'I looked at these girls with little scruple—they looked at me with still less', is his account of his first encounter with the pupils at the Pensionnat (77); 'they talked to me . . . with their eyes, by means of which organs they could . . . say very audacious and coquettish things', but he answers 'the glance of vanity with the gaze of stoicism' and emerges victorious (108). 'I watched her as keenly as she watched me,' he says of Mdlle. Reuter; and the struggle for power they engage in is conducted by means of looks: 'Her eye, fastened on my face, demanded of every feature the meaning of my changed and careless manner. "I will give her an answer," thought I, and, meeting her gaze full; arresting, fixing her glance, I shot into her eyes from my own a look where there was no respect, no love, no tenderness, no gallantry' (103).

But more often looking is less a mode than a refusal of interaction. When others threaten to impinge Crimsworth makes them objects of observation. Thus, he tells of a moment when the 'disgust' inspired by his brother threatens his self-command. 'I looked at him', he recounts, 'I measured his robust frame and powerful proportions'; and the reader's momentary anticipation of incipient physical combat stresses the violence implicit in the objectification of this other with which the paragraph concludes: 'I saw my own reflection in the mirror over the mantelpiece; I amused myself with comparing the two pictures . . . his cold, avaricious eye, his

stern, forbidding manner told me he would not spare' (13). 'Her gaze was ever waiting for mine, and it frequently succeeded in arresting it', he says of Adèle, his
'Gorgon-like' pupil; but rather than allowing himself to be petrified he reads the
face before him as a series of physiognomical signs (91).[10] He is stirred and intrigued
by Hunsden; but instead of betraying feeling he employs himself in a 'rapid scrutiny
of his physiognomy', reading the marks of character in his face (29). When this disturbing other visits him in Belgium, Crimsworth's first act is to polish his spectacles,
'to get a clear notion of his mien and countenance'. 'I was sitting . . . with my back
to the light, and I had *him* vis-à-vis', he says: 'a position he would much rather have
had reversed, for at any time, he preferred scrutinizing, to being scrutinized' (186).
Even—especially—when moved by passion, Crimsworth adopts this strategy. 'On
the brink of falling in love' with Zoraïde, he renews his 'observations' of her. 'She
knows that I watch her; how calm she is under scrutiny!' he marvels; and he spies on
her, unobserved (99). Such imagery reaches its climax in his account of his developing relation to the woman who becomes his wife. She first appears as a shadowy
figure, of whom 'I never had more than a passing glimpse'; 'I had no opportunity of
studying her character, or even of observing her person much' (94). 'Today I had on
my spectacles,' he remarks a little later; 'her appearance therefore was clear to me at
the first glance'. Now, characteristically, he reads her physiognomy, attempting to
'decipher' her 'sentiments . . . in her countenance' (124). When she looks at him, his
response is to scrutinize her—'She looked at me; her eye said most plainly, "I cannot follow you"'; when she 'appeals' to him, he 'disregards' the appeal. (113). And
these preliminaries are succeeded by a series of scenes in which he spies on his
beloved—watching her grief in the cemetery: 'eavesdropping' on her singing; when
he takes his friend Hunsden to meet her, placing himself in a 'position [from which]
I could see them both'; even, years afterward, following and observing as she bids
her son goodnight.

   Crimsworth's is not presented as a peculiar or eccentric stance, but as endemic to
the world through which he moves. Observation and objectification of the other are
central to the dynamics of the society of the novel, from the factory counting-house
with its vigilant 'taskmaster', to the schoolrooms of Belgium with their
institutionalized surveillance,[11] to the pedagogy that the narrator proposes for his
son. For the novel's concern is not merely with the psychology of its teller—
Crimsworth's half-denied eroticism, his thwarted desire for tenderness, his recurrent 'Hypochondria'—but with the implications of the strategies that his case
exemplifies. The fundamental premise of his narrative—the primacy of the
perspective of the antagonistic individual, a perspective opposed to rather
than modified by that of others—is emphasized in a way that exceeds psychological

---

[10] On 'phrenological contemplation' of the other as a means of asserting 'social and psychological
dominance' in *The Professor*, see Shuttleworth, *Charlotte Brontë and Victorian Psychology*, 125–7 and
132–5.
   [11] 'I . . . took possession of the empty chair and isolated desk raised on an estrade of one step high, so
as to command one division; the other division being under the surveillance of a Maîtresse, similarly elevated,' says Crimsworth of his first day in Mdlle. Reuter's Pensionnat (74).

realism, underlined in the novel's imagery, writ large in its form. And it is interrogated with an irony akin to that of Glass Town, an irony that is directed not merely against this narrator, but against the ideology that his narrative inscribes.

For the individual thus defined appears in *The Professor* as a problematic entity. Thus, Crimsworth describes his first day in his brother's counting-house:

A sentiment of keen pleasure accompanied this first effort to earn my own living—a sentiment neither poisoned nor weakened by the presence of the taskmaster who stood and watched me for some time as I wrote. I thought he was trying to read my character but I felt as secure against his scrutiny as if I had had on a casque with the visor down—or rather I shewed him my countenance with the confidence that one would show an unlearned man a letter written in Greek—he might see lines, and trace characters, but he could make nothing of them—my nature was not his nature, and its signs were to him like the words of an unknown tongue; erelong he turned away abruptly, as if baffled, and left the counting-house. (17)

Ostensibly, the moment is one of 'keen pleasure': that satisfied awareness of self-dependence familiar in stories of self-help. But Crimsworth's description focuses less on his own activity than on evasion of this other's 'scrutiny'. Even positive feeling here takes on the character of antagonism—'neither poisoned nor weakened'; the moment becomes a battle which he must face with his 'visor down'. As the narrator asserts his impregnable independence, the prose in which he does so registers a more disquieting state of affairs. For the paragraph and the chapter end not with an account of this 'effort to earn [his] own living', or the 'pleasure' and 'security' he claims to feel, but with an almost obsessive concentration on the antagonistic other of this scene:

he returned to it but twice in the course of that day—each time he mixed and swallowed a glass of brandy and water—the materials for making which, he extracted from a cupboard on one side of the fireplace; having glanced at my translations—he could read both French and German—he went out again in silence.   (17)

Nothing comes of this confrontation; it ends, like most such in this novel, with an abrupt turning away. And the next chapter opens, not—like one of Craik's or Smiles's biographies—by describing the young clerk's labours, but with an account of those about him, and their insistent but ineffectual attempts to find him out:

Mr Crimsworth watched sharply for defects but found none; he set Timothy Steighton, his favourite and head man, to watch also, Tim was baffled . . . Mr Crimsworth made enquiries as to how I lived, whether I got into debt . . . Mr Crimsworth employed Tim to find out whether my landlady had any complaint to make on the score of my morals; she answered that she believed I was a very religious man, and asked Tim, in her turn, if he thought I had any intention of going into the church some day.   (18)

The taskmaster's watchfulness, his brother's enquiries, his landlady's speculations, Hunsden's curiosity—all these receive more attention than his own 'punctuality' and 'diligence'; such satisfaction as he has derives not from what he accomplishes but from evasion of their scrutiny (18).

It is an achievement, in this world, to present 'a calm and sober surface' (2). Crimsworth greets his brother 'with a quiet and steady phlegm', betraying no 'warmth', no 'enthusiasm' (8). He becomes a 'statue' in face of 'the Millowner's blasphemous sarcasms' (19); when Mdlle. Reuter woos him 'like a fascinated bird', he finds himself transformed to 'a rigid pillar of stone' (118). 'I masked my visage with indifference' he says of his interest in Frances (116). He shows 'no eagerness' when he goes to court her; 'she took her cue from me,' he says, and 'evinced no surprise' (201). Mdlle. Reuter keeps 'her temper calm, her brow smooth, her manner tranquil' (95), and Crimsworth marvels at her 'wondrous self-control' (104). Even when her feelings are most turbulent, 'her face and forehead, clothed with a mask of purely negative expression' are 'as blank of comment as her lips' (138). And if in her he condemns this as hypocrisy—'the broad, sober-hued flag of dissimulation . . . hung low over the citadel' (146)—he praises a similar impassivity in Frances, 'personification of discretion and forethought, of diligence and perseverance, of self-denial and self-control' (156).

Yet as Crimsworth sits in self-contained silence, awaiting his first meeting with his brother, the prose is convulsive, not calm:

I anticipated no overflowings of fraternal tenderness—Edward's letters had always been such as to prevent the engendering or harbouring of delusions of this sort. Still, as I sat awaiting his arrival, I felt eager—very eager—I cannot tell you why; my hand, so utterly a stranger to the grasp of a kindred hand, clenched itself to repress the tremor with which impatience would fain have shaken it.   (7)

'Her present demeanour towards me was deficient neither in dignity nor propriety', he says of Mdlle. Reuter, disappointed in her designs; but he looks forward to the moment when this propriety will be shattered. 'Decorum now repressed, and Policy masked it, but Opportunity would be too strong for either of these—Temptation would shiver their restraints' (173). Even as he admires Frances's 'self-denial and self-control' (156) he sees 'with a sort of strange pleasure , revolt, scorn, austerity, bitterness lay energetic claim to a place in her feelings and physiognomy' (185). For his is a narrative concerned less with 'decorum' and indifference than with the violence of repression by which they are produced; less with the surface of 'self-control' than with the 'agitation' beneath (2).

Crimsworth's 'professes' to be a tale of self-dependence and self-sufficiency, of effort that issues in satisfaction and success. But syntax, imagery, and narrative structure tell a rather different story: not of triumphant achievement, but of thwarting and conflict, not of security arrived at, but of continuing, irresolvable unease. Certainly, he presents the negation of impulse as a positive assertion of choice and control. Discovering that Mdlle. Reuter is secretly 'affianced' to his employer, he adopts a position of lordly self-restraint. 'I had no intention,' says the penniless English master, 'of getting up a scene with M. Pelet, reproaching him with perfidy, sending him a challenge or performing other gambadoes of the sort' (102). To reject and deny is to exercise power—over one's actions, over one's feelings, over others. It is the primary assertion of individuality: that which enables the public mask to be different from the private self. Yet, as Freud has famously argued—and as the example just given demonstrates—the denial of an intention reveals its unconscious presence. In literature, alone among the arts, that which is negated can be given its full imaginative weight. And in this novel dominated by negatives Charlotte Brontë exploits this fact to striking effect. The repeated use of the negative, here and throughout Crimsworth's narrative, gives a peculiar fictional life to the seething drama of impulse denied that 'propriety' must conceal.

The façade Mdlle. Reuter presents to the world is one of impassivity: 'As neither surprise, pleasure, approbation nor interest were evinced in her countenance, so no more were disdain, envy, annoyance, weariness' (138). But the effect of this description is not one of tranquillity. Its subject appears less as a coherent individual than as a collection of potentialities—that succession of conflicting feelings which the reader of the sentence is invited to entertain. 'What are you then?' demands Hunsden, rebuking the narrator's apparent passivity:

You sit at that desk in Crimsworth's Counting-house day by day and week by week; scraping with a pen on paper, just like an automaton; you never get up, you never say you are tired, you never ask for a holiday, you never take change or relaxation; you give way to no excess of an evening; you neither keep wild company nor indulge in strong drink.   (30)

And the sequence of negatives opens up a series of rejected possibilities, enacting in miniature the strategies of denial, of repression of impulse and refusal of expressiveness, through which the man he addresses defines and maintains his social identity. 'A professor does not meet his pupil to see her . . . with hair perfumed and curled, neck scarcely shaded by aerial lace,' says Crimsworth:

it is not his business to whirl her through the waltz, to feed her with compliments, to heighten her beauty by the flush of gratified vanity. Neither does he encounter her . . . clad in her becoming walking dress—her scarf thrown with grace over her shoulders, her little bonnet scarcely screening her curls, the red rose under its brim adding a new tint to the softer rose on her cheek . . . it is not his office to walk by her side, to listen to her lively chat, to carry her parasol. (109)

And his extended negative description throws an ironic light upon his subsequent assertion of 'the integrity and moderation of my conduct at Mdlle. Reuter's Pensionnat de demoiselles' (110). It is not merely that in the world of *The Professor* impulses are restrained. The 'integrity' of self itself is questioned in this peculiar centrifugal prose.

'I met him collectedly,' Crimsworth reports, of his second meeting with his brother (12), and his adverb picks up the sense implicit in much of his narrative, of 'I' not as singular, but plural: a mass of conflicting possibilities, which must be corralled together to compose a public self. 'Mdlle. Reuter turned her eye laterally on me, to ascertain probably whether *I was collected* enough to be ushered into her sanctum sanctorum,' he tells of the moment when she introduces him to her class. 'I suppose she judged me to be *in a tolerable state of self-government*, for she opened the door and I followed her through' (74). When M. Pelet speaks of the attractions of his Belgian pupils, 'the question *discomposed me*,' he says (86, my italics throughout).

For Crimsworth, as for those about him, self-reliance—not being indebted to or dependent upon others—is not merely the key to success: it is essential to his whole mode of being. The words he uses to describe this desirable state—keywords of early Victorian economic individualism—are charged with existential resonances. To be economically self-sufficient is to possess a 'competency' (32, 167)—not merely enough to live on, but also the capacity to act. To have an income is to have an 'independency' (229)—not simply financial resources, but autonomy as well. When Crimsworth is penniless, his plight presents itself as 'a pang of *mortification* at the humility of my position and the inadequacy of my means; while with that pang was born a strong desire to do more, earn more, *be more*, possess more' (161, my italics). But the mode of being thus defined appears in his telling as a problematic one. Within the world he describes, economic self-sufficiency is dependent on self-denial: 'as it had ever been abhorrent to my nature to ask pecuniary assistance, I had early acquired habits of self-denying economy; husbanding my monthly allowance with anxious care; in order to obviate the danger of being forced, in some moment of future exigency, to beg additional aid' (18). The feeling is less of autonomy than of continual, anxious defence against perpetually present threat. Just so, the repeated entertainment of denied possibility by which Crimsworth's narrative proceeds complicates the onward thrust of his story with a constant, undertowing sense of energies repressed. The self whose mode of existence is one of abnegation and refusal appears within this prose as neither expressively self-actualizing nor freely self-determining. That which it is not, or cannot or will not do, seems altogether more potent than that which it does or is. It is less an independent agent than the tensely held-together product of a whole constellation of antagonistic relationships.

The 'self-made man' of this narrative is ineluctably social: this is the 'infernal' import of Crimsworth's 'plain and homely' tale. He praises the 'British English' in the girls' school where he teaches for their 'general air of native propriety and decency'; by this, he declares, 'I could at a glance distinguish the daughter of Albion and nursling of Protestantism from the foster-child of Rome' (94). The imagery surrounding this passage underscores and elaborates a primary, now rare or obsolete, meaning of 'propriety'—'the fact of belonging or relating specially to a particular thing or person', 'essence or individuality' (*OED*). The self is here a private possession, to be defended against attack and preserved distinct and inviolable: 'proud, too, was the aspect of these British girls—at once envied and ridiculed by their continental associates, they *warded off* insult with *austere* civility and met hate with mute *disdain*; they *eschewed company-keeping* and in the midst of numbers seemed to dwell *isolated*' (94, my italics). But this constellation of meanings is almost the reverse of that which the word had come to bear by Charlotte Brontë's time, and which she emphasizes, equally tellingly, elsewhere. 'I thought I had never seen two such *models* of propriety', says Crimsworth of Hunsden's first meeting with Frances, 'for Hunsden (thanks to the *constraint* of the foreign tongue), was *obliged to shape* his phrases and *measure* his sentences with a *care* that *forbade any eccentricity*' (217, my italics). Here, the stress is not on individuality but on its antithesis—conformity to others' rules and requirements. In both cases the restraint of free expressiveness is the same, as is the word that is chosen to describe it—'propriety'. The sense of self as 'isolated', quintessentially private property, appears as inextricable from its opposite—a sense of self as constrained by convention, and not independent at all. Unobtrusively but precisely the novel seems to be pointing to a fundamental contradiction in that self-sufficient individualism which Crimsworth seeks to affirm. It is a play with significations that echoes that other, economic, irony which runs through Crimsworth's story: that his vaunted independent 'exertion' is in fact wage slavery.[12]

Crimsworth's is a rhetoric of will-power, exertion, perseverance: one that expresses and underlines the 'self-help' message that success in life is under the individual's control. Yet like that of individual 'independence', this rhetoric is undermined in his narrative by a fundamental irony, which can likewise be focused in the novel's play with a single word. 'My path was gradually growing smooth before me,' says Crimsworth. 'I, in a few weeks, conquered the teasing difficulties inseparable from the commencement of almost any career' (59). The last word in his sentence is usually used today to mean 'a course of professional life or employment, which affords opportunity for progress or advancement in the world' (*OED*). But that meaning was, in the mid-nineteenth century, a relatively recent one. Its primary meaning—one with a far longer history—is of 'a running, a course (usually implying swift motion)' (*OED*)—like a comet's course through the heavens, with an impetus of its own. A 'career' in this sense has connotations of speed, of unstoppability; it is seen from a distance, rather than experienced from within. The suggestion—underlined in colloquialisms such as 'in full career'—is not of individual control. And it is this constellation of meanings that is stressed in Crimsworth's narrative. If he uses the word in its 'modern' sense—looking at the smoky town of 'X—' as 'the scene of his life's career' (12); feeling, when he gains employment at Mdlle. Reuter's school, 'as if some cheerful, eventful, upward-tending career were even then opening to me' (72)—its older connotations keep coming to the fore. Thus, he asks himself whether his brother's bearing towards him 'shall turn me at once aside from the path I have chosen'; and his reply to himself momentarily configures a process that is independent of him: 'No—at least, ere I deviate, I will advance far enough to see *whither my career tends*' (16–17). Thus, the major part of his story of effort and achievement is imaged as a 'Progress' in which he and his wife are swept unresisting along:

---

[12] As Mary Poovey points out in *Uneven Developments: The Ideological Work of Gender in Mid-Victorian England* (London: Virago, 1989), the notion of the 'proprietary self' formulated by Locke in his *Second Treatise of Government*—'every man has a property in his own person'—'structurally . . . amounted to every individual being constituted as a divided subject: this internal difference was the basis for the 'free' exchange of labor and therefore the production of surplus value, but it was also the basis for the alienation every man experienced in the market economy. Because his labor could be expropriated . . . for someone else's profit, and because a man's gain was subject to both the dictates of other people and the vicissitudes of the economy, the individual could experience himself as hostage to incomprehensible forces and frustrating restraints' (76).

Ten years rush now upon me with dusty, vibrating, unresting wings; years of bustle, action, unslacked endeavour; years in which I and my wife, having launched ourselves in the full career of Progress, as Progress whirls on in European Capitals, scarcely knew repose, were strangers to amusement, never thought of indulgence, and yet, as our course ran side by side, as we marched hand in hand, we neither murmured, repented, nor faltered.

'Success', he says, ' bestowed every now and then encouraging reward on diligence' (230); but the sense is less of 'endeavour' bringing about achievement than of the unpredictable appearance of fortune's occasional gifts. It is a sense that is underlined not merely by the repeated disruptive appearance of Hunsden like a wild card in Crimsworth's story, but by the recurrence within that story of an equally disruptive language of chance and contingency.

'I had not forced Circumstances, Circumstances had freed me': this is Crimsworth's reflection on leaving his brother's mill (39). 'Circumstances must guide me,' he says to himself, as he wonders what to do about Pelet's 'perfidy' (102–3). 'Our likings are regulated by our circumstances,' he observes, thinking of 'the charms that attract his notice and win his regard' (110). He rebels, 'almost ungovernably' against remaining in Pelet's service: 'but who is free from the constraint of circumstances?' he asks (171). Such remarks as these provide a constant, subversive counterpoint to his narrative of agency; and their implications are picked up and writ large in more florid images of fate. The hero of the self-help narratives takes advantage of accident and seizes control of destiny. 'Fortune is usually on the side of the industrious,' Samuel Smiles declares.[13] And it is in the spirit of such heroes that Crimsworth seeks employment: 'no disappointment arrested me; defeat following fast on defeat served as stimulants to will. I asked, I persevered, I remonstrated, I dunned. It is so that openings are forced into the guarded circle where Fortune sits dealing favours round' (196). But the sense more often is less of effective self-help than of helpless subjection to chance. 'The current of life and the impulse of destiny had swept her forever beyond my reach,' he says, of the disaster of Frances's disappearance (155); 'at that hour my bark hung on the topmost curl of a wave of fate, and I knew not on what shoal the onward rush of the billow might hurl it,' of the uncertainties that attend a hiatus in his 'career' (198). His search for new employment is a period of 'many alternations', during which, he says, his 'existence . . . resembled a sky . . . haunted by meteors and falling stars': 'Hopes and fears, expectations and disappointments descended in glancing showers from zenith to horizon; but all were transient, and darkness followed swift each vanishing apparition' (196). A rhetoric of fortune, quite different from that of self-making, here comes flooding into his narrative: indeed, the passage is later to be echoed in a different key in Lucy Snowe's description of the lottery—'the alternations of hope and fear raised by each turn of the wheel' (V 222). 'At the very crisis', Crimsworth concludes, 'when I had tried my last effort and knew not what more to do, Fortune looked in at me one morning . . . and threw a prize into my lap' (197). The description is less of an active struggle to

---

[13] Samuel Smiles, *Self-Help. With Illustrations of Conduct and Perseverance* (London: John Murray, 1907), 111.

'master . . . the ascent of the hill of Difficulty' (1) than of a far less heroic submission to what life chances to bring. The narrator's 'career' appears at such moments as these less as a self-determined progress into an expansive future than as constrained and determined by the turning of fortune's wheel. This sense is precisely imaged, with characteristic Brontëian literalism, in Crimsworth's peculiar view from his room at M. Pelet's: 'I had now only the option of looking at a bare gravelled court, with an enormous "pas de géant" in the middle and the monotonous walls and windows of a boys' school-house round' (59). A 'pas de géant' was a pole with ropes attached to a revolving wheel at its head. Propelling or being propelled (the ambiguity is suggestive), those who held on would take 'giant strides' in a circle around.

For if Crimsworth's is a linear story, in which effort leads to success, the logic of that story seems to be a circular one. It begins with an account of an oppositional 'friendship' and of a family divided by hostilities; and it ends with a similar, if more ambiguous, set of images. Crimsworth's domestic idyll is shot through with a kind of amorous antagonism. His wife, we are told, loves her English professor 'too absolutely to fear him *much*'. She would 'vex, tease, pique me', he says; and he responds with 'chastisement' (233, my italics). The only fruit of this union is named, suggestively, Victor; he, like his father, is to be sent to Eton, where he will be 'soundly disciplined' and given a radical grounding in 'the art of self-control' (245). If this tale of success is also, ostensibly, one of the achievement of domestic happiness, it ends, as it began, with an isolated watching individual: one who spies upon his wife and relates to his child by attempting to break his will.

The private sphere appears in this novel less a space of possibility than a peculiarly tense enclosure, which mirrors rather than opposes the conflicts of society at large. Such images of that society as are offered are of estrangement and conflict rather than connectedness. The England of *The Professor* is a place of cut-throat commercial enterprise, in which 'Concern' has a one-dimensionally economic meaning (12); a place not of living affective ties but of atomized individuals; thus, 'X—' is described as 'a mushroom place . . . concerning whose inhabitants it was proverbially said, that not one in a thousand knew his own grandfather' (23). Belgium likewise seems dedicated to the competitive pursuit of self-interest: to 'get on' means to gain and maintain the 'advantage' over others likewise intent. One is reminded of a famous passage from Carlyle's *Past and Present*, published in 1843: 'We call it a Society; and go about professing openly the totalest separation, isolation. Our life is not a mutual helpfulness; but rather, cloaked under due laws-of-war, named 'fair competition' and so forth, it is a mutual hostility.'[14] Just so, in *The Professor*, there is repression and repulsion instead of mutuality; instead of a connecting energy, the hostile tension of impulse denied. Instead of Dickens's great metaphors of circulation and stoppage, or George Eliot's of the social web, there is a singular story of individual self-help. Yet this appears to be less the result of a fail-

---

[14] 'Gospel of Mammonism', *Past and Present*, in Alan Shelston (ed.), *Thomas Carlyle: Selected Writings* (Harmondsworth: Penguin, 1971), 277.

ure on Charlotte Brontë's part to imagine a social world than the precise artistic expression of her view of the logic thereof. For what she suggests, with an exactitude
that echoes Carlyle's outrage, is that a 'Society' composed of competing, self-
interested individuals has no larger coherence at all.

The world of *The Professor* is one of ominous instability. This sense, which runs
through Crimsworth's story, comes to the fore in the final chapter, where he portrays the success to which his efforts have led. In the closing pages of the novel there
are a series of disquieting images of violence and unease. The narrator interrupts his
portrait of marital bliss to ask what his wife might have been 'had she married a
harsh, envious, careless man; a profligate, a prodigal, a drunkard or a tyrant' (235).
Their friend Hunsden visits because, 'according to him, it gets on time to work me
into lunacy by treading on my mental corns, or to force from Mrs Crimsworth, rev-
elations of the dragon within her, by insulting the memory of Hofer and Tell' (239).
He shows them the portrait of the woman he loved but '*could* not' marry: 'I am sure
Lucia once wore chains and broke them', is Frances Crimsworth's 'strange' response (241). 'I never saw a child smile less than he does', says Crimsworth of his son
(242); and he notes the 'ominous sparks' emitted by Victor's 'electrical ardour and
power' (245). 'Oh papa! I'll never forgive you! I'll never forgive you!' declares the
boy, when his father shoots his rabid dog (243). 'He must soon go to Eton', says his
father, looking forward with 'strong repugnance' to this 'fearful operation', which
will mean 'utter wretchedness' for the boy (245). Victor's 'preference' for the provoking Hunsden alarms his father and causes his mother 'unexpressed anxiety':
whilst he is by, 'she roves with restless movement round like a dove guarding its
young from the hovering hawk' (146). And as the novel draws to an end, the 'hawk'
breaks in upon domestic peace: 'But Hunsden comes—I hear his step and there he
is, bending through the lattice, from which he has thrust away the woodbine with
unsparing hand—disturbing two bees and a butterfly' (246).

Like the unanswered letter of the opening chapter, these final images are more in-
tegrally related to the rest of the novel than might at first appear. They are prefigured in the 'Hypochondria' that 'accosts' and 'tyrannizes' Crimsworth; in the
unexplained tears that Frances sheds on the morning of her wedding day, in the 'eccentric vigour' that she occasionally, disconcertingly, displays. And they are prefigured perhaps more pervasively in passages such as the following, where the
narrative's agitated entertainment of what does not or should not take place takes
on a frenzied life of its own:

we . . . rarely suffer the acrid bitterness of hopeless anguish; unless indeed, we have plunged
like beasts into sensual indulgence, abused, strained, stimulated, again overstrained and at
last destroyed our faculties for enjoyment . . . Our agony is great and how can it end? We have
broken the spring of our powers; life must be all suffering—too feeble to conceive faith—
death must be darkness—God, spirits, religion can have no place in our collapsed minds
where linger only hideous and polluting recollections of vice; and Time brings us on to the
brink of the grave and Dissolution flings us in—a rag eaten through and through with disease, wrung together with pain, stamped into the churchyard sod by the inexorable heel of
Despair. (147)

Such passages as these underscore the irony of that Preface in which Charlotte Brontë announced her intention to deal with the sober 'real'. This 'plain and homely' tale of self-sufficiency and success contains, it seems, another story, far 'stranger', more 'startling', more 'harrowing' (1–2), a story less of straightforward progress than of constant, tense self-discipline. For the world configured in this novel is one in which the 'fierce revolt' of feeling must be constantly subdued by violence: not merely by the inner violence of self-government and self-restraint, but by an external violence whose nature is focused and imaged in Crimsworth's reflections on his son.

The presence of that child in the concluding pages of *The Professor* provides a suggestive key to the import of the whole. This is not merely the story of a singular individual, but of how the world he inhabits is sustained and reproduced. Crimsworth's triumphant narrative of self-defence and independence leads inexorably to an image of defencelessness and dependence; not of a self-made man, but of the upbringing of a child. Such an image has no place in the classic self-help narrative. Childhood there is dealt with perfunctorily; as preliminary to, not part of, the real business of life. Crimsworth barely mentions his 'lonely, parentless' boyhood (211): his aim is to chart his progress towards 'independence' and success. Yet his treatment of his son, exactly mirroring his own self-suppression, brings to the fore the logic of the story he has told. Victor, he says, has 'a something in [his] temper' that Hunsden 'calls . . . his spirit and says . . . should not be curbed'. 'I call it the leaven of the offending Adam', says Crimsworth, 'and consider that it should be if not *whipped* out of him, at least soundly disciplined; and that he will be cheap of any amount of either bodily or mental suffering which will ground him radically in the art of self-control.'[15] The child must, he says, be separated from his mother, for she will 'accustom him to a style of treatment, a forbearance, a congenial tenderness, he will meet with from none else.' Within the family, Victor may be 'subjugated' by love. But love is a poor preparation for life in this society. For as Crimsworth asks, with a bleak directness that irradiates not merely his own assumptions but the world that sustains and is shaped by them, 'will reason or love be the weapons with which in future the world will meet his violence?' (245). His victory in life's struggle has led not to an affirmation of that achieved self-sufficiency which his narrative seeks to celebrate, but to a disconcerting confrontation with the violence within and without on which that achievement is based.

What we have been tracing in *The Professor* is not clumsy self-expressiveness, but a highly intellectual art. For Brontë's first, stubbornly defended, novel evinces a striking development from her youthful literary play. The ironic treatment of the narrator, pivotal in her early writings, has become an incisive, pointed questioning of the central presuppositions of one of the most prominent discourses of her time; the self-reflexive comments on the nature of the fictional enterprise that punctuate Glass Town and Angria, an assured exploitation of some of narrative's most dis-

---

[15]   On the links between evangelical doctrine and commercial success in this period, see Boyd Hilton, *The Age of Atonement: the Influence of Evangelicalism on Social and Economic Thought, 1795–1865* (Oxford: Clarendon Press, 1988), 32.

tinctive possibilities. This is a novel quite different from those that Brontë's contemporaries were writing in these years. The moral concerns that shape, for instance, Dickens' explorations of the nature of the self-made man—his tracing of the tragedy of Dombey, with his 'stiff-necked sullen arrogance', his bleakly comic exposure of the dreadful Josiah Bounderby—are notably absent here. The logic of *The Professor* is less moral or exploratory than demonstrative. Succint and unaccommodating, it foregrounds contradiction rather than developing character; it demands intellectual grasp rather than imaginative sympathy. With its almost 'theoretical' economy, its peculiar half-suppressed tension, its emphatically constricted viewpoint, it is a novel of a kind that Charlotte Brontë was not to attempt again. But the sharp analytic intelligence that is evident within it informs her later works.

CHAPTER THREE

Triumph and Jeopardy:
The Shape of *Jane Eyre*

Charlotte Brontë's account of what her first novel was not could serve as a description of her second. Those 'sudden turns' denied to Crimsworth—unearned wealth, a transformative marriage, excessive happiness—are central to Jane Eyre's story. This is no chilly narrative of self-help, but a much more compelling tale of the 'wild wonderful and thrilling', the 'strange, startling and harrowing';[1] of starvation and destitution, and the glamour of aristocratic life. The awkward abrasiveness of that earlier novel is here replaced by a passionate directness, 'more imaginative and poetical', 'more consonant with . . . sentiments more tender—elevated—unworldly' (*P* 1–2) than the cool, unromantic irony with which Edward Crimsworth was seen.

Indeed, *Jane Eyre* seems hardly to question its narrator's point of view. There is nothing here like that deliberate refusal of intimacy with the reader with which *The Professor* opens, nothing like Crimsworth's constant denial of feelings evoked in the prose. As generations of readers have attested, identification with Jane is difficult to resist—not least because she first appears not as an unattractively defensive adult, but as a vulnerable, mistreated child. 'You are a dependant, mama says; you have no money; your father left you none; you ought to beg, and not to live here with gentlemen's children like us,' John Reed tells Jane (11). 'You are under obligations to Mrs Reed: she keeps you,' warns Bessie. 'If she were to turn you off, you would have to go to the poor-house' (13). The England depicted here is that of the New Poor Law, in which the cold calculations of political economy have replaced the traditional conception of 'charity' as a God-given responsibility to help the less fortunate; and the 'poorhouse' is a place of deterrence, not a refuge for those in need.[2] 'Charity', here, is something chilling and mystifying, less to be welcomed than feared. 'It is partly a charity-school,' says Helen Burns, seeking to explain Lowood Institution to the bewildered child who has just begun to experience its rigours (50); 'cold charity must be entreated before I could get a lodging', Jane

---

[1] 'The feeling was not like an electric shock; but it was quite as sharp, as strange, as startling', says Jane of the moment when she hears Rochester's call (419).

[2] The debates surrounding the introduction of the New Poor Law were familiar to Charlotte Brontë, both through *Blackwood's Magazine*, which had in the 1820s and 1830s championed the old Poor Laws; and more immediately through her father, who had in the late 1830s played an active part in local opposition to the Poor Law Amendment Act of 1834. (Barker, 265–9).

agonizes, on her flight from Thornfield (323); when her parents die, it is 'Charity . . . cold as [a] snowdrift' that receives the infant Jane (379). Orphans, here, are abused and starved, and the destitute treated with hostile suspicion; those without power or position seen as hardly human at all. A 'rat', John Reed calls his cousin (11); 'like a mad cat', says Bessie (12); ten years later her aunt recalls the fear the child's outburst inspired in her— 'as if an animal that I had struck or pushed had looked up at me with human eyes and cursed me in a man's voice' (239). A governess is a mere 'creature', able to 'bear anything'—thus, even the amiable daughters of the Eshton family (178). And the workings of the larger society seem merely the large-scale expression of such dehumanizing habits of thought. 'Brought face to face with Necessity', Jane sums up its measure of human value in a telling series of appositions: 'I stood in the position of one without a resource: without a friend; without a coin' (326). The world through which she journeys, alone and destitute, is one in which there can be no reliance on others; in which want is met with suspicion and it is humiliating to ask for aid. 'I blamed none of those who repulsed me,' she says. 'I felt it was what was to be expected' (328). As she lies perishing of 'want and cold' (330)— within sound of a church-bell, at the door of a parsonage, in a 'civilized' Christian country—her plight becomes the index of a whole society's failure to sustain the values of community.

It appears that in this, her second novel, Charlotte Brontë is deliberately choosing to emphasize the dark underside of that gospel of self-sufficiency which Crimsworth sought to celebrate in his tale of successful self-help. Here, early nineteenth-century English society is seen not from the point of view of one of its makers and shapers, but from that of one whose claims on human existence it would deny. Yet from a twenty-first century perspective, it is hard to see in Jane's narrative the straightforward 'moral Jacobinism' that one contemporary found. For this heroine's account of her sufferings is shaped by her society's assumptions, even as her experiences might seem to question them. Thus, as she wanders starving on the moor, one voice within her insists on her right—indeed, her duty—to preserve life: 'But I was a human being, and had a human being's wants: I must not linger where there was nothing to supply them . . . Life . . . was yet in my possession, with all its requirements, and pains, and responsibilities. The burden must be carried; the want provided for; the suffering endured; the responsibility fulfilled' (324–5). But this voice is countered by another, with a different definition of 'right': one that judges human interaction by the standards of an instrumental calculation: 'I wandered away: always repelled by the consciousness of having no claim to ask— no right to expect interest in my isolated lot . . . As to the woman who would not take my handkerchief in exchange for her bread, why, she was right, if the offer appeared to her sinister, or the exchange unprofitable' (327, 329). That sense of 'dependence' as shame that was instilled in the child in the opening pages is echoed here, as the narrating Jane unquestioningly equates need with debasement. Her frantic efforts to obtain work and food are to her a 'moral degradation'; to 'ask relief for want of which I was sinking' is, to her, to be 'brought low' (327–8). 'I felt it would be degrading', she says, 'to faint with hunger on the causeway of a hamlet' (325):

privation, it seems, must be hidden from others' gaze. If this is psychologically realistic, it is from the perspective of hindsight hardly the voice of that revolutionary anger which some contemporaries found in the novel—'the tone of the mind and thought which has overthrown authority and violated every code human and divine abroad, and fostered Chartism and rebellion at home' (*CH* 109–10).

Of course, in presenting the story of a *woman*'s struggle for independence, Charlotte Bronte was offering a much more overt challenge to early Victorian expectations than she had in *The Professor*'s masculine tale of self-help. Sixty years after the publication of *Jane Eyre*, Marianne Farningham, author of a best-selling book of advice for girls, was to recall of her girlhood in the 1840s:

My father gave us two monthly magazines published by the Sunday School Union, the 'Teacher's Offering' and the 'Child's Companion'. In one of these was a series of descriptive articles on men who had been poor boys, and risen to be rich and great. Every month I hoped to find the story of some poor ignorant girl, who, beginning life as handicapped as I, had yet been able by her own efforts and the blessing of God upon them to live a life of usefulness, if not of greatness. But I believe there was not a woman in the entire series.[3]

The view that woman was not formed for independence was propounded again and again in early nineteenth-century England, not so much as an economic doctrine (for it was acknowledged that in unfortunate circumstances even the middle-class woman might be forced to earn her own living), but as a moral, religious, or psychological truth. 'All independence is unfeminine: the more dependent that sex becomes, the more will it be cherished,' declares the anonymous author of *Woman as She Is and As She Should Be* (1835);[4] 'If the Bible did not say that she was created for man, and that the wife ought to be in subjection to her husband, her nature would testify no less plainly that she yearned to be dependent on, and, by consequence, subject to, the other sex,' opines William Landels, a quarter of a century later, in *Woman's Sphere and Work Considered in the Light of Scriptures* (1859).[5] Such views found a different, but perhaps even more compelling, inflection in the language of Byronic romantic love:

> ... she was one
> Made but to love, to feel that she was his
> Who was her chosen: what was said or done
> Elsewhere was nothing
>   (*Don Juan*, Canto II, 202)

And they were, as we have seen, writ large in the marriage laws, which made of the wife a *femme coverte*, whose legal identity was 'covered' by that of her husband.

Small wonder, then, that Jane's insistence that 'I care for myself' was deplored by some early reviewers; or that twentieth-century feminist critics hailed her as a fem-

---

[3] Marianne Farningham, *A Working Woman's Life. An Autobiography* (London: James Clarke, 1907), 44.

[4] Anon., *Woman: As She Is and As She Should Be* (2 vols.; London: James Cochrane & Co., 1835), ii. 37.

[5] William Landels, *Woman's Sphere and Work Considered in the Light of Scriptures* (London: James Nisbet, 1859), 27.

inist heroine. Yet in many ways, it is as difficult to see her thus as it is to see her as a 'moral Jacobin'. When she returns to Rochester as an 'independent woman', it is not as one of the anomalous, self-supporting kind. She seems anxious, indeed, to define herself as more proper than other women: her tale is populated by warning images of those who have lacked self-control—the maniac Bertha, the demi-mondaine Céline (from likeness to whom the 'lively' Adèle must be carefully trained away), the 'showy' and 'striking' Blanche Ingram, all rivals for Rochester's love. The woman who as a child of 10 gave her 'furious feelings uncontrolled play' (37), and who says of herself at 18 that 'the restlessness was in my nature' (109), be-comes a disciplinarian—instructing the pupils in her school 'in doing their work well; in keeping their persons neat; in learning their tasks regularly; in acquiring quiet and orderly manners' (366), supervising the education that makes Adèle an 'obliging companion: docile, good-tempered, and well-principled' and corrects her 'French defects' (450). Despite her impassioned paean on behalf of 'women'— 'they need exercise for their faculties, and a field for their efforts as much as their broth-ers do' (109)—she is only too happy to end her days in quiet domestic seclusion, far from that world whose rigours her story has exposed. Most problematically of all, this 'independent' heroine is peculiarly susceptible to the attractions of masculine power. In love with her employer, she finds his face and features 'full of an interest, an influence that quite mastered me,—that took my feelings from my own power and fettered them in his' (174–5). As her handsome, 'heroic' cousin urges her to go to India, she feels 'his influence in my marrow—his hold on my limbs', and con-templates 'the possibility of conceiving an inevitable, strange, torturing kind of love for him' (406, 416) . And on suddenly hearing a 'mysterious summons' from him whom she calls her 'Master', she abandons 'free and honest' self-sufficiency for the promptings of romantic love (359). As twentieth-century critics—less concerned with propriety than with ideological correctness—have not been slow to point out, the contradictions that emerge in her story—between her rhetoric of equality and her acceptance of social distinction, between her romantic desire for self-fulfilment and her deference to 'laws and principles . . . preconceived opinions, foregone de-terminations' (317) are, in the end, smoothed over. Her problems are resolved by a series of fairy-tale coincidences—a fortunate legacy, a luckily discovered family, a convenient death. *Jane Eyre* came to be seen by critics of the twentieth century as a novel in which the ideological assumptions and social arrangements of early nine-teenth-century England are ultimately not questioned, but endorsed.

Yet *Jane Eyre* has never been *felt* to be a conformist work. And analyses such as these—focusing as they do on that central character Jane, her choices, her attitudes, her development—seem hardly to capture what is most distinctive in the novel: the prose within which what the reader constructs as 'character' is created; and within which, as we have begun to see, the coherent, unified selfhood presupposed by the novel's subtitle is interrogated in unexpected ways. For that which can be traced at a microlevel is writ large in the 'melodrama and improbability',[6] the Gothic and

---

[6] [G. H. Lewes], review of *Jane Eyre*, *Fraser's Magazine* 36, December 1847 (*CH* 85).

fairy-tale suggestions that run through Jane's narrative . This is a novel that seems quite deliberately to flout the 'realist illusion' which—as one of the finest of its critics has suggested—it also consummately creates.[7] For it is one within which both 'dependence' and 'independence' appear in configurations more violent, more extreme, more disquieting, than a realist reading can contain.

Unlike Crimsworth's, Jane's story begins in childhood. Yet if this might seem to signal a new kind of emphasis on psychological development, the expectation is not exactly fulfilled. There is nothing in *Jane Eyre* like that sense of a childish consciousness coming into focus with which *Great Expectations* begins:

My first vivid and broad impression of the identity of things seems to me to have been gained on a memorable raw afternoon towards evening. At such a time I found out for certain, that this bleak place overgrown with nettles was the churchyard . . . and that the low leaden line beyond, was the river; and that the distant savage lair from which the wind was rushing, was the sea; and that the small bundle of shivers growing afraid of it all and beginning to cry, was Pip.

Unlike this uncertain 'bundle of shivers', whose development into a moral agent the novel goes on to trace, Jane is there from the beginning, distinct and defiant, not gradually gaining a sense of herself and her world but insisting on her own point of view. To that first crushing denial she opposes her own negative energy: 'I was glad of it: I never liked long walks'. She is, indeed, an oddly undetermined entity. If others are prominent in her narrative, she herself does not appear shaped by her relations with them. In this, *Jane Eyre* stands in striking contrast not merely to such later Victorian novels of childhood as *David Copperfield* and *The Mill on the Floss* but also to that with which its author was most familiar, her sister Emily's *Wuthering Heights*. That sense, expressed by Catherine Earnshaw, that the self is fundamentally defined by the earliest childhood ties ('My great miseries in this world have been Heathcliff's miseries, and I watched and felt each from the beginning . . . If all else perished, and *he* remained, I should still continue to be') is strikingly absent here. So also is that Wordsworthian concern with the conflict between loyalty to the personal past and aspiration beyond it which Dickens and George Eliot were to explore in their later novels. Jane's trajectory points all one way. There is little in her childhood that demands her fidelity. The Reeds are not her family, as the Tullivers are Maggie Tulliver's or the Dorrits are Amy Dorrit's: she is not held to them by the difficult bonds of love. Rather, she insists on her difference even from those to whom she is closest as a child. Both Helen Burns and Miss Temple definitively disappear from her narrative: their influence passes with them, and self reasserts itself unchanged. Likewise—indeed, more extremely—she is independent of her adversaries: if she is confronted by a number of hostile descriptions of herself—a 'dependant', 'less than a servant', 'an underhand little thing', 'not quite the character and disposition I could wish'—such characterizations are bafflingly alien, to be rejected, rather than assimilated, as her narrative proceeds. 'All said I was

[7] Sally Shuttleworth, *Charlotte Brontë and Victorian Psychology* (Cambridge: Cambridge University Press, 1996), 1–3.

wicked and perhaps I might be so', she thinks to herself in the red-room; but her development consists less in negotiating any very deeply internalized awareness of others' views than in gaining the power to assert her own perspective in opposition to theirs.

Here, as in *The Professor*, relations with others are figured as sites of antagonism. The love between Jane and Rochester is portrayed less as a growing concord than as a continual struggle for dominance. In their early days together, she 'delights' in sparring with him. 'I knew the pleasure of vexing and soothing him by turns . . . Beyond the verge of provocation I never ventured; on the extreme brink I liked well to try my skill' (158). 'Soft scene, daring demonstration, I would not have; and I stood in peril of both,'she says of her affianced lover; 'a weapon of defence must be prepared.' And she holds him at a distance with the 'needle of repartee' (273). 'I felt an inward power; a sense of influence, which supported me,' she tells of her ultimate resistance. 'The crisis was perilous; but not without its charm' (302). Such exchanges as these are pleasurable, even at moments of extremity.[8] As Rochester's speeches make clear, a dynamic of conquest and submission is inscribed in the commonplace clichés of Byronic romantic love: 'You please me, and you master me—you seem to submit, and I like the sense of pliancy you impart . . . I am influenced—conquered; and the influence is sweeter than I can express; and the conquest I undergo has a witchery beyond any triumph *I* can win' (260–1). Yet in *Jane Eyre* such clichés as these are emphasized in a way that led Mrs Oliphant to complain in 1855 that the novel portrayed romantic love as 'a battle . . . deadly and uncompromising, where the combatants, so far from being guided by the old punctilios of the duello, make no secret of their ferocity, but throw sly javelins at each other, instead of shaking hands before they begin'.[9]

Here, as in *The Professor*, the self is most fully itself in so far as it is impervious to others'—even beloved others'—influence. But here the sense is less of guarded self-defensiveness than of a more heroic endeavour. 'My mind had put off all it had borrowed of Miss Temple', says Jane, of her beloved teacher's departure, 'and . . . now I was left in my natural element; and beginning to feel the stirring of old emotions' (84). The idiom is not that of 'self-help'—an individualistic determination 'to do more, earn more, be more, possess more' (*P* 161)—but of romantic self-assertion; of a self more essential, more 'natural', more gloriously unsubmissive, than can be accommodated within the social world. And throughout the novel, this idiom merges with and is reinforced by another (also, it seems, unironized): an idiom of spiritual struggle in which Jane, like Bunyan's Christian, struggles to preserve herself in face of temptation and threat. Here the echoes of *Pilgrim's Progress* are more pervasive and less sardonic than they are in *The Professor*. Jane's resistance to Rochester is portrayed in biblical terms, as a 'soul'-securing victory: 'physically, I felt, at the moment, powerless as stubble exposed to the draught and glow of a furnace—mentally, I still

---

[8] On the 'erotics of power' in such scenes, see Shuttleworth, *Charlotte Brontë and Victorian Psychology*, 170–3.

[9] *CH* 312–13.

possessed my soul, and with it the certainty of ultimate safety' (317).[10] 'Conqueror I might be of the house', he says of her imagined surrender; 'but the inmate would escape to heaven before I could call myself possessor of its clay dwelling-place' (318). There is nothing here like *The Professor*'s peculiar exposure of the contradictions inherent in its narrator's stance: romantic and religious suggestions merge to underwrite rather than question Jane's stubborn assertion of self. For if Crimsworth's insistence on his own 'independence' is exposed in *The Professor* as a process of self-division, Jane's is seen as a struggle, in face of assault and temptation, to preserve an apparently unambiguously valued integrity. And if Crimsworth's narrative bespeaks the contorted deadlock of impulse denied, the inward-turned energy of 'self-control', Jane's is framed in a language of expressiveness, liberty, transcendence: a language not of repression, but of power.

Like Crimsworth's, Jane's drive towards 'independence' is inscribed most intimately in her narrative: everything in her world is seen from her controlling point of view. But where that earlier narrator was portrayed, ironically, as a self-defensive spy, there seems to be no such questioning of Jane's perspective in *Jane Eyre*. It is true that those who threaten Jane most are distanced throughout her narrative by a cool, analytic observation. 'I knew he would soon strike,' she says of the bully John Reed, 'and while dreading the blow, I mused on the disgusting and ugly appearance of him who would presently deal it' (10). 'His face riveted the eye', she confesses of St John Rivers; but compulsion becomes a categorizing power as she proceeds to anatomize his appearance: 'It was like a Greek face, very pure in outline; quite a straight, classic nose; quite an Athenian mouth and chin' (345). Left alone, as a child, with the forbidding Mrs Reed, she occupies herself in 'watching her . . . I examined her figure; I perused her features' (35). (In a review that connected this sharpness of observation with deplorable 'want of feeling', the *Christian Rembembrancer* complained that Jane's aunt's 'unrepentant' deathbed was 'described with as deliberate a minuteness and as severe a tranquillity as a naturalist might display in recording the mortal orgasms of a jelly-fish').[11] But if this objectifying of others is reminiscent of Crimsworth, the world through which Jane moves is more passionate and more threatening than that place of mutual surveillance in which he defends himself. At Lowood, accused of being a liar, she feels the eyes of the school 'directed like burning-glasses against my scorched skin' (66). 'The fiery eye glared upon me' is her worst, fragmented memory of the crazed Bertha's murder attempt (284). 'He searched my face with eyes that I saw were dark, irate and piercing,' she tells of her first evening at Thornfield with Rochester (121); 'he seemed to devour me with his flaming glance', of the moment in which she flees from him (317). If her vision, like Crimsworth's, is a weapon, it is wielded in a fierier, more heroic struggle than his.

And that 'vision' is not questioned or ironized, but figured throughout in images of romanticism, creativity, transcendence. She who as a child took care that her book 'should be one stored with pictures' (7), who longed to examine the design on

---

[10] The reference is to Isaiah 5: 24.   [11] *Christian Remembrancer*, 15 (1848), 399.

a pretty plate (20), who even in hunger notes first 'how pretty . . . the china cups and bright teapot look' (72), sees her world with an artist's eye: again and again in her narrative, scenes, faces, rooms appear in pictorial terms. Thus, she describes the 'rude noise' of Rochester's horse approaching and disturbing the evening peace, 'as, in a picture, the solid mass of a crag, or the rough boles of a great oak, drawn in dark and strong on the foreground, efface the aërial distance of azure hill, sunny horizon and blended clouds, where tint melts into tint' (111–12): his face, first seen, is 'like a new picture introduced to the gallery of memory; and . . . dissimilar to all the others hanging there' (115).The child who on her first evening at Lowood 'puzzl[es] to make out the subject of a picture on the wall' (43), who feasts in her dormitory bed 'on the spectacle of ideal drawings' (74), grows into a woman accomplished in drawing and painting. And this sense of the narrator as artist carries with it suggestions of her superior, visionary power—a power that seems, magically, to penetrate to the essence of things and, at crucial points in the novel, to point prophetically forward. The fairy-tale horror with which her childish gaze invests Brocklehurst— 'What a face he had, now that it was almost on a level with mine! what a great nose! and what a mouth! and what large, prominent teeth!' (32)—is not, like Pip's first, appalled vision of Magwitch, replaced by the clearer vision of maturity: it is proved true by subsequent events, and echoed as Jane's story unfolds. 'What a hot and strong grasp he had!' she says, as she recalls Rochester's demeanour at the altar on their bigamous wedding day, 'and how like quarried marble was his pale, firm, massive front at this moment! How his eyes shone, still watchful, and yet wild beneath!' (289). Hers is a vision quite different from Crimsworth's—revelatory, transformative, creative, surrounded by suggestions of prophecy and preternatural power. It is closer to that of the Genii than to the perspective of the creatures of Glass Town.

For there is nothing like it in the novel. The logic of Crimsworth's watchfulness is objectified in the unresting mutual surveillance, the constant suspicion and antagonism, of the world that he confronts. But Jane's vision is not thus mirrored; and Jane's story—framed in the language of heroic struggle, of romantic love, of creative freedom—does not seem to offer this kind of implicit judgement on its narrator's existential stance. Her eye remains pre-eminent. Her viewpoint is confirmed, even celebrated. Hers is an extreme, absolutist version of that which is to some extent implicit in all first-person narrative: the power of the teller to shape the fictional world. In *The Professor* the narrator's announced 'independence' was fictionally undermined. But there is no such narrative irony in *Jane Eyre*. The story that unfolds from Jane's perspective is one in which her view of her world is unequivocally confirmed, and she assumes a position of unassailable power. Those others who have threatened her are one by one themselves confounded. Investigation into the affairs of Lowood produces 'a result mortifying to Mr Brocklehurst' (83); John Reed's is a 'shocking' death, and his mother's a desolate one. The Reed sisters are disposed of, the one to a loveless marriage with a 'worn-out man of fashion', the other to be 'walled up alive in a French convent' (242); Bertha Rochester perishes; the 'glorious sun' of St John Rivers 'hastens to its setting' as the novel ends. Less violent offenders are chastened. Little Adèle, 'who had been spoiled and indulged, and therefore was sometimes wayward', is made tractable to Jane's influence (108, 450); her rival, Blanche Ingram, is categorically dismissed by the man she has sought to entrap. Rochester is blinded, injured, and domesticated: no longer the figure with the 'flaming glance' (317) who offered 'glimpses' of a wider world to an 'honoured' and 'gratified' Jane (146), but dependent on her both for 'vision' and for his 'right hand' (451). Jane's friends, on the other hand, prosper. The Rivers sisters share her inheritance; Miss Temple marries 'an excellent man, almost worthy of such a wife'; even Helen Burns's grave is now marked by 'a grey marble tablet . . . inscribed with her name, and the word "Resurgam"' (82). The logic is that of fairy tale, in which moral complexity is replaced by an absolute opposition between the deserving who succeed and the bad who get their just deserts. And of this tale Jane is the triumphant heroine—the Cinderella who surpasses her ugly sisters and stepmother, and receives unlooked-for fairy gifts; the Bluebeard's wife who survives to tell her story; the changeling who is recognized by her kinsfolk; the Beauty who finally tames the Beast. By the end, she is paramount: those who have sought to wrong her are punished, her decisions are vindicated and her desires fulfilled. Hers is a trajectory more violent, more extreme than that of the conventional *Bildungsroman*, in which subjective desires are countered and tempered by the world into which the protagonist goes.

Yet it is no less questioned than Crimsworth's, though in an entirely different way. For if Jane's uncontested narrating voice, rewarding her friends and punishing her enemies, oddly recalls the great Genii of Glass Town, much that is most distinctive in *Jane Eyre* evokes also the quite different viewpoint of their creatures. From the opening chapter, where the terrorized child fantasizes about the 'death-white realms' depicted in the book on her lap, to the closing paragraphs, in which 'Jane Eyre' has become Jane Rochester, this tale of egocentric triumph is counterpointed by another story, in which the protagonist is not all-powerful, but precarious, powerless, threatened: one that speaks not of self-confirming triumph, but of uncertainty and impotence. It is a story that begins in very first sentence of the novel, with its uncompromising negative—'There was *no possibility* of taking a walk that day'. This is quite unlike the negatives with which Crimsworth opens his tale. For that which is here configured is not simply or primarily an oppositional stance, but the intransigence of a world beyond the narrator's control. Jane's first direct statement of feeling—'I was glad of it: I never liked long walks'—is less assertive than reactive: it is succeeded by a series of clauses in which her impotence is stressed: '*dreadful to me* was the coming home in the raw twilight, with *nipped* fingers and toes, and a heart *saddened* by the chidings of Bessie, the nurse, and *humbled* by the consciousness of my physical inferiority to Eliza, John, and Georgiana Reed' (my italics). Where, at the opening of *The Professor*, others' words were reported by a controlling narrative voice, here they loom larger, unmediated, imperfectly understood. Others, in these opening pages, speak not so much *to* Jane as *of* her:

> 'She never did so before,' at last said Bessie, turning to the Abigail.
> 'But it was always in her,' was the reply. 'I've told Missis often my opinion about the child,

and Missis agreed with me. She's an underhand little thing: I never saw a girl of her age with so much cover.' (12)

'Mr Brocklehurst, I believe I intimated in the letter which I wrote to you three weeks ago, that this little girl has not quite the character and disposition I could wish.' (33)

To such characterizations, it seems, there can be no reply, any more than there could be a reply to the murmuring voices of 'Strange Events'. Indeed, it is in words that echo Lord Charles Wellesley's that the narrator describes her habitual childish awareness of this weight of others' speech: 'I had nothing to say to these words: they were not new to me: my very first recollections of existence included hints of the same kind. This reproach of my dependence had become a vague sing-song in my ear; very painful and crushing, but only half intelligible' (13). Others are not here rejected, as they are in *The Professor*, in a movement of antagonism. They are 'painfully' and 'crushingly' unanswerable: for the order of being they occupy is— like that of the mighty other whom Lord Charles Wellesley sees—more effective, more definitive than that of the helpless protagonist.

The hostile others who inhabit Jane's world are far more substantial than she. The physical and moral violence of John Reed and of Mr Brocklehurst is made worse by their grotesque solidity. John Reed is 'large and stout for his age', with 'thick lineaments in a spacious visage, heavy limbs and large extremities': he 'gorge[s] himself habitually at table' (9). Mr Brocklehurst has the surrealistic rigidity of 'a black pillar! . . . standing erect on the rug'; his 'grim face' is 'like a carved mask, placed over the shaft by way of capital' (31). St John Rivers, ascetic as he is, has a different, but comparable solidity: his face is 'like chiselled marble' (377): at the fireside he appears like 'a cold cumbrous column, gloomy and out of place' (393). John Reed's sisters grow up into women much larger than Jane: 'Miss Reed is the head and shoulders taller than you are; and Miss Georgiana would make two of you in breadth,' Bessie tells her (90). Mrs Reed has a 'stony eye—opaque to tenderness, indissoluble to tears' (231). Bertha Rochester is 'a big woman . . . and corpulent besides', her 'lurid visage' and 'bloated features' make her like a 'clothed hyena' (293). Rochester has a 'square, massive brow . . . strong features, firm, grim mouth,—all energy, decision, will' (174).

And if such presences seem larger, more unyielding, more grossly material than life, they have also a preternatural potency. The world through which Jane moves is one of fairy-tale malevolence: a place of spells, of curses, of charms. 'What a face he had, now that it was almost on a level with mine! what a great nose! and what a mouth! and what large, prominent, teeth!' exclaims Jane of Mr Brocklehurst (32). 'What a pigmy intellect she had, and what giant propensities!' says her husband of Bertha Rochester. 'How fearful were the curses those propensities entailed on me!' (306). At Gateshead, a 'switch' lurks in a corner, 'waiting to leap out imp-like and lace my quivering palm or shrinking neck' (230); at Thornfield a raving lunatic is 'prompted by her familiar to burn people in their beds at night, to stab them, to bite their flesh from their bones' (301); in face of St John's importunings, Jane feels 'as if an awful charm was framing round and gathering over me: I trembled to hear some fatal word spoken which would at once declare and rivet the spell' (402). 'Like a giant', her cousin appears, on the final page of the novel, 'hew[ing] down the prejudices' that 'encumber' 'his race' (452).

Jane, however, is evanescent: as she puts it, 'like nobody there' (15).[12] 'A strange little figure ... like one of the tiny phantoms ... Bessie's evening stories represented,' she appears to herself in the red-room mirror (14); to Rochester, years later, she is a 'mocking changeling' (438), 'a strange . . . almost unearthly thing' (255), like one who comes 'from the abode of people who are dead' (245). 'I hardly know what thoughts I have in my head,' she says to him on their wedding eve. 'Everything in life seems unreal' (279). If the fairy-tale portents, prefigurative metaphors, and premonitory dreams that punctuate her story seem to underwrite her progression to triumph, they also question and qualify that narrative of effective self-making implied by its 'autobiographical' form. For even at decisive moments, she is figured less as shaping her own destiny than as propelled by mysterious powers—by the 'fairy' gift of a suggestion (86), by a strange 'human form ... in the azure' (319), by a supernatural call that makes the 'flesh quiver on the bones' (419). Indeed, this sense of self as passive object, rather than as active subject, runs in a different way through her most private self-communings. For the Jane who insists so urgently on her right to self-determination is repeatedly portrayed as the helpless, imperilled object of forces beyond her control; at the mercy not merely of more powerful others, but of a whole constellation of emotions that threaten and assail her from within. Her feelings are represented less as impulses emanating from herself than as entities with lives of their own. 'A hand of fiery iron grasped my vitals,' she says, of her resistance to Rochester. 'My very Conscience and Reason turned traitors against me, and charged me with crime ... They spoke almost as loud as Feeling: and that clamoured wildly. "Oh, comply!" it said' (315, 317). Like the external world through which she moves, this inner landscape has the malevolence of fairy tale. 'Something of vengeance I had tasted for the first time; as aromatic wine it seemed on swallowing, warm and racy: its after-flavour, metallic and corroding, gave me a sensation as if I had been poisoned' (38). 'Oh, that fear of his self-abandonment ... how it goaded me! It was a barbed arrow-head in my breast: it tore me when I tried to extract it; it sickened me when Remembrance thrust it further in' (321); 'My iron shroud contracted round me: persuasion advanced with slow sure step' (404).[13]

The others who populate Jane's narrative are not merely more solid, more effective, than she: they are actively persecutory. Each of those on whom she is dependent threatens her very existence; not metaphorically, but literally. Mrs Reed, like a fairy-tale evil stepmother, has her taken away and locked up, giving her 'nerves' such a

---

[12] For a suggestive discussion of this 'remoteness of that very "I" which dominates the novel' see Karen Chase, *Eros and Psyche: The Representation of Personality in Charlotte Bronte, Charles Dickens, George Eliot* (London: Methuen, 1984), 70–9.

[13] The 'iron shroud' is the subject of a *Blackwood's* tale of terror with which Brontë had probably been familiar since childhood—William Mudford's 'The Iron Shroud' published in August 1830, in which a prison cell contracts and crushes its occupant to death. (See J. M. S. Tompkins, 'Jane Eyre's "Iron Shroud", *Modern Language Review*, 22 (1927), 195–7).

'shock' that even the phlegmatic Bessie is afraid that 'she might die' (19–20). 'What did they do with her at Lowood?' Jane's aunt wonders on her deathbed. 'The fever broke out there, and many of the pupils died. She, however, did not die: but I said she did—I wish she had died!' (232). 'I must keep in good health, and not die,' Jane tells Mr Brocklehurst; but 'How can you keep in good health?' he asks, unanswerably, in reply (32). His 'institution' is a place of death, in which she is starved and frozen, and threatened with hell-fire. The 'master' into whose employment she goes likewise jeopardizes her life. His house is a 'Bluebeard's castle' where a 'Vampyre'-like figure tries to kill her; his attempts to persuade her to stay with him turn her 'stone-cold with ominous terror' (316); and the flight to which he drives her is figured as a dreadful death: 'He who is taken out to pass through a fair scene to the scaffold, thinks not of the flowers that smile on his road, but of the block and axe-edge; of the disseverment of bone and vein; of the grave gaping at the end' (321). Reduced, by that flight, to destitution, she almost dies of 'want and cold' (330). Her rescuer, St John Rivers—Jane's only living male relative, and hence her natural protector—proves, as his sister warns, 'inexorable as death' (356). His proposal of marriage appears as a threat to her very life: 'I felt how—if I were his wife—this good man, pure as the deep sunless source, could soon kill me, without drawing from my veins a single drop of blood, or receiving on his own crystal conscience the faintest stain of crime' (411). More prosaically, Jane reflects on his desire to conscript her as a missionary: 'if I go to India, I go to premature death' (404).

Above all, perhaps, Jane's account of her love for Rochester is informed throughout by a sense of her own precariousness and of this other's potency. Her 'master' is her employer; she is his 'paid subordinate' (134). He is accustomed to possess and control (124); she is effective, if at all, only in a contracted sphere. He has travelled throughout Europe, 'provided with plenty of money, and the passport of an old name' (311); she gazes yearningly outwards towards the wider world. Like a Genie, he offers to transform her life—'I shall waft you away at once to town . . . I shall bear my treasure to regions nearer the sun' (259)—and to load her with fairy gifts. 'I will myself put the diamond chain around your neck, and the circlet on your forehead . . . and I will clasp the bracelets on these fine wrists, and load these fairy-like fingers with rings' (259). Such promises, to Jane, pose a threat to her very being: 'And then you won't know me, sir; and I shall not be your Jane Eyre any longer, but an ape in a harlequin's jacket,—a jay in borrowed plumes' (259). From the clichés of his love-song—'My love has sworn, with sealing kiss, | With me to live—to die'—she extracts, half-humorously, a serious meaning, 'I should . . . not be hurried away in a suttee' (273). And as he responds to her greeting—'It is Jane Eyre, sir'—with 'Soon to be Jane Rochester', she feels 'something stronger than was consistent with joy—something that smote and stunned: it was, I think, almost fear' (258). In an access of triumphant possessiveness, Rochester repeats her future, altered name. But Jane's response—'It can never be, sir: it does not sound likely'—hints at a darker feeling. 'It can never be': for to conceive of the subject 'Jane Eyre', becoming that other-defined object, 'Jane Rochester', is as impossible as imagining her own death, her replacement by another—'not I, but one Jane Rochester'—one who will displace her as surely as 'garments said to be hers had already displaced my black stuff gown and Lowood bonnet' (275).

A heroic 'determined revolt' (400) against the violence of such monstrous figures as a Mrs Reed or a Mr Brocklehurst is comparatively easy. Those to whom Jane is drawn pose a far more insidious threat. As she gazes unobserved at Rochester, she feels 'a precious yet poignant pleasure; pure gold, with a steely point of agony: a pleasure like what the thirst-perishing man might feel who knows the well to which he has crept is poisoned, yet stoops and drinks divine draughts nevertheless' (174); on the eve of her wedding, she tells him, 'I cannot see my prospects clearly to-night ... Everything in life seems unreal' (279). 'I was tempted', she says of St John Rivers, 'to cease struggling with him—to rush down the torrent of his will into the gulf of his existence, and there lose my own' (418). Again and again in her narrative the image reappears of a potent, compelling other engulfing independent self. Thus, she finds Rochester's features 'full of an interest, an influence that quite mastered me,—that took my feelings from my own power and fettered them in his' (175); thus, on the morning of the abortive wedding, 'my heart was with my eyes; and both seemed migrated into Mr Rochester's frame' (287). Thus, St John Rivers' 'influence' takes over and shapes her own purposes— 'My work, which had appeared so vague, so hopelessly diffuse, condensed itself as he proceeded, and assumed a definite form under his shaping hand' (404). Thus, Rochester, even in absence, is able to dominate and control:

His idea was still with me; because it was not a vapour sunshine could disperse; nor a sand-traced effigy storms could wash away: it was a name graven on a tablet, fated to last as long as the marble it inscribed. The craving to know what had become of him followed me every-where: when I was at Morton, I re-entered my cottage every evening to think of that; and now at Moor House, I sought my bedroom each night to brood over it.   (399)

Here, as when she was a child at Lowood, Jane is less agent than sufferer, 'nipped' by 'cold without' and 'gnawed' by 'hunger within'—though here the cold is not literal cold, but the icy passion of St John Rivers, and the hunger not literal hunger, but a 'craving' to know what has happened to her beloved. At this stage in her narrative, she has arrived at a much surer identity than that bewildered charity-child. An heiress, and now herself a 'benefactress', she is living amongst kinsfolk. '*I* care for myself' she has insisted to the man she loves (317). Yet like that literal 'stone-tablet', the mere 'idea' of this other seems more persisting, more unquestionable, more potent than the ineffectual, helplessly driven self.

That sense of egocentric omnipotence which is in one way inscribed in *Jane Eyre* is, then, counterpointed throughout by a sense of absolute jeopardy: one that culminates, indeed, in the disappearance of 'Jane Eyre'. For as the novel draws to a close, and the narrator becomes 'not I, but one Jane Rochester', that embattled, precarious 'I' is transmuted into a 'we':

I am my husband's life as fully as he is mine. No woman was ever nearer her mate than I am: ever more absolutely bone of his bone, and flesh of his flesh. I know no weariness of my Edward's society: he knows none of mine, any more than we each do of the pulsation of the heart that beats in our separate bosoms; consequently, we are ever together.   (450)

And Jane's description resonates not merely with the biblical account of the creation of Eve as Adam's helpmeet,[14] but also with Milton's far darker portrayal of
Adam's appalled confrontation of their inescapably conjoined doom:

> flesh of flesh
> Bone of my bone thou art, and from thy state
> Mine never shall be parted, bliss or woe.
> (*Paradise Lost*, 9. 914–16)

This is a curious ending to that story of a singular self, desperately 'tenacious of life'
(121) which is inscribed in the novel's imagery of basic biological need. The sparring
opposition between Jane and Rochester here gives way to the image of a union in
which each of those striving egos disappears: 'We talk, I believe, all day long: to talk
to each other is but a more animated and an audible thinking. All my confidence is
bestowed on him; all his confidence is devoted to me: we are precisely suited in
character; perfect concord is the result' (451). And the absence of the desperate
struggle that has animated Jane's story contributes at least as much to the feeling of
an energy gone from these passages as does the more overt fact of Rochester's blind
and crippled state. Like that informing imagery of two becoming one flesh, this insistence on a unity that denies division ('all . . . all . . . precisely . . . perfect') works
oddly against the narrator's protestations of happiness. The intimation that 'Jane
Eyre' has gone is reinforced by the hints of death that play through the novel's descriptions of what becomes her final home. Ferndean is a 'desolate spot', with 'dark
and green . . . decaying walls', which has long been unlettable because of its 'ineligi-
ble and insalubrious site'. 'Can there be life here?' asks Jane (430). Her expansive
reaching out for 'all of incident, life, fire, feeling, that I desired and had not' has contracted to a single object—'loving him, being loved by him' (367); her longing for a
'power of vision' that might 'overpass' bounding 'limits' has ended in viewless retirement, deep in a 'gloomy wood' with 'no opening anywhere' (430).

   Throughout the novel, then—not merely at those points at which its heroine almost perishes (from 'a species of fit' at Gateshead, from typhus at Lowood school,
at the hand of the mad Bertha, from starvation on the moor, by choosing to go to
India) but even in her account of her love for Rochester—runs the constant suggestion that the narrating 'I' is in imminent danger of extinction. Even in the final
pages this sense remains, complicating and questioning that story of desire fulfilled
which Jane's 'independent' return to the dependent Rochester in one way seems to
be. It is a sense that is underwritten by the novel's closing paragraphs, where that
'we' who live in satisfied retirement (broken only by letters and visits and consulta-
tions with oculists) give way to an as yet unsatisfied 'I', who labours undaunted in a
wider world, urged onward in his 'high ambition' by all that self-assertive energy
which has vanished from its heroine's tale; one whose assured invocation of the
supreme authority of Scripture emphasizes that hers is a choice of finite, earthly
'blessedness'. 'No fear of death,' says Jane, 'will darken St John's last hour'; and the

---

[14] Genesis 2: 23.

insistent third person of the sentence that follows—'*his* mind will be unclouded; *his* heart will be undaunted; *his* hope will be sure; *his* faith steadfast' (452, my italics)—suggests that there may be no such confidence for her.

This final, troubling image of one other than the narrator seems less to turn away from the questions raised in her story than to focus the contradictions that its conformations emphasize. That longing to break the bounds of a confined existence which propelled Jane away from Lowood, which unsettled her at Thornfield, is echoed here in St John Rivers's hunger for immortality; that impulse towards subjugation of the other which surrealistically shapes her narrative has its counterpart here in his imperializing zeal. That sense of self as annihilable and of other as all-powerful which quite differently haunts her story is paralleled here by his evangelical self-surrender: his final call to his yearned-for 'master' resonates with hers. Like the intimations of violence that disrupt Crimsworth's closing descriptions of domestic bliss, this strange, suggestive portrait appears less as an irrelevant coda to an already finished narrative than as an emphatic, final image of that peculiar double logic that is inscribed in it throughout.

It is a doubleness very different from *The Professor*'s two-dimensional irony. *Jane Eyre* tells not a single, fictionally undermined story, but two opposing and incommensurate ones. The self at the centre of each appears in a radically different way: in one, as magically omnipotent, triumphing absolutely; in the other, as insubstantial, the constantly jeopardized object of forces beyond its control. And as the suspense that attends even repeated re-readings suggests, these conflicting stories can hardly be reconciled by reading the novel as an account of the 'resolution' arrived at by the developing character Jane. Those opposing configurations of triumphant omnipotence and imminent annihilation which animate her narrative remain to the end unresolved: indeed, they are brought together and imaged in the potent yet death-bound figure both of romantic self-assertion and of evangelical self-immolation who has the novel's final word. And in this these final paragraphs of *Jane Eyre* point not away from but towards the mid-nineteenth-century world.

CHAPTER FOUR

'Dreadful to me':
Jane Eyre and History (1)

I

'It has no learning, no research, it discusses no subject of public interest,' wrote Charlotte Brontë shortly after the publication of *Jane Eyre*.[1] Even the novel's admirers have been inclined to echo this view. 'Of the novels included here' Kathleen Tillotson announces categorically, in her *Novels of the Eighteen-Forties*, '*Jane Eyre* has the least relation to its time.'

Such social commentary as it may offer is oblique, limited, incidental. It is both in purpose and effect primarily a novel of the inner life, not of man in his social relations; it maps a private world . . . A love-story, a Cinderella fable, a Bluebeard mystery, an autobiography from forlorn childhood to happy marriage: this novel makes its appeal first and last to 'the unchanging human heart'.[2]

For *Jane Eyre*'s fairy-tale shapings, its archetypal themes of search for love and escape from danger, above all, perhaps, its representation of childhood suffering, do seem to point away from its specific historical moment, and towards areas of experience which all can readily understand. 'Who that remembers early childhood, can read without emotion the little Jane Eyre's night journey to Lowood?' asked Sydney Dobell, in an early review.[3] 'Passages read like a page out of one's own life', G. H. Lewes declared.[4] And generations of girls have thrilled, with similar empathy, to Jane's story of passionate love.[5] The meanings its critics have traced in it may have changed with changing *mores*, but in its evocation of vulnerable childhood, its representation of desire, *Jane Eyre* has seemed to speak less of historical difference than of its readers' most intimate concerns.

Yet it was with regard to its handling of those universal themes of childhood suffering and passionate love that the question of the novel's historicity was first most sharply posed. In 1857, when Elizabeth Gaskell's *Life of Charlotte Bronte* had familiarized readers with the real-life 'originals' of Mr Brocklehurst and Lowood school,

---

[1] Charlotte Brontë to W. S. Williams, 28 October 1847 (*CBL* i. 554).
[2] Kathleen Tillotson, *Novels of the Eighteen-Forties* (Oxford: Clarendon Press, 1954), 257–8.
[3] [Sydney Dobell], *The Palladium*, 1 (1850), 171.
[4] 'Recent Novels: French and English', *Fraser's Magazine*, 36 (1847), 691–2.
[5] For a suggestive account of the history of such response, see Patsy Stoneman, *Brontë Transformations* (Hemel Hempstead: Harvester Wheatsheaf/Prentice Hall, 1996).

a review in the *Christian Observer* attacked Charlotte Brontë for her depiction of them: 'her picture is that of a morbid fancy, mixing up fiction with fact, and traducing, with a random pen, an Institution to which she and her family were wholesale debtors'.[6] From June to August of the same year, a controversy raged in the correspondence columns of the *Halifax Guardian* as to the accuracy of the novel's 'picture' of the Clergy Daughters' School.[7] Ex-pupils wrote in defending its diet and discipline; Charlotte Brontë's widower replied with counterexamples. Neither side seems to have doubted that here, at least, Charlotte Brontë was addressing herself to a subject of considerable 'public interest'. Similarly, and no less confidently, the novel's unprecedented emphasis on a woman's passionate desire was explicitly measured against its first critics' views of 'real life'. 'It is not thus that generous men make their advances, or that women worthy of the name are won,' wrote William C. Roscoe, of Brontë's depiction of courtship.[8] 'Passion occupies too prominent a place in her pictures of life', Harriet Martineau complained, in her otherwise admiring obituary; in representing 'love' as women's 'whole and sole concern', the author of *Jane Eyre* had given a quite false view of their lives.[9] 'The author has struck only one chord of the human heart ... and has set it vibrating alone, to the exclusion of all the rest', echoed Émile Montégut in 1857. '*Jane Eyre* is a passionate dream, a perfect castle in Spain.'[10] To some, at least, of its earliest readers, it seems, this 'Cinderella fable' spoke controversially of contemporary actualities, rather than of universal truth.

The correspondents who disputed the details of the regime at Cowan Bridge school in the *Halifax Guardian* may have had rather naïve notions of the relation between fact and fiction. But their argument over *Jane Eyre*'s 'truthfulness' does point towards that which its author's apologetic sense that 'it discusses no subject of public interest' obscures. In her representation of Jane's childhood—to which a third of the novel is devoted—Charlotte Brontë is dealing with a set of power relations no less socially significant than those issues of class and gender and race with which recent critics have been concerned. Here, that which appeared so disquietingly as a coda to Crimsworth's story—the figure of the subjugated child—occupies the centre of the stage. It is not here distanced into the third person, as it was in *The Professor*, or as it had been in Dickens' *Oliver Twist*, first published in serial form ten years before. Jane tells of her childhood sufferings with an intimacy and a directness hitherto unparalleled in fiction; and the shape they assume in the telling is a quite distinctive one.

'There was no possibility ...', Jane begins; and in the novel's very first paragraph, before the reader learns her name, she records that of one whose authority prescribes the limits of her world. If hers is an urgent, first-person voice, it is not exactly a freely expressive one. In face of this forbidding other, the narrating 'I' is not a sub-

---

[6] *Christian Observer* NS 234 (June 1857), 428.   [7] Reprinted in *LL* iv. app. 1.

[8] William C. Roscoe, 'The Miss Brontës', *Poems and Essays*, ed. R. H. Hutton (2 vols.; London: Chapman & Hall, 1860), ii. 350.

[9] *CH* 302.   [10] *CH* 372.

ject but an object, awkwardly prominent, as Jane is in her exclusion: 'Me, she had dispensed from joining the group'. The direct voice of the child, 'saddened', 'humbled', excluded, gives way to the speech of one whose pronouncements have the force of general laws:

saying, 'She regretted to be under the necessity of keeping me at a distance; but that until she heard from Bessie, and could discover from her own observation that I was endeavouring in good earnest to acquire a more sociable and child-like disposition, a more attractive and sprightly manner,—something lighter, franker, more natural as it were—she really must exclude me from privileges intended only for contented, happy, little children.'   (7)

Like the text-bearing tablet that Jane is later to confront at Lowood, Mrs Reed's words are mystifyingly incontestable: apparently impersonal, yet violent in their alienation from the child. The inverted commas, the formality, the use of the third person all draw attention to this discourse, so different from that of the opening sentences: it is objectified, placed on display. Jane's reply to this speech—'What does Bessie say I have done?'—punctures with its childish directness the balloon of this other's pomposity; but the power of the discourse that places her by no means ends there. Instead of an answer to her question there is a refusal of dialogue: 'Jane, I don't like cavillers or questioners.' The urgent first-person voice of the opening is met by condemnatory judgement—a configuration that is to recur throughout *Jane Eyre*.

This opening opposition between Jane's baffled subjectivity—suffering, fearful, desperate, longing—and the disciplinary injunctions, the condemnatory judgements, of others soon becomes actual violence: hands holding her down, bonds being prepared, darkness and imprisonment. The sense, powerfully conveyed through all the resources of a preternaturally suggestive prose, is of a world that poses a threat to the protagonist's very being. Of course, the young Jane's story is also one of rebellion, 'fierce speaking' and 'fiendish feeling' (47). Her angry outburst against her bullying cousin is the originating moment of that narrative of self-assertion which is one way of reading *Jane Eyre*. But that sense of a self in jeopardy and a persecutory reality which informs the novel's opening portrait of the 'dependent', threatened child is not transcended as Jane matures, but articulated throughout, a powerful undertow to its 'Cinderella-fable' of survival, happiness, success. The world through which this heroine moves is not merely repressive and disheartening, but a murderous place in which her survival is at stake.

It is a sense that seems to exceed even the bleakest construction of the material conditions of life in early Victorian England. Yet it is one that the novel from its opening locates within the discourses and the practices of a sharply seen actual world. For if Mrs Reed is a monstrous figure, her speech is of a kind that would have been quite familiar to the novel's first readers. Thus, for example, Mrs Chapone's much-reprinted *Letters on the Improvement of the Mind* (1773), on which the relatively liberal curriculum of Roe Head School, where Charlotte Bronte was both pupil and teacher, was based: 'To make you the delight and darling of your family, something more is required than barely to be exempt from ill-temper and troublesome humours. The sincere and gentle smiles of complacency and love must adorn your countenance. . . . Conversation . . . must be cultivated with the frankness and openness of friendship.'[11] In the face of such discourse as this, the child is not a thinking, feeling subject but a creature to be disciplined and trained. This is the characteristic language of much early nineteenth-century English pedagogy. But *Jane Eyre* traces a darker logic in that pedagogy than many of its more well-meaning practitioners might have been prepared to admit.

Even as Jane is scolded and bullied, unjustly accused and punished, excluded and 'kept at a distance', her tormentors portray themselves, mysteriously, as her 'benefactors'. 'What we tell you is for your good,' says Bessie, as she enjoins the child to 'try to be useful and pleasant'. 'if you become passionate and rude, Missis will send you away, I am sure.' 'Besides,' said Miss Abbot, 'God will punish her: he might strike her dead in the midst of her tantrums, and then where would she go?' (13). Miss Abbot's is no general threat, but the quite distinctive discourse of a specific ideology. As the Reeds, with their punishments and humiliations, are succeeded by that 'pillar' of society, Mr Brocklehurst, and by the institutionalized violence of his 'evangelical, charitable establishment' (63), it becomes evident that in her depiction of Jane's traumatic childhood Charlotte Brontë is responding to a major social and cultural fact of early nineteenth-century England, which she herself had known in an especially extreme manifestation: that distinctive pedagogy which had developed out of the evangelical revival of the eighteenth century and which by the nineteenth was enshrined in schools such as those at Kingswood and at Cowan Bridge and promulgated in hundreds of tracts and articles, sermons and stories—which had become, indeed, in more or less modified form, probably the most powerful ideology of child-rearing in early Victorian England.[12] When one contemplates the surviving records of that pedagogy, the 'strange, startling and harrowing' configurations of Jane's story begin to appear less as the work of a 'morbid fancy' than as an emphatic invocation of some of the key terms and concepts of a well-known contemporary discourse; as familiar to the author of *Jane Eyre* as the teapot in the Bronte household, with its sombre, gilt-lettered text: 'For to me to live is Christ, and to die is gain.'

---

[11]   Hester Chapone, *Letters on the Improvement of the Mind. Addressed to a Lady*, new edn. (London: Harvey & Darnton, 1820), 117. The Parsonage Museum at Haworth possesses a copy of this pedagogical guide and advice book for young ladies, presented to Charlotte Brontë's friend Ellen Nussey as a 'prize for good and ladylike conduct' at Roe Head School.

[12]   On the nature and importance of evangelical pedagogy see Paul Sangster, *Pity My Simplicity* (London: Epworth Press, 1963); David Grylls, *Guardians and Angels: Parents and Children in Nineteenth-Century Literature* (London: Faber, 1978); Margaret Nancy Cutt, *Ministering Angels: A Study of Nineteenth-Century Evangelical Writing for Children* (Broxbourne: Five Owls Press, 1979); Doreen M. Rosman, *Evangelicals and Culture* (London: Croom Helm, 1984). Other late 18th- and early 19th-cent. systems of child-rearing, even 'liberal' ones, seem to have shared many of the characteristics of this pedagogy. On Rousseau, for example, see Alice Miller, *For Your Own Good: The Roots of Violence in Child-Rearing* (London: Virago, 1983), 97: or, for a contemporary view, Mrs Gaskell's account of her aunt's upbringing by a disciple of the 'enlightened' Thomas Day (Gaskell, 87–8).

In evangelical thinking,[13] the child was a being very different from the innocent child of Romanticism: not a unique individual, whose potentialities should be allowed to unfold in as unobstructed a way as possible, but a creature of 'inbred corruption',[14] destined for hell. 'You are a sinner, and without a gracious Saviour you must perish!': such is the tenor of the great evangelical Legh Richmond's letters to his children, reprinted in a book that 'strongly attracted and strangely fascinated' Charlotte Brontë when she read it at the age of 21.[15] It is this constellation of feeling that Jane Eyre invokes, in describing her childish resistance to John Reed as 'roused by the same sentiment of deep ire and desperate revolt which had stirred *my corruption* before' or her departure from Gateshead as marked by 'a sense of outlawry and almost of *reprobation*' (27, 227, my italics):[16] it is to this that Brocklehurst appeals, when he declares 'we are not to conform to nature: I wish these girls to be the children of Grace' (64). From the perspective of such thinking, the child was less a being to be respected, or even acknowledged, than one whose 'self-will' needed, for his or her own sake, to be 'broken' by rigorous discipline, whose 'passions' had to be curbed. The authority of parent or teacher was absolute, and unquestionable. In Mrs Sherwood's best-selling evangelical novel for children, *The Fairchild Family*, the paterfamilias reminds his son, 'I stand in place of God to you, whilst you are a child.'[17] 'A wise parent . . . should begin to break [his child's] will the first moment it appears', wrote John Wesley. 'In the whole art of Christian education there is nothing more important than this. The will of a parent is to a little child in place of the will of God.'[18]

Evangelical beliefs were not merely articulated as doctrine: they found expression and reinforcement in a range of child-rearing practices. The evangelical child

---

[13] As Boyd Hilton notes, evangelicalism was 'not a precise phenomenon', and 'Evangelical attitudes' may be 'attributed to many who would not have been regarded as "Evangelicals" with a capital "E"' (*The Age of Atonement: The Influence of Evangelicalism on Social and Economic Thought, 1795–1865* (Oxford: Clarendon Press, 1988), 7, 29); for this reason I shall not in this chapter capitalize the word. In essence, evangelicalism was a world-denying theology, distinguished by its emphasis on the need for redemption, and on original sin. The evangelical Christian was not at home in this world, and was not expected to look for temporal happiness. The only lasting joys were heavenly joys, and the main purpose of the Christian's sojourn in this world was to prepare for death. Such beliefs were not, Michael Wheeler suggests, confined to any single group, but 'exploited by preachers and teachers of many different persuasions': 'God's wrath and the possibility of imminent judgment were central to orthodox Christian teaching, and were widely accepted commonplaces of popular belief' (*Death and the Future Life in Victorian Literature and Theology* (Cambridge: Cambridge University Press, 1990), 117).
[14] *Christian Observer* (1806), quoted in Grylls, *Guardian Angels*, 48.
[15] Legh Richmond, *Domestic Portraiture; or, The Successful Application of Religious Principle in the Education of a Family Exemplified in the Memoirs of Three of the Deceased Children of the Rev. Legh Richmond* (London: R. B. Seeley & W. Burnside, 1833), 76. For Charlotte Brontë's reading of this work, see CBL i. 171.
[16] 'Corruption' was the 'original Adam', the sinful nature of man; 'reprobation' the state of being rejected by God, and condemned to eternal perdition.
[17] Mrs Sherwood, *The History of the Fairchild Family, or The Child's Manual*, 14th edn. (London: J. Hatchard & Son, 1841), pt. I, 260.
[18] Quoted in Philip Greven, *The Protestant Temperament: Patterns of Child-Rearing, Religious Experience, and the Self in Early America* (New York: Alfred A. Knopf, 1977), 37. Wesley's own mother, Susannah, had brought him up according to this system.

was the object of constant surveillance: that officious supervision which Mr Brock-lehurst enjoins the Lowood teachers to practice—'Teachers, you must watch her: keep your eyes on her movements, weigh well her words, scrutinize her actions, punish her body to save her soul' (66)—and of which Mr Brocklehurst's prototype, Carus Wilson, had been especially proud. 'It was often said of me', he is reported as saying, 'that I had eyes in every part of me: and . . . I have no hesitation in saying that herein consisted one of the chief services I rendered to the School.'[19] Legh Rich-mond advocated education at home, in small groups, to facilitate closer observa-tion—'two or three may be watched every hour—evil checked as it arises—every occurrence improved—religion infused into every pursuit and instruction'; 'I see more and more, daily,' he wrote to his wife, 'how desirable my own presence is, and that continually.' 'Such was his vigilance', his biographer reports, 'that if a friend in-troduced his son under circumstances of common courtesy, he appeared restless and uneasy if the young people were left together without superintendence for a few moments.'[20] 'Vigilance' such as this was to the evangelicals merely an earthly re-minder of the unceasing scrutiny of the all-seeing, eye of God. Thus Carus Wilson's *The Friendly Visitor*, 'published in monthly Tracts during the Year 1821', and de-signed for very young children, contains a chilling little dialogue, in which Mr S. tells his godson Charles of a book that God keeps, in which all the child's sins are set down:

C.—Then God remembers the lie I told you before, when I was quite a little boy; and how I fell into a passion, and pushed my little cousin Margaret off the bank, and had nearly killed her.
Mr S.—Yes, God remembers all this.
C.—O dear! I shall be sadly frightened when the day of judgment comes. I was in hopes that every body had forgot about my being naughty, since you and Mr Wilson never say anything about it now.
Mr S.—God forgets nothing, my dear.

THE END

'Our mother', wrote the novelist Charlotte Elizabeth Tonna of her childhood, 'had taken infinite pains to assure us of one great truth—the omniscience of an Om-nipresent God—and this I never could for a moment shake off.'[21] 'Remember! the eye of God is upon you in every place', Legh Richmond instructed his son. 'Be where you will, do what you will, you may always say with Hagar in the wilderness—"Thou God seest me".'[22]

A similar vigilance was expected of the child himself. He or she was trained in the art of self-examination: a kind of spiritual account-keeping, in which every motive, every action, every moment, was monitored with care:[23]

---

[19] Clement Carus-Wilson Shepheard-Walwyn, *Henry and Margaret Jane Shepheard: Memorials of a Father and Mother* (London: Elliot Stock, 1882), 113.
[20] Richmond, *Domestic Portraiture*, 15, 62.
[21] Charlotte Elizabeth Tonna, *Personal Recollections* (London: R. B. Seeley & W. Burnside, 1841), 17.
[22] Richmond, *Domestic Portraiture*, 55.
[23] See Leonore Davidoff and Catherine Hall, *Family Fortunes: Men and Women of the English Middle Class 1750–1850* (London: Hutchinson, 1987), 88.

>Every morning must begin
>With resolutions not to sin;
>And every evening recollect
>How much you've failed in this respect.[24]

'Teach [children] to render an account of all their thoughts to God', M. A. Stodart advised in *Principles of Education* (1844). 'They will not then shrink from the piercing eye, the close observation of their fellow creatures.'[25] 'I am . . . slatternly; I seldom put, and never keep, things in order; I am careless; I forget rules; I read when I should learn my lessons; I have no method; and sometimes I say, like you, I cannot *bear* to be subjected to systematic arrangements': thus Helen Burns presents her spiritual account to Jane Eyre (56). The fictional Lucy Fairchild, in *The Fairchild Family*, is given a diary, and told to keep 'an account of what passed in her heart, that she might learn more and more to know and hate her own sinful nature'.[26] The diary of Margaret Gray, 17-year-old daughter of an evangelical family in York, tells how, on 1 January 1826, she began to use the Biometer, a chart in which the thoughts and employments of every day were to be recorded with 'extreme minuteness'. Twelve days later, she was suffering from 'giddiness': this was succeeded by 'inflammation of the brain', 'extreme restlessness' and—on the last day of the month—by death.[27]

Evangelical condemnation was directed most particularly at the sins of vanity and of lying—seen as perhaps the two worst examples of that 'self-will' which had to be broken in the child. The 'worldly sentiment of pride' that Mr Brocklehurst seeks to 'mortify' in the pupils at Lowood (34) is attacked again and again in evangelical writings. In Carus Wilson's *Friendly Visitor* for 1821 there is a report of an inquest on a servant who hanged herself after getting into debt through love of dress, and girl readers are warned:

We are hurt to see your love of dress, and we reprove you for your smart clothes and fine curls. . . . We have lived a little longer in the world than you; and we have seen the end of many a poor girl who was fond of dress; and in pity to your souls we warn you. We wish to nip the evil in the bud. Bad habits, if not checked, will be sure to grow. You will covet finery which you see others have. In order to purchase it, you are tempted to steal. The next step perhaps is the gallows.

'Each of the young persons before us has a string of hair twisted in plaits which vanity might have woven,' splutters Brocklehurst. 'My mission is to . . . teach them to

   [24] 'The Way to Cure Pride', Ann and Jane Taylor, *Hymns for Infant Minds* (1808), in *The Poetical Works of Ann and Jane Taylor* (London: Ward, Lock, & Tyler, 1877), 25.
   [25] M. A. Stodart, *Principles of Education Practically Considered; with an Especial Reference to the Present State of Female Education in England* (London: R. B. Seeley & W. Burnside, 1844), 130.
   [26] Sherwood, *The Fairchild Family*, pt. I, 82–9.
   [27] Mrs Edwin Gray, *Papers and Diaries of a York Family 1764–1839* (London: Sheldon Press, 1927), 256–9. The work in question was entitled, 'Biomêtre ou Mémorial Horaire, servant à indiquer le nombre des heures données par jour à chacune des divisions. Par M. A. Jullien, de Paris, Auteur de l'Essai sur l'emploi du Temps'. For a less extreme, but still tormented, example of such a diary, kept in the late 1830s, see Anthony Kenny (ed.), *The Oxford Diaries of Arthur Hugh Clough* (Oxford: Clarendon Press, 1990).

clothe themselves with shame-facedness and sobriety, not with braided hair and costly apparel' (64). If Jane, at Lowood school, is forced to display herself as 'a liar!' on a 'pedestal of infamy' (66–7) such punishment was not, in evangelical circles, unusual, or even unusually extreme. The novelist Elizabeth Missing Sewell tells in her *Autobiography* how, at the school she attended in the 1820s,

> ... if a child told a lie, she was not allowed any reward for three months, and was obliged to stand up in the schoolroom for several hours with a long black gown on, and a piece of red cloth—cut in the shape of a tongue, and on which the word 'Liar' was worked in white letters—fastened round the neck so as to hang down in front. The awe which fell upon the school when Miss Crooke in a solemn voice said, 'Put on the Gown and the Liar's tongue', was indescribable.[28]

The issue of Carus Wilson's *Children's Friend* that appeared in June 1847, a few months before *Jane Eyre*, contains a story whose title tells all—'The Liar's Mouth Sewn Up': it is illustrated by a graphic woodcut. And the tract on the Liar that Mr Brocklehurst gives to Jane has its prototype in dozens of such stories, by Carus Wilson and by others, in which liars meet dreadful earthly punishments, or go to everlasting perdition. The message was driven home with singular ferocity. 'All Liars shall have their part in the lake which burneth with fire and brimstone', Rowland Hill warns his infant readers; 'and how grievously they are tormented you will see in the picture.'[29] 'Then let me always watch my Lips,' resolves the child speaker of Isaac Watts' 'Against Lying':

> Lest I be struck to Death and Hell
> Since God a Book of Reckoning keeps
> For every Lye that Children tell.[30]

'I was thunderstruck and almost distracted', declared one early nineteenth-century father, of his discovery that his 3-year-old son had told a lie, 'for the information seemed to blast my most cherished hopes. This might, I thought, be the commencement of a series of evils for ever ruinous to our peace. . . . I am not sure that my agony, on hearing of his death, was much more intense than that which I endured, from an apprehension of his guilt.'[31]

Evangelical children were not simply watched and warned. They were subjected also to a rigorous discipline, aimed at subduing the desires of the flesh, instilling humility and obedience, and fitting them for eternity. This was most famously institutionalized, of course, in schools such as Kingswood and Cowan Bridge, with their monotonous, exacting routines—like the 'rules . . . lessons . . . method . . . systematic arrangements' (56) of the Lowood regime—in which every moment of the day had its allotted task, and children were uniformly attired, given the plainest food,

[28] *The Autobiography of Elizabeth Missing Sewell,* edited by her niece, Eleanor L. Sewell (London: Longmans, Green & Co., 1907), 13–14. On such punishments as 'standard practices', see Barker, 125.
[29] Quoted in Sangster, *Pity My Simplicity,* 139.
[30] Isaac Watts, *Divine Songs, Attempted in Easy Language for the Use of Children,* facs. reproduction of 1st edn. of 1715 (London: Oxford University Press, 1971), 23.
[31] *Eclectic Review,* 2nd ser. 18 (1822), 71.

and severely punished for their faults. Yet schools such as these merely provided spectacular, public examples of a discipline that was practised to greater or lesser extent in hundreds of thousands of early Victorian homes. Daily life was closely regulated, Sabbath observance rigidly enforced, and even on weekdays prohibitions and restrictions were plentiful. The child's friendships and reading-matter were censored and controlled; and he or she was made to learn hymns and large portions of Scripture by heart. (A prominent item in Mr. Brocklehurst's cautionary repertoire is the paragon of 'infant piety' who receives gingerbread-nuts in return for learning psalms). Catechizing, which had begun to be outmoded, was revived in the early years of the century. Evangelical catechisms were advertised in Hannah More's *Cheap Repository Tracts* and praised in the *Evangelical Magazine*.[32] Such catechisms recur in *Jane Eyre*. At Jane's first meeting with the black marble Brocklehurst she is subjected to a form of catechizing; Sunday evenings at Lowood are spent 'in repeating, by heart, the Church Catechism' (60); later, St John Rivers is reported to have gone to Morton school to give a daily catechizing class.

Formal catechizing was, however, but the public, ritual face of much more intimately intrusive inquisitorial practices. The evangelical child was constantly questioned as to the state of his or her soul: parental letters to their children are filled with urgent interrogations. 'It is time you seriously reflected on eternity, and the value of your soul', Legh Richmond urged one son after another's death. 'You are a sinner; and without a gracious Saviour you must perish. Do you pray in Christ's name? and that earnestly, for the pardon of your sins? . . . Do you think of [your brother's] last words to you . . . ? Have you written down his dying words, as I desired you?'[33] For evangelical discipline was not merely an external regime: it extended like rapine into the most private areas of the psyche. Richmond's lengthy description of his son Wilberforce's death today makes harrowing reading, not least because of the evidence it provides of the boy's desperate attempts to preserve an area of privacy in face of his father's equally desperate questioning. Indeed, the entire volume in which that account appears offers an (unintentionally) chilling picture of what the psychodynamics of a family life motivated by evangelical ideology might be. Richmond was not merely 'very attentive to [his children's] regularity, neatness and good manners': 'when he perceived youthful spirits rising to excess, he would throw in a remark to check the exuberance'.[34] 'While at home as well as when abroad', his biographer writes of him, 'he kept up a correspondence with his family, which he used to call his *Home Mission*'—a correspondence motivated largely by his confessed inability to initiate 'close personal conversation' with them. 'When I begin, they are silent,' he admits; 'and it is not long before I also feel tongue-tied; yet I cannot be easy without ascertaining the effect of my instructions, and hence I have been driven to use my pen, because I could not open my lips.' Richmond never used 'corporal chastisement'. Like Mrs Reed, though no doubt from higher spiritual

---

[32] Sangster, *Pity My Simplicity*, 40. See e.g. Mrs Sherwood, *Stories Explanatory of the Church Catechism* (Wellington, Salop: F. Houlston & Son, 1821) and [Eliza Smith], *Chapters on the Shorter Catechism, a Tale for the Instruction of Youth*, 2nd edn. (Edinburgh: Paton & Ritchie, 1850).
[33] Richmond, *Domestic Portraiture*, 76.   [34] Ibid. 70.

motives, he 'kept the offender at a distance, or separated him from the society of his family, as one unworthy to share in their privileges and affections'—his 'countenance' meanwhile expressing 'the deepest anguish' at the sense of himself as 'the author of a corrupt being'. The result appears to have been acquiescence: or, as his admiring biographer puts it, 'Perhaps there never was a family where the reign of love suffered less interruption.'[35]

'Love' was certainly often invoked as the mainspring of evangelical pedagogy. The claim—very often sincere—was that those who thus watched and punished their little ones were acting for their 'own good', striving to ensure their salvation from a terrible doom. 'Remember that your parents are commanded by God to correct your faults,' enjoined John Angell James; 'that they are actuated by love in performing this self-denying duty, and that it costs them more pain to inflict it, than it does you to endure it.'[36] 'I wished every stroke had been a stab', says Charlotte Elizabeth Tonna, describing the whipping her father gave her for telling a lie. 'I wept because the pain was not great enough; and I loved my father at that moment better than even I, who almost idolized him, had ever loved him before.'[37] 'A poor little girl who had been taken into a school was whipped', tells Carus Wilson, in *The Children's Friend*, apparently of a child at Cowan Bridge school. 'She asked, "If they love us, why do they whip us?" A little girl of six replied, "It is because they love us, and it is to make us remember what a sad thing sin is. God would be angry with them if they did not whip us."'[38] ('Cruel? Not at all! She is severe: she dislikes my faults,' says Helen Burns (55), of the terrible Miss Scatcherd.) 'Precious, no doubt, are these little ones in your eyes; but if you love them, think often of their souls', exhorted J. C. Ryle, in a sermon preached a year before the publication of *Jane Eyre*:

No interest should weigh with you so much as their eternal interests. No part of them should be so dear to you as that part which will never die . . . To pet and pamper, and indulge your child, as if this world was all he had to look to, and this life the only season for happiness; to do this is not true love but cruelty.[39]

Yet if evangelical teaching was often sincerely motivated by a desperate desire to save the 'little ones' at whom it was directed, its God was less a God of love than a God of vengeance:

> Two sinners God's just vengeance felt
> For telling one presumptuous lie:
> Dear children, learn to dread his wrath,
> Lest you should also sin and die.[40]

---

[35] Richmond, *Domestic Portraiture*, 73, 81.

[36] John Angell James, *The Family Monitor, or A Help to Domestic Happiness* (Birmingham, 1828), 179.

[37] Tonna, *Personal Recollections*, 18–19.   [38] Quoted in *LL* i. 72.

[39] J. C. Ryle, 'Train up a Child in the Way He Should Go', *A Sermon for Parents preached in Helmingham Church* (1846), quoted in Elisabeth Jay, *The Religion of the Heart: Anglican Evangelicalism* (Oxford: Clarendon Press, 1979), 137.

[40] Rowland Hill, quoted in Sangster, *Pity My Simplicity*, 134.

And it was enforced by a programme of coercion and punishment, intimidation and humiliation, which—however it might be softened by affection or (as it was for the young Brontës) countered by other influences—was expressly designed to break the 'spirit' of the child.

For evangelical discipline was aimed, above all, at the subjugation of self: not merely that denial of the flesh which might, in extreme cases, lead to actual death (as at Lowood), but also, and most centrally, the 'mortification' of worldly impulses and desires (*JE* 76). The child's will had to be broken, lest he or she be damned: the successfully reared evangelical child was one who—like Helen Burns—had internalized the self-suppression thus imposed. This was a project far more extreme than that character-building 'self-control' seen as essential to success in early nineteenth-century England which Brontë had portrayed in Crimsworth.[41] For its explicit aim was self-annihilation; and it was both motivated and mirrored by the evangelical emphasis on death.

'God has spared you', declares Carus Wilson, in a New Year address to a child whose 'little companion' has died: 'Why? That you may get ready to die. He has let you see a new year. Why? Because he wants you to seek a new heart and so be prepared for heaven.'[42] To the evangelicals, life on earth was a mere preparation for the hereafter: death, therefore, was its climactic point—the moment of entry into bliss or perdition. When the 10-year-old Maria Brontë was questioned by her father as to 'what was the best mode of spending time', hers was the orthodox response of the ideal evangelical child: 'By laying it out in preparation for a happy eternity.'[43] Long before she embarked on the use of the Biometer, the youthful Margaret Gray had recorded her grand aim in life: 'to be deeply impressed with the vanity and unsatisfactory nature of all earthly things; to have realizing views of eternity; to look steadily to the near approach of death; to hold converse with heaven'.[44] In 1797 the *Evangelical Magazine* printed a Spiritual Barometer, an aid to self-examination, by the use of which the child could monitor the state of his soul: its point of highest spiritual excellence was 'Desiring to depart, to be with Christ.'[45] Just such a 'point of spiritual excellence' is prominently figured in the letter Jane quotes from St John Rivers at the ending of *Jane Eyre*.

Death, indeed, was the central theme of evangelical pedagogy. The aim of the myriads of tracts and stories directed in these years at little children was to convince the child of the inevitability of death and of the dreadfulness of the punishment awaiting sinners. One such tract, 'containing 'an account of the awfully sudden death of Martha G—, a naughty child addicted to falsehood and deceit' (35) is presented by Brocklehurst to Jane: later, she tells how the pupils at Lowood were subjected to 'evening readings from books of his own inditing, about sudden deaths

[41] See Sally Shuttleworth, *Charlotte Brontë and Victorian Psychology* (Cambridge: Cambridge University Press, 1996), ch. 7, for an illuminating discussion of *The Professor* and 'the art of self-control'.
[42] *The Children's Friend*, January 1845.   [43] Gaskell, 94.
[44] Gray, *Papers and Diaries of a York Family*, 249.
[45] Reproduced in Sangster, *Pity My Simplicity*, 147. Near the bottom of the scale, amongst the activities leading to perdition, is listed 'love of novels'.

and judgments, which made us afraid to go to bed' (123). Carus Wilson's actual output certainly conforms to this description. *The Child's Magazine, and Sunday-School Companion* for July 1824, which appeared the month before the 8-year-old Charlotte Brontë entered Cowan Bridge school, and is likely to have formed part of her reading there, contains an article entitled 'On Man's Mortality', which instructs its young readers that 'of nothing can we be more certain, than of this, however we may strive to forget it, we must die', and calculates the numbers of people dying throughout the world:

Each year Thirty-three millions three hundred thousand
Each day Eighty-three thousand
Each hour Three thousand four hundred and fifty
Each minute Fifty-seven
Which amounts almost to One each second.

'If the mortality be so great each year, and even each day', it concludes, 'is it not more than probable that some one of our fellow-creatures is this moment departing from the world? And before an hour has elapsed, more than three thousand souls who are still inhabitants of time will have passed into eternity! What a motive to induce us to think frequently and seriously upon death, and to live in a state of continual preparation for our solemn change!' Each issue of this journal—as of *The Children's Friend*—contains at least one account of an early death. Some describe the edifying deaths of pious children—those who have internalized evangelical strictures so effectively that all desire for self-preservation (at any rate in this world) has been obliterated in them. One such anecdote, which appears in *The Children's Friend* for 1826, is of particular interest, in that it concerns a girl who was a contemporary of Charlotte Brontë's at Cowan Bridge, entering the school in February 1824 at the age of 9 (the 8-year-old Charlotte was to join her in August of the same year) and dying at the age of 11 in 1826:

On the 28th of last September died in the Clergy School at Cowen Bridge [*sic*] Sarah Bicker, aged 11 years. . . . Her complaint was inflammation in the bowels, and her sufferings were very great. . . . I had heard from her teachers that she had expressed a desire to depart and to be with Christ and I was anxious to assure myself that her hopes were well founded . . . I bless God that he has taken from us the child of whose salvation we have the best hope and may her death be the means of rousing many of her school-fellows to seek the Lord while he may be found.

Before her holy death, Sarah Bicker had (it is reported) urged a naughty companion to 'humble her pride and pray to God, and he would be sure to take away her heart of stone and give her a heart of flesh': her words are echoed in Mr Brocklehurst's injunction to Jane Eyre: 'You have a wicked heart; and you must pray to God to change it: to give you a new and clean one: to take away your heart of stone and give you a heart of flesh' (33). (The allusion, in both cases, is to Ezekiel 11: 19.) Other stories—like that of 'the sudden death of the Liar', which Brocklehurst gives to Jane (67)—recount the dreadful deaths of the unrepentant. One such, in *The Child's First Tales*, describes that of a boy who skated on the sabbath, fell through the ice, and was drowned: 'He left his school. He took his play on the Sunday. And he thought he should go to hell for this. I fear he would go there. How sad it is to think of!'[46] Another, recounted in monosyllables for infant readers, tells of a little girl of 3, who flew into a violent 'pet' with her mother:

She was in such a rage, that all at once God struck her dead . . . No time to pray. No time to call on God to save her poor soul . . . And oh! where do you think she is now? . . . We know that bad girls go to hell . . . I do not think that this poor girl's rage is now at an end, though she is in hell. She is in a rage with her-self.[47]

For if for the regenerate death was the gateway to eternal bliss, no evangelical child could be safe from fear of the terrible alternative. Even the saintly Wilberforce Richmond was tormented by doubts on his deathbed. 'I often think how shocking it would be to go to hell,' confided the 11-year-old Margaret Gray to the diary of self-castigation she kept for her mother's perusal, in 1820. 'I can't bear the thought of it; and I think sometimes, suppose I was to die, where should I go to?'[48] To the child Jane, locked in the red-room at Thornfield, a dreadful question presents itself: 'Was I fit to die?' (48). Sophisticated theologians might differ on the subject,[49] but the notion of everlasting punishment was prominent in evangelical writings for children in the first half of the nineteenth century. Thus, the evangelical catechism 'For Children of Tender Years':

Q. What sort of a place is Hell?
A. A dark and bottomless pit, full of fire and brimstone.
Q. How will the wicked be punished there?
A. Their bodies will be tormented by fire.[50]

Thus Legh Richmond, to his 11-year-old son: 'You have need to flee from the wrath to come. Repent, for the kingdom of heaven is at hand. The wicked and all the people that forget God, shall be turned into hell. Dear Willy, if you forget him, what will be your portion?'[51] And thus Carus Wilson, in a memorable formulation:

> 'Tis dangerous to provoke a God
> Whose power and vengeance none can tell;
> One stroke of his almighty rod
> Can send young sinners quick to hell.[52]

Jane's 'ready and orthodox answer' to Mr Brocklehurst's query, 'Do you know where the wicked go after death?' could have come from any one of hundreds of evangelical tracts, with their graphic depictions of that fearful 'pit full of fire'. Her progress through the novel is attended by threats of Hell and damnation, from Miss

---

[46] William Carus Wilson, *The Child's First Tales* (Kirkby Lonsdale: A. Foster, 1836).
[47] Carus Wilson, *The Child's First Tales*, 47.   [48] Gray, *Papers and Diaries of a York Family*, 250.
[49] See Geoffrey Rowell, *Hell and the Victorians: A Study of the Nineteenth-Century Theological Controversies Concerning Eternal Punishment and the Future Life* (Oxford: Oxford University Press, 1974).
[50] Quoted in Sangster, *Pity My Simplicity*, 139.
[51] Richmond, *Domestic Portraiture*, 210.
[52] *The Children's Friend*, quoted in *LL* i. 71.

Abbot's awful question (reminiscent of Carus Wilson)—'God . . . might strike her dead in the midst of her tantrums, and then where would she go?' (13)—to Brockle-hurst's—'And should you like to fall into that pit and to be burning there for ever?' (32); from the terrible temptation of Rochester's 'flaming glance', before which she is 'powerless as stubble exposed to the draught and glow of a furnace' (317) to St John Rivers's pointed reading of 'the lake which burneth with fire and brimstone, which is the second death' (417).

If Jane's is an extreme example of a 'universal' experience of childish vulnerabil-ity and humiliation, it has, then, a quite particular cultural inflection. Indeed, much in these early chapters of *Jane Eyre*—the injunctions and warnings directed at Jane; the discipline institutionalized at Lowood school, with its surveillance, its regimen-tation, its punishments and privations; the caricature-portrait of Mr Brocklehurst and his publications; Helen Burns's pious (if slightly unorthodox) death—seems designed to offer less a peculiar, private nightmare-vision than a hostile but realis-tic portrayal of the ethos of evangelicalism. Brocklehurst's words virtually echo the published writings of his real-life prototype:[53] the punishments inflicted on Helen and Jane can be paralleled by the (often far worse) punishments suffered by disobedient children in hundreds of evangelical tracts. And if, as Carus Wilson's supporters indignantly noted, the depiction of the Lowood regime amounts to a 'wholesale' attack on the methods of evangelical pedagogy, more subtly, but just as trenchantly, Jane's narrative challenges the values it sought to inculcate. The 'res-traint' and 'chastisement' to which she is subjected are opposed by the 'liberty' for which she strains, the 'praise' she longs for; the acceptance and forbearance preached to her by those about her by the 'rebellion and rage' that impels her on. Unmoved by threats of hellfire, and with remarkably little inner struggle, she makes her choice of earthly happiness: a choice whose difference from the path of evan-gelicalism is emphasized in her narrative's closing contrast between the mutuality of her life with Rochester and St John Rivers's 'undaunted' aspiration towards death.

Usually, *Jane Eyre*'s relation to the religious discourses on which it draws has been seen in a more positive light. Jane's refusal to depart from paths of virtue, the echoes from *Pilgrim's Progress* she repeatedly invokes, have seemed, to many, to sig-nal a reworking of that Bunyanesque narrative of a journey through perils to 'blessedness' which was evangelicalism's message of hope to the child. If Brockle-hurst's religiosity, Helen Burns's self-immolation, the icy sternness of St John Rivers are all rejected as paths to salvation, *Jane Eyre*, it is argued, does not reject that narrative: rather, it reinflects it, to suggest that the claims of nature and of Grace, of this world and the next, can finally be reconciled.[54] And much in the novel itself ap-pears to support this view. Certainly, Jane's account of her progress towards happi-

---

[53] See, for examples, Rev. Angus Mackay, 'The Brontes at Cowan Bridge', *The Bookman*, October 1894, reprinted in *LL* i. 71–5.

[54] For examples of this kind of reading, see Barry V. Qualls, *The Secular Pilgrims of Victorian Fiction: The Novel as Book of Life* (Cambridge: Cambridge University Press, 1982), 51–69, and Thomas Vargish, *The Providential Aesthetic in Victorian Fiction* (Charlottesville: University Press of Virginia, 1985), 58–67.

ness seems to be shaped and underwritten by conformations prominent in evangelical writings. Like theirs, her moral universe is one without nuance or ambiguity: a place of black-and-white judgement, where the good and the bad respectively receive their just deserts. John Reed, with his 'shocking' end, Helen Burns, with her pious resignation, could be exemplary figures from evangelical tracts; so could the libertine Rochester, restless and unhappy in his search for worldly satisfaction, and condemned to a biblical punishment for his 'offence' against God's law.[55] The nodal, epiphanic moments in which it is revealed to Jane what she must do—to 'flee temptation' (319) or to 'advertise' for a situation (86), the magical solutions that appear to her dilemmas (her discovery of her family, her uncle's legacy, Bertha's convenient death, even her 'call' to return to Rochester) likewise have their parallel in evangelical writings: the *Methodist Magazines* Brontë knew as a child recorded dozens of examples of such Special Providences, or minor miracles performed for his chosen by God.[56] Here, as in puritan autobiography or evangelical tract, the social world appears as a place of solitary pilgrimage, and the self as a radical isolate, pursuing its own separate path to its own peculiar end. If this is most obviously true of those more or less orthodox Christians, Helen Burns and St John Rivers—characters whose 'ends' are figured prominently as images of solitary transcendence[57]— it may also be seen as in some respects true of Jane. 'I still possessed my soul', she asserts, as she describes her flight from Rochester, 'and with it the certainty of ultimate safety' (317). Like Bunyan's Christian, she struggles against temptation and defends her integrity: and like an exemplary figure in an evangelical tract, she is rewarded with perfect happiness—though in this world, rather than the next.

Yet the configurations of evangelicalism appear in *Jane Eyre* not merely, or even mainly thus, but distinctively, disconcertingly, to quite opposite effect. Jane's, as we have seen, is a story not merely of survival and triumph, but of constant, imminent jeopardy. As a child, she is subjected to others' authority—inquisitorial, judgemental, punitive; she is beaten, starved, frozen; warned both of death—'Children younger than you die daily' (32)—and of the dangers of hellfire. And that which at first appears as a realistic, if negative, representation of evangelical doctrines and practices is inscribed surrealistically throughout: in a plot in which, again and again, the other appears as dreadful in potency and the teller is threatened with extinction, and in a prose that repeatedly represents self as impotent, endangered and persecuted, not merely from without, but from within. Feelings, in this narrative, have something of the autonomous energy of the figures who populate Bunyan's allegory. 'As to my own will or conscience, impassioned grief had trampled one and stifled the other: I was weeping wildly as I walked along my solitary way; fast, fast I went like one delirious' (321). Self appears less as the agent of its own destiny, developing, acting, choosing, than as having its fate appointed for it—a sense that is

---

[55] Matthew 5: 28–30.

[56] Jay, in *Religion of the Heart*, 97 ff., traces the considerable controversy over this doctrine in the first half of the 19th cent.

[57] St John 'aims to fill a place in the first rank of those who are redeemed from the earth' (452); Helen's grave is marked 'Resurgam' (82).

reinforced by the premonitions and portents that punctuate Jane's narrative of ostensible self-making and choice.[58] If that 'Providentialist' narrative of temptations withstood and salvation arrived at owes its conformations to the discourse of evangelicalism, so too does this other story, of ultimate powerlessness and irresolvable threat. That confrontation between the defenceless child and the persecutory other which is portrayed in the novel's opening pages resonates throughout—through its figures, its images, through the very syntax in which that story is framed.

These features of the novel were seen, by early readers, as 'the work of a morbid fancy', 'most extravagantly improbable'.[59] Yet that 'morbidity' is inscribed in the surviving documents of the period. The records of those who subjected little children to a regime designed to break their wills and terrify them into submission testify to the actual, substantial existence in early Victorian England of a reality that might well appear 'extravagantly improbable'. Of course, not all came under the sway of a Carus Wilson. But, as *Jane Eyre*'s echo of Mrs Chapone indicates, even more benign pedagogies partook of his methods.[60] The 'context of living fear' engendered by that lurid, familiar, intimidating world of early nineteenth-century evangelicalism must for many have been a paramount subjective fact.[61] For its pedagogy was one of the most extreme forms imaginable of that regulatory system of control by which, it is argued, bourgeois order was established in nineteenth-century England: a stringent form of disciplinary power, exercised upon those least able to resist or even question it; one that seems to have operated in more or less

---

[58] For a suggestive discussion of signs and portents in *Jane Eyre*, and their relation to the 'essentially theological' and pre-novelistic' allegory of the emblem books, see Hermione Lee, 'Emblems and Enigmas in *Jane Eyre*', *English*, 30 (1981), 233–55.

[59] *Christian Observer* NS 234 (June 1857), 428; unsigned review in *Christian Remembrancer*, quoted in *CH* 90.

[60] If Carus Wilson seems an extreme figure, it is noteworthy that his school had the support of most of the progressive educationists of the day; and that the initial list of subscribers included not merely such prominent Evangelicals as William Wilberforce, Hannah More, and Charles Simeon, but local Members of Parliament and neighbouring clergy; its regime, according to Juliet Barker, 'was no worse, and in some respects more lenient, than at other comparable schools' (Barker, 119–27). The Brontës, of course, not least through their experience as governesses, were familiar with quite other modes of child-rearing: thus Charlotte Brontë writes to Ellen Nussey in 1840 of the 'unruly, violent family of Modern children' with whom her sister Anne has had to contend (*CBL* i. 210). A recurring figure in their fiction is the indulged, usually upper-class child, like 'Eliza, John, and Georgiana Reed'. Less repressive attitudes—such as Brontë was to observe in the family of Mrs Gaskell—are represented in *Jane Eyre* by Miss Temple, and by Jane's treatment of Adèle. But the concern in *Jane Eyre* is not with presenting a 'fair' or balanced picture of life in early 19th-cent. England, but with tracing the logic of the ideology that the narrating Jane confronts.

[61] The *Dictionary of National Biography*'s claim that 'most children of the English middle classes, born in the first quarter of the nineteenth century, were brought up on *The Fairchild Family*' is borne out by F. J. Harvey Darton. In the Introduction to his *Life and Times of Mrs Sherwood* (London: Wells Gardner, Darton, 1910), he records that 'a prominent literary journal' had, ten years earlier, asked 'prominent men of the day' to name the two books of their childhood that they 'remembered most vividly, or which had in one way or another impressed [them] most strongly': 'Much divergence was discovered as regards the second of the two books named in each instance; but respecting the first there was agreement little short of unanimity. Practically all those who voted had been brought up, in the fifties of the nineteenth century, and earlier, on *The Fairchild Family*. They did not all like the book, but they had read it, and, it appeared, had read it thoroughly.'

extreme form throughout large sections of the society,[62] and reached into the deepest layers of the individual psyche.[63] Its surveillance extended to the most intimate recesses of the personality, its discipline to the regimentation of every moment, its sanctions to the threat not merely of death but of eternal perdition. Within the context of its writings, that sense of ever-present existential threat which attends Brontë's heroine's progress seems the stuff less of timeless fantasy than of historical actuality: not a remote fairy tale, but the texture of life as it was actually presented to and experienced by hundreds of thousands of children in the England of its time.

'Crowds and crowds of little children are strangely missing from the written record,' writes Peter Laslett in *The World We Have Lost*; 'nearly half the whole community living in a condition of semi-obliteration.'[64] *Jane Eyre* portrays early nineteenth-century England from the perspective of one such oppressed and 'semi-obliterated' child. Its concern is not with the psychological costs of evangelical pedagogy, like such other mid-century fictions as Dickens' *Bleak House* and *Little Dorrit* or Kingsley's *Alton Locke*. If Jane speaks of the 'morbid suffering' to which she is 'a prey' (22), and attributes her habitual childhood mood of 'humiliation, self-doubt, forlorn depression' (23) to her 'life of ceaseless reprimand and thankless fagging' (20), the ease with which she leaves each stage of her life behind seems indeed to point away from any such concern. The child is not here treated as a psychological case, or seen from the point of view of a later, more 'realistic' maturity. Rather, as Doreen Roberts suggests, the young Jane's 'magnified vision . . . establishe[s] the dominant viewpoint and prepare[s] the reader for the persistent distortion which is the essence of the book's method'.[65] For with its opening emphasis on the repressive, death-directed practices and doctrines of early nineteenth-century evangelicalism and its closing image of the missionary St John Rivers, dying to this world, ambitious for the next, the novel draws attention to the reality in which its 'melodrama' is based: not merely the manifest reality of privation and punishment epitomized by 'Lowood Institution', but the more insidious reality of that self-subjugating discipline, that ideology of death and judgement, promulgated in the writings of Carus Wilson and his like. This 'mere domestic novel' is not, it would appear, simply a striking rendition of an individual subjectivity. In its distinctive

---

[62] On the extraordinarily widespread circulation of evangelical tracts, and the manner in which they were distributed (through just one of the many agencies devoted to such purposes), see William Jones, *The Jubilee Memorial of the Religious Tract Society* (London: Religious Tract Society, 1850) and Samuel Green, *The Story of the Religious Tract Society* (London: Religious Tract Society, 1899). Carus Wilson's *The Friendly Visitor* was first issued in 1819, *The Children's Friend* in 1824. The latter ran for forty years, and even achieved an Arabic edition in 1870. According to Sheila A. Egoff, 'over 50,000 copies of [*The Children's Friend*] and his adult publications, *The Friendly Visitor* and *The Christian Guardian*, were sold each month' (*Children's Periodicals of the Nineteenth Century. A Survey and Bibliography*, Library Association Pamphlet No. 8 (London, 1951), 9).

[63] For a detailed account of the lifelong effects of evangelical pedagogy see e.g. Elizabeth Missing Sewell's *Autobiography*, cited above.

[64] Peter Laslett, *The World We Have Lost: England Before the Industrial Age* (New York: Charles Scribner's Sons, 1965), 104.

[65] 'Jane Eyre and the Warped System of Things', in Heather Glen (ed.), *Jane Eyre: New Casebook* (London: Macmillan, 1997), 147.

representation of the world as experienced by and presented to the child, it offers a powerful realization of some of the most fundamental processes whereby a whole society conceived of and constructed itself.

II

The injunction to die to self, to submit to a more powerful other, was not, in early Victorian England, confined to evangelical teaching. If a middle-class boy could expect to grow beyond the powerlessness of childhood, and appear, at least, 'to have his fate in his own hands' (as Elizabeth Gaskell remarked of the young Branwell Brontë)[66]—for a middle-class girl the experience of childhood was more likely to be reinforced than transcended in adulthood. 'From their early childhood, girls are accustomed to fill an inferior place, to give up, to fall back, and to *be as nothing* in comparison with their brothers,' observes Sarah Ellis in 1843 (my italics).[67] 'Woman has been and is even yet too often told that in herself she can be nothing; that she is in fact a mere relative being, dependent entirely upon man for her happiness,' writes Anne Richelieu Lamb in the following year.[68] For this was a society in which masculine power was paramount. And the model of womanhood approved by its moralists, underwritten by its laws, and inscribed more enticingly in its rhetoric of romantic love was one of 'subordination and dependence',[69] rather than of self-assertion.

'The Lowood constraint still clings to you somewhat;' says Rochester to Jane, one evening early in her stay at Thornfield, 'controlling your features, muffling your voice, and restricting your limbs; and you fear in the presence of a man and a brother—or father, or master, or what you will—to smile too gaily, speak too freely, or move too quickly' (138). His words signal the homology between the 'disciplined and subdued character' required of the evangelical child and the behaviour expected of the governess—that 'refined propriety' which in the model Miss Temple 'precluded deviation into the ardent, the excited, the eager' (73). Rochester, of course, is no advocate of such 'propriety'. 'You are not naturally austere,' he assures his 'paid subordinate'. 'In time I think you will learn to be natural with me, as I find it impossible to be conventional with you; and then your looks and movements will have more vivacity and variety than they dare offer now' (138). But the ironic echo here of Mrs Reed's first mystifying pronouncement, and the rapidity with which the language of emancipation ('a man and a brother')[70] slides, on Rochester's lips, into

---

[66] Gaskell, 197.

[67] Sarah Ellis, *The Wives of England, their Relative Duties, Domestic Influence, and Social Obligations* (London: Fisher, Son, & Co., 1843), 68.

[68] [Anne Richelieu Lamb], *Can Woman Regenerate Society?* (London: John W. Parker, 1844), 3.

[69] M. A. Stodart, *Every Day Duties; In Letters to a Young Lady* (London: R. B. Seeley & W. Burnside, 1840), p. vii.

[70] This phrase was a famous one in early 19th-cent. England, and cannot have failed to carry this resonance for the novel's earliest readers. 'Am I not a man and a brother' appeared as a legend on a cameo produced by Josiah Wedgwood, depicting a kneeling negro slave in chains; it became a catch-phrase of

that of patriarchy and class ('or father, or master'), draws attention to the fact that the world through which Jane moves is one whose inequities cannot be transcended by this kind of drawing-room egalitarianism. If as a child she was labelled 'an inter-loper and an alien' and 'exposed to general view on a pedestal of infamy' (67, 68); so later, as a governess, she is singled out as the object of the condemnatory gaze of those more privileged than she. 'I noticed her:' says Lady Ingram. 'I am a judge of physiognomy, and in hers I see all the faults of her class' (177). But unlike that earl-ier, terrorized child, Jane no longer sees her lot as a shamefully singular one. In words that resonate with her childhood experience, she has linked her own 'doom' to that of 'millions', protesting not merely against the hardships and frustrations of the governess, but against the model of proper womanhood which that 'anathema-tized race' (177) was expected to exemplify and inculcate: '. . . Women are supposed to be very calm generally: but women feel just as men feel . . . they suffer from too rigid a restraint, too absolute a stagnation, precisely as men would suffer; and it is narrow minded . . . to say that they ought to confine themselves to making puddings and knitting stockings' (109).

A major early Victorian cultural phenomenon is evoked in these references to what 'women' are 'supposed to be' and what they 'ought to' do. 'The press has lately teemed with works treating of the condition, the destiny, the duties of women,' the art historian Anna Jameson had written, in an essay published the year before *Jane Eyre*. 'The theme, however treated, is one of the themes of the day.'[71] Such 'works', addressed on the whole to the women of the middle classes, ranged from the overtly misogynistic, such as *Woman: As She Is and As She Should Be* (published anony-mously in 1835) to more or less explicitly feminist tracts, such as Anne Richelieu Lamb's *Can Woman Regenerate Society?* (1844) and Marion Reid's *A Plea for Woman* (1843).[72] Somewhere in the middle were the best-selling advice books of Mrs Sarah Stickney Ellis, today often cited as the unquestioned voice of the age.[73] Book-length treatises on womanhood were merely the tip of an iceberg. Pro-nouncements upon and advice to women abound in the periodicals of the period, both those explicitly directed at them and also those aimed at a general readership. As E. M. Palmegiano points out, in her useful bibliography of the subject, 'the ma-jority of authors inferred that they knew better than most women what constituted womanhood and how best to express it. This implicit desire to train the sex may be

the anti-slavery movement. For a suggestive account of Branwell Brontë's interest in this image in 1845, see Christopher Heywood, ' "Alas! Poor Caunt!" Branwell's Emancipationist Cartoon', *BST* 21: 5 (1995), 177–85.

[71] ' "Woman's Mission" and "Woman's Position" ', in Anna Jameson, *Memoirs and Essays: Illustra-tive of Art, Literature and Social Morals* (London: Richard Bentley, 1846), 215.

[72] Mrs Hugo Reid, *A Plea For Woman: Being a Vindication of the Importance and Extent of Her Nat-ural Sphere of Action; with Remarks on Recent Works on the Subject* (Edinburgh: William Tait, 1843).

[73] Immensely successful as she was, Mrs Ellis was also the butt of considerable criticism. The publi-cation of her advice books—*The Women, The Wives, The Daughters, The Mothers* of England—in a cheap series in 1845–6 provoked *Punch*, for instance, to considerable hilarity at her expense. (See Catherine Peters, *Thackeray's Universe: Shifting Worlds of Imagination and Reality* (London: Faber, 1987), 126).

more significant than anything that was actually written about it.'[74] If writers on the 'Woman Question' were not entirely agreed as to what woman was, or should be, there can be no question as to the intensity of attention to which she was subjected in the period, the assiduity with which her 'nature' was explained and her conduct prescribed.[75]

Many of these writers on womanhood were in fact evangelicals; and some voice sentiments that would not be out of place in evangelical tracts. 'We all have an hereditary propensity to evil', proclaims *Woman's Worth: or, Hints to Raise the Female Character*, published in 1844.[76] But they speak on the whole of 'faults' rather than of 'sins': religion for them is more taken for granted than stressed.[77] Thus, in her Preface to *The Women of England* Sarah Ellis (married to an evangelical missionary) announces that her concern is not with her readers' salvation, but with 'those domestic habits, and relative duties, which in after life will materially assist the developement [*sic*] of the Christian character';[78] it is thus that, in a later work, she defends her attention to 'the minute and homely details of woman's daily life'.[79] 'The present time only is our own—the next hour we may be numbered with the dead,' points out the author of *Woman's Worth*, but the reader's attention is directed not to the fate of the imperilled soul but to the practical duties of every day:

It is a wise arrangement to divide the day into sections, and to allot a given time to every occupation. By this method, every duty would have the proper time allotted to it, and there would be no fear that one which afforded pleasure would be followed to such a length as to leave no time for another which might be regarded as less agreeable.[80]

The effective time-management here recommended is rather different from the self-castigation expected of the evangelical child. For these moralists of womanhood are less concerned with the annihilation of self than with techniques for self-construction and self-discipline. Their titles speak for themselves: *Thoughts on Self-Culture, Hints to Raise the Female Character, Letters on the Improvement of the*

---

[74] 'Women and British Periodicals 1832–1867: A Bibliography', *Victorian Periodicals Newsletter* 9 (1976), 5. On the attention paid to 'woman' in medical and social scientific texts, see Jill L. Matus, *Unstable Bodies: Victorian Representations of Sexuality and Maternity* (Manchester: Manchester University Press, 1995).

[75] See Judith L. Newton, ' "Ministers of the Interior": The Political Economy of Women's Manuals', in *Starting Over: Feminism and the Politics of Cultural Critique* (Ann Arbor: University of Michigan Press, 1994), 125–47, for a thoughtful analysis of the role of advice books for women in consolidating middle-class values.

[76] *Woman's Worth: or, Hints to Raise the Female Character* (London: H. G. Clarke & Co., 1844), 218. On the evangelical model of womanhood in the period, see Leonore Davidoff and Catherine Hall, *Family Fortunes: Men and Women of the English Middle Class 1780–1850* (London: Hutchinson, 1987), 114–18.

[77] In 1846, indeed, an anonymous reviewer of the 6th edn. of Mrs John Sandford's *Woman in her Social and Domestic Character* complained that, in the writings of 'the great modern writer upon women, who has hold of the present attention of the sex, the incomprehensibly popular Mrs Ellis', 'the condemnation of the world is faint' ('Englishwomen of the Seventeenth and Nineteenth Centuries', *English Review*, 6 (1846), 285–8).

[78] Sarah Ellis, *The Women of England: Their Social Duties and Domestic Habits* (London: Fisher, Son, & Co., 1838), p. iv.

[79] Ellis, *Wives of England*, 237.   [80] *Woman's Worth*, 156, 158.

Mind.[81] To them, a girl is not an inherently sinful creature whose will must be broken, but a moral being for whom 'the work of individual self-formation' is 'a peremptory, and . . . urgent duty'.[82] 'How necessary it is,' Sarah Ellis urges *The Wives of England*, 'for women to have learned to manage themselves before undertaking the management of a household, for the charge is both a serious and a comprehensive one.'[83]

For women appear in these writings not as the passive objects of a disciplinary process, but as active participants in the regulation of everyday life.[84] 'A young girl marries, and on a sudden she rises from a state of submission to one of command,' writes the author of *Woman's Worth*. 'Her domain may be but a limited one, but over this she has almost absolute sway, for home and the things of home are under her complete control.'[85] 'She no sooner takes upon herself the duties of a mistress,' says Sarah Ellis, 'than she becomes in a great measure responsible for the welfare of every member of the family over which she presides. And not only is this her situation in the ordinary course of things, but in all extraordinary occasions, she must be at the same post, ever on the alert, prompt to direct, and ready with expedients suited to every emergency that may occur.'[86] If woman's moral 'influence' was seen, idealistically, 'as oil cast on the waters, smoothing down the billows, till the troubled ocean of life changes within her immediate sphere of action, into a sweet and holy calm, reflecting back the blue face of the unclouded heavens', she was urged also to function 'as oil applied to a machine, enabling all parts to work easily and harmoniously, well-directed towards a rightly chosen end'.[87]

Such writings are altogether milder, less menacingly coercive than those addressed to the evangelical child. Within them, women are seen—albeit within a circumscribed 'sphere'—as agents, rather than as objects to be disciplined and controlled; not as creatures of corruption whose spirits must be broken, but as responsible beings who 'can accomplish great and glorious purposes, supported and carried forward by that most valuable of all faculties—*moral power*'.[88] Sometimes, indeed, they are hailed as the moral conscience of the nation, 'the prime agents of God in the regeneration of mankind'.[89] 'Shall it be said that women have no political existence, no political influence, when the very germs of political regeneration

---

[81] Emily Shirreff and Maria Grey, *Thoughts on Self-Culture: Addressed to Women* (London: Moxon, 1850) is probably the volume that appears as 'Self-Culture' in a 'List of Books from Smith & Elder March 18th. 1850' found in Charlotte Brontë's desk (*CBL* ii. 361 and 362 n. 5).

[82] Sarah Lewis, *Woman's Mission* (London: John W. Parker, 1839), 97–8. For an extensive discussion of this work—a part translation, part adaptation of the Rousseauian Louis Aimé Martin's *De l'éducation des mères de famille, ou la civilisation du genre humain par les femmes* (1834)—and its reception, see Elizabeth K. Helsinger, Robin Lauterbach Sheets, and William Veeder, *The Woman Question: Society and Literature in Britain and America, 1837–1883*, i. *Defining Voices, 1837–1883* (2 vols; Manchester: Manchester University Press, 1983), ch. 1.

[83] Ellis, *Wives of England*, 246.

[84] On this subject, see Newton, ' "Ministers of the Interior" ' and Elizabeth Langland, *Nobody's Angels: Middle-Class Women and Domestic Ideology in Victorian Culture* (Ithaca and London: Cornell University Press, 1995), ch. 2.

[85] *Woman's Worth*, 95.   [86] Ellis, *Wives of England*, 247.   [87] Stodart, *Every Day Duties*, 106.

[88] Ellis, *Women of England*, 49.   [89] Lewis, *Woman's Mission*, 20.

may spring from them alone, when the fate of nations yet unborn may depend on the use which they make of the mighty influences committed to their care?' asks 'Sarah Lewis', perhaps the most forceful exponent of this view, in her popular *Woman's Mission*.[90] 'You have deep responsibilities; you have urgent claims; a nation's moral worth is in your keeping,' Sarah Ellis adjures her readers.[91] 'It is a vast and substantial influence which woman exerts,' declared *Woman's Worth* in 1844, 'and none the less real because unseen.'[92]

Despite Jane Eyre's outspoken criticism of her society's pronouncements on womanhood, in many ways her narrative appears to endorse this womanly ideal.[93] When the angry child of the opening pages learns to curb her passions, and achieves 'better regulated feelings' (84), she is believed by her teachers, respected by her acquaintances, approved, and eventually esteemed. Unlike Blanche Ingram, with her 'meretricious arts and calculated manoeuvres' (187), she behaves with propriety and restraint, and wins the love of one whom others desire. She resists temptation in the manner recommended in advice books: 'Fix therefore in your mind, as deeply as possible, those rules of duty and prudence which now seem reasonable to you, that they may be at hand in the hour of trial, and save you from the miseries, in which strong affections, unguided by discretion, involve so many of our sex.'[94] And, as in an improving fable, she not only avoids such 'miseries,' but becomes happy, well-connected, and rich. Indeed, her trajectory is not merely one of virtue rewarded; she comes to exercise an effective womanly power. She who was disciplined grows up to discipline others—the little coquette Adèle, the 'heavy-looking, gaping rustics' who fall to her charge at Morton—into a similar mould: 'charmed and benefited' by this (366), they 'repay' her with 'grateful attention' and 'general regard' (450, 366). She who was presented with the tract about the Liar peoples her own later narrative with other, more varied, cautionary figures—Adèle, with her 'superficiality of character' (145); Céline Varens, 'frivolous, mercenary, heartless, and senseless' (143); Blanche Ingram, 'showy, but . . . not genuine' (185); the Reed young ladies, opposing caricatures of asceticism and indulgence: it is as she distinguishes herself from these that her own self-discipline, modesty, diligence, uprightness are defined. For the darkest and most dreadful of these others is one who at once recalls and in her contrast points to how far this narrator has come from that childish 'fury' (11) which caused others both to doubt her 'sanity' (12) and to fear she was destined for hell—a literal 'fury' (310) and a madwoman, whose dreadful fate is akin to that of the Liar.

Yet if the success of the character Jane Eyre depends on her differentiating herself from a series of unapproved (and punished) others, *Jane Eyre* as a novel is altogether darker in its vision of how, in the world it depicts, the identity of a 'proper

---

[90] Lewis, *Woman's Mission*, 67.   [91] Ellis, *Women of England*, 13.   [92] *Woman's Worth*, 26.
[93] For this view, see Jina Politi, '*Jane Eyre* Class-ified', in Glen (ed.), *Jane Eyre: New Casebook*, 78–91; and (more extremely) Bette London, who reads the novel *as* 'a nineteenth-century deportment book, offering its readers—within and outside the text—lessons in the proper forms of feminine conduct' (Bette London, 'The Pleasures of Submission: *Jane Eyre* and the Production of the Text', *ELH* 58 (1991), 209).
[94] Chapone, *Letters on the Improvement of the Mind*, 96–7.

woman' is constituted and maintained. For, as we have seen, Jane's exemplary narrative of successful self-formation is counterpointed by another story of imminent
annihilation, which charges even frequent re-readings with cliff-hanging suspense.
And to turn to the moralists of womanhood from the perspective provided by this
other story is to perceive in them emphases rather different from their overt messages of exhortation or advice.

For if woman as these moralists present her might partake of a heroic agency denied to the evangelical child, she appears within their writings also in disquietingly
contradictory guise. Whatever potency they might assign to her influence, such
writers had to acknowledge that woman's scope for activity was in actuality confined to 'the narrow and quiet sphere', or, as a critic expressed it, the 'prison' of
home.[95] If the model child was one whose will had been broken, the ideal woman
was one whose expressiveness was curbed. 'Woman ... must not be *on the look-out
for excitement* of any kind,' pronounces Mrs John Sandford. 'She ... must find her
pleasures as well as her occupation in the sphere which is assigned to her' (my italics).[96] And the insistence of her imperatives, her sober Latinate prescriptions, cannot quite counter her lively sense—registered in that colloquialism—of the
impulses that need to be kept down. Others are more explicit about the paradoxical
nature of their advice. 'It *is* an apparent inconsistency,' admits Sarah Lewis, 'to rec-
ommend at the same time expansion of views and contraction of operation; to
awaken the sense of power, and to require that the exercise of it be limited; to apply
at once the spur and the rein.'[97] Where the evangelical child was disciplined and
humiliated, woman was expected to be modest, submissive, restrained. For her
'character'-construction was explicitly conceived as a project of subjugation of
'self'. *Thoughts on Self-Culture*, for example, devotes its whole first chapter to a description of the 'Instruments of Moral Discipline' that its readers are exhorted to
use: among the headings listed are 'Management of Temper', 'Self-correction',
'Habitual Self-examination', and 'the habit of keeping the mind in subjection to
certain principles'—or 'Self-control'. The sense is of a reining in of energies, a turning upon the self, that is analogous to the self-mortification required of the evangelical child.

Self-management, in such writings, implies self-presentation. Woman is enjoined
never to forget that she is an object of observation: but the concern is less with the all-
seeing eye of God than with the judging eyes of the world. Even comparatively progressive writers advise their readers to speak with sense and dress with propriety.
More conservative moralists prescribe 'artless' behaviour in ways which evoke Mrs
Reed. 'There should be gentleness of manner', pronounces *Woman's Worth*, three
years before the publication of *Jane Eyre*; 'and, at the same time, it should be artless
and free ... unconstrained and frank, without ostentation or a vain attempt at

---

[95] Anon., 'Englishwomen of the Seventeenth and Nineteenth Centuries', 327; [Lamb], *Can Woman
Regenerate Society?*, 8.
[96] Mrs John Sandford, *Woman, in her Social and Domestic Character* (London: Longman, Rees,
Orme, Browne, & Green, 1831), 169.
[97] Lewis, *Woman's Mission*, 49.

display.'[98] In *The Women of England*, Mrs Ellis exhorts her readers not to 'regard as insignificant the smallest of those means by which a woman *can render herself an object* either of affection or disgust' (my italics).[99] 'Display' of accomplishments was, on the whole, deplored; but the woman reader was urged to develop instead qualities that could make her more solidly approved. 'Either she is a mere toy, the plaything of an hour ... or she is a gem, the brilliancy of which fades not by long possession, and the preciousness of which is not determined by fashion or caprice,' writes Mrs John Sandford in 1836.[100] Just so, Rochester figures Jane not as a 'bloom' which is likely to 'fade', 'but rather the radiant resemblance of one ... an indestructible gem' (314).

If man could strive to succeed, woman had to 'strive to oblige'.[101] Like the evangelical injunction not to displease the Creator, this was an imperative underwritten by gross inequality of power. All the moralists of womanhood, conservatives and progressives alike, write of a world in which woman's position is subordinate to that of man. Like the evangelical child's, hers is a state of subjection; like the evangelical parent's, his authority is absolute. 'Next to pleasing God, a woman's first duty is to please man,' writes the author of *Woman: As She Is and As She Should Be*:

> Before the altar must she swear to love, *serve*, honour, *and obey* ... there is *one* sole interest that is to absorb all others. Duties, wishes, habits,—all must be molten into the stream of affection; and she must unceasingly strive to oblige, with all *her* soul, that man who has made her a present of his own. ... she must learn and adopt his tastes, study his disposition, and submit, in short, to all his desires.[102]

And if for this writer such submission seems rendered even pleasurable by the all-dissolving 'stream of affection', others cannot but register that it might be less easy than this. 'As a wife, woman should place herself, instead of running the risk of *being placed*, in a secondary position,' Sarah Ellis suggests, with a significant emphasis on the risk to which she refers.[103] 'Undisputed power to will, and to act, is often accompanied by a kind of moral majesty, which a weaker spirit never can attain, while *kept in bondage, either by fear or absolute restraint,*' she elsewhere opines, of the difference between husband and wife (my italics): she follows this up with a vision of the husband's wrath as akin to the wrath of God: 'What then, if by perpetual provocation she should awaken the tempest of his wrath! We will not contemplate the thought, for there is something as fearful in his indignation, as there is attractive in his kindness, and flattering in his esteem.'[104] The threat is not of eternal punishment but of the loss of approbation: for this, like that of the evangelical tracts, is a discourse that invokes 'love'. And here, as in the evangelical tracts, transgression means annihilation. 'The wife who has lost her husband's love by mere carelessness of the common and familiar means of giving pleasure' is portrayed by Sarah Elllis in the most popular of her

---

[98] *Woman's Worth*, 67.   [99] Ellis, *Women of England*, 128.

[100] Mrs John Sandford, *Female Improvement* (2 vols.; London: Longman, Rees, Orme, Browne, &d Green, 1836), 22–3.

[101] *Woman: As She Is, and As She Should Be*, ii. 272.   [102] Ibid. 271–2.

[103] Sarah Ellis, *The Mothers of England: Their Influence and Responsibility* (London: Fisher, Son, & Co., 1843), 27.

[104] Ellis, *Wives of England*, 85–6.

advice books, as standing 'amidst her family like a living statue amongst the marble memorials of the dead—instinct with life, yet paralyzed with death—the burning tide of natural feeling circling round her heart—the thousand channels frozen, through which that feeling ought to flow.'[105]

Where the evangelical child's will was broken, woman was urged to 'yield up her own ways and will'.[106] Some saw such self-abnegation as woman's natural bent. 'There is in the warm fond heart of woman a strange and sublime unselfishness', writes W. R. Greg, in an article on prostitution, 'which men too commonly discover only to profit by,—a positive love of self-sacrifice,—an active, so to speak, an *aggressive* desire to show their affection, by giving up to those who have won it something they hold very dear.'[107] Others were more inclined to deplore the psychological distortions the ideal of 'selflessness' imposed. '[Women] have no independent exercise of either the senses or the intellect,' lamented one Owenite writer. 'Hence they become lame, mutilated beings, unable to provide for their own happiness ... The sympathetic part of their nature only, is cultivated; and they are rendered utterly dependent on others . . . varnished over with an affectation of self-sacrifice ... and ... possessed by a weakness which makes them throw away their individuality, and the very privileges and powers of humanity.'[108] 'The old prejudices regarding woman convert the noble duty of self-renunciation into a most criminal self-extinction,' wrote Marion Reid.[109] But despite such dissentient voices, the dominant image of the ideal woman was of one who sacrificed self—as Sarah Ellis portrays her, in a striking series of negatives, one 'whose deepest enjoyments are all relative; who has nothing and is nothing of herself; whose experience, if unparticipated, is a total blank ... who, in her inexhaustible sympathies can live only in the existence of another, and whose very smiles and tears are not exclusively her own'.[110]

'The legal position of woman is a most anomalous one ... Political existence she has none,' declared Edwin Hood of the mid-nineteenth-century woman. 'Widow or spinster, she is no citizen, and as a wife her whole being is merged in the being and existence of her husband.'[111] The legal non-existence of women is a subject to which writers on women in the period return again and again. The metaphor seems to compel them, is pondered, elaborated, explored. And as they do so it becomes a potent figure for the darker implications of womanly 'dependence,' the more than metaphoric annihilation implied by the clichés of romantic love. For like the jeopardized evangelical child, constantly threatened with death, woman appears in these writings as by definition a provisional being: one whose very existence is an ambiguous, uncertain thing.

---

[105] Ellis, *Women of England*, 375. [106] Stodart, *Every Day Duties*, 194.
[107] W. R. Greg, 'Prostitution', *Westminster Review*, 53 (1850), 244.
[108] *Monthly Repository*, 10 (1836), 426–7.
[109] Reid, *A Plea for Woman*, 28. [110] Ellis, *Daughters of England*, 126.
[111] Edwin Paxton Hood, *The Age and its Architects: Ten Chapters on the English People in Relation to the Times* (London: Charles Gilpin, 1850), 389–90.

> Man's the Lord of creation, the head and the boast
> But woman's a Cipher, a cipher at most,

proclaimed a rhyme copied into early nineteenth-century commonplace books; and the force of the observation is not quite undermined by the wit of the couplet that follows:

> A Cipher when placed at the right hand just so
> Makes a figure just ten times the value, you know.[112]

'Women are, in fact . . . strictly speaking, relative creatures,' Sarah Ellis reminds her readers. 'Without the faculty of instrumentality, they are only as dead letters in the volume of human life, filling what would otherwise be a blank space, but doing nothing more.'[113] 'She can have no will in her half-sort of existence, is utterly without power, a mere derivative, scarcely held responsible for her own actions! Surely the state of the much-ridiculed spinster is better than this very equivocal position, in which there is a great risk of losing our very identity,' the feminist Lamb protests. The woman whose mind is 'fettered and chained', whose 'sphere' is 'a prison', must become, 'like the generality of prisoners . . . a heartless, listless, apathetic being, hoping for nothing; or . . . enduring much, and fearing more': such an existence leads, inexorably, to 'petrification of the mind' and 'all but annihilation of the soul'.[114]

And if the discourse of 'womanhood' in early nineteenth-century England is haunted by images of the annihilation of those who are its subjects, in another, and almost entirely unspoken way,[115] the threat of death attends its rhetoric. For central to that discourse is the idea of motherhood as woman's highest calling: that which at once enshrines her as guardian of 'the moral world' and demands her most 'unselfish devotedness'.[116] 'The grand function of woman, it must always be recollected, is, and ever must be, Maternity,' wrote G. H. Lewes, in an unsigned review of *Shirley*.[117] 'THE MOTHER, it has been said, IS THE DEITY OF INFANCY,' declared Edwin Hood. 'The cradle and the fireside are hers, and committed therefore to her trust, is a power far beyond that delegated to any earthly ruler; mind is hers to kindle, almost to create.'[118] 'I still think that as a wife, woman should place herself . . . in a secondary position,' writes Sarah Ellis. 'As a mother, I do not see how it is possible for her to be too dignified, or to be treated with too much respect.'[119]

---

[112] Quoted in Davidoff and Hall, *Family Fortunes*, 452.

[113] Ellis, *Women of England*, 150, 209–10.

[114] [Lamb], *Can Woman Regenerate Society?*, 109, 8–9.

[115] Sarah Ellis's *The Mothers of England* contains no reference to maternal mortality or to the inroads on maternal health caused by repeated child-bearing: neither—perhaps because they were intended to encourage rather than alarm the women who read them—do such medical manuals on pregnancy and child-bearing as Thomas Bull's *Hints to Mothers for the Management of Health* (1837), P. H. Chavasse's *Advice to a Wife on the Management of her own Health, and on the Treatment of some of the Complaints Incidental to Pregnancy, Labour and Suckling* (1839), and J. T. Conquest's *Letters to a Mother* (1848). Within such works, the disorders 'incidental to pregnancy' appear as minor complaints, easily dealt with by the woman's proper self-management.

[116] Lewis, *Woman's Mission*, 130, 24.

[117] *CH* 161.   [118] Hood, *The Age and its Architects*, 385.   [119] Ellis, *Mothers of England*, 27.

Yet such idealization can hardly have obscured what for most women must have been an all-too-familiar knowledge: the fact that in the most literal sense maternity in early nineteenth-century England posed a threat to women's lives.[120] Most would have known at least one woman who had died as a result of childbirth;[121] Patrick Brontë's opposition to his daughter's marriage seems to have been partly motivated by a (tragically justified) fear that she herself would meet this fate.[122] Woman's 'grand function' must even for the most privileged have been attended by apprehension and dread. Thus, after the birth of her first grandchild in 1859, Queen Victoria writes of looking forward to seeing her daughter 'without that load of anxiety and uncertainty which we have carried about with us since last May!' and describes the relief she herself 'always' felt from 'the mornings of anxious expectation, of dread and anxiety' once she was safely confined.[123] For that majority of women who managed to escape 'this . . . deep, dark and continuous stream of mortality'— as William Farr, Compiler of Abstracts to the General Register Office, was to call it in 1877[124]—very real physical anxieties remained, to underscore, in a manner hardly imaginable today, that loss of the body's autonomy, that deeper psychic challenge to self-sufficient identity, perhaps implicit in all childbearing. 'For twenty years of the best years of their lives . . . women are mainly occupied by the cares, the duties, the enjoyments and the sufferings of maternity,' G. H. Lewes writes, reviewing *Shirley*. 'During large parts of these years, too, their bodily health is generally so broken and precarious as to incapacitate them for any strenuous exertion.'[125] Or as Queen Victoria wrote to her daughter:

[120] On maternal mortality in the period, see William Farr, *Vital Statistics: A Memorial Volume of Selections*, ed. Noel A. Humphreys (London: Edward Stanford, 1885), 270–81; Anthony S. Wohl, *Endangered Lives: Public Health in Victorian Britain* (London: Dent, 1983), 346 n. 16; Roger Schofield, in 'Did the Mothers Really Die? Three Centuries of Maternal Mortality in "The World We Have Lost"', in L. Bonfield, R. Smith, and K. Wrightson (eds.), *The World We have Gained: Histories of Population and Social Structure* (Oxford: Basil Blackwell, 1986), 231–60. In *Death in Childbirth: An International Study of Maternal Care and Maternal Mortality, 1800–1950* (Oxford: Clarendon Press, 1992), Irvine Loudon points out that death in childbirth seems to have seared the popular imagination with especial force, for it 'was the only major cause of mortality that was not a disease, and in that way it stood apart. . . . When a maternal death occurred it was swift, unexpected, and a sudden and brutal disruption of a family' (164); something of the shock he describes is registered in ch. 3 of *Mary Barton*, published the year after *Jane Eyre*. One can only conjecture what contribution the (much greater) expectation of infant mortality had on women's perceptions of child-bearing in these years; at the very least, it must, as Margaret Homans suggests, have led them to 'associate it with death' (*Bearing the Word: Language and Female Experience in Nineteenth-Century Women's Writing* (Chicago: University of Chicago Press, 1986), 88–9; see also Carolyn Dever, *Death and the Mother from Dickens to Freud: Victorian Fiction and the Anxiety of Origins* (Cambridge: Cambridge University Press, 1998).

[121] Sarah Ellis, who was herself childless, as a young woman watched two of her three sisters die shortly after childbirth (*The Home Life and Letters of Mrs Ellis*, compiled by her nieces (London: J. Nisbet & Co., 1893), 9–11, 29–32.

[122] Gérin, *Charlotte Brontë*, 440, 471, 518. 'Mr Brontë', reports Mrs Gaskell, felt his children's 'frequent appearance on the scene as a drag on his wife's health' (Gaskell, 86). 'I always told you Martha', he said to the servant after Charlotte Brontë's death, 'that there was no sense in Charlotte marrying at all, for she was not strong enough for marriage' (Gérin, *Charlotte Brontë*, 566). On the probable cause of Charlotte Brontë's death, see Barker, 967–8 n. 96.

[123] Roger Fulford (ed.), *Dearest Child: Letters Between Queen Victoria and the Princess Royal 1858–1861* (London: Evans, 1964), 170.

[124] William Farr, *Vital Statistics*, 279.   [125] *CH* 161.

in a physical point of view . . . if you have . . . (as I had constantly for the first 2 years of my marriage)—aches—and sufferings and miseries and plagues—which you must struggle against . . . you will feel the yoke of a married woman! . . . I had 9 times for 8 months to bear with those above-named enemies . . . one feels so pinned down—one's wings clipped—in fact, at the best . . . only half oneself.[126]

In the most immediate and (as the Queen put it) 'animal' sense, motherhood in early nineteenth-century England meant a literalization of the figures of that discourse of self-abnegation which ran through its writings on womanhood. 'Indeed—indeed Nell—it is a solemn and strange and perilous thing,' wrote Charlotte Brontë to her unmarried friend, Ellen Nussey, nine months before her own death in pregnancy, 'for a woman to become a wife.'[127]

The hints and intimations inscribed in the writing of the period that the construction of proper womanhood might mean the annihilation of self are in *Jane Eyre* picked up and writ large. That which the novel delineates is less the smooth construction of an acceptable femininity through a successful process of 'self-formation' than a world of internal and external coercion in which self is perpetually at risk. For the menacing configurations of Jane's world of childhood are not left behind, but repeated, confirmed, and intensified, as the novel goes on to tell of her later life. If as a child she is subjected to actual and psychological violence, as a woman she feels the more seductive, but no less sapping, pressures of male social, economic, and psychological power. 'I am used to say "Do this", and it is done,' says Rochester (124); 'When he said "go" I went; "come," I came; "do this," I did it' says Jane of St John Rivers (398).[128] Where the child was locked up and disciplined, the superficially freer young woman is no less surely confined. Her captivity at Lowood, with its 'high and spike-guarded' walls (75), gives way to 'the viewless fetters of a uniform and too still existence' at Thornfield (116), to the narrow duties of the schoolroom at Morton, and finally to domestic immurement at Ferndean, 'deep buried in a wood' (429): her circumscribed sphere is, in each case, emphatically contrasted with the apparent freedom of one who is other, and male. The surveillance to which she was subjected as a child is replaced, as her story goes on, by a more impassioned, more intimately threatening scrutiny: John Reed's prying, Mr Brocklehurst's all-seeing eyes give way to St John Rivers's 'curious intensity of observation', his 'ever-watchful blue eye . . . searching me through and

---

[126] Fulford (ed.), *Dearest Child*, 77–8. For the more general picture, see Davidoff and Hall, *Family Fortunes*, 335–8, and Roy Porter and Dorothy Porter, *In Sickness and in Health: The British Experience 1650–1850* (London: Fourth Estate, 1988), 86.

[127] A few sentences before, she had written: 'As far as my experience of matrimony goes—I think it tends to draw you *out of, and away from yourself*' (*LL* iv. 145; my italics).

[128] 'I really seem to have had scarcely a spare moment since that dim quiet June Morning when you, E.Nussey and myself all walked down to Haworth Church,' wrote Charlotte Brontë to Miss Wooler on 22 August 1854: 'Not that I have been wearied or oppressed—but the fact is my time is not my own now; Somebody else wants a good portion of it—and says we must do "so and so". We *do* "so and so", accordingly; and it generally seems the right thing—only I sometimes wish that I could have written the letter as well as taken the walk' (*LL* iv. 148).

through' (397), the 'devouring' menace of Rochester's 'flaming glance' (317). The hands that bullied and held her down are succeeded by the 'iron grasp' of Rochester at the altar; the bonds that intimidated her by more metaphorical, but no less alarming, threats. 'When once I have fairly seized you, to have and to hold, I'll just—figuratively speaking—attach you to a chain like this' (270), says Rochester. 'A hand of fiery iron grasped my vitals,' she says, of her departure from him. 'Terrible moment: full of struggle, blackness, burning!' (315). Her 'iron shroud' contracts around her as her cousin attempts to persuade her to become his wife—'the sole helpmeet I can influence efficiently in life, and retain absolutely till death' (404, 406). And if she escapes the 'monstrous martyrdom', the 'premature death' of a loveless marriage to him (405), her story ends with the more subtly disquieting erasure of individuality, difference, of 'Jane Eyre' herself, in her life at Ferndean with Rochester. 'Ever more absolutely bone of his bone and flesh of his flesh', says Jane, of her marriage; and the image is reminiscent of William Blackstone's elaboration of the doctrine of *coverture*: that husband and wife are in law one flesh, 'and that flesh is the husband's'.[129]

In each case, except perhaps the last, the character Jane asserts her will, controls her passions, survives. Yet if in this she is akin to the exemplary woman of the advice books, the novel in which she appears seems less to be 'appropriating their strategies'[130] than highlighting a darker logic in those strategies than many might, in early Victorian England, have been willing to admit. Here, that confinement of women to the domestic sphere, that unquestioning acceptance of male social, economic, emotional power, that feminine self-suppression of which contemporary writers speak appear in shapes of Gothic extremism. More subtly, but no less disquietingly, that which is implicit or metaphoric in early Victorian models of womanhood configures the novel in central and peculiar ways. Jane distinguishes herself most sharply from those figures of advice-book opprobrium—the shallow drawing-room creature, the mere displayer of accomplishments, she who gives herself over to baser appetites. And that which the advice books characterize in general terms assumes, in her story, monstrous corporeal shape: the 'majestic', 'showy' Blanche Ingram (173, 185); the 'full-blown, very plump' Georgiana Reed (228); Bertha Rochester—'a big woman, in stature almost equalling her husband, and corpulent besides' (293).

In one way, of course, this grossly material imaging of the repudiated other can be seen as a fundamental strategy of Jane's autobiographical 'self-formation', an assertion of the narrating subject's objectifying power.[131] But it is a strategy whose less than straightforwardly triumphalist implications are realized in one of the most

---

[129] Quoted in Helena Michie, 'Under Victorian Skins: The Bodies Beneath', in Herbert F. Tucker (ed.), *A Companion to Victorian Literature and Culture* (Oxford: Blackwell, 1999), 420.

[130] London, 'The Pleasures of Submission', 198.

[131] See ch. 2, n. 10. On the repudiation of the body implicit in the construction of proper bourgeois subjectivity, see M. M. Bakhtin, *Rabelais and His World*, trans. H. Iswolsky (Bloomington: Indiana University Press, 1984), and Peter Stallybrass and Allon White, *The Politics and Poetics of Transgression* (Ithaca: Cornell University Press, 1986).

distinctive features of *Jane Eyre*. For that which Jane repudiates looms large in her narrative: not merely distanced and caricatured, but more sharply defined, more substantial, more powerful than she. Like the ideal Victorian woman, Jane Eyre resists temptation, controls her passions, waits for Providence to bestow a fortune, a family, an eligible mate. But it is Bertha Rochester, figure of an anger unrestrained by propriety, a sensuality unbridled by principle, who appears in the novel as an agent—attempting to murder her rival, burning down Thornfield Hall. She who follows the path of propriety is an insubstantial and uncertain presence; imperilled, not strengthened, by her difference; shadowy, tenuous, unreal. Indeed, Jane's reflections on the eve of her marriage—'Mrs Rochester! She did not exist... garments said to be hers had already displaced my black stuff Lowood frock and straw bonnet: for not to me appertained that suit of wedding raiment; the pearl-coloured robe, the vapoury veil' (275) resonate with suggestions of that 'crisis in the integrity of the body' which Helena Michie has charted in the passage from maidenhood to wifehood in the period: 'upper middle-class honeymoons, replete with their consuming rituals of tourism, sex and shopping, produced, when successful, a different woman in a different body and different clothes, who answered with new knowledges to a new name'.[132] The 'relative creature' of the advice books, she who 'has nothing and is nothing of herself', who 'can live only in the existence of another', whose utmost fulfilment lies in 'the renunciation of self', here keeps coming, distinctively, disquietingly, to the fore, in the figure of one ambiguously poised between 'substance and shadow' (245); who seems to herself 'the image of a stranger' (286); whose first person is finally submerged in a symbiotic 'we'. And that largely unspoken 'shadow side' of the Victorian woman's life, with its attendant 'dread and anxiety', here comes into focus, in a series of disturbing dreams, in which Jane is 'burdened with the charge of a little child', her 'movements ... fettered', her 'voice ... inarticulate' (281); dreams that reach a kind of narrative fulfilment when she who eventually has a child is almost effaced from the story—no longer Jane Eyre, but 'one Jane Rochester', one oddly peripheral to the patriarchal line of descent.[133]

The story I have been tracing in Jane's narrative of childhood, her account of her young womanhood, is one of objectification and powerlessness, of vertiginous insecurity, of disconfirmation and dread. It is a story more extreme, more 'extravagantly improbable', than that psychologically realist narrative of development as which *Jane Eyre* is often read. It is certainly very different from those that shaped public versions of reality in early nineteenth-century England—the romantic story of human possibility, the progressive idea of effective individual agency, which were celebrated in so many of that culture's official fantasies and enshrined in the 'autobiographical' form. Yet *Jane Eyre* speaks of realities intimately known to 'millions' in early nineteenth-century England—the prescriptive, self-abnegating, death-shadowed world of its ideal 'womanhood', the coercive, persecutory, death-dominated world presented to the evangelical child. The opening chapters of the

---

[132] Michie, 'Under Victorian Skins', 420, 421.

[133] Thus Jane describes the birth of her son: 'When *his* first-born was put into his arms, he could see that the boy had inherited *his own* eyes, as they once were—large, brilliant, and black' (451, my italics).

novel and the surrealistic narrative into which they lead are charged with a knowledge which the records of the period suggest was neither extraordinary nor simply private: a sense of life as a constant threat of obliteration, of the world as a place of awful danger, of the self as a relative creature, of power as residing elsewhere. In giving voice to that knowledge *Jane Eyre* articulates a cultural unconscious that the realism of its period could not express. And in doing so it offers as powerful a diagnostic vision of the devastating costs and conditions of life in early nineteenth-century England as that offered by Dickens in *Bleak House.*

CHAPTER FIVE

'Incident, life, fire, feeling':
Jane Eyre and History (2)

> ... the Queen of Angria was sitting close by a large bright fire. Her sofa was covered with many beautiful little volumes, bound in white & crimson & green & purple Russia. Some were open, displaying exquisite engravings on silver paper & fair type on a surface almost like ivory. One had dropped from her hand & lay at the footstool at her feet & she was leaning back with her eyes closed & her thoughts wandering in day-dreams ...
>
> (*Passing Events*, 1836)[1]

I

Yet the Jane Eyre of most readers' memories is not the subjugated child of the evangelical tracts, or the 'relative creature' of whom the moralists of womanhood speak, but a figure of a very different kind. If Jane's realist 'autobiography' is disrupted by intuitions of self as jeopardized object it is disrupted also, as we have seen, by a figuring of self-assertive power. By the end of her story, Jane has magically assumed a position of unchallenged 'ascendancy' (420); her enemies are confounded; every other significant character is in some way dependent upon her. Indeed, if that narrative of jeopardy is articulated through the language of evangelicalism, so partly— but almost blasphemously—is this opposing narrative of power. Jane's desperate prayer to heaven—'Shew me—shew me the path!'—is answered not by God, but by the voice of her beloved: her response to his call—'I am coming ... I will come!'— sacrilegiously prefigures those words of Christ that St John Rivers quotes at the end (419–20). Listening to the humbled Rochester, she likens herself to Mary, the mother of God: 'I kept these things, then, and pondered them in my heart' (448).[2] Indeed, as 'the alpha and omega' of her lover's 'heart's wishes' (447), she stands for him in place of God himself.[3]

Of course, in one way, Jane's 'ascendancy' might be assimilated to an unexceptionable early nineteenth-century model of redemptive feminine power. When *The*

---

[1] Charlotte Brontë, *Five Novelettes*, ed. Winifred Gèrin (London: Folio Press, 1971), 55.

[2] The echo is of Luke 2: 19.

[3] See Heather Henderson, *The Victorian Self: Autobiography and Biblical Narrative* (Ithaca: Cornell University Press, 1989), 186–9, for an intriguing discussion of the way in which *Jane Eyre* likens Jane to Christ—and usually to Christ triumphant.

New Female Instructor or, Young Woman's Guide to Domestic Happiness (1819), says 'it were easy to multiply instances of the ascendancy which WOMEN OF SENSE have always gained over men of feeling'; when Sarah Lewis portrays woman's 'mission on earth' as 'not only to shine, to please, to adorn, but to influence, and by influencing to regenerate'; when Anne Richelieu Lamb argues that 'The greatest love is shown in not yielding to weak, foolish, or unjust demands, but in *resolutely opposing them* . . . that woman is the most faithful wife or mistress, who seeks to elevate and ennoble the mind of her husband or lover, though he may not in his momentary blindness think so,'[4] their voices resonate with Jane's. The modest, hardworking governess, who holds by her principles and wins domestic happiness might be seen as just such a figure of moral authority. And Rochester's transformation from wandering Don Juan to domesticated moral being seems to offer a striking example of what woman's 'influence' can achieve.

But there is much in *Jane Eyre* that works against such a reading. The power that Jane most covets is not that of moral influence; and her trajectory is not exactly presented as a process of moral growth. When as a young woman she finds that her Reed cousins have lost their erstwhile power to oppress her, the reason she gives has little to do with the maturity she has acquired: 'within the last few months feelings had been stirred in me so much more potent than any they could raise . . . that their airs gave me no concern either for good or bad' (229). Contemplating Blanche Ingram, she feels a peculiar, hectic 'agitation', as she is drawn into an excited sense of how her rival's romantic campaign might more successfully be pursued (186–7). Refusing to live with her lover, she thinks less of the 'laws and principles' to which she later appeals than of avoiding the hapless fate of the succession of discarded mistresses who have preceded her (312). Reunited with him at Ferndean, she shows considerably more interest in provoking his sexual jealousy than in ensuring that he is reformed (441–3). Indeed, there is little in the novel to suggest that her influence over him is a moral one. Her principled departure drives him not to repentance, but to despair. The remorse that he comes to feel is prompted not by Jane's example but by the awful hand of God. And the earthly agent of the 'justice' that 'humbles him for ever' (446) is not she, but Bertha Rochester: one very far from that 'WOMAN OF SENSE' of whom the moralists approved. Jane and her beloved do, it is true, end in virtuous, contented domesticity. But despite Jane's 'kindness' to Adèle, her visits to her married cousins, her correspondence with St John Rivers, the feeling is of retreat. That sense, articulated by some of the moralists of womanhood, that the 'influence' of woman might extend beyond the domestic sphere and 'regenerate' society is notably absent here. The Jane who longed for 'practical experience' and 'intercourse with [her] kind' (109) has submerged her whole existence in 'attendance' on one other (451). And the suggestions of stasis and constriction that attend

---

[4] *The New Female Instructor or, Young Woman's Guide to Domestic Happiness, Being an Epitome of all the Acquirements Necessary to Form the Female Character in Every Class of Life* (London: Thomas Kelly, 1819), 2; 'Lewis', *Woman's Mission*, 119; [Anne Richelieu Lamb], *Can Woman Regenerate Society?* (London: John W. Parker, 1844), 95.

her descriptions of Ferndean are underlined by the novel's final, contrasting image of St John Rivers's heroic ambition and urgent, open-ended desire.

Above all, perhaps, that view of feminine nature propounded in advice books of the period—'Women cannot have the same degree of excitement as men, but neither do they require it. Less active and enterprising by nature, they do well in a more confined sphere of action'[5]—is quite directly challenged, as, at a pivotal moment in the novel, Jane tells of her inability to be satisfied with 'tranquillity':

Who blames me? Many no doubt; and I shall be called discontented. I could not help it: the restlessness was in my nature; it agitated me to pain sometimes. Then my sole relief was to walk along the corridor of the third story, backwards and forwards, safe in the silence and solitude of the spot, and allow my mind's eye to dwell on whatever bright visions rose before it—and certainly they were many and glowing; to let my heart be heaved by the exultant movement which, while it swelled it in trouble, expanded it with life; and best of all, to open my inward ear to a tale that was never ended—a tale my imagination created, and narrated continuously; quickened with all of incident, life, fire, feeling, that I desired and had not in my actual existence.   (109)

Her confession presents a peculiar challenge not merely to the conservative moralists of her day, but also to those who were questioning the constrictedness of 'woman's sphere'. For if this is a passage whose tenor—'ardent . . . excited . . . eager'—is at odds with self-discipline and propriety (73), it is equally at odds with that of the following paragraph:

Women are supposed to be very calm generally: but women feel just as men feel; they need exercise for their faculties, and a field for their efforts as much as their brothers do; they suffer from too rigid a restraint, too absolute a stagnation, precisely as men would suffer; and it is narrow-minded in their more privileged fellow-creatures to say that they ought to confine themselves to making puddings and knitting stockings, to playing on the piano and embroidering bags.   (109)

Others in the mid-nineteenth century were speaking of women's frustrations, of their consciousness of feelings and capacities that they could not actualize. 'From the period of leaving school to that of marriage', writes one anonymous author three years before the publication of *Jane Eyre*,

the life of a female is generally little more than a blank. She leaves school with expanded faculties, high hopes, beating expectations, and ardour of application, but not a suitable object upon which to expend them—and thus she wastes lofty thoughts, and brilliant purposes, and surprising powers, on the dull earth or the deaf air.[6]

'Why', asks Florence Nightingale in 1852, 'have women passion, intellect, moral activity—these three—and a place in society where no one of the three can be exercised?'[7] 'Success and hope are two indispensable elements in human happiness,' writes Emily Shirreff six years later:

[5] *Woman's Rights and Duties Considered with Relation to Her Influence on Society and on Her Own Condition* (2 vols.; London: John W. Parker, 1840), i. 243.

[6] *Woman's Worth*, 201.

[7] Florence Nightingale, *Cassandra*, with an introduction by Myra Stark (New York: Feminist Press, 1979), 25.

They are absent from the lives of those who have no positive occupations in the present, and no definite object to look forward to as the reward of exertion. Before we condemn women who sink in listless depression under the burden of years so spent, let us try to fancy for a moment what would have been the mental condition of the great body of men who are now acquitting themselves honourably in different active careers, if they had been confined within these narrow and sterile bounds.[8]

When Jane Eyre argues that women need 'exercise for their faculties, and a field for their efforts' because they, like 'their brothers', are 'human beings', her voice chimes with voices such as these. Yet, as Virginia Woolf complained, this moment sits oddly in her narrative; there is an 'awkward break' somewhere here. That 'break', however, lies less, I think, in that turning away from 'her story . . . to attend to some personal grievance'[9] which Woolf attributes to Brontë here than in the difference between the sobriety of Jane's plea for opportunities for women and the passion of the paragraph before. For there she speaks not of measured sufficiency ('exercise for their faculties and a field for their efforts') but of Utopian limitlessness and absolute plenitude—'a tale that was never ended', 'all . . . I desired and had not'; not of sober effort (seeking 'to do more or learn more than custom has pronounced necessary for their sex') but of potent energy and achievement—'a tale my imagination created, and . . . quickened with all of incident, life, fire, feeling, that I desired'. And she offers not rational argument but a compelling articulation of desire.

Jane's polemic on behalf of 'women' is neither out of character nor unprecedented in the novel. It has its roots in that insistence on her rights as a human being which shapes her revolt against the Reeds. That harnessing of frustration into effective self-assertion which makes up a large part of her story, and has caused her to be appropriated as a feminist heroine, underwrites the cool rationality of her argument for her sex. The angry, bewildered child learns to '[avail herself] fully of the advantages offered her' (84), and grows into 'a specimen of a diligent, orderly, energetic woman'—or so St John Rivers says (375). She gains a good education, earns her own living, and becomes, eventually, mistress of her own school. From the perspective of maturity she passes judgement on her childish self; she asserts her spiritual equality with the man she loves; she retains her integrity by resisting his importunings. As an 'independent woman', *she* marries *him.* Yet again and again in her story the discourse of sober achievement is supplanted by a different, and much more compelling, one. Each of her three employments—'the office of teacher' which she 'discharge[s] with zeal for two years' at Lowood (84); her 'smooth career' as a governess at Thornfield (108); and her 'honourable exertion' as a schoolmistress at Morton (366)—gives but limited satisfaction, a satisfaction that is each time only cursorily described. Each time, this exercise for her faculties and field for her efforts leads not to fulfilment but to 'restlessness'. Each time, the interest of the narrative is less in rational enterprise, self-discipline, and achievement, than in an urgent, unfocused, but quite distinctive configuration of desire.

---

[8] Emily Shireff, *Intellectual Education* (London: John W. Parker & Son, 1858), 399.
[9] Virginia Woolf, *A Room of One's Own* (1929) (London: Hogarth Press, 1991), 68.

When her beloved Miss Temple leaves Lowood, Jane, by now 'to the eyes of others, usually even to my own . . . a disciplined and subdued character', 'tires of the routine of eight years in one afternoon'. Her story of self-management is disrupted by more impassioned, more expansive images. 'Now I was left in my natural element; and beginning to feel the stirring of old emotions . . . it was not the power to be tranquil which had failed me, but the reason for tranquillity was no more' (84). As 'better regulated feelings' depart, others assert their claims with the force of 'natural' law. 'Liberty, Excitement, Enjoyment: delightful sounds truly; but no more than sounds for me': these are the almost unimaginable contraries of that restriction, deprivation, privation which have constituted her world. Yet as Jane tries to conceive of ways of actualizing these longings, the parameters of what is become evident and close about her. The desire for 'liberty' shrinks to a prayer for 'change, stimulus' and finally to one for 'a new servitude'. Images of boundless yearning contract into practical possibilities: 'Those who want situations advertise: you must advertise in the —shire Herald' (86). The trajectory figured is one not of purposeful accomplishment but of desire banalized and contained.

Jane's account of her 'smooth career' at Thornfield follows a similar course. Here, as before, her tale is of discipline and achievement. Her 'plans' for her pupil's 'improvement' succeed; the child becomes 'obedient and teachable' (108). But here, as before, satisfaction gives way to agitation and yearning. Here, once again, images of boundlessness, of escape, of unknown sensation and experience come flooding into her narrative, as she tells of a longing for 'a power of vision which might overpass that limit'; for 'more . . . than was here within my reach'; 'all . . . that I desired and had not' (109). Here, once again, no object appears to answer to the urgency of these feelings. For the desire Jane has articulated is not for the 'reasonable progress' she enables in her pupil, nor yet for the 'degree of attachment' she feels for the inhabitants of Thornfield (108); not even 'to do more or learn more than custom has pronounced necessary for [her] sex'. It is one that aspires instead towards energy, excitement, intensity—an 'incident, life, fire, feeling' that indeed enters the novel a few pages later, as Rochester's return to his home, marked by the lighting of 'a genial fire' (117) brings to it 'incident' (115) and life (181).

The same configuration returns when Jane describes her 'calm . . . useful existence' as the mistress of Morton school. Here, once again, the discourse of duty and discipline, of rational application and moderate satisfaction, gives way to a more potent language of energy and desire. The Jane who tells of her pride in seeing her pupils 'doing their work well . . . keeping their persons neat . . . learning their tasks regularly . . . acquiring quiet and orderly manners' (366) tells also of how she 'used to rush into strange dreams at night: dreams many-coloured, agitated, full of the ideal, the stirring, the stormy—dreams where, amidst unusual scenes, charged with adventure, with agitating risk and romantic chance, I still again and again met Mr Rochester, always at some exciting crisis' (366–7). The self who emerges each morning, 'punctually opening the school; tranquil, settled, prepared for the steady duties of the day', seems quite other than that which asserts itself in the absence of restraint. Yet here, once again, the novel's imaginative focus is less on that achieved social mask than on the turbulent energies it conceals. For the remainder of this chapter is devoted not to an account of those 'duties', but to a charged description of St John Rivers's suppressed passion for a 'Peri'-like beauty, his 'unlimited' ambition and 'insatiable' desire (375). And Jane portrays herself not engaged in 'honourable exertion', but 'thrilling in artist-delight' as she paints a romantic portrait, and 'eagerly glancing at the bright pages of *Marmion*' (369, 371).

Passages such as these speak of expressiveness and expansiveness rather than of purposive self-control, not of energies reined in, but of 'transforming', 'exultant' life. That embryonically threatening sense of the potency that comes from a refusal to acquiesce in the given implicit in Jane's image of women's rebellious frustration—'they must have action; and *they will make it if they cannot find it*' (my italics)—is here realized in a series of figures of autonomous imaginative power— the inner voice of the first passage, the 'bright visions' and endless 'tale' of the second, the elaborated 'dreams' of the third. Self here is not the embattled, imperilled object of the evangelical tracts, or a 'disciplined and subdued character', but an aspiring, heroic subject, whose 'restlessness' to go beyond restrictive limits—the 'rules and systems' of Lowood (84–5), the 'viewless fetters of a uniform and too still existence' at Thornfield (116), the 'steady duties' of Morton (367)—has the peremptoriness of 'nature' itself.

Yet if this language of desire is different from that of the rational moralists of womanhood, both progressive and conservative, it would not have been unfamiliar to the novel's earliest readers. Again and again in these years, indeed, Mrs Ellis and her counterparts register a sense that that which they seek to inculcate is neither 'natural' nor habitual to the young women whom they address—nor that which attracts them most. 'The female mind' is 'especially' given to 'resigning itself . . . to the vivid and glowing illusion of romance', writes the author of *Woman: As She Is and As She Should Be*.[10] 'By far the greater portion of the young ladies . . . of the present day, are distinguished by . . . a constant pining for excitement, and an eagerness to escape from everything like practical and individual duty,' Sarah Ellis declares. 'The natural versatility of her mental faculties . . . the multiplicity of her floating ideas . . . the play of her fancy, and . . . the constant overflow of her feelings' mean that the female reader is especially in need of disciplinary advice.[11] Yet such advice, these writers acknowledge, is certainly not their culture's most seductive offering to 'young ladies'. For if woman's dangerous predilection for romance had for many years been a familiar theme in conduct manuals, and, indeed, amongst feminist writers,[12] it is one

---

[10] Anon., *Woman: As She Is and As She Should Be* (2 vols.; London: James Cochrane & Co., 1835), 156.

[11] Sarah Ellis, *The Women of England: Their Social Duties and Domestic Habits* (London: Fisher, Son, & Co., 1838), 12, 277. See Karen Chase and Michael Levenson, *The Spectacle of Intimacy: A Public Life for the Victorian Family* (Princeton: Princeton University Press, 2000), ch. 3, for a suggestive discussion of the tension between romanticism and evangelicalism in Mrs Ellis's work.

[12] Most discussion of this subject has centred on women as novel readers. For a brief, more broadly based account, see John Brewer, 'Culture as Commodity: 1660–1800' in Ann Bermingham and John Brewer (eds.), *The Consumption of Culture 1600–1800: Image, Object, Text* (London: Routledge, 1995), 354–8. On 18th-cent. opposition to women's novel-reading, see Jane Spencer, *The Rise of the Woman Novelist: From Aphra Behn to Jane Austen* (Oxford: Basil Blackwell, 1986), ch. 6; Peter de Bolla, *The*

that receives a new inflection in the first half of the nineteenth century, when we find Mrs John Sandford complaining that young women are 'always inditing sonnets or reciting Lord Byron',[13] Mrs Ellis, rather desperately, asking the daughters of England 'sometimes to leave the Corsairs of Byron to the isles of Greece, and the Gypsies of Scott to the mountains of his native land ... [and] ... look into the page of actual life ... [for] ... experiences as richly fraught with interest, as ever glowed in verse, or lived in story', and Robert Southey advising the 20-year-old Charlotte Brontë that 'the day dreams in wh you habitually indulge are likely to induce a distempered state of mind, & in proportion as all the "ordinary uses of the world" seem to you "flat and unprofitable", you will be unfitted for them, without becoming fitted for anything else'.[14]

Such voices bear witness to a cultural phenomenon that Jane, in her only other extended address to the reader, unequivocally extols. 'He laid on the table a new publication—a poem: one of those genuine productions so often vouchsafed to the fortunate public of those days—the golden age of modern literature.' Thus she recalls her delight, as a lonely village schoolmistress, at her cousin's gift of *Marmion*: she goes on to offer a passionate paean to the 'liberty' and 'strength' of 'poetry' and 'genius', their capacity to 'reign, and redeem' (370). As the specificity of that gift suggests, the 'golden age' to which she looks back is not a timeless ideal but a particular historical moment: that era of high romanticism epitomized by the enormously popular writings of Byron and of Scott.[15] Works such as *Marmion* and *Childe Harold* spoke not of 'steady duties' but of 'excitement', adventure, and 'incident'; not of domesticity but of exoticism and alterity; of a desire in excess of the socially possible, a 'Liberty, Excitement, Enjoyment' at odds with the world of fact. It is against romantic dreams like these that advice-book writers later in the century warn. For despite the passing of that 'golden age' such dreams were in the 1830s and 1840s not merely severely castigated. They were also glamorized and promoted in extraordinarily seductive ways.

In 1813, the 25-year-old creator of those wildly popular 'Corsairs' had written in a private letter of the 'restless doctrines' that informed his art:

The great object of life is Sensation—to feel that we exist—even though in pain—it is this 'craving void' which drives us to Gaming—to Battle—to Travel—to intemperate but keenly felt pursuits of every description whose principal attraction is the agitation inseparable from their accomplishment.... You don't like my 'restless' doctrines—I should be very sorry if *you*

Discourse of the Sublime: Readings in History, Aesthetics and the Subject (Oxford: Basil Blackwell, 1989), 252–78; and Gary Kelly, 'Unbecoming a Heroine: Novel Reading, Romanticism, and Barrett's *The Heroine*', *Nineteenth-Century Fiction*, 45 (September 1990), 220–41. On feminist opposition to 'romance' in the early 19th cent. see Cora Kaplan, 'The Thorn Birds', in *Sea Changes: Essays on Culture and Feminism* (London: Verso, 1986), 121–5.

[13] Sandford, *Woman, in her Social and Domestic Character*, 111–12.
[14] Ellis, *Daughters of England*, 153–4; Robert Southey to Charlotte Brontë, 12 March 1837 (*CBL* i. 166).
[15] *Marmion*, published in 1808, sold 13,000 copies in the first six months and six editions by the end of the year. '"The Lay" converted thousands, and "Marmion" tens of thousands, and the *whole* world read poetry,' *Blackwood's* recalled in 1817 (*Blackwood's Magazine* 1 (1817), 516).

did—but *I* can't *stagnate* nevertheless—if I must sail let it be on the ocean no matter how stormy—anything but a dull cruise on a level lake without ever losing sight of the same insipid shores by which it is surrounded.[16]

To Byron, as to Jane at Thornfield, to chafe against limits is as natural as the instinct for life itself. Yet even as he insists on the inevitability of that impulse, he signals in no uncertain terms to the woman who was to become his wife ('You don't like my "restless" doctrines—I should be very sorry if *you* did') that it is not, in the early nineteenth century, one that women are supposed to feel. The images towards which such 'restlessness' turned in the period were almost inevitably those of masculine achievement—romantic heroism, stirring adventures, military conquest, literary fame. If such images bore little relation to the possibilities open to middle-class men in early nineteenth-century England,[17] they were starkly opposed to that dependence and confinement which constituted the middle-class ideal of 'woman's sphere'. For a woman to lay claim to them, even in 'day dream', was, as Southey warned the young Charlotte Brontë, to 'unfit' herself for the 'duties' to which she was 'called'.

Yet it is a suggestive sociological fact that in early nineteenth-century England women were the chief inheritors and carriers of that structure of feeling which we might loosely call Byronic romanticism. Indeed, Eric Hobsbawm has argued that 'Romanticism entered middle class culture' in this period 'perhaps mostly through the rise in day-dreaming among the female members of the bourgeois family'.[18] Unlike their industrious menfolk, many such women had ample leisure for 'day-dreaming', and all too little other scope for their faculties—or, as one contemporary put it, they had 'more time as well as more inclination to indulge in reveries'.[19] Receiving 'none of the wholesome checks which a man receives in the course of his active career, among the realities and actual struggles of life', woman's mind was, it seemed, all too likely to 'acquire a restless agitation, fretting against the restraints imposed on its outward action, and ending in settled contempt for all the real duties of its station, disguised under a longing for others of a nobler cast, and seemingly more congenial to its capacities'.[20] But if the lives of women of the privileged classes were thus conducive to a 'dissatisfaction with the actual', a readiness 'to sacrifice the useful and the true for the dazzling and romantic',[21] it was not

[16] Byron to Annabella Milbanke, 6 and 26 September 1813, in Leslie A. Marchand (ed.), *Byron's Letters and Journals* (12 vols.; London: John Murray, 1974–82), iii. 109, 119.

[17] Charlotte Brontë's awareness of this is evident in her sardonic banishment of all suggestions of 'romance' from Crimsworth's sober tale. On Byron's access, through money and rank, to 'a world closed off to most of his readers', see Andrew Elfenbein, *Byron and the Victorians* (Cambridge: Cambridge University Press, 1995), 51–2.

[18] E. J. Hobsbawm, *The Age of Revolution: Europe 1789–1848* (London: Weidenfeld & Nicolson, 1962), 272.

[19] 'The Moral and Political Tendency of Modern Novels', *Church of England Quarterly Review*, 11 (1842), 278.

[20] Emily Shirreff and Maria Grey, *Thoughts on Self-Culture: Addressed to Women* (2 vols.; London: Moxon, 1850), ii. 213–14.

[21] Ibid. 214.

merely—or even, perhaps, especially—those condemned to 'bored leisure'[22] who were drawn to romantic dreams. In 1836 the 20-year-old Charlotte Brontë, struggling to earn her living in a Yorkshire school—'Stupidity the atmosphere, school-books the employment, asses the society'—writes in an autobiographical fragment of her own frustrated sense of what her hero Byron called the 'craving void':[23]

Now I should be agonised if I had not the dream to repose on—its existences, its forms its scenes do fill a little of the craving vacancy Hohenlinden! Childe Harold! Flodden Field! The Burial of Moore! why cannot the blood rouse the heart the heart wake the head the head prompt the head [*sic*] to do things like these?[24]

That to which Brontë looks in an effort to assuage her feelings is, however, suggestively different from Byron's casual catalogue of his own 'intemperate' pursuits—the 'Gaming', 'Battle', 'Travel' in which he actually spent much time. The images she summons—that touchingly uncritical litany of the literary monuments of a heroic, masculine romanticism—seem to evoke in her a peculiar sense of impotence. But if the fragmenting objectification of her own self-image here ('the heart', 'the head') registers her actual distance from the heroics of which she dreams, it is also striking that her outburst has none of Byron's flippant world-weariness: these images retain their bright promise perhaps because of their re-moteness from any experience she might really or possibly have. Just so, it is in the same terms as Byron but with an urgency quite different from his that the governess Jane Eyre gives voice to her impatience with the 'stagnation' of an existence whose 'bounds' are all too evident, her longing for 'all of incident, life, fire, feeling, that I desired and had not'.

For in Jane's account this 'restlessness' appears not as a self-indulgent 'doctrine', the egocentric pursuit of a pleasurable 'agitation', but as tormenting, and in-escapable: 'the restlessness was in my nature; *it agitated me* to pain sometimes' (my emphasis). The moment is one of confessional privacy. But Jane's voice is not, like Byron's, arrogantly singular and self-dramatizing. Unusually in her narrative, she connects her own feelings with that which others feel: 'Millions are condemned to a stiller doom than mine, and millions are in silent revolt against their lot . . . Women are supposed to be very calm generally: but women feel just as men feel' (109). She speaks here quite straightforwardly of a much remarked social fact. For if the feelings she attributes to 'women' are very different from those that writers such as Mrs Ellis approve, they are, as we have begun to see, reflected in the records of the period—even in the writings of Mrs Ellis herself. Such 'restlessness' as this, it appears, was widespread amongst women of the middle classes in early nineteenth-century England: so widespread, indeed, as to seem to such moralists—as to Jane Eyre in a very different key—intrinsic to woman's 'nature'. And the 'day-dreaming'

---

[22] Hobsbawm, *Age of Revolution*, 272.

[23] The common source is probably Pope's 'Eloisa to Abelard'—'no craving Void left aking in the breast' (94). Pope was one of the 'first rate' poets recommended by the 18-year-old Charlotte to her friend Ellen Nussey in July 1834—'if you will though I don't admire him' (*CBL* i. 130).

[24] Roe Head Journal fragment, 'I'm just going to write because I cannot help it', *c.* October 1836, MS Bon 98 (7), BPM.

in which it found expression was not, in early nineteenth-century England, merely a private indulgence, but—as writers on 'woman' complain—given considerable cultural nurturing. Indeed, for twenty years before the wildfire success of *Jane Eyre* images of 'incident, life, fire, feeling' had been produced for and presented to women on an unprecedented scale.

II

In 1822 the book- and print-seller Rudolph Ackermann had issued for the Christmas market a tiny, prettily bound gift volume containing selections from the fashionable authors of the day and illustrated by twelve fine engravings. *Forget Me Not: A Christmas and New Year's Present for 1823* was to be the harbinger of an extraordinary publishing phenomenon—that of the best-selling 'annuals', which throughout the 1820s, 1830s, and 1840s found their way into most polite households, even the remote parsonage at Haworth.[25] The success of *Forget Me Not* led to a proliferation of similar volumes, produced, usually, for the Christmas trade, and containing a similar blend of fine engravings and literary contributions. Beautifully bound in coloured glazed paper, watered silk or gilt-stamped leather, and 'embellished' with delicate steel engravings, the annuals were designed first and foremost as sentimental gifts for ladies.[26] Their titles—keepsake, token, souvenir, offering, pledge—indicated their purpose, as did the famous motto for the *Forget Me Not*—'Appealing, by the magic of its name, | To gentle feelings and affections; kept | Within the heart like gold'—taken from a poem by L.E.L. Many, indeed, included an engraved 'Presentation Plate', on which the donor's and recipient's names might be inscribed. Each volume contained between twelve and twenty fine engravings (reproductions of fashionable portraits, romantic landscapes, and scenes of sentiment or of heroism), and a motley collection of short stories and poems—usually by various hands, sometimes, in the later annuals, the work of a single 'editor'—loosely designed to accompany these. Despite the high costs of production, these diminutive volumes were extremely lucrative for their publishers—'Infinite profit in a little book', as Leigh Hunt puts it, mockingly, in an essay on 'Pocket-books and Keepsakes' in *The Keepsake* for 1828. And their vogue was no nine days' wonder: it lasted for thirty years, well into the 1850s. During its heyday, there were 200 different 'annuals', some of which had first editions of over 10,000, followed a few weeks later by a second issue of several thousands more.[27]

[25] Christine Alexander, 'The Influence of the Visual Arts on the Brontës', in Christine Alexander and Jane Sellars, *The Art of the Brontës* (Cambridge: Cambridge University Press, 1995), 15.

[26] 'The annuals', wrote Southey as early as 1828, 'are now the only books bought for presents to young ladies' (quoted in Anne Renier, *Friendship's Offering: An Essay on the Annuals and Gift Books of the Nineteenth Century* (London: Private Libraries Association, 1964), 16).

[27] Frederick Winthrop Faxon, *Literary Annuals and Gift Books: A Bibliography 1823–1903* (1912; rpt. Pinner, Middx.: Private Libraries Association, 1973). For sales of the annuals, see 'The Annuals of Former Days', *Bookseller*, 29 (November 1858), 493; A. Bose, 'The Verse of the English "Annuals"', *Review of English Studies*, NS 4 (1953), 50 n. 2; Richard Altick, *The English Common Reader: A Social History of the Mass Reading Public, 1800–1900* (Chicago: University of Chicago Press, 1957), 362.

They seem to have catered immensely successfully to the taste of their mainly feminine recipients—far more successfully, their sales suggest, than the writings of Mrs Ellis and her ilk.[28]

Yet if the annuals were hugely popular, they were also sternly castigated. 'There are the *Friendship's Offering* embossed, and the *Forget Me Not* in morocco; *Jennings's Landscape* in dark green, and the *Christian Keepsake* in pea'; thus Thackeray in 1837. 'Nothing can be more trumpery than the whole collection—as works of art, we mean. . . . such a display of miserable mediocrity, such a collection of feeble verse, such a gathering of small wit, is hardly to be found in any other series.'[29] The very appearance of these little volumes—exquisitely bound, gorgeously 'embellished'—emphasized their commodity status in the most obvious way. 'They are a' just metempsychoses of the golden calf; for here ye see 'em, calves and gilding,' the Modern Pythagoras declares of them, in a *Fraser's* dialogue in 1834.[30] Many appealed quite openly to snobbery, engaging titled editors and contributors; their engravings of society figures, of the houses of the aristocracy, and of exotic places to which only the rich could afford to go, offered their readers potent images of a way of life of which most could only dream.[31] Their authors, often writing-to-order to 'illustrate' the engravings provided, were (as the career of L.E.L. was most poignantly to illustrate) more like commercial hacks than romantically free cultural agents. It is hardly surprising that they attracted the full force of that scorn of the market which had been one of the hallmarks of high romanticism. 'I hate the paper, the type, the gloss, the dandy plates, the names of contributors poked up into your eyes in 1st page, and whistled thro' all the covers of magazines,' wrote Lamb.[32] 'It would disgrace any name to appear in an annual,' Wordsworth roundly declared.[33] And such voices are echoed, in a different key, by the author of *Woman: As*

---

[28] By the mid-1840s, indeed, the publishers of the advice manuals were attempting to emulate the attractiveness of the annuals. *The Women, Daughters,* and *Wives of England* could all, by 1844, be purchased in a variety of bindings—cloth, silk, or morocco : the last-named was available in a 'Marriage-day Present Edition, elegantly bound in White Morocco', at 21s. (advertisement in *Fisher's Drawing Room Scrap Book,* ed. Mrs Ellis, for 1844).

[29] *Fraser's Magazine* 16 (1837), 757.

[30] 'Two Articles on the Annuals', *Fraser's Magazine,* 10 (November 1834), 602.

[31] On the annuals as enabling the middle-class project of 'cultural emulation', see Glennis Stephenson, *Letitia Landon: The Woman Behind L.E.L.* (Manchester: Manchester University Press, 1995), 126–37. The attraction to aristocratic mores may be seen also in the silver-fork novels of the 1820s and 1830s, and in the increasing popularity, in the 1830s and 1840s, of etiquette books familiarizing middle-class readers with the manners of fashionable society. (On the latter, see Michael Curtin, *Propriety and Position: A Study of Victorian Manners* (New York: Garland, 1987).)

[32] Charles Lamb to Bernard Barton, 11 October 1828, in E. V. Lucas (ed.), *The Letters of Charles and Mary Lamb 1821–1842* (2 vols.; London: Methuen, 1912), ii. 833.

[33] Alan G. Hill (ed.), *The Letters of William and Dorothy Wordsworth: The Later Years, Part II, 1829–1834,* 2nd edn. (Oxford: Oxford University Press, 1979), 275–6. As with most writers of note in the period—including Scott, Moore, Coleridge, Lockhart, Mary Shelley, Tennyson, Bulwer, Landor, Dickens, Thackeray, Ruskin, Elizabeth Barrett, Hogg, Mrs Hemans, Hood, Campbell, James Montgomery, Laetitia Landon, and R. H. Horne—this opinion did not stop him succumbing to the high fees offered and publishing in an annual. (See Peter J. Manning, 'Wordsworth in the *Keepsake,* 1829', in John O. Jordan and Robert L. Patten (eds.), *Literature in the Marketplace: Nineteenth-century British Publishing and Reading Practices* (Cambridge: Cambridge University Press, 1995), 44–73).

She Is and As She Should Be, who finds in the Annuals 'melancholy proof, that . . . the intellectual is superseded by the *visible. Volumes intended for sale* must be embellished . . . they have now become *beaux,* basing their claims upon garniture and a gilded outside.'[34]

'Filled with contributions from all the most famous names, and illustrated with the most wonderful of engravings on steel, and all the triumphs of typography,' Mrs Oliphant was to recall the annuals after a space of fifty years, 'yet, perhaps, more surely destined to the contempt of oblivion than almost any production of the press.'[35] And her view has, by and large, been that of subsequent historians. Unlike the advice books, the annuals have received little serious consideration.[36] Their success has usually been seen as an especially florid example of the commodification of romanticism; their contents dismissed as mere 'show and emptiness'.[37] As Jerome McGann suggests, they have become a 'synonym for bad and sentimental writing': 'literary history pigeonholed them years ago'.[38] Yet missing from such accounts is one crucial point of view. It is the point of view of those whom such critics portray as the mere dupes of the market—those who seem to have been delighted to receive the annuals, and whose sense of these little volumes might have been rather more complicated than this.

The annuals were produced not for instruction, but for enjoyment. The exciting stories and mellifluous verses they contained were as different from the rational arguments of the advice books as were their gorgeous bindings and exquisite illustrations from the latter's sober garb. If the standard of their literary contributions was, on the whole, not high, the engravings that were their primary attraction were often of exceptional quality. At a time when opportunities for seeing original paintings, or even reproductions, were limited, such images would have been of absorbing interest.[39]

---

[34] *Woman: As She Is and As She Should Be,* i. 159 n. 2.

[35] Margaret Oliphant, *Annals of a Publishing House, William Blackwood and his Sons, their Magazine and Friends* (3 vols.; Edinburgh and London: William Blackwood, 1897–8) i. 509.

[36] For general accounts, see Renier, *Friendship's Offering,* and Alison Adburgham, *Silver Fork Society: Fashionable Life and Literature 1814–1840* (London: Constable, 1983), ch. 18. Peter J. Manning, 'Wordsworth in the *Keepsake,* 1829', discusses the annuals as a commercial and entrepreneurial project and the ways in which 'luminaries' were acquired to write for them; and Margaret Linley, 'A Centre that Would Not Hold: Annuals and Cultural Democracy', in Laurel Brake, Bill Bell, and David Finkelstein (eds.), *Nineteenth-Century Media and the Construction of Identities* (Basingstoke and New York: Palgrave, 2000), 54–74, offers a thoughtful exploration of some of their cultural meanings.

[37] Charles Lamb to Bernard Barton, in Lucas (ed.), *Letters of Charles and Mary Lamb,* 833.

[38] Jerome McGann, 'The Rationale of Hypertext', http://jefferson.village.virginia.edu/public/jjm2f/rationale.html, last accessed 11 May 2002.

[39] The introduction of the steel plate in 1823 had made possible not merely a large number of impressions, but also a very fine image. Some of the most famous annuals—Heath's, Fisher's, and Finden's—were, indeed, named after their engravers. 'It cannot be denied', says the editor of the *Forget Me Not* in the Preface to the 1832 volume, 'that to the excellence of their embellishments the Annuals owe the greatest portion of their popularity; sets of the engravings are sold at a higher rate than the entire volume, from which they have been separated; and it is well known that single proof impressions of particular plates have obtained a price superior to that of the complete work.' Others besides the young Brontës seem to have copied the engravings from the annuals: readers of *Forget Me Not,* for example, were invited to subscribe to a print-library, from which they might borrow prints of Ackermann's engravings for copying.

The young Brontës certainly found them so: a manuscript dated 30 September 1830 contains the youthful Charlotte's detailed notes on several of the illustrations in *Friendship's Offering* for 1829,[40] and careful copies were made by Charlotte, Emily and Branwell Brontë from engravings in this and two other annuals—the *Literary Souvenir* for 1830 and *Forget Me Not* for 1831.[41] For that to which they were introduced in these beautiful little books was entirely different from that with which they had been confronted in Carus Wilson's tracts:[42] a world not of discipline and death, but of exoticism, adventure, and feeling; not of repression but of romantic expressiveness; not of deliberate austerity, but of glamorous 'display'.

That world is a potent presence in *Jane Eyre*. It is true that the annuals, with their hackneyed sentiments, their engravings of society beauties, and their unabashed appeals to the snobbery of their readers, may at first seem very far from this novel's passionate unconventionality, its insistence on the claims of a heroine who is 'insignificant, poor and plain'. Yet much of the reason for *Jane Eyre*'s immediate success—certainly that which distinguishes it from its unpublishable predecessor—lies in its evocation of the 'strange, startling, and harrowing', the 'imaginative and poetical', 'wild, wonderful, and thrilling' configurations of that distinctive romanticism which, promulgated in the annuals, had proved so compelling to hundreds of thousands of young women for twenty years before it appeared. These are the images that sweep aside Jane's sober satisfaction in the rational duties of a calm existence: images of an intensity, an expressiveness, an aesthetic pleasure, quite at odds with the disciplined domesticity of 'woman's sphere'. Like the gazer at the annuals, the frustrated young governess pacing the corridor at Thornfield allows her 'mind's eye' to 'dwell' on 'bright visions': like the engravings in the annuals, those 'bright visions' lead to a 'tale' more stirring, more expansive, more 'richly fraught with interest' than anything to be found in 'the page of actual life'.[43] The jumbled exoticism of the world into which Jane goes—its imagery of 'Italian days' (247), of Eastern sultans and slaves and seraglios, of Turkish and Persian despots, of Continental mistresses and Indian suttee, of jewellery, silks, and finery—is similar to that

---

[40] 'Campbell Castle', *EEW* i. 281–3.

[41] For Charlotte's copies, see Alexander and Sellars, *Art of the Brontës*, entries 35, 38, 39, 40, 41, 102, 110. By 1834, the year of the creation of Angria, the Brontës were copying engravings not merely from the annuals, but also from Thomas Moore's *Complete Works of Byron*, which Patrick Brontë had acquired in 1833.

[42] Evangelicals did try to enter the market opened up by the annuals, producing a succession of religious annuals, with such titles as *The Protestant Annual, The Christian Souvenir, The Sacred Iris, The Sacred Lyre*. But the tendency in these publications is for the message to be transformed by the medium, rather than vice versa. Thus, a long poem on 'The Crucifixion' in *The Amulet; A Christian and Literary Remembrancer* for 1830 presents its subject more as a stirring spectacle—'And thousands, tens of thousands, still | Cluster round Calvary's wild hill'—than as an occasion for the believer's self-abasement: it is illustrated by a Martin engraving, and followed in the volume by a 'Turkish Tale' of adventure and some secular verses by L.E.L. Similarly, *The Christian Keepsake and Missionary Annual*, edited during the 1830s by William Ellis (who married Sarah Stickney in 1837), caters to the annual-buyers' taste for exciting stories and exotic locations rather than attempting to inculcate dogma: its chief difference from other annuals lies in the fact that here the heroes are missionaries, and the 'embellishments' are engravings of these heroes and of the benighted regions into which they take God's word.

[43] Ellis, *Daughters of England*, 154.

of the annuals; like theirs, it tantalizes and thrills. Her narrative's fascination with drawing-room 'display'—from 'the beautiful books and ornaments on the consoles and chiffonières' at Thornfield (121) to the 'rich foreign lace', the 'gold-wrought Indian fabric', the 'satin robe of changeful sheen' that the ladies in Rochester's party wear (171–2), its detailed description of society figures, even the artificiality of its conception of 'high life', is likewise akin to theirs. Blanche Ingram has the dark imperiousness of the exotic womanhood in their engravings; Rosamond Oliver—described, in annual terms, as a 'Peri' (363)—the fairness of the society beauties they portray.[44] Their verses are evoked in the songs that punctuate Jane's story: Bessie's ballads of sentiment and romance (21–2); Adèle's 'canzonette' (102); Blanche Ingram's 'sentimental tunes and airs' (189); 'the Corsair-song' that Rochester sings 'con spirito' (179); the love-song he sings, at the 'hour of romance', to Jane (271). Their plates are figured in a different way, in the novel's frequent references to drawing and to painting; and in the visual set-pieces, both of 'portraits' and of 'scenes', that recur throughout Jane's narrative. Above all, that affirmation of the claims of feeling inscribed throughout the annuals is echoed, in a quite different key, in *Jane Eyre*'s passionate insistence on the absolute necessity of love.

Of course, as that gift of *Marmion* suggests, the annuals were by no means women's only pleasurable reading in early nineteenth-century England. 'Romanticism' fed their 'day-dreams' and 'entered middle class culture' in many other, and arguably much more distinguished, forms. Charlotte Brontë's early delight in the *Arabian Nights*, her adolescent passion for Byron, her later interest in de Staël and George Sand, were shared by tens of thousands of her contemporaries; and the impact of each is evident in *Jane Eyre*.[45] But the annuals over which she had pored as a child, with their varied contents and their emphasis on visual representation, seem more centrally, pervasively evoked in the novel than any of these. To come to *Jane Eyre* from these hugely popular volumes is to see how closely the novel registers the widespread feminine 'dreaming' of its time. And *Jane Eyre* in its turn might lead us to look at the annuals in a rather different way: not as depressing evidence of the 'complicity between Romantic idealism and the commercial world',[46] but as offering some access, however speculative, to the subjectivity of those 'millions' who responded to Jane's story with excited recognition, as an articulation of their own intimate dissatisfactions and desires.

For the feelings celebrated in the annuals are suggestively different from those that the moralists of early nineteenth-century England deemed proper to woman's

---

[44] 'Young Peri of the West!' Byron hails his Ianthe, in the dedication to *Childe Harold's Pilgrimage*, which was reprinted in the *Literary Souvenir* for 1830 and illustrated by an engraving that was copied—apparently more than once—by Charlotte Brontë (Alexander and Sellars, *Art of the Brontës*, 19).

[45] For an account of the importance of *The Arabian Nights* for Georgian and Victorian children, see Harry Stone, *Dickens and the Invisible World: Fairy-Tales, Fantasy, and Novel-Making* (Bloomington: Indiana University Press, 1979), 25 ff. On de Staël, see Ellen Moers, *Literary Women* (London: Virago, 1978), ch. 9; on George Sand, Patricia Thomson, *George Sand and the Victorians: Her Influence and Reputation in Nineteenth-Century England* (London: Macmillan, 1977). On Byron's popularity in the period, see Davidoff and Hall, *Family Fortunes*, 159 ff.; and on his significance for Charlotte Brontë, Winifred Gérin, 'Byron's Influence on the Brontës', *Keats-Shelley Memorial Bulletin*, 17 (1966), 1–19.

[46] John O. Jordan and Robert L. Patten, 'Introduction' to *Literature in the Marketplace*, 5–6.

sphere. On the surface, it is true, the annuals are quite conventional: women appear within them as guardians of the domestic affections, men as the makers and shapers of the public world. 'What have we to do with ambition?' reflects the heroine of a story in *The Keepsake* for 1830. 'It is the distinguishing attribute of the other sex—it mingles in their sports of childhood, and lingers amidst the decay of age.—The insignia of power are with them at once the bauble of the boy and the pride of after-life.—The empire of the head we resign to man—the *heart* belongs to us . . . Woman's life is love.'[47] Yet the experience the annuals offered their recipients was more potent and more varied than this. Despite their purpose as romantic gifts, love was by no means their only theme;[48] indeed, their most striking characteristic, to the twenty-first century reader, is the energy with which they point away from 'woman's sphere'.[49] 'Are thy thoughts wandering in the mazes mild | Of old romance?' asks a poem in a *Forget Me Not* apparently possessed by the Brontës, accompanied by a picture of a day-dreaming girl.

> for, on thy placid brow,
> And in thy dark eyes, beautiful and mild,
>   Thoughts lie like blissful dreams. Or haply thou
> Call'st up with memory's spell some distant scene,
> Where thou with thy heart's cherish'd one hast been;
> Some valley of that Transatlantic world
> Where Albion's ships have gallantly unfurl'd
> Her conquering pennon[50]

To those 'unacquainted with the world' the annuals offered highly pleasurable 'glimpses of its scenes and ways' (*JE* 146). Their stories and verses told of foreign places and of far-off times; of 'incident' and 'excitement', heroic exploits, thrilling escapes, 'agitating risk and romantic chance' (*JE* 366). Most of their engravings were of unfamiliar but striking scenes, and of women whose beauty was often of an eastern (or at least a southern) type. So customary was this, indeed, that the editor of *Finden's Tableaux* for 1841 presents as a novelty an annual devoted, for once, to 'the simple representation of English Country Life'—though the images of romanticized rusticity that follow bear little relation to actual life in the mid-nineteenth-century countryside.

---

[47] 'The Prophet of St Paul's', by Lord Normandy.
[48] The most prolific of their female contributors, L.E.L., was famed for writing of love. But if 'love' was the central theme of much of her earlier poetry, the subjects of her poems in the annuals are extraordinarily various, ranging from shipwreck and famine in exotic locations to ballads on chivalry and the supernatural. This kind of variety can be found in all the annuals. The *Forget Me Not* for 1833, for instance, contains stories set in 12th-cent. Verona and in ancient Egypt, an engraving of a scene from the *Odyssey*, an engraving and description of Nuremberg, and a poem on 'Liberty' by Captain Calder Campbell: whilst that that for 1834 includes stories set in the reign of Edward III, during the Napoleonic wars, in the Tyrol, and in 16th-cent. Paris, and verses on 'a legend of Dalmatia', a Brazilian convent, on nature, and on 'Aspiration' (quoted below).
[49] Indeed, as Glennis Stephenson notes, 'the one aspect that the annuals always ignore is the practical matter of running a household' (*Letitia Landon*, 143).
[50] 'A Noontide Retreat', by Mrs C. G. Godwin, *Forget Me Not*, 1831.

Fascinated by 'high life', destined for boudoir or drawing-room, the annuals are marked throughout by those prejudices of class, race, and gender that have troubled critics of *Jane Eyre*. Yet their glimpses of glamour and luxury, their portraits of beautiful women, their images of the exotic, cannot quite be reduced to these. Another way of seeing them is suggested by a traveller's words in an article in the *Oriental Annual* for 1839: 'every sense delighted with the novelty and foreign aspect of the place' (5). The catchwords of much of their writing (illustrated in the case of this annual by Finden's fine engravings)[51] are those of expansive wonder—'striking', 'grand', 'admiration', 'excitement'—rather than of complacent superiority. As William Whewell was to put it, in his Inaugural Lecture on the Great Exhibition, '*Oriental* magnificence is still a proverbial mode of describing a degree of splendour and artistical richness which is not found among ourselves.'[52] The sense is of a longing for something other—more various, more compelling, more full of possibility—than the familiarity of the known. For if the annuals' overt message is often that home is better than adventure, that the English is superior to the foreign, their imaginative pull is all the other way. The world presented within them is infinitely more seductive and more glamorous than that with which Mrs Ellis urged her readers to be satisfied. And it seems expressly designed to cater to those desires for 'incident, life, fire, feeling', for 'Liberty, Excitement, Enjoyment', that receive a different kind of articulation in *Jane Eyre*.

The focus of the annuals is on the forceful, the rousing, the thrilling. Even Mrs Hemans, that 'icon of female domesticity',[53] characterizes 'the themes of song' in an annual poem in these terms:

> Where shall the minstrel find a theme?
> Where-e'er, for freedom shed,
> Brave blood hath dyed some ancient stream
> Amidst the mountains, red. . . .
> The heart that burns, the cheek that glows,
> The tear from hidden springs,
> The thorn, and glory of the rose—
> These are undying things. [54]

When annual authors deal with conventionally Christian themes, they speak of expressiveness rather than self-discipline:

---

[51] The *Oriental Annual* was perhaps the most magnificent of all the annuals. 'The golden elephant, with the golden howdah and its golden occupants; the camel all of gold, with its golden driver under the golden tree, running up the back of the volume—are quite sufficient to remind us of the *Arabian Nights' Entertainments*, or the ingenious signs which used to flare over the shops of our grocers', muses Barry Cornwall of it, in his half-sardonic 'Judgment of the Annuals' (*Fraser's Magazine* 10 (1834), 605).

[52] William Whewell, *The General Bearing of the Great Exhibition on the Progress of Art and Science*, Inaugural Lecture as Master of Trinity College, Cambridge, 26 November 1851, 8.

[53] Anne K. Mellor, *Romanticism and Gender* (London and New York: Routledge, 1993), 123.

[54] 'The Themes of Song', *The Amulet*, 1829.

Tears at each pure emotion flow
They wait on Pity's gentle claim,
On Admiration's fervid glow,
On Piety's seraphic flame.[55]

The emphasis throughout is on foregrounded, intense emotion and on liberation from constraint. Thus, the opening poem in *Friendship's Offering* for 1829 announces that 'each glowing picture' in the volume is designed to allow the free play of the reader's imagination—'That fancy here may gaze her fill | Forming fresh scenes and shapes at will'; one contributor speaks of longing 'To live alone with Nature; to unfold | Her seeming mysteries; to rove at will | Through her untrodden haunts'; while a third declares that

Without resolve that mocks controul,
A conscious energy of soul
That views no height to human skill,
Man never excelled and never will.[56]

In the *Forget Me Not* for 1833 a poem entitled 'Aspiration' (by James Wilson Esq.) calls for

the sea-bird's wing to roam
The infinite waters as my home,
To soar from the Ocean's wild embrace,
And pierce the eternity of Space!

Such images as these—commonplace in the annuals—speak not of confinement to a 'proper sphere', but of freely aspiring subjectivity; not of rational self-management, but of soaring, transcendent desire. And such paeans as these to imaginative potency would have been reinforced for the female reader by the prominence in the annuals of such figures as L.E.L. For if woman appeared in their plates as a beautiful object, she also appeared on their pages as active, creative subject—not as displayer of accomplishments, but as possessor of real professional skills.[57] With their many female contributors and their famous female editors (Mary Russell Mitford, L.E.L, Caroline Norton, Mrs Gore, Mary Howitt, the Countess of Blessington), the annuals bore eloquent testimony to woman's potential for achievement in that sphere of 'Poetry and Genius' which—like Jane Eyre reflecting on *Marmion*—they unequivocally glorified:

---

[55] Lord Morpeth, 'The Use of Tears', *The Keepsake*, 1831.

[56] 'The First Leaf of an Album', by James Montgomery, Esq.; 'Nature', by Miss Jeffrey; 'The Minstrel Boy', by 'the Ettrick Shepherd'; all *Friendship's Offering*, 1829. This is one of the volumes from which the young Brontës copied plates.

[57] On this subject see Margaret Reynolds, 'Introduction I', Angela Leighton and Margaret Reynolds (eds.), *Victorian Women Poets: An Anthology* (Oxford: Blackwell, 1995); Angela Leighton, *Victorian Women Poets: Writing Against the Heart* (Hemel Hempstead: Harvester Wheatsheaf, 1992), 49–50; Mellor, *Romanticism and Gender*, 111–12; and Sonia Hofkosh, 'Disfiguring Economies: Mary Shelley's Short Stories', in Audrey A. Fisch, Anne K. Mellor, and Esther H. Schor (eds.), *The Other Mary Shelley: Beyond Frankenstein* (Oxford: Oxford University Press, 1993), 205–8.

The Poet, too, who, borne along
   In thought to distant time,
Pours forth his inmost soul in song,
   Holds fast this hope sublime!
He would a glorious name bequeath,
   Oblivion shall not blot,
And round that name his thoughts enwreath
   The words—'Forget-Me-Not!'[58]

If the annuals spoke of and celebrated Liberty and Excitement, they also enshrined Enjoyment: a quite immediate enjoyment of a sensuous and aesthetic kind.
'The fair inhabitant of the loneliest hamlet receives from them an idea of the power
which can give form and multiplied existence to gentle thoughts and images,' writes
one contemporary of them, in 1829. 'It is next to impossible that any one should have
looked at the engravings of these volumes, and endure anything either common or
vulgar for the remainder of the year.' Despite that final sentence, the value ascribed
to the annuals here lies less in their appeal to their readers' snobbery than in their capacity to expand their horizons and make them in some way acquainted with art's
'diviner power'.[59] It is of enjoyment like this that Ruskin speaks, when he writes in
Praeterita that 'the really most precious, and continuous in deep effect on me, of all
gifts to my childhood, was from my Croydon aunt, of the Forget-me-not of 1827,
with a beautiful engraving in it of Prout's "Sepulchral monument at Verona" ';[60] it is
to enjoyment like this that the young Brontës' painstaking copies of images from the
annuals bear eloquent testimony. But even for those less concerned with higher aesthetic pleasure, the annuals brought 'enjoyment' of an undeniable kind. From their
first inception as gift-books, they were designed above all to be attractive: as the years
passed, they became more and more sumptuous in appearance, with bindings of
plush, velvet, satin, ornately decorated silk. 'If publications of this nature proceed as
they have begun', wrote Leigh Hunt sardonically, at the beginning of the annuals'
hey-day, 'we shall soon arrive at the millenium of souvenirs. Instead of engravings,
we shall have paintings by the first masters; our paper must be vellum; our bindings
in opal and amethyst; and nobody must read us except in a room full of luxury, or a
bower of roses'.[61] Yet others, in these years, were less dismissive than this. 'Why,
Book-binding has become a beautiful art!' writes John Wilson in an article in *Blackwood's* which the Brontës almost certainly knew: and the language in which he
describes the Christmas annuals points forward to *Jane Eyre*:

---

[58] These verses were published in the *Forget Me Not* for 1824, at the very beginning of the vogue of the
annuals.

[59] *Monthly Review*, NS 12 (1829), 435.This reviewer goes on to celebrate the fact that 'the daughters of
tradesman and manufacturers' will by 'forming a good taste' acquire the 'best and most valuable adornment, next to the moral ones, of woman'. But he is not, as Peter J.Manning suggests, speaking
of fashion plates, which would enable 'the beholder to behold herself as she wished to be', or of the
dissemination of a 'fashionable ideal' ('Wordsworth in the *Keepsake*, 1829', 57). The engravings that
he extols are engravings of works of art, with which 'the inhabitants of the provinces' will be able to 'console' themselves 'for the want of exhibitions and rare collections', such as Charlotte Brontë longed to see.

[60] John Ruskin, *Praeterita* (Oxford: Oxford University Press, 1978), 81.

[61] 'Pocket-books and Keep-sakes', *The Keepsake*, 1828.

all those duodecimos, post-octavos, quartos, and folios, of kid, calf, silk, satin, velvet, russia, morocco,—white, grey, green, blue, yellow, violet, red, scarlet, crimson . . . all the Souvenirs—There they go, one after another—like so many birds of soft or bright plumage . . . Our old eyes are dazzled with the splendour, and are forced to seek relief and repose on the mild moreen of those window curtains, whose drapery descends as simply as the garb of a modest quakeress. Even then, all the colours of the rainbow continue dancing on their orbs.[62]

Fourteen years later, Branwell Brontë was to write with more critical fascination of 'the magnificent engravings that flash from the pages of those hundred "Books of Beauty"—of "Flowers"—"of Affections," &c. &c. blazing forth every season, with a glitter as fair as it is fleeting'.[63] For, however 'fleeting' the annuals' 'glitter' (this article of Branwell's extols the superior merits of Bewick's 'unpretending' wood engravings), their allure was undeniable. To those who gazed at their plates and fingered their opulent bindings, they brought a taste of a richness, an elegance, a luxury that contrasted markedly both with the pleasure-denying discipline of evangelicalism and with the sobriety that the moralists of womanhood approved.

But the annuals did not merely speak to their readers of an excitement, an exoticism, a power, and a pleasure largely absent, for most of them, from 'the page of actual life'. Their very existence held out the promise that the women who were their chief recipients might experience satisfactions quite different from those towards which the advice books exhorted them to look. Whereas writers of these latter again and again deplore woman's 'selfish desire to stand apart from the many; to be something, of, and by, herself; to enjoy what she does enjoy, and to appropriate the tribute society offers her', it was the manifest purpose of the annuals to cater to precisely this.[64] As gift-books, designed to be given to young ladies by their masculine admirers, they were above all intended to assure the recipient that she had, indeed, been singled out from the 'many' to receive a 'tribute' of a particularly pleasurable kind. And in this they bear witness to the fact that in early nineteenth-century England, romantic love was one sphere—far more headily potent than that of 'woman's mission'—within which women might experience excitement, intensity, admiration, enjoyment; might above all gain and exercise a power denied to them in the public world.[65]

---

[62] 'Christmas Presents', *Blackwood's Magazine*, 23 (1828), 7–13. This long description of the annuals, with its verbal echoes of *Jane Eyre*, is the companion article to 'Christmas Dreams', one of the articles that Branwell Brontë, in a letter to the editor of *Blackwood's* in 1835, speaks of having 'read and re-read while a little child' (Oliphant, *Annals of a Publishing House*, ii. 178).

[63] Patrick Branwell Brontë, 'Thomas Bewick: "Flumina amem sylvasque inglorius"', *Halifax Guardian*, 1 October 1842; reprinted in Victor A. Neufeldt, 'A Newly Discovered Publication by Branwell Brontë', *BST* 21: 1 (April 1999, 11–15).

[64] Ellis, *Daughters of England*, 234.

[65] The annuals were, on the whole, too proper to present unlawful passion, though their images of beautiful women had considerable erotic appeal. For a suggestive discussion of the way in which, in some at least of the annuals, 'the sentimental image of the female domestic ideal . . . is set against the contesting image of the sexualised woman', see Stephenson, *Letitia Landon*, 160–5; and, for a more negative view of 'the disavowed erotic saturation that surfaces throughout the *Keepsake* and in the discourse surrounding the annuals', Manning, 'Wordsworth in the *Keepsake*, 1829', 65.

For if 'love' is by no means the only theme of the annuals, 'love' is prominent within them; and prominent in ways subversive of the moralists' womanly ideal. Most obviously, perhaps, it appears in the shape of that straightforward romantic conquest implicit in their 'tribute' form. Thus, the *Keepsake* for 1828 is adorned by a series of exquisite engravings of society ladies: its dedicatory poem, illustrated by one of these, offers a stirring image of 'beauty' as a 'sovereign' power:

> Then, because beauty is the soul of song,
> We bring to thee (the beautiful), to thee,
> The tributory lay of many a tongue;
> Acknowledgement of beauty's sovereignty

A story in the 1831 volume apostrophizes 'Woman' as the 'inspiration of passionate thought', the 'bestower of delight'. In the *Forget Me Not* for 1830, a poem entitled 'Verses On the Portrait of a Spanish Princess', illustrated by an engraving from a Wilkie painting, calls upon readers to

> gaze again
> Upon the picture, and admire the power
> Of woman's beauty. O it hath a charm
> With which the Great Artificer endues
> Nought else of his creation!

Another ('The Chain Broken') more darkly laments—

> Alas! The hour
> When Beauty in her scorn
> Walks forth to triumph in her pow'r,
> And mock at hopes new born;
> The freshest garland on her bow'r
> Has poison in its thorn!—

Passages such as these—commonplace in the annuals—speak not of selflessness, but of self-affirming admiration; of the fiery excitements of emotional adventure, the triumphs of fashionable display.[66] For girls confined to lives of 'bored leisure' they must have held a peculiar potency. There are, it is true, other depictions of love in the annuals. There is some lip-service to the domesticated, self-denying 'woman's love' extolled in the advice books; L.E.L. famously specialized in portraying suffering womanhood. But on the whole, the message of these little volumes is of a markedly different kind. 'Love' appears, in their pages, as pivotal, and empowering: it is the highest expression of free subjectivity, the prize of the conqueror, the goal of the wanderer; not luxury, but necessity. 'Of all the various inherent energies of the human mind, none is stronger than love', proclaims a story

---

[66] The contradiction between the celebration of 'feeling' and attachment, and the idealization of isolation and autonomy ('liberty'), heroic agency and excitement ('incident') is hardly explored or even confronted in the annuals—or indeed in the high romanticism on which they draw. But it is—as we shall see—central to *Jane Eyre*.

in the *Forget Me Not* for 1830. 'It cannot be constrained by mastery'.[67] 'There is *nothing* which can fill the place of engrossing love within the human soul,' declares a piece called 'Love's Memories', from *The Keepsake* for 1828. Such pronouncements might, of course, be seen as enjoining that narrowing in of all desire to a single goal which Freud was later to see as the hallmark of a conventional femininity. Yet there is much in the annuals that invites one to read them in a different spirit: as offering powerful alternative images to those of female subordination and passivity, and affirming the central importance of that which the culture of early nineteenth-century England relegated to 'woman's sphere'. And in this, they point towards *Jane Eyre*.

III

It is not surprising that the annuals were seen by many as symbols of fashionable decadence. Their open appeals to their readers' snobbery, their celebration of feminine beauty, their very purpose as romantic gifts, promoted exactly that which the advice books disapproved: an ideal of woman as shining in society, rather than devoting herself to the sober duties of the domestic sphere. More than twenty years after *Jane Eyre* was published, George Eliot was to portray the shallow, romantically deluded Rosamond Vincy delighting in the latest 'Keepsake', 'the gorgeous watered-silk publication which marked modern progress at the time': she is, we are told, 'not without relish' for those doyennes of the annuals, Lady Blessington and L.E.L.[68] Such ironic treatment of fashionable pretension is, indeed, prominent in *Jane Eyre*. The over-indulged and pampered Reed children come to deplorable ends; there is a scathing portrait of the Brocklehurst women, 'splendidly attired in velvet, silk, and furs'; the guests at the houseparty at Thornfield are exposed as heedlessly showy and thoughtlessly cruel. Blanche Ingram—who 'doat[s] on Corsairs', appears almost as a parody-embodiment of the evils of 'display': 'she played: her execution was brilliant: she sang: her voice was fine . . . both her words and her air seemed intended to excite not only the admiration, but the amazement of her auditors: she was evidently bent on striking them as something very dashing and daring indeed' (173, 179). The implicit comparison, of course, is with the sharply observing, undesigningly 'genuine', and apparently unregarded Jane, who is both competent to judge these 'attainments' and innocent of any such blatant desire to be admired.

Yet the world in which Blanche shines is not in *Jane Eyre* seen simply through the prism of moralizing judgement. Superficial, artificial, unfeeling, it may be; but it also shimmers with beauty. 'Her purple riding-habit almost swept the ground, her veil streamed long on the breeze; mingling with its transparent folds, and gleaming through them, shone rich raven ringlets': this is Jane's first glimpse of her rival

---

[67] The reference is to Chaucer's *The Franklin's Tale*, l. 764—'Love wol nat ben constreyned by maistrye', though Chaucer's ironies are wholly absent here.
[68] *Middlemarch* (1871–2), iii. ch. 27.

(166). Later, Blanche sits 'with proud grace at the piano, spreading out her snowy robes in queenly amplitude' (179): if this image is undercut by Jane's sardonic observation—'she appeared to be on her high horse tonight'—its impact nevertheless remains. 'Each came out gaily and airily, with dress that gleamed lustrous through the dusk,' she tells, of Rochester's house-guests: 'They . . . descended the staircase almost as noiselessly as a bright mist rolls down a hill . . . All had a sweeping amplitude of array that seemed to magnify their persons as a mist magnifies the moon . . . They dispersed about the room; reminding me, by the lightness and buoyancy of their movements, of a flock of white plumy birds' (167–71). Thornfield, too, has a ravishing luminosity. 'What a beautiful room!' exclaims Jane, when Mrs Fairfax first shows her the dining-room. 'I thought I caught a glimpse of a fairy place: so bright to my novice-eyes appeared the view beyond.' What she sees 'beyond' is a drawing-room 'ceiled with snowy mouldings of white grapes and vine-leaves, beneath which glowed in rich contrast crimson couches and ottomans; while the ornaments on the pale Parian mantel-piece were of sparkling Bohemian glass, ruby red; and between the windows large mirrors repeated the general blending of snow and fire' (104). If the dryness with which Blanche Ingram is observed (and the housework at Thornfield described) recalls the debunking satire of Glass Town and of Angria, passages such as these point back to those rather different moments in their author's early writings that display an apparently uncritical delight in the *mores* of fashionable life. In *High Life in Verdopolis* (1834), Charles Townshend quotes Zamorna: 'I like high life: I like its manners, its splendors, its luxuries, the beings which move in its enchanted sphere.' If Brontë, through her narrator, here ironically distances herself from this 'tone of feeling', she is also humorously aware that it gives her licence for lavish description of 'high life'.[69] Two years later, the youthful author was to dwell more directly on her pleasure in her Angrian creations: 'I know their parks, their halls, their towers, I The sweet lands where they shine'.[70] This frank attraction to 'elegance', to glamour, and to beauty is evident throughout the novelettes of her twenties; and it is brought distinctively into focus in *Jane Eyre*. The feeling is quite different from the announced anti-romanticism of *The Professor*, the 'unromantic' coolness of *Shirley*, the disillusioned clarity of *Villette*. Yet it is in *Jane Eyre* by no means simply ingenuous. For within the novel one can trace a more perspicacious engagement with the seductive world of early nineteenth-century female 'day-dreaming' than might at first appear.

That engagement is signalled on the very first page of Jane's story. 'I soon possessed myself of a volume, taking care that it should be one stored with pictures,' she tells. And the resonant image of that child, sitting 'cross-legged, like a Turk', and entering freely into a 'strangely impressive' imaginary world, is as pivotal in the novel as that other opening image of the 'saddened', 'humbled' 'dependant', condemned to a situation she is powerless to change or to understand. If that downtrodden

[69] 'High Life in Verdopolis, by Lord C. A. F. Wellesley' (1834), *EEW* ii. 4–5.
[70] 'Long since as I remember well', 265–6, in *CBP* 283.

child compels the reader's sympathy, the child who gazes at Bewick invites a more intimate identification: she, like the novel's reader, is 'turning over the leaves of [a] book'. The book over which Jane pores is not, of course, an annual. But the 'day-dreaming' here imaged—not merely a withdrawal from social demands and relations, but an entry into realms of passionate private enjoyment, of stirring subjective freedom—evokes precisely the experience that the annuals invited their readers to have.[71] And it evokes it in a manner quite different from the way in which such 'day-dreaming' was usually portrayed.

The youthful female reader, carried away in fantasy, was a familiar literary character in the eighteenth and nineteenth centuries. From Charlotte Lennox's 'female Quixote' to Jane Austen's Catherine Morland (and, indeed, to Joyce's Gertie McDowell), she was seen almost invariably from the perspective of a more knowing, more disillusioned realism, as one whose book-induced day-dreams are destined to be corrected, ironically or tragically, by experience of the world. Charlotte Brontë herself had, indeed, created just such a figure in Caroline Vernon, the last of her Angrian heroines—a girl who worships 'Lord Byron & Bonaparte & the Duke of Wellington & Lord Edward Fitzgerald', and sits 'pondering over a reverie of romance' as her maid dresses her hair:

... something so delicious—yet so undefined—I will not say that it was all Love—yet neither will I affirm that Love was entirely excluded there-from—something there was of a Hero—yet a nameless, a formless, a mystic being—a dread shadow—that crowded upon Miss Vernon's soul—haunted her day & night when she had nothing useful to occupy her head or her hands—I almost think she gave him the name of Ferdinand Alonzo FitzAdolphus, but I don't know ... whether he was to have golden or raven hair or straight or aquiline proboscis she had not quite decided—however, he was to drive all before him in the way of fighting—to conquer the world & build himself a city like Babylon—only it was to be in the moorish style—& there was to be a palace called the Alhambra—where ... she, Miss C. Vernon ... was to be his chief Lady & to be called the Sultana Zara-Esmerelda—with at least a hundred slaves to do her bidding—as for the gardens of roses & the Halls of Marble & the diamonds & fine pearls & the rubies—it would be vanity to attempt a description of such heavenly sights—the reader must task his imagination & try if he can conceive them.[72]

Jane Eyre, however, is quite unlike the soon-to-be-disillusioned Caroline: and *Jane Eyre's* portrayal of its heroine's dreams is quite different from this. The difference is worth exploring, for in it lies the clue to much of the novel's subversive originality.

Ten years after the publication of *Jane Eyre*, Flaubert, in perhaps the most famous of all literary evocations of this disparaged feminine 'day-dreaming', writes of another heroine's encounter with the annuals:

Some of her companions brought back keepsakes presented to them at the New Year, and there was a great business of hiding them away and reading them in the dormitory. Delicately

---

[71] At the age of 16, Charlotte Brontë had written eloquently of the exhilarating power of Bewick's 'enchanted page', its 'pictured thoughts that breath and speak and burn': see her 'Lines on Bewick' (*CBP* 138–40). On her copies of engravings from Bewick, see Alexander and Sellars, *Art of the Brontës*, 22, 160–1.

[72] 'Caroline Vernon', in Brontë, *Five Novelettes*, 312–13.

fingering their lovely satin bindings, Emma gazed in wonder at the unknown signatures beneath the contributions—mostly Counts and Viscounts.

She thrilled as she blew back the tissue paper over the prints. It rose in a half-fold and sank gently down on the opposite page. Behind a balcony railing a young man in a short cloak would be pressing to his heart a girl in white with an alms-purse at her waist. Or it would be an unnamed portrait of an English milady with golden curls, looking at you with her big bright eyes from under a round straw hat. Other ladies lolled in carriages, gliding through the park with a grey-hound leaping in front of the horses and two little postilions driving them along at a trot . . . And the Sultans, with their long pipes, swooning in arbours in the arms of dancing girls! The Giaours, the Turkish sabres, the Greek fezzes! And all those pallid landscapes of dithyrambic regions, depicting often palms and pines together, with tigers on the right and a lion on the left, Tartar minarets on the horizon, Roman ruins in the foreground, and some kneeling camels in between: the whole framed by a well-kept virgin forest, with a great perpendicular sunbeam quivering on the water, and, at isolated points on its steel-grey surface, a few white scratches to represent swans floating.[73]

Emma Bovary, enthralled by a succession of manufactured images, yields deliciously to their power. Her naïvely narcissistic relation to the unreal world they depict carries her, in a movement that is to be repeated throughout the novel, from her initial position as viewing subject to that of viewed object: 'an English milady with golden curls, *looking at you*' (my italics). If the prose at such moments as this registers the extent of her absorption, it nevertheless maintains an ironic detachment from her. The images that charm her are set before the reader in a mocking Rabelaisian catalogue, as the frankly ersatz products of a synthetic romanticism. Here, as throughout *Madame Bovary*, the world of feminine day-dreaming is distanced and anatomized as a phenomenon of the boudoir, disabling the one who indulges in it for any more authentic life.

There is nothing of this feeling in *Jane Eyre*. It is not so much that Jane Eyre, the presented character, is more resistant than Emma to the thrilling allure of 'high life'; that unlike Flaubert's heroine, she demonstrates the bourgeois virtues of self-discipline and self-control. The dreams that compel her are quite differently seen. To Flaubert, Emma's desire is 'a highly intelligible cliché',[74] bounded by the frames of the pictures at which she gazes, the repetitive scenarios of the fiction that she reads. Again and again in the novel her engrossing, escapist longings contract to a single theme. As a schoolgirl, she finds 'an unlooked-for delight' in the sermons she hears, with their 'metaphors of betrothed, spouse, heavenly lover, marriage everlasting'; the novels she keeps in her apron pocket are 'all about love and lovers, damsels in distress swooning in lonely lodges, postilions slaughtered all along the

[73] Gustav Flaubert, *Madame Bovary*, trans. Alan Russell (Harmondsworth: Penguin, 1950), 50–1. Subsequent page references in the text are to this edition. On the French 'keepsakes' (modelled, as their name suggests, on the English), see Bernard-Henri Gausseron, *Les Keepsakes et annuaires illustrés de l'époque romantique: Essai de bibliographie* (Paris: Librairie A. Fontaine, E. Rondeau, successeur, 1896), 203–51, and Frédéric Lachèvre, *Bibliographie sommaire des keepsakes et autres recueils collectifs de la période romantique 1823–1848* (2 vols.; Paris: L. Giraud-Badin, 1929).

[74] Leo Bersani, *A Future for Astyanax: Character and Desire in Literature* (London: Marion Boyars, 1978), 95.

road, horses ridden to death on every page, gloomy forests, troubles of the heart, vows, sobs, tears, kisses' (49, 50). If her love affair appears to open up 'a marvellous world . . . where all was passion, ecstasy, delirium . . . and ordinary life was only a distant phenomenon', the incipient expansiveness of this is narcissistically closed off, as she becomes 'a part of her own imaginings, finding the long dream of her youth come true as she *survey[s] herself* in that amorous role she ha[s] so coveted' (50, 175; my italics). In *Jane Eyre*, however, Jane's longing is imaged as a yearning to see beyond the horizons that limit her vision; and the desires that animate her story are by no means confined to 'love'. The objects that evoke her wonder are not mockingly enumerated, but recalled in all their vividness: Bewick and *Gulliver's Travels*; Helen and Miss Temple conversing 'of nations and times past; of countries far away' (73); the drawing-room at Thornfield; the 'bright pages of *Marmion*'; even the dresses she refuses to allow her lover to buy—the one a 'superb pink satin', the other a 'rich silk of the most brilliant amethyst dye' (268). Emma's vision of the yearned-for life of society and of luxury is clichéd, banal, one-dimensional; it is simply the necessary backdrop for a single repetitive dream:

Sighs in the moonlight, long embraces, hands at parting bathed with tears, all the fevers of the flesh and the languid tenderness of love—these could not be separated from the balconies of stately mansions, the life of leisure, the silk-curtained boudoir with a good thick carpet, full flower-bowls and a bed on a raised dais, nor from the sparkle of precious stones and shoulder-knots on servants' livery. (72)

But the world of 'high-born elegance' (*JE* 168) at which the governess Jane Eyre gazes flashes, gleams, and shines. And the images to which it gives rise—'as noiselessly as a bright mist rolls down a hill'; 'a sweeping amplitude of array that seemed to magnify their persons as a mist magnifies the moon'; 'reminding me by the lightness and buoyancy of their movements, of a flock of white plumy birds'—are not constrictingly predictable, but instinct with burgeoning life.

   For the desire of which *Jane Eyre* speaks in passages such as these is not deluded and delusory but seminal, subversive, challenging. Where Emma 'gazes in wonder' (and soon becomes, in fantasy, not gazer but object of the gaze), Jane enters unknown realms and 'form[s] an idea of [her] own'. She is not the helpless victim of a disabling, clichéd fantasy: she 'draws parallels in silence', which inspire her, decisively, to act (11). If she 'feasts', as a child at school, 'on the spectacle of ideal drawings', these consolatory images are 'all the work of [her] own hands' (74). When she opens her 'inward ear' to 'a tale . . . of incident, life, fire, feeling' it is one that is 'created . . . narrated . . . quickened' by her own imagination; not a series of stereotyped images, but a story that never ends (109). Emma's fantasies centre on and return always to herself. But Jane longs for 'an existence more expansive and stirring than my own' (280). And it is as she speaks of such desires as these that at two key moments in the novel she connects her own singular story to that of a wider world. Thus, as she tells of 'eagerly glancing at the bright pages of *Marmion*'—'one of those genuine productions so often vouchsafed to the fortunate public of those days'—she insists that even now, in the world of her maturity, 'poetry' and 'genius' not only live, but reign and redeem' (370–1). Thus, remembering how, as a governess, she allowed her 'mind's eye to dwell on whatever bright visions rose before it', she aligns herself with the 'millions' who are likewise 'in silent revolt against their lot' (109).

Flaubert's disparaging view of feminine day-dreaming has become more or less institutionalized in our culture.[75] Yet if his ironic view of his heroine bespeaks an easy assumption of masculine authority, there is an equal, and by no means negligible, authority in Jane Eyre's generalization from her own situation to a larger experiential reality: a reality usually discounted because 'silent' and issueless, but here passionately invoked. That dissatisfaction with the quotidian, that longing for something other—elsewhere, more intense, more satisfying—deplored by moralists and denigrated by realists in the early years of the nineteenth century here appears not as a feminine weakness, but as the mark of an essential humanity, which strains to be delivered from 'restraint' and 'stagnation' in all their oppressive forms. There is assurance as well as defiance in Jane's affirmation that 'women', no less than men, are 'human beings', who 'feel just as men feel'; that their 'silent revolt' is at one with all the unknown 'rebellions' that 'ferment in the masses of life which people earth' (109). Some, indeed, have found, in these references to a 'revolt' amongst 'masses', a rhetoric of class rebellion—what one critic in 1848 called 'the tone of the mind and thought which has overthrown authority and violated every code human and divine abroad, and fostered Chartism and rebellion at home'.[76] Yet this passage, with its emphasis on an enforced 'tranquillity' (rather than compulsion to labour) and a desire for 'action' (rather than a demand for rights) is far more directly evocative of the 'bored leisure', the 'silent' escapist dreams, of those women of the polite classes whose frustrations posed no such obvious political threat. And its challenge to its readers lies precisely in its insistence that this, too, is a 'rebellion' of an extensive and significant kind. This is very far from the accepted early nineteenth-century characterization of such day-dreaming: far, indeed, from the way in which even those 'women' of whom Jane speaks usually saw their dreams.[77] Yet the excitement with which *Jane Eyre* was received suggests that it struck a chord in 'millions'. And those to whom it most immediately spoke were those whose dreams, like its author's, were fed by the best-selling annuals, those gorgeous products of a burgeoning consumer culture so deflatingly evoked by Flaubert.

For from the perspective provided by *Jane Eyre*, the annuals appear in quite a different light. At first sight, it is true, these lavishly produced little volumes, full of portraits of beautiful women, designed as romantic gifts, might lead one to agree

[75] On the pejorative modernist construction of 'mass culture' as essentially feminine, and on *Madame Bovary* as one of the 'founding texts' of this view, see Andreas Huyssen, 'Mass Culture as Woman: Modernism's Other', in Tania Modleski (ed.), *Studies in Entertainment: Critical Approaches to Mass Culture* (Bloomington: Indiana University Press, 1986), 188–207.

[76] Elizabeth Rigby, quoted in *CH* 109–10; for a recent example, see Cora Kaplan, 'Pandora's Box', in *Sea Changes*, 173.

[77] 'We fast mentally, scourge ourselves morally, use the intellectual hair-shirt, in order to subdue the perpetual day-dreaming, which is so dangerous!' Florence Nightingale was to write five years later. 'We . . . endeavour to combat it. Never, with the slightest success' (*Cassandra*, 27–8).

with their critics that they 'promoted' simply what Emma Bovary finds in them: 'an image of the ideal woman ... as the object rather than the owner of the gaze'.[78] But in another, and by no means trivial, sense—a sense foregrounded by *Jane Eyre*—they 'promoted' quite the opposite. It is not merely that many of their most prominent editors and contributors were women. The women who were their chief recipients were themselves invited to be 'gazers', to turn the pages, study the engravings, enter the world they presented, and to entertain feelings of a rather different kind from those deemed appropriate to their sex. Of course, such gazing might in practice simply have enabled the entertainment of narcissistic fantasies such as Emma Bovary's. But that seminal image of the child Jane Eyre, 'shrined in double retirement' and projecting extraordinary vistas of distant regions and strange emotions from the 'vignettes' at which she peers, suggests that it might also be a way of withdrawing from the demands of duty and society into a charged and privileged space—a space whose potentialities her creator had pondered for years.

   In a manuscript written some four or five years after she first began to copy their engravings, Charlotte Brontë hints at the connection between the burgeoning world of her creation and the annuals that had fed her youthful dreams. 'A Peep into a Picture Book' records the musings of Lord Charles Wellesley as he turns the pages of one of 'three large volumes' with 'green watered-silk quarto covers and gilt backs', and comments on the plates it contains. (The 'picture book' of the title—'Tree's Portrait Gallery of the Aristocracy of Africa'—is perhaps based less on the actual annuals than on the lavish 'Elephant-Folios' of engravings, such as *Finden's Portraits of the Female Aristocracy* or *Finden's Byron Beauties* which during the 1830s appeared with them as drawing-room books.) 'I will raise first from the shadow of gossamer paper, waving as I turn it like a web of woven air, the spirit whosoever it be, male or female, crowned or coronetted, that animates its frontispiece,' Lord Charles begins; and anticipation is answered with an awesome immediacy: 'A mighty phantom has answered my spell, an awful shape clouds the magic mirror. Reader, before me I behold the earthly tabernacle of Northangerlands unsounded soul! There he stands!'[79] Lord Charles, like Emma Bovary, is seen with an ironic eye. Yet the moment of unfolding possibility of which he grandiloquently speaks is quite different from Flaubert's cool depiction of his heroine's ingenuousness. There is a deflating insistence on the flat materiality of the 'keepsake' at which Emma 'thrills': 'at isolated points on its steel-grey surface, a few white scratches to represent swans floating'. But the portrait that Brontë's Lord Charles beholds is 'animated' by a 'spirit' which the gazer, Genie-like, can 'raise'. ('I have looked at you', he later says of the portrait of Zamorna, 'until words seem to issue from your lips').[80] To Flaubert that 'tissue

---

[78] Anne Mellor, *Romanticism and Gender* (London: Routledge, 1993), 111. For a similar view, see Hofkosh, 'Disfiguring Economies', 205–8.

[79] 'A Peep into a Picture Book', in *EEW* ii. 2, 86.

[80] Ibid. 93. In *The Female Thermometer: Eighteenth-Century Culture and the Invention of the Uncanny* (New York and Oxford: Oxford University Press, 1995), Terry Castle suggests that in the early 19th cent. 'reading in general' was increasingly seen as 'a phantasmagoric process ... Medical writers ... frequently warned that excessive reading—and especially reading books of a romantic or visionary nature—could send one into morbid hallucinatory states' (242 n. 54).

paper'—one of the hallmarks of the annuals[81]—represents the world of commodified luxury for which his heroine yearns.[82] But for Lord Charles it is a 'charmed
medium',[83] instinct with genii-magic, 'waving as I turn it like a web of woven air'.
And his image points forward to a poem that his youthful creator was to write in the
following year, celebrating the 'mighty phantasm' that had evolved from the Glass
Town 'plays'.

For the origins of Glass Town and Angria lay not merely in the ironies of *Blackwood's* and of *Fraser's*, but also in uncritical wonder, such as seems to have led the
young Brontës to copy the annual engravings, transmuting their subjects from
romanticized peasants and society figures into Mina Laury, the Duke of Zamorna,
Alexander Soult. And as Brontë at 20 looks back to the beginnings of their
'phantasm' she reworks Lord Charles's image into a subtly different one:

> We wove a web in childhood
> A web of sunny air

As for him that 'shadow of gossamer paper' was charged with possibility, so for her
that dream swells into reality 'now', in once undreamed-of ways:

> Faded! the web is still of air
> But now its folds are spread
> And from its tints of crimson clear
> How deep a glow is shed.
> The light of an Italian sky
> Where clouds of sunset lingering lie
> Is not more ruby-red.[84]

The gauzy paper, the exotic landscapes of the annuals lie somewhere behind these
lines. But this is a world that has far transcended its origins; vivid with colour, as the
illustrations in the annuals were not;[85] and expanding—as the stanza breaks the
mould of the quatrains that precede it—beyond any limiting frame.

Charlotte Brontë must have been one of the most extraordinary of those myriads
of readers whose day-dreams were fired by the annuals. But *Jane Eyre*'s opening
image of the lonely child gazing at Bewick and 'form[ing] an idea of [her] own', Jane's
invocation of the 'millions' who share her 'silent revolt' (109), her later passionate
insistence on the 'redeeming' power of romance (371), open up questions about them

---

[81] In his ironic article on the annuals, Barry Cornwall singles out their 'gauze paper, or, as the best public instructors call it, "flimsy" ' as one of their most striking features ('Judgment of the Annuals', 606).

[82] As Carol Rifelj points out, this moment is echoed later in the novel, when M. Lheureux tries to
tempt Emma to buy some shimmering Algerian scarves (' "Ces tableaux du monde": Keepsakes in
Madame Bovary', *Nineteenth-Century French Studies*, 25 (1997), 378). On the 'erotic thrill' of that tissue
paper, see Tony Tanner, *Adultery in the Novel: Contract and Transgression* (Baltimore: Johns Hopkins
University Press, 1979), 285–6.

[83] 'The glamour of inexperience is over your eyes, and you see it through a charmed medium,' says
Rochester to Jane, when she tells him Thornfield is a 'splendid mansion' (215).

[84] 'We wove a web in childhood', 19 December 1835, in Juliet Barker (ed.), *Charlotte Brontë: Juvenilia
1829–1835* (London: Penguin, 1996), 262.

[85] All but one of Charlotte Brontë's surviving copies of engravings from the annuals are, however, in
'glowing' watercolour (Alexander and Sellars, *Art of the Brontës*, nos. 35, 38, 39, 40, 102, 110).

that are hardly raised by the rather less captivating women's advice books, or, indeed, by evangelical tracts. Were the recipients of the annuals always the unwitting dupes of artificially constructed desires? Might not the annuals' very 'trashiness'—their variegated contents, their instantaneous appeal—have enabled a less compliant, more undisciplined kind of reading than that respectful assent which more serious literature seemed to require? Did the girls who gazed at them identify only with their pictured beauties, becoming in fantasy, like Emma Bovary, 'the object rather than the owner of the gaze'?[86] Did they, as they turned those alluring pages, align themselves, always, with the passive, waiting heroines of their stirring rhymes and stories, and not with their images of adventure, heroism, self-assertive power?[87] Might not their experience of the annuals have been rather more complicated—more full of potentiality—than their detractors allow?[88] To begin to answer such questions properly would require a sociological, even psychoanalytic, analysis of the responses of actual readers that is, of course, impossible at such a distance in time.[89] But even to raise them is to

[86] For the debates in film theory that have established the notion of the gaze as always male, see Laura Mulvey, 'Visual Pleasure and Narrative Cinema', *Screen* 16: 3 (1975), 6–18, and 'Afterthoughts ... Inspired by *Duel in the Sun*', *Framework*, 15–17 (1981), 12–25; Teresa de Lauretis, *Alice Doesn't: Feminism, Semiotics, Cinema* (Bloomington: Indiana University Press, 1984); and Mary Anne Doane, *The Desire to Desire: The Woman's Film of the 1940s* (Bloomington: Indiana University Press, 1987). For a thoughtful counter-view, see Jackie Stacey, 'Desperately Seeking Difference', in *The Sexual Subject: A Screen Reader in Sexuality* (London: Routledge, 1992), 244–57.

[87] 'In song and story', says Simone de Beauvoir, 'the young man ... slays the dragon, he battles giants: she is locked in a tower, a palace, a garden, a cave, she is chained to a rock, a captive, sound asleep: she waits' (*The Second Sex*, trans. H. M. Pashley (New York: Random House, 1974), 328). But, as Barbara Sichtermann suggests, 'Even in daydreams it is often a good idea to check whether the longing and object of that longing, and then perhaps subject and object again, should not be interchanged before the message will make any sense' (*Femininity: the Politics of the Personal*, ed. Helga Geyer-Ryan (Oxford: Polity, 1983), 83). Just so, in *Jane Eyre*, Charlotte Brontë (who, as 'Strange Events' suggests, had at 14 a sophisticated sense of self both as subject and as object) portrays Jane dreaming of saving Rochester 'at some exciting crisis'; and offering an extended narrative 'illustration' of her approach to Ferndean as that of 'a lover' approaching an apparently sleeping 'mistress' (367, 424). Brontë's interest in what has come to be called 'cross-gender identification' is signalled by the prominence, within her novels, of various episodes of cross-dressing (from Rochester as gipsy to de Hamal as nun), and of figures (such as Hunsden and Shirley) who strongly embody qualities culturally assigned to the opposite sex. For recent discussion of women's relation to 'masculine' cultural images see Cora Kaplan, 'The Thorn Birds', in *Sea Changes*, 118–20, and Kate Soper, 'Stephen Heroine', in *Troubled Pleasures: Writings on Politics, Gender and Hedonism* (London: Verso, 1990), 246–68.

[88] For a fascinating exploration of such issues in relation to the 20th-cent. toy and media industry for children, see Mary Hilton (ed.), *Potent Fictions: Children's Literacy and the Challenge of Popular Culture* (London: Routledge, 1996); and, on this issue more generally, John Fiske, *Understanding Popular Culture* (London and New York: Routledge, 1989).

[89] The nature and significance of even contemporary readers' responses to another mass cultural phenomenon—20th-cent. popular romantic fiction—has been the subject of considerable debate: see e.g. Tania Modleski, *Loving With a Vengeance: Mass-Produced Fantasies for Women* (London: Methuen, 1984); Janice Radway, *Reading the Romance*, new edn. (London: Verso, 1987); Bridget Fowler, *The Alienated Reader: Women and Popular Romantic Literature in the Twentieth Century* (Hemel Hempstead: Harvester Wheatsheaf, 1991). On the complexities of determining how such fiction is actually read, even when readers can be interviewed, see especially Radway, *Reading the Romance*, 4–15, 209–22. Radway's careful, detailed, empirical work poses a powerful challenge to the notion that any group of cultural texts can be seen in any simple way as 'constructing subjectivity' for actual, rather than implied, readers. For a more general exploration of these issues see Jonathan Rose, 'Rereading the English Common Reader: A Preface to a History of Audiences', *Journal of the History of Ideas* 53 (1992), 47–70.

begin to move beyond the condescending reductiveness of Flaubert, and closer to what appear to have been the actual, and much more complex, possibilities for middle-class feminine subjectivity in early nineteenth-century England: possibilities that are realized and contemplated in that best-seller of the era of the annuals, *Jane Eyre*.[90]

IV

Certainly, in one conspicuous way, Jane Eyre appears, throughout the novel which bears her name, as the owner rather than the object of the gaze.[91] Just as her creator, as a short-sighted schoolgirl in an isolated country parsonage, had spent many hours copying images of a glamorous unknown world, so this unregarded governess devotes a large portion of her narrative to detailed 'portraits' of the characters and delineations of the 'scenes' of a life that she cannot share. 'The pictures stand out distinctly before you: they are pictures, and not mere bits of "fine writing",' wrote G. H. Lewes in an early review. 'The writer is evidently painting by words a picture that she has in her mind.'[92] But *Jane Eyre*'s is not an unconsidered realism. The novel is more reflective about this strategy than Lewes's observation suggests.

If all within Jane's narrative is seen from her point of view, that point of view is figured in emphatically visual terms. Again and again in the novel, the world that threatens and marginalizes the narrator appears as a series of 'portraits' and 'scenes', composed by her shaping eye. 'The new face, too, was like a new picture introduced to the gallery of memory' she thinks, after first meeting Rochester (115); Blanche, prefigured by the 'picture' Jane has painted, answers to it, 'point for point' (172); St John Rivers is imaged in her first extended description of him 'sitting as still as one of the dusky pictures on the walls'. 'It is seldom, indeed, an English face comes so near the antique models as his,' says Jane, as she tells of 'examining' its Grecian 'outline' and its 'blue, pictorial-looking eyes' (344-5). The festivities at Thornfield are portrayed as aesthetic spectacles: 'The curtain was swept back from the arch; through it appeared the dining-room, with its lit lustre pouring down light on the silver and glass of a magnificent dessert-service covering a long table; a band of ladies stood in the opening; they entered, and the curtain fell behind them' (171). Here, as in *The Professor*, an unchosen exclusion is appropriated as a position of advantage. Thus, as the guests approach Thornfield, Jane takes care 'to stand on one side, so that, screened by the curtain, I could see without being seen' (166). For her,

---

[90] Certainly, other women in these years write of their earliest 'day-dreaming' in terms akin to Charlotte Brontë's portrait of the child Jane Eyre. See e.g. Charlotte Elizabeth Tonna, *Personal Recollections* (London: R. B. Seeley & W. Burnside, 1841), 7, 63; 'The History of a Child', in L.E.L., *Traits and Trials of Early Life* (London: Henry Colburn, 1836), 301–4; and Lamon Blanchard, *Life and Literary Remains of L.E.L.* (2 vols.; London: Henry Colburn, 1841) i. 14–24.

[91] For a differently focused discussion of this, see Peter J. Bellis, 'In the Window-Seat: Vision and Power in *Jane Eyre*', *English Literary History* 54 (1987), 639–52.

[92] *CH* 86.

as for Crimsworth, 'seeing' is a strategy of control. Yet her 'seeing' shapes her narrative in a way quite different from his. For the sentence just quoted is the prelude not to a hostile depiction of an antagonistic world, but to a Byronically romantic vision of an approaching 'cavalcade'—'fluttering veils and waving plumes', 'young, dashing-looking . . . cavaliers', and a lady with veil streaming 'long on the breeze' (166). Jane's is neither a defensive nor a coolly appraising eye, but the eye, the power of the artist. And that which is inscribed in her mode of telling is objectified and contemplated in the novel's depiction of her art.

For Jane does not merely observe, she draws: and her drawing gives her a potency undreamed of in Crimsworth's narrative. It is prominent, indeed, in her narrative of social success. When Bessie comes to Lowood to bid her former charge farewell, Jane can prove herself 'quite a lady' by pointing to one of her watercolours on display—'as fine a picture as any Miss Reed's drawing-master could paint' (92). Later, her haughty Reed cousins are gratifyingly 'suprised at [her] skill': each 'sits for a pencil outline', and the fashionable Georgiana asks for a drawing for her album (234). Diana and Mary Rivers are 'surprised and charmed' by her ability, 'greater in this one point than theirs' (350): whilst the heiress Rosamond Oliver, impressed by her sketches—'Had I done these pictures? Did I know French and German?'—seeks out her acquaintance and invites her to her home (369).[93] Yet Jane's artistic skill is more than a mark of gentility. It is to feed her 'inward cravings' as a lonely child at school that she first begins to feast on imagined 'ideal drawings', which she pictures in touching detail as 'all the work of my own hands' (74). The 'peculiar' pictures she shows to Rochester were done with no intent to impress, but 'in an artist's dreamland' when she was entirely alone. 'I was absorbed . . . and I was happy', she tells her surprised employer. 'To paint them was to enjoy one of the keenest pleasures I have ever known' (126). 'What did it signify that those young ladies turned their backs on me?' she asks, as she gazes at her sketch of her beloved. 'I smiled at the speaking likeness: I was absorbed and content' (234). The sense is less of that dependence on others' opinions implied in the acquisition of 'accomplishments' than of triumphant self-sufficiency.

This repeated, emphasized figure of a woman observing, controlling, configuring her own images seems a deliberate riposte to that familiar stereotype of feminine susceptibility, the woman held in thrall by the images she confronts. But the triumphant female agency that may be traced in scenes such as this is by no means unequivocally celebrated in *Jane Eyre*. For the novel's portrayal of its heroine's artistic power is, when more closely examined, a critically inflected one. If Jane's 'vision' is mostly portrayed in a language of romantic creative transcendence, her attempts to bend it to the purposes of her world appear, like Crimsworth's drive to succeed, in a somewhat darker light. Three times in the course of her story she tells of drawing a face. Each time, it is a portrait of a kind familiar in the annuals. Each

---

[93]   On painting and drawing as desirable feminine accomplishments in early Victorian England see Christine Alexander, 'Charlotte Brontë's Paintings: Victorian Women and the Visual Arts' (Canberra: Australian Academy of the Humanities, 1993), 4–12.

time, the novel configures her act as one of aggressive enclosure rather than transformative power.

Confronted with the fact of a rival, Jane takes the finest tools of her trade and
devotes a fortnight to an 'ivory miniature of an imaginary Blanche Ingram'—'an
accomplished young lady of rank'. The ostensible object is to compare this face with
her own, hastily sketched in chalk—'Portrait of a Governess, disconnected, poor,
and plain'; and to 'force' her 'feelings to submit' to a 'course of wholesome discipline' (161–2). This she presents to the reader as an exercise in 'self-control' (162). Yet
the novel's depiction of the episode is somewhat stranger than this. For the narrative space given up to a description of the rival's pictured charms—'the raven
ringlets, the oriental eye . . . the Grecian neck and bust . . . the round and dazzling
arm . . . aërial lace and glistening satin, graceful scarf and golden rose'—is suggestive of something other than ascetic self-restraint. The sense is less of feeling disciplined than of feeling elaborately entertained; less of the acceptance of limits than of
the assertion of power—and power far in excess of that required for 'self-control'.
For if Jane has '*forced* her feelings to submit' she has also '*given* force and fixedness
to the new impressions I wished to stamp indelibly on my heart' (162; my italics).
And the generative potency thus signalled is underwritten by her narrative.
Blanche, when she appears, is simply the embodiment of this prefiguring 'picture'
(172): her charms are impotent to impress. But the narrating Jane is not confined by
the 'harsh lines' of her own self-portrait: she ceases to be 'a governess', acquires
'connections' and a fortune, and, beloved by one who has rejected this beauteous
rival, looks at her face in the glass and feels herself 'no longer plain' (257). The
'wholesome discipline' that she claims to have undergone is countered in her narrative by the undisciplined absoluteness of the victory she achieves.

Later, called away from Thornfield, Jane draws a 'speaking likeness' of the 'master' she has grown to love. Here, as before, she has a rational intention: to 'amuse'
herself and assert her independence of the supercilious Reeds (233–4). Yet here, as
before, the scene evinces a power in excess of this. For here Jane reverses that
subjection to her master's 'influence' which she has confessed to feeling in his presence: 'my eyes were drawn involuntarily to his face; I could not keep their lids under
control' (174). Compulsion is replaced by accomplishment, as she herself shapes the
face that 'took my feelings from my own power and fettered them in his' (175) :

I took a soft black pencil, gave it a broad point, and worked away. Soon I had traced on the
paper a broad and prominent forehead, and a square lower outline of visage: that contour
gave me pleasure; my fingers proceeded actively to fill it with features . . . Now for the eyes: I
had left them to the last, because they required the most careful working. I drew them large;
I shaped them well . . . I wrought the shades blacker, that the lights might flash more bril-
liantly—a happy touch or two secured success. There, I had a friend's face under my gaze.
(233–4)

'Well did I remember Mrs Reed's face . . . How often had it lowered on me menace
and hate!' says Jane a few pages earlier; 'how the recollection of childhood's terrors
and sorrows revived as I traced its harsh line now! . . . I felt a determination to

subdue her—to be her mistress in spite both of her nature and her will' (230–1). Just so, the mastering Rochester's face is now safely 'under' a 'gaze' quite different from that former agonized, involuntary one. And here, once again, the act of drawing is charged with prophetic potency. For here, the controlling artist leaves those challenging eyes 'to the last'; the effect for a moment, as Hermione Lee points out, is 'of an eyeless face'.[94] Jane's successful drawing of her 'master' does not merely cheer and console her: it prefigures his ultimate fate.

The third of Jane's portraits is that of Rosamond Oliver: a finely drawn likeness of a beautiful, aristocratic young girl. Again the narrative tells of rational pleasure and achievement. Jane feels 'a thrill of artist-delight at the idea of copying from so perfect and radiant a model' (369); she produces, her cousin pronounces, 'a well-executed picture . . . very soft, clear colouring; very graceful and correct' (369). Yet here, again, there is a suggestion of a power beyond that of 'accomplishment'—the daemonic or Genie-like power to bestow life itself: 'It is like!' he continues. 'It smiles!' (371–2). Here, once again, she who has been the victim of uncontrollable feeling—assailed every night by dreams of her lost beloved—assumes, through her drawing, a position of control. But here the power Jane exercises is not, even ostensibly, over her own feelings. The portrait becomes the focus for one of the novel's strangest episodes, as she coolly observes in another 'the burst of passion', 'the convulsion of despair' which—she has just confessed—each night overwhelm her (367). She has a professedly benevolent 'reason' for this: the 'frank discussion' of his feelings that follows brings St John Rivers 'a new pleasure, an unhoped for relief' (372). Yet here, once again, feelings in excess of such 'reason' are brought disquietingly into play. Here a man contemplates a portrait of a woman he desires. But that portrait is the work of a woman, and the masculine gaze is itself the object of a powerful feminine one. 'I knew his thoughts well, and could read his heart plainly', says Jane. 'I had then temporarily the advantage of him' (371). Like those earlier scenes of her portrait painting, this episode leads to an intimation of the triumph that is to be hers. At the end of the scene she herself becomes the object of this other's 'peculiar . . . glance', a glance that bespeaks a knowledge she herself does not possess. Yet in the scheme of the narrative the moment points not to this other's 'ascendancy', but to Jane's. For it is this 'glance' of her cousin's—one which seems 'to take and make note of every point in my shape, face, and dress' (376)—which leads (as her identity is discovered) to her ultimate, victorious empowerment, as 'independent' heiress and benefactress of the man who seeks to find her out.

Jane presents these scenes of her 'drawing' as part of a narrative of success. Self-disciplined, resourceful, beneficent, she negotiates her place in a world of others—teaching herself to subdue her desires, cheering herself in absence from her beloved, offering her cousin an 'unhoped-for relief'. But these charged, disquieting, 'portraits', these scenarios of submerged violence and claustrophobic intensity, of subjugation and control, speak less of cool rationality than of feverish emotion, less of relationship with than of victory over the other, less of maturing character than of

---

[94] Hermione Lee, 'Emblems and Enigmas in *Jane Eyre*', *English*, 30 (1981), 241.

the appropriation of objectifying power. In each, Jane is victorious, but unsatisfied—decently self-controlled, but still yearning for love; independent of her cousins, but still under a 'hostile roof' (227); the cool anatomizer of another's passion, but eaten up with an unconfessed longing of her own. The trajectory of triumph here charted is not an unambiguous one. For if each of these episodes triumphantly reverses that familiar cultural stereotype, enshrined in the portraits in the annuals, of woman as the object of the gaze, each evokes the world of the annuals in much more restrictive ways. Unlike the novel's images of Jane's empowering dreaming—the child gazing out from the window-seat, the governess from Thornfield Hall—these scenes point not away from but towards the drawing-rooms in which the annuals appeared;[95] not towards liberating expressiveness but to a struggle for 'ascendancy', not to expansive possibility, but to that which is bounded and contained. The sense—finely captured in the second of these episodes, where Jane begins by 'sketching fancy vignettes representing any scene that happened momentarily to shape itself in the shifting kaleidoscope of imagination', and ends by portraying Rochester (233)—is of a narrowing in from the strangeness and spontaneity of those ever-varying dreams to a self-assertion of a far from transcendent kind. The 'drawings' on which these scenes pivot—an ivory miniature of 'an accomplished lady of rank', painted with 'delicate camel-hair pencils'; a 'very faithful representation' of a well-known masculine face; a 'copy' in 'careful outline' of a 'perfect . . . radiant . . . model', carefully coloured in—are quite unlike Jane's enigmatic paintings of subjects seen with 'the spiritual eye' (125). 'I was tormented by the contrast between my idea and my handiwork,' she says of these latter; 'in each case I had imagined something which I was quite powerless to realize' (126). But the faces she draws of the glamorous others in her world are finished in every detail, with mimetic accuracy. The suggestion is less of expressiveness than of the control and management of feeling, less of the transcendent romantic imagination than of worldly accomplishment. And the configuration here inscribed is repeated, on a larger scale, as Jane's tale of triumph over others comes to its conclusion with assertions of absolute satisfaction and images of the circumscribed and confined. The sense is of a desire that is bent to the purposes and bounded by the horizons of a less than perfect world.

For despite her yearning for 'loving him, being loved by him', Jane's is a more varied, more energetic, less focused 'restlessness' than Emma Bovary's obsession with love: closer, indeed, to that ungendered matrix of desire—'women feel just as men feel'—of which she so resonantly speaks. Even as she yearns for her lost love at Morton, she dreams not merely of Rochester, but of excitement, adventure, and sensation—'dreams many-coloured, agitated, full of the ideal, the stirring, the stormy'; it is 'always at some exciting crisis' that she imagines meeting her lover, 'amidst

---

[95] Jane's first portrait is prompted by Mrs Fairfax's description of Blanche's drawing-room triumphs at 'a Christmas ball and party Mr. Rochester gave' (159); her 'speaking likeness' of Rochester by the coldness of her cousins in their Gateshead drawing-room. That of Rosamond leads St John Rivers to picture himself 'stretched on an ottoman in the drawing-room at Vale Hall, at my bride Rosamond Oliver's feet' (373).

unusual scenes, charged with adventure, with agitating risk and romantic chance' (366–7). Her desires are not for the quotidian, but for 'incident', variety, intensity; for 'action', expansiveness, 'liberty'; for 'what is bright, and energetic, and high' (252). And from this perspective her story of singular triumph is also a story of loss. Hers is a trajectory of energies contained which has an emphatic parallel in the novel's portrayal of that contrasting other who appears so prominently at its end.

For St John Rivers, so manifestly unlike, is also akin to Jane. Like Jane, he describes himself as 'poor' and 'obscure' (253, 354): like her, he chafes at his 'cramped existence' (362); like hers, his 'energies . . . demand a sustenance they cannot get' (361). 'My powers heard a call from Heaven to rise', he says, as he tells of his missionary vocation (362): '*My* powers were in play and in force', says Jane of her own very different 'call' (420). Each is a figure of 'restlessness' (109, 356), longing for 'sensations and excitements' (85), for 'the more active life of the world' (361). 'In your nature', he tells her, 'is an alloy as detrimental to repose as that in mine' (354). It seems not insignificant that it is as she attempts to turn away from her love for Rochester that this disturbing other with his 'insatiate yearnings and disquieting aspirations' assumes importance in her narrative; or that her account of her own repressed passion is succeeded, immediately, by the image of his refusal to settle for the satisfactions of romantic love. 'He could not bind all that he had in his nature— the rover, the aspirant, the poet, the priest—in the limits of a single passion,' Jane declares, as she contemplates her cousin's refusal of love's 'elysium'. 'He could not—he would not—renounce his wild field of mission warfare for the parlours and the peace of Vale Hall' (368). And the reader is sharply reminded that 'all that he had in his nature'—those 'complicated interests, feelings, thoughts, wishes, aims' (406) that he seeks to harness to the missionary cause—may be traced, in a different inflection, in hers. It is as if to emphasize what has gone from her story that, as her longings reach quiescence in the regained 'elysium' of life with Rochester (352) that the figure of this unquiet other returns, speaking of an aspiration which is as yet unfulfilled.

In the twentieth century it became fashionable to speak of desire as a universal, ahistorical energy repressed by reason, morality, convention, which of its very nature exceeds social possibility, and in its pure form, indeed, refuses to be satisfied.[96] *Jane Eyre*'s resonant final image of this straining solitary figure might at first appear indicative of such an insatiable energy at work within and finally uncontainable by the world Jane's narrative depicts. Yet the novel is more acute and more specific in its social criticism than this. For the desires that animate Jane's story and remain urgent at its end appear not as boundless and timeless energies but in forms that would have been quite familiar to its early nineteenth-century readers. If Jane's gazing towards distant horizons, her yearnings for 'Liberty, Excitement, Enjoyment', for passionate love and 'domestic endearments' compose a configuration—potent, problematic, contradictory—writ large in the best-selling annuals, that evangelistic

---

[96] See e.g. Bersani, *A Future for Astyanax*; Julia Kristeva, *Desire in Language*, trans. Thomas Gora, Alice Jardine, and Leon S. Roudiez (Oxford: Blackwell, 1980).

fervour, that heroic resolution, that burning 'ambition' for the highest place, which, embodied in St John Rivers, both echo and question her desires, are likewise clearly of their time. For these are the matter of countless missionary sermons preached, printed, and circulated in the early nineteenth century, in which Christian self-immolation appears paradoxically as the ultimate fulfilment of self. These two individualistic figures are also, it seems, representative; their aspirations emphatically marked by all the contradictoriness of the well-known discourses within which they are framed. And if those aspirations reach, in their different ways, beyond the confines of the given, they take on, as the novel draws to a close, the contours of social possibility: contours which by its ending have assumed familiar shapes.

Most obviously and most immediately, Jane's marriage for love, St John Rivers's passage to India, might be read as a realistic portrayal of the fate of such 'restlessness' as theirs in the actual world of early Victorian England, with its sharp division of masculine and feminine, public and private, spheres. If the images that allured the early nineteenth-century woman in the pages of the annuals were of soaring aspiration, of exoticism and adventure, her longings were expected to be satisfied by a 'love' enclosed within the family, her activity confined to the duties of domestic life. And if Jane's might be seen as a typical fate, there is a representative realism also in the novel's portrayal of her cousin's missionary destiny, apparently so remote from the excesses of Byronic desire. For in early nineteenth-century England the missionary vocation was not merely the ultimate answer to the evangelical call to die to this world: it was, as Stuart Piggin has noted, one way in which young men without Byron's advantages could assuage a 'restlessness' akin to his.[97] Many aspiring missionaries saw themselves as conquering warrior-heroes (asking, indeed, sometimes, to be sent to places of special danger); theirs was emphatically a calling that did not require them (as Byron put it) to 'stagnate'. 'Well may he eschew the calm of domestic life,' Jane Eyre thinks of her cousin. 'It is not his element: there his faculties stagnate . . . It is in scenes of strife and danger—where courage is proved, and energy exercised, and fortitude tasked—that he will speak and move, the leader and superior . . . He is right to choose a missionary's career' (393). 'My cramped existence all at once spread out . . . my powers heard a call from heaven to rise,' he has, a little earlier, told her. 'Skill and strength, courage and eloquence, the best qualifications of soldier, statesman and orator, were all needed: for these all centre in the good missionary' (362). For many young men such as he the potent 'career' of the missionary enabled a harnessing of energies hitherto unexercised; it was also seen as the path to the highest of destinies. 'The Missionary calling ranks high—yes, the very highest—in the estimation of God; above the cunning artificer, above the eloquent orator; above the poet, the hero, the statesman,' declares a sermon published the year before *Jane Eyre*.[98] 'Let a holy ambition animate your breasts', the Scottish

---

[97] Stuart Piggin, *Making Evangelical Missionaries 1789–1850: The Social Background, Motives And Training Of British Protestant Missionaries To India* (Abingdon: Sutton Courtenay Press, 1984), 47, 133, 135.

[98] 'Missionary Warfare', A Sermon by Rev. Hugh Macneile, preached at St Bride's Church, Fleet St., Monday 5 May 1845, *The Pulpit*, 58 (1846), 187.

Missionary Society advised its candidates.'Be not content with a low seat in heaven. Aim after one of the highest . . . This is the path to one of the brightest crowns.'[99] 'Refuse to be my wife, and you limit yourself for ever to a track of selfish ease and barren obscurity,' St John Rivers warns his cousin (409). His purpose here is to stress the selflessness of the missionary life, but his words betray his sense of its glorious difference from any more obscure and limited fate. If his, as his sister Diana laments, is the chosen path of the Christian martyr—'He will sacrifice all to his long-framed resolves . . . natural affection and feelings more potent still' (356)—his solitary pilgrimage away from human ties and native land, and towards 'a place in the first rank of those who are redeemed from the earth', is redolent also of that romantic egotism of which Byron's biographer, in a book well known to Charlotte Brontë, wrote in 1833:

The truth is, I fear, that rarely, if ever, have men of the higher order of genius shown themselves fitted for the calm affections and comforts that form the cement of domestic life . . . it will be found that, among those who have felt within themselves a call to immortality, the greater number have, by a sort of instinct, kept aloof from such ties, and instead of the softer duties and rewards of being amiable, reserved themselves for the high, hazardous chances of being great.[100]

If St John Rivers seems still at the close of the novel to embody much of that 'restless' aspiration which has informed and is gone from Jane's story, it is an aspiration that is emphatically other, and male.

Indeed, these two contrasting figures appear in these closing pages as prototypes of a 'masculinity' and a 'femininity' whose opposing characteristics are almost aggressively stressed. More adamantly, more abidingly than the shackled, crippled Rochester, St John Rivers stands in the novel as an image of phallic coercive power. In ways that the twentieth-century reader might find hard fully to recognize—but that Jane certainly registers—he is a figure of supreme patriarchal authority. As a vicar of Christ, he commands her 'veneration' (418); his voice, quoting Scripture, has the novel's final word. A figure, also, of imperialistic virility, he 'labours for his race', hewing down all that stands in the way of its 'improvement'; like a chivalric knight, he eschews all consolations that would distract him from his goal. And if, with 'his measured warrior-march' and his 'ineradicable ambition' (407), he is an extreme example of the heroic masculinity admired in early nineteenth-century England, the marriage into which Jane Eyre disappears emphatically assumes the contours of its ideal feminine fate. Her submergence of self in symbiotic union resonates with the language not merely of Bible and prayer book but of contemporary moralists of womanhood; the enclosed satisfaction, the 'perfect concord' of her life with Rochester with their depictions of 'woman's sphere'.

Yet if each sees his or her destiny as the supreme fulfilment—she finding herself 'blest beyond what language can express', he anticipating 'his incorruptible

---

[99]   Quoted in Piggin, *Making Evangelical Missionaries*, 135.
[100]   Thomas Moore (ed.), *The Works of Lord Byron, with his Letters and Journals, and his Life*, 3rd edn. (17 vols.; London: John Murray, 1833) 3, 125–8.

'crown'—each points also to that which is repressed or denied by the other's path. St John Rivers appears in Jane's narrative, and above all at its ending, as heroic, undaunted, indomitable, a 'glorious sun' which she can only regard with awe. But that narrative offers also an analysis of his defects. Sternly despotic, ruthlessly impervious, 'cold, hard, ambitious' (375), 'inexorable as death' (356), he is imaged, again and again, as inhuman and life-denying, a figure of 'marble' or of 'ice', who knows 'neither mercy nor remorse' (402). If he is 'of the material from which nature hews her heroes—Christian and Pagan—her lawgivers, her statesmen, her conquerors: a steadfast bulwark for great interests to rest upon', he is not formed for human relations—'at the fireside, too often a cold cumbrous column, gloomy and out of place' (393). The emphasized reciprocity of Jane's and Rochester's love highlights in its contrast the aggressive egocentricity of his, their unbroken togetherness, 'the cross of separation' he must bear (354). But if Jane's account of her blessedness casts a cold light on his masculine endeavour, her feminine closure appears, beside her portrayal of him, as less than unqualified bliss. It is not merely that St John Rivers's assurance of 'a place in the first rank of those who are redeemed from the earth' (452) bespeaks a standpoint (which many of the novel's first readers must have shared) from which her triumphant assertion, 'I married him', is a choice of a lesser prize. In rather less orthodox ways, his prominence in these closing pages serves to underscore the darkness with which her fulfilment is tinged. 'The family? It is too narrow a field for the development of an immortal spirit,' Florence Nightingale was to declare, in a subversive unpublished manuscript written five years after *Jane Eyre*.[101] Just so, Jane's account of her life with Rochester bespeaks the diminution of powers and contraction of horizons; it is haunted by suggestions of death. She is immured in domestic seclusion, far from that 'busy world' for which she once yearned. But her cousin is not required to be 'satisfied with tranquillity' (109); his energies are all engaged. Her 'time and cares' are no longer her own; 'my husband needed them all' (450). But this other remains, intransigent in his singleness: it is he, rather than she (or even that beloved husband), who retains voice, charisma, energy to the end. Jane Eyre has disppeared, and been replaced by Jane Rochester. But St John continues, undaunted, on the road to his own salvation, his unchanged name already inscribed in 'the Lamb's book of life' (417). And if Jane's repeated assertion that for her no need is left unsatisfied has an oddly paradoxical effect, it is partly because this other's refusal of all earthly, partial fulfilment makes him a symbol of that which 'satisfaction' must relinquish—the potent open-endedness of continuing desire.

Despite the admiration that suffuses Jane's portrait of her cousin, the satisfaction she professes for herself, the novel's depiction of their destinies seems less an idealization of a stereotyped 'masculinity' and 'femininity' than a deliberate, critical foregrounding of what those stereotypes imply and cost. Its ending, so often read as complicitous with the ideology of its time, seems rather to question that doctrine beloved of early nineteenth-century moralists that masculine competitive striving

---

[101] Nightingale, *Cassandra*, 37.

and nurturing feminine domesticity should counterbalance one another as parts of a harmonious whole. It is not merely that the marriage in which Jane's story culminates is markedly not presented as an image of such counterbalancing: that, unlike the ambitious Robert Moore (whose marriage to Caroline Helstone in *Shirley* might indeed be thus seen), Rochester remains crippled and confined. The disruptive reappearance of St John Rivers in the paragraphs that follow means that the novel ends not with an image of union—that coming together in marriage which formed the conclusion of so many Victorian novels—but with one of stark divergence. Each of these two contrasting figures points sharply in a different direction. The suggestion is not of a balancing, but of an opposition. This masculinity cannot form part of a complementarity: 'the parlour is not his sphere' (393). This femininity has little apparent 'influence': it is buried in the midst of a wood, remote from any other 'life'. And neither has much effect on the repressive society the novel has portrayed: the one is self-enclosed, inward-turning, the other aggressively elsewhere.

V

The differing fates of these two 'restless' aspirers, opposed and juxtaposed at the ending of the novel, serve as a stark reminder of the frustrations and repressions, the differently limiting logics, the gender arrangements of early nineteenth-century England actually imposed on the trajectory of desire. Read thus, *Jane Eyre* appears to be offering a more unillusioned view of the dreams of those 'millions' of whom Jane speaks than her invocation of their 'rebellion' might at first suggest. Yet to read the novel merely thus is hardly to begin to account for its extraordinary, and continuing, capacity to stir, to excite, to inspire. For to generations of readers, sophisticated and unsophisticated alike, *Jane Eyre* has appeared quite differently: less as offering a pessimistic analysis of the deforming and limiting shapes into which aspiration was forced in early nineteenth-century England, than as underwriting and affirming its urgent, imperative claims. And if such readings tend to overlook the diagnostic intelligence at work in the novel (simplifying it, usually, into an account of Jane's progress towards happiness), they should by no means, I think, be set aside. For they point also to that in *Jane Eyre* which reaches beyond diagnosis, and sets this novel apart from almost every other of its period: to that quite unironic insistence on fundamental need unanswered, on the importunity of the striving to realize what will answer to desire, which is imaged in those moments when Jane gazes out towards distant horizons—on the window-seat at Gateshead, looking out from the windows of Lowood, on the leads at Thornfield Hall. This is a configuration very different from the triumphant self-assertion focused in those scenes of Jane's drawing. It seems to point not towards, but away from a limiting social world.[102] Yet in

---

[102] 'As someone who has been assigned an unimportant place in the social hierarchy,' argues Janet Gezari, 'Jane repeatedly seeks an eminence from which she can survey the world with a vision that is comprehensive, wide-ranging, and proprietary' (*Charlotte Brontë and Defensive Conduct: The Author*

its own quite different way it resonates, as Jane indicates, with a manifest social fact of the England of its time: that refusal of an unsatisfying reality which for 'millions' found expresssion only in the 'silence and solitude' of dreams (109).

For the records of early nineteenth-century England, like the popularity of *Jane Eyre*, bear testimony to the 'restlessness' of which Jane speaks. The evidences that remain are scattered and indirect—the castigations of the moralists; a few auto-biographical confessions; the once 'bright pages' of Scott and of Byron and of de Staël. They are there perhaps most suggestively in the annuals, whose contents be-speak the potency in the period—especially, it seems, for women—of images of the exotic, of the stirring, of the sublime. The charm that these volumes once held for their readers has now, largely, disappeared. But their extraordinary success attests to the existence, in the England of *Jane Eyre*, of an extensive 'counter-culture of feminine desire'.[103]

'Women dream till they have no longer the strength to dream,' wrote Florence Nightingale of what she called 'the common-place lives of thousands', five years after the publication of *Jane Eyre*: 'dreams against which they so struggle, so hon-estly, vigorously, and conscientiously and so in vain, yet which are their life, with-out which they could not have lived.'[104] Those 'dreams' have long been subjected to what Edward Thompson once in another context called 'the condescension of pos-terity'; a condescension evinced not merely in that persistent trope of the deluded romantic heroine, but also in feminist suspicions of 'day-dream' and 'romance'. But in *Jane Eyre* they are accorded a significance of an unprecedented kind. It is not St John Rivers, the missionary, aiming for a heavenly crown, but the 'discontented' governess, envisaging 'all of incident, life, fire, feeling, that I desired and had not in my actual existence', who is portrayed in the novel as a paradigmatic figure: her longing, not his, is connected to all those unknown rebellions 'which ferment in the masses of life which people earth'. If hers is a singular voice, the frustrations of which she speaks are, she says, shared by 'millions' (109). And the intimate dreams of 'millions' appear throughout the novel in shapes that its earliest readers might have been expected to recognize.

Jane's restless desires for 'incident, life, fire, feeling', that urgent 'need of being loved' which shapes her story, are certainly quite different from the higher moral imperatives of those 'men of wide views' who sought to find an answer to the prob-lems of the England of her time. There is nothing in these 'swift and vehement pages'[105] like Carlyle's sober appeal to 'the imperishable dignity of man', Ruskin's

and The Body at Risk (Philadelphia: University of Pennsylvania Press, 1992). Yet the Jane of these pas-sages is a figure not of proprietorial power but of dissatisfaction and 'restlessness', acutely aware of the horizons that bound her view. And that which she strains to view is not simply the given world, but 'something . . . beyond her situation . . . something not round her nor before her'—as she says of the very differently 'day-dreaming' Helen Burns (52).

[103] I take this phrase from Ian Duncan's brief but suggestive discussion of 18th-cent. opposition to romance reading by women, in his *Modern Romance and Transformations of the Novel: The Gothic, Scott, Dickens* (Cambridge: Cambridge University Press, 1992), 11–12.

[104] Nightingale, *Cassandra*, 49, 30.

[105] The phrase is Eugène Forçade's, from a review in *Revue des deux mondes*, 31 October 1848, quoted in *CH* 101.

to the 'Vital Beauty' of a society that values human life, Dickens's to the redemptive moral force of innocent love. Yet *Jane Eyre* belongs, in ways that have hardly yet been acknowledged, in that great Victorian tradition of imaginative social thought which sought to keep alive the aspirations of romanticism in a changing nineteenth-century world. Indeed, it arguably comes closer to the shapes those aspirations actually assumed for 'millions' in mid-nineteenth-century England than Dickens's appeals to 'fancy', the medievalism of Ruskin and Carlyle. For in reinflecting the familiar language and imagery of the annuals it gives powerful articulation to that 'silent revolt' against the given of which those gorgeous volumes are the lifeless residue.

Commercialized, clichéd, scorned as they were, the annuals spoke to and of desires that were denied by many of the social arrangements of early nineteenth-century England, desires too intransigent to be moralized away. It is true that much in their pages was unoriginal and stereotyped; that their images of fashion, of sexuality, and exoticism reinforced, rather than challenged, contemporary prejudices of class, of gender, of race. Yet their cultural import was—at least potentially—rather more subversive than this. For they posed a specific, seductive challenge to some of the central principles on which the society that produced them was based. Their images of aspiring subjectivity, of the sublime and of the intense were the antithesis of the self-discipline that its moralists of womanhood extolled. Their concern with excitement and adventure spoke of that larger sphere of action denied to the women who were their principal readers; their portrayal of the exotic and the 'natural', of that which lay beyond the imprisoning proprieties of the polite drawing-room. And their emphasis on 'love' points likewise, however naïvely, away from a public world of competitive individualism, and towards a quite different definition of essential human need. The 'artificial paradise' that appeared in their gorgeous pages must have seemed to many to stand in absolute contrast to the 'narrowness and pinched circumstances of their real and immediate life'.[106] If their popularity in one way seems a 'nightmare' example of the commodification of romanticism,[107] it might also be seen as testifying to widespread, if incoherent yearnings for 'Liberty, Excitement, Enjoyment' and 'incident, life, fire, feeling'—for a variety, a vitality and a potency, an aesthetic richness and emotional fulfilment that early nineteenth-century English society seems not to have supplied[108]

It is easy to dismiss the annuals, but it is perhaps less easy to dismiss the real aspirations to which they point. They are aspirations that are by no means dismissed in *Jane Eyre.* For if in its caricature-portrait of Blanche Ingram the novel mocks that craving for pleasure, admiration, and excitement to which the annuals appealed, it

---

[106] Gramsci, on Dumas, in *Prison Notebooks*, quoted in Bridget Fowler, *The Alienated Reader: Women and Popular Romantic Literature in the Twentieth Century* (Hemel Hempstead: Harvester Wheatsheaf, 1991), 32.

[107] The word is Jerome McGann's, in 'Rethinking Romanticism', *ELH* 59 (1992), 746.

[108] For a suggestive discussion of the relation between the appeal of culturally and historically specific forms of 'entertainment' and 'real needs created by society', see Richard Dyer, 'Entertainment and Utopia', *Movie*, 24 (1978), 2–13.

seems also, in Jane, to embody as 'natural' exactly that constellation of longings—
for enjoyment, for recognition, for agency—that such cravings might be seen to bespeak. The deprived young governess takes a sensuous pleasure in colour, beauty,
form. Trained up in the asceticism of Lowood, she revels in her new room at Thornfield: 'bright', 'gay', comfortable, it seems to promise 'flowers and pleasures': 'My
faculties, roused by the change of scene . . . seemed all astir' (98). Knowing only
'school-rules' and 'school-duties', she longs 'to go where there [is] life and movement' (87, 89). 'Unacquainted with the world', she takes ' keen delight' in listening
to her 'master', 'imagining the new pictures he portrayed, and in following him in
thought through the new regions he disclosed' (146). She who is 'small and plain'
desires 'to be tall, stately, and finely developed in figure' (255, 98). She whom society
labels inferior finds 'pleasure' less in moral influence than in power: 'I knew the
pleasure of vexing and soothing him by turns' (158). She who was 'disciplined and
subdued' yearns for expressiveness (84). She who is objectified, defined, and labelled by others—a 'castaway', a 'Liar', a 'mere governess'—yearns to be recognized. She whose story begins in isolation and rejection longs—above all—for love.

The constriction, the 'stagnation', the restriction to narrow horizons endemic to
Jane's world are countered in her narrative by romantic tropes of distance, of the
exotic, of the powerful and the sublime. The evangelical injunction to mortify the
flesh, the more worldly voices of propriety and self-control, are opposed by images
of sensual and aesthetic pleasure: the 'Turkey carpet' and 'Tyrian-dyed curtain', the
'pale Parian mantel-piece' and 'sparkling Bohemian glass' in the public rooms at
Thornfield, the 'dark-blue silk dress' and 'chestnut tresses' of Rosamond Oliver, the
'winter delight' and the Midsummer splendour of the landscapes round Thornfield
Hall. The coercive, death-directed logic of evangelical teaching is answered by a determination to 'keep in good health and not die' (32), the idealized self-extinction
of early nineteenth-century womanhood by a passionate demand for 'a full and delightful life' (252). Most subversively of all, perhaps, the 'cold charity' of the England
of the New Poor Law (323, 379) is answered not by 'moral Jacobinism'—a demand
for social justice—but by an affirmation of the primacy of the need for love.

For if Jane's dreams are not 'all about love', like Emma Bovary's, the longing to
be loved is not disparaged here, as it is in *Madame Bovary*. It seems, rather, to be insisted on in a wholly serious way. It is this emphasis in the novel that has led generations of readers to see it as 'a love-story, a Cinderella Fable':[109] it is this that has
provoked the frequent critical charge that *Jane Eyre* offers a spurious, 'romantic'
resolution to the inequities of its world. And it was this that disturbed some of the
novel's first critics, at least as much as any 'murmuring against the comforts of the
rich and against the privations of the poor'.[110] For the language of romantic love—
so prominent in the annuals—was one of the most well-worn of the period, and one
of the most condemned. Woman's yearning for love was seen by feminists and conservatives alike as not merely the most potent but the most problematic of her

[109] Kathleen Tillotson, *Novels of the Eighteen-Forties* (Oxford: Clarendon Press, 1954), 258.
[110] [Elizabeth Rigby], unsigned review of Jane Eyre, *Quarterly Review*, 84 (December 1848), *CH* 109.

'dreams'. 'Love. What young heart does not throb at the name?' ask Emily Shirreff and Maria Grey, three years after the publication of *Jane Eyre*: 'How large a propor-tion of the thoughts, hopes, and dreams of youth does it occupy? . . . The first notion of a girl . . . is that she must be in love and have a lover. . . . This fictitious sentiment is cherished by idleness, by novel reading, by day-dreams and is made an excuse for the neglect of every active duty.'[111] 'The desire of being beloved . . . who shall record the endless variety of suffering it entails upon woman?' laments Sarah Ellis twelve years earlier. 'Let her seek as she may the admiration and applause of the world, it never satisfies the craving of her soul . . . The world has no wealth to offer, that she would possess alone.'[112] 'Woman . . . is trained up as if for love alone . . . told from childhood on that she must love in order to find happiness . . . that to love comprises her whole destiny,' complains Anne Richelieu Lamb:

This species of feeling is a mere *ignis fatuus*, leading often into all kinds of bogs and morasses, though at the same time a something so beautiful, that in gazing upon it, the gazer seems to lose his senses, or appears as if he had drunk some inchanted [*sic*] wine, which had effect of lifting him above the sordid cares of a prosaic world . . . [such emotions] are too exciting and all-absorbing, and should be but sparingly indulged in . . . We may find in the events of a sin-gle day many channels in which our feelings may flow and with propriety, without need of this especial one which is called love.[113]

These sentiments are echoed, indeed, by Jane Eyre herself, with a verbal exactness that points to her creator's sharp awareness of such arguments as these.[114] Yet 'the desire of being beloved' is urgent in her narrative, displacing, rather than countered by, the soberer satisfactions, the rationality, the religion, to which these writers point.

For Jane's is a world very different from Emma Bovary's. It is not a place of stultifying bourgeois comfort, but one within which life can scarcely be sustained. Her story tells not of entrapping boredom and jaded appetite, but of literal confine-ment and actual starvation; not of social ambition, but of seeking to be acknow-ledged as a human being; not of escapist dreams, but of a desperate will to survive. Most crucially, perhaps, Jane Eyre is portrayed not simply as a woman lured by the *ignis fatuus* of romance. For the whole first third of the novel she appears as a hun-gry, unloved child. It is this that sets this novel apart from every other of its period— except perhaps that which its author knew best, her sister's *Wuthering Heights*. And it is this that most profoundly connects its narrative of constant jeopardy with its story of desire fulfilled. For the 'energy', 'fire', 'life' that Jane feels in Rochester's presence (146, 151, 423) answer not merely to her longings for 'incident, life, fire, feeling' but to the abjection of her state as a child. 'You think I have no feelings', Jane says to Mrs Reed, 'and that I can do without one bit of love or kindness; but *I cannot*

---

[111]   Shirreff and Grey, *Thoughts on Self-Culture*, ii. 268.   [112]   Ellis, *Women of England*, 305.
[113]   [Anne Richelieu Lamb], *Can Woman Regenerate Society?* (London: John W. Parker, 1844), 86–8.
[114]   'It is madness in all women to let a secret love kindle within them, which, if unreturned and un-known, must devour the life that feeds it; and, if discovered and responded to, must lead ignis-fatuus-like, into miry wilds whence there is no extrication,' she tells herself (161).

live so' (36, my italics). It is the child's baffled recognition of this, rather than her angry rebellion, that is the mainspring of the narrative that follows; for the need thus delineated is one that no amount of self-assertion can assuage. Jane's angry 'victory' over her aunt brings her no satisfaction: she is left, she says, in her 'conqueror's solitude', like 'a ridge of lighted heath . . . black and blasted after the flames are dead' (37). 'I cannot bear to be solitary and hated', she says to Helen Burns, 'If others don't love me, I would rather die than live.' 'You think too much of the love of human beings', says Helen (69). But Helen Burns is dying: the thrust of the narrative is with Jane's struggle to survive. For her rhetoric of 'love' is underwritten by the novel's most characteristic and pervasive, yet perhaps least remarked-upon, imagery: that which speaks of something deeper and more unquestionable than any ambition, preference, or desire—of the instinct for life itself.

'You must be tenacious of life,' says Rochester, when Jane tells him that she spent eight years at Lowood school (121). And tenacity to life is a central concern in *Jane Eyre*. 'I must keep in good health, and not die,' is Jane's 'objectionable' reply to Brocklehurst (32). 'How sad to be lying now on a sick-bed, and to be in danger of dying!' she thinks as a child at school, liberated by spring and by the relaxation of the Lowood regime (79). Years afterward she remembers the 'revived vitality' produced by 'the bit of bread, the draught of coffee' that constitute Lowood's meagre supper (54); 'we lived better too,' she says, as she recalls the more plentiful food—'a large piece of cold pie, or a thick slice of bread and cheese'—which 'those who continued well' received when Lowood had 'fewer to feed' (77). 'I felt the reviving warmth of a fire,' she says, of the moment when Rochester takes her down to the library, after her dark night of the soul on what should have been her wedding day. 'He put wine to my lips; I tasted it and revived; then I ate something he offered me, and was soon myself' (299). Such imagery is central to the novel's long description of near-death from starvation and exposure. For here, the narrative emphasis is not on passive suffering but on the instinct to preserve life: 'I *coveted* a cake of bread. With that refreshment I could perhaps regain a degree of energy'; 'I was so sick, so weak, so gnawed with *nature's cravings, instinct kept me roaming* round abodes where there was a chance of food'; 'The girl emptied the stiffened mould into my hand, and *I devoured it ravenously*' (325, 327, 329; my italics). Even in the absence of any conscious desire to live, this instinct remains: 'To die of want and cold, is a fate to which nature cannot submit passively,' says Jane. Throughout, the impulse to life is involuntary, insistent, strong: 'the rain fell fast, wetting me afresh to the skin . . . my yet living flesh *shuddered* to its chilling influence. *I rose* ere long.' 'I tasted what they offered me: feebly at first, *eagerly* soon,' she tells, of her first moments in Moor House; 'look at the *avidity* in her eyes,' Mary Rivers says. By the fourth day there, she has 'eaten *with relish*' and feels 'comparatively . . . revived' (330–1; 337; 339; my italics).

Such imagery as this speaks of basic bodily experience, not of transcendent desire. And it is fundamental to Jane's narrative, throughout reinflecting and reanimating that suspected discourse of 'love'. 'There was a *reviving* pleasure in this intercourse, of a kind now *tasted* by me for the first time,' says Jane, as she tells of her growing acquaintance with her cousins. 'The ease of his manner freed me from painful restraint,' she recalls, of her burgeoning relationship with Rochester. 'My thin-crescent destiny seemed to enlarge; the blanks of existence were filled up; *my bodily health improved; I gathered flesh and strength.*' 'Who would be hurt by my once more *tasting the life* his glance can give me?' she asks, as she returns to him (349, 146, 423; my italics). The notion that love enabled life itself was in the early nineteenth century an utterly conventional one:

> The truest love that ever heart
>   Felt at its kindled core
> Did through each vein, in quickened start,
>   The tide of being pour,

sings Rochester to Jane, in what could be a verse from an annual (271). But the trope he invokes is brought to life in the novel in a quite unconventional way. It is as she is recognized with 'kindness' rather than labelled as a Liar that the child for whom 'the present was vague and strange', who could not remember the past, and could form of the future 'no conjecture' (49), finds her 'memory . . . improved', her 'wits . . . sharpened' and learns 'the first two tenses' of the French verb 'to be' (75). Gazing at her face in the glass, Jane finds 'hope in its aspect, and life in its colour' after Rochester's declaration of love (257). And her account of her marriage—informed though it is by suggestions of self-annihilating symbiosis—appears also as the triumphant culmination of this coming to life through love: 'It brought to life and light my whole nature: in his presence I thoroughly lived; and he lived in mine' (437). Even the dying Helen Burns is kindled into life in 'the presence and kindness of her beloved instructress': 'her spirit seemed hastening to live within a very brief span as much as many live during a protracted existence' (73). 'When once I had pressed the frail shoulder', says Rochester of his first meeting with Jane, 'something new—a fresh sap and sense—stole into my frame' (313); 'Such society revives, regenerates', he declares, of his burgeoning 'acquaintance' with her (218). Even the death-bound St John Rivers, who seeks to 'sacrifice all to his long-framed resolves . . . natural affection and feelings more potent still' (356), comes to life in the face of his beloved—'his cheek would glow, and his marble-seeming features, though they refused to relax, changed indescribably' (367).

Conversely, the absence of love is imaged throughout *Jane Eyre* as an assault on life itself:

Helen Burns was not here; nothing sustained me: left to myself I abandoned myself . . . I had meant to be so good, and to do so much at Lowood; to make so many friends, to earn respect, and win affection . . . now, here I lay again crushed and trodden on: and could I ever rise more? 'Never,' I thought; and ardently I wished to die.   (68)

When Jane contemplates leaving Rochester, 'a hand of fiery iron grasp[s her] vitals' (315). Estrangement from her cousin is 'refined, lingering torture': 'I felt how—if I were his wife—this good man, pure as the deep sunless source, could soon kill me; without drawing from my veins a single drop of blood, or receiving on his own crystal conscience the faintest stain of crime' (411). This kind of imagery, with its life and

death urgency, runs right through *Jane Eyre*. Even when it fixes on the Byronic figure of a Mr Rochester, the longing that animates Jane's story is presented not as a
desire for transcendence but as a longing for life itself:

I love Thornfield:—I love it, because I have lived in it a full and delightful life,—momentarily at least. I have not been trampled on. I have not been petrified . . . I have known you,
Mr Rochester; and it strikes me with terror and anguish to feel I absolutely must be torn from
you for ever. I see the necessity of departure; and it is like looking on the necessity of death.
(252)

And Jane's declaration is underwritten not—as such declarations are, for example,
in the annual verse of L.E.L.—by an account of the sufferings of romantic love, but
by that central, disquieting scenario, in which Jane does leave Thornfield, falls away
from all human recognition—'Alas, this isolation—this banishment from my
kind!' (335)—and faces a lonely, agonizing death.

   For that image of Jane starving on the moor, at the centre of the novel, echoing all
its earlier images of cold, hunger, and isolation, is above all an image of the impos-
sibility of surviving alone. 'Not a tie holds me to human society,', Jane says of her
arrival at Whitcross. 'Not a charm or hope calls me where my fellow-creatures
are—none that saw me would have a kind thought or a good wish for
me' (323). Yet if she turns, romantically, away from 'man' and towards 'the universal mother, Nature', her dreams are dispelled, as she is forced to confront the intimate, internal ravages of a far from benevolent natural law—'I was so sick, so weak,
so gnawed with nature's cravings, instinct kept me roaming round abodes where
there was a chance of food' (327). She is 'a human being', and has 'a human being's
wants': wants that must—as her desperate wanderings around that inhospitable
hamlet suggest—be answered not by nature, but by the human world. 'Man shall
not live by bread alone', says Brocklehurst (63); and despite the novel's emphasis on
the importunity of bodily need, this, it suggests, is true in ways he hardly means. For
Jane is brought back to life not—as she at first believes—by any kindness of
strangers, but by the care of her own near 'kin'. 'That is an *ignis fatuus*,' she thinks,
when she first sees the light of Moor House (330). But it is in fact no '*ignis fatuus*' of
unrequited love, nor yet a 'bonfire' of passion: it is a reliable 'beacon', 'shining dim,
but constant, through the rain' (330–1). From her very first glimpse of these unknown others she feels an affinity with them. 'I had nowhere seen such faces as
theirs: and yet, as I gazed on them, I seemed intimate with every lineament' (332).
This sense is, of course, confirmed by her discovery of actual kinship; but the point
does not seem to be a mystical valorization of blood-relationship. The younger
Reeds, as closely related to Jane as are the Rivers, are opposed to her 'in temperament, in capacity, in propensities' (14). Rather, the notion of kinship works in the
novel as an image of a kind of relation quite different from those of inequality and
obligation that structure its larger world: a relation that is characterized by reciprocity, by 'regard', by recognition and confirmation rather than by the objectifying strategies of power and privilege. 'I do not want a stranger—unsympathizing,
alien, different from me,' says Jane, when St John Rivers speaks of the connections

her money will enable her to make. 'I want my kindred: those with whom I have full fellow-feeling' (388). 'I felt at times as if he were my relation rather than my master,' she tells, of her growing intimacy with her employer (146); when she sees him disguised as a gipsy woman, 'her accent, her gesture, and all, were familiar to me as my own face in a glass—as the speech of my own tongue' (202). Though he moves among those equal to him in 'rank and wealth', he is not, she says, 'of their kind. I believe he is of mine;—I am sure he is,—I feel akin to him . . . I have something in my brain and heart, in my blood and nerves, that assimilates me mentally to him' (175): announcing his intention to marry her, he pronounces Jane 'my equal . . . and my likeness . . . I love you as my own flesh' (254–5). Once past the threshold of the Rivers' house, and 'brought face to face with its owners', Jane is able 'to put off the mendicant—to resume my natural manner and character' (337): conversely, the sharing of her legacy with them enables their return to their natural selves. 'They were under a yoke: I could free them; they were scattered,—I could reunite them' (385); that done, 'the air of the moors, the freedom of home, the dawn of prosperity, acted on Diana's and Mary's spirits like some life-giving elixir' (394).

These images of a 'natural' self, enabled, vivivified, released by love, and of self-confirming, liberating 'kinship', are familiar enough romantic ones,[115] often to be found in the annuals. But they appear in *Jane Eyre* less as conventional tropes than as precisely articulated answers to a deprivation that is sharply and extensively portrayed. For the opening image of the cold, hungry, unloved child, 'an interloper and an alien' (66) who is 'like nobody there' (15), opens up, in the narrative that follows, resonances quite different from those that the figure of the woman longing for love was, in the early nineteenth century, customarily made to bear. In *Jane Eyre* that figure—so familiar, so deplored, in early nineteenth-century England—does not appear as one lured by an escapist dream of romance. Instead, she becomes an image of absolute primary need: one that in a peculiarly embarrassing way questions the terms within which the society presented in the novel conceives of and constructs itself.

' "*I should kill you—I am killing you*": your words are such as ought not to be used: violent, unfeminine, and untrue', says St John Rivers, when Jane refuses his proposal of marriage, on the grounds that he does not love her. And his words prefigure the negative criticism *Jane Eyre* received, from readers as diverse as Elizabeth Rigby and Harriet Martineau. Such critics condemned the novel, centrally, for its offences against 'propriety': its heroine's 'unregenerate and undisciplined' desire for self-fulfilment, its author's 'insistent . . . tendency to describe the need of being loved'.[116] In part, of course, they were responding, in their very different ways, to such obvious challenges to 'conventionality' as Jane's unwomanly expressiveness, her outspoken declaration of desire. As even the feminist author of *Can Woman Regenerate Society?* put it in 1844: 'to go and look at a man straight in the face, and with

---

[115] On romantic 'kinship' see e.g. Shelley, *Epipsychidion*, and Byron, *Manfred*, II. ii. 105–7.

[116] [Elizabeth Rigby], unsigned review, in *CH* 105–12; Harriet Martineau, unsigned review of *Villette*, *Daily News*, 3 February 1853, in *CH* 171–4. Martineau's criticism here—not simply of *Villette*, but of Brontë's 'tendency' as a writer –was to provoke Charlotte Brontë to angry response.

a coaxing tone request him to have the goodness to marry you, would be the most dreadful outrage, the most deadly offence you could commit against propriety and feminine delicacy.'[117] But there is, I think, a deeper logic in their accusations. For 'propriety', as Charlotte Brontë had sardonically indicated in *The Professor*, is a word with ambiguous resonances. It does not merely signify compliance to social conventions: in its root sense of 'essence' or 'individuality' (and perhaps also in its now obsolete meaning of 'property'), it speaks also of the proprietory self of that competitive individualism which underpinned the social arrangements of early nineteenth-century England—the society whose version of 'charity' starves and baffles the child Jane Eyre. And to 'propriety' in this sense *Jane Eyre* offers a distinctive challenge: a challenge quite different from *The Professor*'s irony. Whereas, in the earlier novel, Crimsworth's pretensions to 'independence' are undercut by a prose that registers his intimate implication in that which he rejects, *Jane Eyre*, with its central emphasis on absolute, primary need, more directly, more urgently questions the notion that self is or could be an autonomous entity. This, rather than its 'unfeminine' demand that women should have 'exercise for their faculties and a field for their efforts', or its 'improper' depiction of female sexuality, is its real offence: not merely against the 'proprieties' of early nineteenth-century English society, but even, arguably, against our own.[118]

[117] [Lamb], *Can Woman Regenerate Society?*, 105.
[118] Contemporary theorists still tend to speak of sexuality rather than of love, of desire rather than of need, of the body's pleasures, rather than of its frailty. For a powerful challenge to the Freudian conception of desire as an individual, pleasure-seeking drive, see Ian D. Suttie, *The Origins of Love and Hate* (London, 1936). Suttie's attack on the Freudian assumption that self is a radical isolate, his argument for the primacy of the need to love and be loved, were little taken up at the time, partly because of his untimely death on the day of publication of his book, partly because of his abrasive personal style. (See Foreword by John Bowlby and Introduction by Dorothy Heard to Suttie, *The Origins of Love and Hate* (London: Free Association Books, 1988)). But they have subsequently become accepted and elaborated by the British object relations school of psychoanalysis, who likewise see sociability as a primary rather than a secondary phenomenon. See e.g. Ronald Fairbairn, *Psychoanalytic Studies of the Personality* (London: Tavistock, 1952); D. W. Winnicott, *The Maturational Process and the Facilitating Environment* (London: Hogarth Press, 1965); Michael Balint, *The Basic Fault* (London: Tavistock, 1968); John Bowlby, *Attachment and Loss* (3 vols.; London: Hogarth Press, 1969–80); and (in America) Daniel Stern, *The Interpersonal World of the Infant: A View From Psychoanalysis and Developmental Psychology* (New York: Basic Books, 1985).

CHAPTER SIX

The Terrible Handwriting: *Shirley*

I

'I had drawn parallels in silence, which I never thought thus to have declared aloud': thus Jane Eyre describes her decisive rebellion against John Reed. In one sense, the 'parallels' between inarticulate private suffering and public official history are writ large in *Shirley*. This, it has seemed, is Charlotte Brontë's attempt to write a 'condition-of-England' novel such as other of her contemporaries were producing in these years. Yet the novel has always refused quite to fit that category. Its narrative focus shifts from one subject to another—the curates and their absurdities; the dispute between masters and men; Robert Moore's entrepreneurial ambitions; the story of Caroline Helstone's lonely decline; the aristocratic heiress, Shirley, her governess and her tutor; the extraordinary Yorke family and their concerns. There are chunks of text in foreign languages, old ballads, hymns, poems, even a school essay, interspersed with extended reflections upon such themes as the effects of the war with France and the sufferings of old maids. The whole is, as one contemporary reviewer put it, 'presented to us less in the manner of a continuous tale . . . than in a series of detached and independent pictures, dialogues and soliloquies'.[1]

Jane Eyre's passionate directness has here been replaced by the ironically appraising tones of a markedly unillusioned voice. Whereas the earlier novel offered 'sentiment, and poetry, and reverie', this narrator invites the reader 'back to the beginning of this century' with the distinctly deflationary image of an after-dinner snooze (5). Jane's dreams were subversive and empowering. But here the dreaming Caroline is a stereotyped victim of romance. 'Impossible for her now to suspect that she was the sport of delusion,' remarks the narrator knowingly (99), dismissing her girlish day-dreams as 'the visions we see at eighteen' (97). 'That music stirs my soul', says Shirley, listening to a 'martial tune'. 'I almost long for danger; for a faith—a land—or, at least, a lover to defend.' But the grandeur of this aspiration is punctured by the nature of the occasion that inspires it. 'No foe or tyrant is questioning or threatening our liberty', says Helstone, laughing at her. 'There is nothing to be done: we are only taking a walk' (302). Elsewhere the eponymous heroine's rhapsodies—on the nature of the 'first woman' (320), on 'Genius and Humanity' (489)—are given freer rein. But such 'Titan visions' (322) remain contained within an ironizing narrative quite different from that of *Shirley*'s predecessor—a 'whim'

---

[1] Unsigned review, *Examiner*, quoted in *CH* 127–8.

to be humoured (321), a school essay 'scored' by a 'censor-pencil' with corrections that the student is unable to understand (490).

Religious and political differences, too, are treated with what some contemporaries complained was a 'jesting' irony.[2] Biblical texts are bandied about as counters in ignoble arguments; theological disagreement becomes burlesque in the mock-heroic battle of the Sunday School Whitsuntide feast. Political disputes are diminished into personal animosities. Even the story of class against class that lies at the novel's centre is presented with a curious jauntiness. 'You never heard that sound, perhaps, reader?' demands the obtrusive narrator, as he tells, at the climax of that story, of the 'West-Riding-clothing-district-of-Yorkshire rioters' yell':

> So much the better for your ears—perhaps for your heart; since, if it rends the air in hate to yourself, or to the men or principles you approve, the interests to which you wish well, Wrath wakens to the cry of Hate: the Lion shakes his mane, and rises to the howl of the Hyaena: Caste stands up, ireful, against Caste; and the indignant, wronged spirit of the Middle Rank bears down in zeal and scorn on the famished and furious mass of the Operative Class. It is difficult to be tolerant—difficult to be just—in such moments.   (343–4)

And the distancing personifications, the relativizing gesture at 'the principles you approve, the interests to which you wish well', leave the 'reader' half taunted, half implicated—awkwardly detached from the 'tolerance' to which other writers in these years appeal.

For if the subject-matter of *Shirley* is, as Brontë anxiously registered in the course of writing the novel, akin to that of *Mary Barton*, the peculiar, alienating irony with which it handles that subject is quite unlike Gaskell's earnest attempt to engage her readers' sympathies. Indeed, in the novel's final volume this irony seems explicitly directed at the fictional expectations which *Mary Barton* had raised:

> I doubt not a justice-loving public will have remarked, ere this, that I have thus far shewn a criminal remissness in pursuing, catching, and bringing to condign punishment the would-be assassin of Mr. Robert Moore: here was a fine opening to lead my willing readers a dance, at once decorous and exciting: a dance of law and gospel, of the dungeon, the dock, and the 'dead-thraw'. You might have liked it, reader, but *I* should not: I and my subject would presently have quarrelled, and then I should have broken down: I was happy to find that facts perfectly exonerated me from the attempt. The murderer was never punished; for the good reason, that he was never caught; the result of the further circumstance, that he was never pursued.   (634–5)[3]

This is closer to the flippancies of *Blackwood's* and the early *Fraser's* than it is to the moral seriousness of the condition-of-England novelists. It is certainly very different from the tautness of *The Professor*, the first-person urgency of *Jane Eyre*.

---

[2] Unsigned review, *Atlas*, quoted in *CH* 121; see also *CH* 117, 156, 163.

[3] In February 1849, whilst in the midst of writing *Shirley*, Brontë was 'so dismayed to find [herself] in some measure anticipated both in subject and incident' by *Mary Barton* that she was prompted to submit the first volume of her unfinished novel to her publishers for their opinion (*CBL* ii. 174). This passage from the third volume, much worked over in manuscript, provides suggestive evidence not merely of her continuing anxiety on this subject, but also of her ironic sense of the difference of what she offered from what contemporaries might expect.

A key to the novel can, I think, be found in the writings of Glass Town and Angria. There, too, one finds abrupt shifts of scene and character, anti-romantic irony, and constant self-reflexive commentary on the nature of the fictional enterprise. And there, in ways that are—as we shall see—picked up and writ large in *Shirley*, the fictional world is imaged as a heteroglossic place. The 'anecdotes', the 'Conversations' and the correspondence columns of the early *Young Men's Magazine* were succeeded in the writings of Brontë's early twenties by a series of evocations of 'the talk of coffee-houses . . . the gossip of news-rooms . . . the speculations of public-prints . . . the chit-chat & scandal . . . respecting the characters, ongoings & probable destinies of eminent men'.[4] At the opening of 'The Duke of Zamorna', written in 1838, William Percy tells of the 'anecdotes, tales, stories . . . piquant rumours' from 'servants' halls', 'which in my childhood were rife in every house in the West'. 'What would I have given to cast away the medium and behold the figures face to face,' he exclaims:[5] but a central concern in the writings of Glass Town and Angria is precisely with the 'medium' through which their 'figures' are portrayed. There is a constant play within them with the diverse and conflicting idioms that make up the fictional world. Thus, a comic song in 'The Foundling' is written in 'the old young men tongue' (a language imitating Yorkshire dialect invented by Branwell for the original twelve Young Men); there is parody of the jargon of Methodism in 'The Return of Zamorna' and 'Julia'; Charles Townshend reproduces a fashionable gossip-column in 'Stancliffe's Hotel'.

Here, too, as later in *Shirley*, sardonic narrative voices mock romantic expectation and depict heroic passions in less than heroic guise. 'One cannot continually keep one's feelings wound up to the pitch of romance and reverie,' declares Charles Townshend, in 'The Duke of Zamorna': 'I began this work with the intention of writing something high and pathetic . . . Let it suffice to say that I found this pitch far too high for me. I could not keep it up. I was forced to descend a peg.'[6] 'How do you know whether the sentimentality is in jest or earnest?' he demands, as he concludes a lengthy paean in praise of the love of his life. 'Aint it very probable that I may be bamming you by doing a bit in the soft line?'[7] This kind of debunking self-reflexiveness recurs throughout these youthful writings. It is there in the voice of Charles Townshend, observing the world of Angrian passion with a coolly cynical eye; in the exaggerated mock-heroics of such early stories as 'Albion and Marina'; in the *Don Juan*-like shifts of tone of the later 'Stancliffe's Hotel':

'Charles,' said my fair companion in her usual voice, half a whisper, half a murmur. 'Charles, what a sweet night—a premature summer night! It only wants the moon to make it perfect . . . How many fond recollections come on us at such a time as this! Where do you think my thoughts always stray on a summer night? What image do you think "a cloudless clime & starry skies" always suggests?'

---

⁴ 'Passing Events' (1836), in Winifred Gérin (ed.), *Five Novelettes* (London: Folio Press, 1971), 54.
⁵ 'The Duke of Zamorna', in Thomas Wise and John Symington (eds.), *The Miscellaneous and Unpublished Writings of Charlotte and Patrick Branwell Brontë* (2 vols.; Oxford: Shakespeare Head, 1938), ii. 348–9.
⁶ Ibid. 373, 375.   ⁷ Ibid. 391.

'Perhaps,' said I, 'that of the most noble Richard Marquis of Wellesley as you last saw him reposing in gouty chair and stool, with eyelids gently closed by the influence of the pious libations in claret with which he has concluded the dinner of rice-currie, devilled turkey and guava.'[8]

It is there in their comic treatment of the extravagances of Methodism and of the failings of the Anglican clergy;[9] and more subtly, more pervasively, in the coolly analytic detachment with which passionate feeling is described. And it can be traced in a different way in the often humorous emphasis on the narrative activity itself:

let [Richton] write so well that each separate voice shall speak out of the page in changeful tone, the word passing from mouth to mouth, the flexible lip & the rapid tongue of Edward Percy succeeding in raised bass the energetic silver dictum of Howard Warner ... Let Richton do this & astonish us & let Hastings familiarise us with the terms & tactics of war, let him stir us up with the sweet & warlike national airs of Angria ... Sublime!—but stop, my recollections of Hastings have led me too far astray. let the Earl & the Major say I dilate on these things, let them rush upon that noble quarry, they are eagles, let them travel that broad road, they are mounted on chargers of the Ukraine. for me I am but a crow, so I must be well content in the rookeries that shade Africa's ancestral Halls. I have but my own shanks to go on ...[10]

A novel can scarcely be called a novel unless it ends in a marriage, therefore I herewith tack to, add and communicate the following *postscriptum*.[11]

Throughout, the sense is less of a world of feeling uncritically indulged than of a cool, critical, sometimes sardonic observation of feeling; less of an expressive outpouring of emotion than of a rather more self-conscious play with the fictional medium itself. It is a 'play' that is evident also in *Shirley*'s ironic, distancing, self-referential narrative stance.

But in *Shirley* this stance has become part of a much more coherent fictional enterprise than it is in the loosely structured writings of its author's formative years. The banter of the opening page ('If you think, from this prelude, that anything like a romance is preparing for you, reader, you never were more mistaken') has an echo in the novel's closing words: 'The story is told. I think I now see the judicious reader putting on his spectacles to look for the moral. It would be an insult to his sagacity to offer directions. I only say, God speed him in the quest!'[12] The family jokes of the juvenilia have here been replaced by a deliberate, framing emphasis on the resistance of this 'story' to the kinds of interpretation its 'reader' is likely to attempt. And that earlier narrative stance of detached, sardonic observation has developed into a distinctive, obtrusive insistence on the externality of the perspective from which the fictional world is seen:

---

[8] BPM: MS Bon 114 (my punctuation).

[9] On the portrayal of Methodism in these writings, see Valentine Cunningham, *Everywhere Spoken Against: Dissent in the Victorian Novel* (Oxford: Oxford University Press, 1975), 116–19.

[10] 'Passing Events', in Winifred Gérin (ed.), *Five Novelettes*, 35–7.

[11] 'The Spell: an Extravaganza', *EEW* ii. pt. 2, 236.

[12] Cf. Byron's similarly flippant taunt, in *Don Juan*, at readers who 'cry that they the moral cannot find' (Canto I. 208–9).

It is probable that the three there present felt this charm: they all *looked* happy.   (88)

Moore seated himself at his desk, broke the seals of the documents, and glanced them over. They were all short, but not—*it seemed*—sweet; *probably* rather sour on the contrary, for as Moore laid down the last, his nostrils emitted a derisive and defiant snuff; and, though he burst into no soliloquy, there was a glance in his eye which *seemed* to invoke the devil.   (125)

An acute observer *might have* remarked.   (456) [my italics throughout]

Jane Eyre's vision could penetrate the inner truth of her world. But such passages as these delineate a more resistant set of appearances. Here, that controlling auto-biographical eye/I, irresistably insisting that the reader 'see what she sees',[13] is re-placed by a foregrounded process of inference and conjecture. 'His station . . . you could not easily determine by his speech or demeanour; perhaps the appearance of his residence may decide it' (42); 'Does he feel the chaste charm nature wears tonight? . . . Impossible to say; for he is silent, and his countenance does not speak' (567). Even where the reader is invited to share a more intimate knowledge, it is an invitation of a strangely voyeuristic kind. When Caroline will not stay to listen to Robert and Shirley, 'the reader is privileged to remain, and try what he can make of the discourse' (235). 'Come near, by all means, Reader: do not be shy: stoop over his shoulder fearlessly, and read as he scribbles': thus the narrator introduces the jour-nal of Louis Moore (521). At such moments the narrative stance seems closer to that of the eavesdropping, spying Charles Townshend than to the passionate inward-ness of *Jane Eyre*.

Shirley, like Glass Town and Angria, is full of opinion and conjecture. Thus, the first mention of Louis is as one who 'was *said* now to be tutor in a private family' (64); 'I've *heard* he's an honest man,' Moore says, of the workman Farren (162); '*People say* you are miserly,' Caroline reproaches her mother (448); '*Everybody said* it was high time for Mr Moore to return home,' remarks the narrator, of Moore's 'strange absence' after the attack on his mill. 'All Briarfield wondered at his strange absence, and Whinbury and Nunnely brought each its separate contribution of amazement' (529; my italics). Such references are pervasive, and they are under-lined throughout. For from the opening portrait of the curates, with their Babel-ish 'confusion of tongues' (12), to the legends and reminiscences of the 'old house-keeper' at its close, there is in this novel an emphasis quite different from anything in *The Professor* or *Jane Eyre* on that constant verbal interaction which, more prominently than work, constitutes its social world. 'Talking a bit! Just like you!' says Shirley, goodhumouredly, to the crowd of 'milk-fetchers' at Fieldhead, on the morning after the attack on the mill. 'You *talk* if anybody dies suddenly; you *talk* if a fire breaks out; you *talk* if a mill-owner fails; you *talk* if he's murdered' (355). The novel is full of references to such 'talk', from the curates' disputations over 'minute points of ecclesiastical discipline' (12), to 'disaffection . . . heard muttering to him-self' and swearing 'ominous oaths over the drugged beer of alehouses' (528); from the ladies 'at Whinbury' who sit 'in a corner of the drawing room talking about'

---

[13] Virginia Woolf, '*Jane Eyre* and *Wuthering Heights*', *The Common Reader*, First Series (London: Hogarth Press, 1925), 197.

Moore (156) to the 'gabble' of the guests at the Rectory tea (116). Moore deplores the 'ridiculous gossips of Whinbury and Briarfield' (25); Caroline fears the 'tomahawk tongues' of 'certain ladies' of the parish (171); 'I hate to be . . . a theme for village-gossip', Shirley says (508). Yet 'village-gossip' is portrayed as a powerful force. The public perception of Helstone has been coloured by the 'rumours . . . rife in the neighbourhood' after the death of Mary Cave (53). 'The disaffected here are in cor-respondence with the disaffected elsewhere', says Robert Moore to Shirley. 'The long-threatening storm is sure to break at last' (291). More comically, 'the news of what happened at the Hollow' is 'spread all over the neighbourhood', with a Chinese-whispers effect: within a very short time, rumour has solidified into wildly exaggerated fact (353).

Jane Eyre's undisputed, singular voice has here been replaced by a host of sharply characterized voices, whose divisive cacophony is stressed. From the 'uproar' of the curates in Mrs Gale's parlour to the Methodists' 'shouts, yells, ejaculations, frantic cries, agonized groans' (145), from Hortense's scolding to Rose Yorke's 'ranting and spouting' (401), from the 'confusion of tongues' at the Whit-Tuesday feast (292) to the 'rioter's yell' that signals the attack on Hollow's Mill, the novel is alive with verbal noise. Different accents and inflections signal differences of gender, of region, of race, of creed, of class.[14] Thus, the reader is told that Malone's 'high Celtic voice' (10) 'proclaims him at once a native of the land of shamrocks and potatoes' (8), that Moore's 'outlandish accent . . . grates on a British . . . ear' (27), that Mr Yorke's 'York-shire burr' is 'as much better than a Cockney's lisp, as a bull's bellow than a ratton's squeak' (50). Cyril Hall, that 'fluent . . . agreeable talker' (271) speaks in a 'broad, northern tongue' that is at first almost incomprehensible to Mrs Pryor (449). 'I like your southern accent', says Caroline to her mother. 'It is so pure, so soft. It has no rugged burr, no nasal twang, such as almost every one's voice here in the north has' (449). 'One would think that when I open my lips in company, I speak English with a ridiculous accent, whereas I am quite assured that I pronounce it properly', declares Hortense (66). 'Northern ears receive with singular sensations' Donne's elaborately 'genteel' 'utterance of certain words' (288); whilst Mrs Pryor's quite different 'correctness', her 'formal . . . accent and language', provoke Helstone into pretending to be deaf (195–6). Again and again, the narrator offers to translate that which might otherwise be 'unintelligible to some readers' (547): the 'peculiar orthography' of the Luddite note left for Moore (40); the conversation 'in French' between Moore and his sister (72); the *devoir* of Shirley's that Louis repeats aloud (547). But the effect of such moments is less to inspire confidence in the mediating powers of 'translation' than to indicate difference and uinintelligibility. 'We hardly speak in the same tongue,' says Shirley to her uncle (557). Here, as in Glass Town and Angria, speech makes for Babel-like division rather than communal accord.[15]

---

[14] In 'A Yorkshire Burr: Language in *Shirley*', *Studies in English Literature 1500–1900*, 27 (1987), 637–43, Susan Belasco Smith points to the accuracy with which different dialects and accents are represented in the novel.

[15] Indeed, an early reviewer complained that 'the first volume will be unintelligible to most people, for it is half in French and half in broad Yorkshire' (*Fraser's Magazine* 40 (1849), 693).

Here, more sustainedly than in those youthful writings, language itself is a central object of concern. 'It was no gift, but the confusion of tongues which has gabbled me deaf as a post', says Helstone, hailing his curates as 'three presumptuous Babylonish masons' (12–13); and the images of Pentecost and Babel recur ironically throughout. From the novel's opening pages, dense with ironic echoes of the Bible, to the closing paragraphs, in which the narrator glosses the old housekeeper's archaisms, there is an emphasis, unparalleled in any of Brontë's other novels, on the recalcitrance of the medium within which the narrative is framed. ' "C'en est trop," she would say, if she could speak French', says the narrator of Mrs Gale (8): 'I put that in French', he adds in parentheses, 'because the word "effleurer" is an exquisite word' (584). Elswhere, 'reflet' is left untranslated; the narrator remarks in a footnote: 'Find me an English word as good, reader, and I will gladly dispense with the French word. Reflections won't do.'[16] Prominent throughout the novel is the image of the alien word: most obviously in its frequent references to learning and speaking a foreign tongue, more pervasively in its constant, estranging insistence on language not as a universally available, always amenable tool, but as freighted with social meanings in problematizing ways. 'You scornfully enclose the word ['sentiment'] in quotation marks' wrote Charlotte Brontë to Lewes, in January 1848: maintaining the quotation marks, she goes on to offer her own more positive definition of the word.[17] And repeatedly, in the novel she began to write that month, words—including that of which she is speaking here—are 'scornfully' or estrangingly placed in quotation marks. ' "Inverted commas" ', says Geoffrey Hill, 'can be used as tweezers, lifting a commonplace term out of its format of habitual connection'; and again and again in *Shirley* words thus marked (or italicized) become within the narrative objects of discussion and dispute.[18]

In Gaskell's *Mary Barton*, too, there is a central concern with language—the difference of the 'work-people' 's language from that of the middle-class reader; the novelist's stated anxiety to give some 'utterance' to their agony.[19] But the nature of that concern is an entirely different one. Gaskell's explanatory glosses on the character's dialect words, citing examples from Anglo-Saxon, Chaucer, and

[16] *Shirley*, ed. Margaret Smith and Herbert Rosengarten (Oxford: Clarendon Press, 1979), 644. In an article in *Blackwood's* for April 1839, which Brontë may well have known, de Quincey defends the use of French words in English novels where 'the English could not have furnished a corresponding phrase with equal point or piquancy—sometimes not at all' ('The English Language', *Blackwood's Magazine* 45 (1839), 460).

[17] *CBL* i. 14.

[18] Geoffrey Hill, 'Our Word is Our Bond', in *The Lords of Limit: Essays on Literature and Ideas* (London: André Deutsch, 1984), 142–3. In the *Fraser's* of the 1830s, well known to the young Brontës, key words in polemical articles are disputatiously or ironically italicized or placed in quotation marks: see e.g. the reviews of Thomas Chalmers's *On Political Economy* in some of the first issues received in the Parsonage, those for August and September 1832 (*Fraser's Magazine* 6 (1832), 113–18, 239–48). Words treated thus in *Shirley* include '*brutally*' (59); *hankering* (16); 'sentiment' itself—which Mark Yorke looks up in the dictionary (159); '*living*' (375); 'down-draughts' (383); '*incapable*' (529).

[19] See Gillian Beer, 'Carlyle and *Mary Barton*: Problems of Utterance', in Francis Barker (ed.), *The Sociology of Literature 1848: Proceedings of the Essex Conference on the Sociology of Literature, July 1977* (Colchester: University of Essex, 1978), 242–55.

Shakespeare, work, as Stephen Gill has suggested, to 'show Mrs Gaskell's educated reader that . . . the poor speak the language that is the common heritage of all Englishmen'.[20] Quotation and allusion in *Mary Barton* point to community of feeling: the mottos that head the chapters suggest to a middle-class readership that the lives being depicted, so remote from polite experience, nevertheless partake of a common humanity. At the climax of the novel, Mr Carson in his study reads his Bible, 'understanding for the first time the full meaning', as John Barton lies on his deathbed, recalling his youthful efforts 'at following th' Bible myself': the two are brought together in a reconciliatory deathbed scene.[21] In *Shirley*, however, there is no such undisputed 'full meaning'. The same texts are interpreted in radically different ways. Caroline and Robert disagree over *Coriolanus* (91–4);[22] Rose Yorke reads *The Italian* with an excitement no longer possible to Caroline (398–9); Shirley takes exception to Milton's version of Eve (320). Yorke and Moore invoke Exodus to argue opposing points of view (39). The Bible is put to all manner of uses, from Helstone's jibes at the curates to Rose Yorke's interpretation of the parable of the talents to Michael Hartley's antinomian prophecies. 'It would be possible, I doubt not, with a little ingenuity,' says Caroline, in reply to Joe Scott's quotation from St Paul, 'to give the passage quite a contrary turn' (330).

Implicit in those quotation marks, foregrounded in those arguments, is the pervasive, ironic sense that, as Bakhtin was later to argue, 'every discourse has its own selfish and biassed proprietor; there are no words with meanings shared by all.'[23] This sense in Charlotte Brontë dates from childhood. It is writ large in the distancing humour of those youthful writings in which she objectified, contemplated, and played with the discourses that shaped her world. But it comes to the fore in a quite new way in *Shirley*, not merely in those recurrent images of Babel division, but in a distinctive and innovatory play with the novel form.

The romantically expressive individualism of a Caroline, a Shirley, is countered in the novel by the emphasized sense that they inhabit a world of others' words. 'When I meet with *real* poetry, I cannot rest till I have learned it by heart, and so made it partly mine,' says Caroline (95). When Louis recites a passage 'deliberately, accurately, with slow impressive emphasis', Shirley takes 'the word up as if from his lips . . . his tone . . . his very accent . . . his manner, his pronunciation, his expression', and finds 'lively excitement in the pleasure of making his language her own' (493–4). There is a succession of more extended images of recitation and of reading. Sometimes, at such moments, others' words become a vehicle through which repressed emotion can be expressed: Caroline's recitations of 'La Jeune Captive' (94)

---

[20] Elizabeth Gaskell, *Mary Barton*, ed. Stephen Gill (Harmondsworth: Penguin, 1970), 474 n. 8. The 5th edn. of *Mary Barton* (1854) included as an appendix *Two Lectures on the Lancashire Dialect* by Mrs Gaskell's husband, Revd William Gaskell.

[21] Gaskell, *Mary Barton*, 440–1.

[22] *Coriolanus* was a much disputed text in the early 19th cent. See e.g. the opposing political readings debated in the *Monthly Repository*, 8 (1834), 41–54, 76–81, 129–39, 190–202, 292–9.

[23] M. M. Bakhtin, *The Dialogic Imagination: Four Essays* (Austin, Tex., and London: University of Texas Press, 1981), 401.

and 'The Castaway' (226);[24] Shirley's singing of 'snatches of sweet ballads' (225); Martin Yorke's solitary reading of fairy tales (567–8). Those words may, indeed, be enriched in the process, as Shirley's singing breathes life into Sir Philip Nunnely's song (544). But perhaps more prominently there is difficulty: 'She began to read. The language had become strange to her tongue; it faltered: the lecture flowed unevenly, impeded by hurried breath, broken by Anglicised tones' (484).

Again and again in the novel, that which is here called 'lecture' has an oddly disruptive effect. Hymns, an essay, a diary, snatches of poetry and song are interpolated into the narrative, signs of that Babel division which fractures the fictional world. Again and again, others' words appear intransigent in their difference, giving utterance to voices and perspectives that cannot be contained within the narrative frame. Samples of each of the 'different strains' of the Methodists' hymns are given for the reader's perusal; their peculiar jauntiness, their paradoxical violence, their lurid biblical shorthand an abrupt and startling contrast to the ironies of the narrative voice (144–6). The novel's description of Caroline's most intimate humiliation is interrupted by an extract from an 'old Scotch ballad, written I know not in what generation nor by what hand'; the reprinted stanzas with their dialect 'images of horror' bring bursting into the novel a resentful energy quite at odds with the psychic economy of the represented world. 'But what has been said in the last page or two is not germane to Caroline Helstone's feelings', remarks the narrator, disingenuously (106). But the represented 'misery' remains, to colour and complicate the narrative, much as the painting of a 'night-eruption of Vesuvius' 'blazes' and 'glows' in the sitting-room at Briarmains (147). Thus, differently, but no less tellingly, the hymn that Mrs Pryor sings in her 'fading' daughter's sickroom erupts into the novel with a strangely disturbing force, opening up perspectives quite different from those of that domestic scene. Here, there is no difference of register or of dialect: Watts's stanzas are familiar, requested, known. But the vision of time and change they evoke is one that cannot be incorporated into the fictional world. Caroline makes no comment, but asks for another song: her uncle, overhearing, hastens to escape (431). And here, as elsewhere, the narrating voice makes no attempt (as Gaskell would) to explain: the sense, rather, is of an otherness—social, psychic, cosmic—that the narrative cannot contain.

'In *Shirley* all unity . . . is wanting . . . It is not a picture; but a portfolio of random sketches,' complained George Henry Lewes in a review.[25] Yet this lack of 'unity' is, it is beginning to seem, less a sign of authorial ineptness than expressive of the novel's vision of the nature of its world. For the society presented here is not merely a chaos of competing voices: it is one that different voices configure in radically different ways. 'Young parsons and grand folk fro' London is shocked at wer "*incivility*",' says Joe Scott, early in the novel. 'It's sport to us . . . to hear 'em say, nipping off their

---

[24] 'Cowper's poem, "The Castaway", was known to them all, and they all at times appreciated, or almost appropriated it,' Mary Taylor recalled of the young Brontës (Gaskell, 580).

[25] Unsigned review, *Edinburgh Review*, quoted in *CH* 164–5.

words short, like—Dear! dear! Whet seveges! How very corse!' (59). 'Certain sets of human beings are very apt to maintain that other sets should give up their lives to them and their service,' reflects Caroline. 'They call them devoted and virtuous' (174). Language here is a weapon in social struggle. 'You shall hear from us again,' the Luddites threaten, in a note to 'the Divil of Hollow's-miln' (33). 'I've no grand words at my tongue's end, Mr Moore,' says the pacific William Farren, 'but I feel that it wad be a low principle for a reasonable man to starve to death like a dumb cratur' . . . I'll talk,—I'll mak' as big a din as ever I can' (137). More comically, the Dissenters' 'dolorous canticle' gives way in the face of their opponents' singing of 'Rule, Britannia'. 'The enemy was stung and stormed down . . . as far as noise went, he was conquered,' is the narrator's sardonic remark (304). Indeed, the novel's most violent moment—the sound of the 'volley of musketry' from the attacked mill—is greeted by one of several ironic invocations of the image of Pentecost: 'Moore speaks at last! . . . and he seems to have the gift of tongues; for that was not a single voice' (344).

The public world of *Shirley* is a world made up of words. 'Nothing can happen that is not sure to get into a newspaper,' declared an article in *Fraser's* for January 1848, the month in which the novel was begun. 'Newspapers contain every thing, and are found every where. The threads of newspaper correspondence enclose the whole globe in a net-work of espionage.'[26] When Moore and Helstone quarrel at a public meeting, their dispute is continued in 'some pungent letters in the newspapers' (168). Moore, visiting Shirley, brings with him 'a batch of newspapers, containing . . . accounts of proceedings in Nottingham, Manchester, and elsewhere' (248). 'This was known at Briarfield: the newspapers had reported it: the "Stilbro' Courier" had given every particular, with amplifications,' the narrator reports of the sentence on the attackers of Moore's mill (528). 'Women read men more truly than men read women,' declares Shirley. 'I'll prove that in a magazine paper some day when I've time' (352). 'I should think you read the marriages, probably, Miss,' says Joe Scott, patronizingly, as she boasts of her newspaper-reading (327); and the novel's account of its heroine's marriages is in the language of newspaper report (645).

In the course of planning *Shirley*, Mrs Gaskell tells, Charlotte Brontë sent for the files of the *Leeds Mercury* of 1812–14.[27] This has usually been taken as indicative of her desire to acquire more detailed information about the historic events with which her novel was to be concerned. Yet from childhood the author of *Shirley* had been rather more canny than this. 'We take 2 and see three Newspapers as such we take the Leeds Inteligencer party Tory and the Leeds Mercury Whig': thus wrote the 13-year-old Charlotte in 1829.[28] It seems that the impulse that led her, twenty years later, to turn once again to the *Mercury* 'in order to understand the spirit'[29] of the

---

[26] 'Current History', *Fraser's Magazine* 37 (1848), 113.   [27] Gaskell, 378.

[28] 'The History of the Year', 12 March 1829, in Juliet Barker (ed.), *Charlotte Brontë: Juvenilia 1829–1835* (London: Penguin Classics, 1996), 2.

[29] Gaskell, 378.

times of which she was to write was less a simple desire to acquaint herself with the 'facts' than a more sophisticated awareness that 'facts' are refracted, always, through differing voices and perspectives; that information is a contested, opinion a constructed thing. For in *Shirley,* the 'issues of the day'—Luddite insurrection, the position of women, the progress of the war with France—appear not as unmediated 'facts' but as objects of discussion and report. 'Sich paragraphs as we could contrive for t'papers!' cries Mr Yorke, fantasizing a victory over 'these starved ragamuffins of frame-breakers'. 'Briarfield suld be famous; but we'se hev a column and a half i' th' *Stilbro' Courier* ower this job, as it is, I daresay: I'se expect no less.' 'And I'll promise you no less, Mr Yorke, for I'll write the article myself,' the militant Helstone replies (41). 'Lord Wellington's own despatches in the columns of the newspapers' are per-used in quite different ways by the 'high Tory' Helstone and the 'bitter Whig', Robert Moore (102, 168). Even that question of the fate of single women which calls up Caroline's most intimate fears appears not merely as a subject for private reflec-tion but also—indeed, most strikingly—as a theme of public talk. Both Caroline's solitary musings and Shirley's pronouncements on the subject are shot through with an awareness of that which others are wont to say: 'other people solve it by say-ing, "our place is to do good to others" ' (174); 'hard labour and learned professions, they say, make women masculine, coarse, unwomanly' (229); 'Lucretia . . . and Solomon's virtuous woman, are often quoted as patterns of what "the sex" (as they say) ought to be' (392). 'I often wish to say something about the "condition of women" question,' Charlotte Brontë had written in to her publisher in May 1848; 'but it is one respecting which so much "cant" has been talked, that one feels a sort of reluctance to approach it.'[30] Some of that 'cant' is directly reproduced in her next novel's most ironic invocation of the public press: its verbatim quotation of phrases from the hostile review that *Jane Eyre* had received in the *Quarterly Review* (376–7).[31] Here, in a manner unintended by the character who quotes them, those magisterial strictures appear in a mockingly critical light. The novel itself takes its place in the midst of that 'wordy combat' (56) which is its image of the social world.

For in *Shirley* authoritative discourse is objectified and ironized not merely by the characters but also by the narrative voice. Thus, for example, the novel's ac-count and explanation of the social unrest with which it deals:

The 'Orders in Council', provoked by Napoleon's Milan and Berlin decrees, and forbidding neutral powers to trade with France, had, by offending America, cut off the principal market of the Yorkshire woollen trade, and brought it consequently to the verge of ruin. Minor for-eign markets were glutted, and would receive no more. The Brazils, Portugal, Sicily, were all overstocked by nearly two years' consumption. At this crisis, certain inventions in machin-ery were introduced into the staple manufactures of the north, which, greatly reducing the number of hands necessary to be employed, threw thousands out of work, and left them

---

[30] Charlotte Bronte to W. S. Williams, 12 May 1848 (*CBL* ii. 66).
[31] Charlotte Brontë's own Preface to the novel, rejected by her publishers, was a more extended, elab-orately comic riposte to this same review: entitled 'A Word to the Quarterly', it is reprinted as Appendix C to *Shirley,* ed. Herbert Rosengarten and Margaret Smith (Oxford: Clarendon Press, 1979).

without legitimate means of sustaining life. A bad harvest supervened. Distress reached its climax. Endurance, overgoaded, stretched the hand of fraternity to sedition; the throes of a sort of moral earthquake were felt heaving under the hills of the northern counties. But, as is usual in such cases, nobody took much notice. When a food-riot broke out in a manufacturing town, when a gig-mill was burnt to the ground, or a manufacturer's house was attacked, the furniture thrown into the streets, and the family forced to flee for their lives, some local measures were or were not taken by the local magistracy; a ringleader was detected, or more frequently suffered to elude detection, newspaper paragraphs were written on the subject, and there the thing stopped. As to the sufferers, whose sole inheritance was labour, and who had lost that inheritance—who could not get work, and consequently could not get wages, and consequently could not get bread—they were left to suffer on, perhaps inevitably left; it would not do to stop the progress of invention, to damage science by discouraging its improvements; the war could not be terminated, efficient relief could not be raised; there was no help then, so the unemployed underwent their destiny—ate the bread, and drank the waters of affliction.   (30–1)

This might at first seem a straightforward—indeed, emphatic—expression of what one early reviewer called Charlotte Brontë's 'rational acquiescence in the inevitable tendencies of society'.[32] Social and economic processes are figured, here, as abstract and inexorable law, rebellion as natural disaster ('the throes of a sort of moral earthquake'), and suffering as the will of God. If here, as elsewhere in *Shirley*, the voice that speaks echoes those of others, here all seem to speak in unison, rather than oppose. The sonorous periods of historical summary ('the "Orders in Council", provoked by Napoleon's Milan and Berlin decrees'), the deterministic axioms of political economy ('it would not do to stop the progress of invention'), the repetitive reports of those ineffective 'newspaper paragraphs' ('some local measures were or were not taken by the local magistracy'), the mystifying rhetoric of political generalization ('the war could not be terminated, efficient relief could not be raised'), the pontifical pronouncements of tract and sermon ('so the unemployed underwent their destiny—ate the bread, and drank the waters of affliction') chime together in a series of confirming appositions, just as, in the actual England of 1811, the progressive arguments of the political economists, the laissez-faire doctrines of the Whigs, and the nostalgic conservatism of a Toryism supported by faith in a divinely ordained order of things all concurred to produce 'no help'.[33]

---

[32] Unsigned review, *Examiner*, quoted in *CH* 128.
[33] Several important studies have, indeed, quoted this passage as straightforwardly expressive of its author's point of view. Thus, Terry Eagleton complains that 'the novel's attitude to the working class wavers . . . between panicky contempt and paternalist condescension. The workers' plight is regretted, but nothing can be done: it is sad that those thrown out of work are left to suffer, but they are "perhaps inevitably left: it would not do to stop the progress of invention, to damage science by discouraging its improvements" ' (*Myths of Power: A Marxist Study of the Brontës* (London: Macmillan, 1975), 49–50). See also Patrick Brantlinger, *The Spirit of Reform: British Literature and Politics, 1832–1867* (Cambridge, Mass., and London: Harvard University Press, 1977), 125; Rosemarie Bodenheimer, *The Politics of Story in Victorian Social Fiction* (Ithaca and London: Cornell University Press, 1988), 42–3; Patricia Ingham, *The Language of Gender and Class; Transformation in the Victorian Novel* (London: Routledge, 1996), 34–5.

Yet the novel's insistent concern with the linguistic construction of its world might alert us to read this less as the complacent voice of an unexamined determinism than as a more critically inflected representation of some of those chiming or conflicting languages through which Charlotte Brontë's contemporaries sought to make sense of the society in which they lived. It is not merely that sonorous generalization—'the throes of a sort of moral earthquake were felt heaving under the hills of the northern counties'—is undercut in a debunking change of register—'But, as is usual in such cases, nobody took much notice.' Syntax and imagery throughout seem half parodically to emphasize the fatalistic view of social process to which the passage gives voice. Thus, the insistent nominalizations and passivizations configure a world in which abstract entities ('the Orders in Council', 'minor foreign markets', 'certain inventions in machinery', 'some local measures', 'distress', 'endurance', 'the thing') take on a strange life of their own, and the sources of agency are obscure. Here, as in the novel's later description of the repeal of the Orders in Council (in a chapter called 'The Winding Up'), the long pseudo-logical sentences convey a sense not merely of a train of events that all are powerless to change, but also of a logic running away with itself. Here, the Orders in Council appear not as an act of national self-assertion, but as a mere reaction 'provoked by Napoleon's Milan and Berlin decrees': they lead only to the denial and suppression of action and transaction—they 'forbid', they 'offend', they 'cut off'. Even the ostensibly powerful are peculiarly ineffective—'some local measures were or were not taken by the local magistracy; a ringleader was detected or more frequently suffered to avoid detection': the images—underlined by the tolling negatives of the final sentence—are all of impotence, stalemate, hopelessness. This seems less a straightforward expression than a marked stylization of the fatalism implicit in the languages of social explanation which the passage orchestrates. And this sense comes to the fore as the paragraph draws to a close. 'As to the sufferers . . . they were left to suffer on,' the narrator concludes; 'perhaps inevitably left'. In the wake of the emphatically deterministic language of the preceding paragraph, that 'perhaps' has a peculiar force. For it is through the chink thus opened in the seamlessness of the analysis that the 'inevitabilities' that condemn the 'sufferers' to their 'destiny' appear, as the sentence proceeds: not as 'open-faced facts'[34] but through a series of modal verbs—'*It*

---

[34]   The phrase is Edward Thompson's, from his account of the same historical moment, in *The Making of the English Working Class* (Harmondsworth: Penguin, 1968), 224–5: 'The Orders in Council had in 1811 brought certain trades almost to a standstill . . . the power-loom competed with the hand-loom. But even these open-faced facts, with their frank credentials, deserve to be questioned. Whose Council, why the Orders? . . . The raw fact—a bad harvest—may seem to be beyond human election. But the way that fact worked its way out was in terms of a particular complex of human relationship: law, ownership, power. When we encounter some sonorous phrase such as 'the strong ebb and flow of the trade cycle' we must be put on our guard. For behind this trade cycle there is a structure of social relations, fostering some sorts of expropriation (rent, interest, and profit) and outlawing others (theft, feudal dues), legitimizing some types of conflict (competition, armed warfare) and inhibiting others (trade unionism, bread riots, popular political organization)—a structure which may appear, in the eyes of the future, to be both barbarous and ephemeral.' *Shirley*, as Thompson complains (613), contains none of this kind of questioning of the immutability of circumstance. But, as I have been suggesting, it is in a different way 'on guard'.

would not do to stop the progress of invention'; 'the war *could not* be terminated'; 'efficient relief *could not* be raised'—that signal the defensive or sardonic distance of the narrative voice from the positions it entertains.

This is hardly the voice of protest: the 'would' and 'could' of others' opinions hardens, inexorably, here, into the 'was' of incontestable fact. But the passage is more subversive than might at first appear. As the narrator speaks of the 'sufferers . . . who could not get work, and consequently could not get wages, and consequently could not get bread', the repetition of 'consequently' draws attention not merely to the inexorability of 'progress', but also to the mode of explanation focused in the word. This is the impersonal, 'objective' language of causality: 'consequently' is, after all, a logical term. Yet here it is charged with a far from dispassionate awareness of how and why it was actually used in early nineteenth-century England, and by whom. Such causal connectives as this were prominent in the discourse of political economy: they could be deployed with confidence by those who were in a position to offer an authoritative analysis of their world. 'Have you taught them the science of consequences?' Mrs Gaskell asks in *Mary Barton*, as she describes the bewilderment of the starving, helpless to understand the forces that keep them down.[35] Yet that distancing authority had, in the early nineteenth century, been challenged, in ways of which Charlotte Brontë seems to have been aware.[36] Thus, for example, her childhood hero Byron, in his famous maiden speech in the House of Lords, delivered at the height of the Luddite agitation in the debate on the Frame-Work Bill, addresses himself to the fact that 'improvements' in technology have 'superseded the necessity of employing a number of workmen, who were left *in consequence* to starve . . . The rejected workmen, in the blindness of their ignorance, instead of rejoicing at these improvements in arts so beneficial to mankind, conceived themselves to be sacrificed to improvements in mechanism' (my italics).[37] 'In consequence' here shocks, and it is clearly meant to shock; much as Pope's polite—but devastatingly rhymed—'observe', shocks in his third *Moral Essay*:

> What Nature wants, commodious Gold bestows,
> 'Tis thus we eat the bread another sows:
> But how unequal it bestows, observe,
> 'Tis thus we riot, while who sow it, starve.[38]

---

[35] Gaskell, *Mary Barton*, 219.

[36] She would have been familiar with the extensive attacks on and burlesques of the arguments of the political economists that appeared in *Fraser's Magazine* (taken in the Parsonage) during the 1830s. Thus e.g. 'Morgan Odoherty' (William Maginn) in *Fraser's*, 9 (1834), 322: 'Abstract doctrines of democracy and political economy are endowed with the sole control of public affairs, to the exclusion of all interference on the part of national conviction and desire. Institutions and laws—property and subsistence—trade, currency, and finance—religion and morals—are placed under rules as arbitrary as those of arithmetic and geometry.'

[37] Byron's speech is reprinted as an Appendix to Michael Foot, *The Politics of Paradise: A Vindication of Byron* (London: Collins, 1988), 398–404.

[38] Alexander Pope, *Moral Essays. Epistle III. To Allen Lord Bathurst*, 21–4, in John Butt (ed.), *The Poems of Alexander Pope* (London: Methuen, 1963), 572.

Byron, like Pope, is concerned not merely with the fact that his is a world in which the 'advantage' of some means the starvation of others, but with the smoothness with which the rhetoric of impartial analysis ('considerable injury has been done to the proprietors') and suave generalization ('these improvements in arts so beneficial to mankind') can accommodate such a fact.[39] And the sardonic irony with which he inflects that rhetoric is focused most sharply, here, in the blandly explanatory 'in consequence' by which he offers to connect two incommensurable realities—the abstract 'necessity' of economic progress and the actual plight of those who are 'left' in its wake. The ingratiating language of economic expediency—an 'advantage', 'the necessity'—is disrupted by an abrupt confrontation of an all-too-material 'consequence': the workers have been 'left . . . to starve'. 'Left'—a word which, like 'consequently', Charlotte Brontë repeats in the final sentence of the passage we have been considering—indicates the distanced perspective of privilege from which he and his audience ('the polished part of society', as the Nottingham Framework-Knitters were to call them)[40] are considering their plight.

Yet if there is a similar critical inflection of those 'polished' idioms in *Shirley*, here it seems to be pointing towards rather different concerns. Byron's 'modest impudence' is informed and underwritten by an urgent sense, here and throughout his speech, of the claims of real men to be regarded not as expendable objects of others' calculations but as of 'consequence' in themselves.[41] Against the impersonal summations of economic analysis, he sets the 'foolishness' of the 'rejected workmen', who 'imagined that the maintenance and well-doing of the industrious poor were objects *of greater consequence* than the enrichment of a few individuals by any improvement in the implements of trade' (my italics).[42] In doing so, he invokes a perspective quite different from that of the 'glib economists', and a scheme of value that poses—however impotently—a radical challenge to theirs. But this perspective and this challenge seem curiously peripheral in *Shirley*. The arguments of the workers are, it is true, portrayed. Moore's peroration on the resistless march of progress—'Suppose that building was a ruin and I was a corpse, what then? . . . would that stop invention or exhaust science?—not for the fraction of a second of time!' (136)—is answered by William Farren's simple observation, 'Invention may

[39] It is hard to know which angered Byron the more: the outrages themselves or the excuses . . . he heard from the ministers or their supporters,' observes Michael Foot (*The Politics of Paradise*, 137).

[40] 'It is true that Government has interfered in the regulation of wages in times long since gone by; but the writings of Dr Adam Smith have altered the opinion, of the polished part of society, on this subject. Therefore, to attempt to advance wages by parliamentary influence, would be as absurd as an attempt to regulate the winds' (United Committee of Nottingham Framework-Knitters, quoted in Thompson, *The Making of the English Working Class*, 586). As Geoffrey Hill remarks of this passage, 'the framework-knitters of 1812 know that the polish is that of adamant' ('Redeeming the Time', in *The Lords of Limit*, 86–7).

[41] 'I spoke very violent sentences with a sort of modest impudence, abused every thing & every body, & put the Ld Chancellor very much out of humour,' wrote Byron to Francis Hodgson of this speech (Leslie A. Marchand (ed.), *Byron's Letters and Journals* (12 vols.; London: John Murray, 1973), ii. 167).

[42] Foot, *The Politics of Paradise*, 399. 'We must not allow mankind to be sacrificed to improvements in Mechanism,' Byron was to write to Lord Holland on 25 February 1812. 'The maintenance & well doing of ye. industrious poor is an object of greater consequence to ye. community than ye. enrichment of a few monopolists by any improvement in ye. implements of trade' (*Byron's Letters and Journals*, ii. 165).

be all right, but I know it isn't right for poor folks to starve' (137): the entrepreneur's frustration—'I cannot get on—I cannot execute my plans' (25)—is tellingly echoed in a clergyman's question to a starving family, 'How do you get on?' (139). Indeed, the rebuke that might be presented to the standpoint of the polite by those who were the objects of their arguments is focused, later in the novel, in a more explicit consideration of 'consequently' itself. 'I see a great deal of distress', says Farren to Shirley. 'And consequently, there is still discontent, I suppose?' she asks. '*Consequently*—ye say right—*consequently*,' he replies, ironically repeating and emphasizing the word. 'In course, starving folk cannot be satisfied or settled folk. The country's not in a safe condition;—I'll say so mich!' (325). And the difference to which he points, between the decorous language of polite rational explanation ('*Ye* say') and the starker, more violent idiom of the dispossessed ('*I'll* say so mich'), is writ large when Moore's polished arguments are answered not merely by the voice of antinomian prophecy but by the 'fierce flash and sharp crack' of the bullet that lays him low.

Yet if such moments as these indicate Charlotte Brontë's familiarity with the questions on which Byron's irony turns, that concern is undeveloped in *Shirley*. There is remarkably little, here, of that sense of the 'consequence' of the disregarded which animates Byron's arguments, and of which other novelists were, in the middle years of the century, most eloquently to speak. The 'starving' are scarcely mentioned in the novel's final volume: when they do appear, in the closing pages, it is simply as objects of the manufacturer's altered ambition, grateful denizens of his successful new mill-town. Moore's reformation—which might have provided the 'moral' of a more conventional 'condition-of-England' novel—is dealt with perfunctorily, and is reported, rather than seen. Most disquietingly of all, perhaps, precisely those questions that for others in these years were the subject of urgent debate are evoked, and left suspended—'Let us hope they have enough to eat; it would be a pity were it otherwise' (62); 'as to the sufferers . . . they were left to suffer on, perhaps inevitably left' (30)—in a manner that suggests a deliberate refusal to deliver what the reader of a work on such a subject would expect. As the narrator remarks sardonically in the novel's concluding words: 'I think I now see the judicious reader putting on his spectacles to look for the moral . . . I only say, God speed him in the quest!'

That refusal is not, however, mere frivolity or evasiveness. For, as that closing jibe reminds us, a novel is not, like a speech in parliament, directed towards an end. If *Shirley*'s ironies are more elusive than Byron's impassioned conviction, the issues to which they point are subtly yet decisively different from those with which he is concerned. For the world the novel delineates is less that place in which some hold power and others do not of which Byron's ironies speak than one which even those who act most decisively are impotent to change. The repetition of 'consequently' in the passage I have been considering signals not merely that opposition between the arguments of economic expediency ('in consequence') and the claims of humanity ('of consequence') which is the mainspring of Byron's invective, but a rather different concern: a multiply inflected awareness of untranscendable determinism, which is reinforced and underlined throughout. It is this, rather than the rhetoric of moral responsibility, that throughout the novel most fundamentally questions the aspirations and ambitions that drive the characters forward. And it is in this that one can trace *Shirley's* essential difference from the 'condition-of-England' novels with which it is so often compared.

II

That difference is perhaps most strikingly evident in the novel's portrayal of Robert Moore, figure of a thrusting ambition—shared, it is said, by 'thousands besides'—that seeks its fulfilment at others' expense. *Shirley's* interest here is not, it seems, primarily in an ethical judgement of the mill-owner, such as one finds, for instance, in *Mary Barton* and *North and South*. Gaskell's questioning of entrepreneurial 'independence' through her heroine, Margaret Hale, is prefigured, it is true, in *Shirley*, in Caroline's questioning of Robert Moore. But Caroline's consciousness is not the voice of the novel; and her criticisms of her lover are peripheral to its central imaginative thrust. The shaping interest is less in 'whether his advance was or was not prejudicial to others' (29) than in a wholly different kind of challenge to that ambivalently seen 'advance'. 'At the time this history commences, Robert Moore had lived but two years in the district, during which period he had at least proved himself possessed of the *quality of activity*' (29; my italics). The energy that drives Moore forward is figured, strikingly, as a noun—a passive attribute, rather than an active force. And that which is foregrounded here is implicit in the novel as a whole. Moore enters the narrative less as an independent agent than as one who is subject to a causality beyond his control. In the paragraphs that introduce him the striving entrepreneur is described in terms that emphasize passivity and unfreedom. 'Trade' is not for him a chosen occupation but a 'hereditary calling'. He is the inheritor of traits which (probably) determine his actions ('A hybrid in nature, it is probable he had a hybrid's feeling on many points'); the victim of 'by-past circumstances' not of his own making; his mind 'impressed in no golden characters' by 'a childhood passed ... under foreboding of coming evil, and a manhood drenched and blighted by the descent of the storm' (27–8).

That which is inscribed in the narrator's account of Moore is writ large in the novel's plot. This 'thoroughgoing progressist' (31) is one whose progress is 'checked' (29). 'Curbed by poverty', 'rendered ... prone' by 'circumstances' to 'confine his attention and efforts to the furtherance of his individual interest', he is 'baffled at every turn' by 'the untoward effects' of a political situation beyond his control (29, 167, 25). *Shirley's* imaging of this is more resonant and more developed than *The Professor's* ironic interrogation of Crimsworth's pursuit of success. Moore's most urgent desire is portrayed as a desperate drivenness: 'straitened on all sides as I am, I have nothing for it but to push on' (162). His most defiant assertion—'Here I stay; and by this mill I stand'—carries a darker, more desolate charge: '*Suppose that building was a ruin and I was a corpse*, what then? ... would that stop invention or exhaust science?—Not for the fraction of a second of time! Another and better gig-mill would rise on the ruins of this, and perhaps a more enterprising owner come in my place' (136; my italics). Moore is described by the narrator—with suggestive ambiguity—as a 'man of determined spirit';[43] he breasts 'the storm of unpopularity with gallant bearing and soul elate' (529). But again and again he is figured less as heroic subject than as replaceable object, a mere cog in a process of technological advance that continues heedless of his, or any individual's, agency, and regardless of his, or any individual's, fate.[44]

Some such sense indeed in these years formed the basis of the manufacturers' case against the workers' demands. 'When you talk of the working classes not being independent, but being in the hands of the masters, on the other hand do you conceive the masters to be independent?' demanded the counsel questioning Richard Oastler before a Select Committee of the House of Commons in 1832;[45] and his words are echoed in *Shirley* by the 'baffled' mill-owner Moore: 'if I stopped by the way an instant, while others are rushing on, I should be trodden down. If I did as you wish me to do, I should be bankrupt in a month: and would my bankruptcy put bread into your hungry children's mouths?' (138). Yet the novel's emphasis on Moore's unfreedom goes beyond such reasoned arguments. That tension between aspiration and the determining force of circumstance which is focused in the image of the 'baffled' entrepreneur is echoed and confirmed throughout, in its depiction of desires and energies quite different from his. Louis Moore, his brother, is a 'satellite of the house of Sympson'; 'his faculties seemed walled up in him' (455); the young Henry Sympson 'burns day and night . . . to be—to do—to suffer', but his mind 'lies in physical bondage' within a crippled frame (465). Moore's ambition and his impotence are paralleled by Caroline's fruitless longings and enforced passivity. If he is 'curbed' by poverty, her feelings are 'curbed and kept down' (347). 'I see no more light than if I were sealed in a rock', says he, of his business prospects (163); her life calls up the image of 'the toad's, buried in marble . . . for ever shut up in that glebe-house—a place . . . like a windowed grave' (399). And if her romantic dreams are seen more sympathetically than his entrepreneurial ambitions, the sense of entrapment here imaged is confirmed in her case too by the narrating voice. For she—in marked contrast to Jane Eyre—is presented from the perspective of a knowing disenchantment, as one about to submit to the 'resistless' authority of Experience (98), whom the promise that 'Reality' holds out (97) is doomed, inevitably, to disappoint. 'Impossible for her now to suspect that she was the sport of delusion:

---

[43] The phrase is used twice in the narrator's account of Moore's reaction to the smashing of the frames (32) and again of Moore in the discussion of *Coriolanus* (93).

[44] The terms in which he presents himself are ironically reminiscent of those in which the displacement of the skilled 'artisan' by the mere replaceable 'operative' was, in the early 19th cent., being deplored by Tory commentators. Thus e.g. Edward Edwards speaks in *Blackwood's Magazine* for 1830 of the way in which the 'labouring classes' are 'in many places as much parts of machinery as are spindles. Thousands are but cogs' ('The Influence of Free Trade Upon the Condition of the Labouring Classes', *Blackwood's Magazine*, 27 (1830), 582).

[45] Quoted in Catherine Gallagher, *The Industrial Reformation of English Fiction: Social Discourse and Narrative Form 1832–1867* (Chicago and London: Chicago University Press, 1985), 27.

her expectations seemed warranted, the foundations on which they arrested appeared solid' (99): the ordinary past tense of narrative here takes on a bleaker significance. Like the romance of Mrs Radcliffe's of which she speaks to Rose Yorke (400), hers is not a story that opens out into possibility, but one whose ending is already known.

The novel's other heroine at first appears quite different. Less constrained than Moore by economic necessity, more defiant than Caroline of conventional 'womanliness', she counters the narrow individualism of economic self-interest with the aristocratic assertion of a self free from all control. Hers is the compelling 'freedom' of a Byronic aspiration that refuses to submit to constraints that others obey. If the 'pictures' filling Caroline's dreams are all simply 'images of Moore' (173), hers have the 'genii-life' of a more transcendent desire (387). Yet by the end she is 'vanquished and restricted . . . like any other caged denizen of deserts', 'conquered by love, and bound with a vow' (637). More extremely than Moore's or than Caroline's, her trajectory seems to speak of the emptiness of fulfilment: that sense that the dream might be 'firmer or at any rate brighter than its realization'[46] which hovers in the novel's closing image of the promised mill-town is writ large in her warning to her lover, as he pleads with her to 'fix our marriage-day'—'You don't know how happy you are!—any change will be for the worse!' (631). And the novel's account of her reveries speaks not of power, but of impotence: 'her eye seeks, and her soul possesses, the vision of life as she wishes it. No—not as she wishes it; *she has not time to wish*: the swift glory spreads out, sweeping and kindling, and multiplies its splendours *faster than Thought can effect his combinations, faster than Aspiration can utter her longings*' (387; my italics). Shirley's is a dreaming that can find no realization, even in the world of 'Thought'; in which the dreamer herself is effaced. The narrative voice describes her with a cool, analytic detachment, and moves on to distance the moment into the completed past:

Had she a little more of the organ of Acquisitiveness in her head . . . she would . . . write plainly out . . . the story that has been narrated, the song that has been sung to her, and thus possess what she was enabled to create. But . . . she does not know, has never known, and *will die without knowing*, the full value of that spring whose bright fresh bubbling in her heart keeps it green.   (388; my italics)

If that reference to her dreams as a 'genii-life' is, for those who know Glass Town, charged with remembered excitement, it carries also a more chilling reminder of promise blasted and hopes destroyed. The narrator's 'she will die without knowing' is to be echoed later in the novel, in 'He shall die without knowledge'—the 'peculiar' words of prophecy that precede the shooting of Moore (543). That sense of opening possibility which shaped the young Jane Eyre's story is here replaced by a different feeling: the future is not unknown, but all too decisively foretold.

Like those of *The Professor* and *Jane Eyre*, *Shirley*'s is a world of urgent striving. But here the third-person narrative allows that striving to be seen in quite a differ-

---

[46] Ernst Bloch, *The Principle of Hope*, trans. Neville Plaice, Stephen Plaice, and Paul Knight (3 vols.; Oxford: Blackwell, 1986), ii. 181.

ent way. For here, the portrayal of aspiration is countered by an estranging sense of the characters *as* characters, objectified and distanced by a more knowing narrative voice. In each of those earlier novels, the thrust of the narrative is forward; there is little sense, at the opening of either, of where its story will lead. But the opening paragraphs of *Shirley* speak of a present day that is 'dusty, sunburnt, hot, arid': this novel will tell of a 'dawn' whose promise has not been fulfilled. Here, as in *Don Juan*, the narrator looks back, ironically, on the world of thirty years before: here, as there, the sense is less of contemplating a past whose conflicts are now resolved, than of a sardonic undercutting of that hopeful aspiration which, in the form of the characters' schemes and desires, will drive the narrative forward. It is a sense that is emphasized and confirmed as *Shirley* comes to an end.

In the novel's closing paragraphs, those whose desires and energies have animated the narrative are distanced into the past of a 'story' that is told. Here, the narrative time becomes that of 'the other day', and the narrator-figure enters the novel, listening to his 'old housekeeper' 's stories of the neighbourhood. The moment recalls that in which Lockwood, at the ending of *Wuthering Heights*, listens to Nelly Dean's account of the tales of 'the country folks' (*WH* 336). Yet like most such echoes in Charlotte Brontë, it speaks of difference from her sister, rather than of similarity.[47] Indeed, in *Shirley*'s brisk 'winding-up' of loose ends, its stress on finality and pastness, one might well trace a sombre, ironic riposte to that sense of conflicts unresolved and a yet-continuing tale with which *Wuthering Heights* had closed. The revenant dead, the perhaps unquiet graves, of that earlier novel have here been replaced by the speeded-up time of a stark modernity. The emphasis is not on renewal, but on despoliation and loss: not on open-ended possibility, but on a process of disenchantment. Memory is not collective—outlasting individual life, pointing into an ongoing future—but private, and disappearing. As the narrator's obtrusive glosses on the housekeeper's words insist, even language is an obsolescent thing. If the ending of *Wuthering Heights* points ambiguously outwards and forwards, *Shirley*'s seems designed to produce a precisely opposite effect.

The closing chapter does tell of a series of ' "good" outcomes' to the dilemmas the novel has portrayed.[48] The paralysis imposed by the Orders in Council is ended; Caroline attains her desires; Robert Moore's 'day-dreams' are realized; the workers are employed. But each of these resolutions appears in an ambiguous light. The 'prosperity' brought by the repeal of the Orders in Council is described with a deflating irony:

all, like wise men, at this first moment of prosperity, prepared to rush into the bowels of speculation, to delve new difficulties, in whose depths they might lose themselves at some future day. Stocks, which had been accumulating for years, now went off in a moment, in the twinkling of an eye; warehouses were lightened, ships were laden; work abounded, wages rose: the

---

[47] 'Charlotte told me, that the remarks made had seldom any effect in inducing her to alter her work,' says Mrs Gaskell, of Brontë's descriptions of the sisters' nightly readings to one another of 'the stories they were engaged upon' (Gaskell, 307–8).
[48] Eagleton, *Myths of Power*, 47.

good time seemed come. These prospects might be delusive, but they were brilliant—to some they were even true.   (637)

This speeded-up picture of uncontrollable, unpredictable economic process, within which men are helpless dupes rather than effective agents—more like the surrealism of Pope's third *Moral Essay* than the realist nineteenth-century novel— underwrites, rather than answers to, that sense of human powerlessness inscribed in *Shirley*'s presentation of the public world. And there is a similar ironic perfunctoriness in the novel's account of the marriages in which its heroines' stories end: 'This morning there were two marriages solemnized in Briarfield church,—Louis Gérard Moore, Esq., late of Antwerp, to Shirley, daughter of the late Charles Cave Keeldar, Esq. of Fieldhead: Robert Gérard Moore, Esq., of Hollow's mill, to Caroline, niece of the Rev. Matthewson Helstone, M.A., Rector of Briarfield' (645). In a striking reversal of Jane Eyre's self-affirming 'I married him,' Caroline and Shirley are objectified and distanced by the reporting narrative voice, even their names swallowed up in a patriarchal litany. Once again, the feeling is less of satisfaction and completion than of a peculiar, mocking dismissal of that disruptive subjective immediacy that has marked their stories throughout.

This brisk 'winding-up' of the novel's romantic plot is succeeded by an account of a different kind of 'fulfilment': one that is likewise questioned even as it is portrayed. 'I suppose', says the narrator, 'Robert Moore's prophecies were, partially, at least, fulfilled' (645). The Hollow has become a mill town. But the emphasis is less on achievement than on usurpation and desolation. There is little sign, here, of that succour once promised for 'the houseless, the starving, the unemployed': the manufacturer's 'day-dreams' are 'embodied'[49] not in bread, but in stone. The 'unmolested trees' of the spot where Caroline and her mother walked (372) have given way to 'stone and brick and ashes': a 'cinder-black highway' runs through 'the romantic Hollow' which only 'tradition' now recalls as 'once green, and lone, and wild'. The Hollow, now dominated by the Urizenic arrogance of 'a mighty mill, and a chimney, ambitious as the tower of Babel', is less a place of thriving life than a monument to one man's dreams. And this sense of history not as progress but as loss is underwritten in the closing paragraphs, as the future to which the characters looked becomes the completed past, and the narrating voice gives way to the housekeeper's longer view. Those who have occupied the foreground become mere vanishing memories, as the process of 'alteration' (646) moves imperviously on.

Others in the mid-nineteenth century were responding to the march of industry in apparently similar terms. 'The pastoral scene, the ancient association, the romantic solitude, fly before . . . the forges, the hammers, and the looms of industrial prowess,' Edwin Hood was to write in the following year:

every thing speaks of the conquest of the old order of things—the stream is stained with the refuse of a hundred mills—the atmosphere is heavy and dark—the green turf, the meadow,

---

[49] Charlotte Brontë's desire to convey a sense of lifeless materiality here is evident in her substitution of this word for 'realized' in the MS (Clarendon edn., 739).

the glistening plough-share, are all gone; that great sorcerer man, the labourer, has transformed the whole scene, and because he has done so, some imagine that our whole world is locked outside the very gates of Providence [*sic*].[50]

'He solemnly informed me that hell was foreordained my inevitable portion; that he read the mark of the beast on my brow,' says Robert Moore of Barraclough (238), and *Shirley*'s description of the 'altered' Hollow, like many contemporary accounts of the fast-industrializing landscape, is touched with suggestions of hell.[51] He who was called by the Luddites 'the Divil of Hollow's-miln' (40) and a 'Lucifer' by Shirley (536), whose look the narrator described as seeming 'to invoke the devil' (125), has achieved the 'smooth descent' of his prophecies—a 'broad, black, sooty road, bedded with the cinders from my mill'(644). Even the 'cottage-gardens', which are the only signs of life, are mentioned simply as part of a catalogue of 'change'.[52] 'You will change our blue hill-country-air into the Stilbro' smoke atmosphere', Caroline has lamented, as Robert promises to turn the 'lonely watercourse' by which they once walked together (234) into 'the waters of Pactolus' and 'the green natural terrace' of the Hollow into a 'paved street' (644).[53] Yet the sense in *Shirley*'s closing paragraphs is not simply or even centrally of a natural paradise lost. It is darker, more ironic than this.

Here, even the achievements of industry are impermanent. If the Hollow has been 'altered' beyond recognition within the space of living (or at least remembered) memory, the alterations themselves have a strangely ephemeral air. The abrupt materialization of that which a few pages earlier has been articulated as 'prophecy' has the effect of an 'all but miraculous creation' (as one contemporary described the coming of the machine).[54] But it also has the effect of making the phenomena it

---

[50] Edwin Paxton Hood, *The Age and its Architects: Ten Chapters on the English People in Relation to the Times* (London: Charles Gilpin, 1850), 122–3.

[51] On the early 19th-cent. rhetoric of the industrial landscape as hell, see Francis D. Klingender, *Art and the Industrial Revolution*, revd. edn. (London: Paladin, 1968), 104–7; Humphrey Jennings, *Pandaemonium: the Coming of the Machine as Seen by Contemporary Observers, 1660–1886* (London: André Deutsch, 1985).

[52] 'Nor is there much satisfaction in contemplating the world with nothing left to the spontaneous activity of nature,' John Stuart Mill had written in the preceding year: 'with every rood of land brought into cultivation, which is capable of growing food for human beings; every flowery waste or natural pasture ploughed up . . . every hedgerow or superfluous tree rooted out, and scarcely a place left where a wild shrub or flower could grow without being eradicated as a weed' (*Principles of Political Economy* (1848), Book IV ch. 6 para. 3, in *Collected Works of John Stuart Mill*, gen. ed. J. M. Robson (20 vols.; Toronto: University of Toronto Press, 1965), iii. 756).

[53] Her protest prefigures Ruskin's warning to the political economists that 'there are three material things, not only useful, but essential to life . . . these are Pure Air, Water, and Earth'. *Fors Clavigera*, Letter V (1 May 1871), in E. T. Cook and Alexander Wedderburn (eds.), *Library Edition of the Works of John Ruskin* (39 vols.; London: Allen, 1912), xxvii. 91–2. And it has a curious antecedent in 'Sir—it is well known that the Genii', a Glass Town fragment dated 14 July 1829, apparently a letter to the editor of the *Young Men's Magazine*, describing the 'impudent' claim of the Genii 'that by their magic might they can reduce the world to a desert, the rivers to streams of livid poison and the clearest lakes to stagnant waters, the pestilential vapours of which shall slay all living creatures. . . . But in the midst of this desolation the Palace of the Chief Genii shall rise sparkling in the wilderness' (*EEW* i. 39).

[54] J. R. McCulloch, 'Philosophy of Manufacturers', *Edinburgh Review*, 61 (1835); cited in Judith L. Newton, 'Sex and Political Economy in the *Edinburgh Review*', *Starting Over: Feminism and the Politics of Cultural Critique* (Ann Arbor: University of Michigan Press, 1994), 119.

describes seem independent of human control. And the suddenly expanded time-scheme within which the manufacturer's achievements are placed brings with it the suggestion that these things, too, will in their time disappear. One is reminded of Engels's observation, in *The Condition of the Working Class in England in 1844*, that 'the workers' housing, built by speculators for fast profits, was constructed to last for only forty years';[55] one is reminded too of Shirley's earlier reference to 'that mill—your Moloch!' (535), and of the fate of those cities where sacrifices to Baal and to Moloch were made.[56] And this sense of the ultimate impotence of the ambitions here writ large is focused in the image of a 'chimney mighty as the tower of Babel' with which the narrator's description ends.

Partly, that resonant image points back to the 'wordy combat' in which the novel began. If the 'brick and ashes', the 'cinder-black highway' recall Milton's description of the building of Babel—

> a black bituminous gurge
> Boils out from underground, the mouth of hell
> Of brick, and of that stuff they cast to build
> A city and tower, whose top may reach to heaven
> (Book 12. 41–4)

—here, as in *Paradise Lost*, that description is succeeded by the 'jangling noise of words unknown' (55). Here, characteristically, the register is prosaic: simply a few words of the housekeeper's whose meanings have to be explained. Unobtrusively but decisively, they signal linguistic division, and hint—against those high-speed accounts of peace concluded and marriages made—that perhaps the conflicts the novel has portrayed will never be reconciled. But the image of the Tower of Babel has significances beyond this: significances that Brontë had been pondering for over twenty years.

For that Tower had been a potent symbol in the Brontës' youthful 'plays'. To children steeped in the Bible, the creation of that 'mighty phantasm' must have seemed liked the building of Babel described in Genesis 11: 6: 'this they begin to do: and now nothing will be restrained from them, which they have imagined to do'. Their joking awareness of this is indeed registered early in the 'plays', when 'the Tower of Babylon' appears as the mightiest of the buildings of Glass Town.[57] Later,

---

[55] Marshall Berman, *All that is Solid Melts into Air: The Experience of Modernity* (London and New York: Verso, 1983), 99 n. 'The pathos of all bourgeois monuments', writes Berman, 'is that their material strength and solidity actually count for nothing and carry no weight at all, that they are blown away like frail reeds by the very forces of capitalist development that they celebrate.'

[56] See e.g. Hosea 2: 8–13; Jeremiah 19: 8; 32: 35–6. Such prophecies were of new interest in the early years of the 19th cent. because of the archeological excavations for the first time being made at the cities of which they spoke.

[57] It appears as 'the Tower of Babylon' amongst the Advertisements in *Blackwood's Young Men's Magazine* for December 1829 (*EEW* i. 97). 'I lay awake for the whole night on the morrow of which I might expect to catch the first glimpse of Babel', recalls a character in the August 1830 number of the same journal (*EEW* i. 224). In another early fragment, Glass Town is described as Babylon, and the Tower of All Nations is shrouded in the fog that emanates from 'her huge furnaces and great thunder-shaken edifices, misnomered mills' (*EEW* i. 334). An untraced manuscript, entitled 'A Book of Rhymes',

as the Tower of All Nations, it was to come to serve as an image of the chaos of competing voices—'the dissonant cries of all nations, kindreds and tongues, congregated together'[58]—that made up the fictional world. But this was the least of its meanings. For the Tower spoke also of the irony which informed those youthful 'plays': their constant undercutting awareness not merely of the aspiring energies but also of the ultimate impotence of those whom the Genii had made. In the early Glass Town writings, it is mainly in a comic spirit that this meaning of the Tower is evoked. Thus, the young Charlotte writes expansively of 'the Glass Town, of whose splendour, magnificence and extent, power, strength and riches, occasional tidings came from afar'. 'But', she continues,

to most of the inhabitants of [England] it bore the character of a dream or gorgeous fiction. They were unable to comprehend how mere human beings could construct fabrics of such a marvellous size and grandeur as many of the public buildings were represented to be; and as to the Tower of All Nations, few believed in its existence. It seemed as the cities of old Nineveh or Babylon with the temples of their gods . . .[59]

'Oh, thou great, thou mighty tower!' she apostrophizes it, more humorously, in a poem written on October 7, 1829:

> Thou seem'st, as silently I gaze,
>   Like a pillar of the sky:
> So lofty is thy structure grey;
>   So massive, and so high!

And grandiosity is abruptly punctured by the poem's closing lines—

> And such a charming doggerel
>   As this was never wrote
> Not even by the mighty
>   And high Sir Walter Scott.

—with their comic sense (not unrelated to the sardonic self-reflexiveness of the final paragraph of *Shirley*) of the dependence of this mighty edifice, indeed, the whole world of Glass Town, upon the writing child.

Yet such jokes about fictionality had, even from the beginning, darker resonances than this. 'I found myself lifted by a hand wide enough almost to grasp the Tower of all Nations': if Lord Charles Wellesley's disconcerting experience testifies to the mighty power of the Genii, it opens up also a perspective very different from theirs—one writ large in the image of the Tower that the Brontë children knew best. In the heady years of the building of Glass Town, a mezzotint of John Martin's *Belshazzar's Feast* hung in Haworth Parsonage; it hung there still as Charlotte

---

listed in the fourteen-year-old Charlotte Brontë's *Catalogue of my Books with the periods of their completion up to August 3, 1830*, includes a poem entitled 'On Seeing the Ruins of the Tower of Babel' (*EEW* i. 214).

[58] 'The Bridal', 20 August 1832, *EEW* i. 338.
[59] 'Albion and Marina', A Tale by Lord Wellesley, 12 October 1830, *EEW* i. 290–1.

Brontë finished *Shirley* in the summer of 1849.[60] In this image, the Tower of Babel has a peculiar, eerie centrality. The foreground is taken up by the lavish, interrupted feast, the diminutive forms of a terrified multitude, dwarfed by colossal architecture, overshadowed by a gathering storm. But the 'perspective of feeling', as Martin called it,[61] draws the observer's eye ever inwards to the background, where the Tower, surrounded by lightning, trembles on the brink of destruction, a doomed, ambiguous figure of the immensity of human aspirations, the futility of human schemes. The most striking feature of the painting—more striking, indeed, in the mezzotint—is the way in which the whole is lit up by the glaring writing on the wall.[62] That writing, being interpreted, spelt mortality: it would hardly have been possible for Charlotte Brontë to use the image of the Tower in the summer after her sisters' deaths without calling this to mind. 'Worse than useless did it seem to attempt to write what there no longer lived an "Ellis Bell" to read,' she was to write of her struggle to finish *Shirley.* 'The whole book with every hope founded on it, faded to vanity and vexation of spirit.'[63] Just so, in the novel's final paragraphs, and perhaps in implicit rejoinder to the lost 'Ellis Bell', *Shirley*'s world of desire and enterprise is 'faded' into the distance of a vanished past.[64] Perhaps it is not too fanciful to see, playing through the novel's description of the manufacturer's ambitious 'schemes', an ironic reference to the potency of that brighter 'darling dream';[65] in their embodiment in 'a mill . . . mighty as the tower of Babel', a hint of that shared 'mighty phantasm', always instinct with an awareness of its own insubstantiality, and now forever gone.

Yet freighted though they are with private memories, these closing pages of the novel are not an artless expression of its author's subjective despair. Here, the Tower is a mill-chimney, familiar emblem of that 'progress' which was transforming the Pennine landscape in the years in which the Brontës grew up. Looming in the once-green hollow, it is a precise and telling reminder of the novel's informing concerns—the heterogeneous voices, the antagonisms and divisions, that fracture its social world; the powerful yet doomed aspirations that drive the characters for-

[60] *Belshazzar's Feast* was exhibited in Leeds from 1 November 1823 to the end of January 1824, when Patrick Brontë may have bought the mezzotint, which was still in the Parsonage at his death (Barker, 213–14; Joanna Hutton, 'The Sale at Haworth Parsonage', *BST* 14: 75 (1965), 46–50).

[61] Quoted in William Feaver, *John Martin 1789–1854* (Catalogue sold in aid of the National Art-Collections Fund, Loan Exhibition of Oil Paintings, Water Colours, Prints at Hazlitt, Gooden & Fox, 30 October–21 November 1975), 6.

[62] This effect was noted by contemporaries, and stressed in Martin's descriptions. Indeed, as an advertisement, he displayed an enamel-painting of the subject on glass in the Strand, 'inserted in a wall so that the light was really transmitted through the terrible handwriting' (Richard Redgrave, *Century of Painters of the English School* (1865), quoted in Thomas Balston, *John Martin 1789–1854: His Life and Works* (London: Gerald Duckworth & Co., 1947), 58).

[63] Charlotte Brontë to W. S. Williams, 16 April 1849 (*CBL* ii. 203).

[64] In the autumn of the following year, in her 'Biographical Notice' of Emily, she was to attack her sister's critics by developing an extended image of Belshazzar's feast and the writing on the wall ('Biographical Notice of Ellis and Acton Bell', in Emily Brontë, *Wuthering Heights*, ed. Hilda Marsden and Ian Jack (Oxford: Clarendon Press, 1976), app. 1. 438).

[65] 'We wove a web in childhood', 19 December 1835, in Barker (ed.), *Charlotte Brontë: Juvenilia*, 264.

ward. The constellation of feeling signalled by its figuring as Babel is certainly rather different from the moral concern with the social consequences of industrialism that shaped the condition-of-England novels of these years. Yet it was by no means merely a private, eccentric one. For as the presence of that mezzotint in the Parsonage at Haworth suggests, it was prominent within the culture in which Charlotte Brontë grew up.[66]

John Martin's prodigious canvasses spoke of that soaring ambition, that attempted 'mastery' of nature, writ large in the mighty constructions and unprecedented transformations of the advancing industrial age.[67] Yet they were also disquieting images of the comparative impotence of man. The Tower of Babel in his *Illustrations of the Bible* (1835)—a series apparently known to the Brontës—was based on an engraving of Lymington Iron Works on the Tyne: it portrayed ant-like figures toiling to tend vast furnaces, dwarfed by an enormous tower.[68] Martin's human figures were not triumphant achievers, but helpless pawns of the Almighty, dwarfed amidst mighty landscapes, threatened and overwhelmed: his subjects the collapse of civilizations—Babylon, Nineveh, Jerusalem—or disasters cosmic in scale. Such were the prints that hung in the Parsonage, the three great mezzotints by which the painter first made himself a household name: *Belshazzar's Feast, The Deluge, Joshua Commanding the Sun to Stand Still*. Each, with its striking images of the awesome power of the Almighty, made its own unanswerable comment on that confidence that man can shape the world according to his own desires inscribed in the march of industry and in the artist's own progressive 'schemes'.[69]

What Martin offered the Brontë children was less a vague sense of 'grandiose achievement'[70] than a vision of aspiration shot through with apprehensions of doom. Central to their construction of their imaginary world was a sense of—indeed a play with—the contradictions of his. That sense must for them have been reinforced by their youthful reading of Byron,[71] the other great shaping influence

---

[66]   When *Belshazzar's Feast* was first exhibited at the British Institution in 1821, it had to be cordoned off from the enthusiastic crowds: because of its popularity, the exhibition was kept open for three extra weeks (Balston, *John Martin*, 58). On Brontë's response to Martin, see Winifred Gérin, *Charlotte Brontë: The Evolution of Genius* (Oxford: Oxford University Press, 1967), 43–50; Christine Alexander, ' "The Burning Clime": Charlotte Brontë and John Martin', *Nineteenth-Century Literature* 50: 3 (December 1995), 285–321.

[67]   Martin's Babylonian vistas, indeed, inspired industrial architecture, and he himself spent most of his time and his income on a series of ambitious 'schemes' of his own for London's water supply and sewage, not unlike Robert Moore's plans to 'pour the waters of Pactolus through the valley of Briarfield' (644), though on a far grander scale (Feaver, *Art of John Martin*, ch. 6).

[68]   Feaver, *Art of John Martin*, 143–4; Alexander, 'The Burning Clime', 294–5.

[69]   Alexander and Sellars, *Art of the Brontës*, 12. These , produced between 1826 and 1828, were the first three of Martin's large mezzotints.

[70]   Gérin, *Charlotte Brontë*, 43.

[71]   Along with Milton and the Bible, Byron formed Martin's chief reading-matter throughout his life, and many of his paintings were on Byronic themes (Balston, *John Martin*, 175). On the use of Martin's images in the staging of Byron, see Martin Meisel, 'The Material Sublime: John Martin, Byron, Turner and the Theater', in Karl Kroeber and William Walling (eds.), *Images of Romanticism: Verbal and Visual Affinities* (New Haven and London: Yale University Press, 1978), 211–32.

on their adolescent 'plays'.[72] Charlotte Brontë's passion for Byron is perhaps most obviously evident in the 'high life' settings, the love-wracked heroines, the defiant, immoral, irresistible heroes of the fictions of her later teens. But Byron's legacy to the young Brontës (and, indeed, to the culture at large) was rather more complex than this. For within his writings heroic ambition and passionate desire appear, again and again, from a perspective of diminishing irony. *Childe Harold* and *Don Juan* speak not simply of quest and conquest. The former's plangent questions,[73] the latter's brilliant flippancies, in their different ways articulate a darker, more ironic, vision of human insignificance and the transience of earthly things. More suggestively yet, perhaps, for the reader of *Shirley*, Byron's dramas offer not simply a seductive entry into a world of eastern exoticism, but awful glimpses of a limitless universe within which 'men walk darkling to their doom'.[74] Martin's *Belshazzar's Feast* and *Fall of Nineveh* had indeed been prefigured in Byron's 'Vision of Belshazzar' and *Sardanapalus*; Martin's yawning gulfs and awful vistas by those cosmic visions of human littleness, *Heaven and Earth* and *Cain*; Martin's magnificent cities, poised on the brink of destruction, by Byron's dramatic images of aspiration swallowed up in 'vast desolate night'.[75]

If both Martin and Byron were disapproved by critics, both were immensely popular. Even the spartan Parsonage at Haworth possessed three large Martin mezzotints and (as the Bill of Sale for the Parsonage puts it) several costly 'Byron books'. For that excitement of aspiration, that terror of insignificance inscribed in Byron's comic and tragic ironies, writ large in Martin's canvasses, can be traced throughout the records of the time. On the one hand, those records evince a seemingly unprecedented exhilaration at human achievements and confidence in human powers. 'Man in the civilized world feels a kind of omnipotence', Edwin Hood proclaimed, a year after *Shirley* appeared:

he knows that, either by speculation or action, industry has wrought all the marvels of which civilization makes its boast; he tore up the forest that the carriage might move through it, made a highway through the old granite rock, called up the city from the desolation of the desert, with the sound of whirring wheels, tall chimnies, and smoky skies . . . Magic! Wizardry! Who ever heard of magic like that of industry?[76]

---

[72] Byron was known to Charlotte Brontë as early as 1829: as Winifred Gérin points out, she quotes from both *Manfred* and *Cain* in her 'Tales of the Islanders' of that year (*Five Novelettes*, 13). But, as Gérin suggests, he becomes a major presence in her writings only after 1833, when Patrick Brontë's edition of the *Collected Works* appears to have been purchased (*Emily Brontë* (Oxford: Oxford University Press, 1978), 44).

[73] See e.g. Canto V of *Childe Harold* , which seems to have been in Charlotte Brontë's mind in the months after her siblings' deaths. She rewrites stanza 141, with its image of prying into the abyss—'To gather what we shall be when the frame | Shall be resolv'd to something less than this | Its wretched essence; and to dream of fame, | And wipe the dust from off the idle name | We never more shall hear'— in a tenderer, less egocentric key, in the closing words of her Biographical Notice of her sisters: 'This notice has been written, because I felt it a sacred duty to wipe the dust off their gravestones, and leave their dear names free from soil'; and she quotes from the preceding stanza (describing the death of the Gladiator), in her description of William Farren's tears in *Shirley* (139).

[74] *Heaven and Earth* (1821), I. 3. l. 285, in Ernest Hartley Coleridge (ed.), *The Works of Lord Byron* (5 vols.; London: John Murray, 1898), v. 303.

[75] *Cain* (1821), I. i. 330, *Works of Lord Byron*, v. 222.   [76] Hood, *The Age and its Architects*, 13, 19.

In the year of Charlotte Brontë's death, Mrs Gaskell was to portray her heroine in *North and South* as thrilling to 'the exultation in the sense of power' that the manufacturers of Milton feel: 'they seemed to defy the old limits of possibility, in a kind of fine intoxication, caused by the recollection of what had been achieved, and what yet should be'.[77] Yet such 'exultation' is countered in the writing of the period by intuitions of a rather different kind. 'We penetrate the earth, we turn the course of rivers, we exalt the valleys and bow down the mountains; and we die and return to our dust, and they remain and remember us no more,' writes Fanny Kemble, after a visit to the Thames Tunnel in December 1827.[78] 'We stand in a Presence which has not, nor ever shall have one sympathy with ourselves', declares Thomas Hawkins, of the bones of an ichtyosaurus found in Somerset: 'those Worlds, those antipodal Populations, that Presence passionless, and silent dead; I say the instruments of a few bones verify a Sublimity before which no man can stand unappalled.'[79] 'Every person probably feels, at first, lost, confounded, overwhelmed, with the vastness of this spectacle,' confesses William Whewell, as he speaks of the vistas of time and space opened up by the advance of science, 'and seems to himself, as it were, annihilated by the magnitude and multitude of the objects which thus compose the universe.'[80] This sense of the puniness of human life can be traced in phenomena as various as the legacy of evangelicalism, with its constant reminders of human mortality and the awful omnipotence of God;[81] in the widespread interest in the excavation of Nineveh and Pompeii, whose ruins spoke of the impermanence of human achievements;[82] in the emerging sciences of geology and paleontology, with their evocation of vistas that eclipsed human aspiration;[83] in the development of an

---

[77] Elizabeth Gaskell, *North and South*, ed. Dorothy Collin (Harmondsworth: Penguin, 1970), 217.

[78] Frances Ann Kemble, *Record of a Girlhood* (3 vols.; London: Richard Bentley & Son, 1878), i. 196.

[79] Thomas Hawkins, *The Book of the Great Sea-Dragons: Icthyosauri and Plesiosauri* (London: W. Pickering, 1840), 15.

[80] William Whewell, *On Astronomy and General Physics Considered with Reference to Natural Theology* (*The Bridgewater Treatises on the Power, Wisdom and Goodness of God as Manifested in the Creation: Treatise III*); 7th edn. (London: William Pickering, 1839), 280. Whewell goes on to counter this sense, by invoking 'Divine care': but here and throughout his works, as throughout those of other scientific writers at this time, the more negative perception remains. For a fascinating discussion of this, see Susan Gliserman, 'Science Writers and Tennyson's *In Memoriam*: a Study in Cultural Exchange', *Victorian Studies*, 18: 3 (March 1975), 276–308.

[81] 'We have just seen something of the mighty power of God: he has unsheathed his sword, and brandished it over our heads, but still the blow is suspended in mercy—it has not yet fallen upon us,' Patrick Brontë had written of the bog-burst that the Brontës had witnessed as children in *A Sermon Preached in the Church of Haworth, in Reference to an Earthquake, in 1824* (J. Horsfall Turner (ed.), *Brontëana: The Reverend Patrick Brontë's Collected Works* (Bingley: T. Harrison & Sons, 1898), 218).

[82] Austen Layard's *Nineveh and its Remains* (described by *The Times* as 'the most extraordinary work of the present day') appeared in 1848–9, and caused an immediate public sensation: an abridgement was selling in railway bookstalls by 1851. Bulwer Lytton's *The Last Days of Pompeii* (1834) was one of the 'top ten' novels listed by W. H. Smith for 1848 (Raymond Williams, 'Forms of English Fiction in 1848', *Writing in Society* (London: Verso, n.d.), 151). The month after *Shirley* was finished, a long article appeared in *Fraser's* on 'the vestiges still remaining upon the site at Babel', enquiring into the motives of the builders of the tower. ('Babel', *Fraser's Magazine* 40 (1849), 318–27).

[83] No educated reader of the periodical press in the first half of the 19th cent. could have been unaware of the emerging—and theologically challenging—evidence from fossils and geological strata that 'mightier things have been extinct' (*Cain*, II. i), or of the immense amount of scientific speculation on

increasingly secular, scientific view of nature as a vast mechanism of which man was but a tiny part. Each of these cultural phenomena also bespoke a will to power: that evangelical ambition expressed (for example) in the rhetoric of missionary sermons; the Smilesian enterprise with which archeologists were succeeding in uncovering the secrets of the ancient world; the palaeontologists' ambition to 're-vivify the whole Universe that is gone' and enshrine it in a museum which will lead to the improvement of the race;[84] the aspiration to scientific and clinical authority in the professionalization of science and of medicine. Yet against the mighty ambition, the massive triumphs of the emerging industrial age each sets a differently inflected sense of the littleness of human life, against that attempt to assert domination over nature writ large in the 'alteration' of the landscape, a counter-awareness of perspectives within which man shrinks into insignificance, and of powers before which all inescapably must bow.

It is of this constellation of feeling, enshrined so compellingly early in the century in the works of Martin and of Byron, that *Shirley* in its own way speaks. There is, of course, nothing in this novel like the vast disquieting vistas of *Heaven and Earth* or of *Cain*, nothing like Martin's images of disaster and apocalypse. The references in the opening paragraphs to cooking, to ironing, to the nursery, give notice that this will be an 'unromantic' world. Yet with a characteristic irony *Shirley* signals that the great contradictions that Byron and Martin configure are also its concern. For their mighty visions appear within it, diminished, emasculated, contained. The eruption of Vesuvius, subject of one of John Martin's famous early images of catastrophe, is glimpsed as a picture in the sitting-room at Briarmains—albeit the 'most sinister' object in the room (147, 150).[85] 'The passage of the Red Sea', of which the Brontë family possessed a framed John Martin engraving, is more extensively evoked, as Yorke and Moore argue over the Peninsular wars: that which Martin portrayed with visionary grandeur has become an example to clinch an argument, over which two half-ridiculed figures squabble like dogs over a bone (39). 'I suppose you fancy the sea-mammoths pasturing about the bases of the 'everlasting hills', devouring

the subject of the pre-Adamite world. See Charles Coulston Gillispie, *Genesis and Geology: A Study in the Relations of Scientific Thought, Natural Theology, and Social Opinion in Great Britain, 1790–1850* (New York: Harper & Row, 1959); Milton Millhauser, *Just Before Darwin: Robert Chambers and Vestiges* (Middletown, Conn.: Wesleyan University Press, 1959); James A. Secord, *Victorian Sensation: The Extraordinary Publication, Reception, and Secret Authorship of Vestiges of the Natural History of Creation* (Chicago and London: University of Chicago Press, 2000). John Martin, who had a lively interest in palaeontology, illustrated Gideon Mantell's *The Wonders of Geology* and engraved the frontispiece to Hawkins's *Book of the Great Sea-Dragons.*

[84] Thus Hawkins, of his reconstructions of primeval creatures from their bones (*Book of the Great Sea-Dragons*, 20). For the desire to educate through museum-displays, see Thomas Hawkins, *Memoirs of Ichthyosauri and Plesiosauri* (London, 1834), 29–30; and Gideon Mantell, *Petrifications and Their Teachings; or, a Hand-book to the Gallery of Organic Remains of the British Museum* (London: Henry G. Bohn, 1851).

[85] Martin's *The Destruction of Herculaneum and Pompeii* (1822) was one of a number of artistic depictions of its subject during the early years of the century. 'Pompeii', argues Laurence Goldstein, 'became a symbolic code word for what Madame de Staël calls 'death's abrupt invasion'. It fostered a dark literature of premature burial, natural calamity, and universal extinction' ('The Impact of Pompeii on the Literary Imagination', *Centennial Review*, 23 (1979), 229).

strange provender in the vast valleys through and above which sea-billows roll,' says Shirley, playfully, to Caroline (245): the colossal primeval creatures that fired contemporary fantasies are here mere fanciful images, enlivening a conversation between two gently bred girls. Even the familiar images of *Belshazzar's Feast* are comically redeployed. The heiress's uncle is silenced by 'something in Shirley's face,—a very awful something—inscrutable to him as the writing on the wall to Belshazzar', and is 'moved more than once to call Daniel, in the person of Louis Moore' (547). And these teasing reminders of Martin are accompanied by others, of Byron. Shirley's Titan vision of Eve as possessing 'the daring which could contend with Omnipotence: the strength which could bear a thousand years of bondage,— the vitality which could feed that vulture death through uncounted ages' (320) would, for the mid-nineteenth-century reader, have been full of tantalizing echoes of his heretical, provocative, but immensely popular *Cain*:[86]

> Souls who dare use their immortality—
> Souls who dare look the Omnipotent tyrant in
> His everlasting face, and tell him that
> His evil is not good! [87]
>
>   for to give birth to those
> Who can but suffer many years, and die,
> Methinks is merely propagating death . . .[88]

'You have got such a hash of Scripture and mythology into your head that there is no making sense of you', remarks the listening Caroline, in an affectionately deflating way (321). And the same domesticating ironies surround the novel's more explicit allusions to *Cain*'s sequel, *Heaven and Earth*. For as some, at least, of *Shirley*'s contemporary readers would have noted with a shock, the epigraph and subject of Shirley's school-essay are those of that mighty drama of primeval disaster and doom: 'And it came to pass . . . that the sons of God saw the daughters of men that they were fair; and they took them wives of all which they chose.[89] 'She felt the world, the sky, the night, boundlessly mighty. Of all things, herself seemed to herself the centre,—a small, forgotten atom of life . . . now burning unmarked to waste in the heart of a black hollow,' writes Shirley of her heroine (487), recalling *Cain*'s desolate vision of a world of 'animated atoms | All living, and all doom'd to death, and wretched';[90] its stage-direction '—The Abyss of space'.[91] Where *Cain* ends in disaster, and *Heaven and Earth* in the Deluge, Shirley's heroine achieves triumphant 'immortality'. But as that sardonic chapter-title, 'The First Blue-Stocking', suggests, this feminist attempt

---

[86] 'A magnificent poem,' the 18-year-old Charlotte Brontë had termed it, in a letter to Ellen Nussey on 4 July 1834 (*CBL* i. 128). On *Cain*'s popularity in the period, see Samuel Chew, *Byron in England: His Fame and After-Fame* (London: John Murray, 1924).

[87] *Cain*, I. i. 177–80, *Works of Lord Byron*, v. 218.   [88] *Cain*, II. ii. 77–9, ibid. v. 235.

[89] For a suggestive account of the relation between Byron's dramas (especially *Heaven and Earth*) and Emily Brontë's *Wuthering Heights* see Stevie Davies, *Emily Brontë* (Hemel Hempstead: Harvester Wheatsheaf, 1988), 121–5.

[90] *Cain*, II. i. 53–4, *Works of Lord Byron*, v. 234.   [91] *Cain*, II i. ibid. v. 233.

at the sublime is emphatically circumscribed. It appears, indeed, in a shape that expressly signals breeding and accomplishment—a *devoir* composed in order to improve a young lady's proficiency in French. Cosmic vision here has shrunk to the contours of a schoolgirl exercise, remembered for sentimental reasons and recited (somewhat improbably) by the tutor whose 'censor-pencil' once 'scored it with condemnatory lines' (490).

The romanticism here invoked is quite different from that which is invoked in *Jane Eyre*: that of Martin's apocalyptic landscapes rather than of Finden's beauties, the Byron of ironic deflation and cosmic darkness rather than of exotic promise and aristocratic allure. And it is invoked in quite a different way. In *Jane Eyre*, a highly popular, much-disparaged constellation of feeling was rescued from condescension and given serious weight. Here, the visionary is ironized and contained. Just as, in the actual world of early nineteenth-century England, Byron's and Martin's images of catastrophe, of the vastness of time and space, were softened and commodified into 'poetic gems' and fashionable songs, reproduced, diminished, and framed, as 'illustrations' in the fashionable annuals or to decorate drawing-room walls,[92] so here they appear as a detail in a 'back-parlour', a fantastic day-dream, an essay in an old copy-book, the subject of teasing badinage or serio-comic dispute. There is an echo here of the mock-heroics of Glass Town—those childish jokes through which the four Chief Genii articulated their awareness of the gulf between the actual circumstances of their 'plays' and the materials on which they drew. Yet images as familiar as these might—as the Brontë children's play with that of the tower of Babel suggests—be parodied, domesticated, ridiculed, and still not lose their serious force. Indeed, as their reading of Byron must have taught them, the irony might itself be part of the point. For if this structure of feeling is quite unlike that of *Jane Eyre*, it is one that is no less echoed by the imaginative shape of the novel in which it appears. Whereas *Jane Eyre* points forward, throughout, to an as yet unreached future (a trajectory that is emphasized in St John Rivers's closing plea), the ironized visions of *Shirley* are echoed in an irony of structure, a constant placing movement of retrospect. Here, that earlier novel's compelling realization of the utopian import of 'dreams' has been replaced by a darker configuration: one that speaks not of possibilities denied by the conditions of life in early nineteenth-century England, but of a quite untranscendable reality.

---

[92] In the eleven years between 1826 and 1837 John Martin's work appeared twenty-seven times in various annuals: from 1835 until his death numerous engravings after his work appeared not only in the annuals but in a variety of other books. He attained his greatest popularity through his prints, which were not merely produced in large runs, but also much copied and pirated. See William Feaver, Introduction to *John Martin 1789–1854*, 15, 17, 9. On the commodification of Byron in the early 19th cent., see Peter Manning, 'Childe Harold in the Marketplace: From Romaunt to Handbook', *Modern Language Quarterly*, 52 (1991), 170–90 and Andrew Elfenbein, *Byron and the Victorians* (Cambridge: Cambridge University Press, 1995), ch. 4.

III

In 1850, Charlotte Brontë, on a visit to London, was taken to the Royal Academy, where she was particularly struck by two canvasses: 'a large one by Landseer of the Duke of Wellington on the field of Waterloo, and a grand, wonderful picture of Martin's from Campbell's poem of the "Last Man", showing the red sun fading out of the sky, and all the soil of the foreground made up of bones and skulls'.[93] The contrast between those two paintings—the one an image of the foremost living Englishman, recounting his mightiest triumph on that field of lasting fame; the other that of one left utterly desolate, bereft of all social ties—may well have spoken to her poignantly of her own situation: on the one hand, successful and celebrated beyond her youthful dreams, on the other, 'stripped and bereaved' of those she loved most on earth.[94] Yet each of these immensely popular paintings resonated, too, with more than private significances: significances writ large in the novel that she had completed in the preceding year.

Landseer's *Dialogue at Waterloo* had been produced to cater to that hero-worship which was, in these years, still centred—albeit ambivalently—upon the Duke of Wellington.[95] It depicts an aged but imposing figure on horseback, occupying a commanding position in the landscape at which he points: not merely a hero, but a patriarch, with his daughter-in-law, the beautiful Marchioness of Douro (object of many of Brontë's youthful fantasies) at his side. The image is of potency in all its senses: of one whose effectiveness is unquestioned, whose posterity and fame are assured. Yet the picture is not without its ambiguities—some, perhaps, of an unintended kind. Landseer's patron, Robert Vernon, had originally commissioned 'a grand canvas' of the actual battle of Waterloo, to be engraved and afterwards donated to the nation as part of a larger bequest. But Landseer found it difficult to paint battles, or any such crowded scene. In this case, he was eventually forced to abandon the attempt, and to produce instead this rather wooden 'dialogue', with its far smaller group of figures and its aged, reminiscing Duke.[96] The suggestion, inevitably, is that martial triumph has become a tale of the past. The other figures in the painting are a ploughman—symbol of the peace that Wellington has ensured in Europe—and a group of souvenir sellers, such as by now were to be found peddling mementos of his victory on the field of Waterloo. And if these may be taken as suggesting that this victory still has meaning, they are images that suggest, also, that remembered glory has given way to a mercantile world.

It is a configuration of feeling not unlike that of *Shirley*. Indeed, it is in its depiction of the figure portrayed in this painting, hailed by the narrator as a 'demi-god',

---

[93] Charlotte Brontë to Revd Patrick Brontë, 4 June 1850 (*CBL* ii. 411).
[94] Charlotte Brontë to W. S. Williams, 13 June 1849 (*CBL* ii. 220).
[95] Even before it was finished its subject meant that 'drawing room walls throughout the land were screaming for the engraving' (Campbell Lennie, *Landseer: the Victorian Paragon* (London: Hamish Hamilton, 1976), 151).
[96] Ibid. 151.

that one finds that novel's least equivocal celebration of heroic human agency, its most unironic account of what such agency can achieve: 'In this year, Lord Welling-ton assumed the reins in Spain: they made him Generalissimo, for their own salva-tion's sake. In this year, he took Badajos, he fought the field of Vittoria, he captured Pampeluna, he stormed St. Sebastian; in this year, he won Salamanca.' But in *Shirley* this litany of victories is likewise a tale of the past: 'Lord Wellington is, for you, only a decayed old gentleman now' (636). And the aftermath of his triumphs—the repeal of the Orders in Council—is portrayed in terms that ironically stress that which the Landseer perhaps unconsciously registers: that the brave new world he has ushered in is one not of heroes but of 'Merchants and Manufacturers' (636).

Yet if, in its refusal or failure to glamorize its subject, Landseer's painting suggests that *Shirley*'s disenchanted perspective was shared by others at this time, Martin's, with its remoter subject-matter, offers perhaps the more revealing insight into the contemporary fantasies and realities of which the novel speaks. Here, the viewer is confronted by a lone human figure, not dominating but dwarfed by the landscape in which he appears. This is no conqueror showing the scene of his triumph to an admiring young woman, but one who gestures impotently towards the indifferent sun. The image is not of peace and plenty, but of a world turned to ash and ruin; not of fame (however ambiguous), but of finality. Yet it is an image less remote from the actualities of life in early nineteenth-century England than might at first appear. For if Martin's painting, like Landseer's, was inspired, partly, by fashion, it was also a re-sponse to all-too-material fact. He had painted a *Last Man* (this one in water-colours) in 1832—the year of the first great British epidemic of cholera, 'one of the most terrible pestilences which have ever desolated the earth'.[97] And when he re-turned to the subject, it was at a time when dread of 'pestilence' once again domin-ated public consciousness and shaped private imaginings—during the cholera epidemic of 1848–9. The fleeing hordes of his great biblical subjects were in this painting replaced by a single isolated figure, the grandeur of Babylonian architec-ture by a waste of bones and skulls. Yet this last survivor of humanity is not, like the lonely heroes of Martin's earlier romantic landscapes (Sadak, Manfred, the Bard), the only figure in the composition. Beside him, on the ground, is the lifeless body of a girl. It is an arresting image of the most intimate, least assimilable meaning of Martin's great visions of unavoidable doom. And it is an image that points towards *Shirley*. For if there is nothing in *Shirley* of Martin's visionary vastness, at two key moments in the novel the reader is suddenly confronted, as Martin here confronts the viewer, with an image of the death of a girl, and a prospect of the future as not open, but closed. They are moments that interrupt, rather than contribute to, the narrative. But they are directly expressive of an awareness that shapes the whole.

Twice, in the midst of a description of a lively social scene, the novel looks for-ward to the future, and to the death of one of the most vital participants: little Jessie Yorke, 'gay and chattering, arch—original', 'as hearty a little Jacobin as ever pent a free mutinous spirit in a muslin frock and sash' (149, 407). Each time, the narrator

<hr>

[97] Feaver, *Art of John Martin*, 187; *Quarterly Review*, 46 (1832), 170.

intervenes directly: in the first, offering Jessie's father a 'magic mirror' that will disclose his daughter's destiny—the grave in a foreign cemetery that will be hers within twenty years (149);[98] in the second (407–8) with a diary-like immediacy that has led one twentieth-century commentator to describe it as 'a direct and startling impression of the author actually at work writing, looking out on the church-yard at Haworth',[99] and another, more critically, to complain that 'the continuity of the scene is broken . . . and whatever emotion is felt is diverted from the real theme'.[100] The effect—reinforced by Jessie's marginality within the narrative—is certainly of disruption. These are not conventional prolepses, which describe events that will be dealt with more fully later in the narrative: they point quite out of the novel's frame. Yet the effect is less of a change in narrative perspective than of a vivid realization of that which is implicit throughout. For here, that ironic movement which again and again in the novel places the characters' strivings and desires within a wider determining frame comes to the fore, as Jessie's vitality is curbed, not by her controlling mother, but by a voice that foresees her future and relegates it to the past. The fictive illusion that the narrated present is progressing towards an open future is punctured with disconcerting suddenness. And the abruptness is part of the point. The concern that is focused here is not with the questioning and tempering of subjective purposes by a social world to which they must be accommodated, but with their absolute defeat in death.

It is a concern that is registered in the novel with an almost flippant literalism, as each of the four main characters is threatened with extinction: Caroline struck low by a mysterious fever, Moore cut down by a would-be assassin, Louis succumbing to illness and 'obliged to keep his chamber' (479), Shirley bitten by an apparently rabid dog. But on a quietly realistic level, too, death is an everyday feature of the novel's social world. 'There are two funerals', Cyril Hall says casually, as he speaks of the duties for which he must leave 'the cozy circle' around 'the bright little school-room fire' (470). 'Consumption or decline would close the chapter', says Mrs Pryor, as she describes the fate of the 'broken down' governess. 'Such is the history of many a life' (378). People observe how others are 'altered' by illness: the signs of mortality are everywhere read. If Helstone does not, others perceive the signs of Mary Cave's 'lingering decline' (53). When they observe those 'reduced to pallor, debility, and emaciation', 'people think . . . that they will soon withdraw to sickbeds, perish there, and cease' (191). Miss Mann's 'corpse-like' aspect, her 'bloodless pallor of complexion', give evidence of 'cruel, slow-wasting, obstinate sufferings'—a

[98] The *Literary Souvenir* for 1830, from which Charlotte Brontë copied two plates, contained a poem by Mrs Hemans, entitled 'The Magic Glass', which envisages such a 'magic mirror'. The feeling here, however, is closer to that of a passage from *Suspiria de Profundis*, published in *Blackwood's Magazine* for July 1845, in which de Quincey considers 'the past viewed not *as* the past, but by a spectator who steps back ten years deeper into the rear in order that he may regard it as a future,—the calamity of 1840 contemplated from the station of 1830,—the doom that rang the knell of happiness viewed from a point of time when as yet it was neither feared nor would even have been intelligible.' (David Masson (ed.), *The Collected Writings of Thomas de Quincey* (14 vols.; Edinburgh: A. & C. Black, 1897), xiii. 352).
[99] Margaret Smith, Introduction to *Shirley*, p. xxi.
[100] Rebecca West, 'Charlotte Brontë', *The Great Victorians*, ed. H. J. Massingham and Hugh Massingham (London: Nicholson & Watson, 1938), 73.

'canker . . . deeply corroding' of a quite literal kind (201–2). When Caroline begins to decline, the 'change' in her looks is noticed by 'everyone': 'most people said she was going to die' (214); 'Miss Keeldar . . . had at first entertained no fears at all for her friend; but seeing her change and sink from time to time when she paid her visits, alarm clutched her heart' (424). The change that comes over Shirley herself is remarked by those about her: 'Now that her face showed thin, and her large eye looked hollow, there was something in the darkening of that face . . . which touched as well as alarmed' (498). 'I assure you she is wasting: her hands are growing quite thin, and so is her cheek', says Henry Sympson, confiding his fears for her life (503).

'Today you see them bouncing, buxom, red as cherries, and round as apples; to-morrow they exhibit themselves effete as dead weeds, blanched and broken down', remarks Helstone, irritably, of women, as he confronts his declining niece. 'With-out his being aware of it, the rose had dwindled and faded to a mere snowdrop: bloom had vanished, flesh wasted; she sat before him drooping, colourless, and thin' (189). 'She wasted like any snow-wreath in thaw, she faded like any flower in drought', says the narrator of Caroline's decline (424). But despite these images of drooping flowers, illness in this novel is no metaphor. Throughout, there is an em-phasis on the humbling reality of the perishable body, which no amount of heroism can deny. Even Shirley, who is 'fearless, physically', observes, 'we have none of us long to live' (266, 267); the Titan 'vitality' she imagines simply feeds 'that vulture death' (321). Napoleon can be repelled by Wellington, the Luddites by military force, but there is no defence against 'the yellow taint of pestilence, covering white English isles with the poisoned exhalations of the East' (421). Each of those two as-pirers—Shirley, the fiery dreamer, Moore, the ambitious manufacturer—is felled; not in heroic combat, but by vulnerable flesh and blood. The proudly defiant Shirley is reduced to 'a strange quietude' by 'something between a burn and a cut'— 'a mark in her white arm' (497, 508). Robert's confident assertions that he can 'con-quer' and 'rule' his impulses are abruptly broken off, as an unseen assassin's bullet lays him prostrate in the dust (542–3). Even the most indomitable have no control over this, their ultimate fate. As the narrator remarks of Helstone's fearlessness in face of Luddite threat: 'such death had for his nerves no terrors: it would have been his chosen—*might he have had a choice*' (384; my italics).

Of course, in *Shirley*, famously, each of the protagonists recovers. Indeed, as crit-ics have argued, the experience of illness is instrumental in solving the dilemmas each has to face.[101] Yet this emphasis on the manifest plot has tended to divert at-tention from those less conspicuous but arguably more powerful configurations in the novel that reinforce rather than counter a sense of the human being as 'sentient target of death'.[102] 'I am obliged to look forward to a possibility that has its terrors'

---

[101]   For a reading of *Shirley* along these lines, see Miriam Bailin, *The Sick Room in Victorian Fiction: the Art of Being Ill* (Cambridge: Cambridge University Press, 1994), 59–65.

[102]   The phrase is Charlotte Brontë's, from a letter to W. S. Williams, 12 April 1850: 'what the blood rushes through, what is the unseen seat of Life and the sentient target of Death—*this* Miss Austen ig-nores' (*CBL* ii. 383).

says Shirley (577); and if her immediate fears prove groundless, the novel again and again draws attention to the fact that that 'possibility' will come as a certainty to all. 'Shirley . . . does not know, has never known, and *will die without knowing* the full value of that spring whose bright fresh bubbling in her heart keeps it green,' the narrator pronounces inexorably (388, my italics). Caroline's liveliest moment is placed, by that narrating voice, as a fleeting, finished thing: 'once gone, no more to be reproduced . . . than the glancing ray of the meteor . . . the colour or form of the sun-set cloud' (91). 'There is no such ladies now-a-days', the old housekeeper remarks in closing, as she recalls the bright eyes with which Shirley once 'pierced a body through' (646).

Such intimations of mortality are underwritten in the novel by the movement of retrospection that by the end has relegated all the characters and their strivings to the past of a story that is done. And they are likewise echoed, tellingly, as the characters look forward. 'Suppose that building was a ruin and I was a corpse, what then?' demands Robert Moore: his defiant stand against his workers is also a prefiguring of death (136). 'He will come when they have laid me out,' thinks Caroline, less metaphorically, 'and I am senseless, cold, and stiff' (427). This 'tale of the perfect tense'[103] is punctuated by images of futurity, whose import is as desolate as that of Martin's glaring writing on the wall. For the future to which they point is one that holds not possibility, but that sentence which none can avert. 'I thought I should die. The tale of my life seemed told', says Caroline of her illness '. . . the book lay open before me, at the last page where was written "Finis".' 'You speak my experience,' says Robert (583). If each of the central characters recovers from immediate danger, the world at THE END of the novel is one from which all are gone.

'The future sometimes seems to sob a low warning of the events it is bringing us,' announces the narrator, at the opening of the novel's third volume. And in the course of the paragraph that follows that future is imaged in steadily more appalling shape. The conventional image of 'gathering storm' gives way to a more concrete and—in 1849—more topical one: that of 'fog' bringing 'the yellow taint of pestilence, covering white Western isles with the poisoned exhalations of the East, dimming the lattices of English homes with the breath of Indian plague'.[104] 'At other times,' the narrator continues, 'this Future bursts suddenly, as if a rock had rent, and in it a grave had opened, whence issues the body of one who slept. Ere you are aware, you stand face to face with a shrouded and unthought-of Calamity—a new Lazarus' (421). The passage remains metaphorical, but startling in its physicality. The image is not of a raising to life, but of a dreadful opening of the grave: an image more immediately disturbing to the novel's original readers than is

---

[103] This was the subtitle of Charlotte Brontë's 'The Green Dwarf ' (1833), which opens with a description of the now-deserted Genii's Inn, kept by 'the four Chief Genii, Tallii, Brani, Emi and Anni' in Glass Town 'twenty years since', which 'now stands silent and lonely in the heart of great Verdopolis'. 'But our business is with the past, not with the present day', the narrator continues, prefiguring the opening of *Shirley*. 'Therefore, let us leave moping to the owls, and look on the bright side of matters' (*EEW* ii. 1, 132).

[104] '*Shirley* was evidently written during the recent pestilence,' declared a reviewer in December 1849 (*CH* 151).

easily imaginable today.[105] The final phrase, added in manuscript, is a bitterly ironic one. This is a new kind of Lazarus: 'a shrouded and unthought-of Calamity' that speaks—unlike the Gospel story—not of hope, but of mortality.

Much of *Shirley* was indeed written, as Charlotte Brontë was later to put it, 'under the shadow of impending calamity': 'calamity' that by the time its last volume was begun had become all too terribly real.[106] 'When I close my eyes I seem to see poor papa's epitaph in black letters on the white marble. There is plenty of room for other inscriptions beneath', Caroline muses on 'the Helstone monument' (430), recalling to the reader familiar with Gaskell's *Life* of her creator that crowded monument in Haworth church, whose inscriptions had in time to be more closely 'pressed together', and which, when *Shirley* was completed, had no room for more names beneath.[107] But *Shirley*'s emphasis on mortality cannot be seen as simply a response to personal tragedy. It is integral to the novel's precisely articulated vision of what it meant to live in the England of its time.

The deaths that devastated the Brontë family were, after all, part of a much wider history: a history of disease and death to which the demographic records of the period all too eloquently point. Indeed, the very existence of those records testifies to the fact that such subjects were in these years not merely private calamities but matters of public concern.[108] Birth and death rates and quantification of causes of death were now, for the first time, being calculated with some accuracy. By 1849, the year of *Shirley*'s publication, William Farr, of the Registrar-General's office, was able to announce with authority, 'since 1816 the returns indicate a retrograde movement. The mortality has apparently increased.'[109] For many, such dismal statistics pointed not to despair but to action: they were, as Farr put it, an 'arsenal for sanitary reformers to use'.[110] The

[105] The idea of 'an opened grave' provoked considerable public anxiety in the early years of the 19th cent. Ruth Richardson, *Death, Dissection and the Destitute* (London: Routledge, 1987), offers a definitive account both of the controversy over the supply of corpses for medical dissection, which culminated in the Anatomy Act of 1840, and of its larger sociocultural significance. The Brontë children's fascination with the 'resurrection men' is evident throughout their Glass Town writings: Doctor Hume Bady, Young Man Naughty, and Ned Laury, body-snatchers and dissectors, are prominent figures there. Indeed, the dissecting room is the subject of a couple of jokes in *Shirley* (179, 643). That sense of corpses out of place that was stirred by the resurrection men was by the time of the publication of *Shirley* being underlined by the attempts of the sanitary reformers to draw attention to the the appalling risks to health imposed by the condition of urban burial grounds, and by their graphic descriptions of the ways in which the physicality of the corpse obtruded, unwanted, into early Victorian life. This was a subject on which Charlotte Brontë, whose home was almost surrounded by graves, can hardly have been unmoved. It was, indeed, to figure largely in Benjamin Herschel Babbage's *Report to the General Board of Health on a Preliminary Inquiry into the Sewerage, Drainage, and Supply of Water, and the Sanitary Condition of the Inhabitants of the Hamlet of Haworth* (London: HMSO, 1850), which recommended the churchyard's immediate closure.

[106] Charlotte Brontë to James Taylor, 5 September 1850 (*CBL* ii. 461).   [107] Gaskell, 493.

[108] The census of 1831, which drew attention to an increase in national mortality rates, led to a rapid growth in statistical studies, culminating in the establishment of the office of the Registrar-General in 1837: see M. J. Cullen, *The Statistical Movement in Early Victorian Britain: the Foundations of Empirical Social Research* (Hassocks: Harvester, 1975).

[109] Quoted in George Rosen, 'Disease, Debility and Death', in H. J. Dyos and Michael Wolff (eds.), *The Victorian City: Images and Realities* (2 vols.; London: Routledge, 1973), ii. 626–7.

[110] Quoted in Anthony S. Wohl, *Endangered Lives: Public Health in Victorian Britain* (London: J. M. Dent, 1983), 145.

1840s saw the beginning of that bureaucratic and legislative programme for the improvement of public health which was to affect the daily lives of English men and women more widely than any other government action in the first half of Queen Victoria's reign. The promise of the sanitary reformers, proclaimed in Chadwick's epic *Report on the Sanitary Condition of the Labouring Population of Great Britain* (1842), was that better ventilation and hygiene, improved drainage schemes and water supplies, would lower the death rate and increase life expectancy: their campaigning was to issue, the year before the publication of *Shirley*, in the Public Health Act of 1848.[111] 'Sanitary statistics' became the basis for a developing system of 'medical policing'—a programme of social action for the improvement of the nation's health. This was accompanied by a steady rise in the status of the medical profession. Between 1801 and 1850, over 8,000 university-educated men in Great Britain became doctors—more than in all previous history.[112] In the novels of the 1850s, indeed, the doctor begins to appear as a hero—a figure not merely of healing, but for the conquest of much larger social ills.[113] 'Providence has appointed diseases and plagues to commit their ravages upon us in order to rouse us from ignorance and barbarity; to stimulate us to use our faculties for their prevention, and for the elevation of our physical and moral nature', declared one actual campaigning doctor in 1845.[114] The fight against 'diseases and plagues' was conducted with heroic energy—an energy reflected in the literature of the time. 'What a yet unspoken poetry there is in . . . sanitary reform! It is the great fact of the age. We shall have men arise and write epics on it', declares Bracebridge, in Kingsley's *Yeast*.[115] And if no such epics appear to have eventuated, it does seem that the strategies of enquiry that were institutionalized and developed in the campaign for public health were to decide the thematic concerns and shape the narrative methods of many of the greatest novels of these years.[116]

Yet *Shirley* speaks, it seems, of a different awareness. It is not merely that the novel contains no such authoritative doctor-figure as Dickens's Allan Woodcourt or

---

[111] 'It establishes a central authority, it appoints superintendent inspectors, organises a local executive body with ample powers, imposes upon it some wholesome checks, and appoints a corps of useful officials:—in a word, it is an Act which . . . is capable of working a complete physical revolution in the disease-smitten towns of England', *Fraser's* commented, as the Act was passed. ('The Public Health Bill: Its Letter and Its Spirit', *Fraser's Magazine*, 38 (1848), 444).

[112] Bruce Haley, *The Healthy Body and Victorian Culture* (Cambridge, Mass.: Harvard University Press, 1978), 5.

[113] See 'The Symbolic Function of the Doctor in Victorian Novels', in F. R. and Q. D. Leavis, *Dickens the Novelist* (London: Chatto & Windus, 1970), 242–7; Lawrence Rothfield, *Vital Signs: Medical Realism in Nineteenth-Century Fiction* (Princeton: Princeton University Press, 1992).

[114] William Strange, MD, *An Address to the Middle and Working Classes on the Causes and Prevention of the Excessive Sickness and Mortality Prevalent in Large Towns* (London, 1845), 19.

[115] 'Write one yourself, and call it the *Chadwickiad*', the hero, Lancelot, rudely replies. But Kingsley's agreement with Bracebridge's view is evident throughout, not least in Lancelot's eventual conversion to the cause. This passage is in ch. 5 of the first version of the novel, which appeared in parts in *Fraser's Magazine* between July and December 1848: it is in ch. 6 of the novel as it was eventually published in 1851.

[116] See David Trotter, *Circulation: Defoe, Dickens and the Economics of the Novel* (Basingstoke: Macmillan, 1988), 61–133; Simon During, *Foucault and Literature: Towards a Genealogy of Writing* (London: Routledge, 1992), 55–67; Rothfield, *Vital Signs*.

Kingsley's Tom Thurnall (or even the more ambivalently regarded John Graham Bretton); that it shows little interest in that possibility of social transformation which such figures metaphorically represent. The emphasized, ironic distance of the narrating voice throughout seems less controlling than impotent. Even on the level of manifest plot the novel makes its own dark comment on the public health campaigners' battle against mortality. Shirley, Caroline, Robert recover, but by the end all are dead. The novel's constant pointers to unsurmountable mortality are quite at odds with the rhetoric of sanitary reform. 'If this generation has not the power to call the Dead up from their graves, it can close thousands of graves now opening,' William Farr, the Registrar-General, proclaimed in his *Tenth Annual Report*, the year before *Shirley* was begun.[117] But *Shirley*'s striking image of the 'Future' as a body bursting from the tomb is a shocking reminder of 'realities' that posed in their intransigence as stark a contradiction to the optimistic image of the age as did those facts of social deprivation and division upon which reformers focused, and on which twentieth-century historians have dwelt.

For even to the fortunate in early nineteenth-century England the knowledge of illness and death came in ways quite other than those developed by sociological report and statistical enquiry, or by the clinical gaze. For the middle-class Victorian family, death was a fact of daily life to an extent difficult to imagine today. It almost always took place at home, rather than in the sanitized separateness of a hospital, 'the awe and trouble of the death-scene' unsoftened by effective medication, undistanced by institutional routine.[118] (The physical details of her siblings' deathbeds—Branwell's 'twenty minutes' struggle' in the 'last agony' of death, 'the spectacle of his pale corpse'; Emily 'torn conscious, panting, reluctant . . . out of a happy life' ; 'the long desolate hours' of Anne's 'patient pain and fast decay'—haunted Charlotte Brontë for years.)[119] After death, the corpse lay at home, and was prepared for burial there.[120] Deathbeds were public events, described and remembered: they were followed by elaborate mourning rituals—funeral sermons, black-bordered notepaper, mourning clothing worn for carefully specified periods—that kept the fact of mortality constantly before the public gaze.[121] Most important of all was the simple fact that in mid-nineteenth-century England death

---

[117]   Quoted in Edwin Chadwick, *Report on the Sanitary Condition of the Labouring Population of Great Britain*, ed. M. W. Flinn (Edinburgh: Edinburgh University Press, 1965), 29.

[118]   The 'awe and trouble of [Branwell's] death-scene—the first I had ever witnessed' brought on a crisis of illness in Charlotte Brontë (*CBL* ii. 122).

[119]   Ibid., 126, 200, 216.

[120]   See Julian Litten, *The English Way of Death: The Common Funeral since 1450* (London: Hale, 1991), 124. *Shirley* tells that Mary Cave's housekeeper and nurse 'gossiped together over the corpse' (53); 'Let [Mrs Gill] lay me out, if I die,' is one of Shirley's requests (512). Both Branwell's and Emily's bodies lay in the Parsonage for several days after death; it would have been difficult for anyone in a house of this size to have been unaware of the details of the process of laying-out (Richardson, *Death, Dissection and the Destitute*, 21). 'Ere he could be interred I fell ill', Charlotte Brontë was later to write of the days following Branwell's death (*CBL* ii. 190).

[121]   See John Morley, *Death, Heaven, and the Victorians* (London: Studio Vista, 1971). Even in the relatively spartan Brontë household, such customs seem to have been kept (Barker, 941 n. 33).

was far more likely than it is today to occur before the end of the allotted span.[122] The figures being produced in these years by the sanitary statisticians gave, indeed, cause less for encouragement than for concern. The mortality rate was virtually immobile in the decades between 1830 and 1870 (in the later 1840s it actually rose appreciably): in the words of a modern historian, 'sanitary reform . . . was just holding the line'.[123] Those figures, it seems, bear witness not merely to the energy of the contemporary determination to conquer this last of human enemies,[124] but also to what, for many besides Brontë, were quite unconquerable realities.

It is true that in Haworth this general history had an extreme, local inflection. In 1850 Benjamin Babbage was to find that in the preceding ten years 41.6 per cent of the population of the village had died before reaching the age of 6. In the overcrowded churchyard, onto which the windows of the Parsonage looked, over 1,344 burials had taken place since 1843.[125] 'The Passing-Bell was *often* a dreary accompaniment to the day's engagements', Ellen Nussey recalled, 'and must have been trying to the sensitive nervous temperaments of those who were always within sound of it, as the Parsonage inmates were':

but *everything* around, and in *immediate vicinity* was a reminder of man's last bourne, as you issued from the Parsonage gate, you looked upon the Stone-cutter's chipping shed which was piled with slabs ready for use, and to the ear there was the incessant sound of the *chip, chip* of the recording chisel as it graved in the In Memoriams of the departed.

From the Parsonage-windows the first view, was the plot of grass edged by a wall, a thorn tree or two, and a few shrubs and currant-bushes that did not grow; next to these, was the large and half-surrounding church yard, so full of grave-stones that hardly a strip of grass could be seen in it.[126]

But if the Brontë family lived in the midst of death, in this they were not unique. 'Our homes are literally built in a charnel or a sepulchre,' wrote Edwin Hood in 1850 of the conditions prevailing in English towns.[127] Nor were they especially singled out for tragedy. Each of their individual deaths may be seen as part of a more general experience—experience of which the surviving sibling was all too sharply aware. The registers of the Clergy Daughters' School at Cowan Bridge record that of the fifty-three pupils at school with the four eldest Brontë girls, eleven left school in ill health and six were to die shortly afterwards. One, Sarah Bicker, died at school. If Carus Wilson's 'institution' was perhaps an extreme example, illness and death were common features of nineteenth-century boarding-school life.[128] Amongst the sparse details recorded of each new pupil on her entry to the school at Cowan Bridge

---

[122]   See M. J. Cullen, *The Statistical Movement*, chs. 2 and 3; and, for a different kind of discussion, Geoffrey Rowell, *Hell and the Victorians: A Study of the Nineteenth-Century Theological Controversies Concerning Eternal Punishment and the Future Life* (Oxford: Oxford University Press, 1974), 13.

[123]   F. B. Smith, *The People's Health, 1830–1910* (London: Croom Helm, 1979), 197.

[124]   1 Corinthians 15: 26: 'The last enemy that shall be conquered is death.'

[125]   Babbage, *Report on the Sanitary Condition of Haworth*, 19.

[126]   Ellen Nussey, 'Reminiscences of Charlotte Brontë by a Schoolfellow', *CBL* i. 604. In *Shirley* there is discussion of 'the graves under the Rectory back-kitchen' (240, 245).

[127]   Hood, *The Age and its Architects*, 163.   [128]   Barker, 127 and 858 n. 47.

are inoculations against measles, chicken-pox, and whooping-cough. The importance attached to this is borne out by the Brontës' experience: it was because they had succumbed to these illnesses, in the Haworth epidemics of the previous year, that Maria and Elizabeth Brontë arrived at Cowan Bridge in a fatally weakened state.[129] 'Consumption'—the disease of which they were to die—is the cause of death most frequently mentioned in the registers of the school for the 1820s:[130] it accounted for a third of all deaths from disease during Victoria's reign. Although, like most other maladies, it affected the poor most severely, it was also a scourge of the middle class, thriving in the insanitary conditions of Victorian households and institutions, and killing with what seemed frightful rapidity, for it was usually only in in its final stages that a diagnosis was made.[131] Similarly, the 'typhus' epidemic that broke out during Charlotte's last months at the school was but a small-scale example of a familiar catastrophe. In the year before *Shirley* was begun, there was an epidemic of 'Irish fever'—typhus that began amongst starving immigrants from Ireland—in which 30,000 died.[132] Yet if 'typhus' and 'consumption' were terrifying, the dread visitation that had inspired Martin's painting was by far the most potent figure for the shock of mortality in these years. During the time of the writing of *Shirley*, the second great cholera epidemic claimed over 50,000 lives. And its impact was greater, even, than such statistics might suggest. As Henri Blanc was later to declare, 'the very name of cholera inspires a deadly fear'.[133] Cholera struck swiftly and suddenly, raising local death rates dramatically, if ephemerally: its cause was unknown, and there was no known cure. *Fraser's* review of *Shirley*, in 1849, was succeeded by a long article, entitled 'Cholera Gossip', noting the 'wider prevalence' and 'increased fatality' of the disease.[134]

---

[129]   Gérin, *Charlotte Brontë*, 6.   [130]   Barker, 858 nn. 47 and 48.

[131]   René and Jean Dubos, *The White Plague: Tuberculosis, Man and Society* (London: Gollancz, 1953), 203–5. Charlotte Brontë writes of 'the fearful, rapid symptoms which appalled in Emily's case' (*CBL* ii. 172), and of 'the terrors of the swift messenger which snatched Emily from us—as it seemed—in a few days' (*CBL* ii. 174). But she had been familiar with the symptoms of 'consumption' since childhood. Thus, in an Angrian story of 1834, her Duke of Zamorna thanks his mistress for nursing his infant son as he dies of the disease: 'Your work is nearly completed. It has been a hard task to preserve what destiny had marked for decay . . . Let me hear nothing from you . . . till you think the scene is about finally to close, when he seems to have no more than perhaps a week's strength in him, that is to say, my girl, when respiration begins to rattle in his throat and the infernal brightness dies off his cheek, and his flesh (the little that remains) grows perfectly transparent, shewing no blood, but bones ('The Spell: an Extravaganza,' *EEW* ii. pt. 2, 153).

[132]   Haley, *The Healthy Body and Victorian Culture*, 7. 'Typhus' was, in these years, a generic term used of a number of differing epidemic diseases with similar symptoms.

[133]   *Cholera: How to Avoid It and Treat It* (London: H. S. King, 1873), 33.

[134]   'Cholera Gossip', *Fraser's Magazine*, 40 (1849), 702–11. Between 1845 and 1856, indeed, over 700 works on cholera were published in London (Wohl, *Endangered Lives*, 121): the contents page of *The Lancet* for the year of *Shirley*'s publication—which includes 'Report of a Case of Cholera Treated by Transfusion'; 'Treatment of Cholera by Small and Repeated Doses of Calomel'; 'On the Employment of Embrocations and Injections of Strong Liquid Ammonia in the Collapse Stage of Cholera', 'On the Production of Cholera by Insufficient Drainage, with Remarks on the Hypothesis of an Altered Electrical State of the Atmosphere'—speaks eloquently of the absence of any consensus as to either treatment or cause.

To write of illness in 1849 was not simply to speak of private misery, but to address a burning issue of the day.[135] Of course, the composition of most of *Shirley* was attended by more immediate personal anxieties, as the author's horizons contracted to the question of her sisters' health. 'Now when I hear Anne cough as Emily coughed, I tremble', she wrote in the winter of 1849:

However I must not look forwards, nor must I look backwards. Too often I feel like one crossing an abyss on a narrow plank—a glance round might quite unnerve . . . All the days of this winter have gone by darkly and heavily like a funeral train; since September sickness has not quitted the house—it is strange—it did not use to be so—but I suspect now all this had been coming on for years: unused any of us to the possession of robust health, we have not noticed the gradual approaches of decay; we did not know its symptoms; the little cough, the small appetite, the tendency to take cold at every variation of atmosphere have been regarded as things of course—I see them in another light now.[136]

Yet even this darkness of dread was but an extreme form of a much more general experience. On the most intimate level, life in early Victorian England was attended by a continual, gnawing uncertainty, a sense of its vulnerability to potentially terminal threat, difficult, perhaps, to imagine today. Different seasons brought different varieties of danger. 'This is autumn, a season fertile in fevers,' says Louis Moore, seeking to explain his illness (480). Warmer weather might bring 'the yellow taint of pestilence', like the typhus at Lowood school, 'quickening with the quickening spring' (*JE* 76). Winter, on the other hand, took its toll of the old and the feeble and the victims of lung disease: as Charlotte Brontë's letters attest, a cough or shortness of breath were viewed with well-founded apprehension.[137] 'I had been wishing to hear from you for some time before I received your last,' she writes to her former teacher, before her three last siblings' deaths. 'There has been so much sickness during the past winter, and the influenza has been so severe and so generally prevalent, that the sight of suffering around has frequently suggested fears for absent friends.'[138] In her early twenties, she had written to one such friend of her concern at another's 'pain in her chest, and frequent flushings of fever'. 'I cannot tell you what agony these symptoms give me. They remind me so strongly of my two sisters whom no power of medicine could save.'[139] 'Could we only reckon upon another year I

---

[135] Mayhall's *Annals of Yorkshire* regularly reports epidemics of cholera, typhus, and influenza amongst its other news of the years between 1820 and 1850. *Fraser's* account of current events in the month in which *Shirley* was begun reports not merely on the current 'commercial crisis', which has brought about a standstill in trade, causing the bankruptcy of many 'houses of the first respectability' and widespread suffering amongst the poor, but also that, in the preceding year, 'our towns and villages have undergone a visitation of sickness which is without parallel since the days of the great plague. Last spring seemed to let loose upon us a twofold amount of catarrhs and intermittent fevers. . . . with winter, influenza in its worst form set in. It is now aggravated by a species of fever which partakes largely of the character of the pest. We believe that the mortality in London has well-nigh doubled, within the last two months, that of any similar period of time in living memory' ('Current History', *Fraser's Magazine*, 37 (January 1848), 115).
[136] Charlotte Brontë to W. S. Williams, 18 January 1849 (*CBL* ii. 168).
[137] See e.g. *CBL* ii. 130, 147, 152, 168.   [138] 31 March 1848 (*CBL* ii. 47).
[139] 9 June 1838 (*CBL* i. 179). She is referring here to Maria and Elizabeth Brontë.

should be thankful', she writes ten years later, of the last of her surviving siblings. 'But can we do this even for the healthy?'[140] 'I dare communicate no ailment to papa', she confides to Ellen Nussey. 'His anxiety harasses me inexpressibly'.[141] Such comments recur in her letters, not merely at this dark period but throughout. They speak not merely of private anxiety, but of a far more widespread awareness, shared by Brontë and her correspondents, of the frailty of human life.

If mortality was high in the early years of Victoria's reign, the experience of debilitating illness was widespread.[142] The Revd Patrick Brontë's heavily annotated copy of Thomas John Graham's *Modern Domestic Medicine* (1826) testifies to some of the most pressing occasions of concern. His reading of that volume must have been accompanied by poignant private memories of those 'whom no power of medicine could save'.[143] But his notes speak too of the absence of effective cure for what today are 'minor' ailments, and of a variety of sufferings that were an all too familiar part of 'domestic' experience throughout the land. In 1836, T. R. Edmonds calculated that of persons between 15 and 60 '30 per cent . . . are yearly attacked by sickness'; nearly thirty years later, G. H. Lewes observed that 'few of us, after thirty, can boast of robust health'.[144] For whatever its claims to authority, medicine could offer little help either to explain or to alleviate any of the great killer diseases—typhus, cholera, scarlet fever, influenza, and tuberculosis—that swept through the nation in these years. And whatever the promises of the public health campaigners, few families could escape an untimely and intimate acquaintance with 'that terrible handwriting of human destiny, illness and death'.[145]

Of course, as those campaigners insisted, in early Victorian England that 'handwriting' was shaped most decisively by class. 'Comparative statistics' were deliberately presented in ways that drew attention to the connections between poverty and disease.[146] Such statistics comprised a compelling indictment of the state of the nation: more compelling, indeed—because they applied more generally—than that exposure of conditions in the factories which has been taken as paradigmatic of social 'protest' in these years. 'Fever and cholera are . . . God's handwriting on the wall against us, for our sins of filth and laziness,' declared Kingsley, in a sermon preached at the height of the cholera epidemic in 1849. That 'handwriting', he averred, could be answered only by a programme of radical social reform.[147] And the imagery of death and disease is prominent not merely in his novels—*Yeast, Alton Locke*, and *Two Years Ago*—but in the works of those other novelists who sought to confront their privileged readers with the appalling social divisions of

---

[140] 30 January 1849 (*CBL* ii. 173).   [141] 14 July 1849 (*CBL* ii. 230).
[142] See James C. Riley, *Sickness, Recovery and Death: A History and Forecast of Ill Health* (London: Macmillan, 1989).
[143] The volume was published in 1826. All Patrick Brontë's notes must have been made after the deaths of his wife and two elder daughters.
[144] 'Statistics of the London Hospital, with Remarks on the Law of Sickness', *Lancet*, 2 (1835–6), 778; Lewes, 'Training in Relation to Health', *Cornhill*, 9 (1864), 219.
[145] George Eliot, *Amos Barton* (1857), ch. 9.   [146] Cullen, *The Statistical Movement*, 146.
[147] Charles Kingsley, 'First Sermon on the Cholera', *Sermons on National Subjects, Preached in a Village Church* (London: John J. Griffin & Co., 1852), 183.

the advancing industrial age. Thus, with detailed, almost documentary realism, Elizabeth Gaskell spells out, in *Mary Barton*, the connection between poverty and death. Thus, in Dickens's novels of the late 1840s and 1850s, the facts to which the sanitary reformers drew attention and that he himself had as a campaigning journalist exposed are transformed into resonant symbols. Contagion and filth, sickness and its scars, appear as signs of a diseased society; disease itself becomes a striking metaphor for the spread of social ills.[148] But dark as their vision of their society is, inscribed in the works of both—as in Kingsley's more programmatic novels—is a kind of confidence (however uncertain, however minimal) in the possibility of change. 'How little can the rich man know | Of what the poor man feels!' declares the 'Manchester song' that stands as epigraph to the chapter of *Mary Barton* describing Ben Davenport's death: but Mrs Gaskell's whole project is designed to acquaint her middle-class readers with 'what the workman feels and thinks',[149] and thus to awaken the sympathies that might work towards the amelioration of the sufferings she describes. 'Oh for a good spirit who would take the house-tops off . . . and show a Christian people what dark shapes issue from amidst their homes', cries Dickens, in *Dombey and Son*, and implicit in the cry is the hope that if 'a Christian people' could see, they would be moved to reform.[150]

Yet the 'social problem' novelists' concern with poverty and deprivation is curiously absent from *Shirley*. If illness and death loom large in this novel, those gross inequalities that others exposed are barely touched upon here. The Farrens, it is true, have some conventional pathos. But the other starving workers are distanced, by the narrator, into those who 'eat the bread and drink the waters of affliction'; and in the novel's third volume even such generalized images as this almost disappear. If the fever that afflicts Louis Moore, the bullet that strikes Robert down, come from these wretched others—the one, 'perhaps caught . . . in one of the poor cottages of the district' (479), the other, a more deliberate instrument of the workers' revenge—the concern is not here (as in Gaskell's depiction of Carson's murder, or Dickens's of the infection that comes from Tom-all-Alone's) with the social divisions and connections that are thereby made manifest. What assumes narrative importance is the laying low of the sufferer: the risk to life, rather than its cause. The 'spark' of Caroline's illness is 'fanned' to flame by her 'mental excitement', but its ultimate source is a mystery. 'How she had caught the fever . . . she could not tell. Probably in her late walk home, some sweet, poisoned breeze, redolent of honey-dew and miasma, had passed into her lungs and veins' (422). Shirley,

---

[148] Thus, the chapter of *Little Dorrit* that describes the 'moral infection' emanating from the banker Merdle is entitled 'The Progress of an Epidemic'. In 1880 Ruskin was to argue that the nine deaths in *Bleak House* were less the melodramatic expression of a peculiar pessimism than 'a properly representative average of the statistics of civilian mortality in the centre of London' at the time. ('Fiction, Fair and Foul' in *Library Edition of the Works of John Ruskin*, xxxiv. 272). For two rather different views of this kind of imagery in Dickens, see A. Susan Williams, *The Rich Man and the Diseased Poor in Early Victorian Literature* (London: Macmillan, 1987), 82–7, and Trotter, *Circulation*, chs. 5–7.

[149] Gaskell, *Mary Barton*, 60.

[150] Charles Dickens, *Dombey and Son*, ed. Peter Fairclough, with an introduction by Raymond Williams (London: Penguin, 1970), 738.

even more arbitrarily, is bitten by an apparently rabid dog. The sense, again and again, in the novel's depiction of these events, is of something striking from outside, rather than socially determined: of a 'calamity' in which each becomes a victim of forces beyond any human control.

It is an emphasis distinctively different from that of a Kingsley, a Gaskell, a Dickens, those contemporary 'condition-of-England' novelists whose work Charlotte Brontë knew. Indeed, Brontë's difference of perspective may have been a quite conscious one. *Yeast* was appearing in parts in *Fraser's* whilst she was writing *Shirley*. Its final instalment was published in December 1848, the month in which her sister Emily died. *Shirley*, it appears, was then laid aside; but when Brontë returned to the novel, after her sister Anne's death, it is likely that this issue of *Fraser's* would have been much in her mind. For it contained a poignant reminder of the literary aspirations that she and her sisters had shared: on the reverse of the final page of the concluding chapter of *Yeast* is printed a poem by Acton Bell. And the rousing Christian optimism of that chapter—called 'The Valley of the Shadow of Death'—is countered point by point in *Shirley*. Indeed, it is hard not to see, in Charlotte Brontë's choice of its title for that of the opening chapter of her own novel's final volume, something like a riposte. Kingsley's heroine dies: Caroline Helstone lives. But Kingsley's striking figure of spiritual renewal—dry bones shaking and clashing together, the Spirit entering into them, and bringing them to life[151]—is replaced, in Brontë's 'Valley of the Shadow', by that image of the Future as a 'shrouded' corpse, an 'unthought-of Calamity' (421). Kingsley offers a progressive vision of a 'nobler, more chivalrous, more god-like' England—of 'railroads, electric telegraphs, associate lodging-houses, club-houses, sanitary reforms, experimental schools, chemical agriculture, a matchless school of inductive science, an equally matchless school of naturalist painters,—and all this in the very workshop of the world!'[152] But *Shirley* ends with a darker portrait of a chimney 'mighty as the tower of Babel', and a landscape irrevocably despoiled.

'It is difficult now to recapture the visionary quality of their early programme,' writes a modern historian of the sanitary reformers.[153] And in this, those reformers might be seen as paradigmatic figures of that progressive energy which fired such novelists as Kingsley, and which Brontë was differently to image in her manufacturer's 'schemes'. For the facts that they emphasized were facts they believed could be remedied. The fantasy was even of a kind of mastery over death. 'All this death, and all this sickness, with their attendant misery, wretchedness, poverty, pauperism, immorality, and crime, are in our power wholly and entirely to prevent,' declared Hector Gavin, MD, FRCSE, Lecturer on Forensic Medicine at Charing Cross Hospital, in a lecture delivered in 1847.[154] At the end of his *Report on the Sanitary Condition of the Labouring Population of Great Britain*, Edwin Chadwick voices

---

[151] *Yeast, Fraser's Magazine*, 37 (1848), 708.   [152] *Yeast, Fraser's Magazine*, 37 (1848), 708–9.
[153] Smith, *The People's Health*, 195.
[154] Hector Gavin, *Unhealthiness of London, and the Necessity of Remedial Measures, a lecture delivered at the Western and Eastern Literary and Scientific Institutions, Leicester Square and Hackney Road* (London, 1847), 65–6.

the utopian hope that the establishment of 'Boards of Health, or Public Offices for the Prevention of Disease' will lead to 'the approach of those times when, after a life spent almost without sickness, we shall close the term of an unharrassed existence by a peaceful euthanasia'.[155] As the millenarian preacher John Cumming put it in 1848: 'Our sanitary improvements, the most proper and the most laudable, are pointed to by some as if they could bid defiance to the judgments of God, and even to death itself.'[156] Within the prosaic provisions of the Public Health Act of 1848 a curious confidence is inscribed: if the death rate exceeded 23 per 1000, or where 10 per cent of the inhabitants asked for it, an inquiry could be held and something could be done.

Such plans as these for the control and defeat of disease, even death, were, to the author of *Shirley*, a matter of domestic familiarity. For it was to this provision of that Act of 1848 that the Revd Patrick Brontë—bereft, within the preceding year, of three of his last four children—appealed on behalf of the villagers of Haworth as his daughter finished *Shirley* in the summer of 1849. On the day following that on which she wrote to her publishers to announce the novel's completion, he forwarded a petition—organized by himself and signed by the two local surgeons, as well as by other ratepayers in the village—to the General Board of Health in London, asking for 'an authorized Agent, to come and look into our situation' with a view to 'assisting us, in making improvements here'.[157] If Patrick Brontë's long campaign, conducted with characteristic energy, to obtain a 'supply of pure water' for Haworth did not bear fruit until almost the end of his life, he seems never to have abandoned his belief that the sufferings he saw around him could be alleviated by the detailed schemes for 'improvements' he proposed.

Yet, as the case of Haworth all too clearly shows, that faith in preventive measures which fired the work of the early sanitary reformers was repeatedly challenged in these years by the experience of the nation of which they wrote. The letters that Patrick Brontë sent to the General Board of Health on this subject offer a glimpse not merely of the ignorance, inefficacy, or simple inertia even of that body,[158] but also of the actualities with which it manifestly failed to deal. His efforts were clearly prompted by his own all too intimate acquaintance—as attender at deathbeds, conductor of funerals—with the illnesses and epidemics that swept through the village, owing to bad sanitation and the absence of any 'pure water supply'. And they were accompanied always by a pressing awareness that, as his biographers put it, 'all the

---

[155] Chadwick, *Report*, 410. He is citing remarks made by one Dr Wilson at the conclusion of his *Report on the Sanitary Condition of the Labouring Population of Kelso*.

[156] John Cumming, *Apocalyptic Sketches; or Lectures on the Book of Revelation* (London: Hall & Co., 1848), 493.

[157] John Lock and Canon W. T. Dixon, *A Man of Sorrow: The Life, Letters and Times of the Rev. Patrick Brontë 1777–1861* (London: Nelson, 1965), 432–3. The petition was dated 28 August 1849: the day before, Charlotte Brontë had written to William Smith Williams, of *Shirley*, 'The book is now finished (thank God!)' (*CBL*, ii. 241).

[158] If the campaign for public health reached its climax of propaganda activities during the 1840s, effective action was slower to implement (see Smith, *The People's Health*, 199). There was also, throughout the country, local opposition to reform. On such opposition in Haworth, see Lock and Dixon, *Man of Sorrow*, 435–8; on the country more generally, Smith, *The People's Health*, 215–18.

time the cottagers . . . remained without water or sanitation, and continued to die'.[159] 'Summer is approaching, and all that we petition for . . . will be most urgently needed,' he was to write, on 1 April 1851. 'There has already been long, and tedious delay—there has been a deal of sickness amongst us . . . which ills might have been prevented, or palliated, had the remedial measures we hope for, been duly applied,' he continues (into what seems to have been silence) on 10 July 1851. Through these irritated formalities one traces not merely impatience, but something one can only describe as an urgent sense of the precariousness of human life—a sense, indeed, of shared mortality that is usually suppressed in the sanitary reformers' analyses of others' deaths.[160] For the state of affairs those reformers exposed was disturbing in ways that they themselves hardly chose to confront. It was not merely that the reforms they urged were brought about slowly, in piecemeal fashion, and obstructed by interest and ignorance: the dry statistics they recorded spoke less of the invincible power of human agency than of humanity as impotent and at risk. What in their own public self-imagings, and often, indeed, in retrospect, may appear as a history of improvement, of confidence and control, was, even for the more fortunate, an experience of dreadful apprehension and often of absolute defeat.

The contrast between the energy of aspiration exemplified in Patrick Brontë's schemes and the fact of ultimate human powerlessness of which the silent parsonage all too eloquently spoke is a contrast rather different from that division between privileged and unprivileged of which the 'condition-of-England' novelists were writing in these years. Yet it was one that was no less central to early Victorian experience: indeed, it was arguably more central to the experience of the early Victorian middle class. It is a contrast writ large in *Shirley*. And it is in this that the novel's real originality lies.

It is not that mortality is unregistered by the 'condition-of-England' novelists: indeed, to each of them death is a prominent social fact. In *Yeast*, in *Mary Barton*, in *Hard Times*, in *Bleak House*, major characters die and deathbed scenes are graphically portrayed. Yet in each of these works, rather differently, death is imaged not as an absolute check to individual and communal life but as enabling a recognition of bonds that social divisions deny. Sometimes, such moments are reconciliatory (the death of John Carson in *Mary Barton*, of Stephen Blackpool in *Hard Times*); sometimes, death exposes a common humanity with accusatory, retributive force. (Thus, in the final instalment of *Yeast*, the heroine dies of the typhus she has contracted in the hovels that her father refused to improve: thus, in *Bleak House*, the 'corrupted blood' of Tom-all-Alone 'propagates infection and contagion' even to 'the highest of the high'). But if scenes such as these point out of this world, they point back also into it. The euphemisms prominent within them—familiar currency in early Victorian England—may appear sentimental evasions, psychological

---

[159] Lock and Dixon, *Man of Sorrow*, 438.
[160] Ibid. 432–9. The Parsonage water supply came from a well fed from the hillside above, and was far safer than that for the village, but he still speaks of the villagers as 'us' in these appeals.

mechanisms for denying the reality of death. But within these novels of social division they speak powerfully also of the positive ideological function such mechanisms might serve: of how the rituals used by survivors to soften the fact of severance might point towards the reaffirmation of fundamental social bonds.[161] Indeed, Dickens's enormously popular deathbed scenes seem to have worked in this way on his mid-Victorian audience, by constructing a cohesive readership out of readers from widely divided social groups. (Or, as Ruskin was more cynically to remark, 'Nell was simply killed for the market, as a butcher kills a lamb'.)[162]

Yet *Shirley*'s prophetic description of the death of Jessie Yorke is markedly different from this:

But, Jessie, I will write about you no more. This is an autumn evening, wet and wild. There is only one cloud in the sky; but it curtains it from pole to pole. The wind cannot rest: it hurries sobbing over hills of sullen outline, colourless with twilight and mist. Rain has beat all day on that church-tower: it rises dark from the stony enclosure of its graveyard: the nettles, the long grass, and the tombs all drip with wet. This evening reminds me too forcibly of another evening some years ago: a howling, rainy autumn evening too—when certain who had that day performed a pilgrimage to a grave new-made in a heretic cemetery, sat near a wood-fire on the hearth of a foreign dwelling. They were merry and social, but they each knew that a gap, never to be filled, had been made in their circle. They knew they had lost something whose absence could never be quite atoned for so long as they lived; and they knew that heavy falling rain was soaking into the wet earth which covered their lost darling; and that the sad, sighing gale was mourning above her buried head. The fire warmed them; Life and Friendship yet blessed them; but Jessie lay cold, coffined, solitary—only the sod screening her from the storm.   (407–8)

There is no reference here to the hope of a future life;[163] nothing of Wordsworth's sense of the 'community of the living and the dead'.[164] The stress is on finality and severance. Jessie, buried 'under the sod', is utterly alone. There are no comforting

---

[161] Michael Wheeler, *Death and the Future Life in Victorian Literature and Theology* (Cambridge: Cambridge University Press, 1990), 25–65, offers a thoughtful account of early Victorian euphemisms for death. Peter L. Berger and Thomas Luckman, in *The Social Construction of Reality* (Harmondsworth, Middlesex: Penguin, 1967), 118 ff., discuss the fundamental importance for any institutional order of 'the integration of death within the paramount reality of social existence'. For a more individualistic view, see Ernest Becker, *The Denial of Death* (New York: Macmillan, Free Press, 1975), ch. 4. On the Burkeian and Wordsworthian sense of mourning as constituting national community, see Esther Schor, *Bearing the Dead: The British Culture of Mourning from the Enlightenment to Victoria* (Princeton: Princeton University Press, 1994).

[162] Quoted in William R. Clark, 'The Rationale of Dickens' Death Rate', *Boston University Studies in English*, 2: 3 (1956), 127. On the representation of death in the Victorian social problem novel, see Alexander Welsh, *The City of Dickens* (Oxford: Clarendon Press, 1971); Andrew Sanders, *Charles Dickens: Resurrectionist* (London: Macmillan, 1981); Garrett Stewart, *Death Sentences* (Cambridge, Mass.: Harvard University Press, 1984); Michael Wheeler, *Death and the Future Life*, ch. 6.

[163] Contrast Charlotte M. Yonge's description, in her best-selling *The Heir of Redclyffe* (1853), of her hero's last resting-place in a foreign land: 'It was a distant grave, far from his home and kindred, but in a hallowed spot, and a most fair one; and there might his mortal frame meetly rest till the day when he should rise, while from their ancestral tombs should likewise awaken the forefathers whose sins were indeed visited on him in his early death; but, thanks to Him who giveth the victory, in death without the sting' (ch. 36).

[164] Wordsworth, first *Essay Upon Epitaphs* (1810); see also *Excursion*, V. 903–27.

euphemisms: unobtrusively but distinctly, the passage counters them. Instead of those 'soothing' analogies with the ongoing processes of nature of which Wordsworth had written in his 'Essay upon Epitaphs', there are images of natural bleakness: 'nettles' in a 'stony enclosure', 'heavy falling rain soaking into the wet earth'.[165] Death here is no consummation but absolute extinction: all the 'humour' and 'piquancy' that once individualized Jessie are now forever gone.[166] The shock of mortality here does not affirm community. It severs social ties; Jessie, once 'loved' and 'loving', is separated forever from her 'merry and social' friends. Indeed, that oddly jarring momentary glimpse of the group around the fire underlines the absolute contrast between the living survivors and the one beneath the earth. If their 'merry' sociability might appear to suggest a drawing together in the face of loss, there is in this passage a quiet but decided repudiation of any consolatory notion that lasting bonds might be forged by the shared memory of the dead.[167] 'Life and Friendship *yet* blessed them', observes that unsparing, retrospective voice (my italics): and the reader is sharply reminded of the transience not merely of individual life, but also of the 'Friendship' here evoked. For the narrator, remembering Jessie, is now quite emphatically alone: no longer part of that 'circle', but gazing at a desolate graveyard, as the novelist herself must have gazed. The shared social world of the novel—which clergy and manufacturers and landowners see themselves as shaping, in which the children of Briarmains each jostle for a place, within which women and Luddites each differently strain to be heard—suddenly appears ephemeral: a fragile, temporary defence against that which is signified by that relentlessly beating rain.

'Brethren, our faith tells us one thing, and our sensations tell us another', Frederick W. Robertson was to confess, in a sermon preached in 1857, 'When we die, we are surrendering in truth all that with which we have associated existence. Talk as we will of immortality, there is an obstinate feeling that we cannot master, that we end in death.'[168] This 'feeling' was reinforced for many in the early nineteenth century by sharp experience of that 'mortal conflict' before which euphemism seemed powerless.[169] For even the firmest hope of salvation could not blur the physical facts. 'Somebody *must* cheer the rest,' writes Charlotte Brontë, shortly after Emily's death:

---

[165] Wordsworth, *Essay Upon Epitaphs* (1810). For a discussion of such analogies, see Wheeler, *Death and the Future Life*, 59–64.

[166] Contrast Michel Foucault's rather more sanguine account of 'the perception of death . . . in the nineteenth century' as 'constitutive of singularity': 'the dull, common life becomes an individuality at last; a black border isolates it and gives it the style of its own truth' (*The Birth of the Clinic: An Archaeology of Medical Perception*, trans. A. M. Sheridan (London: Tavistock, 1973), 171).

[167] Schor, in *Bearing the Dead*, traces this function of mourning from the Enlightenment through to the Romantic period.

[168] Wheeler, *Death and the Future Life*, 27.

[169] 'I try with all my might to look beyond the grave, to follow my dear Sisters and my poor brother to that better world where—I trust—they are all now happy,' she wrote to a friend in March 1850; 'but still . . . I cannot help recalling all the details of the weeks of sickness, of the mortal conflict, of the last difficult agony' (*CBL* ii. 373).

So I will not now ask why Emily was torn from us in the fullness of our attachment, rooted up in the prime of her own days in the promise of her powers—why her existence now lies like a field of green corn trodden down—like a tree in full bearing—struck at the root; I will only say, sweet is rest after labour and calm after tempest and repeat again and again that Emily knows that now.[170]

And that which she will not allow herself to ask is figured far more powerfully in those concrete images of devastation than the platitudes she repeats 'again and again' like a lesson to be learned by rote.

Such difficulties in accepting conventional consolations were not peculiar to Brontë. Mortality and its meanings were questions as urgent in the period as that of the 'condition of England'; and debated just as much.[171] Even within theology there was not consensus but controversy; and theological controversy was but the rational, public face of what seem to have been, for many, irresolvable anxieties. In *Jane Eyre*, the fate of the soul is for Jane an open question: ' "One lies there," I thought, "who will soon be beyond the war of earthly elements. Whither will that spirit— now struggling to quit its material tenement—flit when at length released?" ' (*JE* 237). But the shape such speculations assume in *Shirley* is a quite different one. Jane's images of death as 'release' echo those in which she portrays her desire to reach beyond the 'limit' of an actual constraining life. But Caroline Helstone's torrent of questions—'*Where is* the other world? In *what* will another life consist?'— contains no such hint of liberation: 'What is that electricity they speak of, whose changes make us well or ill; whose lack or excess blasts; whose even balance revives? What are all those influences that are about us in the atmosphere, that keep playing over our nerves like fingers on stringed instruments?' (427). Hers is a language not of subjective potency, but of passivity in face of natural law. Death as envisaged here is no act of aspiration. It 'bursts' upon the powerless subject, as that calamitous Future has, a few pages earlier, been imaged 'burst[ing] suddenly' like a corpse from an opened grave.

'Have I not cause to think that the hour is hasting but too fast when the veil must be rent for me? Do I not know the Grand Mystery is likely to burst prematurely on me? Great Spirit! in whose goodness I confide; whom as my Father I have petitioned night and morning from early infancy, help the weak creation of thy hands! Sustain me through the ordeal I dread and must undergo! Give me strength! Give me patience! Give me—oh! *give me* FAITH! (427–8)

The novel's insistent underwriting of this sense of human impotence—no less than the prominence within it of the 'dark recollection' of an earthly 'Father' in whose

---

[170] Charlotte Brontë to W. S. Williams, 25 December 1848 (*CBL* ii. 159).

[171] Caroline's 'musing about remnants of shrouds, and fragments of coffins, and human bones and mould' (245) may, as Shirley says, be morbid, but it is entirely characteristic of the time. On 'the Victorians' obsessive interest in death', see Wheeler, *Death and the Future Life*, ch. 1. *In Memoriam*, the most popular poem of the mid-century, was merely one example of a vast literature on the subject, ranging from tracts and sermons to quasi-religious works such as Elizabeth Rowe's *Friendship in Death: Twenty Letters from the Dead to the Living* (a survival from the 18th cent., owned by Caroline Helstone) to much more secular genres: indeed, as Boyd Hilton has shown, thoughts of a life beyond the grave informed even economic thought (*The Age of Atonement: The Influence of Evangelicalism on Social and Economic Thought 1795–1865* (Oxford: Oxford University Press, 1988), 3).

'goodness' there could be no confidence (102)—drains this prayer of solace: it remains a 'strange soliloquy', delivered into a void.

It is a moment of quite private panic. *Shirley*'s concern, however, is not merely with such feeling, but with the powerlessness against it of larger cultural forms. A few pages later, Caroline asks her mother to sing 'that hymn which begins,—

> Our God, our help in ages past,—
> Our hope for years to come . . .'

The request seems to be for consolation. Yet the verses that Mrs Pryor sings, and which are reprinted in the novel, are very much bleaker than this: indeed, Charlotte Brontë omits two somewhat softer ones.[172] Those that are actually given configure a disquieting vision of vast impersonal vistas, within which the individual lifespan shrinks into insignificance, and nations and generations appear as transient as dreams:

> Thy word commands our flesh to dust,
>   'Return, ye sons of men':
> All nations rose from earth at first
>   And turn to earth again.
>
> A thousand ages in thy sight
>   Are like an evening gone;
> Short as the watch that ends the night
>   Before the rising sun.
>
> Time, like an ever-rolling stream,
>   Bears all its sons away;
> They fly, forgotten, as a dream
>   Dies at the opening day.
>
> Like flowery fields, the nations stand,
>   Fresh in the morning light;
> The flowers beneath the mower's hand
>   Lie withering ere 'tis night.

It is true that the final stanza that is sung calls upon a God whose paternal care might answer the anxieties such images arouse:

> Our God, our help in ages past,—
>   Our hope for years to come;
> Be thou our guard while troubles last,—
>   O Father, be our home!

It is perhaps because those anxieties are so powerfully stirred, and, in the end, so calmly resolved, that Watts's hymn in its entirety is such a compelling one. But here, selectively quoted and ironically contextualized, it works to quite different effect. It

---

[172] See Wheeler, *Death and the Future Life*, 45–6, on the more usual 'consolatory discourse' of mid-19th-cent. deathbed hymns. The omitted verses of Watts's hymn are the second and third, which speak of God as enduring forever, and of 'our defence' as 'sure'.

brings flooding into the novel a vision of a universe alien to human purposes, of expanded and destructive time, of the greatest human achievements as frail and temporary things. This, of course, was the message of geology, paleontology, astronomy, archeology to the early nineteenth century.[173] In this domestic sick-room setting, the intimate challenge thus presented to human purposes and meanings—a challenge taken up by the most famous poet of the day—is sharply, dramatically realized. But *Shirley*'s concern with this subject—wittier, more detached than Tennyson's—is less with individual emotional response and intellectual speculation than with the impact of this awareness on the shared social world.

For as Mrs Pryor begins to sing, the narrative focus shifts, away from mother and daughter, to 'old Helstone', the parish priest. He, whose avoidance of feeling has chilled his niece and is reputed to have killed his wife, at first stops to listen and then hastens to get away:

> Why it reminded him of his forgotten dead wife, he could not tell; nor why it made him more concerned than he had hitherto been for Caroline's fading girlhood. He was glad to recollect that he had promised to pay Wynne, the magistrate, a visit that evening. Low spirits and gloomy thoughts were very much his aversion: when they attacked him he usually found means to make them march in double-quick time. The hymn followed him faintly as he crossed the fields: he hastened his customary sharp pace, that he might get beyond its reach. (431)

It is immediately after this description that the novel quotes those four bleakest stanzas of the hymn—stanzas implicitly sounding in his retreating ears. The point is not merely an exposure of the psychological limitations of this half-ridiculed 'little man' (37). The 'warlike' pillar of the church (37), fleeing across the fields, becomes a resonant image of an irony implicit throughout. Authority and assertiveness disintegrate and retreat in the face of that to which Watts's pursuing hymn gives 'classic' expression:[174] the fact of human creaturehood, which even the most powerful cannot ultimately evade.

The moment offers a disquieting glimpse of the precariousness of that confidence which in early nineteenth-century England underpinned the public world. In this, it focuses and images that which is implicit in the novel's more extended puncturing portrayal of that representative contemporary hero, the ambitious entrepreneur, baffled in his desire to 'get on', brought low by a fanatic's bullet, his ambitions finally realized in ambiguous, Babel-like shape. For in *Shirley* obduracy and enterprise appear less as heroic and effective than as dependent upon a denial of those intransigent facts of experience that threaten the illusion that the world can be mastered and controlled. This sense is articulated in a different way, unobtrusively but distinctly, in the novel's representation of Caroline Helstone's decline.

---

[173] 'Our space is a point, our time a moment, our millions a handful, our permanence a quick decay', William Whewell had declared, in the third of the Bridgewater Treatises, designed to demonstrate 'the Power, Wisdom and Goodness of God' (*Astronomy and General Physics*, 201).

[174] It has, says Donald Davie, 'attained the ultimate classic status of being known to, and sometimes quoted by, people who know not what it is, nor who it is, that they quote' (*A Gathered Church: The Literature of the English Dissenting Interests, 1700–1930* (London: Routledge & Kegan Paul, 1978), 21).

For even as it depicts her unhealthy lack of 'self-possession', the narrative voice quietly questions that powerful contemporary normative rhetoric of 'health': 'Collected, she was not yet; perhaps healthy self-possession and self-control were to be hers no more; perhaps that world the strong and prosperous live in had already rolled from beneath her feet for ever' (426–7). Caroline is not pathologized as 'morbid'. Rather, the demonstrative 'that' distances the world of the 'healthy', and aligns the narrative perspective with hers. And the imagery of the hymn that follows, echoing as it does this account of her state of mind—'Time, like an ever-rolling stream | Bears all its sons away'—underwrites her point of view. The lonely, painful experience of bodily decline is presented as giving access to a truth that the project of world-making must repress.Caroline's world is not 'that' sphere of exertion and self-assertion that Moore and Helstone and Shirley each differently occupy. Hers is a different knowledge, of powerless, finite creaturehood. But it is this that is presented in the novel as the reality that all, inescapably, share.

Shirley is certainly very different from the 'condition-of-England' novels with which it is often compared. It is not, as has sometimes been argued, a clumsy or ideologically blinkered attempt to deal with the questions with which novelists such as Gaskell and Kingsley were concerned. The questions with which it engages are distinctively different from theirs. The 'story' to which its absence of 'moral' points is as subversive of that faith in 'progress' which shaped the world of mid-nineteenth-century England as any moral exposure of the consequences of industrialism. It is a 'story' not of progress and improvement, of medical authority and clinical control, but of the hidden, undermining experience of the imperilled body, with its inescapable message of the finitude of earthly life;[175] not of the transcendent hope of an unquestioned faith, but of the open-endedness of unknowing; not of a triumphant project of social construction, but of ultimate impotence. Unsparing, ironic, unillusioned, refusing the consolations of politics or religion, it offers a vision of the nature of the social world that is sharply, suggestively different from that of any other novel published in England in these years.

---

[175] As Charles Kingsley was to observe, one of the main, if often unacknowledged, benefits of good health is that it 'makes one unconscious of one's own body' (quoted in Haley, *The Healthy Body*, 5).

CHAPTER SEVEN

'Entirely bewildered': *Villette* and History (1)

I

After the expansive social landscape, the flexible third-person narrative of *Shirley*, *Villette* seems oppressively constricted. Here, more extremely than in any of Brontë's previous novels, the viewpoint is confined to that of an individual sensibility—a sensibility more eccentric than Crimsworth's, less expressive than Jane Eyre's. 'Hope smiles on Effort!' Crimsworth had proclaimed, invoking the certainties of an enterprise culture (*P*166). But to Lucy Snowe, whose story ends in shipwreck and defeat, 'Hope' is 'a false idol—blind, bloodless, and of granite core' (160). Like *Jane Eyre*, *Villette* explores the plight of a woman who is 'insignificant, poor and plain'. But it offers a far darker view of the possibilities for such a one. Lucy, like Jane, is an orphan; her family are hinted at only in images of disaster and loss. But she finds no congenial kinsfolk: at her story's end, she is alone. If like Jane she must earn her own living, she must do so to the end. She, like Jane, lacks beauty; but hers, for most of the novel, is the more usual fate of the unattractive and obscure. *Jane Eyre* ends with assertions of fulfilment, in this world or the next: Jane's account of her married happiness, St John Rivers's confident expectation of the coming of his Lord. But there is no such consummation, either actual or anticipated, here.

Yet *Villette* has none of the melodramatic darkness of *Jane Eyre*. Instead of those images of elemental nature that gave Jane's story cosmic urgency, here there are images of banal, domesticated space.[1] The keynote is struck in the novel's opening paragraphs. 'My godmother lived in a handsome house in the *clean* and ancient town of Bretton,' Lucy commences; and the word I have italicized, which recurs in the paragraph that follows, immediately punctures any incipient suggestions of romance. The monstrous Reeds and Brocklehurst are replaced, in this novel, by more ambiguous figures: the obtuse but benevolent Brettons, the 'acute and insensate' Madame Beck (74). Jane Eyre was threatened with literal death—from cold, from hunger, at the hands of the hostile others in her world. *Villette*, however, portrays no such extremity: indeed, the Gothic sensationalism of that earlier novel

---

[1] The classic account of *Jane Eyre*'s 'elemental' imagery is David Lodge, 'Fire and Eyre: Charlotte Brontë's War of Earthly Elements', in *The Language of Fiction* (London: Routledge & Kegan Paul, 1966). On *Villette* and domesticity see Tony Tanner, Introduction to *Villette* (Harmondsworth: Penguin, 1979), 12.

seems here half-comically recalled. In *Jane Eyre*, the 'well-known scent' of Rochester's cigar heralds his approach and his proposal, in an 'Eden-like' garden on midsummer eve (*JE* 248). But Lucy describes how M. Paul leaves her gifts that '*smell of cigars*'. 'This was very shocking, of course', she continues, in a tone quite unlike Jane Eyre's. 'I . . . used to open the window with some bustle, to air my desk, and with fastidious finger and thumb, to hold the peccant brochures forth to the purifying breeze' (343). 'The drug and the pastille' are powerless, at Lowood, to 'overcome the effluvia of mortality' (*JE* 77). At the Pensionnat Beck, by contrast, a handsome young doctor is summoned to write 'harmless prescriptions'; his patient eats 'like a raven' whilst gambolling 'day and night in her bed' (97). A madwoman is incarcerated for ten years in the attic at Thornfield Hall; but Lucy is locked up by an officious 'little' man in an attic for an afternoon. Jane tells how, dying of starvation, she 'coveted a cake of bread' (*JE* 325); but Lucy finds herself longing for a 'petit pâté à la crème' (137). In *Jane Eyre*, an unknown woman, hideous as 'the Vampyre', visits Jane's room by night and tears her wedding-veil in two. But Lucy's nocturnal visitant is a rather more prosaic figure—'a dumpy, motherly, little body, in decent shawl and the cleanest of possible nightcaps', who inspects her belongings 'impartially' and with 'exemplary . . . care' (118). The omnipotent 'hand of God' smites and humbles Rochester (*JE* 446); but M. Paul is rendered 'blind and helpless' when Lucy breaks his treasured 'lunettes' (326). The desire and the threat that informed *Jane Eyre* are here, it seems, being contemplated in a rather different way.

Here, as in *Shirley*, there is a distinctive, mock-heroic domestication of 'the issues of the day'. The ignominious quarrels between the curates, the unseemly fracas of the Sunday-school outing, which seem in the earlier novel to evoke and to parody mid-nineteenth-century religious dispute, have their parallels in *Villette*'s comic representation of Anglo-Gallic differences—in Lucy's sardonic account of the attempt to convert her to Rome (413), her description of Madame Beck as 'a little Bonaparte in a mouse-coloured silk gown' (143), her histrionic school-room defence of 'l'Angleterre, l'Histoire et les Héros!' (341). But in *Villette* this irreverence of tone is more radical, more pervasive than in *Shirley*. No character appears in the unironically romantic guise of a Caroline or a Shirley: none is entirely undiminished by Lucy's narrating voice. Dr John may be perilously attractive, but he is figured too as a kind of expensive animal: 'without thought of the price of provender, or care for the cost of keeping it sleek and high-pampered', he 'delights' in feeding his 'masculine self-love' (197). Paulina Mary Home de Bassompierre is 'delicate, intelligent, and sincere': she evokes from Lucy a declaration of 'admiration' that 'I have not often made concerning my acquaintance, in the course of this book' (371). But she is seen, also, momentarily but tellingly, in a more disconcerting light: as akin to the 'small spanieless' that adores M. Paul, 'a . . . loving, and loveable little doggie . . . looking with expressive, attached eyes into his face; and whenever he dropped his bonnet-grec or his handkerchief . . . crouching beside it with the air of a miniature lion guarding a kingdom's flag' (411). M. Paul is constantly, farcically, characterized by his garments, a 'bonnet, a paletot': the 'details' of his appearance are 'so domesticated' in Lucy's memory, 'and so knit with many a whimsical association, as almost by this their sudden apparition, to tickle fancy to a laugh' (310). 'The little man looked well, very well', she notes of him on his fête-day, with a flippancy akin to Lord Charles Wellesley's. 'His figure (such as it was, I don't boast of it) was well set off by a civilized coat and a silken vest quite pretty to behold' (338). This is very different from Caroline's view of Robert, or Shirley's of Louis Moore.

Yet if in one way the ironies of *Villette* are more puncturing than those of *Shirley*, in another, they are less extreme. There is nothing here like the earlier novel's disquieting portrayals of Jessie Yorke's death, or of Helstone fleeing from Mrs Pryor's song. The ambitions portrayed in *Shirley* ended in a ravaged landscape and a chimney like 'the tower of Babel'. But *Villette* opens with images of 'peaceful' well-being and confident, purposeful life. Instead of the 'stone, brick and ashes' of Robert Moore's mill-town, there are 'large' rooms, with 'well-arranged furniture' and 'clear wide windows'; instead of his 'cinder-black highway' a 'clean pavement' and a 'fine antique street'. This is not *Shirley*'s 'Monday morning' world of aspiration and striving, but a place where 'Sundays and holidays seemed always to abide'. And those for whom it is home are thriving, flourishing figures; their authority and 'vivacity' are by no means ironically seen (5). Indeed, they are strangely impervious to that which threatens in *Shirley*. The 'alacrity and power of five-and-twenty still breathed from her and around her,' says Lucy of Louisa Bretton; at 50, 'good health and an excellent temperament' keep her 'green as in her spring' (180, 173). Madame Beck's 'unfaded hair, her eye with its temperate blue light, her cheek with its wholesome fruit-like bloom—these things pleased in moderation, but with constancy' (102). The troubles that come to the Brettons seem effortlessly surmounted. 'Adversity gave me and my mother one passing scowl and brush, but we defied her . . . and she went by' (250). 'Doubtless,' says Lucy, John Bretton and his wife 'knew crosses, disappointments, difficulties; but these were well borne'. By such as these, it appears, even death can be transcended: 'others sprang healthy and blooming to replace the lost' (436). Buoyant in face of reversal, 'a man of luck—a man of success' (318), Dr Graham is not, like Robert Moore, a figure of aspiration checked. 'I was going to write *mortal*,' says Lucy, as she tells of his courtship of Paulina, 'but such words ill apply to one all living like him' (433).

But if in *Villette* 'that world the strong and prosperous live in' (*S* 427) appears more impregnable than in *Shirley*, the distancing implied by that demonstrative is here much more centrally inscribed. 'My godmother lived in a handsome house in the clean and ancient town of Bretton,' Lucy's narrative opens. 'Her husband's family had been residents there for generations, and bore, indeed, the name of their birthplace—Bretton of Bretton: whether by coincidence, or because some remote ancestor had been a personage of sufficient importance to leave his name to his neighbourhood, I know not.' The trailing negative in which she introduces herself to the reader is quite unlike the negatives in which, at the outset of their stories, Crimsworth and Jane announced their resistance to, refusal of their worlds. Here, these others whose name is triply emphasized occupy the centre of the stage. The narrator remains obscure, unnamed until the second chapter; if she tells of the pasts and the futures of others, of her own she has little to say. And this opening configuration is repeated in the novel's closing paragraphs, which refuse to disclose the end of her story, and name those others who 'prosper' as apparently she does not.

Yet this shadowy, reticent narrator is a potent presence in *Villette*. Her inner life is figured in a lurid, metaphoric language, full of personified abstractions and biblical allusions, which seems to speak of energies that threaten to burst the bounds of realism: excitement, anxiety, panic, dread, desolation, uncertainty, despair. Indeed, to many, this story of aberrant subjective feeling has seemed the essential *Villette*. 'Why is *Villette* disagreeable?' asked Matthew Arnold, shortly after its publication. 'Because the writer's mind contains nothing but hunger, rebellion and rage, and therefore that is all she can, in fact put into her book.'[2] ' "Currer Bell" here afflicts us with an amount of subjective misery which we may fairly remonstrate against,' Harriet Martineau declared. 'An atmosphere of pain hangs about the whole, forbidding that repose which we hold to be essential to the true presentment of any large portion of life and experience.'[3] 'The method of *Villette*,' pronounced Raymond Williams, more than a century later, 'is the fiction of special pleading... that fiction in which the only major emotion, and then the relation with the reader, is that exact stress, that first-person stress: "circumstanced like me".'[4] Each of these critics—eloquent though he or she is in praise of Brontë's achievement[5]—sees that achievement as limited by her choice of an urgent, monologic fictional voice: a choice that to them bespeaks a failure to take a larger, more balanced view. 'The stress is this really,' says Williams, seeing only that first-person singular. 'The world will judge me in certain ways if it sees what I do, but if it knew how I felt it would see me quite differently.'

Villette is certainly quite different from those novels of the mid-nineteenth century which seem to offer a wider view of the society of which they speak—*Pendennis, Bleak House, North and South*. 'My observation cannot penetrate where the very deepest political and social truths are to be learnt,' Brontë had written to her publisher after the publication of *Jane Eyre*. 'I must guess, and calculate, and grope my way in the dark and come to uncertain conclusions unaided and alone.' It was different, she said, for 'such writers as Dickens and Thackeray', who had 'access to the shrine and image of Truth, have only to go into the temple, lift the veil a moment

---

[2] *CH* 201.   [3] *CH* 172.
[4] Raymond Williams, *The English Novel from Dickens to Lawrence* (London: Chatto & Windus, 1973), 73–4.
[5] Martineau, Brontë, and Arnold all met at Loughrigg Holme, the home of the Quillinan family on 21 December 1850. The two survivors were to write two of Brontë's most moving obituaries, Martineau's appearing in the *Daily News* of 6 April 1855 and Arnold's elegy 'Haworth Churchyard' in *Fraser's Magazine* for May 1855 (Kathleen Tillotson, ' "Haworth Churchyard": the Making of Arnold's Elegy', *BST* 15: 2 (1967), 105–22). My own debt to Williams's attempt, in several brief but suggestive discussions, to read these novels of 'intense personal feeling' as part of a radical tradition of insistence on human need should be evident throughout this book. For a perceptive discussion of Williams's pioneering work in this sphere, see Cora Kaplan, ' "What We Have Again to Say": Williams, Feminism, and the 1840s', in Christopher Prendergast (ed.), *Cultural Materialism: On Raymond Williams* (Minneapolis: University of Minnesota Press, 1995), 211–36.

and come out and say what they have seen'.[6] Yet *Villette* is more assured, and very much more sophisticated, than this disclaimer might suggest. For Lucy's narrative is by no means merely a psychological one. With a comic banality reminiscent of the jokes of the juvenilia, the novel itself signals this. The Nun that haunts this narrator is by no means merely the product of her 'highly nervous state' (248): it is concrete objective evidence of a love affair in which she has no part. Those peculiar shifts of tone between 'personifications of passion' and the 'deliberately prosaic' are not the marks of clumsiness, but disconcertingly significant.[7] Moreover, the 'over-wrought writing' that Martineau deplored in the novel is very much more precise than its critics appear to have perceived.[8] To take just one example: the import of the passage that Raymond Williams quotes as an illustration of its limiting 'first-person stress' is, in fact, rather different from the gloss that he provides. 'Circum-stanced like me,' says Lucy, 'you would have been, like me, wrong' (157). Here, using a word that is prominent in her narrative, she directs the reader's attention not to-wards her 'feelings' but to the 'circumstances' in which she is placed.[9] And in doing so she indicates that which is evinced in *Villette*'s distinctive emphasis on bourgeois solidity and confidence: a central fictional concern not merely with singular 'pain', but with a sharply seen social world.

'I should much—very much like to take that quiet view of the "great world" you allude to,' Charlotte Brontë had written to her publisher when he suggested a visit to London after the publication of *Jane Eyre*. 'Ellis, I imagine would soon turn aside from the spectacle in disgust . . . his reason may be in advance of mine, but certainly it often travels a different road.'[10] And in pointing to her difference from her sister, she indicates the 'road' her own imaginative 'reason' was increasingly to take. In the months in which she was projecting *Villette* she was at last to take that 'quiet view of the "great world"' which her publisher had urged upon her in happier days. And she was, it seems, pondering deeply the issues that 'spectacle' raised. 'The state of Society in our days is, of all possible states, the least an unconscious one,' Carlyle had written in an essay that Brontë read in 1849. 'This is specially an Era in which all manner of Inquiries into what was once the unfelt, involuntary sphere of man's ex-istence find their place, and as it were, occupy the whole domain of thought.'[11] Charlotte Brontë's letters in the years that preceded the publication of *Villette* evince her lively interest in 'Inquiries' such as these. She read the fictions concerned

---

[6] Charlotte Brontë to W. S. Williams, 28 January 1848, *CBL* ii. 23.

[7] 'The personifications of passion are unnatural, and clumsily patched upon the tale,' 'It is the fiery spirit of the mind and the pen, that bursts through the deliberately prosaic nature of the incidents and situations': thus, two contemporary reviews of *Villette*, each taking a rather different view of which is pre-eminent (*CH* 215, 200).

[8] *CH* 172.

[9] *Villette* is less than 10,000 words longer than *Jane Eyre*, but 'circumstances' or 'circumstanced' are used four times as often. The sense that 'feelings' are rather different from 'circumstances' is registered early in the novel in a distinction that Lucy makes—'my state of mind, and all accompanying circum-stances' (49).

[10] Charlotte Brontë to W. S. Williams, 25 February 1848, *CBL* ii. 28.

[11] Thomas Carlyle, 'Characteristics' (1831), in *Critical and Miscellaneous Essays: Collected and Repub-lished*, 3rd edn. (4 vols.; London: Chapman & Hall, 1847), ii. 396.

with social issues that her contemporaries were bringing out—Dickens's *David Copperfield* and *Bleak House*, Thackeray's *Pendennis*, Kingsley's *Alton Locke*, and Mrs Gaskell's *Ruth*.[12] Her reading included, too, a number of more analytic discussions of social problems, ranging from Carlyle's *Critical and Miscellaneous Essays* and Ruskin's *Stones of Venice*, to such surveys of the state of contemporary society as Elizabeth Whateley's *English Life, Social and Domestic, in the Middle of the Nineteenth Century, Considered in Reference to our Position as a Community of Professing Christians* (1847) and John Stores Smith's *Social Aspects* (1850); and a variety of speculative articles on social, moral, and theological questions in the journals that she regularly received—G. H. Lewes's new *The Leader* and her old favourite, *Fraser's Magazine*.[13] Moreover, and perhaps most significantly, two of the closest intellectual friendships that she made in these years of her fame were with women who were in different ways centrally concerned with the question of how society might be understood. In her first novel, *Mary Barton*, Elizabeth Gaskell had drawn on her own close knowledge of the lives of the Manchester poor in order to 'write truthfully' about the conditions in which the working classes lived.[14] *Ruth*, which she completed whilst Charlotte Brontë was struggling to finish *Villette*, sought to change public opinion on an issue of 'public interest' of a yet more controversial kind.[15] Harriet Martineau was the author of a pioneering work on the methodology of social observation:[16] she was now one of the most prominent social analysts of the day. 'Both these ladies are . . . certainly far my superiors in attainments and experience—I think I could look up to them if I knew them,' Charlotte Brontë had written to her publisher in November 1849.[17] She was, in fact, to know them, and to visit and correspond with them, whilst projecting and writing *Villette*. And she was, it seems, thinking deeply about the differences between her view of the world and theirs.

For there is evidence of that thinking everywhere in *Villette*. 'The good of *Villette* in my opinion Miss is a very fine style; and a remarkably happy way (which few female authors possess) of carrying a metaphor logically through to its conclusion,' wrote Thackeray to a female correspondent just after the novel appeared.[18] The man may have been avuncular, yet the novelist in him recognized this novel's

---

[12] 'I have read "David Copperfield"; it seems to me very good—admirable in some parts. You said it had affinity to "Jane Eyre": it has—now and then—only what an advantage has Dickens in his varied knowledge of men and things!' (to W. S. Williams, 13 September 1849; *CBL* ii. 251). On *Bleak House*, see *LL* iii. 322; on *Pendennis*, *CBL* ii. 148, 351, 358–9; on *Alton Locke*, *CBL* ii. 488; on *Ruth*, *LL* iii. 332; iv. 34–5, 48–9.

[13] Carlyle, *Critical and Miscellaneous Essays*, 3rd edn. (1847) were mainly on literary subjects, but they included two seminal essays on the state of English society—'Signs of the Times' (1829) and 'Characteristics' (1831), quoted above; Brontë read them with 'great interest' in 1849 (*CBL* ii. 197, 202). On her reading of Ruskin, see below. She read Mrs Whateley 'with pleasure' in September 1849 (*CBL* ii. 251) and Smith's 'deeply interesting' book in July 1850 (*CBL* ii. 429).

[14] See John Geoffrey Sharps, *Mrs Gaskell's Observation and Invention* (Fontwell: Linden Press, 1970), 51–67.

[15] Charlotte Brontë to Mrs Gaskell, 26 April 1852, *LL* iii. 332.

[16] Harriet Martineau, *How to Observe. Morals and Manners* (London: Charles Knight, 1838).

[17] *CBL* ii. 285–8.   [18] *CH* 197.

extraordinary artistry. In the precision of its language, in its 'carrying through' of its metaphors, there is, I shall be suggesting, an analytic power more acute, more exploratory, more disciplined, than the authoritative generalizations of such 'men of wide views' as he. This is no 'fiction of special pleading', but a precisely articulated vision of the mid-nineteenth-century world, quite different from those that others were offering in these years: Brontë's most provocative, most powerful reflection not merely on social issues but also on the ways in which her contemporaries thought about them.

II

'Withdrawing to a quiet nook, whence unobserved I could observe—the ball, its splendours and its pleasures passed before me as a spectacle' (142). Thus Lucy Snowe, of the evening of Madame Beck's fête. And the cool survey of Ginevra's frivolity, of Dr John's weakness, of Madame Beck's tactics that she offers in the rest of this chapter is reminiscent both of Crimsworth's 'scrutiny' and of Jane Eyre's more impassioned but also objectifying gaze. For that sense of vision as control which shaped those earlier novels is emphatically marked in this.[19] The world into which Brontë's narrator goes is one of spying and counter-spying, of wielded or evaded supervisory power. Mme Beck's 'watch-words' are 'espionage' and 'surveillance' (72); she 'listen[s] and peep[s]' through a spy-hole' at her teacher conducting a class (81). Dr John's clinical observations are no less invasive in effect. 'I look on you now from a professional point of view, and I read, perhaps, all you would conceal', he says, as he catalogues the visible signs of Lucy's distress (248). At Lucy's first meeting with M. Paul he inspects her countenance for evidence of her character (66): later, he reads her letters, examines her desk, spies on her on her solitary walks, and reveals that he hires a room in which 'I watch you and others pretty closely, pretty constantly, nearer and oftener than you or they think' (363). Such imagery reaches its climax in the appearance within the novel of that object of so many mid-nineteenth-century paranoid fantasies—the 'surveillance of [the] sleepless eye' of the Roman Catholic Church (409).

Yet the threatening 'surveillance' of others is viewed with rather more irony here than it is in *The Professor* or *Jane Eyre*. When Lucy finds Madame Beck 'hard at work' inspecting her possessions, she watches her with 'secret glee' (118). 'I know not whether I was more amused or provoked,' she says, as she tells of M. Paul's 'solemn' warning that 'he had his eye on me' (302). She reports Dr John's diagnosis,

---

[19] There is an extensive critical literature on *Villette* and 'surveillance'. See e.g. Janet Gezari, *Charlotte Brontë and Defensive Conduct: The Author and the Body at Risk* (Philadelphia: University of Pennsylvania Press, 1992); Joseph A. Boone, 'Depolicing *Villette*: Surveillance, Invisibility, and the Female Erotics of "Heretic Narrative"', *Novel*, 26: 1 (Fall 1992), 20–42; Margaret L. Shaw, 'Narrative Surveillance and Social Control in *Villette*', *Studies in English Literature*, 34: 4 (Autumn 1994), 813–34; Nicholas Dames, 'The Clinical Novel: Phrenology and *Villette*', *Novel*, 29: 3 (Spring 1996), 367–90; Sally Shuttleworth, *Charlotte Brontë and Victorian Psychology* (Cambridge: Cambridge University Press, 1996).

deflatingly, as cliché—'it was all optical illusion—nervous malady, and so on'; 'doctors are so self-opinionated, so immovable in their dry, materialist views' (257). 'In her single person', we are told, Madame Beck 'could have comprised the duties of a first minister and a superintendent of police' (74). But it is with sardonic amusement that Lucy portrays her 'stealing like a cat round the garden' (114), 'glid[ing] ghost-like through the house, watching and spying everywhere, peering through every key-hole, listening behind every door' (73), found out, in this last, by an 'irrepressible sneeze' (125). 'It was very much his habit to wear eyes before, behind, and on each side of him', Lucy remarks, derisively, of M. Paul (232):[20] and the farcical comedy implicit in her description is emphasized by the novel's literalization of this figure in the image that becomes his hallmark—that of his treasured, flashing 'lunettes'. Even the novel's most melodramatic example of 'surveillance'—the 'quick-shot and crafty glance of a Jesuit-eye' (394)—is hardly treated with the gravity that the subject might have seemed to contemporaries to demand.[21] If the convent, the confessional, the 'junta' of Jesuitical plotters are all prominent in Lucy's narrative, it is in a spirit rather different from that in which they were being imaged in other novels in these years.[22] The attempt to convert the heroine to Rome—a subject that evoked much Gothic horror in such works—is seen through the prism of a deflating common sense. 'It was a canting, sentimental, shallow little book ... He that had written it was no bad man ... His judgment, however, wanted surgical props; it was rickety,' Lucy says, of the tract urging 'the Protestant' to 'turn Papist' left for her by M. Paul (413). The Nun who haunts this narrator makes her final appearance not as a figure of horror but as 'a long bolster dressed in a long black stole, and artfully invested with a white veil' (470). And Lucy's visit to the confessional leads her not to the rigours of a convent but to a 'cosy arrangement of the cushions' on a sofa in an English drawing-room (175).

---

[20]   The joking reference, much more likely to be picked up by contemporary than today's readers, is to Revelation 4: 6: 'round about the throne, were four beasts full of eyes before and behind'.
[21]   The Pope's decision to establish Roman Catholic bishoprics in England had caused a crescendo of anti-Catholic feeling in 1850–1; the so-called 'Papal Aggression' was one of the most prominent topics of the day. See Robert James Klaus, *The Pope, the Protestants, and the Irish: Papal Aggression and Anti-Catholicism in Mid-Nineteenth-Century England* (New York: Garland, 1987), and D. G. Paz, *Popular Anti-Catholicism in Mid-Victorian England* (Stanford: Stanford University Press, 1992). For the local situation in Leeds, and its reporting in the Leeds press, see Shuttleworth, *Charlotte Brontë and Victorian Psychology*, 225.
[22]   All three of these subjects fascinated anti-Catholic writers. 'This season [ladies] have been greedy in the demand for *The Female Jesuit*,' observed a writer on railway reading in 1851 (Samuel Phillips, 'Literature of the Rail', *The Times*, 9 August 1851). His reference is to Mrs S. Luke's *The Female Jesuit: or the Spy in the Family. A True Narrative of Recent Events in a Protestant Household* (London, Partridge & Oakley, 1851), which was followed by *A Sequel to The Female Jesuit; Containing Her Previous History and Recent Discovery* in 1852. Other anti-Catholic novels of the mid-century in which such themes are prominent include William Sewell, *Hawkstone* (London: Murray, 1845); Elizabeth Missing Sewell, *Margaret Percival* (London: Longman, 1847); *The Convent: A Narrative, Founded on Fact* (London: Aylott & Jones, 1848); and most famously (or notoriously), *The Awful Disclosures of Maria Monk* (London: Harper, 1836), frequently reprinted throughout the century. The figure of the plotting Jesuit recurs in two more serious novels, both of which Brontë read: Kingsley's *Yeast* (1849) and Thackeray's *Henry Esmond* (1852).

'Surveillance', it seems, is invoked in *Villette* only to be mocked and marginalized. But the 'splendours' and 'pleasures' that pass before Lucy 'as a spectacle' might alert us to the prominence in the novel of a different kind of visual imagery, which seems to signal a different centre of concern. Unlike the dangerous places through which Jane and Crimsworth journey, the world this narrator confronts is one of emphasized 'public display' (134). In the well-lit classrooms at the Pensionnat Beck, examinations are public events, taking place before a 'large audience' (155): 'A *showy demonstration*—a telling *exhibition*—must be got up for *public view*, and all means were fair to this end' (153). 'I would pay a fine, or undergo an imprisonment, rather than write *for a show* and to order, perched up *on a platform*,' Lucy protests, ineffectually, when urged to undergo this ordeal (357). 'I saw at a glance that it lacked none of those finishing details which cost so much, and give to *the general effect* such an air of tasteful completeness,' she says, of Ginevra's evening dress. 'She turned airily round *that I might survey her on all sides*' (88). Sexual attraction, here, is a matter of 'tasteful'—or titillating—presentation and display. Madame Beck's pupils are shown off, at her fête, to an audience of 'jeunes gens', invited not as participants but as 'spectators': 'a sort of cordon stretched before them' separates them from the 'belles blondes' or 'jolies brunes' on show (143). In the picture-gallery Lucy visits, a 'cordon stretched before it' likewise protects the spectacle of a well-fed and indolent femininity from 'worshipping connoisseurs' (199). Even Graham Bretton's love for Paulina partakes of the logic of show. 'He was not the man who, in appreciating the gem, could forget its setting,' remarks Lucy. 'In his victrix he required all that was here *visible*—the imprint of high cultivation, the consecration of a careful and authoritative protection, the adjuncts that Fashion decrees, Wealth purchases, and Taste adjusts.' And if Paulina acquires value from the context in which she is displayed, her suitor, too, must be seen in a satisfactory light: 'To satisfy himself did not suffice; society must approve—the world must *admire* what he did' (369–70; my italics throughout).

Such metaphors and moments are not incidental to the novel. They are focused and objectified in a series of images of actual spectacles, exhibitions, and shows. At the Pensionnat Beck, the mistress's fête is the occasion for a showy presentation, a theatrical performance, a splendid ball. When Dr John seeks 'to give pleasure' to Lucy he takes her sightseeing, to 'places of interest in the town' (196); when he writes to her, 'he dwells with sunny satisfaction on scenes which had passed before his eyes and mine' (244). The second and third volumes of *Villette* tell of a succession of such 'scenes': 'a picture of pretentious size, set up in the best light' in a gallery, with 'a cushioned bench' for viewers set in front of it (199); a concert in 'a great illuminated building', where Lucy sits in a place 'commanding a good general view' of a 'vast and dazzling . . . hall' (210); the ceremony of presentation of prizes at the principal college of Villette, and the public lecture that follows; the 'marvellous sight', the immoral 'spectacle' of a theatrical performance of a peculiarly striking kind (258). M. Paul's feast-day is celebrated by 'a pretty spectacle' (327)—the offering of flowers and their ceremonious arrangement into a 'blooming pyramid' (338). He arranges Lucy's present of a watch-guard 'splendidly across his chest, displaying as much and suppressing as little as he could' (346). 'I was shown the Papal ritual and ceremonial. I looked at it,' Lucy says, of the church whose 'painted and meretricious face' is 'unveiled' for her 'admiration'. 'Many people . . . have felt this display impressive', she admits: the 'swarming tapers . . . ecclesiastical millinery . . . celestial jewellery' leave her, however, unmoved (420–1). She finds more to 'charm' and to 'marvel' at in the 'spectacles, decorations, and illuminations' on the night of the city's 'great fête' (453).

Unlike the worlds of either of Brontë's two previous first-person novels, *Villette*'s is one of leisure, of plenitude, comfort and ease. The 'long and difficult' lessons that Jane Eyre found at Lowood are unknown at Madame Beck's school. Here, there are prizes, not punishments; 'life, movement and variety' rather than monotony, confinement, and death (75). 'No minds were overtasked; the lessons were well distributed and made incomparably easy to the learner; there was a liberty of amusement, and a provision for exercise which kept the girls healthy; the food was abundant and good' (73). Here, the schoolrooms—their glass doors opening onto a pretty garden filled with 'orange-trees . . . cacti . . . camelias' (411)—are places not of asceticism, but of agreeable aesthetic display. The icy schoolroom at Lowood is lit by the 'dim light' of 'dips' (*JE* 43), but the *grande salle* at the Pensionnat Beck boasts a 'pair of many-branched chandeliers' (342); 'glowing stoves' bring 'a sense of comfort' and even 'over-heat' the class (231, 353). Instead of the strictures against curls and braids directed at the pupils of Lowood, here there is a 'coiffeur', summoned to arrange the girls' hair (130); instead of the nauseous fumes of burnt porridge, the tempting 'fragrance of baked apples' cooked with 'a little spice, sugar, and a glass or two of vin blanc' (355). This 'flourishing educational establishment' is 'a complete and most charming contrast to many English institutions of the same kind' (75).

Yet if the mores of Villette are strange to the English, Protestant reader, they are, the novel suggests, not as distant from those of England as might at first appear. The ease, the comfort, the pleasantness that Lucy finds in this foreign place are prefigured at the opening of her story: in the 'well-arranged furniture' and 'clear wide windows' of those 'large peaceful rooms' in which the confident Brettons of Bretton, quintessential figures of Englishness, are cheerful, prosperous, at home.[23] This too is a place of health and equanimity, where 'shipwreck' is unknown, and 'eccentricities' concealed (32). Here, 'time always flows smoothly' (6); problems are calmly dealt with; unobtrusive servants are despatched to carry out tasks. The essential configuration is not of aspiration and striving, but of ease, of competence, of assurance; not of intensity and uncertainty, but of moderation, security, success. And this configuration remains unchanged—indeed, it is yet more evident—when the household of the Brettons is reconstituted in Villette. This is surely part of the point of that scene at the opening of the second volume where the familiar things of Bretton appear with a quite new sharpness of detail in this unfamiliar place. Where the pleasant ease of Bretton was figured in a metaphor from Bunyan, the 'material

---

[23] 'Clear wide windows' were a sign of material prosperity, as the window-tax was not abolished until 1851.

comforts' (284) of La Terrasse are more solidly specified. This is a place of cosy meals, bright fires, and ample curtains: it is cushioned, carpeted, insulated against the shocks of the outside world. Here, once again, there are servants—'housemaid steps on the stairs' (181), the 'bonne' who 'place[s] a screen' between Lucy and the lamp (168), the hands that lift her 'from the carriage . . . and put [her] in at the door' (274). Here, distant storms sound 'only like murmurs and a lullaby' (181): here, once again, the 'eccentricity' of powerful feeling is unknown (176). For here, as in Madame Beck's school, there is agreeably unobtrusive order; neither asceticism nor indulgence, but pleasant liberality; variety, rather than monotony, and pleasure, rather than pain. There is nothing, here, like Crimsworth's striving, or the frustrated entrepreneurial 'ambition' that fires Robert Moore. 'In the profession he had adopted, his success was now quite decided,' says Lucy of the young doctor. All that he does is 'accomplished with the ease and grace of all-sufficing strength' (177, 196). 'Hard-worked, yet seldom over-driven', he has time for 'beneficial enjoyment', returning home each night in a 'kindly, pleasant mood' (196, 272). His 'mellow voice' never has 'any sharpness in it'; it is 'calculated . . . to soothe' (182). Here, as in Bretton, the household revolves around this emphatically masculine figure; here, as there, he comes and goes whilst his womenfolk wait at home. But the qualities he embodies are not, in *Villette*, peculiar to masculine privilege. For his mother, too—'little changed' (171) since those former days in Bretton—is 'busy and happy' in her life at La Terrasse' (272). She, no less than her son, seems of a different species from Lucy: 'a stately ship, cruising safe on smooth seas' (181), 'well fitted to fight a good fight with the world, and to prevail' (177).

Of course, it was 'pain' that early reviewers discerned most sharply in *Villette*. But much of the novel's distinctiveness lies in the fact that the world that meets this tormented narrator's gaze is emphatically one of plenitude, of solid prosperity, and ease. It is a world on display, lit up by oil-lights (469), by gas-light (401–2) and 'lustres' (137), by dazzling chandeliers. 'Villette is one blaze, one broad illumination . . . The town, by her own flambeaux, beholds her own splendour' in the scene that brings to a climax the novel's imagery of show (452). It is a world in which things go smoothly: if Lucy's characteristic posture is one of anguished suspense, waiting to gain admission or to hear the ring of the bell, in the company of the Brettons she experiences the magic of the opening door (198, 209). And it is a world that is filled with objects—'crochet, guard-chains, cookery, and dress', a contemporary reviewer remarked disapprovingly[24]—minutely particularized, copiously described. Jane Eyre paints visionary watercolours, but Lucy is the maker of 'handscreens' decorated with 'elaborate pencil-drawings finished like line-engravings' (166), of a 'pin-cushion . . . of crimson satin, ornamented with gold beads and frilled with thread-lace' (169), of a watchguard 'glossy with silk and sparkling with beads' (346), which she encloses in 'a small box I had bought for its brilliancy, made of some tropic shell of the colour called "nacarat," and decked with a little coronal of sparkling blue stones' (335). Jane tells the reader that she went to Lowton 'to get

---

[24] *Eclectic Review*, quoted in *CH* 196.

measured for a pair of shoes' (*JE* 87), but Lucy of shopping for the 'wools, silks, embroidering thread, etcetera, wanted in the pupils' work', of 'choosing and matching ... silks and wools', of selecting 'the slides and the tassels for ... purses', 'the patterns for ... slippers ... bell-ropes ... cabas' (386–7). Jane Eyre speaks simply of 'dark handsome new carpets and curtains', of 'old mahogany and crimson upholstery' when she tells of refurnishing Moor House (*JE* 391). But the school M. Paul gives to Lucy is very differently described:

> There was a little couch, a little chiffonière—the half-open, crimson-silk door of which, showed porcelain on the shelves; there was a French clock, a lamp; there were ornaments in biscuit china; the recess of the single ample window was filled with a green stand, bearing three green flower-pots, each filled with a fine plant glowing in bloom; in one corner appeared a guéridon with a marble top, and upon it a work-box, and a glass filled with violets in water. (485)

The triple repetition of 'filled' underlines the effect of crowdedness: no container here is left empty, no surface bare. The list-like catalogue of objects and the absence of striking adjectives to suggest an organizing consciousness create a sense, not unlike that of contemporary pre-Raphaelite painting, of an almost incoherent proliferation of things.

It is a sense which—along with those other, shaping emphases on prosperity on display, on bourgeois comfort and ease—comes most sharply into focus in that pivotal scene in which Lucy tells of her awakening at La Terrasse. For here, that 'calm and decorated' drawing-room (29), that quiet bedroom in Bretton of which the opening chapters speak, suddenly appear as rooms filled with furniture, every surface 'covered', every article abundantly 'finished' and 'adorned'. Things in these rooms are loaded with ornament, 'myriad gold leaves and tendrils'; 'bordered with ... foliage', or 'frilled with thread-lace', 'worked with groups of brilliant flowers'; 'curtained', 'cushioned', 'smooth', 'shiny', 'polished', 'foliated', 'carved' (166–70). Here, there is a thickness of description unlike anything in Brontë's earlier fiction; a superfluity like the 'gorged designs' of high Victorian domestic art.[25] If the splendours of *Jane Eyre*'s Thornfield—its 'Tyrian-dyed curtains' and 'Parian mantelpiece', its 'crimson couches and ottomans' (*JE* 104)—evoke an exotic world of romance, familiar from the sub-Byronic annuals, this prosaic collection of domestic objects, bewilderingly out of place, points, like the novel's descriptions of Madame Beck's school and of the Brettons and de Bassompierres, towards a less poetic, more solidly material reality: that mid-nineteenth-century world of bourgeois

---

[25] Thus Ralph Nicholson Wornum, disparagingly, in his Prize Essay on the Great Exhibition (quoted in Asa Briggs, *Victorian Things* (Harmondsworth: Penguin, 1990), 53). 'There is always abundant space for the display of much elegant decoration', declared *The Art Journal Illustrated Catalogue of the Great Exhibition*. (London: George Virtue, 1851). 'Ornamental articles now meet the eye at every turn' (51, 86). The fashion for stylized patterns from nature—differently evoked by Dickens, in Mr Gradgrind's interrogation of Cissy Jupe—is reflected here in the 'autumn-tinted foliage' bordering the table-cover, the wallpaper where 'a slight but endless garland of azure forget-me-nots' runs 'mazed and bewildered amongst myriad gold leaves and tendrils', the 'brilliant flowers' worked on the seats and the backs of the chairs.

confidence and affluence enshrined and celebrated in the Great Exhibition, which Charlotte Brontë visited five times whilst she was conceiving *Villette*.

'Yesterday I went for the second time to the Crystal Palace', she wrote to her father, from London, on 7 June 1851. 'It is a wonderful place—vast—strange new and impossible to describe.'[26] The letter in which she describes this visit is full of prefigurations of *Villette*: pearls of great price, precious objects stored in 'caskets', the transporting power of the eastern Genii, a sound 'like a tide retiring from a shore of the upper world' (*V* 427, 243, 167, 181). Other of her letters from London at this time describe other 'wonderful sights', which appear transmuted in the novel—Thackeray's lectures; the 'impiously theatrical' scene of a Roman Catholic confirmation held by Cardinal Wiseman ; the fine 'collection of pictures' in Lord Westminster's 'splendid Gallery'; Rachel's acting ('a wonderful sight . . . I shall never forget it—she made me shudder to the marrow of my bones').[27] Less strikingly, but most suggestively, they tell of Brontë's new familiarity with affluent middle-class life—of her stay with George Smith and his mother in their comfortable house in Gloucester Terrace, and of Mrs Gaskell's 'large—cheerful airy house' in Manchester, to which she paid her first visit en route from London to home.[28] Of course, *Villette*'s foreign setting is more explicitly drawn from its author's two sojourns in Brussels, in 1842 and 1843.[29] But even as the nature of the Bretton world comes into focus for Lucy ten years later, and in another place, so in this last of Charlotte Brontë's novels features of that time in Brussels hardly touched on in *The Professor* assume a prominence that connects them with those new experiences of 1851.The emphasis here is not on privation and struggle, but on ostentatious comfort and ease; not on work, but on its results—a hand-screen, a pin-cushion, a watch-guard—on display. Instead of *Jane Eyre*'s 'incident, life, fire, feeling', *Shirley*'s aspiration and conflict, there are obtrusive material objects, an increased elaboration in the prose.[30] The configuration signals *Villette*'s imaginative engagement with a central 'issue of the day'.

The middle years of the nineteenth century saw a remarkable transformation in English society. This was a period of steadily increasing national prosperity, of

[26] Charlotte Brontë to her father, 7 June 1851 (*CBL* ii. 630).

[27] Charlotte Brontë to her father, 31 May 1851; to Ellen Nussey, 24 June 1851 (*CBL* ii. 625, 648).

[28] Charlotte Brontë to George Smith, 1 July 1851 (*CBL* ii. 655). 'Haworth Parsonage is rather a contrast,' she wrote to Mrs Smith, on the same day (*CBL* ii. 654). Winifred Gérin provides a suggestive description and photograph of Mrs Gaskell's 'famous drawing-room', 'to our modern eyes, overcrowded with bric-a-brac, ornaments and cabinets; but . . . to the taste of the day, with its heavily draped and curtained windows and doors' (*Charlotte Brontë: The Evolution of Genius* (Oxford: Oxford University Press, 1967), 488).

[29] Gérin, *Charlotte Brontë*, 209–10, 235, 237–9, 243–4, 248–52.

[30] Robert Heilmann has pointed to the 'sensory and architectonic elaborateness' of *Villette*: its 'insistent alliteration', its 'subtle patterns of repetitive sound', the 'new euphuism' of its 'Johnsonian effects, the Latinistic and epigrammatic', its 'parallel and antithetical structures . . . pervasive alliteration and related sound effects', its 'personifications . . . figurative language . . . mythological references' ('Tulip-Hood, Streaks, and Other Strange Bedfellows: Style in *Villette*', *Studies in the Novel*, 14 (1982), 235–7). These features of the novel, it might be argued, are an exact stylistic equivalent of that intricate ornamentation, that adoption of spurious historical styles, that unnatural use of nature, which distinguished so many of the artefacts on display in the Great Exhibition.

imperial and commercial expansion, of rapid urban growth.[31] New kinds of public buildings were now being constructed—railway stations, department stores, exhibition halls: 'massive monuments to wealth, imperial glory and commercial supremacy, self-important spectacle productions in real . . . brick . . . iron, and glass'.[32] 'Go to the most insignificant country town', enjoined a writer in 1850. 'It has its elegant houses, perhaps its monuments and squares . . . its shops bear the evident stamp of taste and fashion . . . In the great metropolis . . . the evidences of social prosperity become still more ample and imposing, refinements and splendours are poured all round with a most unsparing affluence, graceful buildings meet us in every prominent street . . . proofs of the most unbounded wealth astonish us.'[33] The increasing number and variety of manufactured goods meant that the middle-class home was filled with comforts and gadgets of hitherto unknown kinds. It was cushioned, curtained, carpeted, upholstered; its bright fires burnt in redesigned grates; its walls were covered with wallpaper; its furnishings with veneer.[34] John Stores Smith, who in 1850 admiringly presented Charlotte Brontë with a copy of his *Social Aspects* (and received an approbatory letter in reply),[35] speaks in that work of 'an entire change in the whole aspect of middle-class life'. 'A young man must plunge into married life at full gallop,' he reports. 'He must have a house replete with elegancies, with plate, pier glasses, pictures, and all the paraphernalia of a drawing-room of fashion'; for this is an age of 'superfluities' and 'extravagant display'.[36] 'A London drawing-room fitted up without regard to expense', observes Thackeray, more ironically, in *Pendennis*, 'is surely one of the noblest and most curious sights of the present day.'[37]

Prosperity was far more visible now than ever before. Dress, especially for women, became more ostentatious; it was decorated with flounces, ruching, trimmings; rich new fabrics such as gauze and organdy, velvet and brocade, began to be used. During the 1850s the slim lines of the sentimental style gradually gave way to more inflated sleeves and skirts, and brilliant, often violently contrasting, colours replaced paler tints. If the woman of the 1830s and 1840s had been slender, unob-

---

[31] J. F. C. Harrison, *Early Victorian Britain 1832–51* (London: Fontana, 1979), 32, 36). For the larger European picture, see Eric Hobsbawm, *The Age of Capital 1848–1875* (London: Weidenfeld & Nicolson, 1975), ch. 13.

[32] Michael R. Booth, *Victorian Spectacular Theatre 1850–1910* (London: Routledge & Kegan Paul, 1981), 3.

[33] Hood, *The Age and its Architects*, 28–9.

[34] This latter indeed (as Dickens was famously to register) became a disapproving shorthand for meretricious 'show and display'; the age, *Fraser's Magazine* complained in a series of articles between September 1850 and September 1851, was becoming an 'age of veneer'. On the cult and the actualities of the middle-class 'home' in this period, see Harrison, *Early Victorian Britain*, 32–45; Davidoff and Hall, *Family Fortunes*, 375–95; and, for a detailed account of the 'substantial comfort' of high Victorian life, John Gloag, *Victorian Comfort: A Social History of Design from 1830–1900* (London: A. & C. Black, 1961).

[35] Charlotte Brontë to John Stores Smith, 25 July 1850; to Ellen Nussey, 1 August 1850 (*CBL* ii. 428–9, 433). See also Kathleen Tillotson's account of Smith's subsequent visit to Charlotte Brontë, 'A Day with Charlotte Brontë in 1850', *BST* 16: 1 (1971), 22–3.

[36] John Stores Smith, *Social Aspects* (London: Chapman, 1850), 40, 45.

[37] William Makepeace Thackeray, *The History of Pendennis*, ed. Donald Hawes (Harmondsworth: Penguin, 1972), 399.

trusive, and delicate, the fashionable woman of the 1850s was imposing, colourful, difficult to overlook.[38] 'The ladies, in their bescented pomp, with their many-flounced distended dresses, their jewels and camellias, and the gentlemen, with their broidered fronts and fashionable extravagancies, strut the rooms, self-satisfied,' wrote John Stores Smith of this 'age of . . . immense and brilliant assemblies'; for him, the marks of the period were 'épergnes, ottomans, chandeliers, pier glasses, and champagne'.[39] In London, where once 'a few blinking oil-lamps just sufficed to render the darkness visible', an observer in the mid-1850s remarked that 'broad streams of gas flash like meteors into every corner of the wealth-crammed mart'.[40] The houses of the middle classes, too, lit up: wax candles, then oil lamps, replaced the rush lights and tallow dips of former years.[41] Shopkeepers were beginning to try the new 'expedient of giving brilliancy and apparent vastness by clothing wall and ceiling with looking-glass, and causing these to reflect the light from the rich cut-glass chandelier'.[42] 'When we arrive at St. Paul's Churchyard', declared *Knight's Cyclopaedia of London* in 1851—noting there the new glass-fronted shops, lit from outside 'with a reflector so placed as to throw down a strong light on the commodities in the window'—'we come to a very world of show'.[43]

Charlotte Brontë had first encountered something of this bright new world of conspicuous consumption and display in the Brussels of 1842–3. But by the time she began to write *Villette*, its impact was being felt in the details of her life at home. For if the once lively Parsonage was now a place of 'hush and gloom',[44] it was also beginning in these years to acquire comforts hitherto unknown. In 1850 its roof was removed and extensive internal alterations made: the dining-room around which the sisters had paced together became a larger sitting-room, for Charlotte's solitary use.[45] 'The parlour has been evidently refurnished within the last few years,' Mrs Gaskell observed in 1853, 'since Miss Brontë's success has enabled her to have a little more money to spend.'[46] Curtains and furniture were purchased;[47] framed portraits of the Duke of Wellington and of Charlotte herself arrived to hang on the

[38] C. Willett Cunnington and Phillis Cunnington, *Handbook of English Costume in the Nineteenth Century*, 3rd edn. (London: Faber, 1970), 420–62.

[39] Smith, *Social Aspects*, 52, 55.

[40] Charles Manby Smith, *The Little World of London; or, Pictures in Little of London Life* (London: Arthur Hall, Virtue, & Co., 1857), 324–5.

[41] Something of the impact of such changes on those used to darkness is registered in *Jane Eyre*. 'She ushered me into a room, whose double illumination of fire and candle at first dazzled me,' Jane says of her arrival at Thornfield, 'contrasting as it did with the darkness to which my eyes had been for two hours inured' (95). 'I had fires in my bedroom evening and morning, two wax candles—&c. &c.', wrote Charlotte Brontë to her friend Ellen Nussey of her first visit to the Smiths' house in December 1849 (5 December 1849, *CBL* ii. 299): 'a tall waxlight' stands 'on each side the great looking-glass' in the 'little sea-green room' at La Terrasse where Lucy and Paulina renew acquaintance after ten years (*Villette*, 343).

[42] Charles Knight (ed.), *Knight's Cyclopaedia of London* (London: Charles Knight, 1851), 761.

[43] *Knight's Cyclopaedia of London*, 761.

[44] Charlotte Brontë to W. S. Williams, 26 July 1849 (*CBL* ii. 232).

[45] Jocelyn Kellett, *Haworth Parsonage: The Home of the Brontës* Keighley: Brontë Society, 1977), 39–46.

[46] Gaskell, 506.

[47] Charlotte Brontë to Ellen Nussey, 8 December 1851 (*CBL* ii. 726). There had been no curtains at all prior to this (see Ellen Nussey's 'Reminiscences of Charlotte Brontë', *CBL* i. 599).

walls.[48] That 'little more money' was spent, too, on numerous other things. Nearly every letter from Brontë to her friend Ellen Nussey in the years between the composition of *Shirley* and the publication of *Villette* contains some discussion of clothing, or of other shopping commissions—'a patent shower-bath' in 'a huge Monster-package' from Nelsons of Leeds; 'a boa and cuffs'; furs both 'sable' and 'squirrel'; 'patterns' for dresses; a 'card-case' intended as a wedding gift: a flowery cushion for embroidering; a plait of false hair; '3 yds of brown satin ribbon'; 'some chemisettes of small size'.[49] Even such a secluded life as Brontë's was not, it seems, untouched by the proliferation of British consumer goods—or their export to the furthest quarters of the globe. In 1849 her publishers, Smith & Elder, expanded their export trade to include a variety of manufactures: in one humorous letter, prefigurative of *Villette*, Brontë depicts the gentlemen of the firm trying on 'a selection of ladies' bonnets for East-Indian exportation':

A gentianella blue satin is found most becoming to Mr T—y—r; Mr W—m's artist's eye finds a 'special' charm in the rich tint of a 'chapeau grenat' (anglice a garnet-coloured velvet bonnet) while Mr G—e S—th divides his preference between the prettiest little pink drawn-silk and the neatest white chip with a single drooping ostrich feather.[50]

In April 1851 Brontë asks Ellen Nussey 'to do a small errand' in Leeds: 'in case you chanced to be in any shop where the lace cloaks black and white, of which I spoke, were sold, to ask their price.'[51] Later, she writes that she purchased 'one of the black lace mantles', but that, finding 'it looked somewhat brown and rusty' against her 'black satin dress', she has exchanged it for a white one, 'pretty, neat and light'.[52] 'I went to Hunt & Hall's [in Leeds] for the bonnet', she confesses on 10 May,

and got one which seemed grave and quiet there amongst all the splendours—but now it looks infinitely too gay with its pink lining—I saw some beautiful silks of pale sweet colours but had not the spirit or the means to launch out at the rate of 5s. per yd and went and bought a black silk at 3s. after all.[53]

Yet if that scene of the trying-on of bonnets and these latter, much pondered purchases seem to point quite directly towards Mrs Bretton's joking adornment of her son with a sky-blue turban, and to that 'third person in a pink dress and black lace mantle' who sees herself in a 'a great mirror' at the concert in Labassecour (262), *Villette* is by no means simply a fictional exploration of its author's private concerns. Here, as in each of Charlotte Brontë's earlier novels, one finds a quite original reflection upon that much wider experience of which her own partook: a

[48] Charlotte Brontë to George Smith, 1 August 1850; Patrick Brontë to George Smith, 2 August 1850 (*CBL* ii. 433–5).

[49] *CBL* ii. 233, 249, 250, 265, 367, 395, 602.

[50] Charlotte Brontë to George Smith, 26 December 1849 (*CBL* ii. 318).

[51] Charlotte Brontë to Ellen Nussey, 12 April 1851 (*CBL* ii. 601–2).

[52] Charlotte Brontë to Ellen Nussey, 23 April 1851 (*CBL* ii. 608). The mantle, a wide-sleeved, semi-fitting overgarment, became very popular in the 1850s: see Sarah Levitt, *Victorians Unbuttoned: Registered Designs for Clothing, their Makers and Wearers, 1839–1900* (London: Allen & Unwin, 1986), 71.

[53] *CBL* ii. 613.

wider experience being focused, contemplated, celebrated in a great new national symbol in the months in which *Villette* was conceived.

To the surviving creator of Glass Town, the Great Exhibition, in its palace of glass, must have been an evocative sight.[54] 'It is such a Bazaar or Fair as eastern Genii might have created', Charlotte Brontë wrote to her father, whom she may well have expected to catch her allusion to the 'plays'.[55] Even its official title—the Great Exhibition of the Works of Art and Industry of All Nations—could hardly have failed to prompt poignant memories of the Tower of All Nations that had dominated the Glass Town world. For this, too, was hailed as the pinnacle of human achievement: an 'image of the world and its arts . . . exhibited before [the] bodily eye in a vast crystal frame'.[56] Here, the multifarious was made intelligible and ordered: the catalogues and the categories, the 'jurors' and the medals all test-ified to the triumph of taxonomy, of the organizing, judging gaze. Yet the records of the period suggest that many, including Brontë, saw the Exhibition in a rather different way.

In a world of show and display, this was the quintessence of spectacle. For those who held season tickets it was, 'first and foremost a lounge and a panorama un-equalled for comfort, splendour and variety'.[57] Charles Babbage described it as a 'Diorama of the peaceful arts'.[58] A culture of enjoyable spectacle—of which the Great Exhibition was merely one massive example—is inscribed in such visual metaphors. Indeed, the word 'panopticon', once synonymous with disciplinary surveillance, was in 1850 adopted as the title of one of the many 'shows of London' that the Exhibition spawned.[59] The Royal Panopticon of Science and Art was an in-stitution very different from Bentham's 'Inspection House'. A display of handi-crafts, manufactured goods and scientific discoveries, housed in an imposing Saracen-style building, it was intended as 'a source of recreation' for 'all classes of the community'. 'We know of no more delightful lounge in London, whether the taste of the pleasure-seeker . . . finds its gratification in fine music, in large fountains, in interesting experiments, or even in shopping', *The Athenaeum* proclaimed of it

---

[54] For a suggestive discussion of Glass Town as a 'proleptic vision' of the Crystal Palace, and of *Vil-lette*'s relation to this, see Isobel Armstrong, 'Charlotte Brontë's City of Glass', The Hilda Hulme Memo-rial Lecture, 2 December 1992 (London: University of London, 1993).

[55] Charlotte Brontë to Patrick Brontë, 7 June 1851 (*CBL* ii. 631). For Patrick Brontë's 'lively interest' in his children's amusements, see Barker, 109.

[56] William Whewell, *The General Bearing of the Great Exhibition on the Progress of Art and Science*, In-augural Lecture as Master of Trinity College, Cambridge, 26 November 1851, 5.

[57] *Athenaeum*, 7 June 1851, 605.

[58] Charles Babbage, *The Exposition of 1851; or, Views of the Industry, the Science and the Government of England* (London: John Murray, 1851), pp. v–vi.

[59] This was the year of the Deed of Settlement of the Royal Panopticon of Science and Art, though the institution itself was not opened until 1854. *OED* cites this as the first use of the word as meaning 'in which all is seen' rather than 'all-seeing'. But an article in *Fraser's* for June 1845—which Brontë probably read with interest—deploring 'the great increase of *display* as a motive in modern women', also uses the word in this sense: 'They are brought up in a sort of panopticon; everything they can do must be pinned to their shoulders, that the world may be advertised of their merits.' ('An Inquiry into the State of Girls' Fashionable Schools', *Fraser's Magazine*, 31 (1845), 703).

in April 1854.[60] Of course, such shows as these bore testimony to work. The Great Exhibition's medals were inscribed 'Pulcher et ille labor palma decorare laborem': at the Royal Panopticon, 'busy artisans' were prominently on display.[61] But even at the 'Palace of Industry' (as the Great Exhibition was sometimes called), 'the aesthetics of the place, its artistic arrangement, its beauty and satisfaction to the outward sense were the chief attractions' for the crowds.[62] 'A show got up for the pleasure of the People', an article in *The Leader* called it in 1851.[63] The *Illustrated London News* complained that in order to 'divert the dazzled multitude from [its] more utilitarian and instructive purposes', 'everything was sacrificed to show'.[64]

It is just such a world of enjoyment, of pleasurable spectacle that Lucy confronts in *Villette*. At the Pensionnat Beck she sees 'the thriving outside of a large and flourishing educational establishment', whose pupils gain knowledge 'by a marvellously easy method, without painful exertion or useless waste of spirits', where even the teachers, who do 'the real head-labour' have 'their duties so arranged that they relieved each other in quick succession whenever the work was severe' (75). Her sojourn with the Brettons is a time of 'pleasant recreation'; Dr John takes her to every 'object worth seeing', 'every museum . . . every hall sacred to art or science', to 'galleries, salles and cabinets' (196).[65] The lure of Rome is displayed before her in 'flowers and tinsel . . . wax-lights and embroidery' (421). Venturing forth to the public park on the night of the city's great fête, she finds herself—in a moment that recalls the extraordinary anthropological jumble on display in the Crystal Palace—'Indian Pagodas and Chinese Idols', 'crucifixes, rosaries'[66]—in 'a region, not of trees and shadow, but of strangest architectural wealth—of altar and of temple, of pyramid, obelisk, and sphynx' (453).

For the Great Exhibition was not simply a 'famous and wonderful sight';[67] it was an enormous collection of things. There were works of art and exotic artefacts and a multitude of useful objects—both the ordinary appurtenances of bourgeois life, and bizarre, ingenious inventions—a 'masticating knife and fork for the toothless' (from Yarmouth), a collapsible piano for gentlemen's yachts, a silent alarm clock that turned one's bed on its side (noted by Charlotte Brontë),[68] a sheet of paper 'not less than 2500 yards long'. Many of these things were copiously decorated, often

---

[60]   *Illustrated Handbook of the Royal Panopticon of Science and Art; An Institution for Scientific Exhibitions, and for Promoting Discoveries in Arts and Manufactures* (London, 1854), Introduction, 8, 5, 9. For a fuller account of the Royal Panopticon, see Richard Altick, *The Shows of London* (Cambridge, Mass.: Harvard University Press, 1978), 491–6.

[61]   'The vast hall filled with objects of fine and industrial Art, its area occupied by scientific machinery and its galleries by busy artisans, forms a coup d'œil unique of its kind' (*The Art Journal* (1854), quoted in Thomas Balston, *John Martin, 1759–1854, His Life and Works* (London: Duckworth, 1947), 231).

[62]   *Tallis's History and Description of the Crystal Palace and the Exhibition of the World's Industry in 1851* (3 vols.; London: John Tallis & Co., 1851), i. 101.

[63]   'What the Great Exhibition will do for us', *The Leader*, 8 February 1851, 126.

[64]   *Illustrated London News*, 18 October 1851, quoted in *The Crystal Palace and its Contents: An Illustrated Cyclopaedia of the Great Exhibition of the Industry of All Nations 1851* (London: W. M. Clark, 1852), 75.

[65]   'Cabinet' is here used in the (obsolete) sense of a museum or picture-gallery.

[66]   Prince Albert, quoted in Briggs, *Victorian Things*, 62.

[67]   Charlotte Brontë to Amelia Ringrose, 7 June 1851 (*CBL* ii. 633).   [68]   See *CBL* ii. 655 and 656 n.

with foliage, fruit, and flower designs. But there were not merely more, and more elaborate things. There was a new kind of focus on things as such. Things were displaced from their contexts, placed in strange juxtapositions, oddly defamiliarized by being put on show. Hitherto unregarded things became strangely prominent. Things 'invariably thrust into some obscure corner' were now being produced in 'artistic-looking designs', which had 'the effect of drawing them from their obscurity, and assigning them an honourable post'.[69] The 'apparently trifling' came to be seen as 'really important':[70] whole sections (and chapters of explanation) in the catalogues were devoted to previously unconsidered objects—spectacles, shawls, cigar-cases; caskets, hand-screens, frames. In *Villette*, too, each of these articles assumes a peculiar importance, whether as object of terror or amazement, conferred with unexpected value, or placed 'bewilderingly' on display (324, 70, 222, 110, 166, 170). For in Lucy's narrative, too, there is a new kind of emphasis on things. Objects are encased, enclosed, and placed in safe receptacles: violets between the folds of a dress (119), a miser's hoard in 'a secret drawer' (126), 'a closely-folded bit of pink paper' in a 'small box of white and coloured ivory' (110), a watchguard in an elaborate box pronounced 'a superb bonbonnière' (335, 346). A hidden letter is relished as 'that treasure in the case, box, drawer upstairs' (242).[71] Paulina's entry into the novel is signalled by 'a small crib, draped with white' and a 'tiny rosewood chest' (6). A pink dress, a turban, a handkerchief are invested with fetishistic significance. Lucy picks up a love-letter addressed to '*la robe grise*' (110). 'A paletôt, and a bonnet grec, filled the void', is her description of M. Paul's unexpected appearance (133): 'the wild inburst of a paletôt' (398) summons her to be examined by Monsieurs Boissec and Rochemorte. 'Some object drop[s] prone at [her] feet' as she walks in the garden at evening (110): things 'magically grow' in her desk, presents from M. Paul (343). And her narrative is punctuated by a series of images of things out of place: a cigar-case and a lady's blue turban, distributed as prizes in a lottery; 'the wonders and the symbols of Egypt' which appear in the park of Villette (453); that collection of well-known furniture filling an unknown room.

'Had a Genius . . . borne me over land and ocean, and laid me down quietly beside a hearth of Old England?' Lucy wonders, as she confronts this last bewildering 'assemblage'; and her exclamation echoes what many at the Great Exhibition seem to have felt. 'The observer is, as it were, carried away by magic, from country to country, from east to west, from iron to cotton, from silk to wood, from machines to manufactures, from implements to produce,' reported one French visitor.[72] A sense of 'magic' recurs in contemporary accounts. *The Arabian Nights' Entertainments*—that favourite of many early Victorian childhoods—was constantly invoked. The swift construction of Paxton's building seemed like the work of the genii. 'When first I saw it glittering in the morning sun, I felt as if Aladdin and the

---

[69] *Art Journal Catalogue*, 32: the particular object of discussion here is the coal-scuttle.
[70] *Tallis's History*, i. 207.
[71] On the 19th-cent. bourgeois obsession with containers, see Walter Benjamin, *The Arcades Project*, trans. Howard Eiland and Kevin McLaughlin (Cambridge, Mass.: Harvard University Press, 1999), 220.
[72] M. Blanquin, quoted in *Tallis's History*, i. 199.

Jin who was the slave of the lamp must have been at work on it,' recalled Lord Redesdale in his *Memories*. 'No mere human hands and hammers and builders' tools could have wrought such a miracle.'[73] 'With two common materials—glass and iron—he raised the palace of the genii,' declared Charles Reade in a novel published in the same year as *Villette*.[74] And if the glittering Crystal Palace seemed to speak of magical achievement, so too did the great array of commodities it contained. Even to the prosaic Queen, the interior, filled with 'all sorts of objects of art, manufactures, etc', 'looked quite like fairyland'.[75] Here were marvels of technology incomprehensible to the uninitiated: 'the great steam-hammer, which forges an anchor, or cracks an egg-shell, with an equal regulation of its power . . . the hydraulic machine, which lifted the mighty tubes of the Britannia Bridge to their high level . . . the Jacquard loom, which can weave such embroidery in an hour as would demand a life-long labour from the nicest sempstress of the Ind'.[76] The achievements not merely of science, but also of capitalist imperialism, here appeared as wonders. 'It seems as if magic only could have gathered this mass of wealth from all the ends of the Earth,' Charlotte Brontë remarked.[77]

Just so, in *Villette*, the world that Lucy confronts seems, often, moved by a 'magic' that she does not understand. 'I hardly noticed by what magic these doors were made to roll back—Dr John managed these points,' she relates, of their visit to the concert (209): 'Of every door which shut in an object worth seeing . . . he seemed to possess the "Open! Sesame",' she recalls (198). And the smoothly running domestic arrangements of the Brettons have a parallel in the perhaps less benevolent 'magic' of the Pensionnat Beck. There, the doors 'revolve noiselessly on well-oiled hinges' (118); 'As I paced the alleys or sat in the berceau, a girl never came to my right hand, but a teacher, as if by magic, appeared at my left' (84). 'Neither masters nor teachers were found fault with in that establishment, yet both masters and teachers were often changed: they vanished, and others filled their places, none could well explain how' (72). Such moments culminate on the night of the city's fête, when the 'great portal' of the Pensionnat Beck 'seems almost spontaneously to unclose' and Lucy, 'with the suddenness of magic', is 'plunged amidst a gay, living, joyous crowd' (451–2).

The 'magic' on show in the Crystal Palace was, however, a magic of a peculiarly disenchanted kind. For it was a magic that was at once displayed and demystified: indeed, a large part of the purpose of the Exhibition was to demonstrate how apparent marvels were achieved. 'When Aladdin raised a palace in one night . . . he accomplished this wonder by the agency of the Slaves of the Lamp', began a description of the Crystal Palace in *Household Words* in May 1851: it went on, however, to offer a detailed account of the building's method of construction.[78] The Exhibition guide-books were filled with lengthy descriptions of how things worked,

---

[73] Quoted in J. B. Priestley, *Victoria's Heyday* (Harmondsworth: Penguin, 1972), 74.
[74] Charles Reade, *Peg Woffington: A Novel* (London: Bentley, 1853), 224.
[75] Quoted in Briggs, *Victorian Things*, 61.
[76] 'Three May-Days in London. III. the May Palace', *Household Words*, 3 (1851), 124.
[77] Charlotte Bronte to Patrick Brontë, 7 June 1851 (*CBL* ii. 631).
[78] 'Three May-Days in London', 121.

and of the materials of which they were made. 'The GLASS FOUNTAIN, by Messrs. OSLER, of Birmingham', explained the *Art Journal Catalogue*, was 'supported by bars of iron, which are so completely embedded in the glass shafts, as to be invisible', and in no way interfere with its 'purity and crystalline effect'.[79] Just so, in *Villette*, mystery is demystified and the magician's tricks revealed. Madame Beck's 'system for managing and regulating' the 'mass of machinery' that comprises her establishment is coolly, sardonically described. 'She would move away on her "souliers de silence", and glide ghost-like through the house, watching and spying everywhere, peering through every key-hole, listening behind every door' (73). Lucy particularly notes 'a clear little oval mirror fixed in the side of the window recess—by the aid of which reflector madame often secretly spied persons walking in the garden below' (98). 'But, Monsieur, you could not from the distance of that window see what passed in this garden at night?' she asks, as M. Paul tells of the 'miracles of discovery' his 'magic lattice' has 'wrought'. 'I use a glass', he responds. 'But the garden itself is open to me. In the shed, at the bottom, there is a door leading into a court, which communicates with the college; of that door I possess the key' (365). 'In five minutes, the secret was mine—the key of the mystery picked up, and its illusion unveiled,' says Lucy, as she tells of the wonders that greet her in the park on the night of the fête. Even the Nun who haunts her is by the end debunked as an artfully contrived 'illusion' (470). It is surely not accidental that Graham, that quintessential figure of bourgeois confidence and efficiency, boasts of his skill in 'sleight of hand'—'I might practise as a conjuror if I liked' (248); or that the 'secret junta' of Lucy's enemies appears at the end as a 'conjuration' (460)—not merely co-conspirators, but performers of magic tricks.

   Yet the world of spectacle and display is not simply demystified in *Villette*. 'I took a revel of the scene,' says Lucy, as she tells of finding herself 'in a land of enchantment, a garden most gorgeous, a plain sprinkled with coloured meteors, a forest with sparks of purple and ruby and golden fire' (453). The streets of Villette, lit up by night, have for her an 'exhilarating charm' (208). 'No matter that I quickly recognized the material of these solemn fragments,' she recalls of the night of the fête; 'the timber, the paint, and the paste-board—these inevitable discoveries failed to quite destroy the charm, or undermine the marvel of that night' (453). And in this, too, *Villette* seems both to reflect and reflect upon a more widely shared experience, one of which the public were by the mid-nineteenth century becoming connoisseurs. The 'general impression' of the Great Exhibition, Lord Redesdale was later to recall, was 'a joyous, sensuous revelling in a palace of light'.[80] 'Look at it from the gallery', a contemporary guide-book urged. 'What a glancing bed of peripatetic flowrets—pinks and roses, and lilies and carnations . . . a kaleidoscopic *parterre* of bright hues and tints, shifting and blending and intermingling like living shot-silk.'[81] 'It is a quadrille of colours—a pool of prismatic rays—which may well turn the Koh-i-noor pale with envy,' *Punch* observed of the 'flying panorama' to be seen from the Shilling

---

[79] *Art Journal Catalogue*, 255.   [80] Quoted in Priestley, *Victoria's Heyday*, 74.
[81] *Tallis's History*, iii. 53.

Gallery.[82] Such descriptions as these remind us that the years leading up to the Exhibition saw the heyday of optical toys and gadgets such as kaleidoscopes, zoetropes, stereoscopes; of the panorama, the diorama, the phantasmagoria, the magic lantern display.[83] Often such scopic devices—like the Great Exhibition—promised to 'instruct' as well as to entertain. But the experience they offered, of pleasurable passivity in face of a flux of visual phenomena, was quite different from that of the categorizing, assessing gaze. It was an experience akin to that of many visitors to the spectacular Crystal Palace, 'fine—gorgeous—animated—bewildering', with its 'blaze and contrast of colours and marvellous power of effect'.[84]

'An attention that pleased and surprised me more I think than any other', Charlotte Brontë wrote of her visit to London in the summer of 1851, 'was the circumstance of Sir David Brewster—who is one of the first scientific men of his day—coming to take me over the Crystal Palace and pointing out and explaining the most remarkable curiosities'.[85] Like Brontë's own soon-to-be-created Mr Home, Brewster was a Scotsman and a scientist. As well as being a publicist and popularizer of new scientific ideas, he was a leader in the burgeoning field of optical research.[86] James Hogg had sketched his portrait as one of *Fraser's* 'Gallery of Literary Characters' in the year in which the magazine was first taken in the Parsonage: the young Brontës must have been intrigued by his account of Brewster's just-published *Letters on Natural Magic*, 'as diverting as so many Arabian tales'.[87] *Letters on Natural Magic* was not, however, a work of fiction, but part of that Enlightenment project of rational demystification which the Exhibition was later to enshrine. It gave scientific explanations of the wonders produced by shamans, 'spectral apparitions' and hallucinations, the 'magic glasses' of *The Arabian Nights*, and other secrets of the occult. In the company of Brewster, Brontë 'began a little better to comprehend' the Exhibition. He 'gave information in the kindest and simplest manner'; months afterwards she was to recall 'hearing in his kindly Scotch accent his lucid explanation of many things that had been to me before a sealed book'.[88]

Yet Brewster's interest in visual experience was by no means confined to scientific research. Thirty years earlier, he had invented the kaleidoscope—'the beautiful little toy, with its marvellous witcheries of light and colour' which had 'spread over Europe and America with a *furor* which is now scarcely credible', as his daughter

[82] 'The Front Row of the Shilling Gallery', *Punch* 21 (1851), 10.

[83] For an extensive account of popular spectacles and entertaining 'shows', designed to delight and to titillate the eye, see Altick, *The Shows of London.* On optical toys, see Susan R. Horton, 'Were They Having Fun Yet?: Victorian Optical Gadgetry, Modernist Selves', in Carol T. Christ and John O. Jordan (eds.), *Victorian Literature and the Victorian Visual Imagination* (Berkeley: University of California Press, 1995), 1–26.

[84] Charlotte Brontë to Patrick Brontë, 31 May 1851, 7 June 1851 (*CBL* ii. 625, 631).

[85] Charlotte Brontë to Patrick Brontë, 26 June 1851 (*CBL* ii. 650).

[86] For an account of optical researches in the early 19th cent., see Jonathan Crary, 'Modernizing Vision', in Hal Foster (ed.), *Vision and Visuality* (Seattle: Bay Press, 1988), 29–44.

[87] *Fraser's Magazine*, 6 (1832), 416.

[88] Charlotte Brontë to Ellen Nussey, 24 June 1851; to James Taylor, 15 November 1851 (*CBL* ii. 648, 718).

was later to recall.[89] By the time of the Great Exhibition he had improved and simplified the stereoscope; his version of this hugely popular optical toy, made by Duboscq of Paris, was there prominently on display. In 1854 he was to help to found the London Stereoscope Company, an enormously successful commercial concern.[90] As a juror of the Exhibition, he took a particular interest in the Koh-i-noor diamond, or 'Mountain of Light'—perhaps the most famous object there. At first, this had been something of a disappointment to viewers, for the position in which it was placed and the manner in which it was cut meant that it emitted little brilliancy. Brewster suggested that 'fifteen or sixteen gas lights' be placed behind it, whereupon 'it threw out a radiance of coloured light which delighted all who saw'.[91] It seems that this eminent scientist (who was also, intriguingly, the son-in-law of Charlotte Brontë's childhood hero 'Ossian') was something of a connoisseur—indeed, an entrepreneur—of 'dazzle'. If his was the authoritative eye of scientific observation, he was also an adept manufacturer of a new, commodified pleasure in a quite different kind of gaze.

And that pleasure was writ large in the Exhibition. For the great glass building, flooded with light and crowded with commodities, was not merely a mighty monument to 'the progress of art and science'.[92] It offered, also, a visual experience of a quite distinctive kind—a visual experience whose nature is indicated by the name by which it came to be known.[93]

> HA! yon burst of crystal splendour,
>   Sunlight, starlight, blent in one;
> Starlight set in arctic azure,
>   Sunlight from the burning zone . . .
>
> Iris and Aurora braided,—
>   How the woven colours shine,—
> Snow-gleams from an Alpine summit,
>   Torchlight from a spar-roofed mine.
> Like Arabia's matchless palace,
>   Child of magic's strong decree,
> One vast globe of living sapphire,
>   Floor, walls, columns, canopy . . .
>
> Dazzling the bewildered vision,
>   More than princely pomp we see;
> What the dome of the Alhambra,
>   Dome of emerald, to thee!

---

[89] Margaret Maria Gordon, *Home Life of Sir David Brewster* (Edinburgh: Edmonston & Douglas, 1869), 95.

[90] Altick, *Shows of London*, 233.   [91] *Home Life of Sir David Brewster*, 213.

[92] This phrase is taken from the title of Whewell's inaugural lecture as Master of Trinity College, Cambridge.

[93] The name 'Crystal Palace' was coined by *Punch* on 2 November 1850, and quickly became common currency.

proclaimed a poem on the subject in the *Quarterly Journal of Prophecy*.[94]And that image of prismatically separated light 'dazzling the bewildered vision' is echoed in more prosaic contemporary accounts. 'The eye is completely dazzled by the rich variety of hues which burst upon it on every side,' the *Art Journal Illustrated Catalogue* observed. 'It is not until this partial bewilderment has subsided, that we are in a condition to appreciate as it deserves its real magnificence and . . . harmonious beauty of effect.'[95] In a comic poem published a week before the Exhibition opened, Thackeray depicts a Hibernian visitor gazing in wonder 'Until me sight I was dazzled quite I And couldn't see for staring'. 'Along the dazzling colonnade, I Far as the straining eye can gaze', he was to proclaim more poetically, in an Ode written for the opening. 'Gleam cross and fountain, bell, and vase, I In vistas bright.'[96] More poetically yet—or at least, more effusively—Samuel Warren recalls 'objects of every form and colour imaginable, far as the eye could reach . . . dazzlingly intermingled . . . bewildered charmingly . . . The Soul was approached through its highest senses, flooded with excitement; all its faculties were appealed to at once, and sank, for a while, exhausted, overwhelmed.'[97] 'I came back quite dead beat and my head really bewildered by the myriads of beautiful and wonderful things, which now quite dazzle one's eyes,' declared Queen Victoria, in her Exhibition Journal.[98] 'The fatigue of even the most cursory survey was indescribable,' Jane Welsh Carlyle complained.[99]

The Exhibition, it seems, presented a peculiar challenge to the 'comparing, judging, scrutinizing' eye which its arrangement and its catalogues presupposed.[100] Indeed, the four volumes of the *Official Catalogue* were far too heavy to carry as a guide, and the shorter version, with its 'curt descriptions', was, as one reviewer remarked, 'consulted with the same feeling of despondency with which one is wont to search the rubrics of that kindred sphinx of railway locomotion—Bradshaw—and in general with the like results'.[101] 'The edifice—the treasures of art collected therein, the assemblage and the solemnity of the occasion,—all conspired to suggest something more than sense could scan,' Queen Victoria remarked of the opening ceremony.[102] 'He stands agape and wondering in pure vacant bewilderment', wrote *Tallis's History* of the characteristic behaviour of the plebeian visitor on a 'shilling day'. 'He has never heard the phrase *embarras de richesses*; but without

[94] 'The Seen and the Unseen', *The Quarterly Journal of Prophecy*, 3 (1851), 422–3.
[95] *Art Journal Catalogue*, p. xxv.
[96] 'Mr Maloney's Account of the Crystal Palace', *Punch*, 26 April 1851; 'May-Day Ode' (May 1851), reprinted in Anne Ritchie (ed.), *The Works of William Makepeace Thackeray* (13 vols.; London: Smith, Elder & Co., 1907), xiii. 65–8.
[97] *The Lily and the Bee: An Apologue of the Crystal Palace* (Edinburgh: Blackwood, 1851), 9. 'If you have read it, you have effected an exploit beyond me', Charlotte Brontë wrote of this panegyric to her friend Ellen Nussey on 8 December 1851. 'I glanced at a few pages and laid it down hopeless' (*CBL* ii. 727).
[98] The Queen's Exhibition Journal, 29 April 1851, quoted in C. R. Fay, *Palace of Industry, 1851: A Study of the Great Exhibition and Its Fruits* (Cambridge: Cambridge University Press, 1951), 45.
[99] 11 May 1851, quoted in Priestley, *Victoria's Heyday*, 81.
[100] Whewell, *General Bearing of the Great Exhibition*, 5.
[101] 'Official Catalogue of the Great Exhibition of the Works of Industry of all Nations, 1851', *Edinburgh Review*, 94 (October 1851), 558.
[102] Quoted in Fay, *Palace of Industry*, 49.

knowing it he feels its meaning . . . The eastern sun is flashing through the long avenues of glittering industry and art, over sparkling jewellery and god-like statues . . . trophies and triumphs of the beautiful and useful . . . and [he] stands petrified in the midst of elaborated chaos.'[103] Even the more sophisticated seem to have shared something of this feeling. 'I find I am "used up" by the Exhibition,' Dickens confessed. 'I don't say there is nothing in it—there's too much. I have only been twice; so many things bewildered me.'[104] 'Do not press me much on the subject of the "Crystal Palace" ', Charlotte Brontë wrote to a friend. 'I went there five times . . . and the "coup d'œil" is striking and bewildering enough—but . . . each renewed visit was made under coercion rather than of my own free will. It is an excessively bustling place.'[105]

The act of seeing evoked in such accounts is scarcely one of visual control. Indeed, it is hardly an act at all. 'As the visitor entered the transept', *Tallis's History* records, 'its full glories burst upon his view':

Every glance revealed some new effect, gorgeous or graceful. His eyes travelled at one moment to the semi-transparent roof, with its delicate arches of blue and white . . . then they rested upon the pendant tapestry above the galleries, the rich carpets and the brocades; or followed the crimson lines of the gallery rails, till they wearied with the luxuriance of colour, animate and inanimate; for all this time, silk, satin, and velvet, plumes and flowers, borne by gazers as curious as ourselves, were streaming all around . . . East and west next challenged attention, the various objects arranged in the centre striking the eye in rapid succession.[106]

This writer speaks not of the deliberate, objectifying, classifying gaze, but of the more transitory, more embodied 'glance'.[107] Some suggested that, given time and 'information', dazzle and bewilderment would subside and rational observations could be made. 'The eye, at first blinded by the immense glare, begins gradually to recover its power, and to settle on distant objects,' pronounced an account in *Punch*.[108] 'Entering . . . the Rotunda, the eye is arrested by objects, which, by their gorgeousness, dazzle, and by their number, bewilder the visitor,' observed the guidebook to the Royal Panopticon in 1854. The visitor, it promises, however, 'can fairly settle down to examine in detail' after a little time has elapsed.[109] But the very architecture of the

---

[103] *Tallis's History*, iii. 54.

[104] Dickens to the Hon. Mrs Richard Watson, 11 July 1851, in *The Letters of Charles Dickens*, ed. Graham Storey, Kathleen Tillotson, and Nina Burgis, Pilgrim Edition 6 (Oxford: Clarendon Press, 1988), 327.

[105] Charlotte Brontë to Margaret Wooler, 14 July 1851 (*CBL* ii. 666).   [106] *Tallis's History*, i. 44–5.

[107] For this distinction, see Norman Bryson, *Vision and Painting: The Logic of the Gaze* (London: Macmillan, 1983). Some 'artizan visitors', who had a practical interest in many of the 'constructions and contrivances' on show, did, *Tallis's History* records, examine and study them in a more purposeful way. But rapidity was essential at the Great Exhibition: the enormous crowds of visitors, and the fact that the Exhibition's police force liked to keep them moving smoothly through the building, meant that (as Thomas Richards puts it) 'visitors were virtually forced to acquire a limited attention span' (Thomas Richards, *The Commodity Culture of Victorian England: Advertising and Spectacle, 1851–1914* (London: Verso, 1990), 35). *Tallis's* account deplores the fact that the holders of expensive season tickets seem not to have cared for 'the details which occurred beyond the first reach of the eye, and which did not form a striking part of the spectacle as seen from any favourite point of view' (i. 101).

[108] 'The Front Row of the Shilling Gallery', 10.

[109] *Illustrated Handbook of the Royal Panopticon*, Introduction, 21.

Crystal Palace baffled attempts to assess and understand. 'Instead of moving from the wall at one end to the wall at the other, the eye sweeps along an unending perspective that fades into the horizon,' one visitor remarked. 'We cannot tell if this structure towers a hundred or a thousand feet above us . . . for there is no play of shadows to enable our optic nerve to gauge the measurements.'[110] 'As in a crystal, there no longer is any true interior or exterior,' declared another. 'The barrier erected between us and the landscape is almost ethereal . . . It is, in my opinion, extraordinarily difficult to arrive at a clear perception of the effect of form and scale in this incorporeal space.'[111] If 'the mighty and multifarious action by which all man's . . . wants are supplied' was here 'brought for the first time into a single point of view', that point of view was, it seems, not easy to achieve.[112] Many visitors seem to have been less edified and educated than 'dazzled', 'exhausted, overwhelmed', 'used up', 'very sufficiently bleached and broken in bits'.[113]

For if those who spoke of being 'dazzled' by the brave new world of display meant that they were 'struck or surprised with splendour' (as Johnson's *Dictionary*, not altogether approvingly, defined the term), their use of the word registered also another feeling, which is indeed quite prominent in their accounts. 'To overpower or confound, as with brilliant or showy qualities or . . . with excess of brightness': this is the second sense of 'dazzle' given in Johnson's *Dictionary*, a definition that echoes Milton's great description in *Paradise Lost* of God as a 'Fountain of light'.[114] In 1851, the connotations of 'dazzle' were, of course, more prosaic. The Crystal Palace reflected its surroundings, so that from outside it was difficult to see what the building contained. 'In order to subdue the intense light' within, 'all the south side of the upright building, and the whole of the angled roof' had to be covered with 'unbleached calico'.[115] But even the prosaic has a metaphoric suggestiveness. And dazzle—in all its senses of admiration, devastation and exclusion—might well be more apt as a metaphor for the face that the world of bourgeois triumphalism presented to many in mid-Victorian England than that celebratory rhetoric of controlling overview. It

[110] Lothar Bucher, quoted in Marshall Berman, *All That Is Solid Melts Into Air: The Experience of Modernity* (London: Verso, 1983), 239.

[111] Richard Lucae, quoted in Wolfgang Schivelbusch, *The Railway Journey: Trains and Travel in the 19th Century* (Oxford: Blackwell, 1980), 53.

[112] *Athenaeum* (3 May 1851), 478. Even the confident observer just quoted remarks at length on the difficulties involved in seeing the approaching procession. 'The eye took measures of distance at this point which were among the most curious experiences of the day . . . the perspective seemed to stretch infinitely away,—and the termination was a point which the eye could not define. When the procession turned this point, the fact could not be ascertained by the unassisted vision—and it had made some progress up the avenue, when it was discovered by means of a telescope' (477). 'Magnifying glasses, working on swivels' were, one contemporary guide-book records, 'placed at short distances, to give additional facility for commanding a perfect general view' (*Guide-book to the Industrial Exhibition; with Facts, Figures and Observations on the Manufactures and Produce Exhibited* (London: Partridge & Oakley, 1851), 11).

[113] The last phrase is Charlotte Brontë's, from a letter describing the Exhibition to her friend Amelia Ringrose, 7 June 1851 (*CBL* ii. 633).

[114] 'Dark with excessive bright thy skirts appear, | Yet dazzle heav'n, that brightest seraphim | Approach not, but with both wings veil their eyes.' (*Paradise Lost*, III. 357–82).

[115] *Guide-book to the Industrial Exhibition*, 11.

is a metaphor which, to appropriate Thackeray's phrase, Charlotte Brontë 'carries out to its conclusion' in *Villette.*

III

Here, as in Charlotte Brontë's previous novels, the language of vision is prominent, shaping, significant—a complex and powerful metaphor for a whole mode of being in the world. 'A *cold* name she must have', Charlotte Brontë wrote of her heroine, 'partly, perhaps, on the *lucus a non lucendo* principle—partly on that of the "fitness of things".' And her words point not merely towards Lucy's inner passion and 'external coldness', but also towards that more complicated constellation of meanings called into play by her resonant Christian name.[116] For if Lucy herself is a figure of obscurity, her name is evocative also of the luminous world of spectacle that passes before her gaze. And the difficulty of her relation to that world is figured in the novel's visual metaphors. Charlotte Brontë must have known that St Lucy, usually portrayed with her eyes upon a plate, is the patron saint of those with defective sight.

In some respects, Lucy's power of vision is keener than the 'common gaze' (179). She prides herself on her 'cool observation' (13), her clear-eyed analysis of others, her superior skill at espionage. Yet throughout *Villette* she is presented as a 'mere spectator', rather than a shaping observer, of the world through which she moves.[117] 'I am so entirely bewildered, I do not know whether I can trust my senses at all,' she declares to Mrs Bretton, on her awakening at La Terrasse (171). Again and again in the novel, the image recurs of the eye less as organizing than as simply receiving impressions, of a world that baffles, bewilders, dazzles, strikes. Things appear before this narrator in ways she cannot control. 'The curtain drew up— shrivelled to the ceiling; the bright lights, the long room, the gay throng burst upon us,' she recalls, of her theatrical performance (140). M. Paul, more than once, erupts

---

[116] Charlotte Brontë to George Smith, 6 November 1852 (*LL* iv. 18). A *lucus a non lucendo* is an etymological contradiction—an attempt to account for words by deriving them from their opposites: according to such explanation, a grove (*lucus*) derives its meaning from the fact of its not being lucent (*lux,* light, *luceo,* to shine).

[117] Whewell, writing of the Great Exhibition, draws attention to the difference between 'the eminent and zealous men in whose wide views it originated ... those who, with scrutinizing eye and judicial mind, compared those treasures and those wonders, and stamped their approval on the worthiest' and his own position as 'a mere spectator—one of the many millions there' (*The General Bearing of the Great Exhibition,* 1). Jonathan Crary suggests that '*spectare*, the Latin root for "spectator" ... carries specific connotations, especially in the context of nineteenth-century culture ... namely, of one who is a passive onlooker at a spectacle, as at an art gallery or theater ... *observare* means "to conform one's action, to comply with", as in observing rules, codes, regulations and practices. Though obviously one who sees, an observer is more importantly one who sees within a prescribed set of possibilities, one who is embedded in a system of conventions and limitations' (*Techniques of the Observer: On Vision and Modernity in the Nineteenth Century* (Cambridge, Mass. and London: MIT Press, 1990), 5–6). The image of an eye bewildered in the absence of guiding conventions is prominent at the opening of the second volume of *Villette.* 'At first I knew nothing I looked on,' says Lucy. 'A wall was not a wall—a lamp not a lamp. I should have understood what we call a ghost, as well as I did the commonest object' (165).

as a 'sudden apparition': 'suddenly, in a second of time, a head, chest and arms, grew above the crimson desk' (310). 'The words "Basseterre", "Guadaloupe" ... ran athwart the darkness around and before me,' Lucy confesses, of the nights in which she contemplates his 'banishment', 'in zig-zag characters of red or violet light' (441). And that sense of the perceiver's passivity implicit in such descriptions is underlined elsewhere by an emphasis—both metaphoric and literal—on the physiology of perception. Lucy speaks not of impersonal overview, but of partial, corporeal vision, and not of visual agency, but of defencelessness in the face of an impinging phenomenal world. 'Its face of enamelled white and single Cyclop's-eye of vermilion-red had printed themselves ... clear and perfect on the retina of an in-ward vision' (238), she says of Dr John's letter. Paulina later praises his 'clean, mellow, pleasant' handwriting—'no pointed turns harshly pricking the optic nerve' (374). Where Jane Eyre is portrayed as actively 'trac[ing] the general points' of Rochester's appearance (*JE* 113), Lucy, seeing her beloved in a doorway, tells that her 'eyes printed upon [her] brain the picture of M. Paul' (480). Vashti's overpowering genius is imaged as 'a rushing, red cometary light—hot on vision and to sensation' (259). The sense, is indeed, often, of an aggressive assault on the eye. 'This cabinet dazzled me, it was so full of light,' says Lucy of the classroom-turned-dressing-room in which she prepares for her part in the play (138): 'all my eye rested on struck it as spectral', she tells, of her awakening at La Terrasse (165). Her 'very eyes ache' at beholding again the handscreens she once so painstakingly finished (166): later, those eyes are more painfully 'dazzled' by the 'gleam' of Justine Marie's 'bright silk robe ... through the flowers and the glancing leaves' (359). When she attempts to 'peep', unseen, at the irascible literature master, her eye is 'transfixed through its very pupil—transfixed by the "lunettes"' (325). And most prominently and floridly, again and again in the novel, her sight is troubled by an actual and quite un-controllable 'apparition': the menacing 'shape' of 'an image like—a NUN' (245).

Much of what 'passes before' Lucy 'as a spectacle' is indeed suggestive less of control than of hallucination. 'These articles of furniture could not be real, solid arm-chairs, looking-glasses, and wash-stands—they must be the ghosts of such articles,' she thinks, as she comes to consciousness at La Terrasse (168). 'Was it ac-tual substance, this appearance approaching me? this obstruction, partially dark-ening the arch?' she asks, when old Madame Walravens emerges, apparently through a picture on a wall (389). 'On this whole scene was impressed a dream-like character; every shape was wavering, every movement floating': thus the sight that greets Lucy in 'the dubious light, now flashing, now fading' of the nocturnal fête in Villette. She has just, in a striking image of enigmatic visual experience, told of 'fathoming the deep, torch-lit perspective of an avenue, at the close of which was couched a sphynx' (453). 'They vanished like a group of apparitions. I scarce could avouch that I had really seen them,' she recalls, of her attempt to follow 'Paulina and her friends' (453). For if in 'the fête-blazing park at midnight ... new and unanticipated splendours' meet her eye (459, 452), the sense that here an inner logic in the narrative is being realized comes not merely from the dream-like appearance before her, one after another, of those others most prominent in her story, but also from the fact that the feeling that is focused in this 'scene' is by no means 'unanticipated' in *Villette*.

Throughout the novel the bourgeois world of solidity and substance appears before the narrator as a series of visual phenomena of a phantasmagoric kind. The pupils arrayed for Madame Beck's fête are a 'diaphanous and snowy mass'; not the stolid young women of Labassecour, but a radiant 'field of light' (131). When Lucy descends to the festivities, 'the long vista of the school-rooms' discloses 'a thronging, undulating, murmuring, waving, streaming multitude, all rose, and blue, and half-translucent white' (137). 'One dense mass of heads, sloping from floor to ceiling,' confronts her gaze at the concert; 'round two grand pianos . . . a flock of young girls . . . had noiselessly poured' (212). 'The long line of gentlemen, breaking into fragments, mixe[s] with the rainbow line of ladies' as the prizes in the lottery are drawn (220). Later, in summer, 'the hues of the walls and the variegated tints of the dresses' seem 'all fused in one warm glow' in the 'carré, filled with pupils and with light' (410). 'Here were assembled ladies, looking by this light most beautiful; some of their dresses were gauzy, and some had the sheen of satin,' is Lucy's first impression of those 'crowded thousands, gathered to a grand concert in the open air' (455). 'This author is able to lend a strange and romantic colour to the most common occurrences of everyday life,' wrote one percipient early reviewer.[118] Yet such moments as these in *Villette* have an import quite different from the transformative vision of *Jane Eyre*.

'Pendant from the dome, flamed a mass that dazzled me, sparkling with facets, streaming with drops, ablaze with stars,' Lucy tells of her arrival at the concert in Villette. 'It was only the chandelier, reader, but for me it seemed the work of eastern genii,' she says, in explanation. 'I almost looked to see if a huge, dark cloudy hand— that of the Slave of the Lamp—were not hovering in the lustrous and perfumed atmosphere of the cupola' (209). If the object, and, indeed, the invocation of *The Arabian Nights' Entertainments*, would have been familiar to that 'reader' from contemporary descriptions of the Great Exhibition,[119] the feeling is not simply of wonder. Hovering in this scene is a cloudy memory of that 'hand wide enough almost to grasp the Tower of All Nations' in which Lord Charles Wellesley once found himself 'raised'. The echo is one of which Charlotte Brontë may not have been conscious, which she certainly would not have expected her readers to share. Yet it is one that signals a 'darkness' within the experience of 'dazzle' that is further developed in this scene. For here, the prismatic refraction of colours ('gorgeously tinted with dews of gems dissolved, or fragments of rainbows shivered') becomes a figure not merely for a world magically, kaleidoscopically defamiliarized—the 'varying light and shade and gradation' that greets Lucy's gaze in 'that vast and dazzling . . . hall'—but also for that decentring of the viewing subject implicit in the image that

[118] Eugène Forcade, in *Revue des deux mondes*, quoted in *CH* 199.
[119] See e.g. the description of the chandelier in *The Crystal Palace and its Contents*, 417; 'Three May-Days in London', quoted above.

'flashes upon her' immediately after this—a momentary, inadvertently 'received' 'impression' of self as other, estranged (209).[120]

'I faced a great mirror, filling a compartment between two pillars,' says Lucy, in explanation. And her words point back to that earlier scene of her awakening at La Terrasse, in which 'a gilded mirror', which 'filled up the space between two windows', offered her a 'spectral' image of her own 'thin and ashen face' (166). There, the sense of hallucination was produced not by the unfamiliar 'dazzle' of a strange and magnificent spectacle, but by the appearance of the familiar in an unfamiliar place. But in that scene too there is an emphasis on the perceiving subject's lack of control over the visual field. 'My eye . . . blinked baffled' says Lucy, as she tells of gazing bewildered at that inexplicable collection of things (168). There is nothing here of the shaping power of the artist's eye with which the narrating Jane composed the drawing room at Thornfield into an aesthetic whole—a 'rich contrast' of white and crimson, a 'general blending of snow and fire' (*JE* 104). Here there is no 'general blending', but things that proliferate, dissociated, distinct. Verbal agency belongs not to the viewer, but to the objects she confronts. Chairs 'dawn' upon her, an armchair 'grows' familiar (166), 'a whole shining [tea]-service glance[s] at her familiarly' (173); things obtrude upon her vision even as she tries to turn away (170). 'Obliged to know', 'compelled to recognize' that which 'hovers before' its 'distempered vision' (169), self is experienced less as subject than as object—'laid . . . on a sofa', reflected in a mirror, 'bewildered', 'harrassed', 'alarmed'.

Moments such as these in *Villette* speak less of a simple equation of vision with power than of visual experience as complex and problematic, and as figuring a problematic relation to the world. 'Intimate as I am myself with the privations attached to enfeebled vision, it is a calamity with which I specially sympathize,' Charlotte Brontë had written to her former teacher the year before she began to write this novel.[121] Her own 'weakness of sight',[122] no less than the threat of blindness that dogged her father throughout most of her adult years, must have given her a deep-rooted sense of vision as provisional, uncertain, unreliable; indicative less of power than of vulnerability. Yet the figuring of that sense in *Villette* is, as we have begun to see, by no means the reflection of a merely personal concern. As the testimony of visitors to the Great Exhibition suggests, the experience of 'dazzle', of

---

[120] Isobel Armstrong has written suggestively of how 'the new production of mass-produced transparency' in mid-19th-cent. England meant that the body could be 'glancingly, inadvertently, reflected back from the environment, belonging to the urban phantasmagoria outside one's control' ('Transparency: Towards A Poetics of Glass in the Nineteenth Century', in Francis Spufford and Jenny Uglow (eds.), *Cultural Babbage: Technology, Time and Invention* (London: Faber & Faber, 1996), 124).

[121] Charlotte Brontë to Margaret Wooler, 14 February 1850 (*CBL* ii. 74). Even as a schoolgirl, Charlotte Brontë was so shortsighted, her friend Mary Taylor recalled, that 'when a book was given her she dropped her head over it till her nose nearly touched it' (quoted in Barker, *The Brontës*, 173). References to visual prostheses recur throughout her letters. 'We waited long—and anxiously for you on the Thursday that you promised to come', she tells Ellen Nussey on 19 July 1841. 'I quite wearied my eyes with watching from the window—eye-glass in hand and sometimes spectacles on nose' (*CBL* ii. 260). 'I saw him very near, and once through my glass', she writes ten years later, of her attempts to scrutinize a prospective suitor just before she began *Villette* (*CBL* ii. 598).

[122] Charlotte Brontë to M. Heger, 24 July 1844, trans. Margaret Smith (*CBL* i. 358).

visual disorientation and bewilderment, was becoming a familiar one in the England of 1851. Moreover, there was a widespread and increasingly sophisticated interest in the nature of visual experience, partly because of the efforts of such figures as Brewster in popularizing their work. 'The more that was learned about vision, the more unreliable it seemed,' remarks one twentieth-century historian: this sense entered popular experience through the optical instruments and toys increasingly being developed on a commercial scale.[123] Devices such as these directly questioned the notion of authoritative visual agency, for each, rather differently, constructed a view that was independent of the viewer's control. In the kaleidoscope, for instance, pattern was created not by the eye of the observer, but by a mechanical trick.[124] Differing visual experiences could be produced by viewing the object through different lenses, or positioning the viewer in a different space. Such gadgets must have brought home to many that sense, being explored by the optical researchers, of vision not as objective and normative, but as subjective, embodied and fallible.[125]

Surviving records provide some tantalizing hints of Charlotte Brontë's growing familiarity with these new technologies of vision in the years before the publication of *Villette*. 'Reader, as yet I have written nothing, I would fain fall into some regular strain of composition, but I cannot, my mind is like a prism full of colours but not of forms ... A Panorama is round me whose scenes shift before I can at all fix their features,' her narrator, Charles Townshend, confesses, in her youthful tale, 'Passing Events' (1836).[126] Ten years later, Jane Eyre tells of 'sketching fancy vignettes' from the 'ever-shifting kaleidoscope' of her own imagination (*JE* 233). There is a shadowy suggestion of the zoetrope (invented in the 1830s) in Lucy Snowe's later image of that which is 'difficult of recall to memory', which 'when reviewed, must strike us as things wildered and whirling, dim as a wheel fast spun' (486). At the end of the 1840s the word 'daguerreotype' enters Brontë's vocabulary. (It is possible that Brontë

---

[123] Susan R. Horton, 'Were They Having Fun Yet?', 3. On the cultural implications of these phenomena see Jonathan Crary, *Techniques of the Observer*; Lindsay Smith, *Victorian Photography, Painting and Poetry: The Enigma of Visibility in Ruskin, Morris and the Pre-Raphaelites* (Cambridge: Cambridge University Press, 1995); and Armstrong, 'Transparency', 142–5.

[124] Its inventor boasted that it possessed 'the character of the highest class of machinery ... It will create in an hour, what a thousand artists could not invent in the course of a year' (David Brewster, *The Kaleidoscope: Its History, Theory, and Construction*, 2nd edn. (London: John Murray, 1858), 136). Ten years later, *The Times* was to take a more pessimistic view: 'Already mechanical science has succeeded in binding down the wings of genius; and carpet-manufacturers and fancy workers no longer consult the taste of artists, but apply to the kaleidoscope to supply them with new patterns' (20 May 1830; quoted in Altick, *Shows of London*, 360). Later yet, Ruskin was to develop this idea as the figure for a larger determinism: 'there is no law of history any more than of a kaleidoscope. With certain bits of glass—shaken so, and so—you will get pretty figures, but what figures, heaven only knows' (John Ruskin to J. A. Froude, February 1864: E. T. Cook and Alexander Wedderburn (eds.), *Library Edition of the Works of John Ruskin* (39 vols.; London: Allen, 1912), xxxvi. 465).

[125] See Jonathan Crary, *Techniques of the Observer*; Jean-Louis Comolli, 'Machines of the Visible', in *The Cinematic Apparatus*, ed. Teresa de Lauretis and Stephen Heath (London: Macmillan, 1980), 123–4; and Martin Jay, *Downcast Eyes: The Denigration of Vision in Twentieth-Century French Thought* (Berkeley, Los Angeles, and London: University of California Press, 1993), ch. 3.

[126] Gérin (ed.), *Five Novelettes*, 38–9.

herself sat for a daguerreotype at around the time at which *Villette* was conceived.)[127] 'An accurate daguerreotyped portrait of a common-place face', she called *Pride and Prejudice* in 1848; 'Memory took a . . . distinct daguerrotype of the two days I spent in Scotland,' she writes in 1850, of a visit she had paid there with George Smith.[128] 'Caroline saw a shape, a head, that, daguerreotyped in that attitude . . . would have been lovely': thus she describes her heroine before the glass in *Shirley.* 'His image struck on her vision with painful brightness, and pictured itself on her memory as vividly as if there daguerrotyped by a pencil of keen lightning,' she writes, of the same character's helpless love for Robert Moore. (*S* 100, 308). And the interest in daguerreotypy hinted at in such figures lies also, perhaps, behind those images of 'sunshine' and 'shadow' which are so prominent in *Villette.*[129] For if Lucy is 'well habituated to be passed by as a shadow' (385), those others of whom her narrative tells stand out beside her in sharp relief, as figures of 'sunny' distinctness. They have connections and resources, and clearly defined identities; they act decisively and effectively; their stories have known beginnings and ends. Lucy, however, is hidden from view, overlooked, insubstantial; her past is undisclosed and her future unknown. It is perhaps not too fanciful to see *Villette*'s distinctive deployment of such imagery as this as informed by the widespread new awareness that the subject had to be unobscured and in sunshine for a daguerreotype image to be produced.

   Certainly, the concerns of the eminent optical researcher who acted as Brontë's guide to the Exhibition—his interest in the 'dazzle' of retinal after-images and the prismatic separation of colours, as well as in 'spectral apparitions'—appear as prominent images in the novel she went on to write.[130] And that novel's interrogation of vision and its meanings is signalled with ironic literalism by the portrayal within it of a series of visual aids and prostheses: the 'reflector' fixed in the side of the window recess, by whose aid Madame Beck 'often secretly spied persons walking in the garden below' (98); the 'glass' de Hamal holds 'to one of his optics' as he gazes at the Cleopatra (205); the eye-glass Ginevra levels 'sarcastically' at Mrs Bretton (217); the spy-glass used by M. Paul (365). M. Paul's intellectual influence is imaged by Lucy as an eye-salve: 'There were few bound and printed volumes that did not weary me— whose perusal did not fag and blind—but his tomes of thought were collyrium to the spirit's eyes' (381). Most strikingly, her narrative is dominated by two recurring images

---

[127] A daguerreotype purported to be of Charlotte Brontë is now in the National Portrait Gallery. See Juliet Barker, 'Charlotte Brontë's Photograph', *Brontë Society Transactions*, 19, (1986), 27–8, and Audrey W. Hall, *A Suspected New Photograph of Charlotte Brontë* (Keighley: J. L. Crabtree, 1991).

[128] Charlotte Brontë to G. H. Lewes, 12 January 1848; to W. S. Williams, 20 July 1850 (*CBL* ii. 427). 'The curates and their ongoings are merely photographed from the life,' she writes to her publisher, of *Shirley* (Charlotte Brontë to W. S. Williams, *c.* 10 February 1849 (*CBL* ii. 181)).

[129] Reflection on 'sunshine' and 'shadow' was by no means new to Brontë. Ackermann's *New Drawing Book of Light and Shadow, in Imitation of Indian Ink*, which she had used as a girl of 13, stressed the 'necessity of learning to reason upon the causes of relief, and the contrasts of light and shadow' (quoted in Alexander and Sellars, *Art of the Brontës*, 40). Such reflection is prominent in *Modern Painters I*, which she read with keen attention in the summer of 1848 (*CBL* ii. 94).

[130] See below, *passim.* One might also compare the reflector and glasses in *Villette* with Brewster's demystifying accounts of the ways in which 'glasses' were used by those professing magical powers.

of disturbed or defective vision—the 'optical illusion' (as she and others term it) of the nun that appears to haunt her—'the vision of the garret, the apparition of the alley' (463);[131] and more banal, but no less prominent, the metonymic detail by which the man she comes to love is figured—those terrifying, vulnerable 'lunettes'.

Such images in *Villette* offer an ironic riposte to that ideal of authoritative overview which had been enshrined in the Great Exhibition two years before the novel appeared. There is a pointed, significant difference between Whewell's commendation of those men of 'wide views' who planned the great display, they 'who, with scrutinizing eye and judicial mind, compared those treasures and those wonders, and stamped their approval on the worthiest', and Lucy Snowe's awkward insistence on the vicissitudes of corporeal sight. She, she says, is 'too weak to scrutinize' (167); she emphatically, even farcically, figures herself as one whose vision is obstructed and disturbed:

Not being quite tall enough to lift my head over his desk, elevated upon the estrade, and thus suffering eclipse in my present position, I ventured to peep round, with the design, at first, of merely getting a better view of his face . . . Twice did I enjoy this side-view with impunity, advancing and receding unseen; the third time my eye had scarce dawned beyond the obscuration of the desk, when it was caught and transfixed through its very pupil—transfixed by the 'lunettes'. (325)

Hers is a perspective very different, too, from that of the freely gazing *flâneur* whom Baudelaire, a few years later, was to liken to a kaleidoscope and portray as the 'passionate spectator' of the mid-nineteenth-century spectacle of bourgeois prosperity.[132] And this is not merely because her solitary wanderings are driven by misery, rather than impelled by interest; not merely, even, because—as is demonstrated on the night of her arrival in Villette—as a woman she is subject to harrassments from which the male wanderer is spared.[133] Throughout *Villette*, 'just looking' is figured as signifying fixity, rather than freedom; a peculiar, painful passivity, rather than pleasurable choice and control. Prominent in the novel are a series of striking images of Lucy's inactivity as a viewer: feigning sleep, as she watches Madame Beck's inspection of her possessions (69); sitting on 'a cushioned bench' designed for those 'who, having gazed themselves off their feet, might be fain to complete the business sitting' (199); gazing, drugged and disorientated, at the 'illuminated park' (479).

---

[131] Dr John dismisses the Nun as 'all optical illusion' (257) and Lucy herself at one point refers to it as 'the curious illusion of vision . . . experienced in that place some months ago' (360). In *Letters on Natural Magic*, Letter III, Brewster offers an account of 'spectral apparitions' as 'illusions of vision' to which those of 'morbidly sensitive imagination' may be prone (Sir David Brewster, *Letters on Natural Magic Addressed to Sir Walter Scott* (London: John Murray, 1832), 48).

[132] 'We might liken him to a mirror as vast as the crowd itself; or to a kaleidoscope gifted with consciousness, responding to each one of its movements and reproducing the multiplicity of life and the flickering grace of all the elements of life' (Charles Baudelaire, 'The Painter of Modern Life' (1859–60), in *The Painter of Modern Life and Other Essays*, trans. and ed. Jonathan Mayne (London, Phaidon: 1964), 9).

[133] On the relation of the image of the *flâneur* to feminine experience, see Janet Wolff, 'The Invisible *Flâneuse*: Women and the Literature of Modernity', *Feminine Sentences* (Cambridge: Polity, 1990) and Deborah Epstein Nord, *Walking the Victorian Streets* (Ithaca and London: Cornell University Press, 1995).

And most extensively and suggestively, in a scene that brings into focus the signific-ance of such images in *Villette*, she appears immobilized, lying on a sofa—the help-less beholder of a baffling spectacle, 'carried' there she knows not how.

Here, Lucy's vision is not obscured; rather, it is all too keen. The domestic ac-coutrements of comfortable bourgeois life—'an easy chair covered with blue damask', 'other seats, cushioned to match', 'a carpet where arabesques of bright blue relieved a ground of shaded fawn; pale walls over which a slight but endless gar-land of azure forget-me-nots ran mazed and bewildered amongst myriad gold leaves and tendrils', a 'scroll-couch' and a 'round centre-table, with a blue covering, bordered with autumn-tinted foliage', 'two little footstools with worked covers', 'a small ebony-framed chair, of which the seat and back were also worked with groups of brilliant flowers on a dark ground', 'a white centre-ornament, a classic group in alabaster, preserved under glass'—appear before her in all their distinctness, 'well lighted', 'clearly . . . seen' (166–7). But there is nothing here of the satirical assurance of Thackeray's description of the high Victorian drawing-room, published three years before *Villette*:

> the carpets were so magnificently fluffy that your foot made no more noise on them than your shadow: on their white ground bloomed roses and tulips as big as warming-pans: about the room were high chairs and low chairs, bandy-legged chairs, chairs so attenuated that it was a wonder any but a sylph could sit upon them, marqueterie tables covered with marvel-lous gimcracks, china ornaments of all ages and countries, bronzes, gilt daggers, Books of Beauty, yataghans, Turkish papooses and boxes of Parisian bonbons. Wherever you sate down there were Dresden shepherds and shepherdesses convenient at your elbow . . . there were muslin curtains and brocade curtains . . . a clock singing tunes on a console-table and another booming the hours like Great Tom, on the mantelpiece—there was, in a word, everything that comfort could desire, and the most elegant taste devise. (*Pendennis*, 1848–50)[134]

Nor is there anything like Gaskell's sense of the social significance of a Manchester drawing-room's aggressive display: 'The apartment blazed forth in yellow silk damask and a brilliantly-flowered carpet. Every corner seemed filled up with orna-ment, until it became a weariness to the eye, and presented a strange contrast to the bald ugliness of the look-out into the great mill-yard' (*North and South*, 1854–5).[135] For this narrator's is emphatically an impotent, rather than a judging, gaze. Here, the eye is not in control, but 'struck', 'bewildered', 'baffled': the viewer positioned not as shaping observer but as one who is compelled to 'take in' that which is before her as 'fact' (166). The things Lucy sees in this 'unknown room' (166) are not, like the things in those other fictional drawing-rooms, imbued with social meaning. Rather, it is their refusal to yield up their meanings that is the centre of narrative concern. In their proliferating intricacy, their hallucinatory sharpness of outline, they are more like the insistent, challenging details of contemporary pre-Raphaelite painting—that 'insanity of realism' which Pater was to find in Rossetti—than to

---

[134] Thackeray, *The History of Pendennis*, 399.
[135] Elizabeth Gaskell, *North and South*, ed. Dorothy Collin (Harmondsworth: Penguin, 1970), 213.

Gaskell's moralizing, Thackeray's satiric, or Dickens's symbolic readings of the mid-Victorian world.[136]

'Of all these things,' says Lucy, 'I could have told the peculiarities, numbered the flaws or cracks, like any *clairvoyante*' (166). This preternatural distinctness of vision has, as she records it, a certain psychological realism. 'Nothing is more notable than the way in which even the most trivial objects force themselves upon the attention of a mind which has been fevered by violent and distressful excitement,' Ruskin was to remark, the following year, of the excessively minute exactitude of another contemporary depiction of a bourgeois drawing-room. 'They thrust themselves forward with a ghastly and unendurable distinctness, as if they would compel the sufferer to count, or measure, or learn them by heart.'[137] But Lucy's 'distempered' vision speaks, here as throughout the novel, not merely of her private pain but of larger collective experience. 'Suppose a modern drawing room, with its sumptuous furniture of velvet, silk, glass, gold, china and rosewood, were to be hermetically sealed up and consigned to the inspection of our descendants some two thousand years yet to come,' hypothesized an article in *The Journal of Mental Pathology* in 1851:

> They would hardly understand its paraphernalia and appointments. It would require time and study to make out the use of this article and the meaning of that. Their minds would be discordant from ours, and the material substances upon which they employed themselves, or by which they signified their wishes, wants or desires, would, in process of time, have become so completely new and foreign that *we* could not understand them, nor *they* us.[138]

The subject under discussion is not a private mental state but a public cultural phenomenon: the baffling array of objects on display in the Crystal Palace. Like other contemporary commentators, this writer goes on to suggest that when properly viewed, by those possessed of 'information', the Exhibition is a completely intelligible one. But his strange and unsettling vision of things emptied of meaning before an uncomprehending gaze is evocative of the 'bewilderment' many visitors seem to have felt.[139] It was not merely that even familiar things were in the Crystal Palace displaced and defamiliarized, often made more rather than less baffling by lengthy catalogue descriptions; that the spectator needed 'time and study to make out the

[136]   Walter Pater, 'Dante Gabriel Rossetti', *Appreciations. With an Essay on Style* (London: Macmillan, 1910), 209. Cf. Nathaniel Hawthorne's remark that the Pre-Raphaelite paintings he saw in Manchester in July 1857 'leave out some medium—some enchantment that should intervene, and keep the subject from pressing so baldly and harshly upon the spectator's eyeballs' (*The English Notebooks*, ed. Thomas Woodson and Bill Ellis (Columbus: Ohio State University Press, 1997), 347).

[137]   He is writing about Holman Hunt's *The Awakening Conscience*, in a letter to *The Times* 25 May 1854. Carol Christ, *The Finer Optic: the Aesthetic of Particularity in Victorian Poetry* (New Haven: Yale University Press, 1975), ch. 1, discusses the ways in which an 'intense consciousness of minute detail' was associated with 'morbidity', isolation, and madness in early Victorian art.

[138]   [Anon.], 'The Great Exhibition of 1851', in Forbes Winslow (ed.), *Journal of Psychological Medicine and Mental Pathology*, 4 (1851), 2.

[139]   'I have always had an instinctive feeling against the Exhibition, of a faint, inexplicable sort', wrote Dickens to W. H. Wills, on 27 July 1851. 'I have a great confidence in its being a correct one somehow or other—perhaps it was a foreshadowing of its bewilderment of the public' (*Letters of Charles Dickens*, vi. 448–9).

use of this article and the meaning of that'. The very presentation of things as spectacle—simply to be looked at—had a curiously estranging effect. 'What spectator is
not more or less distant?' asked one of the most eloquent of its eulogists, even as he
wrote of the Exhibition with proprietorial pride.[140] And the configuration of feeling to which his rhetorical question points is crystallized in this scene of Lucy's
awakening at La Terrasse.

Here, as in the catalogues to the Great Exhibition, a series of disparate objects is
described 'in every minutest detail' (167). Here, as there, these things are displaced
from their contexts, and the familiar is defamiliarized—even objects the viewer
herself has made. And here the alienation implicit in the experience is stressed. For
here 'home' appears, strangely, as a spectacle (as it did, in a sense, in the Crystal
Palace): indeed, this is the more peculiar here because it appears in a foreign land.
It is a moment not of recognition but of baffled, blank dislocation. Like the 'gilded
ornaments' and 'polished floor' of that 'cold, glittering' salon in which Lucy awaits
her first encounter with Madame Beck (65), this world takes no cognizance of the
viewer, but returns her own reflection back. And the self thus reflected is a 'spectral' object—one without place or agency, a stranger even to herself.

This is *Villette*'s distinctive reflection on that public celebration of 'home' in
poems, novels, and visual images, domestic manuals and writings on society in the
middle years of the century which Karen Chase and Michael Levenson have called
'the spectacle of intimacy'.[141] 'It is the domestic character of England—the home
comforts, and fireside virtues for which she is so justly celebrated,' Sarah Ellis had
written in 1839.[142] The names of the Brettons and the Homes, resonant of England
and the domestic sphere, point to Brontë's awareness of the importance of 'home'
in the nation's consciousness of itself. 'The word "home" in the real English sense,
is not more peculiar to the language, than is the word "comfort" itself,' observes
Mayhew in 1852. 'The French people have no terms in their vocabulary to express either notion. The adjective *comfortable*, they have been obliged to borrow to the letter from us, and as for their phrases *à la maison* and *chez nous*, they stand for mere
eating and sleeping places.'[143] In *The Professor*, Crimsworth tells of sitting 'almost
in English comfort' in his employer's private sitting-room in Brussels
(*P* 82); in the Brettons' 'pleasant' parlour, in the Homes' apartments in Villette,
Lucy finds 'an English tea', 'an English fire' (173, 263). As Chase and Levenson
demonstrate, other writers in these years were, in varying ways, registering and exploring the tensions and contradictions that threatened this domestic ideal. Indeed,
at the end of *The Professor*, Charlotte Brontë had done so herself. But in *Villette*, the
emphasis is different. The disaster that destroys Lucy's home remains a shadowy

---

140 Whewell, *The General Bearing of the Great Exhibition*, 6.
141 Karen Chase and Michael Levenson, *The Spectacle of Intimacy: A Public Life for the Victorian Family* (Princeton and Oxford: Princeton University Press, 2000).
142 Sarah Ellis, *The Women of England: Their Social Duties, and Domestic Habits* (London: Fisher, Son,
& Co., 1838), 10.
143 Henry Mayhew, 'Home is Home, be it never so Homely', in Viscount Ingestre (ed.), *Meliora: or,
Better Times to Come. Being the Contributions of Many Men Touching the Present State and Prospects of Society*, First Series (London: J. W. Parker, 1852), 261–2.

metaphor. Instead of those images of violence repressed that come to the fore as Crimsworth portrays the idyll to which his strivings lead, there is at the centre of this novel an alienating confrontation with a 'perfect domestic comfort', 'well lighted ... clearly seen' (173, 167).

From the opening pages, in which the no longer 'noticed' narrator describes the smooth arrangements of Bretton (5), to the night of the fête in Villette, when she is an unseen gazer at 'a familiar and domestic group ... the Brettons and the de Bassompierres' (456), 'home' passes before her as a spectacle, 'well-arranged', comfortable, cheerful, impervious to her. Instead of reciprocity there is the dazzle of excluding surfaces. 'While I waited, I would not reflect. I fixedly looked at the street stones, where the door-lamp shone, and noted ... the glitter of wet on their angles': thus Lucy, of the moment when she stands at the Pensionnat door (64). And her narrative is punctuated by images of such *reflets*.[144] Thus, the child Polly gazes, shut out, at 'the glossy panels of the dining-room door, where the reflection of the hall-lamp was shining' (26); thus Lucy notes of Dr John—as he thinks, oblivious, of another—how 'the reflex from the window ... lit his face' (152). The mirror into which the young Jane looks is 'a visionary hollow' within which she can move (*JE* 14). But in *Villette*, where the walls of the hotel Crecy 'gleam with foreign mirrors' (263), depth is replaced by surface, opening possibility by the baffling already-known. 'Bretton! Bretton! and ten years ago shone reflected in that mirror', says Lucy, of that which meets her 'distempered vision' when she awakens from her swoon (169). Instead of the longed-for 'companionship', 'consolation and support' (156) there is the blank indifference of spectacle; instead of self-confirmation (Lucy is literally unrecognized by those who once knew her well), the dislocated reflection of her own 'spectral' face. In a peculiar ironic comment on that which Ruskin had three years earlier called 'the comfort, the peace, the religion of home',[145] the 'household gods' of Bretton appear before her as recalcitrant material objects, 'mere furniture' in an alien place (167, 169).

The feeling configured here is markedly, provocatively different from that exhilarated pride in achievement, that nationalistic triumphalism, which the display in the Crystal Palace was intended to promote. 'It is not a mere picture of things which are found standing together that we have had presented to us; the great achievement was the bringing them together', William Whewell was to declare: 'By annihilating the space which separates different nations, we produce a spectacle in which is also annihilated the time which separates one stage of a nation's progress from another ... How great and unexampled is the opportunity thus given to us, of taking a survey of the existing state of art in every part of the world.'[146] And his first-person plurals signify a confident identification with the power to 'produce' and to 'survey'; in

---

[144] 'Find me an English word as good, reader,' says Brontë, in a footnote to *Shirley*, 'and I will gladly dispense with the French word. Reflections won't do' (*Shirley*, ed. Margaret Smith and Herbert Rosengarten (Oxford: Clarendon Press, 1979), 644).

[145] Ruskin, 'The Lamp of Memory', III, *Seven Lamps of Architecture* (1849), *Library Edition of the Works of John Ruskin*, viii. 226.

[146] Whewell, *The General Bearing of the Great Exhibition*, 6, 4.

this, his is characteristic of many such accounts.[147] Yet there is no such identification in *Villette*. 'Of what are these things the signs and tokens?' Lucy asks, as a girl in
Bretton, finding, as she enters her bed-room, 'an unexpected change': 'In addition
to my own French bed in its shady recess, appeared in a corner a small crib, draped
with white; and in addition to my mahogany chest of drawers, I saw a tiny rosewood
chest' (6). It is not she, but others, who act, decide, effect: the results of their actions
'embodied' before her in 'visible, material shape'.[148] Just so, at La Terrasse, those inexplicable articles of furniture appear as the 'signs and tokens' of a world that she
does not control. For her, as for Whewell, 'time and space' seem annihilated:
'Where was I? Not only in what spot of the world, but in what year of our Lord?'
(166–7). But for her, the experience speaks less of progress than of a history of loss
and displacement, less of the 'magic' of generalized human achievement than of her
own singular powerlessness, and less of authoritative overview than of vision that is
obstructed by intransigent material fact.

  'My eye, prepared to take in the range of a long, large, and white-washed chamber, blinked baffled, on encountering the limited area of a small cabinet,' recalls
Lucy, of her second awakening at La Terrasse. 'The dimity curtains, dropped before
a French bed, bounded my view' (168). The world configured in *Villette* is one
bounded by materiality, rather than opening into possibility. Jane Eyre told of
'breathing on the frost-flowers with which the window was fretted' at Gateshead,
and 'clearing a space in the glass through which I might look out on the grounds' (*JE*
30), but Lucy speaks more fatalistically of 'stinted narrowness of future prospect'
(298). Jane's desire for 'the view beyond' (*JE* 104) is in this later narrative replaced
by more inflexible images of restriction of vision and obstruction of view. For in
Villette, *Jane Eyre*'s world of opening vistas and distant horizons has become a
world of things. The 'God-bent bow, the arch of hope' that seemed to greet Lucy
as she sailed towards Europe—'grand with imperial promise, soft with tints of
enchantment' (57)—finds its ironic fulfilment in the 'fragments of rainbows
shivered' of a 'gorgeous' chandelier (209). When doors magically open in *Villette*,
it is to reveal 'galleries, salles, and cabinets' (198): not expanding prospects, but
heavily decorated rooms:

a hall . . . whose sweeping circular walls, and domed hollow ceiling, seemed to me all dead
gold (thus with nice art was it stained), relieved by cornicing, fluting and garlandry, either
bright, like gold burnished, or snow-white like alabaster, or white and gold mingled in
wreaths of gilded leaves and spotless lilies: wherever drapery hung, wherever carpets were
spread, or cushions placed, the sole colour employed was deep crimson.   (209)

---

[147] Ruskin, in the Preface to the second edition of *The Seven Lamps of Architecture* (1855), defines this
'Proud Admiration' as 'the delight which most worldly people take in showy, large, or complete buildings, for the sake of the importance which such buildings confer on themselves, as their possessors, or
admirers.' *Library Edition of the Works of John Ruskin*, viii. 8.

[148] 'The eminent and zealous men . . . by whose indomitable energy and perseverance the great
thought of such a spectacle was embodied in a visible, material shape' (Whewell, *The General Bearing of
the Great Exhibition*, 1).

Faced with Rochester's perfidy, with St John Rivers's persuasions, Jane is twice roused to action by an apparently supernatural voice. But Lucy, fleeing from an obscurer—yet no less life-threatening—anguish, wakes to find herself confronted by 'real, solid arm-chairs, looking-glasses . . . washstands' (168): not by an opening future, but by the intractable evidence of a fixed and unalterable past.

Jane's is an artist's eye, transfiguring the world it sees. To her, the ladies at Thornfield are 'a flock of white plumy birds': 'all had a sweeping amplitude of array that seemed to magnify their persons as a mist magnifies the moon' (*JE* 171). But to Lucy, less shaping subject than helpless object, things loom large in quite a different way. 'She had stepped out suddenly,' she recalls of Madame Beck in her fashionable clothing. 'She seemed to magnify her proportions and amplify her drapery; she eclipsed me; I was hid' (444).[149] Where Jane paints visionary watercolours, Lucy makes hand-screens, a pincushion, a lavishly embroidered watchguard, and painstaking copies of engravings, 'tediously working up my copy to the finish of the original, for that was my practical notion of art' (398). Jane creates a 'speaking likeness' of the man she loves, 'actively fill[ing] it with features', exulting in her 'success' (*JE* 233). But Lucy lies prostrate on a couch, unable to 'exclude' the image of one she was powerless to impress. Jane's vision is empowering, retributive, prefigurative. But Lucy's 'necromantic joys of fancy' simply help her to bear her lot (77).

For if each invokes imagination, it is to very different effect. 'Poetry' and 'genius' 'not only live, but reign and redeem', declares Jane Eyre (*JE* 370). Her story is informed by the energies of high romanticism, by its visions of quest, of conquest, of 'incident, life, fire, feeling'—of the aspiring ego, of creative vigour, and of restless desire. But in *Villette* such energies are other, displaced from the narrative voice. And they speak not of power, but of impotence. 'Certain accidents of the weather . . . were almost dreaded by me,' says Lucy, 'because they woke the being I was always lulling, and stirred up a craving cry I could not satisfy':

> the tempest took hold of me with tyranny: I was roughly roused and obliged to live . . . I could not go in: too resistless was the delight of staying with the wild hours, black and full of thunder, pealing out such an ode as language never delivered to man—too terribly glorious, the spectacle of clouds, split and pierced by white and blinding bolts.
>
> I did long, achingly, then and for four-and twenty-hours afterwards, for something to fetch me out of my present existence, and lead me upwards and onwards. This longing, and all of a similar kind, it was necessary to knock on the head. (109)

Here, as elsewhere in the novel, 'longing' is countered with a brutality more extreme than Jane's sternest efforts at self-control. Lucy's 'craving' is not for 'a power of vision' but for 'something to fetch me out': even in 'longing' she is less agent than victim—tyrannized, 'roused', 'obliged to live'. 'I only wished that I had wings and could ascend the gale, spread and repose my pinions on its strength, career in its course, sweep where it swept,' she declares, at a later moment, as she describes her

---

[149] On the increasing size of ladies' skirts throughout the late 1840s and early 1850s, see C. Willett Cunnington and Phillis Cunnington, *Handbook of English Costume in the Nineteenth Century*, 3rd edn. (London: Faber & Faber, 1970), 442, 445.

desperate wanderings through the streets of Villette. And as she evokes *Childe Harold's* transcendent energy of aspiration—

> To act and suffer, but remount at last
> With a fresh pinion; which I feel to spring,
> Though young, yet waxing vigorous, as the blast
> Which it would cope with, on delighted wing,
> Spurning the clay-cold bonds which round our being cling.[150]

—the expansive impulse to identify with the 'blast' is checked by a recognition of her own inescapable subjection to exactly those 'clay-cold bonds'. 'While wishing this, I suddenly felt colder where before I was cold, and more powerless where before I was weak,' she recalls. 'Instead of sinking on the steps as I intended, I seemed to plunge headlong down an abyss' (164).

Once, indeed, in the novel, Lucy speaks of a 'kinder Power', 'softer and better than human reason':

bringing all round her a sphere of air borrowed of eternal summer; bringing perfume of flowers which cannot fade—fragrance of trees whose fruit is life; bringing breezes pure from a world whose day needs no sun to lighten it. My hunger has this good angel appeased with food, sweet and strange, gathered amongst gleaning angels, garnering their dew-white harvest in the first fresh hour of a heavenly day; tenderly has she assuaged the insufferable tears which weep away life itself—kindly given rest to deadly weariness—generously lent hope and impulse to paralyzed despair. Divine, compassionate, succourable influence! When I bend the knee to other than God, it shall be at thy white and winged feet, beautiful on mountain or on plain. (230)

Recent critics have hailed this rhapsody as a triumphant 'feminization' of 'the Romantic Imagination', an assertion of its superiority to masculine 'reason and control'.[151] Yet the difference of Lucy's 'spirit' from the 'Genius' Jane Eyre celebrates might suggest a rather different view. This is not an energizing inner power, but a soothing, calming emissary from another, ideal realm: an 'angel', to be 'worshipped' by the powerless votary. Instead of 'expanding with life' (*JE* 109), it brings sweetness, succour, refreshment. These are gifts that Lucy is later to question as delusive and unsustaining: 'that manna I drearily eulogized a while ago' (239). And they are questioned also by a larger irony, unobtrusively but distinctively inscribed in the novel as a whole. For the terms in which they are imaged are the same as those that configure that ambiguous sphere of 'sunshine' which the fortunate occupy in its world. The 'perfume of flowers which cannot fade' recalls the Bretton of Lucy's youthful visits, like the meadows of *Pilgrim's Progress* 'beautified with lilies all the year round' (6). The 'eternal summer' of this spirit is like her society's 'picture' of the sheltered lives of 'girls and women' as 'warmed with constant sunshine, rocked by breezes indolently soft' (35). Indeed, it has a concrete counterpart in the figure of

---

[150] *Childe Harold's Pilgrimage*, Canto III. 73. 693–8.
[151] Mary Jacobus, 'The Buried Letter: Feminism and Romanticism in *Villette*', in Pauline Nestor (ed.), *Villette: New Casebook* (Basingstoke: Macmillan, 1992), 135–7; Shuttleworth, *Charlotte Brontë and Victorian Psychology*, 233.

'Mrs Bretton—a summer-day in her own person' (274), 'beneficial . . . as the atmosphere of some salubrious climate' (180). This 'food, sweet and strange', this
'dew-white harvest' recur in Lucy's vision of the 'Happiness' that Dr John prescribes: 'a divine dew which the soul, on certain of its summer mornings, feels drop-
ping upon it from the amaranth bloom and golden fruitage of Paradise' (250). And
the softness and sweetness here imaged are like the 'delicious . . . sweetness' of her
dreams of La Terrasse (232). 'It was all of sweetness in life I had to look for', she says,
of her longing to hear from Graham (268); his letter, when it comes, is 'a bubble—
but a sweet bubble—of real honey-dew' (244). 'It was the honey of his temper; it was
the balm of his mellow mood,' she thinks, of his 'benignity'; 'he diffused it about
him, as sweet plants shed their perfume' (362).

'To bright, soft, sweet influences his eyes and lips gave bright, soft, sweet welcome',
says Lucy, not uncritically, of this 'cool young Briton' (259). She later describes him
as one 'eager for nutriment, and alive to gratification when it came' (423). The sweetness, the softness, the brightness of the bourgeois world are not merely metaphors in
Villette. They are portrayed with a deflating literalness which provides a subtly ironic
commentary on the limitations of that world. He who as a boy had a taste for 'sweet
cake' and 'marmalade' (25, 23) comes as a charming young doctor to feed *eau sucrée*
to the little Fifine (95). In the Brettons' 'pleasant parlour' in Labassecour Lucy finds
the same seed-cake as at Bretton, like manna miraculously preserved (173). The unfading flowers and eternal summer that she hails her good angel as bringing have their
material counterparts in the 'endless garland of azure forget-me-nots' on the wallpaper at La Terrasse (166), in the pots of flowers that adorn the Pensionnat Beck, and
the stoves that keep it warm. There is a 'world whose day needs no sun to lighten it' in
Villette's 'radiant park and well-lit Haute-Ville' (468), in the streets at which Lucy
gazes on her way to the concert at night, 'brightly lit, and far more lively now than at
high noon' (208). And there is 'rest to deadly weariness' in the sleeping-draught she
is given in the haven of La Terrasse—'A tide of quiet thought . . . came gently caress-
ing my brain, softer and softer rose the flow, with tepid undulations smoother than
balm' (168). If the 'spirit' she hails is one of sweetness and softness, which comes
bringing longed-for 'rest', the terms in which she images it are charged with ironic
echoes of her taunt to Madame Beck: 'Make your own bed warm and soft; take seda-
tives, and meats and drinks spiced and sweet' (447).

Even that 'spirit''s promise to 'gild' her dreams speaks of the bourgeois world.
'Gilding' was fashionable in the early nineteenth century: Ruskin had described it in
Seven Lamps of Architecture as 'one of the most abused pieces of magnificence we possess'.[152] In the preface to *Jane Eyre* Charlotte Brontë had written in praise of those
who dare 'to rase the gilding, and show base metal under it' (*JE* 4). But here the term
is suggestive less of deception than of a curious impotence. This 'good angel' is not
effective, but beautifying and embellishing—more like fancy than imagination, in
Coleridgean terms. For where *Jane Eyre* invoked the 'golden age' of Poetry and

---

[152] 'The Lamp of Truth', XVII, in *Seven Lamps of Architecture* (London, 1849), *Library Edition of the Works of John Ruskin*, viii. 78.

Genius, *Villette* tells of 'the gilded, not the golden age'.[153] Lucy is to speak, metaphorically, of the refinements of bourgeois breeding as 'gilding' Paulina's 'peculiarities' like 'a fine and even polish' (288). And the image is echoed in the novel in a series of representations of substantial bourgeois things: the 'gilt door' and 'gilded ornaments' in Madame Beck's salon (65), the 'wreaths of gilded leaves' on the ceiling in the concert-hall (209), the 'gilded' mirror at La Terrasse and the 'thin porcelain cups, dark with purple and gilding' which the Brettons use at tea-time (166, 173), that 'broad, gilded picture-frame' around the portrait over which the schoolgirl Lucy dreamed. There are no such gilded objects in *Jane Eyre*. But their prominence in *Villette* provides a suggestive counterpoint to Lucy's transcendent rhapsodies: one that points not away from but towards a substantial material world.

'She saw me weep and she came with comfort,' Lucy says of her 'daughter of Heaven' (230). The original sense of 'comfort' (from the Latin *confortare*—to strengthen) persisted in English until the seventeenth century—and sometimes, indeed, beyond:

> 'Glad comforter! will I not brave,
> Unawed, the darkness of the grave?
> Nay, smile to hear Death's billows rave—
>   Sustained, my guide, by thee?
> The more unjust seems present fate,
> The more my spirit swells elate,
> Strong, in thy strength, to anticipate
>   Rewarding destiny!'

'Never was better stuff penn'd,' Charlotte Brontë wrote on the manuscript of her sister Emily's poem of 1845.[154] But by the nineteenth century 'comfort' more usually meant not to strengthen or invigorate, but to soothe and to console. In *Villette*, Lucy confesses that she is 'perishing for . . . an accent of comfort' (161); Graham's letters bring her 'vital comfort' (253); he is 'a fine-hearted son; his mother's comfort and hope' (372). 'I want to give you an assurance which I know will comfort you—and that is that I find my husband . . . the best earthly comfort that ever woman had,' Charlotte Brontë was to write from her deathbed in 1855.[155] The 'comfort' that Lucy's 'good angel' brings is clearly of this kind. But here, as in the rest of her rhapsody, the word she uses is charged with a sense of its more material meanings—meanings that by the middle of the nineteenth century it was beginning, increasingly, to bear.

In *Pickwick Papers* (1829) Dickens portrays his hero retiring to live in Dulwich in a house 'fitted up with every attention to substantial comfort'; this phrase, says a twentieth-century historian of English taste, 'became the theme song of the Victorian age'.[156] 'The matter of coziness and home comfort has been so studied, and

---

[153] Catherine Gore's Cecil, in *Cecil; or, The Adventures of a Coxcomb* (London: Bentley, 1845), i. 102. For Charlotte Brontë's reading and admiration of Mrs Gore, see *CBL* ii. 455–6, 644–5.

[154] 'Anticipation', *EBP* 13 and 231 n.

[155] C. B. Nicholls to Ellen Nussey, 21 February 1855 (*LL* iv., 175).

[156] Gloag, *Victorian Comfort*, p. xvi.

matured, and reduced to system, that they really have it in their power to effect more, towards making their guests comfortable, than perhaps any other people,' wrote Harriet Beecher Stowe, on a visit to England in the year of the publication of *Villette*.[157] ' "COMFORTS" appear in the windows of the smallest village-shop, or surround the hearth of the humblest cottage ... which the spoiled children of civilization now appropriate as "mere matters of course",' declared another writer, pondering the term, in 1851. And whilst this writer insists that true comfort cannot come from 'mere *material* conveniences', '*comfortable people*', she says, '*have comfortable things about them*'; she praises their sofas, their fires, 'their furniture and household appointments', the 'exhilarating wholesome atmosphere' of their 'regularly and discreetly ventilated' rooms.[158] It is not a long step from such panegyrics as these to the 'large peaceful rooms' and 'well-arranged furniture' of the opening paragraphs of *Villette*, to the smooth arrangements of the Pensionnat Beck, and the 'perfect domestic comfort' Lucy finds at La Terrasse (173)—'the snug comfort of the close carriage' on a chilly evening excursion (208), the 'cosy arrangement of cushions in a corner of the sofa' that Graham makes for her (175).[159] And her paean to imagination is informed with her creator's awareness of the fact that the resonances of 'comfort' had in mid-nineteenth-century England become almost the reverse of the original meaning of the term.[160]

Here, echoes of the Bible are softened, sweetened, prettified. The tree of life is a 'fragrance'; the sustaining 'manna' of the Bible is most unbiblically 'sweet'.[161] 'Comforter' was the epithet applied to the Holy Spirit (John 15: 26), 'The Comforter . . . [is] an indwelling Person, not a vague and transitory influence,' argued F. D. Maurice in a Whit Sunday sermon probably attended by Charlotte Brontë as she began to conceive *Villette*.[162] During the preceding decade, such doctrine had been transmuted in some of the most powerful lyrics of the century into more 'abstract' images of animating energy.[163] 'They stirred my soul like the sound of a trumpet when I read them alone and in secret,' Charlotte Brontë recalled.[164] But in Lucy's Victorian vision the mighty wind of the Spirit has become a refreshing

---

[157] Harriet Beecher Stowe, *Sunny Memories of Foreign Lands* (2 vols.; London: Sampson Low, Son & Co., 1854), i. 13.

[158] 'Comfortable People', in M.B.H., *Home Truths for Home Peace, or 'Muddle' Defeated: A Practical Inquiry Into What Chiefly Mars or Makes the Comfort of Domestic Life*, 6th edn. (London: Longman, Brown, Green, and Longmans, 1854), 164, 171.

[159] See John Gloag, *Victorian Comfort*, ch. 3, for a suggestive account of the padded, cushioned, buttoned plumpness of mid-19th-cent. upholstered furniture.

[160] By the time she came to write *Villette*, Brontë may well have been familiar with Richard Chenevix Trench's discussion of the degeneration of words from their original meanings in his *On the Study of Words* (London: John W. Parker and Son, 1851), 31 ff.

[161] The Bible says it tasted like 'fresh oil' (Numbers 11: 8).

[162] Frederick Denison Maurice, *The Old Testament: Nineteen Sermons Preached in the Chapel of Lincoln's Inn* (London: John W. Parker & Son, 1851), 308. For Brontë's probable attendance at this sermon, which was preached on 8 June 1851, see Marion J. Phillips, 'Charlotte Brontë's Favourite Preacher: Frederick Denison John Maurice (1805–1872)', *BST* 20: 2 (1990), 77–88.

[163] See Lisa Wang, 'The Holy Spirit in Emily Brontë's *Wuthering Heights* and Poetry', *Literature and Theology*, 14: 2 (June 2000), 160–73. The term 'abstract' is Charlotte Brontë's (*CBL* ii. 132, 140).

[164] Charlotte Brontë to W. S. Williams, September 1848 (*CBL* ii. 119).

breeze. Brontë's alertness to this shift from the spiritual to the material is signalled a paragraph later, when her narrator tells of waking and seeking a concrete 'dark comforter' (231)—the stove in the refectory at the Pensionnat Beck.

The 'sweetness', the 'softness', the elaborate allegory of Lucy's vision of imagination are not merely private dreams. Like those solid 'material comforts' (V 284) of which perforce they speak, they belong, quite markedly, to the world of 1851. They were, indeed, prominent features of the Great Exhibition; and they were strikingly exemplified there in an object that Brontë may well have seen. Prominently on display in the main avenue was an upholstered chair in papier-mâché, made by Jennens and Bettridge of Birmingham.[165] This curious artefact—designed, apparently, to appeal to those who were still, at the mid-century, devouring the annuals in ever larger and more opulent shapes—was called the 'Day Dreamer' chair. It was, the catalogue recorded, copiously decorated in 'the Italian style', ornamented at the top by 'two winged thoughts'—the one with bird-like pinions and crowned with roses, representing happy dreams; the other with leather bat-like wings representing troubled ones—with Hope behind them, in the shape of the rising sun. The twisted supports of the back were adorned with poppy, heartsease, convolvulus, and snowdrop, all emblematic of dreaming, and in front of the seat was a shell, flanked by two large figures representing pleasant and unpleasant dreams. 'It is in its woolliness', says Pevsner, 'as typical of the date as is the elaborate allegorical apparatus built up around so utilitarian an object as an easy chair.'[166] In this fantastic object, destined for a lady's boudoir, the feminization of imagination is enshrined. Here, as in Lucy's vision, a 'spirit, softer and better than Human Reason' is intricately allegorized: indeed, some of the details—such as the unfading flowers and angelic wings that signify 'good' dreams—are the same. The material succour, the soothing repose of which Lucy speaks are here made solid and tangible; for the better comfort of the 'dreamer', plump, buttoned upholstery covers the ample seat. And this 'gilded' monument to the dreamer's passivity finds a curious echo in the voice of Lucy's 'good angel': 'Sleep sweetly—I gild thy dreams!'

It is not very likely that Brontë would have admired the Day-Dreamer chair. But it seems right to end with an object, as prospects end in objects in *Villette*. And this

---

[165] In the autumn of 1851, Brontë's friend Harriet Martineau was to write a series of articles for Dickens's *Household Words* in the spirit of the Exhibition's catalogues, for 'instruction and entertainment'. Each contained a lengthy description of some class of manufactured articles and the processes by which they were produced. 'Flower-shows in a Birmingham Hot-house', based on Martineau's visit to the Jennens and Bettridge factory, is an extensive account of the wonders of papier-mâché. 'From end to end of the show-room of this manufacture, there is a refinement of convenience as well as of beauty,' Martineau declares (*Household Words*, 4: 5, nos. 82, 85). It is likely that Charlotte Brontë, who was in close correspondence with Martineau at this time, would have known this article, which was followed in the next issue by one on 'electro-plating and gilding', and eventually by several more on subjects ranging from 'Rainbow-Making' (Coventry ribbons) and 'Birmingham Glass-works' to 'Railway ticket manufacture' (Harriet Martineau, *Autobiography* (2 vols.; London: Virago, 1983), ii. 385–8).

[166] Nikolaus Pevsner, *High Victorian Design: A Study of the Exhibits of 1851* (London: Architectural Press, 1951), 113. The 'Day-dreamer' was not without its critics. One contemporary complained that 'the figures, allegorical of sleep, dreams, good and bad, were too fanciful and too large; and the colour generally was cold and uncomfortable' (*The Crystal Palace and its Contents*, 213).

one may serve as a fitting image of the difference between the landscapes of *Jane Eyre*, where day-dreams open into possibility, and the 'solid material comforts' that Lucy Snowe confronts. For this novel speaks not simply of a different heroine—more 'morbid', less lucky than Jane Eyre—but of a very different world. 'Liberty, Excitement, Enjoyment' have here been replaced by that triumph of the material which at least one contemporary observer saw in the Great Exhibition: 'An importance is given to small, incomplete, and narrow-minded details of physical comfort which in some minds converts the monster advertising show-room, about to open in Hyde Park, into a crisis of sublunary things.'[167] In the words of the 'common saw' that plays ironically through Lucy's ambivalent account of the kindness of the Brettons—'beneficial to me as the atmosphere of some salubrious climate' (180)—we have come 'out of heaven's benediction' and into 'the warm sun'.[168]

IV

In one sense, Lucy is not at all dazzled by the glamour of bourgeois life. She notes Madame Beck's little vanities, the obtuseness of the Brettons and Homes. She anatomizes the defects even of her beloved Dr John. Her cool, unillusioned view of the mores of the Pensionnat Beck, of the comfortable life of the Brettons, is a forceful reminder that 'just looking', that resonant catch-phrase of consumer culture, registers not merely the freedom of the consumer before a prospective purchase, but also an ambivalence: to be 'just looking' is to be not prepared to buy. Yet *Villette* is quite different from those other great novels of the mid-nineteenth century in which privilege and prosperity are critically or ironically portrayed. There is nothing, here, like Dickens's outraged exposure of social ills, or Thackeray's satire of vulgar display. 'My godmother's . . . warm prompt hand, her self-reliant mood, her decided bearing, were all beneficial to me as the atmosphere of some salubrious climate,' says Lucy (180); she is 'eased' and 'soothed', 'pleased and edified' even by Madame Beck (398). Almost, it seems, against her will, she is compelled and preoccupied by 'sunshine'. Even the flirt Ginevra becomes 'a sort of heroine' to her (159). The Brettons, the Homes, the Pensionnat Beck—these dominate her story, not merely as objects of criticism but as types of an effectiveness and fulfilment that she herself is denied.

Ever since *Villette*'s first appearance, this viewpoint has troubled its readers. Whilst they acknowledged the novel's power, its earliest critics expressed unease at the feelings its narrator betrayed. 'Why is *Villette* disagreeable?' Matthew Arnold demanded. 'Because the writer's mind contains nothing but hunger, rebellion and rage.'[169] 'A bitter complaint', the reviewer in the *Spectator* called it, deploring 'the

---

[167] [W. R. Greg], review of William Johnston, *England As It Is; Political, Social, and Industrial, in the Middle of the Nineteenth Century*, in *Christian Remembrancer*, 21 (1851), 401.

[168] *King Lear* II. ii. 155–7. For other instances, see William George Smith, *The Oxford Dictionary of English Proverbs*, 2nd edn, rev. Sir Paul Harvey (Oxford: Clarendon Press, 1948), 480.

[169] Letter to Mrs Forster, 14 April 1853, quoted in *CH* 201.

morbid feeling so predominant in the writer—the hunger of the heart which cannot obtain its daily bread, and will not make-believe that a stone is bread.'[170] More recent critics, responding to a different ideological climate, have been disquieted less by any 'rage' that may be found in Lucy's narrative than by the ways in which her 're-bellion' is complicated by 'hunger'. *Villette*'s 'subcurrent of resentment' is 'stemmed by the overriding need to celebrate bourgeois security', Terry Eagleton argues; its 'final, "official" verdict' springs from its impulse to 'affirm rather than subvert'.[171] 'Brontë's exclusion from social and economic life precluded her free rejection of it,' declare Sandra Gilbert and Susan Gubar;[172] her 'protest stops short', suggests Judith Lowder Newton, 'because it is difficult systematically to criticize what one rejects on one level and longs for on another'.[173] And the elision of Brontë with her narrator in such accounts as these seems to bespeak a widespread sense that what one finds in this novel is an unselfconscious, direct expression of the feelings they disapprove.

Yet Lucy's ambivalent 'longing' is by no means unexamined in *Villette*. Indeed, it is held up to scrutiny at the opening of the second volume, where she tells of lying gazing at a comfortable domestic interior which she must 'perforce . . . recognize and . . . hail' (169). For here she is troubled, tantalized, 'charmed', even as she seeks to turn away:

My bed stood in a little alcove; on turning my face to the wall, the room with its bewildering accompaniments became excluded. Excluded? No! For as I arranged my position in this hope, behold, on the green space between the divided and looped-up curtains, hung a broad, gilded picture-frame enclosing a portrait. It was drawn—well drawn, though but a sketch—in watercolours; a head, a boy's head, fresh, life-like, speaking, and animated. It seemed a youth of sixteen, fair-complexioned, with sanguine health in his cheek; hair long, not dark, and with a sunny sheen; penetrating eyes, an arch mouth, and a gay smile. On the whole, a most pleasant face to look at, especially for those claiming a right to that youth's affection . . . Any romantic little schoolgirl might almost have loved it in its frame.   (170)

Here, the narrative concern with the spectacle of bourgeois prosperity reaches a peculiar climax. That which appears before Lucy's eyes is an imposing decorative object, surrounded by gilding and placed on display: in a striking reversal of ordinary descriptive convention, the 'enclosing' frame takes precedence over the 'portrait' it contains. The image thus framed is a 'pleasant' one, of 'sanguine health' and of happiness, 'speaking', in its sunny animation, of that confidence, potency, belovedness which she—bewildered, powerless, disoriented—so manifestly lacks. 'On the whole a most pleasant face to look at,' says Lucy; and if here, like Thackeray, she echoes Ecclesiastes,[174] it is with none of the *vanitas vanitatum* that informs that

---

[170] *CH* 182.

[171] Terry Eagleton, *Myths of Power: A Marxist Study of the Brontës* (London: Macmillan, 1975), 71, 92.

[172] Sandra M. Gilbert and Susan Gubar, *The Madwoman in the Attic: The Woman Writer and the Nineteenth-Century Literary Imagination* (New Haven and London: Yale University Press, 1979), 402.

[173] Judith Lowder Newton, *Women, Power and Subversion; Social Strategies in British Fiction, 1778–1860* (New York and London: Methuen, 1985), 118–19.

[174] 'Truly the light is sweet, and a pleasant thing it is for the eyes to behold the sun' (Ecclesiastes 11: 7). 'But if a man live many years, and rejoice in them all; yet let him remember the days of darkness; for they shall be many. All that cometh is vanity', continues the next verse.

'Titan'´s vision of the early Victorian world. Yet the qualification that follows—'especially for those claiming a right to that youth's affections'—evokes something more disquieting, perhaps, than ever envisaged by Thackeray: the position of one for whom to 'look' might be a more difficult thing.

For the 'pain' here brought into focus is a subject imaginatively contemplated, not a weakness artlessly betrayed. This 'sunny', alluring, tormenting image resonates with suggestions that are developed throughout *Villette*. Again and again in the novel, John Graham Bretton, his 'face bright with beaming . . . energy' (250), is likened to the sun. 'As the sun to the shivering jail-bird,' Lucy recalls his kindness (247): his 'influence' on her life is like 'the sun' on a 'sad cold dell' (253). 'Beside him was rest and refuge—around him, fostering sunshine,' she remarks of his disposition (223): he thaws the 'self-imposed restriction' of Paulina's 'gentle ice' (424). His, she says, is a temper 'bland, glowing, and genial, within whose influence it is as good for the poor in spirit to live, as it is for the feeble in frame to bask in the glow of noon' (196). 'Really, I seem to live in a sort of moral antipodes,' his mother declares of his homecomings, 'and on these January evenings my day rises when other people's night sets in' (272). Such images as these seem to speak of a 'sunshine' wholly beneficent, 'fostering' life and energy, radiant, beautiful. Yet the metaphor in *Villette* has darker resonances than this.

Since girlhood, Charlotte Brontë had been fascinated by sun-worship. Thomas Moore's 'The Fire-Worshippers' (from *Lalla Rookh*) was known to her in 1834:[175] it clearly made a lasting impression, as it is quoted both in *Jane Eyre* (366) and *Villette* (196). Fired, apparently by this work, she and her brother Branwell had made the rising sun the symbol and god of their newly created Angria. 'Turn from the basilisk Percy!' Zamorna exhorts the Angrians. 'Fix your eyes on my sun and standard till their glory ceases to dazzle you.'[176] The mark of a 'thorough-going Angrian' is 'devoted worship of the Rising Sun'.[177] Such references are frequently ironic. Benjamin Wiggins (Charlotte's comic figure for Branwell) appears in one early story 'fallen upon his face flat as a fluke, motionless as a dead herring, prostrated towards the east like a Parsee worshipping the new risen sun'.[178] 'We are fire-worshippers and would fain make our petitions to the sun, but it dazzles us, so we turn to the moon': thus the Duchess of Zamorna describes the project of those who seek through her to gain favours from the Duke.[179] And it is with a hint of a similar irony that the image of sun-worship reappears twenty years later in *Villette*. 'Temples have been reared to the Sun,' reflects Lucy, as she turns from thoughts of Graham to extol that spirit of imagination 'whose day needs no sun to lighten it', and enjoins herself to hush 'the impulse to fond idolatry' (230–1). The moment points back to her earlier contemplation of this literally dazzling figure—'his hair, whiskers, and complexion . . . of such a tone as a strong light brings out with somewhat perilous force'—where one of the novel's most telling images appears with the force of revelation: 'I was driven to

175 *EEW* ii. 2, p. xx.   176 'Zamorna's Address to the Angrians', *EEW* ii. 2, 300.
177 'My Angria and the Angrians', ibid. 255.   178 'My Angria and the Angrians', ibid. 247.
179 'Corner Dishes: A Day Abroad', ibid. 119.

compare his beamy head in my thoughts to that of the 'golden image' which Nebuchadnezzar the king had set up' (98).[180]

'Idolatry' was a commonplace in nineteenth-century England, used—both flip-
pantly and seriously—to denote that excessive love of the creature against which
Scripture warned.[181]

> Love thee!—'tis more of worship than of love!
>   To thee I bend and bow,
> Firm in idolatry, with hopes above
>   All things less bright than thou.

Thus, a poem called 'Love's Idolatry', in one of the first issues of *Fraser's Magazine*
to come to Haworth Parsonage.[182] 'I could not . . . see God for his creature:
of whom I had made an idol,' Jane Eyre recalls of the heady days of her courtship (*JE*
274). 'You see I still think of Frank more than of God,' Miss Marchmont confesses
to Lucy, 'and unless it be counted that in thus loving the creature . . . I have not . . .
blasphemed the Creator, small is my chance of salvation' (41). Ginevra is Dr John's
'idol' (183), whom he thinks—for 'a moment'—'divine' (218). The term had become newly prominent in the middle years of the century, in attacks both on
Roman Catholicism and on the increasing materialism of the age. Anti-Catholic
writers portrayed the Roman church as 'the old heathen idolatry', dependent for
her power 'not upon the purity of her creed . . . but upon the splendour of her rites,
her crucifixes, her genuflections, her golden shrines'.[183] Excessive love of the goods

---

[180] The reference is to Daniel 3, which recounts how Nebuchadnezzar made an enormous 'image of
gold' and commanded 'every man' to fall down and worship it: the Israelites Shadrach, Meshach, and
Abednego refuse, and are cast into a 'burning fiery furnace' from whose flames they are protected by God.

[181] It became more fashionable in the 20th cent. to speak of 'fetishism' than of 'idolatry', partly because
of Marx's and Freud's appropriation of the former term. (See Emily Apter, Introduction, *Feminism as Cul-
tural Discourse*, ed. Emily Apter and William Pietz (Ithaca: Cornell University Press, 1993), 1–12.) Indeed,
David Simpson suggests that 'in the nineteenth century . . . it frequently seems synonymous with *idolatry*'
(*Fetishism and Imagination: Dickens, Melville, Conrad* (Baltimore and London: Johns Hopkins University
Press, 1982), 9). But the words were not exactly synonymous, and carried quite different resonances.
'Fetishism' entered the English language as a term of anthropological description, denoting naïve worship
of an object as and for itself. Charlotte Brontë could have read of it in the 18-page review of
T. Edward Bowditch's *Mission from Cape Coast Castle to Ashantee* published in *Blackwood's Magazine* in
1819 (Barker, 155). The emphasis in discussions of fetishism is on the tawdriness of the object: the term's
associations with the primitive enabled polite readers in the early 19th cent. to distance themselves from it.
'Idolatry', however, was a theological term. It had become newly topical by the early 1850s, and its meanings
were being explored by such writers as Ruskin and Carlyle. (See e.g. John Ruskin, 'Proper Sense of the Word
Idolatry', *The Stones of Venice* (2 vols., 1851–3), ii. app. 10; Thomas Carlyle, *On Heroes, Hero-Worship and the
Heroic in History* (1841), Lecture IV). Although it had become a cliché in the discourse of romantic love, it
was still believed to be a sin. It was certainly far more likely than fetishism to be seen as an intimate temptation or pain. There is, indeed, a graphic account of the 'intense anxieties and apprehensions inseparable
from all idolatrous attachment' in a book that Brontë seems to have read with attention whilst she was writing *Villette* (Revd Hugh White, *The Gospel Promotive of True Happiness* (Dublin: James McGlashan, 1851),
7; see below, 269–70). And despite the prominence within the novel of fetishistic synecdoche ('paletôt',
'lunettes'), 'idolatry' rather than 'fetishism' is the figure invoked in *Villette*.

[182] *Fraser's Magazine*, 34 (1832), 415. 'Why are we to be divided? Surely, Ellen, it must be because we
are in danger of loving each other too well; of losing sight of the *Creator* in idolatry of the *creature*', writes
Charlotte Brontë to Ellen Nussey, at the age of 21 (*CBL* i. 164).

[183] John Cumming, *Prophetic Studies; or, Lectures on the Book of Daniel* (London: Arthur Hall, 1850), 116.

of this world had long been designated 'Mammon-worship'; and steadily increasing prosperity gave new resonance to such complaints. 'We boast ... of the sins of idolatry among the Romanists, and we send missionaries to the poor unenlightened heathens,' wrote J. A. Froude in a book which Charlotte Brontë read in 1849,

but oh! if you may measure the fearfulness of an idol by the blood which stains its sacrifice, by the multitude of its victims, where in all the world, in the fetish of the poor negro, in the hideous car of Indian Juggernaut, can you find a monster whose worship is polluted with such enormity as this English one of money![184]

Idolatry of both these kinds figures prominently in *Villette*. To Lucy, the 'Moloch "Church"' of Rome (420) is 'a great mixed image of gold and clay' (419); 'full procession ... high mass ... swarming tapers ... swinging censers ... ecclesiastical millinery' appear to her 'tawdry, not grand', 'grossly material, not poetically spiritual' (421). 'The tale is short, and not new,' she declares, as she tells of the 'junta''s schemes. 'Its alpha is Mammon, and its omega, Interest' (461). Madame Walravens is 'as hideous as a Hindoo idol' and possesses 'an idol's consequence'; those interested in her wealth appear as her 'votaries' (461). 'She offered messages and gifts at an unique shrine, and inauspicious seemed the bearing of the uncouth thing she worshipped,' says Lucy of Madame Beck's attendance upon this jewel-bedecked figure (390).

Yet idolatry in *Villette* is not simply a conventional figure. It is more subtly invoked, more deeply pondered, and more central to the novel than this. 'Any romantic little schoolgirl might almost have loved *it in its frame*,' says Lucy, of Graham's image (my italics): and the observation conveys not merely a sardonic sense of the conventionality of his charm, but also, in its emphasis on circumscribed materiality, the suggestion that such 'love' is a form of idolatry. The suggestion is developed in the anecdote that follows, in which Lucy tells how this graven image became to her in girlhood an object of fascination, and how she took the little Paulina to 'test' its effect upon the child. Her description of the portrait as it now confronts her—'fresh, life-like, speaking, animated'—is charged with the same feeling. At first 'it' is inert 'in its frame', but the hint of independent agency implicit in 'penetrating eyes' begins to be developed as, in a series of anxious conjectures, the gazer endows it with life. 'Those eyes looked as if ... they would flash a lightning response to love'; 'his lips menaced, beautifully but surely, caprice and light esteem.' For to look one's fill at an object is to acknowledge that object's power. Even as Lucy tells how she 'used to mount a music-stool for the purpose of unhooking *it*, holding *it* in my hand', the portrait begins to 'glance', to reverse that objectifying gaze.[185]

---

[184] *The Nemesis of Faith*, 2nd edn. (London: John Chapman, 1849), 46–7. The image of Juggernaut in his car—to figure prominently in *Villette*—was a popular one in the period. 'It was the fashion, some years ago, to sneer at Success,' recalled a writer in *The Cornhill Magazine* in 1860. 'Clever men drew pictures of Success, represented by a mighty Juggernaut passing triumphantly over the necks of thousands of prostrate worshippers' ([Sir William Kaye], 'Success', *Cornhill Magazine*, 2 (1860), 729).

[185] 'An idol, technically speaking, is simply an image which has an unwarranted irrational power over somebody; it has become an object of worship, a repository of powers which someone has projected into it, but which in fact it does not possess' (W. J. T. Mitchell, *Iconology: Image, Text, Ideology* (Chicago: University of Chicago Press, 1986), 113.

The moment ends with the admission that she who gazes has been 'charmed'. And the word is here not simply a nineteenth-century romantic cliché, but instinct with its earlier associations of magic and necromancy.

Unlike the shallow Ginevra, the malevolent Madame Walravens, the sunny-haired youth in the portrait is an idol not easily dismissed. 'He was not made of common clay, not put together out of vulgar materials,' Lucy is later to observe (190). Nor is he the object merely of the narrator's singular desire. He is approved, beloved, desired by others: the inheritor and possessor of what Charlotte Brontë once called 'wealth—Appearance Family—and all those advantages which are the acknowledged idols of the world'.[186] A figure of easy assurance, before whom others are supplicants ('claiming a right to [his] affections') he can bestow or withdraw confirmation to delightful or devastating effect. 'Liberal, suave, impressible' (171): if these terms of praise contain also, in their suggestions of smoothness and worldliness, a hint of limitation, judgement is subordinate here to a sense of this other's power. Graham's is a 'pleasant' image of the glamour of self-possession, but it is one that prompts in the viewer an unease amounting to 'pain'. That which this moment configures is no safe critical distance, but a much more dangerous space.

For if John Graham Bretton is likened to the sun, the novel's portrayal of this golden figure is suffused with Lucretius's warning—*Sol etiam caecat, contra si tendera pergas* ('If you persist in gazing at it, the sun will send you blind').[187] Confronted by his youthful portrait, Lucy remembers the child Paulina: 'she . . . gazed long, and at last a darkness went trembling through her sensitive eye, as she said, "Put me down"' (170). The suggestion comes into focus at one of the very few moments in the novel when the narrator allows another to catch a glimpse of what she feels. Paulina—her 'native clear sight' now 'dazzled' by 'cloudless happiness'—begins to discuss her love with her friend, in an exquisitely painful way. 'Do other people see him with my eyes?' she asks, importunately. '*I never see him*', is Lucy's strange and emphatic reply.

'I looked at him twice or thrice about a year ago, before he recognized me, and then I shut my eyes; and if he were to cross their balls twelve times between each day's sunset and sunrise— except from memory, I should hardly know what shape had gone by.'

'Lucy, what do you mean?' said she, under her breath.

'I mean that I value vision, and dread being struck stone blind'.   (424–5)

And the reader is sharply reminded that one is by no means indifferent to that which one is 'dazzled' by.[188]

---

[186] Charlotte Brontë to Ellen Nussey, 24 April 1845 (*CBL* i. 391).

[187] For a discussion of early 19th-cent. optical researchers who damaged their eyes by gazing at the sun in the course of investigating retinal after-images, see Jonathan Crary, *Techniques of the Observer: On Vision and Modernity in the Nineteenth Century* (Cambridge, Mass., and London: MIT Press, 1990), 107–12, 139–42; in 'Modernizing Vision', in Hal Foster (ed.), *Vision and Visuality* (Seattle: Bay Press, 1988), 34, Crary discusses the 'strange intensity and exhilaration' of this research.

[188] The image of being blinded by dazzle recurs not merely at moments of horror—as when Lucy in her delirium sees the 'coronals' on the 'ghastly white beds' in the dormitory as 'sunbleached' skulls, with 'wide gaping eye-holes'—but also in a lighter key. 'I could have exulted to burst on his vision, confront and confound his 'lunettes', one blaze of acquirements' (354), she recalls, of her 'comet-like professor'

The idea of a god-like, masculine sun, dazzling, potent, devastating, was not new to the author of *Villette*. From the very inception of Angria, 'the god-like Zamorna, our idol, the idol of me and all our sex' (as the Duchess of Zamorna calls him) is described as a 'fire rob'd god'.[189] 'Fire! Light! What have we here? Zamorna's self, blazing in the frontispiece like the sun on his own standard,' Lord Charles Wellesley exclaims, as he gazes at his album portrait. 'O Zamorna! What eyes those are . . . Man nor woman could never gather more than a troubled, fitful happiness from their kindest light.'[190] In a wholly different key, such a sun is a central image in some of the most striking of those verses, 'condensed and terse, vigorous and genuine', which Charlotte Brontë had been instrumental in publishing in 1846:

> Blood-red, he rose, and, arrow-straight,
> His fierce beams struck my brow;
> The soul of nature, sprang, elate,
> But *mine* sank sad and low![191]

Emily Brontë's 'dazzling sun' is at once an invigorating force that 'restor[es] our earth to joy', and a burning, 'blinding' 'hostile light', invading intimate private space ('My lids closed down—yet through their veil I I saw him blazing still')[192] and violating the tranquillity of the speaker's 'changeful dreams'. The 'he' of this poem (the masculine pronoun is insistent) is certainly very different from the successful young doctor whose 'firm, marble chin' and 'straight Greek features' compel admiration from one unregarded by him. Yet this sense of a 'dazzling', threatening other is strangely recalled in *Villette*. Indeed, there is perhaps an ironic echo of this poem, whose speaker, in bed in a curtained room, turns her face to the pillow, unable to shut out the light, in that novel's portrayal of Lucy Snowe, turning her face to the wall in a bedroom at La Terrasse and confronted by a 'sunny' image which she is powerless to 'exclude'.[193] That at which Lucy gazes is merely the portrait of a charming youth, who 'menace[s]' nothing worse than 'caprice and light esteem'. Yet the moment is one that evinces less a trivialization of concerns which in Emily

---

(212). 'It is a new thing' for her, she reflects at another moment, 'to see one testily lifting his hand to screen his eyes, because you tease him with an obtrusive ray' (334).

[189] 'The Spell, An Extravaganza' (1834), *EEW* ii. 2, 190; *EEW* ii. 1, xv.

[190] 'A Peep into a Picture Book', *EEW* ii. 2, 86.

[191] 'Stars', *EBP* 5–6. Charlotte Brontë's description of her sister's poetry is in her *Biographical Notice of Ellis and Acton Bell* (1850).

[192] She seems literally to have looked at the sun. For the experience she describes is that of a retinal afterglare, which appears as a spot of darkness when the eye is open, but as light when it is closed. 'If we look at the sun, for example, when near the horizon, or when reflected from glass or water, so as to moderate its brilliancy, and keep the eye upon it for a few seconds, we shall see it even for hours afterwards, and whether the eyes [sic] is open or shut, a spectre of the sun varying in its colours,' writes Brewster in *Letters on Natural Magic* (22).

[193] Her sisters' poetry haunted Charlotte Brontë, she confessed, in the years that followed their deaths. 'In the hill-country silence', she wrote to W. S. Williams on 22 May 1850, 'their poetry comes by lines and stanzas into my mind: once I loved it; now I dare not read it' (*CBL* ii. 403). As Mary Jacobus has noted, Lucy's description of her awakening at La Terrasse 'resembles nothing so much as Emily Brontë's "Prisoner" after visionary flight' (Jacobus, 'The Buried Letter', 135).

Brontë's more 'abstract' poetry are more seriously explored than an acute imaginative intelligence of quite a different kind.[194]

For here, that Apollo-like warrior-god has become an ambiguous figure of mid-nineteenth-century bourgeois prosperity. That which confronts this bed-bound narrator is not a life-giving godlike force, but a 'life-like ... animated' image: an 'idol' which is enlivened by her own worshipping gaze. It is not an elemental energy but a substantial material object, enshrined between 'looped-up curtains', displayed in a 'gilded frame'.[195] Indeed, in its peculiar compound of 'flatness' and 'alluring radiance', its refusal to yield up its pleasure to one who can claim no 'right', it is like the archetypal commodity of burgeoning consumer capitalism, which 'tenderly returns the gaze of every potential customer, while frostily withholding it from the destitute'.[196] Yet the threat to self-possession that this mundane object presents is rather more insidious than that invasion by an unwanted other which is the subject of 'Stars'. For Lucy's description registers a far more intimate conscription than that earlier speaker's defencelessness in the face of aggressive light. 'Those eyes,' she says, revealingly, 'looked as if ... they would flash a lightning response to love'. The idol's unreliable promise is born of the worshipper's longing. 'How was it,' she recalls herself 'pondering', 'that what *charmed* so much could at the same time so keenly pain?' (my italics). And the fact that the verbs now belong to this image rather than to she who gazes renders the moment more sinister than might at first appear. Power has passed to the idol, and been drained from the idolater.[197]

'To honour what has won success is worthy worship, and not to be condemned or restrained,' an essayist was to write in the *Cornhill Magazine* seven years after the publication of *Villette*. 'It is veneration for that type of manhood, which most nearly approaches the divine, by reason of its creative energy. It is a good sign of the times that we appreciate it at its true worth.'[198] Just so, within Lucy's narrative, Graham Bretton appears as a 'true young English gentleman', 'beautiful with a man's best beauty', 'under a ray of special illumination, which shone all partial over his head' (63, 190, 175). Yet the perspective of the 'worshipper' as it is figured in *Villette* is not one of calm 'appreciation' and evaluation of 'worth'. For this gilded youth is not merely an ambiguous, tantalizing image of the good things of this world. He is also

---

[194] 'Because Ellis's poems are short and abstract, the critics think them comparatively insignificant and dull. They are mistaken' (Charlotte Brontë to W. S. Williams, 16 November 1848, *CBL* ii. 140).

[195] 'He looks superb in his beautiful, tasteful, gilded gibbet', Charlotte Brontë was to write, ambiguously, less than a year later, of her publisher's gift of a framed portrait of her erstwhile idol, Thackeray (to George Smith, 26 February, 1853; *LL* iv. 47).

[196] These phrases are taken from Terry Eagleton, *Walter Benjamin: or Towards a Revolutionary Criticism* (London: Verso, 1981), 25, 26, 38.

[197] 'The 'horror' of fetishism,' notes W. J. T. Mitchell, 'was not just that it involved an illusory, figurative act of treating material objects as if they were people but that this transfer of consciousness seemed to drain the humanity out of the idolater. As the stocks and stones come alive, the idolater is seen as falling into a kind of living death ... in which the idol is more alive than the idolater. Marx's claim that commodity fetishism is a kind of perverse "exchange", producing "material relations between persons and social relations between things", employs precisely the same logic' (Mitchell, *Iconology*, 190).

[198] [Sir William Kaye], 'Success', 729. The *Cornhill Magazine*, in the second issue of which this article appeared, was the brainchild of George Smith, the charming, successful, impervious man who seems partly to have inspired Brontë's portrait of Graham Bretton.

the impervious object of a potentially devastating desire. In Lucy's oblique confession of this, the novel brings together two of the most charged, most embarrassing of subjects in mid-Victorian England—the pain of those who did not share in the prosperity so prominently on display, and that other, more intimate, pain, 'forbidden utterance' by social convention, of woman's unrequited love. And in doing so it focuses that which is implicit throughout its distinctive portrayal of the 'sunshine' of the Brettons' world.

The moment when the child Paulina gazes with Lucy at the portrait, with its delicate suggestion of the 'darkness' of idol-worship, is recalled as they discuss its subject many years afterwards. 'To me he seems now all sacred,' says Paulina of her lover; she confides that when she looks at him, she feels 'a sort of fear' (424). From her own very different perspective, Lucy ponders 'that curious one-sided friendship which was half marble and half life' (362). If 'idolatry' is in *Villette* a figure used, pejoratively, to signify the worship of the unworthy—Dr John's passion for Ginevra, the junta's deference to Madame Walravens, even Mrs Bretton's love for her son (187)—it appears most strikingly, most disquietingly, from a perspective usually mocked or reproved: that of the idolator. When the privileged Paulina speaks of her 'fear', hers is the maidenly hesitation of one who is safely loved. But for Lucy the commonplace cliché is charged with more devastating meaning: 'I mean that I value vision, and dread being struck stone blind' (425). 'The spirit of romance . . . would have fashioned a paramount hero, kept faithfully with him and made him supremely "worshipful",' Charlotte Brontë wrote to her publisher, when he expressed dissatisfaction with 'the transfer of interest' away from John Graham Bretton in the final volume of the novel. 'He should have been an idol, *and not a mute, unresponding idol*—either—: but this would have been unlike real Life, inconsistent with Truth—at variance with Probability' (my italics).[199] And in explaining her refusal to be 'more flowery and inviting', she offers a striking image of the constellation of feeling at the centre of *Villette*. The 'pain' that informs the novel—embarrassing, intimate, shocking—is that of idolatry.[200]

'Idolator I knelt to an idol cut in rock!' Brontë had written seven years earlier, apparently of her unrequited love for her teacher, M. Heger:

> I might have slashed my flesh and drawn my heart's best blood:
> The Granite God had felt no tenderness, no shock;
> My Baal had not seen nor heard nor understood.[201]

In *Villette*, idolatry becomes a figure through which that 'hunger' which is usually seen as the novel's weakness is objectified and contemplated. Immured at the Pensionnat Beck for the long vacation, Lucy is seized by the conviction that 'Fate was of

---

[199] Charlotte Brontë to George Smith, 6 December 1852 (*LL* iv. 22–3).

[200] 'Their idols are silver and gold, the work of men's hands. They have mouths, but they speak not: eyes have they, but they see not: They have ears, but they hear not: noses have they, but they smell not: They have hands, but they handle not: feet have they, but they walk not: neither speak they through their throat. They that make them are like unto them; so is every one that trusteth in them' (Psalm 115: 4–8).

[201] 'He saw my heart's woe', *CBP* 244–5.

stone, and Hope a false idol—blind, bloodless, and of granite core' (160). When she tells how she was asked to 'improvise a theme . . . for the pleasure and to the inspiration of a bourgeois of Labassecour', the figure again erupts, bursting the bounds of her sardonic self-irony. The 'Creative Impulse', she says, is 'the most maddening of masters'—more maddening even than the 'master' at whose whim she is urged to perform: 'a deity, which sometimes, under circumstances apparently propitious, would not speak when questioned, would not hear when appealed to, would not, when sought, be found; but would stand, all cold, all indurated, all granite, a dark Baal with carven lips and blank eye-balls, and breast like the stone face of a tomb' (356). Just so, but in a very different key, M. Paul is portrayed on his fête-day, sitting like an idol 'eclipsed' by the 'offerings' of his pupils, who wait for him as the prophets of Baal, having offered up their bullock, waited for their god to speak. 'Voiceless and viewless, stirless and wordless, he kept his station behind a pile of flowers' (339).[202] (Lucy, too, maintains her silence: 'I kept . . . both my box and my countenance, and sat insensate as any stone' (340).) Yet this kind of self-reflexive humour does not diminish the darkness or undermine the import of *Villette*'s recurring figure of the unresponding god. It animates the novel's extraordinary realization of 'private, secret, insidious trauma',[203] the annihilating potential of ordinary, undramatic event. 'He passed me at speed, hardly feeling the earth he skimmed, and seeing nothing on either hand': thus Lucy's account of her invisibility to Graham as, looking 'very handsome' he leaves 'his victrix' Paulina (370). The figure is developed in the novel's final chapter as an image of the larger catastrophe of Lucy's separation from Paul:

The Juggernaut on his car towered there a grim load. Seeing him draw nigh, burying his broad wheels in the oppressed soil—I, the prostrate votary—felt beforehand the annihilating craunch. . . . The great Juggernaut, in his great chariot, drew on lofty, loud, and sullen. He passed quietly, like a shadow sweeping the sky at noon. Nothing but a chilling dimness was seen or felt. I looked up. Chariot and demon charioteer were gone by; the votary still lived. (493)

And the shadowy presence of this trope may be felt within the novel's presentation of Providence itself—from Miss Marchmont's struggles to accept the will of 'Inscrutable God' (40) to that closing image of 'a thousand weepers, praying in agony' for a voice that 'was not uttered—not uttered till, when the hush came, some could not feel it: till, when the sun returned, his light was night to some!' (495).

---

[202] 'And they took the bullock which was given them, and they dressed it, and called on the name of Baal from morning even until noon, saying, O Baal, hear us. But there was no voice, nor any that answered' (1 Kings 18: 26).

[203] Laura Brown, 'Not Outside the Range: One Feminist Perspective on Psychic Trauma', in C. Caruth (ed.), *Trauma: Explorations in Memory* (Baltimore and London: Johns Hopkins University Press 1995), 102.

CHAPTER EIGHT

The Prism of Pain:
Villette and History (2)

a little lady in a black silk gown, whom I could not see at first for the dazzle in
the room

(Mrs Gaskell of her first meeting with Charlotte Brontë)[1]

Lucy Snowe's narrative poses a distinctive challenge to that gospel of effectiveness
and well-being being publicly celebrated, ostentatiously proclaimed in the England
in which *Villette* was conceived. After the insecure 1830s and 1840s, the nation appeared to be entering upon a new period of economic health and social stability; in
which, as one twentieth-century historian puts it, 'contentment as well as prosperity seemed more widely enjoyed'.[2] And the Great Exhibition was a potent symbol of
this optimism. Both the mighty spectacle itself and the 'orderly . . . manageable . . .
good-humouredly amenable' crowds who came to it inspired 'admiration of the
present and confidence in the future'. Both seemed to give evidence that England
was 'moving in a right direction towards some superior condition of society', in
which 'a more refined and fixed condition of happiness' might be universally
shared.[3] The *Westminster Review*, indeed, prophesied that 'new thoughts and imaginations will grow out of it . . . till it shall be an acknowledged practical fact, that
human misery is not a necessity, but a simple ignorance'.[4] 'What luminous and
awakening rays may it not transmit into every nook and cranny of domestic intercourse, lifting even the poor and drudging classes up to a sense of pleasure in the
beautiful, which has hitherto been the exclusive right of the rich?' asked an article in
Fraser's in January 1852. 'Why should not these results ensue to the increase of goodness in the world?'[5]

For the brilliant display in the Crystal Palace was an image not merely of secular
progress and material success. 'Man is approaching a more complete fulfilment of
that great and sacred mission which he has to perform in the world,' proclaimed
Prince Albert at its opening. 'His reason being created in the image of God, he has

---

[1] Mrs Gaskell to Catherine Winkworth, 25 August 1850 (*CBL* ii. 447).
[2] Barry Supple, 'Material Development: the Condition of England 1830–1870' in Laurence Lerner
(ed.), *The Victorians* (London: Methuen, 1978), 56.
[3] *Illustrated London News*, 14 June 1851, 569; 'Three May-Days in London. III. The May Palace', *Household Words*, 3 (1851), 123; 'The Great Exhibition, and the Little One', *Household Words*, 3 (1851), 356.
[4] 'Official Catalogues of the Industrial Exhibition', *Westminster Review*, 55 (1851), 349.
[5] 'Eighteen Hundred and Fifty-one', *Fraser's Magazine*, 45 (1852), 20.

to use it to discover the laws by which the Almighty governs his creation, and, by making these laws his standard of action, to conquer Nature to his use.'[6] 'The sentence has gone forth,' announced F. D. Maurice, in a sermon preached three days later, 'as the profoundest expression of our English faith, in the presence of the representatives of all nations, that knowledge of every kind, which leads to the creation of railways and steam-carriages, as well as the most spiritual, is of God.'[7] 'It is of special use to foreign nations to see for themselves the results of a Protestant faith, of equal laws, and well-regulated liberty, stamped in symbols not to be mistaken,' declared the *Christian Observer*. 'Here they may behold, written as with a sunbeam, that righteousness exalteth a nation, and that happy is the people who have the Lord for their God.'[8] The Bible is quoted in the Exhibition's catalogue, and biblical texts appear on its medals; the building, with its 'nave' and transepts', was laid out like a cathedral and described in ecclesiastical terms. When the sun broke through the clouds at its opening, many saw this as a sign from God. Thus, for example, Thackeray, in lines that Charlotte Brontë admired:

> And see! above the fabric vast,
> God's boundless Heaven is bending,
> God's peaceful sunlight's beaming through,
> And shines o'er all.[9]

Within this rhetoric, the elect have become the successful: those who inherit the earth.

Such imagery as this is prominent in *Villette*: it reaches its climax in Lucy's description of the marriage and subsequent lives of Paulina and Dr John. 'I *do* believe,' she says, at the end of the chapter called 'Sunshine', 'there are some human beings so born, so reared, so guided, from a soft cradle to a calm and late grave, that no excessive suffering penetrates their lot, and no tempestuous blackness overcasts their journey. And often, these are not pampered, selfish beings, but natures elect, harmonious and benign; men and women mild with charity, kind agents of God's good

---

[6] Quoted in *Great Exhibition of the Works of Industry of All Nations 1851. Official Descriptive and Illustrated Catalogue* (3 vols.; London: Spicer Brothers, W. Clowes & Sons, 1851 and 1852), i. 4.

[7] Frederick Denison Maurice, *The Old Testament: Nineteen Sermons Preached in the Chapel of Lincoln's Inn* (London: John W. Parker & Son, 1851), 231–2.

[8] *Christian Observer* 162, June 1851, 437. There were a few who dissented from this view, finding in the Great Exhibition a figure of 'Babel renewed' ('The Prophetic Character of the Great Exhibition', *Quarterly Journal of Prophecy*, III. 272). See also *Tomorrow! The Results and Tendencies of National Exhibitions Deduced from Strict Historical Parallels, by 'Historia'* (London: Saunders & Otley, 1851) and *The Theology and Morality of the Great Exhibition as set forth in certain leading articles which have lately appeared in 'The Times' and 'Record' Newspapers, by a Spiritual Watchman of the Church of England* (London: William Edward Painter, 1851). But such voices appear, perhaps surprisingly, to have been in a minority.

[9] 'May-Day Ode'; Charlotte Brontë to George Smith, 12 May 1851 (*CBL* ii. 614–15). 'When the last echo [of the *Hallelujah Chorus*] died away the gloom which had hung over the scene was suddenly dissipated, a burst of sunlight flashing through the uncovered roof of the transept, and falling full upon the central group,' reports *The Leader* of 3 May 1851. 'The heart, made superstitious by beauty, could not but accept it as a blessing and an omen' that 'just as the cheering without announced the coming of the Queen, the clouds . . . passed away,—and sunlight broke out at once over all the building,' writes the *Athenaeum* on the same day.

attributes' (436). Theirs is a private version of that potent public story of progress and prosperity enshrined in the Great Exhibition; a story of worldly advancement ('he won in moral profit', 'he rose in intellectual refinement' 'she aided in his progress') which in its smooth domesticity ('from a soft cradle to a calm and late grave') evokes that celebration of the comforts of the bourgeois home. 'It was so,' says Lucy, in conclusion, invoking the biblical account of God's creation of the world, 'for God saw that it was good' (437).

Yet the world of the blessed and prosperous is not the whole world of *Villette*. 'But it is not so for all,' the following chapter opens. And the chapter division marks the novel's informing contrast between the 'sunshine' of the fortunate and the 'pain, privation, penury' (229) which are its narrator's lot. It is a contrast that the novel reflects upon as a problem of narratability. Lucy's dark story begins and ends with the more defined narratives of others: named, effective, successful; securely at home in their world. And it is punctuated by invocations of her culture's accepted constructions of the individual life: of the 'women and girls' who are 'supposed to pass their lives . . . as a bark slumbering through halcyon weather, in a harbour still as glass' (35); of those who are 'busy and happy', 'so much sought after, so much engaged' (272); those destined for 'union and a happy succeeding life' (496). Such narratives speak of 'prospects' and 'friends', known pasts and knowable futures; progress, agency, success, fulfilment; the promise of the bourgeois dream. Lucy's 'anomalous' experience fits no such accepted pattern. Her most private misery is shaped by the spectral, confounding assumptions of bourgeois 'normality': 'All at once my position rose on me like a ghost. Anomalous; desolate, almost blank of hope, it stood. What was I doing here alone in great London? What should I do on the morrow? What prospects had I in life? What friends had I on earth? Whence did I come? Whither should I go? What should I do?' (46). For her, the world in which others are at home is uncanny, ambiguous, 'desolate'; fearful, comfortless, 'blank'.[10]

Jane Eyre was 'an autobiography'. But autobiography is hardly possible to such as Lucy Snowe. Her story questions not merely the comfortable clichés that define the 'reality' of the privileged, but that far more sophisticated sense of self as an organically growing entity which others were developing in these years.[11] In *Villette* such self-coherence is a luxury that only the fortunate can afford. 'Her eyes were the eyes of one who can remember; one whose childhood does not fade like a dream,' says Lucy, of the wealthy, beautiful, loved Paulina. 'She would retain and add; often review from the commencement, and so grow in harmony and consistency as she grew in years' (276). But for one in Lucy's position there can be no such 'harmony' as this. 'About the present, it was better to be stoical; about the future—such a future as mine—to be dead' (109). Hers is no 'sunny' progress which builds upon and

---

[10] Charles Taylor, in *Sources of the Self*, speaks of 'this space of questions, which only a coherent narrative can answer. In order to have a sense of who we are, we have to have a notion of how we have become, and of where we are going' (*Sources of the Self. The Making of the Modern Identity* (Cambridge, Mass.: Harvard University Press, 1989), 47).

[11] Charlotte Brontë read *David Copperfield* in September 1849, and *The Prelude* and *In Memoriam* in August 1850 (*CBL* ii. 251, 437, 457). In December 1849 she read Froude's *Nemesis of Faith*, with its suggestive discussion of the connection between personal identity and 'home' (*CBL* ii. 314).

fulfils the promise of earlier years. When the past reappears before her, it is as an un-
bidden spectacle, and its reappearance leads merely to repetition of pain. Much of
her story, it seems, can be told only in the 'darkness' of metaphor (274): 'I must
somehow have fallen over-board . . . there must have been wreck' (35). Like that of
'the half-drowned life-boatman' who 'keeps his own counsel, and spins no yarns'
(181), it is marked by denials, disguises, and silences; bearing witness to 'painful,
unassimilated history', rather than offering a 'continuous, sequential and inte-
grated narrative of the self'.[12]

Yet if Charlotte Brontë's two previous first-person narratives deal, on the
surface at least, with far more culturally normative figures—the self-made man
Crimsworth, the romantic heroine Jane Eyre—it is this 'anomalous' narrator who
insists most frequently and directly that hers is a lot that others share. 'Let us endure
hardness as good soldiers; let us finish our course, and keep the faith,' she exhorts
(438). Her words may recall St John Rivers, 'indefatigable' missionary-warrior; but
this call to solidarity in suffering is quite different from Jane's distancing admiration of her extraordinary cousin's solitary pursuit of 'the path he had marked for
himself' (*JE* 452). 'I see *a huge mass of my fellow-creatures* in no better circumstances,' reflects Lucy, as she thinks of the probable loneliness of her future. '*A great
many men, and more women,* hold their span of life on conditions of denial and privation.' Turning once more to her own story, after the chapter called 'Sunshine',
she makes a yet more sweeping pronouncement: 'Dark through the wilderness of
this world stretches the way for *most of us*' (361, 438, my italics). If *Villette* has customarily been read as a narrative of singular feminine experience, the ungendered
language in which this last assertion is cast makes a rather larger claim. And the repeated first person plurals in this opening paragraph of 'Cloud'—'In fire and in
blood do we trace the record throughout nature. In fire and in blood does it cross
our own experience'—insist on the typicality of this narrator's dark lot. If Lucy's is
an experience obscured from the 'strong and prosperous', it is, she asserts unambiguously, *more* representative than theirs.

Such remarks might appear pious clichés, expressive of resigned acceptance that
this world is a vale of tears. Yet in the context of Lucy's story, so much of which is an
account of 'sunny' prosperity on display, they have far more force than platitudes.
For *Villette* has a good deal to say about the actual 'conditions' and 'circumstances'
of mid-nineteenth-century life. And it tells not merely of that world of 'the strong
and prosperous' at which Lucy gazes 'as a spectacle' but of the rather different reality to which her generalizations here point. Like Crimsworth's, her singular trajectory is also a typical one. She goes to earn a living, however, not in a particular
Brussels, but in the fictional, more generic 'Villette'. And that which confronts her
there is not the workaday world in which Crimsworth makes his way, but the ambiguously dazzling spectacle of bourgeois prosperity. The difference in the novels'

---

[12] These phrases are taken from Jill Matus's incisive discussion of late twentieth-century theories of
trauma, narrative, and history in her *Toni Morrison* (Manchester: Manchester University Press, 1998),
36, 26.

titles signals their different emphases. Where *The Professor* focused on the forging of a social identity, *Villette* tells of dislocation, of an alien public place. And in this, no less than that earlier novel, it speaks of wider social experience—experience that had no place in that story of achievement and confidence which the Great Exhibition enshrined.

For that journey to an unfamiliar city was made by millions in these years. The decades before the publication of *Villette* saw an unprecedented growth in the urban populations of England and France, largely as a result of migration from the countryside. This was becoming 'the age of great cities', not merely of centres of industry, but of 'great capitals' such as London—and Villette (387).[13] In the rapidly expanding cities, those who met one another were strangers; old ties and obligations were gone; social positions not fixed. To Ruskin, the 'crowded tenements of a struggling and restless population', springing up 'in mildewed forwardness, out of the kneaded fields about our capital', were the signs of a 'strange dissolution' of the springs of 'natural affection'.[14] 'Every . . . connexion seems to partake of the uncertain and the transient,' wrote another contemporary observer. 'Uncertainty, with regard to social relationship, is more or less everywhere.'[15] The experience of the city was of 'dazzle', in all its senses: 'the rapid crowding of changing images, the sharp discontinuity in the grasp of a single glance, and the unexpected onrushing impressions' described years later by George Simmel as 'the psychological conditions which the metropolis creates'.[16] 'There every thing deceives us,' writes one commentator on the age, 'and each object is beheld partly in glare and partly in gloom.'[17] Reading character was difficult, and self-disclosure risky. 'In the city most of the men you meet walk with visards—masks on their faces . . . Is it not a solemn thought, that we perhaps walk through a great show-room, where almost every person you meet is other than he or she upon your first acquaintance had been supposed to be?'[18] Self was less a coherent entity, whose history and relations were known, than a presentation for others, fractured into a series of roles. For if the metropolis allowed a new kind of anonymity, within it one was constantly exposed to others' evaluating gaze.

[13] Robert Vaughan, *The Age of Great Cities, or Modern Society Viewed in its Relation to Intelligence, Morals and Religion* (London: Jackson & Walford, 1843).

[14] 'The Lamp of Memory', *The Seven Lamps of Architecture* (1849), *Library Edition of the Works of John Ruskin*, ed. E. T. Cook and Alexander Wedderburn (39 vols.; London: Allen, 1912), viii. 226. Ruskin sees these changes as produced by aspirational tendencies—'when every man's aim is to be in some more elevated sphere than his natural one, and every man's past life is his habitual scorn; when men build in the hope of leaving the places they have built, and live in the hope of forgetting the years that they have lived' (226). Yet Lucy's unchosen migration is arguably more characteristic: 'unutterable loathing of a desolate existence past forbade return' (*V* 49).

[15] Robert Vaughan, *The Age of Great Cities*, 280, 289.

[16] George Simmel, 'The Metropolis and Mental Life', in David Frisby and Mike Featherstone (eds.), *Simmel on Culture* (London: Sage, 1997), 175. On the difference in legibility between London and 'the uniform cities of the Industrial Revolution' see Raymond Williams, *The Country and the City* (London: Chatto & Windus, 1973), 154.

[17] Edwin Paxton Hood, *The Age and its Architects: Ten Chapters on the English People in Relation to the Times* (London: Charles Gilpin, 1850), 175.

[18] Hood, *The Age and its Architects*, 146–7.

The bright new world of the city held out promise of social advancement; the glittering prizes of success were dazzlingly on display. But its 'sunshine' was shadowed by terror—that 'terror of "Not succeeding"' which Carlyle called the 'Hell' of 'the modern English soul'.[19] For the city was also a place of radical insecurity, in which the 'struggle for existence' was severe.[20] Here, the trauma of advancing capitalism was experienced peculiarly sharply. For many, the city was less an arena for effective agency than a place of disorientating complexity in which some seemed simply to 'rise' and others fall. In 'an economic order that neither victims nor victors understood', 'bourgeois respectablity' seemed to be 'founded on chance'.[21] (In *Villette*, for example, Lucy Snowe speaks of the Brettons' 'handsome property', 'invested in some joint-stock undertaking', having 'melted, it was said, to a fraction of its original amount'. 'Even with them, all had not gone smoothly, and fortune had retrenched her once abundant gifts' (35, 177).) Or, as Elizabeth Gaskell put it, in the Preface to *Mary Barton*, 'those who elbowed me daily in the busy streets of the town' seemed 'tossed to and fro by circumstances, apparently in even a greater degree than other men'.

'In a mercantile country like England, people are continually rising in the world,' proclaimed a popular etiquette manual, published in 1836.[22] But individual success stories were contradicted, inevitably, by the experience of the many who failed to attain what Lucy calls 'a happy succeeding life' (492). The ideology of self-making, of the 'career open to talent' was threatened by a lurking sense that success might be a matter of luck rather than of effort and will. 'There are those who fail in life by no fault of their own,' admitted a guide to *Success in Life*, published the year before *Villette*, even as it tried to argue that 'success in life is ... certain ... to him who uses the right means'.[23] Many appeared to be victims of forces over which they had little control. 'The sea of prosperity ebbed, and forthwith the proud vessels, that set sail with such magnificent promise, were left utter wrecks, high and dry, upon the strand,' declared a lecturer to young men of the Railway Mania of 1845: the experiences of many besides Lucy Snowe were figured as 'shipwreck' in these years.[24] 'To

[19]   *Past and Present* (1843), book 3, ch. 2, in Thomas Carlyle, *Selected Writings*, ed. Alan Shelston (Harmondsworth: Penguin, 1971), 277.

[20]   'The severity of the struggle for existence—the strain upon the powers of every man who runs the race of life in this land and age of high excitement ... is a sore evil,' wrote one commentator, who nevertheless defended the state of 'England as it is' ([W. R. Greg], review of William Johnston, *England As It Is; Political, Social, and Industrial, in the Middle of the Nineteenth Century*, *Edinburgh Review*, 93 (1851), 325).

[21]   Richard Sennett, *The Fall of Public Man* (Cambridge: Cambridge University Press, 1977), 19, 138. On the 'precariousness' of the system, and the general lack of understanding of the laws of economic life in the middle years of the century, see Norman Russell, *The Novelist and Mammon* (Oxford: Clarendon Press, 1986), 23.

[22]   *Hints on Etiquette* (1836), quoted in Elizabeth Langland, *Nobody's Angels: Middle-Class Women and Domestic Ideology in Victorian Culture* (Ithaca and London: Cornell University Press), 26.

[23]   *Success in Life: A Book for Young Men* (London:Thomas Nelson & Sons, 1852), 9, 11.

[24]   Rev. John Cumming, 'The Age We Live In', *Lectures to Young Men, delivered before the Y.M.C.A. in Exeter Hall, 1847–8* (London, 1848), 331. On the prevalence of imagery of storm and shipwreck in the economic discourse of the period see Boyd Hilton, *The Age of Atonement: the Influence of Evangelicalism on Social and Economic Thought, 1795–1865* (Oxford: Clarendon Press, 1988), 147–8.

live at all is a struggle,' Mark Pattison was to write in 1877. 'To keep within reach of the material advantages which it is the boast of our century to have provided is a competition in which only the strong can succeed—the many fail.'[25] Yet the public voices of the period could barely admit such knowledge. 'If . . . the industrious, the frugal, and the foreseeing . . . not only cannot maintain their position or rise above it, but are sinking lower and lower in spite of their exertions, then the construction of society is somehow, somewhere in fault,' wrote one contemporary analyst in words that prefigure *Villette*. 'But who will affirm such cases to exist except as rare anomalies?'[26]

Just so, in *Villette*, Lucy's 'position' appears to her 'like a ghost', 'anomalous, desolate, almost blank of hope' (46). Her narrative cannot assume the configurations of a realism that presupposes that all inhabit the same reassuring world. Yet hers is a story that registers, in a quite emphatic way, those features of mid-nineteenth-century life, intimately known to 'many', which the public narrative of optimism defined as 'rare anomalies'. For hers is a paradigmatic story of dislocation and dispossession. When it opens, she is already displaced from her origins; already beginning to be overlooked and unrecognized. News from 'home' she expects to be 'disastrous'; even her 'permanent residence' is a temporary, 'unsettled' one (6). 'Me she had forgotten,' she says, of meeting an old schoolfellow. 'I made no attempt to recall myself to her memory: why should I?' (44). And the chapters that follow chart an intensifying experience of estrangement, as she travels first to London, then Villette. The 'strangeness' and 'vastness' of the 'Babylon and . . . wilderness' of London challenge her 'self-possession' (45); it is here that her first great crisis of identity occurs. As she arrives in Europe, 'homeless, anchorless, unsupported' (51), 'the cloud of doubt' becomes thicker, 'the necessity for exertion more urgent, the peril (of destitution) nearer, the conflict (for existence) more severe' (58). The speech that she heard in London was 'odd as a foreign tongue' (45); here, 'the whole world' is 'gabbling round [her]' in a language she can neither speak nor understand (61). Her earlier sharp observation of her shipboard companions is succeeded by a more desperate reading of the 'countenance, which I am sure wore a light not unbenignant to the friendless' of the 'stranger' whom she has to ask for aid (63, 62). Villette is a grand metropolis. But Lucy's first experience of its 'magnificent' streets and squares (63) is of being 'driven beyond [her] reckoning' by the pursuit of two strange men (64). For if others are signs that she has to decipher, she is also exposed to their gaze. In London she was anxious to establish her 'position' even in the waiter's eyes (48). There, still, a distant memory survives of family and connections (48); but when she

[25] 'The Age of Reason', *Fortnightly Review*, 27 (1877), 357.
[26] [W. R. Greg], review of *England As It Is*, 324. Modern sociologists have analysed the psychologically debilitating implications of the myth of social mobility for those who fail to achieve its promises. The individualistic ethic—enshrined in stories of successful self-help—fixes responsibility for such failure firmly in individual inadequacy; and leads, such writers have argued, to 'fatalism, passivity, and resignation' (Stephan Thernstrom, *Poverty and Progress: Social Mobility in a Nineteenth-Century City* (Cambridge, Mass.: Harvard University Press, 1973), 57–9; cf. also Richard Sennett and Jonathan Cobb, *The Hidden Injuries of Class* (New York: Vintage Books, 1973); Lillian Rubin, *Worlds of Pain: Life in the Working-Class Family* (New York: Basic Books, 1976).

arrives in Labassecour, all sense of 'connection' is gone. Others can 'tell at a glance' that she is 'an individual of no social significance and little burdened by cash' (59). A 'little man . . . in spectacles' is summoned to 'read' her 'countenance' when she arrives at the Pensionnat Beck (66); as she lies, feigning sleep, on her first night there, its mistress inspects her possessions—'to form from the garments a judgment respecting the wearer', and sits for 'a quarter of an hour on the edge of my bed, gazing at my face' (69).

The logic of a social world in which others appear as strangers is explored as the novel proceeds; indeed, it is emphasized in a series of peculiar vignettes. The gaze that objectifies rather than recognizes—judging, evaluating, categorizing—is prominent in Lucy's narrative, from others' misprisions of her 'character'— 'Madame Beck esteemed me learned and blue; Miss Fanshawe, caustic, ironic, and cynical; Mr Home, a model teacher, the essence of the sedate and discreet' (301)— to Dr John's impercipient 'professional point of view' (248). 'Lucy's disadvantages,' says Graham, 'spring from . . . want of colour in character and costume'; M. Paul, however, declares that she dresses with 'too much attention too effect' (333–4). Even her lack of attractions becomes paradoxically conspicuous—'an unwelcome blank on those bright occasions when beauty should shine' (131). A 'sense of shame and fear of ridicule' (208) are Lucy's constant companions. Asked to play a part in the vaudeville, she recoils from 'the public display' (134); at the concert she keeps 'rather in the shade and out of sight, not wishing to be immediately recognized', aware that she sits where she 'must inevitably be seen' (215). Such feelings as these, *Villette* makes clear, cannot simply be pathologized as 'morbid' hypersensitivity: they have concrete social determinants. For from her first arrival in the city, Lucy is presented as one forced to occupy what one twentieth-century social critic has called 'the unremitting hostility of public space'.[27] When she first arrives in Villette as a stranger, she finds herself 'an object of study' (76), even when she retires to bed. As she mounts the 'estrade' on which she is to 'figure' for the first time as a teacher, 'a row of eyes and brows' confronts her (79); later, she is 'fixed in the centre of the grande salle' to undergo a 'show-trial' (399). When she visits galleries and assemblies, she is herself observed. To herself, in one memorable moment, she appears as 'a third person': the publically visible object of her own critically appraising gaze (209).

Yet, as this momentary impression even of self as a 'stranger' suggests, hers is the narrative also of one who is essentially unknown. If she is all too obtrusively visible she is also 'well habituated to be passed by as a shadow in Life's sunshine' (334): a paradox she captures in a striking image—'I well remember feeling myself to be a mere shadowy spot on a field of light' (131). '*Are* you anybody?' asks Ginevra. 'I am a rising character,' Lucy replies ironically, 'once an old lady's companion, then a nursery-governess, now a school-teacher' (309). But the stress throughout her narrative is is less on social mobility than on the precariousness of an identity that is not

---

[27] David Smail, *The Origins of Unhappiness: A New Understanding of Personal Distress* (London: HarperCollins, 1993), 46.

confirmed by others: as Paulina puts it to her, 'I never knew what you were' (285). When old friends meet her they do not know her in the foreign world of Villette. 'To you she is a stranger,' Graham tells his mother (176); his 'entire misapprehension' of her 'character and nature' (318) is preceded by his literal non-recognition of her. For this is a world in which those of unprepossessing 'exterior' can expect no 'notice' or 'consequence' beyond 'what is given to unobtrusive articles of furniture, chairs of ordinary joiner's work, and carpets of no striking pattern' (98). 'Gossip had passed me by; curiosity had looked me over,' Lucy notes with some relief in the time of her 'silent desolation'; Madame Beck's 'whole blind household' has not found her out (448). Yet such overlooking is registered too as trauma: 'Methought the well-loved dead, who had loved *me* well in life, met me elsewhere, alienated' (160); 'that insufferable thought of being no more loved, no more owned' (160); 'it kills me to be forgotten, monsieur' (482). 'It never,' says Lucy of the man she loves, 'occurred to me as possible that he should recognize Lucy Snowe' (176). Central to her narrative is a quite distinctive emphasis on estrangement and alienation, the 'horror of calamity' and 'sick dread of entire desertion' (267) endemic to a world in which one has 'no true home' (361).

Gaskell's acute social observation, Dickens's 'rhetorical totalizing view from outside',[28] Thackeray's assured survey, are here replaced by images of partial, occluded, bewildered vision, of the viewer as powerless in the face of an impinging phenomenal world. The perspective of *Villette*'s narrator is not one of authoritative distance, but located within the world which she seeks to describe. Much in the novel is resonant of the actual perceptual experience of the mid-nineteenth-century city—dazzling, disorienting, baffling: a place whose 'shapes depended on the momentary position of the casual or mobile observer', in which people were 'hard to make out, their gestures and expressions unconvincing, their purposes obscure'.[29] The fragmented vision, the partial glimpses, the misreadings and ambiguities that are part of the texture of urban life do not here, as in Dickens, become repetitive defining gestures: they are rendered with estranging literalism. Again and again intelligibility collapses into sheer appearance. 'At last we were seated in places commanding a good general view', says Lucy of the evening of the concert (210); but 'the vast and dazzling' spectacle that confronts her—though sharply observed and analysed—has its surrealistic strangenesses: 'The semicircle before the stage presented one dense mass of heads, sloping from floor to ceiling' (212); 'some noted singers and musicians dawned upon the platform' (212); the 'sable rank' of gentlemen, 'lining the background' of the royal 'compartment' appear as 'a dark foil to the splendour displayed in front' (214). 'I had already noticed by glimpses, a severe, dark professorial outline . . . seen only in vista,' says Lucy, of an evening assembly (314); at another, 'suddenly, in a second of time, a head, chest and arms, grew above the crimson desk' (310). The 'chance' encounters and re-encounters (369), the

[28] Williams, *The Country and the City*, 159.
[29] T. J. Clark, *The Painting of Modern Life: Paris in the Art of Manet and his Followers* (London: Thames & Hudson, 1985), 3, 48.

uncertain recognitions and perceptions of likeness peculiar to life in the city are writ large in Lucy's narrative.[30] Thus, she tells how on the night of the fête she 'saw a man—a burgher—an entire stranger, as I deemed him for one moment, but the next, recognized in him a certain tradesman . . . a bookseller . . . whom . . . I had ever been disposed to like' (455). 'A recollection which had been struggling to form in my memory, since the moment I heard his voice, started up perfected,' she says of the beginnings of her recognition of Dr John (96). The old priest she meets at Madame Walravens's house begins to appear familiar: 'I became more and more persuaded of his resemblance to my confessor' (392); he is indeed the one whose 'profile and brow' she has glimpsed in the confessional (161). Lucy's pursuers in the streets, 'faces . . . projected in full gas-light from behind the pillars of a portico', reappear as Messieurs Boissec and Rochemorte, her 'moustachioed, sneering' examiners (401–2, 399). 'Dr John' and 'Isidore' turn out to be Graham Bretton, little Polly returns as Paulina Mary Home de Bassompierre. The drawing-room at Bretton and all its original occupants reassemble in Villette. Such moments reach a climax in the phantasmagoric reappearance of the whole cast of characters at the fête in the public park. But the effect is quite different from that of Dickens's dénouements, which snap together to reveal the hidden logic of the society he depicts. Here, there is no such diagnostic triumph; no satisfying sense to be made of a bewildering actuality. For instead of that recognition of 'connection' which points towards change and progress, there is the haunting, unwilled recurrence of a painful, repetitive history, which speaks not of power but of impotence.

Such a narrative might well appear uncongenial to the men of the mid-nineteenth century, that age of practical solutions and reforming zeal. 'It is not enough that the Poet should add to the knowledge of men', wrote Matthew Arnold, authoritatively, in the year in which *Villette* appeared. 'It is required of him also that he should add to their happiness.' And he goes on to argue against the 'painful' representation of those 'morbid' situations 'in which the suffering finds no vent in action; in which a continuous state of mental distress is prolonged, unrelieved by incident, hope, or resistance, in which there is everything to be endured, nothing to be done.'[31] To him, *Villette* was a 'hideous undelightful convulsed constricted novel'—'one of the most utterly disagreeable books I have ever read'.[32] If Harriet Martineau admired the novel more, she, too, deplored its 'subjective misery', its lack of 'that repose which we hold to be essential to the true presentment of any large portion of life and experience', its intolerable 'atmosphere of pain'.[33] Yet from the perspective provided by *Villette*, the insistence of such 'culturally central' figures that literature should energize to action

[30] For Charlotte Brontë's poignant experience of such fragmentary 'recognitions' on one of her visits to London , see her letter to Ellen Nussey of 12 June 1850 (*CBL* ii. 414).
[31] Matthew Arnold, Preface to First Edition of *Poems* (1853), in R. H. Super (ed.), *Matthew Arnold: On the Classical Tradition* (Ann Arbor: University of Michigan Press, 1960), 2–3. Arnold sent Charlotte Brontë a copy of this volume in 1853, but no letter of acknowledgement from her survives (Kathleen Tillotson, ' "Haworth Churchyard": the Making of Arnold's Elegy', *BST* 15: 2 (1967), 118).
[32] Matthew Arnold to Arthur Hugh Clough, 21 March 1853 (*The Letters of Matthew Arnold to Arthur Hugh Clough*, ed. Howard Foster Lowry (London: Oxford University Press, 1932), 132.
[33] Harriet Martineau, quoted in *CH* 172, 174.

and promote hope and happiness begins to seem more problematic than their public assurance might suggest.[34] 'The present age exhibits to the individual man who contemplates it the spectacle of a vast multitude of facts awaiting and inviting his comprehension,' Arnold was to observe, in his inaugural lecture as Professor of Poetry at Oxford in 1857.

An intellectual deliverance . . . is perfect when we have acquired that harmonious aquiescence of mind which we feel in contemplating a grand spectacle that is intelligible to us; when we have lost that impatient irritation of mind which we feel in presence of an immense, moving, confused spectacle which, while it permanently excites our curiosity, perpetually baffles our comprehension.[35]

His imagery is redolent of the accounts of visitors to the Crystal Palace in 1851. And like those accounts it is instinct with an experience quite different from that which it seeks to valorize—a sense of bewilderment in the face of a baffling modernity that was arguably closer to the realities of life for 'many' in mid-Victorian England than the serenity of that privileged perspective of ascent to the overview.[36] It is an experience suggestively akin to that which is charted in *Villette*. 'The style is that of the doctor rather than the explorer,' Arnold was later to remark of this lecture; in his normative insistence on 'cheerfulness', his pathologizing of 'morbidity', he is strangely like *Villette*'s Dr John.[37] And the likeness might serve to alert us to the novel's pre-emptive rejoinder to critics such as he. For that questioning of the authority of the wider, more balanced view that is inscribed in its visual imagery is focused in its portrait of this 'true young English gentleman', fortunate, successful, yet curiously obtuse. (There is even a peculiar anticipation of one of the most famous of Arnold's images in his sharply rendered liking for the comforts of the bourgeois world.)[38] 'I look on you from a professional point of view,' says Dr John

[34] The phrase is Stefan Collini's, in a discussion of Arnold's 1853 Preface (*Matthew Arnold: A Critical Portrait* (Oxford: Clarendon Press, 1988), 67).

[35] 'On the Modern Element in Literature' (1857), in R. H. Super (ed.), *The Complete Prose Works of Matthew Arnold*, i. *On the Classical Tradition* (Ann Arbor: University of Michigan Press, 1960), 20.

[36] *Villette*, 453. The notion of 'wide survey' was deeply attractive to Arnold. 'Our epoch', he argues in this lecture, is distinguished by 'the desire to find the true point of view from which to contemplate this spectacle. He who has found that point of view, he who adequately comprehends this spectacle, has risen to the comprehension of his age' (20). In 'Haworth Churchyard', his elegy for Charlotte Brontë, he praises Martineau who, unlike Brontë, has moved beyond 'Fiction', 'Widen'd her sweep, and survey'd | History, Politics, Mind' (quoted in *CH* 307). Yet his poems of the mid-century—like Martineau's later *Autobiography*—bear eloquent testimony to the private 'morbidities' and 'anxieties' that underlay this public confidence.

[37] Introductory note to 'On the Modern Element in Literature', in Super, *On the Classical Tradition*, 18. 'He who is morbid,' says Arnold, 'is no adequate interpreter of his age' (34), contrasting the 'serious cheerfulness of Sophocles, of a man who has mastered the problem of human life' with the 'weak health' and 'sensitive nature' of Virgil, 'his inadequacy for the thorough spiritual mastery' of 'a great and overwhelming world' (35).

[38] 'He who works for sweetness and light united, works to make reason and the will of God prevail,' Arnold was later to declare, in the Preface to *Culture and Anarchy* (1869). If the Swiftian phrase, 'sweetness and light', came for him to stand for that Hellenic 'clearness and radiancy' which he saw as absent from 'the bad civilization of the English middle class', it is also oddly resonant of Dr John's fondness for sweetcake, his 'enlightened' insistence on reason, his lack of understanding of that which belongs to storm (259–60).

to Lucy, 'and I read, perhaps, all you would conceal' (248); but his authoritative diagnosis of hers as 'a case of spectral illusion' is, as she might put it, 'wrong' (249). The Nun who haunts the Pensionnat Beck has a banal reality; she is not the product of Lucy's unhappiness. Indeed there is a quite direct materialist rebuke to the pathologizing of difference that underlies the confidence of that which Arnold was to call the 'correct point of view'[39] in Lucy's address to the reader earlier in the novel: 'Perhaps, circumstanced like me, you would have been, like me, wrong' (157). Her words are not—as they would be in a novel by Gaskell—an invitation to empathize and understand. Preceded immediately as they are by a characterization of the diversity of actual readers' viewpoints—'religious reader . . . moralist . . . stern sage . . . stoic . . . cynic . . . epicure'—they pose a sharp, recalcitrant challenge to what Stefan Collini has called the 'casual universalism' of the voices of mid-nineteenth-century cultural centrality.[40]

Such voices may be typified by the final paragraph of *Pendennis*, which Charlotte Brontë read as she began to project *Villette*:[41]

If the best men do not draw the great prizes in life, we know it has been so settled by the Ordainer of the lottery. We own, and see daily, how the false and worthless live and prosper, while the good are called away, and the dear and young perish untimely,—we perceive in every man's life the maimed happiness, the frequent falling, the bootless endeavour, the struggle of Right and Wrong, in which the strong often succumb and the swift fall: we see flowers of good blooming in foul places, as, in the most lofty and splendid fortunes, flaws of vice and meanness, and stains of evil; and knowing how mean the best of us is, let us give a hand of charity to Arthur Pendennis, with all his faults and shortcomings, who does not claim to be a hero, but only a man and a brother.[42]

Villette's dark view of life's lottery is very different from this. Indeed, in its closing pages one can perhaps trace a bitter riposte to the tolerant good humour, the suave moral optimism, with which Brontë's once-admired 'Titan' contemplates the injustices of his world.[43] Lucy too speaks of 'untimely' death, of the 'false and worthless' who 'live and prosper'. But Thackeray's consensual first-person plurals, his confident appeal to a shared humanity, are in *Villette* replaced by a taunting, withholding narrator, insisting upon difference; one whose story fits no comfortable paradigm, whom the 'hand of charity' cannot assuage. Thackeray's is the voice of worldly experience ('the best men do not draw the great prizes in life'), the manly urbanity of a subtly consolatory acceptance that 'the way of the world is bad';[44] his pronouncement that his hero is 'a man and a brother' less the rhetoric of emancipation than that of the London club. 'We know it has been so settled by the Ordainer of the lottery', he announces with bland assurance; and even as he asserts that

---

[39] Arnold, 'On the Modern Element in Literature', 25.

[40] Stefan Collini, *Public Moralists* (Oxford: Clarendon Press, 1991), 85.   [41] *CBL* ii. 389 n. 1.

[42] William Makepeace Thackeray, *The History of Pendennis*, ed. Donald Hawes (Harmondsworth: Penguin, 1972), 785.

[43] For Charlotte Brontë's less than admiring view of *Pendennis*, see *CBL* ii. 546.

[44] On 'the element of ratification which lurks in resigned admission of the dominance of evil' see Theodor Adorno, 'Commitment', in *Aesthetics and Politics: Debates between Ernst Bloch, Bertolt Brecht, Walter Benjamin, Theodor Adorno* (London: New Left Books, 1977), 191.

'we' are mere objects of God's purposes his syntax suggests otherwise. Lucy, however, speaks not of confident 'knowledge', but of the limits of 'mortal vision' (179); not with the smoothness of shared cliché but with awful, individual urgency; not of moral choice and effective agency, but of subjection to an inscrutable causality. Hers is a darker, more urgent language, a different kind of first-person plural: 'Dark through the wilderness of this world stretches the way for most of us.'

For *Villette* is not merely more 'morbid' than the reflections of the public moralists of these years. It is framed in very different terms. Its echoes of *Pilgrim's Progress*, its invocations of the Bible, often agonized and extensive, suggest that for this narrator Providence is not the platitude it sometimes seems to be for Thackeray. Yet if the language of Scripture is more prominent here than in any of Brontë's earlier novels, its import is more difficult to grasp. Some have found in Lucy Snowe's story an exemplary narrative of 'pilgrimage', 'informed with portents and signs of a divine plan for the protagonist', in which the narrator's 'courage and strength permit her to accept her allotment', and she at last achieves 'integration, a synthesis of her divided self'.[45] But *Villette* is rather less orthodox and certainly less cheerful than such accounts suggest. There is little indication at the end that Lucy has gained in 'courage and strength', or learned to acquiesce in her lot. If her limited and obstructed vision seems an ironic comment on mid-nineteenth-century injunctions towards the wider, the more balanced view, it comments ironically also on the belief—articulated most powerfully in the mid-nineteenth century by Ruskin—that acute observation could yield spiritual truth. The portents and signs Lucy seeks to read are not merely bleak but inscrutable; again and again in her narrative there is a peculiar emphasis on 'blanks'. Even her most pious pronouncements are not straightforward, but critically inflected, in an insistent fictional questioning of that belief in an overarching Providence which her creator tried to espouse.

'Providence said, "Stop here; this is *your* inn",' says Lucy of her arrival at the Pensionnat Beck. But the language of God's appointment mutates in the next sentence into a very different one. 'Fate took me in her strong hand; mastered my will; directed my actions' (64): if 'Providence' has led her to 'stop', it is Fate that takes active control. 'Providence has protected and cultured you, not only for your own sake, but I believe for Graham's,' she is later to say to Paulina. But here, as elsewhere in the novel, a more secular discourse of fortune counters and relativizes conventional pieties. 'The past has been propitious,' is Lucy's oracular pronouncement; 'Graham's . . . star, too, was fortunate'. She urges the younger woman to entrust events to 'Time and your kind Fate' (376). To the twenty-first century reader, the distinction between Fate or Fortune on the one hand and Providence on the other may seem of little moment. But in the middle of the nineteenth century it was still a charged and significant one.[46]

---

[45] Thomas Vargish, *The Providential Aesthetic in Victorian Fiction* (Charlottesville: University Press of Virginia, 1985), 85, 73; Christina Colby, *The Ends of History: Victorians and 'The Woman Question'* (New York and London: Routledge, 1991), 126.

[46] For Augustine's arguments against both chance and fate see St Augustine, *The City of God Against the Pagans*, trans. William Green (Cambridge, Mass.: Harvard University Press, 1963), ii. 175; and, for the 16th- and 17th-cent. history of the debate, Keith Thomas, *Religion and the Decline of Magic* (London:

'The world rolls on, let what may be happening to the individuals who occupy it,' Harriet Martineau had written in *Deerbrook* (1839). 'It is no wonder that multitudes have formed a conception of Fate—of a mighty unchanging power . . . a huge insensible force.' 'Far higher' and 'far nobler', she says, is the 'conception of a Providence to whom this uniformity and variety are but means to a higher end.'[47] 'No divinity was adored by the Romans . . . under more names than Fortune,' declares the author of *Success in Life*, quoting Michelet. He urges his readers instead to have 'confidence in a superintending Providence, take your circumstances as they are, and make the best of them'.[48] Charlotte Brontë's sharp awareness of such arguments is signalled both in *The Professor*[49] and at a climactic moment in *Jane Eyre*. 'I meant . . . to be a bigamist: but fate has out-manœuvred me; or Providence has checked me,—perhaps the last,' cries Rochester at the altar (*JE* 291); and his shift of register points towards his eventual reform. Yet the weight, in Lucy's narrative, is rather the other way. 'That evening *more firmly than ever fastened into my soul the conviction* that Fate was of stone and Hope a false idol—blind, bloodless, and of granite core,' she says, of the despair that drives her to the confessional. 'I *felt, too*,' she adds, much less strongly, 'that the trial God had appointed me was gaining its climax, and must now be turned by my own hands' (160; my italics). 'With what dread force the conviction would grasp me that Fate was my permanent foe, never to be conciliated,' she declares; and if she goes on to 'conclude' that her sufferings are part of God's 'great plan' (157), this inference has the comparative 'force' of a pious afterthought. 'Conclusions' are based on fallible reason; 'conviction' is overwhelming, and quite unanswerable. In theological discourse, 'conviction' has connotations both of convincing and of convicting: it is the sinner's apprehension of the power of a judging God. But Lucy's is a 'conviction' of implacable blind determinism, without transcendent meaning: a sense that is focused in that moment when, 'snatched' from her gilded dreams by a 'pang . . . like a giant's gripe', she sits down before a too too solid 'dark comforter', to consider 'life and its chances . . . destiny and her decrees' (231).

Yet as the first of those appositions, no less than the banality of that setting, suggests, tragic grandiosity is not the mode of *Villette*. 'The result of circumstances, the fiat of fate, a part of my life's lot', Lucy is to call her sufferings, in another relativizing series (267); and precedent in her list is that ordinary, resonant word whose promin-

---

Weidenfeld & Nicolson, 1971), ch. 4. Charles Manby Smith in *The Little World of London; or, Pictures in Little of London Life* (London: Arthur Hall, Virtue, & Co., 1857), 261, tells of the 'Books of Fate, Universal Dreamers, Universal Fortune-Tellers' still being produced in great quantities in the 1850s by the Seven Dials Press in London. Haworth, J. Horsfall Turner reports, had 'a noted astrologer, who lived near the church' until well after Charlotte Brontë's death (*Haworth, Past and Present* (Brighouse: J. S. Jowett, 1879), 126.

[47] *Deerbrook* (1839; London: Virago, 1983), 358. For Brontë's 'admiration' of this novel, see *CBL* ii. 305 n. By the time she met Charlotte Brontë, Martineau had repudiated Providence: see 275 below.

[48] *Success in Life*, 234. According to the Brontës' classical dictionary, still in Haworth Parsonage, 'Fortuna is blind folded, and generally holds a wheel in her hand as an emblem of her inconstancy' (J. Lemprière, *Bibliotheca Classica* (London: Cadell & Davies, 1798).

[49] 'She had remembered his christian [*sic*] education and had shewn him, with the rooted confidence of those primitive days, relying on the scriptural Jehovah for aid against the mythological Destiny,' notes Crimsworth approvingly, of Frances's essay on Alfred (*P* 123).

ence within the novel I have already remarked upon. 'Man without religion is the creature of circumstances,' pronounced the first page of a book that Charlotte Brontë had read attentively in 1849.[50] If the notion of 'fate' often carries suggestions of meaningful pattern, if the reverses and upturnings of 'fortune' can be conceived as the turning of a wheel, 'circumstances' simply surround; like the novel's end-stopped vistas, in their stubborn materiality they block the larger view. 'Circumstances' is often used, indeed, to signify economic means. Thus, in *Villette*, Lucy speaks of those 'in reduced circumstances' (70), and of the 'stringent necessity of circumstances' suffered by Ginevra's parents (224); when she meets the Homes in Villette, she is embarrassed by the fact that 'Mrs Bretton and her son knew my circumstances; but the Count and his daughter did not' (284). But as legal and popular usage suggest, the term more largely denotes the determining conditions of action: 'circumstances' are the given, over which one has no control.[51] And it is in this sense that the word recurs most tellingly in *Villette*. 'A bitter complaint against the destiny of those women whom circumstances reduce to a necessity of working for a living', the novel was called in one early review.[52] If Crimsworth's was a rhetoric of exertion and self-reliance, Lucy's is a different emphasis: 'Self-reliance and exertion were forced upon me by circumstances, as they are upon thousands besides' (36).

Brontë was probably familiar with Carlyle's resonant assertion that the life of every great man teaches that 'Man is . . . not the thrall of Circumstances, of Necessity, but the victorious subduer thereof.'[53] Yet she had more cause than most to know that such heroic claims as this were for many in mid-nineteenth-century England all too forcibly countered by experience. 'You will say that we ought to have power to bear circumstances, or to bend them . . . but sometimes our best is unavailing,' she wrote to James Taylor in January 1851.[54] And both the moral imperative of which she speaks and a sense of its inefficacy can be traced throughout the writings of others in these years. Thus, in his poem 'Courage', written at the mid-century, Arnold hails 'those sterner spirits' who take command of their destinies, but the curious examplars he chooses—the stoic suicide, Cato, the morally suspect Byron—are far less concretely imagined than his vision of modernity:

> . . . now, when boldest wills give place,
> When Fate and Circumstance are strong,
> And in their rush the human race
> Are swept, like huddling sheep, along . . .[55]

[50] J. C. Hare and A. W. Hare, *Guesses at Truth by Two Brothers*, 3rd edn, 1st series (1847); Charlotte Brontë to W. S. Williams, 13 September 1849 (*CBL* ii. 251).

[51] For the legal resonances in early 19th-cent. England, see Alexander Welsh, *Strong Representations: Narrative and Circumstantial Evidence in England* (Baltimore and London: Johns Hopkins University Press, 1992), ch. 1.

[52] *The Spectator*, quoted in *CH* 182.

[53] Thomas Carlyle, 'Boswell's *Life of Johnson*', in *Critical and Miscellaneous Essays: Collected and Republished*, 3rd edn., (4 vols.; London: Chapman & Hall, 1847), iii. 45. 'Carlyle's Miscellanies interest me greatly,' wrote Brontë to W. S. Williams in April 1849 (*CBL* ii. 2, 197).

[54] *CBL* ii. 554.

[55] 'Courage' (1849–50), in *Poems of Matthew Arnold*, ed. Kenneth Allott, 2nd edn., ed. Miriam Allott (London and New York: Longman, 1979), 147.

More democratically, exponents of 'self-help' sought to argue that circumstances could be transformed: character and effort were all. But their exhortations too are punctuated by glimpses of overwhelming contingency. 'We must indeed be controlled by circumstances,' writes the author of *Success in Life*; 'the man of method and punctuality alone has these under his command.' And that plural 'we' drowns out the hypothetical singular, recalling a powerful image, earlier in his argument, of the 'man without decision' as 'swayed about like a dead log . . . on the tide of circumstances'.[56] 'Surrender yourself to ease, indolence, apathy, and you will be governed not merely by men, but by things,' warned a lecturer in 1848, in the famous YMCA series delivered each year in Exeter Hall. 'You will suffer the indignity of being handed on by circumstances; you will be the weeds, leaves, and straws, floated down the stream of society.'[57] Mr Micawber's 'circumstances beyond my individual control' had, indeed, become a catchphrase of the time.

The voice of cultural authority urged that a man *could* make his own destiny. 'Children of Circumstance are we to be? You answer, *On no wise!*' Thus Clough's Philip, to his moral tutor, in 'The Bothie of Toper-na-Fuosich' (1848).[58] Unobtrusively but distinctly, *Villette* presents the opposite view. Even 'the man of method'[59] is here not superior to circumstances. Paulina's wealth and social position offer 'the state of things . . . the combination of circumstances, at once to attract and enchain, to subdue and excite Dr John' (369). And in her own more painful subjection to far less agreeable circumstance, the novel's narrator is, as she more than once suggests, perhaps closer to the general condition than the effective individual of bourgeois ideology. 'It is a pleasant thing,' pronounced Harriet Martineau in a book that Brontë read as she began to write *Villette*, 'to have a daily purpose of raising and disciplining ourselves, for no end of selfish purchase or ransome, but from the instinctive tendency to mental and moral health.'[60] 'Indeed there was *no way* to keep well under the circumstances,' says Lucy, as if in reply (159; my italics). 'The secret of my success did not lie so much in myself . . . as in a new state of circumstances' (494), is her sharply precise rejoinder to that notion of 'force of character' enshrined in the gospel of self-help[61]—and, indeed, to those more recent critics who have sought to read hers as a narrative of the empowering consolidation of self.

---

[56] *Success in Life*, 191, 138.

[57] Revd John Harris, 'Social Organization', *Lectures to Young Men, delivered before the Y.M.C.A. in Exeter Hall, 1847–8* (London, 1848), 59.

[58] Book 9, l. 75.

[59] 'I can hardly tell how he managed his engagements,' says Lucy of Dr John; 'they were numerous, yet by dint of system, he classed them in an order which left him a daily period of liberty' (196).

[60] Henry George Atkinson and Harriet Martineau, *Letters on the Laws of Man's Nature and Development* (London: John Chapman, 1851), 285. 'Think what an accession [of power] there will be when the cheerfulness of health comes in with its bracing influence,' wrote Martineau in her review of *Villette* (*CH* 174). On 'moral health' in Martineau's writings, see Shelagh Hunter, *Harriet Martineau: the Poetics of Moralism* (Aldershot: Scolar Press, 1995); and on the wider ideology of 'health' in the period, Bruce Haley, *The Healthy Body and Victorian Culture* (Cambridge, Mass.: Harvard University Press, 1978).

[61] 'It was the force of his character that raised him; and this character not impressed upon him by nature, but formed . . . by himself,' writes Samuel Smiles of Francis Horner in *Self-Help* (1859) (*Self-Help, with Illustrations of Conduct and Perseverance*, rev. edn. (London: John Murray, 1907), 451).

This quiet emphasis in *Villette* speaks less of an unexamined 'morbid' fatalism than of an unillusioned awareness of the limits of human agency—an awareness pointedly different from the faith of an Arnold or a Martineau in the 'mastery' to be achieved through disinterested overview.[62] It is an awareness that cannot be dismissed as simply the expression of Charlotte Brontë's recent personal despair. For from her very first attempts at fiction, the author of *Villette* had been pondering the relation between human purposes and a larger determinism. The ironies of her youthful 'plays' with the Genii and the creatures of Glass Town had been succeeded in the novels of her maturity by a more sophisticated articulation of the questions to which those ironies point. Where Arnold links 'Fate and Circumstance' in a vision of tragic determinism, she has a sharper sense of the distinctive resonances of each. If fate and destiny are traditionally personified and seen as makers of meaning, the particularity of 'circumstance' is ignobly arbitrary. Brontë's comic awareness of this is evident in *The Professor*. 'I despise people who are always . . . urging and hurrying circumstances,' says Mdlle. Reuter to Crimsworth:

I like, monsieur, to take my knitting in my hands and to sit quietly down in my chair; circumstances defile past me, I watch their march—so long as they follow the course I wish, I say nothing and do nothing; I don't clap my hands and cry out bravo! How lucky I am! to attract the attention and envy of my neighbours; I am merely passive; but when events fall out ill—when circumstances become adverse, I watch very vigilantly; I knit on still, and still I hold my tongue, but every now and then, monsieur, I just put my toe out—so—and give the rebellious circumstance a little secret push without noise, which sends it the way I wish . . . I mind my knitting, events progress, circumstances glide past . . .   (P 144–5)

'We have . . . explained what circumstances rendered [Moore] specially prone to confine his attention and efforts to the furtherance of his individual interest,' says *Shirley*, rather less playfully (S 167); here, the sense of constraining 'circumstances' leads to a bleaker vision of the limits within which an individual's 'attention and efforts' are inevitably confined. And both comic and tragic inflections play through *Villette*'s repeated invocations of what Brontë's hero Byron had called 'that unspiritual God'.[63] Lucy's dark vision of subjection to an unrelenting necessity is counterpointed throughout by a sharp, sardonic awareness of a nearer, more concrete set of determinants than 'that great abstraction . . . Fate' (185); 'unspeakable oppression' (268) and 'unutterable . . . despair' (160) by an ironically articulated sense of the challenge her lot presents to the generalizing certainties of public morality: 'Perhaps, circumstanced like me, you would have been, like me, wrong' (157).

There is a suggestive indication of the topicality of these issues in a review of a small volume containing two didactic stories that appeared in *Fraser's* in July

---

[62] Arnold, 'On the Modern Element in Literature', 35.
[63] 'Circumstance, that unspiritual God,' *Childe Harold* (Canto IV. 125).

1851, at around the time when Brontë was beginning to write *Villette*.[64] The review would have interested Brontë, for one of the tales was called 'The Young Governess'. The reviewer summarizes and quotes extensively from this story, whose heroine, called Lucy, is forced to leave a home that has become intolerable and go to earn her living on the Continent as a governess. There she receives news that her lover in India has married another. But 'Lucy goes through her hard destiny with a noble resignation, and is rewarded for her sufferings and her patience in the end. Her lover has not been faithless but returns to claim her; and, to crown the happiness which the reader feels she has so well deserved, her father . . . makes a suitable *amende.*'

Thus the reviewer's account of 'the satisfactory termination' of this tale (38). The parallel with *Villette* is intriguing. For Lucy Snowe's narrative, with its darker 'termination', is not merely a riposte to such 'sunny' stories as this: 'Let them picture union and a happy succeeding life' (496). It quite directly counters the message of the volume under review. Its title was *Chance and Choice; or, the Education of Circumstances*, and its purpose, apparently, was 'to illustrate this fact—that through God's Providence, the education of the mind and heart . . . are carried out through those very circumstances which, because they are not caused or foreseen by man, we call *chance*' (37). The interpretation of 'circumstance' as the working of an unseen Providence was, at the time, a standard Christian argument. And it is one of which *Villette* offers a quietly devastating critique. It is not merely that that narrative of 'education' or character development that many still seek to trace in the novel, which this reviewer finds in 'The Young Governess', is subverted throughout by Lucy Snowe's insistence on the determining force of 'circumstances'. The world through which she moves is emphatically portrayed as a place not of meaning, but of 'chance'.

'Happiness is the cure,' says John Graham Bretton to Lucy, when she asks how she might escape the visitations of the Nun. And the exchange that follows is informed by Brontë's sharp awareness of the etymology of that word.[65] 'No mockery in this world ever sounds to me so hollow as that of being told to *cultivate* happiness. What does such advice mean?' demands Lucy. 'How do you manage?' she asks Dr John. 'I am a cheerful fellow *by nature*,' he tells her. 'And then *ill-luck has never dogged me*' (250; my italics). His candour is more subversive than might at first

[64] [Charles Kingsley], 'Little Books with Large Aims' [unsigned review of *Chance and Choice; or, the Education of Circumstances* (London: John W. Parker, 1850)], *Fraser's Magazine*, 44 (July 1851), 26–40.

[65] 'One of the arts of a great . . . writer' Richard Trench had written two years earlier, in *On the Study of Words*, is 'to bring out all the latent forces of his native tongue . . . to reconnect a word by his use of it with its original derivation.' Later in that volume, he discusses the etymology of 'happiness': 'We all know how prone men are to ascribe to chance or fortune those good gifts and blessings, which indeed come directly from God. And this faith of theirs, that their blessings, even their highest, come to them by blind chance, they have incorporated in a word; for "happy" and "happiness" are of course connected with and derived from "hap", which is chance.' (Richard Chenevix Trench, *On the Study of Words* (London: John W. Parker & Son, 1851), 47, 165). Brontë may well have known this popular study, which was admired by Mrs Gaskell and reviewed at length in *Fraser's*.

appear. 'She may feel that she has cause to accuse fate, to account happiness an accident of life to some who are more fortunate than others,' wrote one disapproving contemporary reviewer, quoting this scene in its entirety. 'Exertion is the indispensable condition of all healthy life, mental or bodily; sluggish despondency is nothing but disease.'[66] The ideological imperative—both secular and religious—to argue that 'happiness' was not simply an 'accident' was perhaps especially strong in nineteenth-century England. It was certainly one to which Charlotte Brontë had been exposed from her very earliest years. 'The truth is, that happiness and misery have their origin within, depending comparatively little on outward circumstances,' begins *The Cottage in the Wood, Or the Art of Becoming Rich and Happy*, by Revd Patrick Brontë, published a few months before his third daughter's birth; and his moral tale is designed to give instruction in that 'art'.[67] The connection of happiness with material prosperity made in Patrick Brontë's subtitle was by the mid-nineteenth century writ large in the Great Exhibition: as the rhetoric surrounding that event suggests, 'happiness' was by no means a matter of merely private concern. 'The derivation . . . from 'hap' expressly implies its dependence on external circumstances,' admits the author of *Letters on Happiness*, published three years before *Villette*, but the explicit aim of this work is to teach the reader how to rise above circumstance and 'cultivate' happiness.[68] In 1851 Charlotte Brontë's own publisher published a volume—by a 'Dr John'—on the subject of *Happiness*; 'happiness', it argued, 'results from an active, well-balanced and contented mind—fed by knowledge and engaged in work'.[69] Religious writers still argued that the Christian hope ensured the highest happiness of all. Indeed, one such work, entitled *The Gospel Promotive of True Happiness*, was given to Charlotte Brontë by her former teacher Margaret Wooler whilst she was writing the second volume of *Villette*.[70] 'The book will be precious to me—chiefly perhaps for the sake of the giver, but also for its own sake—for it is a good book,' Brontë wrote in acknowledgement. 'Its perusal came recommended in such a manner as to obviate danger of neglect—its place shall always be on my dressing-table'. But she added, a little more darkly, 'I

---

[66] Unsigned review, *Examiner*, 5 February 1853, *CH* 175–6. 'Every now and then, *in a determined way*, some dirge to the burden of "I can't be happy" sounds from within,' continues this reviewer (my emphasis). Certainly, in *Villette*, the division between 'sunshine' and 'shadow' is repeatedly presented in a language of given, biological inequality. 'He was born victor, as some are born vanquished,' says Lucy of Graham Bretton (443). Hers is 'a soon-depressed, an easily-deranged temperament' (315); but Mrs Bretton is 'constitutionally composed and cheerful' and Graham is 'constitutionally suave and serene' (218).

[67] 'Young women may here especially obtain a knowledge that the path of virtue leads to happiness,' wrote the friend who was to baptize Charlotte in an approving review of this work (John Lock and Canon W. T. Dixon, *A Man of Sorrow: The Life, Letters and Times of the Rev. Patrick Brontë 1777–1861* (London: Nelson, 1965), 169–71).

[68] [S. Warburton], *Letters on Happiness, Addressed to a Friend* (London: Longman, Brown, Green & Longman's, 1850), 15, 16.

[69] Review of John Forbes, MD, *Of Happiness in its Relation to Work and Knowledge* (London: Smith, Elder & Co, 1851), *Athenaeum* (12 April 1851), 1224.

[70] Revd Hugh White, *The Gospel Promotive of True Happiness* (Dublin: James McGlashan, 1851). The volume, which is still in Haworth Parsonage, is inscribed 'Miss Brontë From her affectionate friend MW Sept 3rd 1852'.

wish I may be enabled to read it with some approach to the spirit you would desire.'[71]

If, as she promised her friend, Brontë did indeed read and ponder *The Gospel Promotive of True Happiness* as she struggled on with her novel, it seems to have been not exactly in a spirit Miss Wooler would have approved. For much in the final volume of *Villette* seems like a bleak reply to her friend's well-intentioned gift. Against its bracing contention (for 350 pages) that 'happiness depends more on character than on circumstances'—'a truth, confirmed alike by the testimony of Scripture and the experience of mankind' (115)—we might place *Villette*'s quiet insistence on the determining force of circumstance; against its image of the Christian's 'sweet tranquillity, amidst all the alternations of earthly prosperity and adversity' (96), *Villette*'s recurring emphasis on anxiety and suspense. Where *The Gospel Promotive of True Happiness* warns that 'a storm at sea, or a failure of some hazardous speculation, may in a moment wreck the hopes and happiness of the hitherto highly favoured worshipper of this world's wealth' (67), within the world of *Villette*, the votaries of Mammon triumph. And the earlier volume's portrait of the believer's 'delightful conviction, that he can never be a bankrupt in true happiness, because the vessel which is freighted with his heart's dearest hopes, and most precious treasures, can never be wrecked' (110), is answered, in Lucy's narrative, by the dark suggestion of a shipwreck in which all her hope of happiness is lost. In one climactic paean, the author of *The Gospel Promotive of True Happiness* compares the 'agitating anxieties' of those whose love is fixed on earthly things, to 'the troubled sea, that cannot rest'. 'If there *be* a principle that has power to calm these agitations—if there be a spirit which can say, with a voice of authority, to this troubled sea, "Peace—be still!"—*that* principle must be promotive of true happiness!' (85). That merely rhetorical 'if' becomes in *Villette* the silence that meets 'a thousand' prayers for a voice to utter 'Peace, be still!' (495). And this author's repeated, authoritative pronouncement that 'nothing happens by chance in the providential government of God' (pp. xii, 93) is answered in *Villette* by Dr John's artless admission that 'happiness' indeed depends on luck.

'He is a "curled darling" of Nature and of Fortune,' Charlotte Brontë declared of her hero, as she completed the novel. 'He must draw a prize in Life's Lottery.'[72] The

---

[71] Charlotte Brontë to Margaret Wooler, 21 October 1852 (*LL* iv. 11). Charlotte Brontë's reading of it is indicated by a number of verbal echoes in *Villette* other than those discussed below. 'The desire of the Christian is to realize, by anticipation and foretaste, as much of the happiness of Heaven as can be enjoyed on earth,' declares *The Gospel Promotive of True Happiness* (217). 'Some real lives do . . . actually anticipate the happiness of Heaven,' says Lucy as she describes the 'sunshine' of the fortunate (*V* 436). In a chapter on 'The Domestic Affections', *The Gospel Promotive of True Happiness* exults that even death cannot threaten the 'habitation of the servants of God': with the Christian hope 'soothing the sorrows of separation', 'how the aspect of this king of terrors is changed when he crosses the threshold of such a home!' (328). In *Villette*, Lucy tells how those children of 'sunshine', Paulina and John Graham Bretton, have 'to pay their tribute to the King of Terrors'; but theirs is, significantly, a more earthly consolation: 'others sprang healthy and blooming to replace the lost' (*V* 436). There is even perhaps an echo, in the novel's portrayal of Vashti, of the earlier volume's image (in a chapter on 'Theatrical Amusements') of the theatre as 'the very vestibule of hell' (283).

[72] Charlotte Brontë to George Smith, 3 November 1852, quoted in Barker, 705. The reference is to the description of Desdemona's conventionally eligible suitors in *Othello* I. iii. 67.

image of life as a lottery—invoked at the ending of *Pendennis*—had been a commonplace amongst eighteenth-century writers.[73] It seems to have been reanimated in the early years of Victoria's reign, as the bewildering pace of scientific discovery and social and economic change gave many a sharpened awareness of their lack of control over their lives. 'The system has the fairness of a lottery, in which everyone has the like chance of drawing the prize,' the best-selling, controversial *Vestiges of the Natural History of Creation* (1844) concluded, apparently with intent to reassure.[74] On a less cosmic scale, the gambling metaphor recurs in descriptions of the barely understood mechanisms of advancing capitalism. 'The rashness of speculation, which has been the cause of ruin to thousands, is most earnestly to be deprecated,' writes the author of *Success in Life*, recalling 'the whole gambling system styled "THE RAILWAY MANIA OF 1845"', when 'dishonest speculators . . . realized enormous profits by the mere transfer of bits of paper . . . the conviction gained ground that fortunes were being made at a stroke, that a great legal lottery had been established, in which, any one that chose might realize as high prizes as he pleased'.[75] (The Brontës held shares in the railways, managed by Emily, and observed the 'Railway Mania' anxiously. 'As we have abstained from all gambling, all "mere" speculative buying-in & selling-out—we have got on very decently,' Charlotte Brontë wrote to Miss Wooler at its height).[76] And the lottery was used too as a metaphor for the experience of those with yet fewer choices and even less understanding of the forces that determined their lots. 'Think how mysterious and often unaccountable it is—that lottery of life which gives to this man the purple and the fine linen, and sends to the other rags for garments and dogs for comforters,' wrote Thackeray in *Vanity Fair*.[77] A year later, Elizabeth Gaskell was to speak with less urbanity in the Preface to *Mary Barton* of the feelings of the 'work-people' against 'the rich, the even tenor of whose seemingly happy lives appeared to increase the anguish caused by the lottery-like nature of their own'.[78]

In *Villette* the image of the lottery might seem more trivial than this. An actual 'Lottery' appears in the novel as part of the spectacle of bourgeois life: the drawing of prizes at the concert makes 'an animating and amusing scene'.[79] The moment has a prosaic literalism that is characteristic of *Villette*. The prizes are 'of small value'

---

[73] Thus e.g. Fielding's *The Lottery. A Farce* (London, 1732), 31: 'That the World is a Lottery, what Man can doubt? | When born, we're *put in*, when dead, we're *drawn out*; | And the *Tickets* are bought by the Fool and the Wise, | Yet 'tis plain there are more than ten *Blanks* to a *Prize*.'

[74] [Robert Chambers], *Vestiges of the Natural History of Creation* (London: John Churchill, 1844), 377.

[75] *Success in Life*, 241. The contrast between 'the trickery of the gambler' and 'the reality of noble and honourable enterprise' was a favourite theme of moralizers: see e.g. Revd George Fisk, 'The moral influence of the commercial spirit of the day', in *Lectures to Young Men, delivered before the Y.M.C.A. in Exeter Hall, 1847–8* (London, 1848), from which these phrases are taken, and Revd Thomas Nolan, 'The Fever of Monetary Speculation', in Robert Bickersteth *et al.*, *Twelve Lent Lectures on The Signs of the Times for the Year 1858* (London: John Mills Robeson, 1858).

[76] Charlotte Brontë to Margaret Wooler, 23 April 1845, *CBL* i. 390.

[77] William Makepeace Thackeray, *Vanity Fair*, ed. Peter L. Shillingsburg (New York and London: Norton, 1994), 569.

[78] Elizabeth Gaskell, *Mary Barton*, ed. Stephen Gill (Harmondsworth: Penguin, 1970), 37.

[79] Lotteries had not been held in England since 1826, or in Belgium since 1836.

and tellingly inappropriate—a sky-blue turban for Dr John, a cigar-case for Lucy Snowe. 'As we each held tickets,' says Lucy, 'we shared in the alternations of hope and fear raised by each turn of the wheel' (222). Yet if there is nothing here of the charged 'anxiety', the metaphoric suggestiveness, of other eighteenth- and nine-teenth-century fictional scenes of gambling,[80] the sense of life as a lottery is more in-trinsic to the novel than might at first appear. At the mid-point of her narrative, after the excitement of her visit to the theatre, Lucy tells of being 'dropped out of the memory of [her] friends, the denizens of a freer world'. Those such as she are 'li-able', she says, to 'this long blank of oblivion'; 'Unbroken always is this blank; alike entire and unexplained.' At the end of 'seven weeks as bare as seven sheets of blank paper', she at last admits the 'conviction' that 'these blanks were inevitable . . . a part of my life's lot' (266–7). And the reader is sharply reminded that a 'blank' is not merely an unprinted leaf, or a space void of interest or event; it is a lottery ticket that does not gain a prize.[81]

And Lucy's is a narrative of 'blanks'. If the world at which she gazes is one of 'sunshine' and prizes, in which the strong and prosperous act and are effective, that which she herself occupies is one of 'dead blank, dark doubt, and drear suspense' (385). 'The mid-blank', she says, 'is always a beclouded point for the solitary: his nerves ache with the strain of long expectancy' (267): the observation is that of a connoisseur of such strain. For her, the 'torturing clang' of 'the postman's ring' is 'sure to be followed by . . . blank silence . . . barren vacuum for me' (271); 'the old rack of suspense . . . that corroding pain of long attent' (479) is a customary state. Her at-tempts 'to win from the Creative Impulse one evidence of his presence' are met by a stony inertness like the 'blank eye-balls' of Baal (356). A blank is in one sense a nothing. But in *Villette* it is emphatically something; that which must be lived.[82] No other novel in the language so speaks of the pain of eventlessness. Like the negatives of that 'position' which rises upon her like a ghost, 'anomalous, desolate, almost blank of hope' (46), like the 'unwelcome blank' of the absence of personal attractions 'on those bright occasions when beauty should shine' (131), lack in Lucy's narrative is eloquent in its insistence. And conspicuous within it—from the untold disaster of

[80] Gillian Beer, 'The Reader's Wager: Lots, Sorts, and Futures', *Essays in Criticism*, 40: 2 (April 1990), 109. For a fuller discussion of gambling in 18th- and some 19th-cent. novels, see Thomas M. Kavanagh, *Enlight-enment and the Shadows of Chance: The Novel and the Culture of Gambling in Eighteenth-Century France* (Baltimore and London: Johns Hopkins University Press, 1993), and Justine Louise Crump, 'A Study of Gaming and Eighteeenth-century English Novels', Ph.D. dissertation, University of Cambridge, 1998.

[81] 'As the wheel of fortune turns, her lottery throws up now a prize and now a blank,' Charlotte Brontë had written in *Ashworth* (1840–1). 'Mr Ashworth had got a grievous blank . . . when he lost his house and lands, but now again a prize seemed to have fallen to his lot.' (Charlotte Brontë, *Unfinished Novels* (Stroud: Alan Sutton, in association with the Brontë Society, 1993), 46–7). 'We believe the world has no blanks except to cowards,' Froude had written of youthful hopefulness in a book that Charlotte Brontë had read in 1849. 'And we find, at last, that as far as we ourselves are concerned, it has no prizes' (James Anthony Froude, *The Nemesis of Faith* (London: John Chapman, 1849), 99).

[82] '*My* reserve . . . has its foundation not in design, but in necessity,' Brontë wrote to Ellen Nussey whilst she was writing *Villette*. 'I am silent because I have literally *nothing to say*. I might indeed repeat over and over again that my life is a pale blank and often a very weary burden—and that the Future some-times appals me—but what end could be answered by such repetition except to weary you and enervate myself?' (25 August 1852, *LL* iv. 6).

her girlhood, to that confession unheard by the reader, to that 'pause' at the novel's ending—is a sense of the critical significance of that which is not, cannot be, said.[83] 'As to that week of suspense, with its blank yet burning days, which brought from him no word of explanation—I remember, but I cannot describe its passage,' Lucy says of the week preceding M. Paul's departure (442). 'What might be his private pain or inward reluctance to leave Europe . . . none asked, or knew, or reported. All this was a blank to me' (462). 'When I come back—,' he promises, at her moment of greatest happiness. And Lucy's narrative continues: 'Here he left a blank' (487). Lyndall Gordon has written of how Charlotte Brontë's deletions would in the manuscript of *Villette* 'have been visible to her publisher's eye'. 'In many places Charlotte did not simply cross out; she cut pages and paragraphs, often pasting blank white paper across the back'.[84] Such blanks are very different from that space of possibility which the young Maria Brontë once occupied—'she wrote on its blank leaf'. If the experience of reading a novel is, as Gillian Beer has argued, akin to that of gambling,[85] the reader of *Villette*—from the evasiveness of its opening to its absence of satisfying closure—draws repeated, baffling blanks.

One meaning of 'blank' is a nonplus: a state of perplexity or puzzle, in which, as Arnold might put it, 'there is everything to be endured, nothing to be done'. Thus, for Lucy, powerless to act or protest, the disappearance of her letters is an occasion for 'blank dismay' (292). Yet in *Villette*, as in a lottery, the state that predominates—from those opening images of the child Paulina's anguish to the unresolved suspense of the novel's ending—is not one of calm endurance. '*What* should I do; oh! *what* should I do; when all my life's hope was thus torn by the roots out of my riven, outraged heart?' (445): as Raymond Williams has noted, these questions 'are present and suspended, with almost a pause for response'—or, as we might put it, a blank.[86] Even as Lucy begins to believe in M. Paul's affection, she is 'wasted with hourly torment': 'the persuasion that affection was won could not be divorced from the dread that, by another turn of the wheel, it might be lost' (467). For those 'alternations of hope and fear raised by each turn of the wheel' are repeated in a darker key in 'the rack of expectation, and the sick collapse of disappointment'(267), the 'sick dread' (267) and 'almost certain hope' (271—the blasphemous echo would not have been lost on Brontë's first readers) that Lucy feels at the post-hour; in the 'mighty hope' and 'measureless doubt' between which she helplessly oscillates as she thinks of the prospect of death (421); in the 'joys, griefs, and amazements' that she calls—in an image of the lottery of fortune as well as of visual disturbance—'things wildered and whirling, dim as a wheel fast spun' (486). To the author of *The Gospel Promotive of True Happiness*, Hell is 'a world where hope never comes, but all is wrapped in the blackness of the darkness of despair'.[87]

<hr/>

[83] 'If I could always work—time would not be long—nor hours sad to me—but blank and heavy intervals still occur—when power and will are at variance,' Brontë wrote to George Smith, of her difficulties in finishing *Villette* (*CBL* ii. 720).
[84] Lyndall Gordon, *Charlotte Brontë: A Passionate Life* (London: Chatto & Windus, 1994), 269.
[85] Beer, 'The Reader's Wager'.   [86] *The English Novel from Dickens to Lawrence*, 72.
[87] White, *The Gospel Promotive of True Happiness*, 78. He is quoting from *Paradise Lost*, I. 66.

'I think if Eternity held torment, its form would not be fiery rack, nor its nature, despair,' says Lucy as if in reply, as she images an angel entering Hades, and kindling 'a doubtful hope of bliss to come': 'His legacy was suspense—a worse boon than despair' (445–6). 'Less than ever was a letter probable; still . . . I could not forget that it was possible' (269–70); 'Too poor to lose, God might destine me to gain' (297). Such images of 'hope'—the bell will ring, a letter will come, the pool will stir, the beloved will come—remind us that that which drives a lottery is not resignation or calm endurance, but the 'doubtful hope of bliss to come', the longing for a prize. Intrinsic to the metaphor, as to that other implicit image of idolatry, is the almost shocking acknowledgement of a component of desire.

'These blanks were inevitable,' says Lucy (267). 'Life' in *Villette* is 'so constructed that the event does not, cannot, will not match the expectation' (409). It is not a pilgrimage through a providential universe, but a lottery where few can win. The novel's portrayal of the 'sunshine' of bourgeois normality, the relentlessness of blanks in Lucy's counterpointing experience, make up one overwhelming message: 'dark through the wilderness of this world stretches the way for most of us' (438). Indeed, the figure of the lottery might be seen as underwriting this narrator's claims for the typicality of her sufferings: whilst those who draw prizes are prominent, the majority draw blanks. And it also underwrites the peculiar conjunction of anxiety and fatalism in her narrative: if those who hold tickets in a lottery are held by the 'doubtful hope' of the prize, they can hardly escape the knowledge that they are far more likely not to win. 'Hundreds of the prayers with which we weary Heaven, bring to the suppliant no fulfilment. Once *haply* in life, one golden gift falls prone in the lap' (480; my emphasis). Thus Lucy writes of her chance of happiness; yet this too ends in blank (487). And 'blank' is the novel's image of that which others tried to realize as a 'superintending Providence', 'that mighty unseen centre incomprehensible, irrealizable' (422), its recurrent vision of a world without transcendent meaning—what Brontë had called in an early poem 'the wide blank ocean of pagan night'.[88]

'I try to leave all in God's hands, and to trust in his goodness—but faith and resignation are difficult to practise under some circumstances,' Charlotte Brontë had confessed to Ellen Nussey in October 1848.[89] The myth of Brontë's unswerving faith, promoted by Mrs Gaskell, has been an enduring one.[90] Yet her engagement with her religion was more searching and more strenuous than is now commonly supposed. A visitor to Haworth Parsonage in September 1858, looking at her 'little library, not above sixty or seventy vols in all', and noticing 'amongst others . . . the *Life of Sterling*, *Sartor Resartus*, Newman on the soul, and books of that cast', found there evidence of the 'great revolution her religious views had undergone from that

---

[88] 'Lament', *CBP* 183.   [89] *CBL* ii. 131.

[90] See e.g. Christina Colby, '*Villette* and the End of History', in *The Ends of History: Victorians and 'the Woman Question'* (New York and London: Routledge, 1991); Christopher Ricks, 'E. C. Gaskell's Charlotte Brontë', in *Essays in Appreciation* (Oxford: Clarendon Press, 1996); Marianne Thormählen, *The Brontës and Religion* (Cambridge: Cambridge University Press, 1999).

early time, when she used to correspond with 'E' in the sickly pietistic strain'.[91] Indeed, since adolescence, Charlotte Brontë had been acquainted with free-thinking and atheistic ideas.[92] Their presence in her mind as she wrote *Villette* is signalled by a reference at the climax of one of Lucy's meditations on the unresponsiveness of God: 'To how many maimed and mourning millions is the first and sole angel visitant, him easterns call Azrael' (179). 'We say this world was made by One | Who's seen or heard or known by none' Branwell Brontë had written, in his perhaps most ambitious production, a Byronic epic poem, *Azrael, or Destruction's Eve*, part of which he published in the *Bradford Herald* in 1842.[93] Lucy's bleak vision at this moment in *Villette* of 'dust, kindling to brief suffering life, and, through pain, passing back to dust' certainly recalls that poem's image of humanity as mere 'dust to feed the worm'. By 1851, Charlotte Brontë's faith had been cruelly tested by her brother's and sisters' deaths.[94] And she had begun to read widely and thoughtfully in speculative theological works. If she was familiar with the attempts of such contemporaries as Carlyle and Ruskin to find sacramental meaning in the mid-nineteenth-century world, she was also an avowed admirer of F. D. Maurice, who in the summer of 1851 (when she heard him preach in London) was arguing against analogical and typological schemes.[95] She had found Francis Newman's *The Soul* 'a deep and interesting subject of study'; Froude's *Nemesis of Faith* she thought 'morbid', 'yet in its pages too' she 'found sprinklings of truth'.[96] Each week she read the wide-ranging, sceptical discussion of theological questions in the literary pages of *The Leader*, which she received from its first appearance in March 1850.[97] She was yet more intimately acquainted with her friend Harriet Martineau's 'avowed Atheism and Materialism', as expounded in *Letters on the Laws of Man's Nature and Development* which Martineau and Henry Atkinson had published in 1851.[98] 'She was very far indeed from sympathising in our doctrine,' Harriet Martineau recalled; but Charlotte Brontë was gripped—or, as she put it in another letter, 'partially mesmerized'—by this, 'the first unequivocal declaration of disbelief in the existence of a God or a Future Life—I have ever seen'.[99] The 'impression' the volume made (*CBL* ii. 574) is indicated not merely by a verbal echo in *Villette*,[100] but also, much

---

[91] T. Foley, 'John Elliot Cairnes' Visit to Haworth Parsonage', *BST* 18:4 (1984), 293.

[92] Even in that early correspondence with 'E' she calls Byron's *Cain* 'a magnificent poem' (*CBL* i. 130).

[93] See Barker, *The Brontës*, 399–400.

[94] For the challenge those deaths posed to Charlotte Brontë's religious views see, especially, her letters to W. S. Williams during this period.

[95] For Brontë's reading of Carlyle and Ruskin see *CBL* ii. 94, 197, 202, 546, 593. For her admiration of Maurice, see *CBL* ii. 718 and 719 n.; and, for Maurice's questioning of typology, see e.g. *The Old Testament: Nineteen Sermons*, 238, 286–7.

[96] Charlotte Brontë to James Taylor, *c.* 19 December 1849 (*CBL* ii. 314, 315 n.).

[97] See e.g. its hostile review of *The Hand of God in History; or, Divine Providence Historically Illustrated*, by Hollis Read (1 February 1851).

[98] Charlotte Brontë to James Taylor, 11 February 1851 (*CBL* ii. 574).

[99] Harriet Martineau, *Autobiography* (2 vols.; London: Virago, 1983), ii. 350–2; Charlotte Brontë to George Smith, 7 January 1851, *CBL* ii. 547; Charlotte Brontë to James Taylor, 11 February 1851, *CBL* ii. 574.

[100] 'True seeing,' wrote Atkinson, 'requires harmony within, as well as harmony without, the mind. Otherwise, the mind, as an uneven mirror, or as coloured glass, will distort or colour the object, however beautiful, and torture the truth into hideous and fantastic shapes' (*Letters on the Laws of Man's Nature*

more pervasively, by the prominence in the novel of that sense of 'hopeless blank' and 'unutterable desolation' which Brontë took from it.[101]

For despite her attempts to sustain belief in a superintending Providence, Charlotte Brontë's imagination seems to have 'willed and worked for itself' in the pages of *Villette*.[102] 'When authors write best, or at least, when they write most fluently,' she had written to G. H. Lewes in 1848, 'an influence seems to waken in them which becomes their master . . . dictating certain words, and insisting on their being used, whether vehement or measured in their nature; new moulding characters, giving unthought-of turns to incidents, rejecting carefully elaborated old ideas, and suddenly creating and adopting new ones'.[103] Or, as Lucy Snowe is to put it, in characteristic debunking mode, as she likens Paulina to a spaniel: 'forgive the association, reader, it *would* occur' (415). *Villette*'s 'half atheistical' import was noted more often by contemporaries than it is by present-day readers, to whom invocations of the Bible tend to signify orthodoxy.[104] It is certainly rather at odds with the faith its author professed.

'She believed some were appointed beforehand to sorrow and much disappointment,' Mrs Gaskell reported Charlotte Brontë as saying in 1853; 'that it was well for those who had rougher paths, to perceive that such was God's will concerning them, and try to moderate their expectations, leaving hope to those of a different doom, and seeking patience and resignation as the virtues they were to cultivate.'[105] 'His will be done, as done it surely will be, whether we humble ourselves to resignation or not,' says Lucy Snowe, as if in retort to such pieties:

> The impulse of creation forwards it; the strength of powers, seen and unseen, has its fulfilment in charge. Proof of a life to come must be given. In fire and in blood, if needful, must that proof be written. In fire and in blood do we trace the record throughout nature. In fire and in blood does it cross our own experience. Sufferer, faint not through terror of this burning evidence. (438)

Thus begins what seems to be the novel's most extended attempt to justify the ways of God to man. Yet on closer inspection it is not quite what it appears. The almighty 'will' of which Lucy speaks is quite different from that guiding, protecting, culturing 'Providence' which she elsewhere seeks to invoke (64, 376): indeed, the reiterated impersonal pronoun stresses that 'it' cannot be thus anthropomorphized. The emphasized, foregrounded sense is of 'its' unstoppable movement to 'fulfilment', apparently impervious to that which lies in 'its' path. The relentless present indica-

---

and *Development*, 130). Just so, in *Villette*, Lucy finds her view of what she has seen at the fête clouded by 'the distorting and discolouring magic of jealousy' (479).

[101] *CBL* ii. 574.   [102] This phrase is taken from her editor's Preface to *Wuthering Heights* (1850).
[103] 12 January 1848 (*CBL* ii. 10).
[104] To *The Observer*, the novel was 'half atheistical and half religious' (7 February 1853, 7). The *Christian Remembrancer* objected to the way in which Brontë 'rejects all guide but her Bible, and at the same time constantly quotes and plays with its sacred pages, as though they had been given to the world for no better purpose than to point a witticism or furnish an ingenious illustration' (*CH* 206). 'The religion she invokes is itself but a dark and doubtful refuge from the pain which impels the invocation,' Harriet Martineau observed (*CH* 174).
[105] Gaskell, 510.

tives configure inexorable purpose, before which 'we' are objects—a sense to be echoed, tellingly, in the later, striking image of 'the Juggernaut on his car' (493). And it is against the weight of this vision that Lucy exhorts fellow-'sufferer''s to a 'heroism of endurance' such as Charlotte Brontë had admired in her dying sister Anne.[106] If the imagery that follows is of soldiers, conquerors, victors—'Tired way-farer, gird up thy loins, look upward, march onward'—the effect is hardly one of straightforward triumphalism.[107] In the wake of that opening vision of unbending, absolute purpose, pursuing its unstoppable course, the biblical quotations that fol-low—signalled, as they are not in the closing paragraphs of *Jane Eyre*, by prominent quotation marks—seem less expressive of 'conviction' than fragments desperately shored against an almost overwhelming sense of the 'sufferer''s helplessness. The language of the Scripture is here stylized and objectified, critically inflected and ironized, as other authoritative contemporary discourses had been in Charlotte Brontë's writings since her earliest years. The feeling, as that later echoing image of the Juggernaut picks up, is close to blasphemy.

Far from being a conventional cliché, the notion of suffering on this earth being 'proof of a life to come' was in the mid-nineteenth century a subject of fierce debate. 'The desire of a future existence is mere pampered habit of mind, founded upon the instinct of preservation,' Martineau's friend Henry Atkinson roundly declared.[108] 'He is a Materialist,' wrote Brontë, disturbed. 'He serenely denies us our hope of im-mortality, and quietly blots from Man's future, Heaven and the life to come.'[109] In a book more admired by Charlotte Brontë, Francis Newman had attacked the 'Christian' argument that 'a Future Life . . . is requisite *to redress the inequalities of this*', finding grounds for belief instead in the individual soul's experience—its con-sciousness of its 'union with God' and its 'hope (more or less confident) that that union shall never terminate'.[110] To him, such subjective experience was far super-ior to the 'proofs' and 'evidences' provided by the 'logical demonstrations' of theol-ogy—'the unendurable burden called Christian Evidences . . . a mass of investigation, which, if it is to be calmly and thoroughly judged, requires some ten years' persevering study from a cultivated intellect in its prime'.[111] But such 'proofs'

---

[106] Charlotte Brontë to Ellen Nussey, 13 December 1846 (*CBL* i. 507).
[107] 'While the quoted biblical passages speak of good fights and prizes, none of them fails to empha-sise that it is God alone who saves and succours,' notes Marianne Thormählen in the course of a very dif-ferent reading of *Villette* (*The Brontës and Religion*, 99).
[108] Martineau and Atkinson, *Letters on the Laws of Man's Nature and Development*, 185.
[109] *CBL* ii. 561.
[110] Francis Newman, *The Soul: Her Sorrows and Her Aspirations: An Essay Towards the Natural History of the Soul as the Basis of Theology* (London: John Chapman, 1849), 220, 222. Newman's argu-ments are virtually replicated by his admirer, W. R. Greg, in *The Creed of Christendom: Its Foundations and Superstructure* (London: John Chapman, 1851), whose final chapter, 'The Great Enigma', is devoted to the question of the future life.
[111] *The Soul*, 227 n., 257. 'Instead of heroic martyr Conduct, and inspired and soul-inspiring Elo-quence . . . we have "Discourses on the Evidences", endeavouring, with smallest result, to make it prob-able that such a thing as Religion exists,' complained Carlyle, in another work read by Brontë at this time ('Characteristics', *Critical and Miscellaneous Essays*, ii. 401. Thomas Vargish suggests that in the devo-tional literature of the mid-century the concept of Providence became 'progressively less an image of order, regulation, grand planning, and more an intimate solicitude for individual lives' (*Providential*

and 'evidences' are invoked in *Villette* from a perspective rather more bitter and certainly less hopeful than this. 'Proof of a life to come must be given,' says Lucy, half sardonic, half anguished. And in a series of passive constructions, she presents the 'evidences' of the theologians—that which is 'written' in Scripture, that which is recorded 'throughout nature', that which 'cross[es] our own experience'—as they appear from the perspective of those whose sufferings constitute 'proof'. This is not the judicious voice of theological demonstration, but a more ironic one. And it is not merely ironic: there is a darker feeling in play.

The question of a 'life to come' was one that Charlotte Brontë had pondered with desperate urgency in the years before the publication of *Villette*. 'Had I never believed in a future life before, my Sisters' fate would assure me of it,' she wrote to W. S. Williams shortly after Anne Brontë's death. 'There must be a heaven or we must despair—for life seems bitter, brief—blank.'[112] Assurance is terribly challenged by the shift of modality between those 'musts'—the one ('there must be a heaven') half imperative, half speculative, drawing attention to doubt even as it seeks to assert certainty; the other ('we must despair') signifying the acceptance of an intimate, dark necessity. And 'must' recurs in *Villette*, to rather different effect, as Lucy contemplates the meaning of human suffering: 'Proof of a life to come must be given.' The address to the 'sufferer' that follows is not simply a sardonic commentary on arguments from the 'evidences': it images the 'terror' of subjection to an inscrutable causality. The abstract speculations of a Butler or a Paley are superseded here by more overwhelming immediacies—the 'burning evidence' of pain. 'In fire and in blood, if needful, must that proof be written.' The cool demonstrations of natural religion give way to the more fiery language of prophecy: 'And I will shew wonders in heaven above, and signs in the earth beneath: blood, and fire, and vapour of smoke' (Acts 2: 19). This is the modality of Revelation: 'the Lord God of the holy prophets sent his angel to shew unto his servants the things which must shortly be done' (Revelation 22: 6).

'Of what are these things the signs and tokens?' are Lucy's first spoken words in the novel (6). Hers is a narrative of reading the signs, rather than of confident knowledge; of passivity and 'suspense', not decisive choice and control. 'Speak of it! you might almost as well stand up in an European market-place, and propound dark sayings in that language and mood wherein Nebuchadnezzar, the imperial hypochondriac, communed with his baffled Chaldeans,' she says, as she signals its difference from that story of health and confidence, effectiveness and prosperity

Aesthetic, 21). But Butler's *Analogy of Religion* (1736) and Paley's *Evidences of Christianity* (1794) both remained influential. On Butler, see Matthew Arnold, 'Bishop Butler and the Zeitgeist' (1877) in *Last Essays on Church and Religion*, ed. R. H. Super (Ann Arbor: University of Michigan Press, 1972). Paley's *Evidences* was still a text-book at Cambridge as late as 1884: see e.g. Revd George Fisk (ed.), *Paley's View of the Evidences of Christianity: Comprising The Text of Paley, Verbatim; with Examination Questions, Arranged at the Foot of Each Page of the Text*, 8th edn. (Cambridge: J. Hall & Son; London: Simpkin, Marshall & Co.; Whittaker & Co; and G. Bell & Sons, 1884). It would have been studied there at the beginning of the century by Revd Patrick Brontë, whose copy of Paley's *Horae Paulinae* is still at Haworth Parsonage.

[112] *CBL* ii. 220.

which constitutes the bourgeois norm (273–4). Yet the terms in which she speaks point less towards 'lonely unexpressed feeling'[113] than to a discourse shared by many in mid-nineteenth-century England (one within which, indeed, Nebuchadnezzar was a prominent figure):[114] a discourse that offered to interpret the 'dark sayings' of biblical prophecy and claimed to 'propound' truths that the 'world' was not ready to receive. This was a discourse that spoke not of social effectiveness, but of subjection to an agency baffling to human purposes, not of authoritative 'comprehension' but of the limits of 'mortal vision' (*V* 179); it spoke above all of waiting—for the coming of the Lord. It is evoked with a peculiar inflection in *Villette*.

The history of the upsurge in millenarian speculation amongst the polite classes in mid-nineteenth-century England has yet to be written: there is no space to do so here.[115] 'The religious world teems with new interpretations of the prophecies,' wrote Mill in his 'Spirit of the Age' (1831): throughout the 1830s, 1840s, and 1850s many appear to have felt that history was rapidly approaching the Second Coming of Christ. 'The circle of inquirers is widening every day,' declared Horatius Bonar, editor of the new *Quarterly Journal of Prophecy*, which was to run for twenty-five years, in 1849. 'Interest is rising, prejudices are breaking down, and even the unwilling are compelled to listen.' At the height of the 'Advent Awakening', as it was known amongst the faithful, at least eight periodicals were exclusively or chiefly devoted to the exposition of prophecy; and there was a 'veritable galaxy of premillennial writers', including laymen and clergy, Dissenters and members of the Established Church.[116] 'I have been abstracting the book of Revelation,' wrote Ruskin in his diary on 17 June 1849. 'They say the French are beaten again at Rome, and another revolution in Paris; many signs seem to multiply around us'; in the years that followed he, like thousands of others, attended John Cumming's Covent Garden sermons on millenarian themes.[117] 'Let all who love Christ, and believe his

---

[113] Raymond Williams, *The English Novel from Dickens to Lawrence* (London: Chatto & Windus), 73.

[114] The book of Daniel and the figures of Nebuchadnezzar's dream were favourite subjects of millenarian exegesis: see e.g. John Cumming, *Prophetic Studies; or, Lectures on the Book of Daniel* (London: Arthur Hall, 1850).

[115] I am not concerned here with differences between the various shades of 'futurist', 'historicist', and pre-millennial opinion but with a language and constellation of preoccupations, which include an interest in prophecy, literalism in biblical interpretation, and an overriding concern with the 'last things'. Ernest R. Sandeen, *The Roots of Fundamentalism: British and American Millenarianism 1800–1930* (Chicago: University of Chicago Press, 1970) sketches the general outline. J. F. C. Harrison, *The Second Coming: Popular Millenarianism, 1780–1850* (London: Routledge & Kegan Paul, 1979) discusses popular millenarianism, mainly in the earlier part of the period; though he distinguishes this from 'what may be called respectable, orthodox, scholarly millennialism', the division, as he points out, 'is not hard and fast' (5). Probably the fullest (if somewhat eccentric) account of leading figures and events is LeRoy Edwin Froom, *The Prophetic Faith of Our Fathers* (Washington, DC: Review and Herald, 1946), iii. Robert Metro Kachur, in his unpublished Ph.D. thesis, 'Getting the Last Word: Women and the Authoritative Apocalyptic Voice in British Literature, 1845–1900' (University of Wisconsin, Madison, 1996) discusses the proliferation of commentaries on the Apocalypse written by women in the middle and later years of the century (and offers a rather different view than mine of their relation to *Villette*).

[116] Froom, *Faith of Our Fathers*, 605.

[117] *The Diaries of John Ruskin*, ed. Joan Evans and John Howard Whitehouse (3 vols.; Oxford: Clarendon Press, 1956–9), ii. 389, 467. 'He is, as everyone knows, a preacher of immense popularity, and of the numerous publications in which he perpetuates his pulpit labours, all circulate widely, and some,

word, observe the signs of the times, and remember his repeated exhortations to be ready for his coming,' Catherine Gauntlett urged in her *The Sevenfold Book: Hints on the Revelation*, published in the same year as *Villette*.[118] And the text of which she speaks—'Be ye also ready: for in such an hour as ye think not the Son of Man cometh' (Matthew 24: 44)—is one that for Charlotte Brontë must have been 'printed . . . on the retina of an inward vision' (*V* 341): that inscribed on her mother's memorial tablet in Haworth church.[119]

Charlotte Brontë's earliest surviving writings give considerable evidence of her acquaintance with millenarian ideas. In 'Tales of the Islanders' (1829) the Duke of Wellington describes an apocalyptic vision, in which a monster branded 'bigotry' pursues 'a horrible, old man . . . called the Romish Religion' and spreads pestilence throughout the land.[120] A manuscript diary fragment, dated the following year, tells of a 'fanatical enthusiast' coming to the door of Haworth Parsonage, bearing a message to the Parson from 'the LORD': 'the bridegroom is coming and he must prepare to meet him'. 'I could not,' records the youthful Charlotte, 'forebear weeping at his words.'[121] Theological disputation on millenarian subjects is more ironically invoked in a story of 1834, where Mary, the young Queen of Angria, 'in a tone of assumed solemnity' quotes a series of texts from Daniel and from Revelation: 'the word has been differently explained,' she says, 'by different commentators'.[122] In Brontë's later published writings millenarian ideas are both playfully and seriously entertained. *Jane Eyre's* closing words are a favourite millenarian text: 'that unceasing cry of the Church, which the last words of revelation [*sic*] leave ringing in our ears'.[123] In *Shirley*, Barraclough the antinomian sees 'the mark of the beast' on Moore's forehead and prophesies a judgement to come (*S* 238). Bonaparte's defeat is imaged in the language of those passages of Revelation (16: 1–19) that millenarian writers saw as figuring the Napoleonic wars: 'Three terrible archangels ever stationed before the throne of Jehovah. They stand clothed in white, girdled with golden girdles; they uplift vials, brimming with the wrath of God. . . It is done: the earth is scorched with fire: the sea becomes 'as the blood of a dead man;' the islands flee away; the mountains are not found' (*S* 635–6).[124] 'The Abomination of Desolation was no mystery to them,' remarks the narrator, mockingly, of Shirley's

according to their title-page, have reached the sixteenth thousand,' wrote George Eliot in a scathing review of several of Cumming's works, including his *Manual of Christian Evidences* (*Westminster Review*, NS 8 (October 1855), 438).

[118] [Catherine Gauntlett], *The Sevenfold Book: Hints on the Revelation* (London: Seeleys and Simpkin, Marshall & Co, 1853), 206.

[119] Horsfall Turner, *Haworth, Past and Present*, 97.   [120] 'Tales of the Islanders', *EEW* i. 108.

[121] 'The following strange occurrence', *EEW* i. 177.

[122] 'Corner Dishes: A Day Abroad', *EEW* ii. 2, 118.

[123] William Dodsworth, *The Signs of the Times: Sermons Preached in Advent 1848* (London: Joseph Masters, 1849), 65. The text appeared as epigraph on the title page of Cumming's *Apocalyptic Sketches; or Lectures on the Book of Revelation, Delivered in the Large Room, Exeter Hall, in 1847–48* (London: Hall & Co., 1848).

[124] See e.g. Mrs J. C. Martin, *The Revelation of St John Briefly Explained* (Dublin: James McGlashan, 1851), 178–80, 182–5. The 'vials' of Revelation feature prominently in millenarian writings of the mid-century also as images of the revolutions of 1848.

Sympson cousins (454); the reference is to Daniel 12: 11, much pondered by millenarian writers. 'And you would mate me with a kid,' exclaims the 'leopard' Shirley, scornfully, invoking another such text (Isaiah 11: 6), 'the Millennium being yet millions of centuries from mankind' (*S* 618).

But if Charlotte Brontë's familiarity with the discourses of millenarianism can be traced throughout her works, their characteristic preoccupations—their concern with the biblical books of Daniel and Revelation; their hostility to the Roman Catholic church (in which the Pope appears as Antichrist, and England as his heroic opponent); their figuring of Christian life as a kind of militant submission; even their peculiar literalism—seem much more central to *Villette*.[125] In *Jane Eyre* the pre-millennial hope is a coda to the heroine's story. But in *Villette* the space of waiting is central to the narrative, from those opening vignettes of the child Paulina and Miss Marchmont, waiting for the men they love, to the novel's closing chapters, where Lucy waits for M. Paul. In millenarian writings Christ is figured as the Bridegroom of the waiting church, and his advent is imminent. 'He bids us watch . . . expecting the Bridegroom's coming . . . His bride is now a mourning widow; he calls her as a woman forsaken . . . for the enemies of her absent Lord have usurped his domain, and darkened the earth with heathenism, and polluted it with blood . . . That this time is not now far off, we have abundant proof in the signs that thicken around us,' declared one evangelical writer in 1842.[126] Just so, in the closing pages of *Villette*, the schemes of the junta prosper, and Lucy awaits her Bridegroom. In the last days, it was believed, signs would appear in the heavens, prophesying the coming of Christ (Revelation 6: 12–13; 15: 1). Just so, Lucy reads the signs of the sky, and repeats 'he is coming', 'he is coming', as she watches for the return of her Emanuel.

Yet the 'great city' of the Apocalypse, 'clothed in fine linen, and purple, and scarlet, and decked with gold, and precious stones, and pearls', 'spiritually called Sodom and Egypt' (Revelation 18: 16; 9: 8), is here Villette, a little town. 'A veil, the veil of our own darkened understanding, as yet conceals from us the glory that shall be revealed': thus the resounding cadences of the millenarian hope.[127] But at 'the crisis and the revelation' on the night of the city's fête, that which appears before Lucy is neither glory nor terror, but a 'girl of Villette . . . well-nourished, fair, and fat of flesh' (464). The novel's descriptions of Madame Walravens, a disagreeable old woman, garishly 'decked with ornaments' (405) and attended by a Romish priest, seem like an ironic parody of a favourite millenarian trope, the figuring of the Roman church as the Great Harlot of the Apocalypse.[128] Another favourite trope,

[125] For references to the book of Revelation, see below; for key images from the book of Daniel, see *Villette*, 98, 163, 204, 274.

[126] Charlotte Elizabeth [Tonna], *Principalities and Powers in Heavenly Places* (London: R. B. Seeley & W. Burnside, 1842), 319, 321.

[127] [Tonna], *Principalities and Powers in Heavenly Places*, 287.

[128] 'The gold and precious stones and pearls, with which the woman is decked, most aptly figure the riches, pomp and splendour, the magnificent decorations and costly ornaments of the Romish worship and hierarchy by which they have attracted and attached crowds of ignorant worshippers; gratifying the taste of the refined, and exciting the admiration of the vulgar' (Catherine Gauntlett, *The Sevenfold Book: Hints on the Revelation*, 215).

the overturning of Romanism—depicted in millenarian writings as akin to the fall of Babylon—is likewise mocked and vulgarized in the half-ridiculous moment when Lucy finally dismantles the illusion of 'the NUN': 'Down she fell—down all round me—down in shreds and fragments—and I trode upon her' (470). And the vision of the Holy City in which Revelation culminates is more extensively parodied in the novel's detailed description of the fête in the public park. That city which 'had no need of the sun, neither of the moon, for the glory of God did lighten it' (Rev. 21: 23) is simply the 'well-lit Haute-Ville' (468) in which 'moonlight and heaven are banished' (565), its artificial 'glare' created by 'twinkling' oil lamps (452, 469). The 'voices . . . it seemed to me, unnumbered; instruments varied and countless' which the wondering Lucy hears are not those of 'a great multitude . . . saying Allelulia: for the Lord God omnipotent reigneth' (Rev. 19: 6), but the sound of 'crowded thousands' round 'a sort of kiosk near the park's centre', 'gathered to a grand concert in the open air' (454).[129] Those who bear the Lamb's name 'in their foreheads', standing before his throne (Rev. 22: 4), are here 'assembled ladies' with 'decorated bonnets', sitting on 'little light park-chairs'; the jasper and sapphire and emerald of the glorious holy city (Rev. 21: 19), the fashionable mid-nineteenth-century glories of 'the silk robe, the velvet mantle and the plumed chapeau' (455).

'Watch as I would,' says Lucy, in an earlier echo of Revelation (3: 3), 'I could not detect the hours and moments of his coming' (343). She is speaking of M. Paul's visits to leave books and papers in her desk. The joke takes on a darker inflection in the novel's later echoes of the language of Apocalypse. That vision of a 'friendly company' of pilgrims, enduring hardness and keeping the faith, in expectation of 'glory', which is Lucy's attempted assertion of the hope of 'a life to come', is immediately succeeded in the novel by the image of quite a different company—'all assembled in class', with 'cleanly-written compositions . . . neatly tied with ribbon', waiting for their teacher, M. Emanuel (438). The resounding cadences of biblical promise, much recalled by millenarians in these years—'The hour is coming, in the which all that are in the graves shall hear his voice' (John 5: 28)—are replaced by a more prosaic invocation of a school timetable: 'The hour was come; we expected the master.'. This expected master is not the Emmanuel promised in Scripture, He for whose coming St John Rivers yearns at the ending of *Jane Eyre*. He is an idiosyncratic, irascible, ridiculous 'little man'. And even this expectation ends in anti-climax: 'Instead of him with his swiftness and his fire, there came quietly upon us, the cautious Madame Beck' (438). 'This morning there will be no lesson of literature,' announces the schoolmistress, speaking, Lucy says, in 'paragraphs'. 'It is probable that the lessons will be *suspended* for a week. I shall require at least that space of time to find a substitute for M. Emanuel. Meanwhile, *it shall be our study to fill the blanks usefully*' (439; my italics). Her words mark out a space that is like a banally secular version of the waiting of the millenarians: that 'space' of 'blank' suspense which dominates Lucy's narrative and is unresolved at its end.

---

[129] See Peter Allan Dale, 'Heretical Narration, Charlotte Brontë's Search for Endlessness', *Religion and Literature* 16: 3 (Autumn 1984), 15–20, for a different reading of these figures.

In the middle years of the century, Boyd Hilton has suggested, millenarian speculation took on a more optimistic tone. Descriptions of the apocalypse became gen-
tler, as the image of the fiery furnace was replaced by 'consoling visions of the
"tranquil and glassy sea" (Rev. 15: 2–3)'.[130] Thus, one prominent preacher speaks of
the 'coming tempest', 'the sea and the waves roaring . . . the stars falling from the
heavens,' and the 'thousand shipwrecks' it will bring; but reassures the believer that
'there are ships which shall . . . be found upon crystal and tranquil waters' when 'the
fury is overpast, and the light of a morning which is to know no light breaks gloriously forth'.[131] Others saw the 'sublunary glory' of the Great Exhibition as a 'humble type' of the New Jerusalem; its 'assembling of men from the east, and the west,
and the north, and the south' as a sign of the 'last days when the Spirit shall be
poured upon all flesh, and when the shattered and for so long severed portions of
the human family shall by the bonds of love be united together in one holy family';[132] or spoke of the contrast between the 'mourning, lamentation and woe' in
store for 'those who have spent their time and talents and thoughts upon the things
of this life' and the lot of the true believer: 'Happy, happy are they that now know
Him; and happy, thrice happy *will* they be, in that great and coming day!'[133] Such
confident predictions would have been familiar to Charlotte Brontë. Yet if there is
a kind of parody of millenarian literalism in 'the hour was come',[134] there is a bit-
terer parody of such prophecies as these in the closing pages of *Villette*. That glorious reunion of 'long severed portions of the human family' which marked the
beginning of the fulfilment of the millenarian hope is here represented by the
markedly unconsoling reappearance of the narrator's 'intimate acquaintance' in
the public park of Villette (456): no affirmation of 'the bonds of love', but a spectacle that excludes her. Instead of the 'constant and delightful anticipation of the day
of Christ's second coming' (or at worst, 'hope deferred') with which believers
looked forward,[135] there is the relentless, repeated past tense of Lucy's description
of her happiness (493–5), the agony of anxiety with which she reads the signs.
Instead of the heavenly marriage, the 'fruition of return' (496) there is one who
waits in vain for the Bridegroom, an Emanuel who does not come. Instead of 'the

[130] Boyd Hilton, 'Whiggery, Religion and Social Reform: the Case of Lord Morpeth', *The Historical Journal*, 37 (1994), 849.

[131] Henry Melvill, 'The greatness and condescension of God', *Sermons preached before the University of Cambridge during the month of February 1836*, quoted in Hilton, 'Whiggery, Religion and Social Re-form', 848.

[132] Revd George Clayton, 'Encouragement and Advantages Connected with the Great Exhibition', *Sermons on the Great Exhibition* (London: Benjamin L. Green, 1851), 34; Revd Stephen Bridge, 'Thoughts on the Exhibition', *The Pulpit*, 60 (1851), 242.

[133] Revd W. Pennefather, 'The Luxury and Worldliness of the Present Age', in Bickersteth *et al.*, *Twelve Lent Lectures on The Signs of the Times*, 99.

[134] 'It became a hallmark of the millenarian party [in the first half of the 19th cent.] that literal rather than figurative or spiritualized fulfilments should be sought for every biblical prophecy. When 'king-doms' were prophesied, for example, literal, historical events involving flesh-and-blood kings ought to be expected rather than the triumph of one or another virtue' (Sandeen, *The Roots of Fundamentalism*, 13).

[135] Hugh White, *The Gospel Promotive of True Happiness*, 113; Christina Rossetti, 'Advent' (1858), *The Complete Poems of Christina Rossetti: A Variorum Edition*, ed. R.W. Crump (2 vols.; Baton Rouge and London: Louisiana State University Press, 1979), i. 68–9.

manifestation of his glory in the destruction of his obstinate enemies' there is the triumph of those who in millenarian terms are 'the worshippers of the beast'.[136] 'The spiritual is the real and abiding; the material, however substantial it may appear to us, passes away like a dream,' declared one millenarian writer, in the year of the publication of *Villette*.[137] But the ending of Lucy Snowe's narrative figures the victory not merely of Romanism, but also of the material: 'Madame Beck prospered all the days of her life.'

Others at the mid-century spoke of 'that 'glorious hope', the 'light of the day of the appearing of Christ'.[138] 'Leave sunny imaginations hope,' says Lucy, pointing towards the paradigmatic narratives of bourgeois prosperity. And the thickening ironic references in the novel's closing pages to that which many at the mid-century saw as the great end of history make this a bleak rejoinder not merely to the sanguine expectations of contemporary novel readers, but to that grandest of teleologies. 'The world will prosper,' proclaimed *The Quarterly Journal of Prophecy*, in an article on the Great Exhibition. 'The elements, the machinery of prosperity are there—look at them. Well, what then? Ask Scripture, what then?'[139] Such writers as this looked forward to the passing away of earthly shows, the coming of a 'holy city' that had 'no need of the light of the sun' (Rev. 21: 20). But to Lucy Snowe's 'What then?' (438) *Villette* supplies no answer. It speaks not of the fulfilment of God's promise, but simply of an earthly sun. And that sense of annihilating dazzle which has informed and shaped the narrative comes to the fore in an image of blinding, blank exclusion: 'till, when the sun returned, his light was night to some'.

[136] [Gauntlett], *The Sevenfold Book*, 185, 186.   [137] Ibid. 254.
[138] *Quarterly Journal of Prophecy*, 6 (1858), 290.
[139] 'The Prophetic Character of the Great Exhibition', ibid. (1851), 271.

Epilogue

> And why do you then blame Turner because he dazzles you? Does not the false-
> hood rest with those who do *not*?
>
> (Ruskin, *Modern Painters* I)[1]

It has come to be customary to read *Villette* as the story of Lucy Snowe: a self-
defensive character, a 'constitutionally nervous' individual (*V* 367), 'a nobody and
a somebody', an exemplary figure of 'woman's growth into self-recognition and
self-sufficiency'.[2] But there is a great deal in the novel that cannot be assimilated to
a narrative such as this. Its images of visual bedazzlement and of devastating idolatry bespeak a different kind of engagement with rather different areas of mid-
Victorian cultural debate. This other face of the novel is, it seems, no less expressive
of Charlotte Brontë's concern with contemporary actualities than that psychologically realistic story which its readers usually abstract.

Indeed, the complexities of 'dazzle'—its challenge to perceptual mastery, its connotations both of splendour and of annihilation, as well as, more particularly, the
blinding light of the sun—were in early Victorian England being pondered in another medium by an artist by whom Charlotte Brontë seems to have been deeply
stirred as she began to conceive *Villette*. 'Who can read these glowing descriptions
of Turner's works without longing to see them?' she had written to W. S. Williams
on reading *Modern Painters* in the summer of 1848.[3] And that 'longing' was assuaged at last in December 1849. 'I have seen a beautiful exhibition of Turner's
paintings', she wrote to her father from London: more than two months later she
was to recall to a friend the impact those paintings had made upon her. Which
paintings she actually saw we may never precisely determine, but they seem to have
included some of those oils of the 1840s before which the eye 'blink[s] baffled' (*V*
168)—visions of blinding luminescence, which appear to compel the viewer to look
straight into the sun.[4] 'His later oil-paintings are strange things—things that baffle

---

[1] E. T. Cook and Alexander Wedderburn (eds.), *Library Edition of the Works of John Ruskin* (39 vols;
London: Allen, 1912), iii. 221.

[2] These are the versions of Lucy Snowe explored in four impressive recent studies: Janet Gezari, *Charlotte Brontë and Defensive Conduct: The Author and the Body at Risk* (Philadelphia: University of Pennsylvania Press, 1992); Sally Shuttleworth, *Charlotte Brontë and Victorian Psychology* (Cambridge:
Cambridge University Press, 1996); Tim Dolin, Introduction to *Villette* (Oxford: World's Classics,
2000); Kate Flint, 'The Business of a Woman's Life', in Heather Glen (ed.), *Cambridge Companion to the
Brontës* (Cambridge: Cambridge University Press, 2002).

[3] *CBL* ii. 94. William Smith Williams of Smith & Elder was a great admirer of Turner, and may have
arranged for Brontë's visit 'to one or two private collections' in the following year.

[4] Of course, through Ruskin's eloquent descriptions, she was familiar with many more paintings than
those she actually saw. 'I have seen the pictures in the National Gallery. I have seen a beautiful exhibition
of Turner's paintings,' she wrote to her father, carefully distinguishing the one from the other: to

description', she wrote to Margaret Wooler, of those extraordinary visual reflections on the devastating force of light.[5]

Brontë's sense that those paintings 'baffle[d] description' was echoed, far less admiringly, by others in these years. Mid-nineteenth-century viewers expected readable pictures.[6] Many were bewildered by the 'dazzling obscurity' of Turner's later oils.[7] Others simply castigated what they saw as clumsy technique. 'Is the picture sublime or ridiculous?' demanded Thackeray of *Slavers*. 'Indeed, I don't know which. Rocks of gamboge are marked down upon the canvass [*sic*]; flakes of white laid on with a trowel; bladders of vermilion madly spirited here and there.'[8] Brontë would have been familiar with such criticism as this, possibly in *Blackwood's* and *Punch*, and certainly in *Fraser's*, where Thackeray, as Michael Angelo Titmarsh, was providing 'Picture Gossip' in the 1840s. She could hardly have failed to be struck by the difference between Thackeray's description of *Slavers*—the most famous of Turner's paintings—and Ruskin's great set-piece description in *Modern Painters I*, which she read in 1849. Indeed, her growing sense of the limitations of her former hero seems to have fed into her portrayal of the successful, obtuse Dr John.[9] 'For what belonged to storm, what was wild and intense, dangerous, sudden and flaming, he had no sympathy, and held with it no communion,' remarks Lucy (259). It is hard not to see this as a figuring of Thackeray's response to Turner. Brontë's own different view is inscribed throughout *Villette*.

For the central concerns of Turner's thinking—familiar to Brontë from Ruskin's 'glowing descriptions' even before she saw his paintings—appear in the novel as informing images: light and shadow, sunshine and cloud, dazzle and storm. Turner's great visions of elemental violence are echoed in the metaphors in which the crises of its heroine's inner life are figured; the death-dealing sea he repeatedly painted in the final, literal ship-wreck in which her hopes of happiness are lost. There is even something Turnerian in that debunking insistence on banal, quotidian realities which punctures *Villette*'s invocations of the high romantic sublime. 'No subject was too low or too high for him,' Ruskin was to write of Turner. 'We find him one

Margaret Wooler, she writes later of having seen 'one or two private collections of Turner's best water-colour drawings' as well as 'his later oil-paintings' (to Patrick Brontë, 5 December 1849 (*CBL* ii. 301); to Margaret Wooler, 14 February 1850 (*CBL* ii. 344)). The collection of B. G. Windus at Tottenham was opened to public view once a week, and contained more than 200 watercolours by 1840: in the 1840s, Windus (a major patron of Turner) began to collect the late oils. The collection of H. A. J. Munro of Novar (hanging in his London home at 113 Grosvenor Square) also contained several late oils.

[5] 14 February 1850 (*CBL* ii. 344).

[6] Judith L. Fisher, 'Magnificent or Mad? Nineteenth-Century Periodicals and the Paintings of Joseph Mallord William Turner', *Victorian Periodicals Review*, 29: 3 (Fall 1996), 242–60. On narrative reading of painting in the mid-19th cent. see Kate Flint, *The Victorians and the Visual Imagination* (Cambridge: Cambridge University Press, 2000), 197–235.

[7] *Spectator*, 8 May 1847.

[8] 'Pictorial Rhapsody', *Fraser's Magazine*, 21 (1840), 731.

[9] For this change in attitude, which seems to have begun in January 1851, see *CBL* ii. 546, 561, 615, 662, 717. 'Great image of Nebuchadnezzar's dream—made up of iron and clay—half strength—half weakness,' Charlotte Brontë called him in May 1851 (*CBL* ii. 615). 'I was driven to compare his beamy head in my thoughts to that of the "golden image" which Nebuchadnezzar the king had set up,' says Lucy of Dr John (*V* 98).

day hard at work on a cock and hen . . . next day he is drawing the Dragon of Colchis. One hour he is much interested in a gust of wind blowing away an old woman's cap; the next, he is painting the fifth plague of Egypt.'[10] Just so, Lucy's narrative at one point focuses on the ridiculous prize in a lottery, the breaking of a pair of spectacles, at another on the cosmic meaning of human suffering. Turner's attempts to render the actual nature of optical experience have a parallel in *Villette*'s concern with the subjective and physiological bases of vision, its images less of visual control than of assault on the eye. Turner's obsession with the sun—both with its transfiguring potency and its annihilating 'Gorgon light'—likewise has an echo in Lucy's bedazzlement by 'sunshine', her dread of 'being struck stone-blind'.[11] And as the novel's doom approaches there is an extraordinary fictional counterpart to those oils of Turner's final decade, in which dazzle and storm and shipwreck are strangely combined:

The skies hang full and dark—a rack sails from the west; the clouds cast themselves into strange forms—arches and broad radiations; there rise resplendent mornings—glorious, royal, purple as monarch in his state; the heavens are one flame, so wild are they, they rival battle at its thickest—so bloody, they shame Victory in her pride. (495)[12]

'Of [Currer Bell's] three books, this is perhaps the strangest, the most astonishing,' declared Harriet Martineau. The narrator, she complains, 'speaks in enigmas or in raillery'; some passages are 'not ... congenial, or very intelligible, in the midst of so much that is strong and clear'.[13] *Villette*'s 'uncongenial' or clumsy refusal to accord with accepted conventions of psychologically realistic narrative is noted again and again in contemporary reviews. There is 'much obscurity from straining after figure and allusion', the *Spectator* reviewer complained.[14] 'When . . . it was in the power of the disposing author of the book to close her story with a charming satisfying picture, which she really does elaborately paint,—she daubs her brush across it, and upon the last page spoils it all for no artistic purpose whatsoever, and to the sure vexation of all lookers-on.'[15]

---

[10] *Pre-Raphaelitism, Library Edition of the Works of John Ruskin*, xii. 368–9.

[11] The phrase 'Gorgon light' is from *Modern Painters V* (1860), *Library Edition of the Works of John Ruskin*, vii. 190. Turner, according to Ruskin, was 'a Sun-worshipper of the old breed', who 'meant it, as Zoroaster meant it' (*Fors Clavigera* (1874) in *Library Edition of the Works of John Ruskin*, xxviii. 147): it was said that on his deathbed he declared that 'The sun is God'. The sun-god Apollo appears in his *Chryses* (1811), *Apollo and Python* (1811), and *Ulysses deriding Polyphemus* (1829). For his interest in heathen sun-worship (accounts of which he read in Richard Payne Knight and William Jones), see John Gage, 'J. M. W. Turner and Solar Myth', in J. B. Bullen (ed.), *The Sun is God: Painting, Literature and Mythology in the Nineteenth Century* (Oxford: Oxford University Press, 1989).

[12] 'We never read one of her descriptions that we do not long for more. This book contains a few that are as good as Turner's to the mind's eye,' wrote the reviewer of the novel in the *Literary Gazette* (*CH* 180). Charlotte Brontë herself clearly thought of the novel in painterly terms. 'I doubt the regular novel-reader will consider . . . the colours dashed on to the Canvass with the proper amount of daring,' she wrote of it to her publisher. 'Still—I feel they must be satisfied with what is offered: my palette affords no brighter tints—were I to attempt to deepen the reds or burnish the yellows—I should but botch,' she wrote to William Smith Williams as she was completing *Villette* in November 1852 (quoted in Juliet Barker, *The Brontës* (London: Weidenfeld and Nicolson, 1994), 706).

[13] *CH* 172–4.   [14] *Spectator*, quoted in *CH* 182–4.   [15] *Examiner*, quoted in *CH* 177.

Charlotte Brontë's response to Turner is a subject for another study. Yet the striking parallels between them highlight the ineptness of such criticisms as these. For those images of disturbed, bewildered, occluded vision that punctuate Lucy's narrative bespeak a fictional project akin to Turner's challenge to the controlling conventions of his time. There is a clear, if indirect connection between Turner's fidelity to what Ruskin called the 'truth' of corporeally situated vision, his images of blinding sunshine and of overwhelming storm, and *Villette*'s 'circumstanced' perspective on the seductive, devastating dazzle of bourgeois prosperity. And this might alert us to the fact that that experience of bedazzlement in all its meanings was in the mid-nineteenth century not an eccentric one. It may, as we have seen, be traced throughout the records of the period—part, as Lucy says, of the experience of 'most of us' (438). Charlotte Brontë's interest in Turner points towards a different kind of valuing of her final masterpiece: not simply as a psychological study in morbidity, but as an equally extraordinary reflection on the mid-nineteenth-century world they shared.

Bibliography

PRIMARY SOURCES

For ease of reference, anonymous works are listed alphabetically; all other works are in date order within each entry.

ANON., 'The Annuals of Former Days', *Bookseller* 29, November 1858.

—— *Art and Faith, In Fragments from the Great Exhibition* (London: Partridge & Oakley, 1851).

—— *The Awful Disclosures of Maria Monk* (London: Harper, 1836).

—— *Cholera: How to Avoid It and Treat It* (London: H. S. King, 1873).

—— *The Convent: A Narrative, Founded on Fact* (London: Aylott & Jones, 1848).

—— *The Crystal Palace and its Contents: An Illustrated Cyclopaedia of the Great Exhibition of the Industry of All Nations 1851* (London: W. M. Clark, 1852).

—— 'Englishwomen of the Seventeenth and Nineteenth Centuries', *English Review*, 6 (1846), 285–8.

—— 'The Great Exhibition of 1851', in Forbes Winslow (ed.), *Journal of Psychological Medicine and Mental Pathology*, 4 (1851), 1–8.

—— *The New Female Instructor or, Young Woman's Guide to Domestic Happiness, Being an Epitome of all the Acquirements Necessary to Form the Female Character in Every Class of Life* (London: Thomas Kelly, 1819).

—— Review of William Johnston, *England As It Is; Political, Social, and Industrial, in the Middle of the Nineteenth Century, Christian Remembrancer*, 21 (1851), 400–28.

—— *Success in Life: A Book for Young Men* (London: Thomas Nelson & Sons, 1852).

—— *The Theology and Morality of the Great Exhibition As Set Forth in Certain Leading Articles which have Lately Appeared in 'The Times' and 'Record' Newspapers, by a Spiritual Watchman of the Church of England* (London: William Edward Painter, 1851).

—— *Tomorrow! The Results and Tendencies of National Exhibitions Deduced from Strict Historical Parallels, by 'Historia'* (London: Saunders & Otley, 1851).

—— *Woman: As She Is and As She Should Be* (2 vols.; London: James Cochrane & Co., 1835).

—— *Woman's Rights and Duties Considered with Relation to Her Influence on Society and on Her Own Condition, By a Woman* (2 vols.; London: John W. Parker, 1840).

—— *Woman's Worth: or, Hints to Raise the Female Character* (London: H. G. Clarke & Co, 1844).

ARNOLD, MATTHEW, *The Letters of Matthew Arnold to Arthur Hugh Clough*, ed. Howard Foster Lowry (London: Oxford University Press, 1932).

—— Preface to First Edition of *Poems* (1853), and 'On the Modern Element in Literature' (1857), in R. H. Super (ed.), *Matthew Arnold: On the Classical Tradition* (Ann Arbor: University of Michigan Press, 1960), 1–15, 18–37.

—— 'Bishop Butler and the Zeitgeist' (1877), in *Last Essays on Church and Religion*, ed. R. H. Super (Ann Arbor: University of Michigan Press, 1972), 11–62.

—— *Poems of Matthew Arnold*, ed. Kenneth Allott, ed. Miriam Allott, 2nd edn. (London and New York: Longman, 1979).

The Art Journal Illustrated Catalogue of the Great Exhibition. 1851 (London: George Virtue, 1851).

ATKINSON, HENRY GEORGE, and MARTINEAU, HARRIET, *Letters on the Laws of Man's Nature and Development* (London: John Chapman, 1851).

AUGUSTINE, ST, *The City of God Against the Pagans*, trans. William Green (Cambridge, Mass.: Harvard University Press, 1963).

BABBAGE, BENJAMIN HERSCHEL, *Report to the General Board of Health on a Preliminary Inquiry into the Sewerage, Drainage, and Supply of Water, and the Sanitary Condition of the Inhabitants of the Hamlet of Haworth* (London: HMSO, 1850).

BABBAGE, CHARLES, *The Exposition of 1851; or, Views of the Industry, the Science and the Government of England* (London: John Murray, 1851).

BAUDELAIRE, CHARLES, 'The Painter of Modern Life' (1859–60), in *The Painter of Modern Life and Other Essays*, trans. and ed. Jonathan Mayne (London: Phaidon: 1964).

—— *Tales of Terror from Blackwood's Magazine*, ed. Chris Baldick and Robert Morrison (Oxford: Oxford World's Classics, 1995).

BLANCHARD, LAMON, *Life and Literary Remains of L.E.L.* (2 vols.; London: Henry Colburn, 1841).

BODICHON, BARBARA LEIGH SMITH, *A Brief Summary in Plain Language of the Most Important Laws Concerning Women; Together with a Few Observations Thereon* (London: 1854).

BREWSTER, DAVID, *Letters on Natural Magic Addressed to Sir Walter Scott* (London: John Murray, 1832).

—— 'Statistics and Philosophy of Storms', *Edinburgh Review*, 68 (1839), 406–32.

—— *The Kaleidoscope: Its History, Theory, and Construction*, 2nd edn. (London: John Murray, 1858).

BRIDGE, REVD STEPHEN, 'Thoughts on the Exhibition', *The Pulpit*, 40 (1851), 241–6.

BRONTË, CHARLOTTE, *The Spell: An Extravaganza*, ed. George Edwin MacLean (London: Oxford University Press, 1931).

—— *The Miscellaneous and Unpublished Writings of Charlotte and Patrick Branwell Brontë*, ed. Thomas Wise and John Symington (2 vols.; Oxford: Shakespeare Head, 1938).

—— *Five Novelettes*, ed. Winifred Gérin (London: Folio Press, 1971).

—— *Unfinished Novels* (Stroud: Alan Sutton in association with the Brontë Society, 1993).

—— *Charlotte Brontë: Juvenilia 1829–1835*, ed. Juliet Barker (London: Penguin, 1996).

BRONTË, PATRICK BRANWELL, 'Thomas Bewick: "Flumina amem sylvasque inglorius"', *Halifax Guardian*, 1 October 1842; reprinted in Victor A. Neufeldt, 'A Newly Discovered Publication by Branwell Brontë', *BST* 21: 1 (April 1999), 11–15.

BRONTË, REVD PATRICK, *Brontëana: The Reverend Patrick Brontë's Collected Works*, ed. J. Horsfall Turner (Bingley: T. Harrison & Sons, 1898).

BULL, THOMAS, *Hints to Mothers for the Management of Health During the Period of Pregnancy and in the Lying-in Room*, 12th edn. (London: Longman, Green, Longman, & Roberts, 1859).

BULWER, EDWARD LYTTON, *England and the English* (1833), ed. Standish Meacham (Chicago and London: University of Chicago Press, 1970).

BYRON, GEORGE GORDON, LORD, *Works of Lord Byron, with his Letters and Journals, and his Life*, ed. Thomas Moore (London: John Murray, 1833).

—— *The Works of Lord Byron*, ed. Ernest Hartley Coleridge (5 vols.; London: John Murray, 1898).

—— *Byron's Letters and Journals*, ed. Leslie A. Marchand (12 vols.; London: John Murray, 1974–82).

CARLYLE, THOMAS, *On Heroes, Hero-Worship and the Heroic in History* (London: Chapman & Hall, 1841).

—— 'Gospel of Mammonism', *Past and Present* (1843), in Alan Shelston (ed.), *Thomas Carlyle: Selected Writings* (Harmondsworth: Penguin, 1971).

—— *Critical and Miscellaneous Essays: Collected and Republished*, 3rd edn. (4 vols.; London: Chapman & Hall, 1847).

CARUS-WILSON, W. W., *A Refutation of the Statements in 'The Life of Charlotte Brontë' Regarding the Casterton Clergy Daughters' School When at Cowan Bridge* (Weston-Super-Mare: n.d.).

CHADWICK, EDWIN, *Report on the Sanitary Condition of the Labouring Population of Great Britain* (1848), ed. M. W. Flinn (Edinburgh: Edinburgh University Press, 1965).

[CHAMBERS, ROBERT], *Vestiges of the Natural History of Creation* (London: John Churchill, 1844).

CHAPONE, HESTER, *Letters on the Improvement of the Mind. Addressed to a Lady*, new edn. (London: Harvey & Darnton, 1820).

CHAVASSE, PYE HENRY, *Advice to a Wife on the Management of her own Health, and on the Treatment of some of the Complaints Incidental to Pregnancy, Labour and Suckling* (London: Longman, 1843).

The Children's Friend [periodical], ed. W. Carus-Wilson (Kirkby Lonsdale: A. Foster, 1826–60).

CLAYTON, REVD GEORGE, *Sermons on the Great Exhibition* (London: Benjamin L. Green, 1851).

CLOUGH, ARTHUR HUGH, *The Oxford Diaries of Arthur Hugh Clough*, ed. Anthony Kenny (Oxford: Clarendon Press, 1990).

CUMMING, JOHN, *Apocalyptic Sketches; or Lectures on the Book of Revelation* (London: Hall & Co., 1848).

—— 'The Age We Live In', *Lectures to Young Men, delivered before the Y.M.C.A. in Exeter Hall, 1847–8* (London: Benjamin L. Green, 1848), 309–336.

—— *Prophetic Studies; or, Lectures on the Book of Daniel* (London: Arthur Hall, 1850).

DE QUINCEY, THOMAS, *The Collected Writings of Thomas de Quincey*, ed. David Masson (14 vols.; Edinburgh: A. & C. Black, 1897).

DICKENS, CHARLES, *The Letters of Charles Dickens*, ed. Graham Storey, Kathleen Tillotson, and Nina Burgis, Pilgrim Edition, 6 (Oxford: Clarendon Press, 1988).

DODSWORTH, WILLIAM, *The Signs of the Times: Sermons Preached in Advent 1848* (London: Joseph Masters, 1849).

ELLIS, SARAH, *The Women of England: Their Social Duties and Domestic Habits* (London: Fisher, Son, & Co., 1838).

—— *The Daughters of England, their Position in Society, Character, and Responsibilities* (London: Fisher, Son, & Co., 1842).

—— *The Mothers of England: Their Influence and Responsibility* (London: Fisher, Son, & Co., 1843).

—— *The Wives of England, their Relative Duties, Domestic Influence, and Social Obligations* (London: Fisher, Son, & Co., 1843).

—— *The Home Life and Letters of Mrs Ellis*, compiled by her nieces (London: J. Nisbet & Co., 1893).

EMERTON, REVD J. A., *A Moral and Religious Guide to the Great Exhibition* (London: Longman, Brown, Green, & Longmans, 1851).

FARNINGHAM, MARIANNE, *A Working Woman's Life. An Autobiography* (London: James Clarke, 1907).

FARR, WILLIAM, *Vital Statistics: A Memorial Volume of Selections*, ed. Noel A. Humphreys (London: Edward Stanford, 1885).

FISK, REVD GEORGE, 'The Moral Influence of the Commercial Spirit of the Day', *Lectures to Young Men, delivered before the Y.M.C.A. in Exeter Hall, 1847–8* (London: Benjamin L. Green, 1848), 271–92.

——(ed.) *Paley's View of the Evidences of Christianity: Comprising The Text of Paley, Verbatim; with Examination Questions, Arranged at the Foot of Each Page of the Text*, 8th edn.; Cambridge: J. Hall & Son; London: Simpkin, Marshall & Co.; Whittaker & Co; and G. Bell & Sons, 1884).

FROUDE, JAMES ANTHONY, *The Nemesis of Faith*, 2nd edn. (London: John Chapman, 1849).

[GAUNTLETT, CATHERINE], *The Sevenfold Book; Hints on the Revelation* (London: Seeleys and Simpkin, Marshall, & Co, 1853).

GORDON, GEORGE, *Town Swamps and Social Bridges* (1859), repr. with an intro. by Anthony D. King (Leicester: Leicester University Press, 1971).

GORDON, MARGARET MARIA, *Home Life of Sir David Brewster* (Edinburgh: Edmonston & Douglas, 1869).

GORE, CATHERINE, *Cecil; or, The Adventures of a Coxcomb* (London: Bentley, 1845).

GRAY, MRS EDWIN, *Papers and Diaries of a York Family 1764–1839* (London: Sheldon Press, 1927).

Great Exhibition of the Works of Industry of All Nations 1851. Official Descriptive and Illustrated Catalogue (3 vols.; London: Spicer Brothers, W. Clowes & Sons, 1851 and 1852).

GREEN, SAMUEL, *The Story of the Religious Tract Society* (London: Religious Tract Society, 1899).

GREG, W. R., 'Prostitution', *Westminster Review*, 53 (1850).

——*The Creed of Christendom; its Foundations and Superstructure* (London: John Chapman, 1851).

——Review of William Johnston, *England As It Is; Political, Social, and Industrial, in the Middle of the Nineteenth Century*, *Edinburgh Review*, 93 (1851), 305–39.

GREY, MARIA, and SHIRREFF, EMILY, *Thoughts on Self-Culture: Addressed to Women* (London: Moxon, 1850).

Guide-book to the Industrial Exhibition; with Facts, Figures and Observations on the Manufactures and Produce Exhibited (London: Partridge & Oakley, 1851).

'M.B.H.', *Home Truths for Home Peace, or 'Muddle' Defeated; A Practical Inquiry Into What Chiefly Mars or Makes the Comfort of Domestic Life*, 6th edn. (London: Longman, Brown, Green, & Longmans, 1854).

HARE, J. C., and HARE, A. W., *Guesses at Truth by Two Brothers*, 3rd edn., 1st series (London: Taylor & Walton, 1847).

HARRIS, REVD JOHN, 'Social Organization', *Lectures to Young Men, delivered before the Y.M.C.A. in Exeter Hall, 1847–8* (London: Benjamin L. Green, 1848), 35–60.

HAWKINS, THOMAS, *Memoirs of Ichthyosauri and Plesiosauri, Extinct Monsters of the Ancient Earth* (London: Relfe & Fletcher, 1834).

——*The Book of the Great Sea-Dragons: Icthyosauri and Plesiosauri* (London: W. Pickering, 1840).

—— *The Wars of Jehovah in Heaven, Earth, and Hell: in Nine Books*, illus. John Martin (London: Francis Baisler, 1844).

HAWTHORNE, NATHANIEL, *The English Notebooks*, ed. Thomas Woodson and Bill Ellis (Columbus: Ohio State University Press, 1997).

HOOD, EDWIN PAXTON, *The Age and its Architects: Ten Chapters on the English People in Relation to the Times* (London: Charles Gilpin, 1850).

Illustrated Handbook of the Royal Panopticon of Science and Art; an Institution for Scientific Exhibitions, and for Promoting Discoveries in Arts and Manufactures (London: 1854).

JAMES, JOHN ANGELL, *The Family Monitor, or A Help to Domestic Happiness* (Birmingham: Benjamin Hudson, 1828).

JAMESON, ANNA, *Memoirs and Essays: Illustrative of Art, Literature and Social Morals* (London: Richard Bentley, 1846).

JONES, WILLIAM, *The Jubilee Memorial of the Religious Tract Society* (London: Religious Tract Society, 1850).

[KAYE, SIR WILLIAM], 'Success', *Cornhill Magazine*, 2 (1860), 729–41.

KEMBLE, FRANCES ANN, *Record of a Girlhood* (3 vols.; London: Richard Bentley & Son, 1878).

KINGSLEY, CHARLES, 'Little Books with Large Aims' [unsigned review of *Chance and Choice; or, the Education of Circumstances* (London: John W. Parker, 1850)], *Fraser's Magazine*, 44 (July 1851), 26–40.

—— *Sermons on National Subjects, Preached in a Village Church* (London: John J. Griffin & Co., 1852).

KNIGHT, CHARLES (ed.), *Knight's Cyclopaedia of London* (London: Charles Knight, 1851).

[LAMB, ANNE RICHELIEU], *Can Woman Regenerate Society?* (London: John W. Parker, 1844).

LAMB, CHARLES, *The Letters of Charles and Mary Lamb 1821–1842*, ed. E. V. Lucas (2 vols.; London: Methuen, 1912).

LANDELS, WILLIAM, *Woman's Sphere and Work Considered in the Light of Scriptures* (London: James Nisbet, 1859).

LANDON, LETITIA [L.E.L.], *Traits and Trials of Early Life* (London: Henry Colburn, 1836).

LATHAM, R. G., *The English Language*, 2nd edn., revd. and enlarged (London: Taylor & Walton, 1848).

LAYARD, AUSTEN, *Nineveh and its Remains* (London: John Murray, 1849).

LEMPRIÈRE, J., *Bibliotheca Classica* (London: Cadell & Davies, 1798).

LEWIS, SARAH, *Woman's Mission* (London: John W. Parker, 1839).

LUKES, MRS S., *The Female Jesuit: or the Spy in the Family. A True Narrative of Recent Events in a Protestant Household* (London: Partridge & Oakley, 1851).

—— *A Sequel to The Female Jesuit; Containing Her Previous History and Recent Discovery* (London: Partridge & Oakley, 1852).

MANTELL, GIDEON, *Petrifications and Their Teachings; or, a Hand-book to the Gallery of Organic Remains of the British Museum* (London: Henry G. Bohn, 1851).

MARTIN, MRS J. C., *The Revelation of St John Briefly Explained* (Dublin: James McGlashan, 1851).

MARTINEAU, HARRIET, *How to Observe. Morals and Manners* (London: Charles Knight, 1838).

—— *Deerbrook* (1839) (London: Virago, 1983).

—— *Autobiography* (1877), ed. Gaby Weiner (2 vols.; London: Virago, 1983).

MAURICE, FREDERICK DENISON, *The Old Testament: Nineteen Sermons Preached in the Chapel of Lincoln's Inn* (London: John W. Parker & Son, 1851).

MAYHALL, JOHN, *The Annals of Yorkshire from the Earliest Period to the Present Time* (Leeds: Joseph Johnson, 1861).

MAYHEW, HENRY, 'Home is Home, be it never so Homely', in Viscount Ingestre (ed.), *Meliora: or, Better Times to Come. Being the Contributions of Many Men Touching the Present State and Prospects of Society*, First Series (London: J. W. Parker, 1852), 258–80.

NEWMAN, FRANCIS, *The Soul: Her Sorrows and Her Aspirations: An Essay Towards the Natural History of the Soul as the Basis of Theology* (London: John Chapman, 1849).

NIGHTINGALE, FLORENCE, *Cassandra,* with an intro. by Myra Stark (New York: Feminist Press, 1979).

NOLAN, REVD THOMAS, 'The Fever of Monetary Speculation', in Robert Bickersteth *et al.*, *Twelve Lent Lectures on The Signs of the Times for the Year 1858* (London: John Mills Robeson, 1858), 87–94.

OLIPHANT, MARGARET, *Annals of a Publishing House, William Blackwood and his Sons, their Magazine and Friends* (3 vols.; Edinburgh and London: William Blackwood, 1897–8).

PATER, WALTER, 'Dante Gabriel Rossetti', in *Appreciations. With an Essay on Style* (London: Macmillan, 1910), 205–18.

PENNEFATHER, REVD W., 'The Luxury and Worldliness of the Present Age', in Robert Bickersteth *et al.*, *Twelve Lent Lectures on The Signs of the Times for the Year 1858* (London: John Mills Robeson, 1858), 95–102.

POE, EDGAR ALLAN, 'How to Write a Blackwood Article' and 'A Predicament' (1838) in Edwin Markham (ed.), *Works of Edgar Allan Poe* (10 vols.; New York: Funk & Wagnall, 1904), 115–44.

REID, MRS HUGO, *A Plea For Woman: Being a Vindication of the Importance and Extent of Her Natural Sphere of Action; with Remarks on Recent Works on the Subject* (Edinburgh: William Tait, 1843).

RICHMOND, LEGH, *Domestic Portraiture; or, The Successful Application of Religious Principle in the Education of a Family Exemplified in the Memoirs of Three of the Deceased Children of the Rev. Legh Richmond* (London: R. B. Seeley & W. Burnside, 1833).

RUSKIN, JOHN, *Library Edition of the Works of John Ruskin,* ed. E. T. Cook and Alexander Wedderburn (39 vols.; London: Allen, 1912).

—— *The Diaries of John Ruskin,* ed. Joan Evans and John Howard Whitehouse (3 vols.; Oxford: Clarendon Press, 1956–9).

—— *Praeterita* (Oxford: Oxford University Press, 1978).

SANDFORD, MRS JOHN, *Woman, in her Social and Domestic Character* (London: Longman, Rees, Orme, Brown, & Green, 1831).

—— *Female Improvement*, 2 vols. (London: Longman, Rees, Orme, Browne and Green, 1836).

SEWELL, ELIZABETH MISSING, *Margaret Percival* (London: Longman, 1847).

—— *The Autobiography of Elizabeth Missing Sewell*, ed. her niece, Eleanor L. Sewell (London: Longmans, Green & Co., 1907).

SEWELL, WILLIAM, *Hawkstone* (London: Murray, 1845).

SHEPHEARD, REVD H., *A Vindication of the Clergy Daughters' School and of the Rev. Carus Wilson from the Remarks in 'The Life of Charlotte Brontë'* (Kirkby Lonsdale: J. Foster, 1857).

SHEPHEARD-WALWYN, CLEMENT CARUS-WILSON, *Henry and Margaret Jane Shepheard: Memorials of a Father and Mother* (London: Elliot Stock, 1882).

SHERWOOD, MARY, *Stories Explanatory of the Church Catechism* (Wellington, Salop: F. Houlston & Son, 1821).

—— *The History of the Fairchild Family, or The Child's Manual*, 14th edn. (London: J. Hatchard & Son, 1841).

—— *The Life and Times of Mrs Sherwood 1775–1851: from the Captain and Mrs Sherwood*, ed. F. J. Harvey Darton (London: Wells Gardner, Darton, 1910).

SHIRREFF, EMILY, *Intellectual Education* (London: John W. Parker & Son, 1858).

SMILES, SAMUEL, *Self-Help. With Illustrations of Conduct and Perseverance* (London: John Murray, 1907).

SMITH, CHARLES MANBY, *The Little World of London; or, Pictures in Little of London Life* (London: Arthur Hall, Virtue, & Co., 1857).

[SMITH, ELIZA], *Chapters on the Shorter Catechism, a Tale for the Instruction of Youth*, 2nd edn. (Edinburgh: Paton & Ritchie, 1850).

SMITH, JOHN STORES, *Social Aspects* (London: Chapman, 1850).

STODART, M. A., *Every Day Duties; In Letters to a Young Lady* (London: R. B. Seeley & W. Burnside, 1840)

—— *Principles of Education Practically Considered; with an Especial Reference to the Present State of Female Education in England* (London: R. B. Seeley & W. Burnside, 1844).

STOWE, HARRIET BEECHER, *Sunny Memories of Foreign Lands* (2 vols.; London: Sampson Low, Son & Co., 1854).

STRANGE, WILLIAM, MD, *An Address to the Middle and Working Classes on the Causes and Prevention of the Excessive Sickness and Mortality Prevalent in Large Towns* (London: Longman, Green & Co., 1845).

Tallis's History and Description of the Crystal Palace and the Exhibition of the World's Industry in 1851 (3 vols.; London: John Tallis & Co., 1851).

TAYLOR, ANN and JANE, *The Poetical Works of Ann and Jane Taylor* (London: Ward, Lock, & Tyler, 1877).

[TONNA], CHARLOTTE ELIZABETH, *Personal Recollections* (London: R. B. Seeley & W. Burnside, 1841).

—— *Principalities and Powers in Heavenly Places* (London: R. B. Seeley & W. Burnside, 1842).

TRENCH, RICHARD CHEVENIX, *On the Study of Words* (London: John W. Parker & Son, 1851).

TURNER, J. HORSFALL, *Haworth, Past and Present* (Brighouse: J. S. Jowett, 1879).

VAUGHAN, ROBERT, *The Age of Great Cities, or Modern Society Viewed in its Relation to Intelligence, Morals and Religion* (London: Jackson & Walford, 1843).

VICTORIA, QUEEN, *Dearest Child: Letters Between Queen Victoria and the Princess Royal 1858–1861*, ed. Roger Fulford (London: Evans, 1964).

WALKER, GEORGE ALFRED, *Gatherings from Grave-Yards; Particularly those of London: with a Concise History of the Modes of Interment among Different Nations, from the Earliest Periods. And a Detail of Dangerous and Fatal Results Produced by the Unwise and Revolting Custom of Inhuming the Dead in the Midst of the Living* (London: Longman, Rees, Orme, Brown, & Green, 1839).

[WARBURTON, S.], *Letters on Happiness, Addressed to a Friend* (London: Longman, Brown, Green, & Longmans, 1850).

WARREN, SAMUEL, *The Lily and the Bee: An Apologue of the Crystal Palace* (Edinburgh: Blackwood, 1851).

WATTS, ISAAC, *Divine Songs, Attempted in Easy Language for the Use of Children*, facs. reproduction of 1st edn. of 1715 (London: Oxford University Press, 1971).

WHATELEY, MRS ELIZABETH, *English Life, Social and Domestic, in the Middle of the Nineteenth Century, Considered in Reference to our Position as a Community of Professing Christians* (London: B. Fellowes, 1847).

WHEWELL, WILLIAM, *On Astronomy and General Physics Considered with Reference to Natural Theology* (*The Bridgewater Treatises on the Power, Wisdom and Goodness of God as Manifested in the Creation: Treatise III*, 7th edn. (London: William Pickering, 1839).

—— *The General Bearing of the Great Exhibition on the Progress of Art and Science*, Inaugural Lecture as Master of Trinity College, Cambridge, 26 November 1851.

WHITE, REVD HUGH, *The Gospel Promotive of True Happiness* (Dublin: James McGlashan, 1851).

WILSON, JOHN ['Christopher North'], 'Christmas Presents', *Blackwood's Magazine*, 23 (1828), 7–13.

WILSON, WILLIAM CARUS, *The Child's First Tales* (Kirkby Lonsdale: A. Foster, 1836).

WORDSWORTH, WILLIAM, *The Letters of William and Dorothy Wordsworth, The Later Years, Part II, 1829–1834*, ed. Alan G. Hill, 2nd edn. (Oxford: Oxford University Press, 1979).

NINETEENTH-CENTURY PERIODICALS

(including a selection of annuals)

The Amulet; a Christian and Literary Remembrancer
Athenaeum
Blackwood's Magazine
Chambers' Journal
The Children's Friend
The Christian Keepsake and Missionary Annual
The Christian Souvenir
Cornhill Magazine
Fisher's Drawing Room Scrap Book
Fisher's Oriental Annual
Forget Me Not
Fraser's Magazine
Friendship's Offering
The Gem
Heath's Book of Beauty
Household Words
The Keepsake
The Landscape Annual
The Leader
Literary Souvenir
Monthly Review
The Picturesque Annual
The Protestant Annual
The Pulpit
Punch
The Quarterly Journal of Prophecy
The Sacred Iris

The Sacred Lyre
The Winter's Wreath

SECONDARY SOURCES

AARSLEFF, HANS, *The Study of Language in England 1780–1860* (Minneapolis: University of Minnesota Press; London: Athlone Press, 1983).

ADBURGHAM, ALISON, *Silver Fork Society: Fashionable Life and Literature 1814–1840* (London: Constable, 1983).

ALEXANDER, CHRISTINE, *The Early Writings of Charlotte Brontë* (Oxford: Basil Blackwell, 1983).

—— 'Charlotte Brontë's Paintings: Victorian Women and the Visual Arts' (Canberra: Australian Academy of the Humanities, 1993).

—— 'Readers and Writers: *Blackwood's* and the Brontës', *The Gaskell Society Journal*, 8 (1994), 54–69.

—— ' "The Burning Clime": Charlotte Brontë and John Martin', *Nineteenth-Century Literature*, 50: 3 (December 1995), 285–321.

——and SELLARS, JANE, *The Art of the Brontës* (Cambridge: Cambridge University Press, 1995).

ALTICK, RICHARD, *The English Common Reader: A Social History of the Mass Reading Public 1800–1900* (Chicago: University of Chicago Press, 1957).

—— *Victorian People and Ideas* (New York: Altick, 1973).

—— *The Shows of London* (Cambridge, Mass.: Harvard University Press, 1978).

ARMSTRONG, ISOBEL, 'Charlotte Brontë's City of Glass', *The Hilda Hulme Memorial Lecture*, 2 December 1992 (London: University of London, 1993).

—— 'Transparency: Towards A Poetics of Glass in the Nineteenth Century', in Francis Spufford and Jenny Uglow (eds.), *Cultural Babbage: Technology, Time and Invention* (London: Faber & Faber, 1996), 123–48.

BAILIN, MIRIAM, *The Sick Room in Victorian Fiction: The Art of Being Ill* (Cambridge: Cambridge University Press, 1994).

BAKHTIN, M. M., *The Dialogic Imagination: Four Essays* (Austin, Tex., and London: University of Texas Press, 1981).

—— *Rabelais and His World*, trans. H. Iswolsky (Bloomington: Indiana University Press, 1984).

BALINT, MICHAEL, *The Basic Fault* (London: Tavistock, 1968).

BALSTON, THOMAS, *John Martin 1789–1854: His Life and Works* (London: Gerald Duckworth & Co., 1947).

BARKER, JULIET, *The Brontës* (London: Weidenfeld & Nicolson, 1994).

—— 'Charlotte Brontë's Photograph', *Brontë Society Transactions*, 19 (1986), 27–8.

BECKER, ERNEST, *The Denial of Death* (New York: Macmillan, Free Press, 1975).

BEER, GILLIAN, 'Carlyle and *Mary Barton*: Problems of Utterance', in Francis Barker (ed.), *The Sociology of Literature 1848*, Proceedings of the Essex Conference on the Sociology of Literature, July 1977 (Colchester: University of Essex, 1978), 242–55.

—— 'The Reader's Wager: Lots, Sorts, and Futures', *Essays in Criticism*, 40: 2 (April 1990), 99–123.

BELLIS, PETER J., 'In the Window-Seat: Vision and Power in *Jane Eyre*', *English Literary History*, 54 (1987), 639–52.

BENJAMIN, WALTER, *The Arcades Project*, trans. Howard Eiland and Kevin McLaughlin (Cambridge, Mass.: Harvard University Press, 1999).

BERMAN, MARSHALL, *All that is Solid Melts into Air: The Experience of Modernity* (London and New York: Verso, 1983).

BERMINGHAM, ANN, and BREWER, JOHN (eds.), *The Consumption of Culture 1600–1800: Image,Object, Text* (London: Routledge, 1995).

BERSANI, LEO, *A Future for Astyanax: Character and Desire in Literature* (London: Marion Boyars, 1978).

BLOCH, ERNST, *The Principle of Hope*, trans. Neville Plaice, Stephen Plaice, and Paul Knight (3 vols.; Oxford: Blackwell, 1986).

BOCK, CAROL, *Charlotte Brontë and the Storyteller's Audience* (Iowa City: University of Iowa Press, 1992).

BODENHEIMER, ROSEMARIE, *The Politics of Story in Victorian Social Fiction* (Ithaca and London: Cornell University Press, 1988).

BOOTH, MICHAEL R., *Victorian Spectacular Theatre 1850–1910* (London: Routledge & Kegan Paul, 1981).

BOSE, A., 'The Verse of the English "Annuals"', *Review of English Studies*, NS 4 (1953), 38–51.

BOWLBY, JOHN, *Attachment and Loss* (3 vols.; London: Hogarth Press, 1969–80).

BRANTLINGER, PATRICK, *The Spirit of Reform: British Literature and Politics, 1832–1867* (Cambridge, Mass. and London: Harvard University Press, 1977).

BRIGGS, ASA, *Victorian Things* (Harmondsworth: Penguin, 1990).

BROWN, LAURA, 'Not Outside the Range: One Feminist Perspective on Psychic Trauma', in C. Caruth (ed.), *Trauma: Explorations in Memory* (Baltimore and London: Johns Hopkins University Press 1995), 100–12.

BRYSON, NORMAN, *Vision and Painting: The Logic of the Gaze* (London: Macmillan, 1983).

CAMPBELL, ELIZABETH, '*Great Expectations* and the Language of Fortune', *Dickens Studies Annual*, 24 (1996), 153–65.

CARPENTER, MARY WILSON, *George Eliot and the Landscape of Time: Narrative Form and Protestant Apocalyptic History* (Chapel Hill and London: University of North Carolina Press, 1986).

CASTLE, TERRY, *The Female Thermometer: Eighteenth-Century Culture and the Invention of the Uncanny* (New York and Oxford: Oxford University Press, 1995).

CHASE, KAREN, *Eros and Psyche: the Representation of Personality in Charlotte Brontë, Charles Dickens, George Eliot* (New York and London: Methuen, 1984).

CHASE, KAREN, and LEVENSON, MICHAEL, *The Spectacle of Intimacy: A Public Life for the Victorian Family* (Princeton: Princeton University Press, 2000).

CHEW, SAMUEL, *Byron in England: His Fame and After-Fame* (London: John Murray, 1924).

CHRIST, CAROL, *The Finer Optic: The Aesthetic of Particularity in Victorian Poetry* (New Haven: Yale University Press, 1975).

CLARK, T. J., *The Painting of Modern Life: Paris in the Art of Manet and his Followers* (London: Thames & Hudson, 1985).

COBB, JONATHAN, and SENNETT, RICHARD, *The Hidden Injuries of Class* (New York: Vintage Books, 1973).

COLBY, CHRISTINA, *The Ends of History: Victorians and 'The Woman Question'* (New York and London: Routledge, 1991).

COLLINI, STEFAN, *Matthew Arnold: A Critical Portrait* (Oxford: Clarendon Press, 1988).

—— *Public Moralists* (Oxford: Clarendon Press, 1991).

COMOLLI, JEAN-LOUIS, 'Machines of the Visible', in *The Cinematic Apparatus*, ed. Teresa de Lauretis and Stephen Heath (London: Macmillan, 1980).

CRARY, JONATHAN, 'Modernizing Vision', in Hal Foster (ed.), *Vision and Visuality* (Seattle: Bay Press, 1988), 29–44.

—— *Techniques of the Observer: On Vision and Modernity in the Nineteenth Century* (Cambridge, Mass. and London: MIT Press, 1990).

—— 'The Blinding Light', in *The Sun is God* (Liverpool: Tate Liverpool, 2000), 19–26.

CROWLEY, TONY, *Language in History: Theories and Texts* (London and New York: Routledge, 1996).

CRUMP, JUSTINE LOUISE, 'A Study of Gaming and Eighteeenth-Century English Novels', Ph.D. dissertation, University of Cambridge, 1998.

CULLEN, M. J., *The Statistical Movement in Early Victorian Britain: the Foundations of Empirical Social Research* (Hassocks: Harvester, 1975).

CUNNINGHAM, VALENTINE, *Everywhere Spoken Against: Dissent in the Victorian Novel* (Oxford: Oxford University Press, 1975).

CUNNINGTON, C. WILLETT, and CUNNINGTON, PHILLIS, *Handbook of English Costume in the Nineteenth Century*, 3rd edn. (London: Faber, 1970).

CURTIN, MICHAEL, *Propriety and Position: A Study of Victorian Manners* (New York: Garland, 1987).

CUTT, MARGARET NANCY, *Ministering Angels: A Study of Nineteenth-Century Evangelical Writing for Children* (Broxbourne: Five Owls Press, 1979).

DALE, PETER ALLAN, 'Heretical Narration, Charlotte Brontë's Search for Endlessness' *Religion and Literature*, 16: 3 (Autumn 1984), 1–24.

DAVIDOFF, LEONORE, and HALL, CATHERINE, *Family Fortunes: Men and Women of the English Middle Class 1750–1850* (London: Hutchinson, 1987).

DAVIES, STEVIE, *Emily Brontë* (Hemel Hempstead: Harvester Wheatsheaf, 1988).

DE BOLLA, PETER, *The Discourse of the Sublime: Readings in History, Aesthetics and the Subject* (Oxford: Basil Blackwell, 1989).

DE LAURETIS, TERESA, *Alice Doesn't: Feminism, Semiotics, Cinema* (Bloomington: Indiana University Press, 1984).

DEVER, CAROLYN, *Death and the Mother from Dickens to Freud: Victorian Fiction and the Anxiety of Origins* (Cambridge: Cambridge University Press, 1998).

DOANE, MARY ANNE, *The Desire to Desire: The Woman's Film of the 1940s* (Bloomington: Indiana University Press, 1987).

DOLIN, TIM, Introduction to *Villette* (Oxford: World's Classics, 2000).

DUBOS, RENÉ and JEAN, *The White Plague: Tuberculosis, Man and Society* (London: Gollancz, 1953).

DUNCAN, IAN, *Modern Romance and Transformations of the Novel: The Gothic, Scott, Dickens* (Cambridge: Cambridge University Press, 1992).

DURING, SIMON, *Foucault and Literature: Towards a Genealogy of Writing* (London: Routledge, 1992).

DYER, RICHARD, 'Entertainment and Utopia', *Movie*, 24 (1978), 2–13.

DYOS, H. J., and WOLFF, MICHAEL (eds.), *The Victorian City: Images and Realities* (2 vols.; London: Routledge, 1973).

EAGLETON, TERRY, *Myths of Power: A Marxist Study of the Brontës* (London: Macmillan, 1987).

—— *Walter Benjamin: or Towards a Revolutionary Criticism* (London: Verso, 1981).

EDGERLY, MRS C. MABEL, 'The Structure of Haworth Parsonage: Domestic Arrangements of the Brontës' Home', *BST* 9: 1 (1936), 27–31.

EGOFF, SHEILA A., *Children's Periodicals of the Nineteenth Century: A Survey and Bibliography*, Library Association Pamphlet No. 8 (London, 1951).

ELFENBEIN, ANDREW, *Byron and the Victorians* (Cambridge: Cambridge University Press, 1995).

FAIRBAIRN, RONALD, *Psychoanalytic Studies of the Personality* (London: Tavistock, 1952).

FAXON, FREDERICK WINTHROP, *Literary Annuals and Gift Books: A Bibliography 1823–1903* (1912; rpt. Pinner, Middlesex: Private Libraries Association, 1973).

FAY, C. R., *Palace of Industry, 1851: A Study of the Great Exhibition and Its Fruits* (Cambridge: Cambridge University Press, 1951).

FEAVER, WILLIAM, *The Art of John Martin* (Oxford: Clarendon Press, 1975).

—— *John Martin 1789–1854* (Catalogue sold in aid of the National Art-Collections Fund, Loan Exhibition of Oil Paintings, Water Colours, Prints at Hazlitt, Gooden & Fox, 30 October–21 November 1975).

FISHER, JUDITH L., 'Magnificent or Mad? Nineteenth-Century Periodicals and the Paintings of Joseph Mallord William Turner', *Victorian Periodicals Review*, 29: 3 (Fall 1996), 242–60.

FISKE, JOHN, *Understanding Popular Culture*, (London and New York: Routledge, 1989).

FLINT, KATE, *The Victorians and the Visual Imagination* (Cambridge: Cambridge University Press, 2000).

—— 'The Business of a Woman's Life', in Heather Glen (ed.), *Cambridge Companion to the Brontës* (Cambridge: Cambridge University Press, 2002).

FOOT, MICHAEL, *The Politics of Paradise: A Vindication of Byron* (London: Collins, 1988).

FOWLER, BRIDGET, *The Alienated Reader: Women and Popular Romantic Literature in the Twentieth Century* (Hemel Hempstead: Harvester Wheatsheaf, 1991).

FREUD, SIGMUND, 'Creative Writers and Daydreaming' and 'The Uncanny', in Albert Dickson (ed.), *The Penguin Freud Library*, 14: *Art and Literature* (London: Penguin, 1990), 129–42.

—— 'Formulations on the Two Principles of Mental Functioning', in Angela Richards (ed.), *The Penguin Freud Library*, 11: *On Metapsychology: The Theory of Psychoanalysis* (London: Penguin, 1991), 29–44.

FROOM, LEROY EDWIN, *The Prophetic Faith of Our Fathers* (Washington, DC: Review and Herald, 1946), iii.

GALLAGHER, CATHERINE, *The Industrial Reformation of English Fiction: Social Discourse and Narrative Form 1832–1867* (Chicago and London: Chicago University Press, 1985).

GAGE, JOHN, 'J. M. W. Turner and Solar Myth', in J. B. Bullen (ed.), *The Sun is God: Painting, Literature and Mythology in the Nineteenth Century* (Oxford: Oxford University Press, 1989), 39–48.

GATES, BARBARA T., *Victorian Suicide: Mad Crimes and Sad Histories* (Princeton: Princeton University Press, 1988).

GÉRIN, WINIFRED, 'Byron's Influence on the Brontës', *Keats-Shelley Memorial Bulletin*, 17 (1966), 1–19.

—— *Charlotte Brontë: The Evolution of Genius* (Oxford: Oxford University Press, 1967).

—— *Emily Brontë* (Oxford: Oxford University Press, 1978).

GEZARI, JANET, *Charlotte Brontë and Defensive Conduct: The Author and the Body at Risk* (Philadelphia: University of Pennsylvania Press, 1992).

GILBERT, SANDRA, and GUBAR, SUSAN, *The Madwoman in the Attic: The Woman Writer and the Nineteenth-Century Literary Imagination* (New Haven: Yale University Press, 1979).

GILLISPIE, CHARLES COULSTON, *Genesis and Geology: A Study in the Relations of Scientific Thought, Natural Theology, and Social Opinion in Great Britain, 1790–1850* (New York: Harper & Row, 1959).

GLISERMAN, SUSAN, 'Science Writers and Tennyson's *In Memoriam*: A Study in Cultural Exchange', *Victorian Studies*, 18: 3 (March 1975), 276–308.

GLOAG, JOHN, *Victorian Comfort: A Social History of Design from 1830–1900* (London: A. & C. Black, 1961).

GORDON, LYNDALL, *Charlotte Brontë: A Passionate Life* (London: Chatto & Windus, 1994).

GREVEN, PHILIP, *The Protestant Temperament: Patterns of Child-Rearing, Religious Experience, and the Self in Early America* (New York: Alfred A. Knopf, 1977).

GRYLLS, DAVID, *Guardians and Angels: Parents and Children in Nineteenth-Century Literature* (London: Faber, 1978).

HALEY, BRUCE, *The Healthy Body and Victorian Culture* (Cambridge, Mass.: Harvard University Press, 1978).

HALL, AUDREY W., *A Suspected New Photograph of Charlotte Brontë* (Keighley: J. L. Crabtree, 1991).

HALTTUNEN, KAREN, *Confidence Men and Painted Women: A Study of Middle-class Culture in America, 1830–1870* (New Haven: Yale University Press, 1982).

HARRISON, J. F. C., *Early Victorian Britain 1832–51* (London: Fontana, 1979).

—— *The Second Coming: Popular Millenarianism, 1780–1850* (London: Routledge & Kegan Paul, 1979).

HEILMANN, ROBERT, 'Tulip-Hood, Streaks, and Other Strange Bedfellows: Style in *Villette*', *Studies in the Novel*, 14 (1982), 223–47.

HELSINGER, ELIZABETH K., SHEETS, ROBIN LAUTERBACH, and VEEDER, WILLIAM, *The Woman Question: Society and Literature in Britain and America, 1837–1883* (2 vols.; Manchester: Manchester University Press, 1983).

HELSINGER, ELIZABETH, 'Turner and the Representation of England', in W. J. T. Mitchell (ed.), *Landscape and Power* (Chicago: University of Chicago Press, 1994), 103–25.

HENDERSON, HEATHER, *The Victorian Self: Autobiography and Biblical Narrative* (Ithaca: Cornell University Press, 1989).

HEYWOOD, CHRISTOPHER, ' "Alas! Poor Caunt!" Branwell's Emancipationist Cartoon', *BST* 21: 5 (1995), 177–85.

HILL, GEOFFREY, *The Lords of Limit: Essays on Literature and Ideas* (London: André Deutsch, 1984).

HILTON, BOYD, *The Age of Atonement: The Influence of Evangelicalism on Social and Economic Thought, 1795–1865* (Oxford: Clarendon Press, 1988).

—— 'Whiggery, Religion and Social Reform: The Case of Lord Morpeth', *The Historical Journal*, 37 (1994), 829–59.

HILTON, MARY (ed.), *Potent Fictions: Children's Literacy and the Challenge of Popular Culture* (London: Routledge, 1996).

HOBSBAWM, E. J., *The Age of Revolution: Europe 1789–1848* (London: Weidenfeld & Nicolson, 1962).

—— *The Age of Capital 1848–1875* (London: Weidenfeld & Nicolson, 1975).

HOFKOSH, SONIA, 'Disfiguring Economies: Mary Shelley's Short Stories', in Audrey A. Fisch, Anne K. Mellor, and Esther H. Schor (eds.), *The Other Mary Shelley: Beyond Frankenstein* (Oxford: Oxford University Press, 1993), 204–19.

HOMANS, MARGARET, *Bearing the Word: Language and Female Experience in Nineteenth-Century Women's Writing* (Chicago: University of Chicago Press, 1986).

HORTON, SUSAN R., 'Were They Having Fun Yet?: Victorian Optical Gadgetry, Modernist Selves', in Carol T. Christ, and John O. Jordan (eds.), *Victorian Literature and the Victorian Visual Imagination* (Berkeley: University of California Press, 1995), 1–26.

HUNTER, SHELAGH, *Harriet Martineau: The Poetics of Moralism* (Aldershot: Scolar Press, 1995).

HUTTON, JOANNA, 'The Sale at Haworth Parsonage, *BST* 14: 75 (1965) 46–50.

HUYSSEN, ANDREAS, 'Mass Culture as Woman: Modernism's Other', in Tania Modleski (ed.), *Studies in Entertainment: Critical Approaches to Mass Culture* (Bloomington: Indiana University Press, 1986), 188–207.

INGHAM, PATRICIA, *The Language of Gender and Class: Transformation in the Victorian Novel* (London: Routledge, 1996).

JACOBUS, MARY, 'The Buried Letter: Feminism and Romanticism in *Villette*', in Jacobus (ed.), *Women Writing and Writing about Women* (London: Croom Helm, 1979), 121–40.

JAY, ELISABETH, *The Religion of the Heart: Anglican Evangelicalism* (Oxford: Clarendon Press, 1979).

JAY, MARTIN, *Downcast Eyes: The Denigration of Vision in Twentieth-Century French Thought* (Berkeley, Los Angeles, and London: University of California Press, 1993).

JENNINGS, HUMPHREY, *Pandaemonium: the Coming of the Machine as Seen by Contemporary Observers, 1660–1886* (London: André Deutsch, 1985).

KACHUR, ROBERT METRO, 'Getting the Last Word: Women and the Authoritative Apocalyptic Voice in British Literature, 1845–1900' (Ph.D., University of Wisconsin, Madison, 1996).

KAPLAN, CORA, *Sea Changes: Essays on Culture and Feminism* (London: Verso, 1986)

—— ' "What We Have Again to Say": Williams, Feminism, and the 1840s', in Christopher Prendergast (ed.), *Cultural Materialism: On Raymond Williams* (Minneapolis: University of Minnesota Press, 1995), 211–36.

KAVANAGH, THOMAS M., *Enlightenment and the Shadows of Chance: The Novel and the Culture of Gambling in Eighteenth-Century France* (Baltimore and London: Johns Hopkins University Press, 1993).

KELLETT, JOCELYN, *Haworth Parsonage: The Home of the Brontës* (Keighley: The Brontë Society, 1977).

KELLY, GARY, 'Unbecoming a Heroine: Novel Reading, Romanticism, and Barrett's *The Heroine*', *Nineteenth-Century Fiction*, 45 (September 1990), 220–41.

KLAUS, ROBERT JAMES, *The Pope, the Protestants, and the Irish: Papal Aggression and Anti-Catholicism in Mid-Nineteenth-Century England* (New York: Garland, 1987).

KLINGENDER, FRANCIS D., *Art and the Industrial Revolution*, revd. edn. (London: Paladin, 1968).

KRISTEVA, JULIA, *Desire in Language*, trans. Thomas Gora, Alice Jardine, and Leon S. Roudiez (Oxford: Blackwell, 1980).

KROEBER, KARL, and WALLING, WILLIAM (eds.), *Images of Romanticism; Verbal and Visual Affinities* (New Haven and London: Yale University Press, 1978).

KUCICH, JOHN, *Repression in Victorian Fiction: Charlotte Brontë, George Eliot, and Charles Dickens* (Berkeley and Los Angeles: University of California Press, 1987).

LANGLAND, ELIZABETH, *Nobody's Angels: Middle-Class Women and Domestic Ideology in Victorian Culture* (Ithaca and London: Cornell University Press, 1995).

LASLETT, PETER, *The World We Have Lost: England Before the Industrial Age* (New York: Charles Scribner's Sons, 1965).

LEAVIS, Q. D., 'The Symbolic Function of the Doctor in Victorian Novels', in F. R. and Q. D. Leavis, *Dickens the Novelist* (London: Chatto & Windus, 1970), 242–7.

LEE, HERMIONE, 'Emblems and Enigmas in *Jane Eyre*', *English*, 30 (1981), 233–55.

LEIGHTON, ANGELA, *Victorian Women Poets: Writing Against the Heart* (Hemel Hempstead: Harvester Wheatsheaf, 1992).

LEIGHTON, ANGELA, and REYNOLDS, MARGARET (eds)., *Victorian Women Poets: An Anthology* (Oxford: Blackwell, 1995).

LENNIE, CAMPBELL, *Landseer: The Victorian Paragon* (London: Hamish Hamilton, 1976).

LEVINE, GEORGE (ed.), *Aesthetics and Ideology* (New Brunswick: Rutgers University Press, 1994).

LEVITT, SARAH, *Victorians Unbuttoned: Registered Designs for Clothing, their Makers and Wearers, 1839–1900* (London: Allen & Unwin, 1986).

LINLEY, MARGARET, 'A Centre that Would Not Hold: Annuals and Cultural Democracy', in Laurel Brake, Bill Bell, and David Finkelstein (eds.), *Nineteenth-Century Media and the Construction of Identities* (Basingstoke and New York: Palgrave, 2000), 54–74.

LITTEN, JULIAN, *The English Way of Death: The Common Funeral since 1450* (London: Hale, 1991).

LOCK, JOHN, and DIXON, CANON W. T., *A Man of Sorrow: The Life, Letters and Times of the Rev. Patrick Brontë 1777–1861* (London: Nelson, 1965).

LODGE, DAVID, *The Language of Fiction* (London: Routledge & Kegan Paul, 1966).

LONDON, BETTE, 'The Pleasures of Submission: *Jane Eyre* and the Production of the Text', *ELH* 58 (1991), 195–213.

LOUDON, IRVINE, *Death in Childbirth: An International Study of Maternal Care and Maternal Mortality, 1800–1950* (Oxford: Clarendon Press, 1992).

LUCKACHER, BRIAN, 'Turner's Ghost in the Machine: Technology, Textuality, and the 1842 *Snow Storm*', *Word & Image*, 6 (1990), 119–37.

MCCOURBREY, JOHN, 'Turner's *Slave Ship*: Abolition, Ruskin, and Reception', *Word & Image*, 14 (1998), 319–53.

MCGANN, JEROME, *The Romantic Ideology: A Critical Investigation* (Chicago: University of Chicago Press, 1983).

— 'Rethinking Romanticism', *ELH* 59 (1992), 735–54.

MACKAY, REVD ANGUS, 'The Brontes at Cowan Bridge', *The Bookman*, October 1894, reprinted in *LL* i. 71–5.

MANNING, PETER J., '*Childe Harold* in the Marketplace: From Romaunt to Handbook', *Modern Language Quarterly*, 52 (1991), 170–90.

—— 'Wordsworth in the *Keepsake*, 1829', in John O. Jordan and Robert L. Patten (eds.), *Literature in the Marketplace: Nineteenth-Century British Publishing and Reading Practices* (Cambridge: Cambridge University Press, 1995), 44–73.

MATUS, JILL L., *Unstable Bodies: Victorian Representations of Sexuality and Maternity* (Manchester: Manchester University Press, 1995).

MEISEL, MARTIN, 'The Material Sublime: John Martin, Byron, Turner and the Theater', in Karl Kroeber and William Walling (eds.), *Images of Romanticism: Verbal and Visual Affinities*, (New Haven and London: Yale University Press, 1978), 211–32.

MELLOR, ANNE K., *Romanticism and Gender* (London and New York: Routledge, 1993).

MICHIE, HELENA, 'Under Victorian Skins: The Bodies Beneath', in Herbert F. Tucker, (ed.), *A Companion to Victorian Literature and Culture* (Oxford: Blackwell, 1999), 407–24.

MILLER, ALICE, *Thou Shalt Not Be Aware: Society's Betrayal of the Child*, trans. Hildegarde and Hunter Hannum (London: Virago, 1985).

MILLHAUSER, MILTON, *Just Before Darwin: Robert Chambers and Vestiges* (Middletown, Conn.: Wesleyan University Press, 1959).

MITCHELL, W. J. T., *Iconology: Image, Text, Ideology* (Chicago: University of Chicago Press, 1986).

MODLESKI, TANIA, *Loving With a Vengeance: Mass-Produced Fantasies for Women* (New York and London: Methuen, 1984).

MOERS, ELLEN, *Literary Women* (London: Virago, 1978).

MONK, LELAND, *Standard Deviations: Chance and the Modern British Novel* (Stanford: Stanford University Press, 1993).

MORLEY, JOHN, *Death, Heaven, and the Victorians* (London: Studio Vista, 1971).

MORRIS, R. J., *Cholera 1832: the Social Response to an Epidemic* (London: 1976).

MULVEY, LAURA, 'Visual Pleasure and Narrative Cinema', *Screen*, 16: 3 (1975), 6–18.

—— 'Afterthoughts . . . Inspired by *Duel in the Sun*', *Framework*, 15–17 (1981), 12–25.

NEWTON, JUDITH LOWDER, *Women, Power and Subversion; Social Strategies in British Fiction, 1778–1860* (New York and London: Methuen, 1985).

—— ' "Ministers of the Interior": The Political Economy of Women's Manuals', in *Starting Over: Feminism and the Politics of Cultural Critique* (Ann Arbor: University of Michigan Press, 1994), 125–7.

NORD, DEBORAH EPSTEIN, *Walking the Victorian Streets* (Ithaca and London: Cornell University Press, 1995).

PALMEGIANO, E. M., 'Women and British Periodicals 1832–1867: A Bibliography', *Victorian Periodicals Newsletter*, 9 (1976), 3–36.

PAZ, D. G., *Popular Anti-Catholicism in Mid-Victorian England* (Stanford: Stanford University Press, 1992).

PETERS, CATHERINE, *Thackeray's Universe: Shifting Worlds of Imagination and Reality* (London: Faber, 1987).

PETERS, MARGOT, *Charlotte Bronte: Style in the Novel* (Madison: University of Wisconsin Press, 1973).

PETERSON, CARLA L., *The Determined Reader: Gender and Culture in the Novel from Napoleon to Victoria* (New Brunswick: Rutgers University Press, 1986).

PEVSNER, NIKOLAUS, *High Victorian Design: A Study of the Exhibits of 1851* (London: Architectural Press, 1951).

PHILLIPS, MARION J., 'Charlotte Brontë's Favourite Preacher: Frederick Denison John Maurice (1805–1872)', *BST* 20: 2 (1990), 77–88.

PIGGIN, STUART, *Making Evangelical Missionaries 1789–1850: The Social Background, Motives And Training Of British Protestant Missionaries to India* (Abingdon: Sutton Courtenay Press, 1984).

POLITI, JINA, 'Jane Eyre Class-ified', in Heather Glen (ed.), *Jane Eyre: New Casebook* (London: Macmillan, 1997), 78–91.

POOVEY, MARY, *Uneven Developments: The Ideological Work of Gender in Mid-Victorian England* (London: Virago, 1989).

PORTER, DOROTHY, and PORTER, ROY, *In Sickness and in Health: The British Experience 1650–1850* (London: Fourth Estate, 1988).

PRIESTLEY, J. B., *Victoria's Heyday* (Harmondsworth: Penguin, 1972).

QUALLS, BARRY V., *The Secular Pilgrims of Victorian Fiction: The Novel as Book of Life* (Cambridge: Cambridge University Press, 1982).

Radway, Janice, *Reading the Romance*, new edn. (London: Verso, 1987).

Renier, Anne, *Friendship's Offering: An Essay on the Annuals and Gift Books of the Nineteenth Century* (London: Private Libraries Association, 1964).

Richards, Thomas, *The Commodity Culture of Victorian England: Advertising and Spectacle, 1851–1914* (London: Verso, 1990).

Richardson, Ruth, *Death, Dissection and the Destitute* (London: Routledge, 1987).

Ricks, Christopher, 'E. C. Gaskell's Charlotte Brontë', in *Essays in Appreciation* (Oxford: Clarendon Press, 1996), 118–45.

Rifelj, Carol, ' "Ces tableaux du monde": Keepsakes in *Madame Bovary*', *Nineteenth-Century French Studies*, 25 (1997), 360–85.

Riley, James C., *Sickness, Recovery and Death: A History and Forecast of Ill Health* (London: Macmillan, 1989).

Roberts, David, 'The Social Conscience of Tory Periodicals', *Victorian Periodicals Newsletter*, 10: 3 (1977), 154–69.

Roberts, Doreen, '*Jane Eyre* and the Warped System of Things', in Heather Glen (ed.), *Jane Eyre: New Casebook* (London: Macmillan, 1997), 34–51.

Rose, Jonathan, 'Rereading the English Common Reader: A Preface to a History of Audiences', *Journal of the History of Ideas*, 53 (1992), 47–70.

Rosman, Doreen M., *Evangelicals and Culture* (London: Croom Helm, 1984).

Ross, Marlon, *The Contours of Masculine Desire: Romanticism and the Rise of Women's Poetry* (New York and Oxford: Oxford University Press, 1989).

Rothstein, Lawrence, *Vital Signs: Medical Realism in Nineteenth-Century Fiction* (Princeton: Princeton University Press, 1992).

Rowell, Geoffrey, *Hell and the Victorians: A Study of the Nineteenth-Century Theological Controversies Concerning Eternal Punishment and the Future Life* (Oxford: Oxford University Press, 1974).

Rubin, Lillian, *Worlds of Pain: Life in the Working-Class Family* (New York: Basic Books, 1976).

Russell, Norman, *The Novelist and Mammon* (Oxford: Clarendon Press, 1986).

St Clair, William, 'The Impact of Byron's Writings: an Evaluative Approach', in Andrew Rutherford (ed.), *Byron: Augustan and Romantic* (London: Macmillan in assoc. with British Council, 1990), 1–25.

Sandeen, Ernest R., *The Roots of Fundamentalism: British and American Millenarianism 1800–1930* (Chicago: University of Chicago Press, 1970).

Sangster, Paul, *Pity My Simplicity* (London: Epworth Press, 1963).

Schivelbusch, Wolfgang, *The Railway Journey: Trains and Travel in the 19th Century* (Oxford: Blackwell, 1980).

Schofield, Roger, 'Did the Mothers Really Die? Three Centuries of Maternal Mortality in "The World We Have Lost" ', in L. Bonfield, R. Smith, and K. Wrightson (eds.), *The World We Have Gained: Histories of Population and Social Structure* (Oxford: Basil Blackwell, 1986), 231–60.

Secord, James A., *Victorian Sensation: The Extraordinary Publication, Reception, and Secret Authorship of Vestiges of the Natural History of Creation* (Chicago and London: University of Chicago Press, 2000).

Sennett, Richard, *The Fall of Public Man* (Cambridge: Cambridge University Press, 1977).

Sharps, John Geoffrey, *Mrs Gaskell's Observation and Invention* (Fontwell: Linden Press, 1970).

SHUTTLEWORTH, SALLY, *Charlotte Brontë and Victorian Psychology* (Cambridge: Cambridge University Press, 1996).

SICHTERMANN, BARBARA, *Femininity: The Politics of the Personal*, ed. Helga Geyer-Ryan (Oxford: Polity, 1983).

SIMMEL, GEORGE, 'The Metropolis and Mental Life', in David Frisby and Mike Featherstone (eds.), *Simmel on Culture* (London: Sage, 1997), 174–85.

SIMPSON, DAVID, *Fetishism and Imagination: Dickens, Melville, Conrad* (Baltimore and London: Johns Hopkins University Press, 1982).

SMAIL, DAVID, *The Origins of Unhappiness: A New Understanding of Personal Distress* (London: HarperCollins, 1993).

SMITH, F. B., *The People's Health, 1830–1910* (London: Croom Helm, 1979).

SMITH, LINDSAY, *Victorian Photography, Painting and Poetry: The Enigma of Visibility in Ruskin, Morris and the Pre-Raphaelites* (Cambridge: Cambridge University Press, 1995).

SMITH, SUSAN BELASCO, 'A Yorkshire Burr: Language in *Shirley*', *Studies in English Literature 1500–1900*, 27 (1987), 637–43.

SOPER, KATE, 'Stephen Heroine', in *Troubled Pleasures: Writings on Politics, Gender and Hedonism* (London: Verso, 1990), 246–68.

SPENCER, JANE, *The Rise of the Woman Novelist: From Aphra Behn to Jane Austen* (Oxford: Basil Blackwell, 1986).

STACEY, JACKIE, 'Desperately seeking difference', in *The Sexual Subject: A Screeen Reader in Sexuality* (London: Routledge, 1992), 244–57.

STALLYBRASS, PETER, and WHITE, ALLON, *The Politics and Poetics of Transgression* (Ithaca: Cornell University Press, 1986).

STEDMAN, JANE, 'The Genesis of the Genii', *BST* 14: 75 (1965), 16–19.

STEEDMAN, CAROLYN, *Strange Dislocations: Childhood and the Idea of Human Interiority 1780–1930* (London: Virago, 1995).

STEIN, RICHARD L., 'Remember the *Téméraire*: Turner's Memorial of 1839', *Representations*, 11 (Summer 1985), 165–200.

STEPHENSON, GLENNIS, *Letitia Landon: The Woman Behind L.E.L.* (Manchester: Manchester University Press, 1995).

STERN, DANIEL, *The Interpersonal World of the Infant: A View From Psychoanalysis and Developmental Psychology* (New York: Basic Books, 1985).

STONE, HARRY, *Dickens and the Invisible World: Fairy-Tales, Fantasy, and Novel-Making* (Bloomington: Indiana University Press, 1979).

STONEMAN, PATSY, *Brontë Transformations* (Hemel Hempstead,: Harvester Wheatsheaf/ Prentice Hall, 1996).

SUPPLE, BARRY, 'Material Development: the Condition of England 1830–1870', in Laurence Lerner (ed.), *The Victorians* (London: Methuen, 1978), 49–69.

SUTTIE, IAN D., *The Origins of Love and Hate* (1936; London: Free Association Books, 1988).

TALLENT-BATEMAN, CHAS. T. , 'The "Forget-Me-Not" ', *The Manchester Quarterly: A Journal of Literature and Art*, 21 (1902), in *Papers of the Manchester Literary Club*, 28 (1902), 78–98.

TANNER, TONY, *Adultery in the Novel: Contract and Transgression* (Baltimore: Johns Hopkins University Press, 1979).

TAYLOR, BARBARA, *Eve and the New Jerusalem* (London: Virago, 1983).

TAYLOR, CHARLES, *Sources of the Self: The Making of the Modern Identity* (Cambridge, Mass.: Harvard University Press, 1989).

THERNSTROM, STEPHAN, *Poverty and Progress: Social Mobility in a Nineteenth-Century City* (Cambridge, Mass.: Harvard University Press, 1973).

THOMAS, KEITH, *Religion and the Decline of Magic* (London: Weidenfeld & Nicolson, 1971).

THOMPSON, E. P., *The Making of the English Working Class* (Harmondsworth: Penguin, 1968).

THOMSON, PATRICIA, *George Sand and the Victorians: Her Influence and Reputation in Nineteenth-Century England* (London: Macmillan, 1977).

THORMÄHLEN, MARIANNE, *The Brontës and Religion* (Cambridge: Cambridge University Press, 1999).

THRALL, MIRIAM, *Rebellious Fraser's* (New York: Columbia University Press, 1934).

TILLOTSON, KATHLEEN, 'A Day with Charlotte Brontë in 1850', *BST* 16: 1 (1971), 22–30.

—— ' "Haworth Churchyard": the Making of Arnold's Elegy', *BST* 15: 2 (1967), 105–22.

—— *Novels of the Eighteen-Forties* (Oxford: Clarendon Press, 1954).

TOMPKINS, J. M. S., 'Jane Eyre's "Iron Shroud" ', *Modern Language Review*, 22 (1927), 195–7.

TROTTER, DAVID, *Circulation: Defoe, Dickens and the Economics of the Novel* (Basingstoke: Macmillan, 1988).

VARGISH, THOMAS, *The Providential Aesthetic in Victorian Fiction* (Charlottesville: University Press of Virginia, 1985).

WANG, LISA, 'The Holy Spirit in Emily Brontë's *Wuthering Heights* and Poetry', *Literature and Theology*, 14: 2 (June 2000), 160–73.

WEBB, IGOR, *From Custom to Capital: The English Novel and the Industrial Revolution* (Ithaca and London: Cornell University Press, 1981).

WELLESLEY, DOROTHY (ed.), *The Annual: Being a Selection from the Forget-Me-Nots, Keepsakes and Other Annuals of the Nineteenth Century*, with an intro. by Vita Sackville-West (London: Cobden-Sanderson, n.d.).

WELSH, ALEXANDER, *Strong Representations: Narrative and Circumstantial Evidence in England* (Baltimore and London: Johns Hopkins University Press, 1992).

WEST, REBECCA, 'Charlotte Brontë', in *The Great Victorians*, ed. H. J. and Hugh Massingham (London: Nicholson & Watson, 1937), 49–62.

WHEELER, MICHAEL, *Death and the Future Life in Victorian Literature and Theology* (Cambridge: Cambridge University Press, 1990).

WILLIAMS, A. SUSAN, *The Rich Man and the Diseased Poor in Early Victorian Literature* (London: Macmillan, 1987).

WILLIAMS, RAYMOND, *The Country and the City* (London: Chatto & Windus, 1973).

—— *The English Novel from Dickens to Lawrence* (London: Chatto & Windus, 1973).

—— 'Forms of English Fiction in 1848', *Writing in Society* (London: Verso, n.d.), 150–65.

WINNICOTT, D. W., *The Maturational Process and the Facilitating Environment* (London: Hogarth Press, 1965).

WINNIFRITH, TOM, *The Brontes and their Background: Myth and Reality* (London: Macmillan, 1973).

WOHL, ANTHONY S., *Endangered Lives: Public Health in Victorian Britain* (London: Dent, 1983).

WOLFF, JANET, 'The Invisible *Flâneuse*: Women and the Literature of Modernity', *Feminine Sentences* (Cambridge: Polity, 1990), 34–50.

WOOLF, VIRGINIA, '*Jane Eyre* and *Wuthering Heights*', *The Common Reader*, First Series (London: Hogarth Press, 1925), 196–204.

—— *A Room of One's Own* (London: Hogarth Press, 1929).

Index

Printed in the United States
74501LV00003B/88

9 780199 272556